"This book has it all."
—Nancy Berry, CFRE, President and CEO,
Guadalupe Valley Hospital Foundation, Seguin, TX

"Debra's current edition is near at hand and will always be. It is my constant companion."
—Dick Zinser, Director of Development,
Conrad N. Hilton College of Hotel and Restaurant Management,
University of Houston, Houston, TX

"Daily use, Post-It Notes, and outline pens have nearly worn out my copy of The Complete Guide to Planned Giving."
—Margaret M. Holman, President,
Holman Philanthropic Consulting, Inc., New York, NY

"… the ultimate 'Bible' on planned giving."
—Jon Calder, Director of Annual and Planned Giving,
Providence Alaska Foundation, Anchorage, AK

"…a one-stop reference guide."
—Deborah Lynn Leeson,
Delynn Consulting, Mililani, HI

"…deserves a place on every gift planner's bookshelf— no on every gift planners desk."
—Mike Patterson, Director of Planned Giving,
Trinity University, San Antonio, TX

"….it is still the first place I turn for information."
—Lynda N. Wright, Director of Gift and Estate Planning,
Iliff School of Theology, Denver, CO

"If I could have one book about planned giving, this would be it."
—Craig Esposito, Vice President for Advancement,
Mitchell College, New London, CT

THE COMPLETE GUIDE TO PLANNED GIVING

Everything You Need To Know To Compete Successfully for Major Gifts

Revised Third Edition

Debra Ashton

Legal Counsel
Jonathan G. Tidd

ASHTONASSOCIATES
24 Robertson Street, Quincy, MA 02169
617.472.9316
debra@debraashton.com
www.debraashton.com

THE COMPLETE GUIDE TO PLANNED GIVING

Everything You Need To Know To Compete Successfully for Major Gifts

Revised Third Edition

Dedication:
This book is dedicated to the memory of
David M. Donaldson, Esq. (1938–1994)
and sadly to my dad, John Thomas Thorburn III (1920–2002)

Copyright © 1988, 1991, 2004 by Debra Ashton
ISBN 0-9705818-0-7

Library of Congress Control Number: 2004090306

Printed in the United States of America

ACKNOWLEDGMENTS

It should come as no surprise that I needed a lot of help to produce this book. Those who took special time to assist me are listed here. Others are mentioned throughout the book. I am grateful to them all. If I missed anyone, forgive me.

I would like to thank my friend VAUGHN W. HENRY of Henry & Associates, Springfield, IL, for being the only person to proofread the entire book. Who would agree to such torture? More than that, I appreciate his extensive advice on content. Thanks to Vaughn, the book has a better balance between the nonprofit and for-profit worlds although his constant yammering about incorporating the advisor's point of view was a real pain in the you-know-what. Vaughn's friends are now laughing because they know exactly what I mean. Thanks, Vaughn.

A big thank you goes to my dear friend JIM POTTER of Planned Giving Resources, Inc., Baker, LA, for help with the Charitable Gift Annuities chapter. His contribution to the content of that chapter was invaluable to me. After reading my chapter, he sent me at least six single-spaced pages of changes and edits. Phew! That is a lesson to me. Don't even dream of asking Jim for help next time because he'll actually take it seriously and do it. Thanks, Jim.

Others who helped me with proofreading and content include my good friends at PG Calc, GARY PFORZHEIMER and HENRIETTA YELLE. In addition, I'm sure I strained the support line at PG Calc while creating many of the examples and illustrations for the book. Thanks to JEFF LYDENBERG, WINSTON JONES, TINA YELLE, BILL LASKIN, DYKE TILT, and ANN MCPHERSON.

My friend, BERNIE FRANK, of Lewis, Rice & Fingersh, St. Louis, MO, read my GST Tax chapter and offered some expertise to fix a few things that needed work. I appreciate his keen eye and expertise. Thanks, Bernie.

JOHN TAYLOR at C.A.S.E., Washington, DC, provided help with crediting guidelines in my chapter on Integrating Planned Giving Into A Campaign and allowed me to use a lot of material from the C.A.S.E. publication on campaign reporting standards. Thanks, John.

ERIC DRYBURGH of Silk, Adler & Colvin, San Francisco, CA, rewrote my very bad summary of Charitable Reverse Split Dollar arrangements in the Life Insurance chapter. Thanks, Eric. That section was really a mess before you fixed it.

To get the business office perspective for my real estate chapter, I enlisted the help of my dear friend and former colleague from Wheaton College, MARGARET CASS FERBER. Peg is VP for Finance and Treasurer at Nazareth College, Rochester, NY. She wrote a whole page about working with the business office and provided some sage advice for my readers. Thanks, Peg.

BILL SULLIVAN of William J. Sullivan Insurance, Milton, MA, worked up two charts for the chapter on Life Insurance so that my readers could have an estimate of how much insurance costs for different size policies in different amounts. Bill is a graduate of the Boston College Class of 1960 and was a great friend, volunteer, and supporter of Boston College while I was Director of Planned Giving. Thanks, Bill.

MARK MORITZ of Custom Estate Planning, PLLC, Scottsdale, AZ, assisted me with my discussion of Crummey Powers in the Life Insurance chapter. He provided advanced content and especially pitfalls of which I had no knowledge at all. That's a scary thought. Thanks, Mark.

My long-time friend from the Planned Giving Group of New England CHARLIE GORDY, now with Bank of New York in West Paterson, NJ, shipped off many specimen documents for the chapter about Managing

Your Planned Giving Assets. You'll agree that these pages about how to put together an RFP are a terrific addition to my new Chapter III-9. Thank you, Charlie.

Another set of fabulous documents were sent to me by **CHARLES STERLING** at State Street Global Advisors, Boston, MA. At the end of my chapter on Real Estate, you'll find Charles' fantastic documents to keep you out of trouble when you are dealing with real estate. Charles allowed me to use his Real Estate Questionnaire in both of my prior two editions. For the new book, Charles went out of his way to help me with all new updated documents. Thanks, Charles.

TOM SMITH of Planned Giving Startup, Middlebury, VT, proofed several of the tax chapters and found numerous typos or content problems that have now been fixed. Thanks, Tom. And, he claims to have a bottle of champagne to uncork with me when the book rolls off the presses.

When I needed real figures to illustrate how important planned giving is in a campaign, I turned to a friend from Harvard, **PETER KIMBALL**, Director of Gift Planning, Faculty of Arts and Sciences. Peter gave me actual figures of planned gift totals in the Harvard Campaign that ended in 2000. Thanks, Peter, for showing us what is truly possible, although you have given most of us an inferiority complex.

Appendix V, Specimen Agreements, was provided by my friend, **EMIL KALLINA**, of Kallina & Associates, LLC, Baltimore, MD. When I blasted off an e-mail to Emil asking if he could help me with this section, he immediately sent 10 custom drafted documents (not I.R.S. prototypes). I am very grateful especially because he did this at year end, the busiest time of the year for a charitable giving tax attorney. Thanks, Emil.

ABBY MASON of Kaspick & Company's office in Boston, MA, sat with me for two hours in her office discussing administrative issues, fiduciary issues, and other considerations for charitable clients. Her advice is woven throughout many sections in Part II. Thanks, Abby.

LYNDA MOERSCHBAECHER, LMNOP Seminars and Publications in Carlsbad, CA, was the attorney for my Second Revised Edition and a long-time friend since then. Spontaneously and without my knowledge Lynda took the piece called "About the Author" from my web site and rewrote it. Lynda's version is at the end of this book. Thanks, Lynda. Having printed her rewrite, I've been pondering whether I should go to confession.

PAUL SCHERVISH, who is a friend and former colleague during my seven years at Boston College, made me so very happy when he agreed to write my Preface. The only problem with having such an eloquent visionary like Paul write my Preface is that the readers will figure out in short order that I am not a writer. I extend my deepest gratitude to Paul.

Very special thanks go out to a long-time friend and leader in the charitable giving community, my attorney, **JONATHAN TIDD** of West Simsbury, CT. Jon has ensured that the book is correct under current tax laws as of its publication date. If you know Jonathan, then you know that he didn't let me say anything that wasn't grounded in law. Thank you, Jonathan, for your friendship, wisdom, advice, and counsel during the writing of this book.

You will notice that the new book has a look and feel of the highest professional standards thanks to **ALVART BADALIAN** of Arrow Graphics, Inc, Cambridge, MA. She and her team are responsible for cover design, typesetting, and print management. I'm sure you will agree that Arrow Graphics did an outstandingly superb job with the Revised Third Edition. Thanks, Alvart.

Finally, I extend my thanks and gratitude to **VICTOR GRAPHICS, INC.**, Baltimore, MD, for the excellent quality of the Revised Third Edition that you are holding now. Tom V. Hicks and his team did a marvelous job producing this book.

TO MY READERS: If you know any of the fine individuals listed here or named elsewhere in the text of the book, please tell them that you know they helped me, and, if it is appropriate, patronize them, for they are all among the best in their respective fields.

TABLE OF CONTENTS

PART III: RUNNING A SUCCESSFUL PLANNED GIVING PROGRAM

PREFACE

All giving is planned giving. By this I mean that every gift made by every person involves reflection about just how much to give, to what cause, in what way, and at what time. In other words, giving is a biographical event in which a donor's self-reflective deliberation goes forward along with the gift into the lives of the beneficiaries.

Historically, the term planned giving has been restricted to gifts with some deferred component. Planned giving is aligned to a subdivision of a development office, as a distinctive program with its own director, officers, and named funds. At the extreme, there is territorial competition for donors and gifts among the units dealing with planned giving, annual giving, major gifts, capital campaign gifts, and so forth. In other words, planned giving is defined by the receiver- or demand-side of the gift relationship and is associated with some combination of how a development office is segmented, the kind of technical vehicle employed, and the title of the fund to which a gift is accredited.

It turns out that when we look a bit more deeply at the customary understanding of planned giving, the *planning* part is really something that charities are doing rather than donors. In the traditional sense, a planned gift is a future oriented gift that can't be spent today, requires technical and legal structures, and is often subject to amendment resulting from unpredictable events or decisions such as interest rate changes, life spans, depletion of estates, new trustee designations, and so forth. Clearly, charities have lots of planning to do, not only about how to attract planned gifts, but also about what to do once they receive them.

Now, my purpose is not to disparage this conventional understanding or to revolutionize the working relations that development offices find suitable. It is, however, to suggest a complementary way to understand the meaning and practice of planned giving, because to do so highlights the subtle yet consequential recasting of gift planning that Debra Ashton embeds throughout this grand book.

What Ashton properly grasps is that planned giving is first to be understood from the donor- or supply side of the gift relationship. But, not because the gift is deferred or has a distinctive legal component. Because the real gift planner is the donor. What other than perhaps some complexity makes a thoughtful pledge of $100 a month to Bread for the World less a planned gift from the point of view of the donor than the establishment of a charitable remainder trust at the Salvation Army? Indeed, what from the donor's perspective makes a gift of $100,000 in appreciated assets to the capital campaign of one's alma mater less a planned gift than designating a $100,000 charitable bequest?

A planned gift is any gift that combines conscientious decisions about how much to give, to whom to give it, and when to give it. As such, virtually all giving, from all people, at all times is planned giving. And the corollary: all development professionals are planned giving officers.

All this, Ashton, understands, and more. The best planned gift for a donor, she explains several times, may in fact be an outright gift. After all, it emerges as much as a gift annuity from a self-reflective discernment about how best to combine aspiration, capacity, and character. Because this is so important, I recommend even to seasoned planned giving professionals that the best place to start reading this book is Chapter I-5 where Ashton rectifies six myths about who is a planned giver, what is a planned gift, and who is a planned giving officer.

For Ashton, then, the unit of analysis for planned giving is not the type of vehicle, the timing of a gift, or the fund to which a gift is attributed. The unit of analysis is the planning donor. All the techniques of planned giving are instruments to achieve what donors choose to do. Given her underlying donor focus, the technical expertise she organizes and communicates so well always remains a means to an end. But, just as medical procedures are means to an end, it is still absolutely crucial that, when called for, those means be scientifically advanced and adroitly executed. In this regard, Ashton is an educator, not a trainer. She discusses the most sophisticated information with clarity, the most complex processes with pace, and the most jeopardizing pitfalls with wisdom.

In the end, Ashton verily does provide a Complete Guide to Planned Giving. It is complete in its donor-side starting point, it is complete in its charity-side methodology, and it is complete in its ability to help development professionals to fulfill their calling to find that golden point of compatibility between the needs of donors and the needs of the causes they serve.

Paul G. Schervish
Boston College
January 2004

INTRODUCTION

Planned giving is the vehicle through which inspired individuals can change society. Unfortunately, planned giving is intimidating to many fund raisers. I see this problem constantly in the workshops I run. As a result, potential gifts remain on the table when there are so many wonderful possibilities for structuring creative gifts that benefit both the donor and the charity.

In its first two editions (1988 and 1991), *The Complete Guide to Planned Giving* helped thousands of people negotiate this most difficult, technical, and intimidating area of fund raising. Now, with the Revised Third Edition in hand, you, too, have the power to help donors change society.

Make no mistake about it; you have the best job on the planet. Regardless of the stress you experience every day, you deal with the best that society has to offer. For, within the context of your work, you link donors to a cause, an ideal, or a mission. Through your efforts, donors voluntarily give away money and assets for a purpose that serves the common good. When a donor decides to make a significant gift, it is a magical moment. The gift creates a bond between the donor and the charity that is pure excitement for both. Most important in the process is the relationship between the charity and the donor. Once that connection is established, donors nearly solicit themselves. But, even though 99% of the process is building the relationship, you need to know how to structure the gift, value the gift, dispose of the gift, and administer the gift. This book tells you how. It is the most accessible, understandable, and practical book on planned giving that has ever been written.

A lot has changed since the Revised Second Edition rolled off the presses in 1991. For one thing, the tax law has changed many times. The flip unitrust did not exist. The words Internet, web site, and e-mail never appeared in the last edition. And, what about the proliferation of state regulations on charitable gift annuities? Moreover, consider the fact that the term principal gifts didn't exist back then. Yes, indeed, the planned giving landscape is very different from what it was in 1991. The Revised Third Edition includes it all, and more.

This book, nicknamed "The Blue Bible" by its readers, has been taken apart, chapter by chapter, completely overhauled, and then updated with the most current strategies and tax information available today in plain understandable English. If you own a tattered and dog-eared copy of either of the last two editions, you can now throw it away.

In spite of the many changes since 1991, some things about our charitable industry remain the same. Competition for philanthropic dollars is fierce. Charities have raised their expectations resulting in campaign goals formerly unimaginable. Therefore, fund raisers live with enormous stress trying to achieve higher and higher gift totals. Without planned giving, they are destined to fail.

The Complete Guide to Planned Giving is a very serious hands-on guide, written for real people like you, charged with the important responsibility of raising money to strengthen your organization so that you can carry on your mission.

But, I warn you. This book is not politically correct. Sometimes irreverent, sometimes too honest, this book tells you what really happens to you day to day, in the trenches, when you are the Director of Planned Giving. It tells you how to survive your daily travails, how to set priorities when multiple tasks compete for your time, and what to do when things go wrong.

With this one volume in your fund raising library, and over 500 ridiculously dense, information-packed pages, you can do planned giving. But, this book is not just for Directors of Planned Giving. This book can also help the following:

- Major gifts, leadership gifts, or principal gifts officers who want to be more effective on a visit;
- Directors of Development or Executive Directors who need to know precisely what to do to start a program and what they can do on their own;

- Trust officers who want to secure more charitable business from either nonprofit organizations as charitable clients or from current personal trust customers;
- For-profit professionals such as attorneys, accountants, or financial advisors who are finding a greater demand from clients on charitable vehicles and options.

Why should you trust me? Simple. I was there. As a director of planned giving at four charities over 22 years, my mistakes (and there were many) are disclosed in this book for your benefit. This book is not merely theory. This book is real life. The Revised Third Edition is unparalleled in the industry for frankness and down-to-earth practical advice, honesty, and guidance.

A review of Appendix III illustrates that there are many resources on planned giving, gift planning, estate planning, philanthropy or charitable giving tax law. But, as far as I can tell, there is nothing quite like this book.

Let me tell you why.

This book takes you through every twist and turn and every decision or action you have to take as a Director of Planned Giving. The detail is relentless and it might even make you tired. But, the detail in this book is what is missing in most books. Like I said earlier, this is not theory, it is real life.

Planned giving is critical to the future of your charitable organization. But, institutions get big gifts when they build relationships with donors, not because development officers know charitable giving tax law.

This book teaches you many things besides the tax consequences of different kinds of gifts. However, tax laws need not intimidate you because that is not why people make gifts. If you can build a solid relationship with your donors, then the type of gift is merely a detail.

If you are a Director of Development or an Executive Director, this book will help you sort out your priorities and get your shop in order or help you hire a Director of Planned Giving. If you are a Director of Planned Giving, this book will help you do your job.

There is a lot of competition out there. If your charity is not engaging in planned giving, then you are behind the eight ball. With this book, you can run a comprehensive planned giving program or you can run only a bequest program or incorporate gifts of securities into your annual giving program.

The choice is yours. Do as much as you can.

With this book, you can change the paradigm for your development office. I hope that you will use this book to raise more money than you ever have before. Just remember that people give to people. Build the relationship and the gift will happen.

About the Index: I have done a nonconventional thing with the index. Since there are some topics that didn't make it into this book, I added items to the Index with a comment "not included" so that you don't have to guess when you can't find a topic. Where this book leaves off, there are many resources in Appendix III to fill in the gaps.

Finally, I want to say that I am not an attorney. The book has been reviewed by tax counsel and it is legally correct as of December of 2003. However, tax laws are complex and you need to keep up with tax changes regularly. This book is not intended to present legal advice. Consult your attorney before engaging in any charitable giving activity with your donors.

Best wishes in your fund raising.

Debra Ashton
Quincy, Massachusetts
December, 2003

PART I

THE PREPARATION STAGE

INTRODUCTION

A lot has changed in the planned giving landscape since the first edition of this book. 1988 was a long time ago. Still, many of the same methods and principles apply to running a planned giving program today. In this part of the book, I cover the things you must do to prepare for your year ahead. To be successful, you have to bring in gifts. But, unless you understand some of the things involved with the nature of your work, the culture of your new environment, and the way charities operate, you are destined to fail.

While getting the gifts is the ultimate focus of your efforts, many fund raisers dwell incorrectly on the gift vehicles as a means to that end. This is wrong. People don't contribute to gift vehicles and they don't give to institutions. People give to people! As with the first and second edition, that is the first lesson of this Revised Third Edition.

The premise of this book is to take you through the entire process of starting a planned giving program. If your organization is already way ahead, then you can skip to other chapters that will be immediately helpful to you. However, many of my readers are faced with starting a program from scratch. Therefore, you are the ones for whom I wrote the first six chapters.

It would be easy to skip some of the information in Part I. Having run four planned giving programs, I take for granted that people arrive at an institution with the knowledge to do what needs to be done. However, during the writing of this Revised Third Edition, I had calls from many people looking for help. In most cases, they were in their first position as a planned giving director wondering where to start. Some of them were working all alone, with no guidance, in a small shop, with no history of planned giving at their institution.

For me, starting a program from scratch is always more fun than squeaking out another few million from an existing mature program. I like the idea of doing it all. If you are in a first-time position as a director of planned giving with an institution eager to start a planned giving program, then you have come to the right place. If you are a veteran financial planner or attorney who has just crossed over from the "dark side" into the nonprofit world, you will also find much help in this book. For you, the culture of a nonprofit organization will be a shock that may put you into therapy if you do not have this book. Actually, the commercial professionals should read all of Part I before doing anything else. The six chapters here will keep you from blowing up in the first two months regardless of how much expertise you have in charitable giving tax law or estate planning. Trust me on this.

The Preparation Stage has six chapters, each of which builds on the one before. Read them in sequence to get the most benefit from them. If you do not have a planned giving program yet, you should read all of Part I before you do anything else. Otherwise, you cannot possibly understand the full scope of what you are about to do, where you can get into trouble, or how to deal with the wide variety of tasks you must juggle simultaneously.

Chapter I-1
If You Do Not Have A Planned Giving Program

The first step in creating a planned giving program is to hire a full-time Director of Planned Giving. That may seem impossible to some institutions and to some harried Directors of Development reading this book. But, it may not be as far out of reach as you think. You might as well read the short chapter and give it your best shot. If you really want to start a planned giving program, get a person on board who will be responsible for doing it.

Chapter I-2
The Role Of The Board Of Trustees

Some of the difficulties you may face or obstacles you may encounter in getting your planned giving program up and running stem from a lack of Board involvement or commitment. You may already know this. In this chapter, I discuss issues and concerns in relation to the Board and suggest some ways to deal with them. If you can get the Board to be active in the development of your planned giving program, you will be much more successful.

Chapter I-3
Do You Need A Fund Raising Or Planned Giving Consultant?

There are many times in the life of a charity when a consultant is brought in. When you are trying to create a new fund raising program, especially one as complex as planned giving, you may benefit from using a consultant to work with the Board. In addition, there are many ways a consultant can assist the Director of Planned Giving.

Chapter I-4
Developing A Master Plan

Getting yourself ready for the year ahead involves organization and vision. If you don't inherit someone else's master plan when you take your position as Director of Planned Giving, you must create one. The master plan includes the detail of your operational objectives, setting dollar and other goals, developing a budget, and laying out a 12-month calendar of activities. The process described in this chapter assumes you are starting from scratch.

Chapter I-5
How To Identify Planned Giving Prospects

If you are starting a planned giving program, chances are the organization is also new to major gift fund raising. Therefore, you need to develop a healthy set of prospects as you move through your first 12 months. This chapter discusses the process for identifying prospects for major gift potential. They may be prospects for major outright gifts or for deferred gifts. The most important thing is to identify a pool of individuals and focus your strategic efforts on them.

Chapter I-6
Selecting Legal Counsel

This chapter is a short one, but it is a very important one. All too often, when small organizations start a planned giving program, they use a board member for legal advice. That practice does not work and it places both the charity and the board member in a vulnerable legal position. This chapter discusses why you need to hire your own outside legal counsel for planned giving. It also covers the considerations for choosing the perfect one for your unique planned giving program.

Good luck as you undertake this wonderful profession we call planned giving.

Chapter I-1

IF YOU DO NOT HAVE A PLANNED GIVING PROGRAM

Fund raising in the new millennium is extremely competitive. And, it will only get worse as each organization launches larger and larger campaigns than ever before. You listen to reports of other organizations' success stories until you are sick to death about how you will ever compete. The good news is that the success you desire is within your reach. But, you must start today.

The large gifts you long to experience for your own institution didn't just happen by accident. They have been made possible by a person just like you. It's true. At every peer institution whose planned giving totals make you jealous, someone said, "We need planned giving." Someone took a stand, possibly risking ridicule or dissension. Someone knew that by putting in place a program to attract tax-related gifts, the donors would respond. Fortunately for you, enough history has passed so that the leap of faith your peers took ten or twenty years ago need not be a leap of faith for you. This is real. The success of planned giving programs across this country has been proven time and time again by thousands of institutions throughout the United States. The success in the United States has been so convincing that Canada, England, Australia, and others are now promoting planned giving. There is no excuse any longer to exist without a full, comprehensive planned giving program. That is the reality of fund raising today. If you are not prepared to take this message very seriously for your current organization, you might as well quit your job and find another job at an organization that already has planned giving. Otherwise, you will be frustrated and unhappy.

Most institutions reporting high totals in planned giving have been promoting planned gifts for a long, long time. But, take heart. Many of the people on your long list of major prospects probably know about planned giving already. *They are being educated by scores of other nonprofit institutions, banks, brokerage firms, and financial professionals. Your immediate challenge is to make a commitment to start a planned giving program, even if you can only start with baby steps for now.*

As executive director, president, or director of development of a nonprofit institution, you are surely feeling pressure to increase the sophistication and effectiveness of your fund raising activities. The goal of starting a planned giving program has probably been on your mind for a long time.

Since every organization is different, it is up to you, with the help of this book, to assess how much planned giving you can manage. Most important is to start today.

The first thing you need to know is that you don't need to be a director of planned giving to get planned gifts. It would probably be more comfortable for you to think so because you will have an excuse not to perform to higher expectations. However, if you can open your mind to some of the strategies in this book, you will accomplish great things for your organization.

For example, let's consider one of the major areas of planned giving—bequests. You can easily encourage donors to provide for your institution in their estate plans. Yes, you can do this. In fact, any member of the fund raising staff can do this.

If you are the Executive Director, President, or Director of Development, all you need to promote bequests is the appropriate wording for a bequest to your organization. (See Chapter II-10 on bequests.)

Or, you can visit one prospect per month toward securing a major outright or deferred gift. With this book, you can do a tremendous amount of planned giving. Or, perhaps you would be happy with four or five gifts of $10,000 to $25,000 in the next year. That, too, you can have if you follow the advice in this book. Or, you may be somewhere in the middle—recognizing the need to expand to the next level of activity but not quite able to hire a full-time director of planned giving. I've provided some guidance in Chapter III–6 on how to make the most of limited resources.

The truth is this: You can incorporate planned giving into many aspects of your program without a full-time Director of Planned Giving. But, let's be realistic. In spite of your best intentions, fund raising is a full-time job. Think for a moment about the steps necessary to solicit just one gift.

Step 1:   You retrieve the prospect's correspondence file in order to review the prospect's gift history and past involvement with your organization.

Step 2:   You read everything in the file.

Step 3:   You discuss the prospect with one or two of your colleagues.

Step 4:   If you have a researcher, you request additional research on the prospect.

Step 5:   You review the research and try to determine the best approach.

Step 6:   You identify the best person to help you solicit the prospect.

Step 7:   You call or write to this potential volunteer asking for help to solicit the prospect. Perhaps you meet with the volunteer to plan a strategy.

Step 8:   One of you contacts the prospect to arrange a meeting. This involves a conversation with the volunteer and possibly a lead letter that you ghost write for the volunteer's signature.

Step 9:   Assuming you get a meeting, you drive to the prospect's office or home. Perhaps you also pick up the volunteer in your car on the way.

Step 10: You meet with the prospect for 1-2 hours. You drive the volunteer back to his home or office and drive yourself back to yours.

Step 11: You send a thank-you note to the volunteer, a follow-up letter to the prospect, and you write a contact report for the visit.

Step 12: Perhaps the prospect is thinking it over. You wait a couple of weeks and telephone the volunteer to discuss follow-up plans. Maybe you invite the prospect to meet you for lunch at your institution to continue the discussion.

Step 13: Before the prospect arrives, you discuss the situation with several people.

Step 14: The day the prospect is coming, you review the file again to make certain you don't forget something. You call the volunteer to discuss the day's strategy.

Step 15: You spend 1-2 hours with the prospect discussing the potential gift.

Step 16: After the prospect leaves, you do another contact report, another letter to the prospect, and discuss the situation with your colleagues.

Step 17: If the prospect has still not made a commitment, you mark your calendar to follow up at an appropriate interval, with more steps, more discussion at prospect meetings, or other action.

Step 18: The prospect makes the gift. (You hope.)

By the time you finally get the gift, you have spent the equivalent of two to three days or more on this solicitation. And, this is just one gift! Now what? This is when long-term cultivation begins. Do you really have the time to maintain regular contact with this donor, to keep him or her up to date on your organization's activities, to plan a stewardship visit in three to six months just to chat? With all of your other responsibilities, exactly how are you going to ensure that this donor will want to contribute again? What if you have five of these, or ten? Within a few months, you will have a major problem.

Don't be discouraged. Any amount of major gift activity is better than none. But, this entire process is extremely time consuming. Sooner or later, you will reach a stage of frustration indicated by one or more of the following problems:

- The solicitations you planned six months ago are still on your "to do" list;

- Several donors are in different stages of cultivation, but you cannot find the time to go see them;

- You have had no personal contact in over 12 months with the donors who contributed last year;

- You still don't have a bequest program;

- Your regular work is backed up;

- You have made several false starts toward developing a gift proposal for a major prospect, but it remains incomplete;

- You have neglected following up some proposals for so long it is now embarrassing for you to call;

- Every day you think about the people you should be visiting, but you can't seem to find the time.

There is nothing wrong with you. Your inability to sustain a healthy level of prospect activity stems in large measure from one basic problem: planned giving is a full-time job. And, after a year or more of false starts and good intentions, you'll probably decide you need a full-time director of planned giving. But, much time will have been wasted.

If you are the executive director, president, or director of development, the above situation may be all too real for you. So now what?

You bought this book because you want to know how to run a planned giving program. So here's what you need to know: a proper program deserves a full-time director of planned giving *and* a full-time secretary dedicated solely to planned giving. Providing a secretary for the director is not an idle suggestion. A secretary is more important for the director of planned giving than for almost any other professional position in the department. Most other fund raising support positions are interchangeable. I don't mean to diminish the skills required for processing annual gifts or in supporting the work of the corporate or foundation solicitors. But, when it comes to running a planned giving program, you need a separate person who can become familiar with the terminology, the different gift vehicles, and the specialized planned giving software in order to provide assistance to donors or prospects when the director is out of the office. The administrative and stewardship factors in planned giving cannot be underestimated. When people make deferred gifts, there are administration considerations that do not exist for other fund raising programs.

The best use of your time in the immediate future is in gaining approval from the board to hire both a director of planned giving and a secretary to the director. Then, allow the director to create the program.

At this early stage, you should not concern yourself with questions relating to the type of gifts your institution should or should not solicit. Those questions will be answered with the help of the director of planned giving.

You need to convince the board that there is a need for two new staff members and a budget sufficient to support their efforts. How are you going to do this and how long will it take? Practically, a charity's budget is set several months before the beginning of the fiscal year. Although some charities provide for a "reserve fund" for unexpected initiatives, most charities cannot find new money for expanding development efforts within the middle of a fiscal year. Therefore, efforts to hire new staff and provide a budget for activities ordinarily will focus on the next fiscal year. That may seem like forever to you, but in the life of the organization, it is a very short time.

Here are some steps that might be effective in moving the board forward toward supporting a planned giving program for your institution. All of this takes time, so be patient.

Step 1: Review the list of board members to locate the following information: What college or university did they attend? On what other boards do they serve as trustees, and especially as campaign volunteers. In nearly every case, your board members have affiliations with other charitable institutions that have planned giving programs and/or capital campaigns in which planned giving is an integral part.

Step 2: Pick three or four who are well connected and set up a meeting one by one. If some are not geographically close, contact them by phone. Explain that you are interested in moving the institution's development efforts into the planned giving area and discuss the board member's knowledge of and participation in the planned giving program of his or her college, or of other organizations with which he or she has an affiliation. Ask the board member if he or she would be supportive of moving your institution into planned giving. Some will probably express latent opinions like "we should have done this a long time ago."

Ask if he or she could get copies of the planned giving or campaign materials from his or her other charities. Ideally, it would be great to get enough copies of brochures so that you could compile for your next board meeting complete packets of sample planned giving brochures from three or four other institutions, all of which are connections to your board members. That may not be practical given the large number of board members you may have. However, perhaps it would be possible to get at least 10 copies of such materials.

Step 3: Include the chairman of the board in the kind of discussion described above. The chairman's support of the effort is critical. Since the board usually meets quarterly, discuss the possibility of saving one of the upcoming board meetings for a discussion of planned giving.

Step 4: Building advocacy for the planned giving program among a limited group of board members is your goal to start. To do this, you can involve them in the process by asking them to play a role in gathering data. For example, make up a list of questions for your board members to discuss with either the director of development or with someone else at his or her college or another charity with which he or she has involvement. Questions to be asked include:

- salary for the director (there may be more planned giving staff, but deal with these two positions);
- salary for the secretary;
- legal fees;
- printing;
- postage;
- travel and entertainment;
- telephone;
- consultant, if necessary;
- planned giving software;
- how long has there been a planned giving program;
- what percentage of the institution's total support comes from planned gifts;

- how has the planned giving program affected annual giving;
- what role do bequests play;
- how has the board been involved;
- how long did it take to see results;
- what is the role of life income gifts.

No doubt, other questions will come to mind. Create your own survey questions including any that would be unique for your type of organization.

Step 5: Compile the comparison data first with the chairman of the board. What conclusions can be drawn from the data and how can the experience of others be applied to your institution?

Step 6: Once the chairman is comfortable with the report, ask him to write a letter to the board members to raise the issue of starting a planned giving program. Along with this letter, the members should receive a copy of the report of comparison data for review in advance of the next regularly scheduled board meeting.

Step 7: At the board meeting, the chairman should take the lead and make some introductory remarks about the importance of planned giving to the future strength of the institution. Then, he or she will introduce the three or four other board members who helped gather the data so that they can provide summary remarks about their conversations with other charities.

The board must achieve several objectives during this meeting:

- Approve the establishment of a planned giving program;

- Approve the hiring of a director of planned giving and approve a salary range for the director;

- Approve the hiring of a secretary to the director and approve a salary range for the secretary;

- Appropriate additional funds for operating expenses of the program;

- Resolve to support the program as it develops and matures, including full involvement in solicitation activities and in financial support;

- Resolve to oversee and monitor the progress of the program.

During this meeting, you may encounter some or all of the following objections. It will be a good idea to review with the chairman in advance the possible objections and your response to them.

1. "Why do we need another fund raising position?"

   We can no longer exist year to year on the income from our annual giving operation. The competition demands that we expand the scope of our development program in order to be able to attract larger, more complex gifts that will strengthen our future.

2. "Why can't the executive director (director of development) do planned giving?"

   A proper planned giving program cannot be run on a part-time basis. In order to generate the kind of commitments that this organization deserves, we need someone who can spend at least 50% of the time out of the office visiting prospects. We need someone who is proficient and competent at discussing specialized, tax-related gifts.

3. "I don't have time to do fund raising. And, I've never been comfortable with it."

The board must lead the way as both an example and as an inspiration for others. Initially, we'll be asking everyone to review or screen a list of names so that we can learn about current connections. Next, we'll create a Development Committee consisting of a smaller group of board members. Each of you can play a role at whatever level makes sense.

4. "We don't know anything about planned giving. How can you expect us to help?"

Of course you don't know anything now. Even I know relatively little about planned giving. But, once the director is in place, we will organize training sessions, and perhaps bring in a consultant to help educate you about planned giving. None of you needs to be a tax expert. You simply must understand some basic concepts.

5. "I can't ask for money. You never told me I'd have to do this when I joined the board."

Before saying no, give us a chance to work with you a little. Even the most experienced fund raisers feel anxious about a solicitation. With help from the development office and with the proper support, most of you can be effective advocates for this institution. Keep in mind that you don't have to do this alone. Once you begin to work with an experienced professional, you'll probably find yourself enjoying both the challenge and the satisfaction of really making a difference for this institution. All of us have an obligation to do the very best we can to ensure that the good work of this institution continues.

6. "We can't afford two new full-time staff members."

Up until now, our institution has survived primarily on a cash basis. We rarely develop new programs because there is no money. Our buildings need renovation. If we have to borrow money from endowment to get this program started, we should do so. Unless we bring this institution into a league with our peers, we'll be hard pressed to continue the quality of our programs. The money we invest in these two new staff members will be returned ten fold. But, we must start now.

7. "Let's just hire a director of planned giving and forego the secretary for now. We don't have any space to put them anyway."

We'll find the space. And that's not the point. To attract the kind of experienced professional who'll have the skills to do what we want, we must provide support staff. Without proper support staff, the director cannot run an effective program. No seasoned professional will take this kind of position without support staff. We want the best person for this job, and this is what it will take.

8. "Why can't we just hire a consultant?"

At some point, we may want to hire a consultant—in addition to hiring a director of planned giving. But, a consultant cannot provide the continuity we need with our donors. The consultant is not an employee of this institution and cannot possibly serve our needs over the long term. And, how long can we continue with just a consultant? I'd rather get the director in place, then, if necessary, retain a consultant for a limited period of time to work with the director and with the board.

If you push hard enough and if the chairman supports your plan, you may grudgingly get approval for your director of planned giving and secretary. You may still find less enthusiasm than you would like (and possibly resistance) with regard to the board's involvement. Another strategy which you can employ at this stage is hiring a planned giving consultant to work with you and to help you secure the commitment of the board. Refer to Chapter I–3 for a discussion about consultants.

SUMMARY

By appropriating the money to hire your new director of planned giving (and by giving that position a full-time secretary), you are well on your way to success. Much work lies ahead, but you should congratulate yourself for accomplishing your primary objective.

Beginning with the next chapter, I will be speaking to the director of planned giving—the person you have just hired. However, this is a book for you, too. Far too many executive directors and other administrators hire a director of planned giving without fully realizing the kinds of activities that will be forthcoming. The director needs full rein to do what has to be done. This includes integrating planned giving with other fund raising activities. This includes working with the board. And, all of the activities discussed in this book require support from you. Otherwise, the results you hope to achieve will never materialize.

Some of the sections that follow are technical and will be most helpful to the director of planned giving. Other chapters outline concepts in fund raising that are essential to the success of any fund raising program. You can gain valuable insight into some of the tricks of the trade by reading this book. You don't need to be a director of planned giving to understand that position's scope.

You can also use it to determine whether the ideas and plans of your director of planned giving have merit. One thing is true. When your director of planned giving enters the office on the very first day, a primary concern will be board commitment. The next chapter explains exactly how important its role will be.

Chapter I–2

THE ROLE OF THE BOARD OF TRUSTEES

You are the person hired as a result of the board meeting in the preceding chapter. Or, perhaps you are someone from the inside who has been chosen to take on planned giving. WELCOME! The executive director, president, or director of development has high hopes for you. Sitting down to make a plan for your program is a daunting task. Where do you even begin? Let's start by reviewing the involvement of the Board of Trustees.

Volumes have been written about Boards. For additional reading, there are books listed in the Bibliography to help you or to help them. Admittedly, I have not read any books about Boards, but, from the experience I've had in four different institutions, I can tell you several things about Boards:

- The board is a volunteer group. Thus, the time each member spends on your organization's matters is in addition to his or her other professional and family obligations. Conduct your business with the board efficiently and professionally. Don't waste its time.

- The board is comprised of individuals with varying degrees of fund raising knowledge or experience. Often, members of the board have never been asked to do fund raising. Even more shocking, many members of a board are not contributors themselves and have not been solicited on an annual basis. Hard to believe, but true.

- Some members of a board do nothing but lend their names to the organization on whose board they sit. There could be two reasons for this. First, they were asked to be on the board because their names add prestige, and there was never an expectation that they would be active. Everyone understands and accepts their inactive status. Second, *they have never been asked*.

- Don't assume even the most sophisticated board members know about planned giving. Few do. Fortunately, with the explosion of planned giving in the last ten years, board members with multiple board positions are hearing about planned giving from their other affiliations. This can help you.

- Don't assume the board members will be willing to accept you, work with you, or deem you credible. Many have been on the board for a long time, have relationships with the president or other high-ranking staff members. Their limited involvement is now threatened by your arrival. Unless you are a very seasoned and experienced planned giving professional, you may not be taken seriously. Even if you are a seasoned and experienced planned giving professional, you may not be taken seriously.

Notwithstanding the reality of daily frustration many organizations experience with their boards, there is also good news. In many organizations, the expectations of a board are beginning to shift. Greater expectations for involvement, peer pressure, and more demanding nominating committees are starting to make a difference. Here are some of the positive things that can result when the Board does its job.

- Adequate funds are allocated to the Development Office, including the planned giving program;

- Board members endorse the planned giving program publicly;

- Board members set an example for others by making leadership gifts;

- Board members assume prospect assignments and actually solicit gifts;

- The Board takes responsibility and ownership of fund raising goals, including planned giving.

The impact of a Board on the fund raising success for both large and small organizations cannot be underestimated. When lackluster results are reported from the planned giving office, complaints like the following are all too common:

- "I have no secretary."
- "I'm too busy working on the Annual Report."
- "I have no budget for legal expenses."
- "I was told we need spendable money now."
- "The campaign doesn't count deferred gifts."

But, regardless of the many reasons for failure—inadequate staffing, inadequate budget, or simply that the organization has "other priorities" this year—the real root of the problem is the lack of board commitment. Vision must start at the top.

If you have been hired to do planned giving, you must be ready to accept unexpected changes in your duties because, all too often, the priorities of the development office become blurred over time. For example, you may have a secretary today; tomorrow, your secretary may be working for someone else, too. You may have a mandate to build the bequest program today; tomorrow, you will be told that you need to focus only on current gifts because bequest intentions don't pay the bills.

When financial problems arise in other areas of the institution, most often it is the planned giving program that gets cut. To minimize the likelihood that your program will disintegrate before your eyes, your work with the board in the first year must be well planned and well executed.

Within your first month on the job, you must determine whether or not the board is available, ready, and accessible to assist you in planned giving. If not, you must take some strategic steps to try to correct the situation.

Your board should be the most visible and influential body of your organization. Its priorities are reflected at every stage of management. Thus, some of the most basic needs for the success of your program may be insurmountable goals—depending on whether or not your board truly understands the importance of planned giving.

For small, start-up programs, unless you have total commitment from the Board, your planned giving program will limp along for years and most likely die before it has ever been given a chance. Still, you will find examples of fairly successful planned giving programs that operate with little or no board involvement; however, closer examination would probably reveal many of the difficulties discussed here. Further, these organizations will never experience the full impact of a program run properly. Thus, they live in perpetual ignorance, complacency, or frustration.

If you run a planned giving program that does not have full board involvement and commitment, you'll find yourself complaining about the following:

- **Inadequate resources**

    Your organization pays for your salary but will not pay for the full-time secretary who is essential if you are to spend the majority of your time out of the office visiting donors. You have no money for brochures and, worse, you are not allowed to hire professional tax counsel. Instead, someone on the board volunteers time to provide legal advice, but is only intermittently available and may not have the proper expertise to support your efforts fully. Or, you are forced to use your general in-house counsel for planned giving questions, a situation that is sorely inadequate.

- **No system support**

  The record keeping for the planned giving program is a patchwork system that is never quite right.

- **Low expectations**

  At your organization, $10,000 is considered a large gift.

- **Little or no volunteer involvement**

  You make all of the solicitations yourself.

- **Limited access to the top prospects**

  The biggest prospects are off limits to you even though gifts from the largest prospects may need to include an element of planned giving.

- **Few gifts**

  It should come as no surprise that you enter each performance review with a list of many goals you planned to achieve, but very few you actually did. There is a big knot in your stomach all the time.

Your resources must be brought to bear to convert a doubtful, disinterested, or ineffective board into becoming the proper advocacy group for your planned giving program. Otherwise, your life as a planned giving officer will produce nothing more than frustration, resentment, poor self-image, and, finally, escape to greener pastures.

Not all planned giving programs have the same problems. Some may actually have adequate funds for support staff, brochures, and legal fees, but may not have the financial support or volunteer time of the board. Others may have full or partial board involvement but inadequate resources for cultivation events, computer support, or travel. Small organizations struggling to get going need to understand that few planned giving programs have everything they need. But, one thing is still true. With the board on your side, you'll have as much as is reasonably possible under the circumstances.

Before you can plan a strategy to secure the involvement of the board, you must first assess where you fit into the larger picture. As I mentioned in the Introduction, for purposes of consistency, my ideal reader is the director of planned giving. In this position, you may be far removed from the policy-making rung of your organization's management ladder. As director of planned giving, you don't automatically have direct access to the board. There are layers to go through and that's not necessarily inappropriate. The pyramid structure works because someone needs to control the information getting to the board. Such a situation can be frustrating, but that's the way it is. As you demonstrate your competence, you will get access to and gain the trust of the board members over time.

Consequently, you cannot, by yourself, initiate a strategy to involve the board. You must work through the proper channels from the bottom up. This starts with your boss, let's say the Director of Development.

Your boss wants to do a good job but is a very busy person. He or she may understand fully the necessity of involving the board, but, unfortunately, has little time to think about or to plan the steps necessary to accomplish this objective. Perhaps it is already clear from prior dealings with the board that involving the members in fund raising will be difficult. Or, perhaps your boss, like the board members themselves, is also one of the problems. That would be very unfortunate for you, but it happens.

Let's assume your organizational chart looks like this:

Chairman of the Board
President or Executive Director
Director of Development or Vice President for Development
Director of Planned Giving (you).

In the above structure, the Director of Development is critical. Frequently, the position of Director of Development is not as powerful a position as it should be. As a result, you may be blocked from effectively working through to the higher levels. Early on, you must have a conversation with the Director of Development to evaluate your situation. (*If you are reading this book prior to taking a planned giving position, you can discuss some of these issues during your interviews.*)

You may encounter the following responses:

- "You know I cannot ask for more money for the planned giving program now. You'll have to get along with what you have."

- "You know we cannot afford a full-time secretary for you. Everyone else shares a secretary; why can't you?"

- "Our Board has never been asked to do fund raising. The President will never agree to this."

- "There are some major issues in front of the Board right now. Planned giving will have to wait its turn."

One must assume that if the above statements come from the Director of Development, there is little hope for you. This is the one person who could have and should have helped you.

In the prior chapter, I discussed the usefulness of having select board members conduct a planned giving survey to gather comparison data on other planned giving programs as part of the strategy that got you hired in the first place. When you realize your biggest obstacle is the Director of Development, you may find it necessary to use the same strategy now. If so, you have an up-hill battle all the way.

HOW TO WIN THE SUPPORT OF YOUR BOARD OF TRUSTEES FOR YOUR PLANNED GIVING PROGRAM

Here are suggested steps to recruit the support and commitment of your Board of Trustees:

- Conduct a planned giving survey;
- Increase your technical knowledge about planned giving;
- Develop a list of leadership prospects;
- Write or acquire appropriate sales materials;
- Establish reasonable goals and objectives;
- Hire a consultant;
- Run a planned giving seminar for the Board.

Conduct A Planned Giving Survey

The best place to start is to survey other planned giving officers to find out how they run their programs. This may be the same strategy that your boss used with the board to get you hired. But *your* survey as the planned giving officer will provide much greater detail about the actual gift options, crediting guidelines, and other policy issues. You should select a diverse group, making certain to include one or two from organizations whose service is similar to yours. If you don't know any planned giving officers, you can probably find some by contacting the development office of local hospitals; colleges, universities, or private schools; cultural organizations like museums or symphonies; historical societies; or nature and conservation organizations. Also, many cities have local planned giving chapters. If you are interested in locating the planned giving chapter nearest you, go to the home page of the National Committee on Planned Giving at www.ncpg.org where you will find links to local planned giving council information. It should be easy to find, but don't hesitate to call NCPG directly if you need help (317-269-6274).

Don't rely on a phone conversation to accomplish this important work unless you have to. I have been called in the past by other development professionals seeking information on the history of my planned giving program. Although I am interested in speaking with them and will share any information I think will help them, there is often no structure to the conversation. In addition, I am usually caught in the middle of a project; therefore, it is hard for me to be as helpful as I would like to be. At the very least, if you find it necessary to conduct telephone surveys, be very organized, have a list of your questions on a form, schedule a telephone appointment in advance, and don't stray far from your list of questions.

You will receive better information if you talk to your colleague out of the office. I would suggest meeting separately with a minimum of seven to ten people (yes, this many) in order to secure good comparative data to bring back to your Board. Always offer to mail a copy of your report to the people who have helped you.

The survey provided at the end of this chapter will help you. If you had either my first edition or my second edition, you'll notice that I have condensed the survey quite a bit from four pages to two because I think the last two versions were a bit overkill. I hope the new one is easier to use.

If necessary, mail this survey to colleagues, but first try to arrange a personal visit. There is a very real value to speaking with individuals in person. Planned giving is not an exact science, and unless you speak with your colleagues in person, you'll miss the chance to ask questions or to clarify some of the less precise aspects of their answers. In addition, although I created the survey myself, I would probably be hard pressed to find the time to complete it myself. Over the years, I have received surveys in the mail from people seeking comparison data. I usually flip through the questions, evaluate how long it would take to complete the survey (frequently, two hours or more), then put it in a pile of "things to do," with every intention of getting back to it. I don't think I have ever completed one of these because the information is not readily available.

Hopefully, you will begin to see some of the possible variations in running a planned giving program simply by reading through the survey questions.

Your interviews with other planned giving officers will generate benefits for you in two ways. First, you will be able to produce a comprehensive report with comparison data. Second, you will gain valuable information from the experience of others, and, one hopes, run a more successful program of your own.

Although each organization is different, the results of your research and interviews will probably lead to some general conclusions like:

- The most successful programs have involvement of the Board;

- In order to conduct the number of personal visits and solicitations required for a successful program, you must have a full-time secretary;

- Gift crediting policies are necessary to maintain fairness and consistency for recognition and campaign crediting;

- Guidelines for acceptance, administration, and investment of planned gifts are extremely important to the performance of the planned giving assets;

- Integrating planned giving into other fund raising activities (annual giving or campaign) will both increase the visibility of the program and enhance the chances for success for all fund raising efforts.

- Retaining independent legal counsel is vital to the integrity of the planned giving program.

- A planned giving consultant can provide objective guidance and advice for an organization seeking to begin or to enhance a planned giving program. A consultant is especially important to a program that needs to mobilize an inactive board.

- Planned giving programs are most successful when the director has access to the leadership (board, trustees, president, principal gifts prospects).

Increase Your Technical Knowledge About Planned Giving

You do not have to become the ultimate tax expert to be successful at planned giving. But, you need a working knowledge of both the tax laws that affect charitable giving and the practical administrative implications of the gift vehicles you intend to offer. You cannot be an effective director of planned giving unless you have mastered the subject. This is your responsibility. This is your job.

There are two ways you can increase your expertise about the subject. First, you can attend any of the dozens of planned giving seminars offered by consultants and fund raising groups nation wide. Many of the consultants listed in Appendix IV run seminars for professionals and will be happy to send you a list of their forthcoming offerings.

Try to attend at least one planned giving seminar each year. Even if you think you know as much about planned giving as you care to, you will always benefit from talking with others who do what you do. Attending seminars and professional conferences is not a luxury; it is part of your job. In addition to learning new techniques and strategies, you can share your successes and frustrations with others who have, no doubt, experienced the same.

Many of you reading this section will surely say, "But, I can't get the money for a seminar. There's just no way my organization can afford it." Or, your organization may have a policy of sending only one person from each department to regional seminars or conferences. Following are a few ideas to get yourself to a seminar this year:

1. **Add the cost of the seminar (including transportation, lodging, and meals) to your planned giving budget for the next year.**

   Newcomers to the business may not think of doing this, but it is an effective way to fund your educational objectives. Let's say, for example, you have $15,000 to spend on planned giving activities this year. Carve out a slice to pay for your conference before allocating the balance to programs, mailings, events, or other activities. Hopefully, you can be creative enough with the rest of your budget to make up for the funds you allocated to your own professional development. (*Remember, this is not a frivolous activity.*)

2. **Get yourself on the program.**

   By doing so, you will usually be allowed to attend the entire conference for free and your travel and hotel fees may be covered by the conference organizers. How does one get oneself recruited as a speaker? First, call the conference organizers and offer a compelling topic for consideration. Most organizers of conferences are eager to find new talent and would welcome your initiative. Second, ask a friend to recommend you as a speaker.

3. **Apply for a scholarship.**

   Many local and national fund raising groups offer scholarships for annual membership or for attending conferences. I have been successful at getting three staff members (including a work-study student) into planned giving workshops or conferences by submitting a scholarship proposal. I did this while working at Wheaton College and also at Boston University.

4. **Plan your prospect visits to a particular city around a conference.**

   Even if you must pay for the full conference registration fee plus air fare and hotel expenses, see if you can combine the trip to a conference with a few days of visiting prospects or donors.

The second way to build your knowledge is to read everything you can get your hands on. This sounds easy, but, unless you schedule time to do this each week, you'll never get to it. Setting aside quiet time for reading is one of the hardest things to do when so many pressures fill your day. Nonetheless, to be the best at what you do you must continue educating yourself about planned giving. Often you will read the same article or chapter of a book more than once before fully understanding the material. Just remember that everyone enters this business with a different set of experiences. There will always be people who know more than you do and others who know less. Some excellent resources are listed in the Bibliography. If you cannot find the time during the day, bring the material home.

Develop A List Of Leadership Prospects

Your board will be more receptive to helping you if you develop a list of prospects who can be approached in the coming year. Give them something to do! And, don't forget that many Board members *are* leadership prospects. Refer to Chapter I–5 for a more complete discussion of how to identify prospects.

Write Or Acquire Appropriate Sales Materials

Board members depend on you to provide clear and concise planned giving materials for use on solicitations. It is natural for board members to feel awkward or uncertain when it comes to soliciting others in such a complicated field as planned giving. You will help them overcome their fears—being asked a question they cannot answer, uncertainty about the exact tax consequences of the proposed gift, inability to state the case effectively—by producing or acquiring planned giving materials. Chapter III–1 guides you through a discussion of print materials—what you need and what you don't need.

Establish Goals And Objectives

Planned gifts aren't going to materialize without a plan. You must develop a plan that includes dollar goals and calendar deadlines for each phase of the program. Chapter I–4 provides guidance and gives you the tools you'll need to structure the next 12 months of work.

Hire A Consultant

You may need some outside help when it comes to asking the board to 1) contribute to the program, and 2) make solicitations on behalf of your organization. Many board members have simply not been involved in fund raising before. They will be afraid, unsure, perhaps even angry when they are asked to help with solicitations. This is where a consultant can make a difference. See Chapter I–3 for a discussion of the proper role of the planned giving consultant.

Run A Planned Giving Seminar For Your Board Of Trustees

Many organizations wishing to educate a Board of Trustees bring in an outside consultant for a Planned Giving Seminar. That might seem unnecessary to you when you are capable of running such a workshop yourself. Still, the impact will be greater if the same information is given by a person not connected to the organization. Many of the consultants listed in Appendix IV hold seminars tailored to the special needs and concerns of a Board of Trustees. Such a session can be enormously helpful and can help bring your board to a new level of understanding, commitment, and confidence.

MAKING YOUR PRESENTATION TO THE BOARD

Surely there has been a good deal of excitement as a result of your arrival. The Board and many of your other colleagues will be keenly interested in your master plan. Assuming you have read the appropriate chapters that relate to getting the Board involved, you should be able to produce the following documents for use during a board presentation:

- a comparison report summarizing the results of your planned giving survey;
- a document outlining your dollar goals and program objectives;
- a calendar of activities for the next 12 months;
- an itemized budget;
- a set of recommendations for gift crediting guidelines;
- a set of recommendations for the gift vehicles you would like to offer.

At this important Board meeting, the Board members see for the first time exactly how the program will unfold. They can compare the figures of other planned giving programs to yours and will be better able to understand why you are recommending certain things. Most important, the board should recognize its role in the master plan. This will become clear from the integration of your solicitation plans in the 12-month calendar of activities.

Other agenda items can also be included in this meeting. One is the selection of legal counsel which is discussed in Chapter I–6. Another relates to the advisability of establishing a pooled income fund or a gift annuity program. These two gift vehicles are described in Part II.

At this early stage, it is probably too soon to begin speaking about solicitation assignments which must be undertaken by the board. Nonetheless, introducing the fund raising plan now is critical.

You do not need a brochure at this early stage. It is not possible for you to create a brochure without first knowing which gift vehicles are appropriate for your institution. When you are ready to think about print materials, turn to Chapter III–1.

SUMMARY

I cannot impress upon you how important the Board is to your program. That being said, you may not be in a supportive environment, and some of the above suggestions will appear impossible. Don't give up. Turning around even a few of the best board members will make a difference. It is surely true that people want to be associated with a winning program. Show them how important planned giving will be. In the unlikely event you cannot, by yourself, for whatever reason, get the board involved, you can still run a good planned giving program. However, the day you are offered a job as director of planned giving for a program that does have board involvement, take it.

The next chapter discusses the planned giving consultant. If you do not need a consultant now, you can skip to Chapter I–4 to learn how to develop objectives, goals, and a budget.

PLANNED GIVING SURVEY

Name of organization _____

Address_____

Director of Planned Giving _____ Phone number _____

Year organization was established _____ Size of constituency (if known) _____

Number/percent contributing annual gift _____ Annual Giving dollars last year _____

Size of endowment _____ Number of board members _____

1. In what year did you first have a full-time director of planned giving?

2. How many paid staff are currently devoted to planned giving (including support staff)?

   List their titles _____

   _____

   _____

3. Does the budget for your planned giving program come from:

   _____ Operating budget
   _____ Matching challenge grant
   _____ Campaign budget
   _____ Endowment income
   _____ Other? _____

4. Who have you used as a planned giving consultant? _____

   Tasks performed by the consultant _____

   _____

   Would you recommend this consultant?   _____ yes   _____ no

5. How has your board of trustees participated in your planned giving program?

   _____ Endorsed the program
   _____ Appropriated budget funds for the planned giving program
   _____ Contributed financially   _____ all   _____ most   _____ few
   _____ Taken on prospect assignments   _____ all   _____ most   _____ few
   _____ Actively monitors the planned giving program
   _____ Not actively involved
   _____ Other? _____

6. What is your planned giving budget excluding salaries?

   Does this amount include: _____ Occupancy   _____ Overhead   _____ General Supplies

   (Optional) Is your salary _____ $35,000 or under _____ $35,000 to $49,999 _____ $50,000 to $64,999

   _____ $65,000 to $79,999 _____ $80,000 to $94,999 _____ $95,000 or over

7. How much do you pay annually for professional tax counsel to advise the program? _____

   How are the fees paid? _____ PG Program Budget _____ Business Office _____ Campaign Budget

8. Are you offering the following kinds of gifts?

	Current Dollars	Managed in-house (Y/N)	Minimum Gift	Fees Paid From Gift Assets (Y/N)
Charitable Gift Annuities	_____	_____	_____	_____
Pooled Income Fund(s)	_____	_____	_____	_____
Charitable Remainder Trusts	_____	_____	_____	_____
Charitable Lead Trusts	_____	_____	_____	_____
Revocable Trusts	_____	_____	_____	_____

9. Do you have a deferred, planned giving, or bequest society? _____ yes _____ no

   What benefits do you provide for the members? _____

   _____

   _____

   Do you include all deferred gifts (life income plans, bequests, *etc.*) _____ yes _____ no

10. If you are in a campaign, what is the goal? _____

    Do life income plans count _____ at face value _____ at remainder value _____ both _____ don't count

    What portion of the goal do you expect from deferred gifts? _____

    Do you allow campaign credit for bequests? _____ yes _____ no

    Describe crediting rules for bequests: _____

    _____

    _____

11. Do you have a planned giving committee? _____ yes _____ no

12. What planned giving software do you use?

13. Planned giving is _____ a service to other staff _____ a program with its own assigned prospects

    _____ both a service department and has its own prospects

14. What is the total dollars received from life income plans, lead trust payments, life insurance gifts (distributions and cash surrender value of outright gifts of life insurance), and bequest distributions for the last fiscal year?

Chapter I–3

Do You Need A Fund Raising or Planned Giving Consultant?

If you have turned to this chapter, chances are, something within the fund raising department is not working. But, depending on who you are, the part of your operation that needs to be fixed will vary.

In this chapter, I will address two different audiences. The first audience is the leadership (Executive Director, President, Director of Development). The second audience is the Director of Planned Giving.

Before separating the discussion for either group, let's talk about some of the general reasons you might need a consultant.

MAKING THE DECISION TO USE A CONSULTANT

As you review your program, consider the advice of Dr. Jeffrey Lant who has an excellent book on consulting. In his book, **TRICKS OF THE TRADE: THE COMPLETE GUIDE TO SUCCEEDING IN THE ADVICE BUSINESS**, Dr. Lant cites seven instances when you need a consultant:

- when you don't have the staff to solve the problem;

- when a tough decision needs to be made and no one wants to be publicly associated with it;

- when staff needs to be trained;

- when senior management has lost its way;

- when you need to change;

- when you want a breather from difficult circumstances and may not want to change at all;

- when you want to see how other people are doing things.

Relating the above general ideas to planned giving, here are some of the reasons you may wish to hire a fund raising or planned giving consultant:

- when the members of your Board of Trustees are uninvolved in the fund raising program and you need a neutral party to suggest a larger role for them;

- when the institution cannot afford a full-time Director of Planned Giving;

- when you wish to integrate planned giving into other fund raising activities (annual giving, a campaign, major gifts, leadership gifts) and you need an outside voice to bring a fresh perspective to other members of the development department;

- when you need to train the Board of Trustees, other colleagues, or a group of donors or volunteers;

- when you need assistance with a complex gift proposal;

- when you want to compare what you are doing with the activities of other institutions;

- when you need to revitalize the planned giving program after a period of disappointing results;

- when you need brochures or other print materials and don't have the time or the expertise to produce them yourself;

- when you need to develop policies for gift acceptance, disposition, and management.

By reviewing the bullets above, you'll find may reasons to hire a consultant.

For The Executive Director, President, Or Director of Development

As Executive Director of a nonprofit organization that intends to start or to revamp a planned giving program, you may need a consultant. An important use of a planned giving consultant is for work with the Board.

If you haven't read the preceding chapter, you should read that first. After you do, you'll know that if you can get the Board committed, you'll have a fairly good chance at hiring a Director of Planned Giving. After all, this is the only way to have a good planned giving program.

But, hiring a consultant to help with the board will not guarantee success. You, also, must be committed to following through with recommendations. Although a consultant can do a lot of things, there is no substitute for the continuity of a permanent planned giving staff member who will carry on long after the consultant has collected his or her fee and departed.

Hiring a consultant does not necessarily imply there is anything wrong. Your organization is ready to take on new challenges and needs a person with new expertise. Neither does hiring a consultant mean the staff is unqualified to do the job.

If you already have a Director of Planned Giving, your director may wonder why you need a consultant. Feelings can be hurt easily and people can feel threatened. But, however skilled he or she may be in the technical aspects of planned giving, the Planned Giving Director may be the wrong person to take on the board. Change is always difficult. Personality differences, territorial issues, and politics come into play whenever a new direction is being charted. Frequently, I have been asked to speak to the Board of Trustees of an organization that has a Planned Giving Director. In these instances, I can help set the stage and the mindset of the Board for a productive working relationship with existing staff. It is interesting to note that during my career as a Director of Planned Giving at four organizations, I made presentations to the Boards of many other charities while my employer periodically hired a consultant to do presentations to my own Board. When you plan to hire a consultant for a planned giving presentation, you ought to involve your own Director of Planned Giving in the discussions so that you won't create unnecessary conflict with your Director.

Here are a few things to keep in mind:

1. Working with a consultant will not lessen your work load or make your job easier. In fact, the organization, planning, and thoughtful restructuring of your work style and habits and of those around you will produce more work than you had before.

2. Working with a consultant will be a waste of your time and money unless you are willing to implement the consultant's recommendations.

3. The consultant will not necessarily tell you anything you didn't know already. In fact, the recommendations may seem absolutely basic—almost too obvious. Most people left to their own

resources probably know exactly what changes need to be made. You probably do, too. But, you might need someone else to tell you what to do and who can take the responsibility off of your shoulders.

Some unexpected guidance from the consultant will be on major institutional issues. For example, you may need to reposition the institution so that your donors will want to support a future-oriented fund raising program. The consultant may even, in rare instances, tell you that you are not ready for planned giving.

At other times, the consultant will assist with technical issues. For example, the consultant can help you develop procedures for accepting, disposing of, and managing various types of gifts. On this topic, my advice would be to hold off on such administrative issues until after you have a Planned Giving Director.

If you haven't worked with a fund raising consultant before, let me tell you that it can be quite refreshing. It may be your only chance at making changes that have been a source of discontent for a long time. You will have a person who will listen to you, empathize with your problems, and be an outside partner to whom you may disclose information confidentially, a very theraputic experience.

For The Director Of Planned Giving

As Planned Giving Director, your needs will be similar to those of the Executive Director, but you are attacking the issues from a more practical approach. Frankly, if you already exist, some of the issues mentioned above have been dealt with prior to your arrival. You should already know how to run the pooled income fund you inherited. You should already know how to run a gift annuity program (or get one started). You should know how to calculate the tax consequences of various gift plans. In many respects, you are well on your way to running a successful planned giving program. Even so, here are six ways a consultant can help you, too:

- to get the board involved,

- to run a seminar,

- to provide print materials,

- to assist with donor solicitations,

- to help get you access to the leadership,

- to help you integrate your program into other fund raising activities.

TO GET THE BOARD INVOLVED

When you do not have the support of the board, and if you have already failed to get its involvement using the strategies in the preceding chapter, you might consider hiring a planned giving consultant. This will not be your decision alone. Most likely, your boss will make this decision and pay for it out of the Development Office budget, but only after a lot of encouragement from you.

Consultants make their biggest impact when they give credibility to your own work. Board members, financial vice presidents, and directors of development generally listen to consultants. Maybe this is because advice seems to be valuable when one pays for it. Equally likely, it is because the consultant has nothing to gain or lose in the outcome. Consultants can speak from the experience of working with others, especially with peer institutions.

Before proceeding further, you must realize that it may very well be the institution's administration—and not the board—that is the real obstacle to planned giving success. Those charged with the responsibility of running the institution may try to prevent you from pointing out weaknesses that have existed for a long time. They will claim that consultants are a waste of time and will dismiss the idea as frivolous or unnecessary. Why? Because the major message a consultant will give to the Board members is that they must step forward with leadership gifts and also assist with fund raising. Oh, no-o-o-o-o-o-o!

Perhaps these fearful and cautious institutions (or the people in charge of them) are afraid of finally confronting and solving the problems which they know full well need to be addressed. Perhaps those in charge already understand the magnitude of the changes that need to occur—some even painful changes—and simply don't have the energy, courage, or personal motivation to see them through.

If your objective is to get a commitment from the board, and, if after making every reasonable argument for the cause, your organization refuses to address the problems you know exist, and further refuses to hire a consultant, you can take one of the following courses of action:

1. **Do nothing.**

   This is your choice. Nobody is forcing you to beat your head against a wall. If you decide to do nothing, don't complain about your situation. Make the most of the resources you have and try to do the best job you can. You can still do a lot of planned giving—even without the Board. This would not be an ideal program, but it can work.

2. **Look for another job.**

   In my earlier years, I was obsessed with getting the Board involved. I was on a mission—for years! Over the years, I stopped fighting that battle because I had been beaten back too often. If this is how you feel, I can relate. After a lot of soul-searching, you may decide it is better to seek another employer than to live with a vision that cannot be satisfied. While you are exploring other opportunities, don't run around bad-mouthing the organization, the Board, or the Director of Development. No one wants to hear your continuing complaints. Put 100% of your effort into the job for as long as it takes to get another one.

On the other hand, let's assume you are successful in gaining approval to hire a consultant. Bravo!

Hiring a consultant does not guarantee success. A consultant can be an invaluable aid but cannot do your job for you. All too often, what begins as an exciting, aggressive planned giving effort ends in disaster. Why? Because shortly after your consultant is off the payroll, your boss loses direction. Then, you are pulled off planned giving and assigned to a new project. Or, your budget is cut because another department has exceeded its budget. Perhaps your board members stop doing whatever they promised to do. "No way!" you say. Believe me. It can happen. It happened to me.

One hopes that these unfortunate regressions do not happen to you.

TO RUN A SEMINAR OR WORKSHOP

If you hold a seminar for donors, board members, or other target groups, the planning of the seminar, including all of the details that go along with it, will consume a disproportionate share of your time. You will need to identify the list of participants, get the list approved by your boss, arrange for the room, equipment, refreshments/food, and invitations. Then, you must plan the actual session including hand-outs and other print materials. An excellent use of your planned giving budget may be to hire a consultant to run the session instead. Many of the consultants in Appendix IV have programs for donors, board members, or for volunteers. They will assume all responsibility for the program and hand-outs, thus they save you considerable time and effort. Each one can work with you to create a session tailored to your audience, and in many cases, can provide expertise beyond your own. Especially when the board is involved, a consultant can enhance significantly the effectiveness of a training session. Most consultants will allow you to audit a session that they are holding for another institution so that you can observe them in action.

TO PROVIDE PRINT MATERIALS

Writing print materials is another task that consumes considerable time. Many consultants offer a wide selection of brochures and direct mail packages that you can use on a one-time basis or in a longer-term direct mail program. Even if you have your own internally-produced brochures, you may periodically wish to send a direct-mail piece to a targeted group of prospects without spending the time to create it yourself.

An excellent use of a consultant is for an estate planning or planned giving newsletter. I have used such a piece from Pentera and Stelter (listed in Appendix IV). For each issue, you select the topic from a menu of many topics, receive a generic draft, then edit it to incorporate a personalized touch for your donors. In addition, you have the option of replacing entire modules with anecdotes or donor profiles from your organization, including photographs, or you can change the examples to suit your needs. If you have no time at all for such personalization, all you really need to do is replace throughout the generic text the words "our institution" with your organization's name. And, *voilà*, you have a newsletter.

Many organizations create their own estate planning newsletters and are putting them on the Internet. Also, there are many vendors now providing excellent web content that can also be coordinated with a direct mail program, too. These are listed in Appendix IV.

For a more complete discussion about print materials, refer to Chapter III-1.

TO ASSIST WITH DONOR SITUATIONS

Especially if you are new to planned giving, you may encounter a complex gift situation that requires a level of knowledge beyond your own. This is okay. In fact, even the most experienced planned giving officers use specialists, attorneys or consultants for unusual cases. In this kind of instance, a consultant, specialist or your legal counsel can accompany you on a visit and assist you in developing a proposal.

Most important, use the consultant's time wisely. Do not enlist a consultant for prospects with whom you have never spoken. Such cold calling is a waste of the consultant's time and also a waste of your money. Further, before taking a consultant with you to visit a prospect, outline the division of responsibilities between the consultant and your organization. For example, who should prepare reports for the prospect? Who is the consultant working for? You or the prospect? Who is paying for the consultant's time?

TO HELP GET YOU ACCESS TO THE LEADERSHIP

It has always been curious to me how important planned giving is to the overall development effort yet how segregated and isolated the planned giving program can be. Does the president go out to visit very serious prospects without consulting you about strategies? Are you part of the team discussing the highest level prospects (major gifts, principal gifts)? Are you invited to meetings of the Development Committee of the Board? If you have answered yes to one or more of the above questions, then something is definitely wrong. And, you probably need a consultant to help you.

TO HELP YOU INTEGRATE YOUR PROGRAM INTO OTHER FUND RAISING ACTIVITIES

Is the Director of Annual Giving willing to put planned giving check-off blocks on the reply cards for direct mail pieces? Are you invited to the major gift, leadership gift, or principal gift meetings? Is the fund raising culture at your organization receptive to collaborative efforts between you and other fund raising staff? Can you get space in the institution's annual report of gifts for a listing of the bequest society or the deferred giving society? Do you have a regular space in the institution's periodic publications for a planned giving ad, article, or other planned giving feature? These issues taken together make the difference between running an integrated program or one that is isolated from mainstream development activities. Therefore, a consultant may be necessary to help you through the battles.

WORKING WITH THE CONSULTANT

Regardless of how you intend to use a consultant, you will want to outline carefully the terms of the consultancy. Questions that need to be asked include:

- What is the time frame of the relationship?

- What is the consultant expected to do? What will the consultant not do?

- Where will meetings be held? How often will meetings be held?

- Who will participate in the meetings? From your institution? From the consulting firm?

- How long will meetings be?

- What is included in the fees quoted? What is extra? How will travel time be charged? Phone conversations? Photocopying or printing? Meals?

- How many copies of reports are expected? What is the format of the materials prepared by the consultant? Flip charts? Slides? Print materials?

- Who owns the copyright on materials produced by the consultancy? How may they be used in the future?

- Who is the primary contact for the consultancy at your institution?

You must determine the answers to these questions in the beginning. The consultant will probably present a contract for your review once the details are worked out. You should review the contract with your legal counsel to ensure sufficient attention has been paid to all contingencies.

FINDING THE RIGHT CONSULTANT

The number of fund raising consultants is growing each year. Many people who were formerly Directors of Planned Giving have retired and become consultants.

The first thing you need to do before you hire a consultant is to determine your needs. Do you want someone to help put together a five-year plan or someone to run one donor seminar? Does the consultant need to work with the Board of Trustees or are you looking for someone to show you how to calculate the tax consequences of a charitable remainder trust? Some consultants perform long-term planning studies but cannot write a gift proposal. Do you need a feasibility study?

Once you have determined exactly what you need, you can begin to develop a list of those who can serve you best. The American Association of Fund-Raising Counsel is one place to start. You can go to their web site for a complete list of members. Not all consultants are members, but there is a summary of the AAFRC Membership Standards on the website that would be helpful for you to read.

The American Association of Fund-Raising Counsel, Inc.
10293 North Meridian Street, Suite 175
Indianapolis, IN 46290
317-816-1613
800-462-2372
317-816-1633 (fax)
www.aafrc.org

Without a personal interview, you will find it very difficult to determine whether a firm or a person is right for you or whether the individual has the skills and the experience you need. Many people or firms look great on paper but may be all wrong for your institution.

You also have to be careful about selecting a firm simply because of its reputation. Many fund raising firms got their start when one dynamic individual decided to offer consulting services. However, while the name of this individual is still part of the name of the firm, you cannot be assured that this person will be responsible for your account. The success of your consultancy will be based in large measure on the close relationship you develop with one person. That person must be the right match for your staff, your board, and for your donors. Otherwise, you will be wasting your money.

The considerations for hiring a consultant include:

- experience with organizations similar in size and mission to your institution. You want to know that the consultant understands your unique problems;

- experience as an actual director of planned giving in a prior life. Consultants who have no hands-on experience running a program cannot possibly know what your job entails;

- proven track record in generating the kinds of positive results you are seeking;

- a flair for public speaking and for making presentations. Your consultant must have the polish necessary to engage an audience and to present a compelling case regardless of the audience—the development staff, the Board, a group of prospects, a volunteer committee;

- ability to be flexible and to tailor presentations to whatever group you have assembled;

- prompt follow up. You want someone who returns your calls immediately, who delivers reports and other work on time;

- ability to lead others. You want someone who can take charge, who can identify a problem and present a solution—someone who is better than you are and who cannot be put off track with unforeseen obstacles;

- integrity. Along with experience, the ideal consultant maintains high personal standards.

The best way to narrow the field of potential candidates is to ask colleagues from other institutions about their experience with consultants. This is a people business, and there is no better way to sort out the good from the bad than by speaking candidly with other professionals.

Here are two other points to keep in mind with regard to hiring a consultant:

1. If you are looking for a consultant to help you conduct a feasibility study or to develop a long-term plan, you'll gain greater acceptance for the process if you create a selection committee comprised of at least two of the board members who will be required to work with the consultant. Adding a member of the development department, or a member of the business office, is also a good strategy.

2. When you are interviewing consultants, you cannot assume that the consultant's time and expense for the interview is free. Find out before you arrange the meeting. For any of the consultants listed as members of the AAFRC, the initial meeting is deemed to be free.

SUMMARY

A consultant can assist you in many ways either for a one-time assignment or for a longer-term project. On the bottom line, however, you are the one who must perform up to the standards expected. The consultant cannot do your job.

Much of the work in the early months of your new program will involve creating a master plan. A consultant can help with this task, too. Or, as is the case with most planned giving programs, the Director of Planned Giving develops the plan. In the following chapter, there is a general explanation about the process necessary to develop your program, a suggested list of activities for the first 12 months, some guidelines about how to develop dollar goals, and a worksheet for creating a budget.

Chapter I–4

DEVELOPING A MASTER PLAN

INTRODUCTION

If you are already running a planned giving program, you know how quickly days, weeks, and even months can slip by, laying waste to the great plans you envisioned at the beginning of the fiscal year. The pressures of the moment are all consuming, and they prevent you from planning or implementing long-term goals. You really did have good intentions and you were very sincere when you drafted your plan. So what happened to it?

Does the following sound familiar?

> The monthly Development Office prospect meeting is tomorrow and you have made little progress on the prospects about whom you reported last time (a month ago). This makes you anxious as you drive to work, but you have the whole day to make calls, set up some visits, maybe try to get an update on a couple of outstanding solicitations. You need to make an action step on enough people so that when it is your turn to report, you will have productive things to say as the names on your list are called. No problem. You have no scheduled meetings today and you'll be able to focus on this prospect activity. Just shut your door all day.

> When you arrive at the office, you see a note taped to your door. Your boss has scheduled you to meet for about 45 minutes with a job candidate who is applying for the position of Director of Annual Giving. You block out the appointment on your calendar and the phone rings. One of the donors in your trust program is out at the reception desk. He dropped by to make a transfer of some securities to his trust and is sitting in the waiting area right now. You forward your calls into voice-mail, tidy up the desk and go out to escort the donor to your office. The donor ends up staying for one hour while you make phone calls to the transfer agent of his dividend reinvestment shares. The donor didn't know that these could not be transferred through DTC. You ghost-write a letter for him to send to the company to accomplish the gift and also make a few calls to locate a bank that will give him a medallion signature guarantee.

> When he leaves, you see the message light on your phone. You call voice-mail and hear the dreaded words, "You have five new messages." The first is from the Director of Development who needs you to run a tax calculation for a trustee. This has to be faxed before 11 am. The trustee's financial advisor will be reviewing with him some gift scenarios that have been on the table for a while. You discuss the details with the Director of Development, go back to your office and run an illustration for a charitable remainder trust. After your secretary faxes the information to the trustee, you settle down to work on your prospects. Whew! It is already 11 am. Shortly after the fax, the phone rings and it is the trustee's financial advisor who keeps you on the phone for 20 minutes discussing the illustration, which, of course, needs to be redone with some new variables. You redo the calculations and get them faxed off just in time for the job applicant's arrival and the interview you are supposed to do. After the interview, there are still four unplayed messages on your voice-mail and you are feeling extremely hassled. You ask your secretary to listen to your messages and to tell you only if there is something that cannot wait. Otherwise, you are going to shut your door with a cup of yogurt and a banana to see what you are going to do about your prospects.

> There is a knock at your door. One of the remaining four messages was about a donor in the gift annuity program who died three days ago and the wake is from 2 p.m. to 4 p.m. today at a location an hour away. This was a person very close to you, and it would be extremely bad

form if you did not make an appearance. You reconcile yourself to leaving the office about 2:30 p.m. to get to the wake by 3:30 p.m. Another message involved a member of your planned giving committee who cannot make the meeting this week and wants to review with you one of her prospects to discuss an important development. She has a lot to do so could you please call before you leave the office today.

To save some time, you open your e-mail while you are chatting with the committee member and see an urgent message from your asset manager. You open the message and see that there was a mix-up with the gift annuity payments and that the checks and electronic transfer notices were mailed by the bank to the annuitants instead of the usual procedure of sending them to you first. This means that the people with seasonal addresses that only your office knows will not get their payments at the right address.

By the time you leave the office for the wake, you have not made one call to a prospect and when you arrive at the prospect meeting tomorrow morning, you have a big knot in your stomach.

Day after day, week after week, the pace is relentless. You finish two tasks and five more find their way onto your "to do" list. How can you ever catch up? And, how do you evaluate where you are in relation to where you should be? Easily. You need a master plan.

Preparing a master plan is like being in a "Catch 22." On one hand, you don't know how much money you're going to spend without knowing the kinds of activities you'll undertake. On the other hand, you cannot determine the scope of your activities unless you know how much money you will be allowed to spend. Most important, you cannot know where you are in relation to your goals and objectives unless you have some.

For most planned giving officers, the size of the budget is not negotiable. If you are taking over an existing planned giving position, the budget is fixed for now. You must live within it until the end of the fiscal year. Budgets usually are adjusted at the beginning of each fiscal year. After that, little can be done to change the dollars allocated to your program. You must take responsibility for your budget and stay within your limits. For new programs, a budget may have been approved, ready for your arrival, but it probably does not relate to the reality of what needs to be done.

When you interviewed for the position, you should have asked how much your budget will be. If you are a financial professional who has just moved into planned giving from another career (life insurance, real estate, banking) you probably did not ask about the planned giving budget during your interview because you simply never thought of it. During your interviews, your only concern was making a career shift to planned giving. Now that you are in the position, you should ask immediately how much you'll have to spend this year.

Once you know your budget, developing a master plan becomes a process of setting priorities—and compromising. The master plan has four parts:

- the program objectives,
- the dollar and other goals,
- the budget,
- the calendar of activities.

THE PROGRAM OBJECTIVES

The best place to start is at the beginning. What do you want to do this year? Get gifts, of course. But, "getting gifts" is not specific enough to carry you very far in developing a master plan. Before you even think about getting gifts, step back from your daily tasks, and take the broadest possible look at the coming year. Exactly what is it you really want to do? What are your program objectives? In planned giving, there are lots of different program objectives.

Certainly, the program objectives of a new, first time ever, planned giving program are far different from those of a mature planned giving program. But, the exercise in developing them is still the same. For the benefit of those who must start a program from scratch, this chapter is really for you.

By the time your organization has reached a commitment to hire you—a full-time director of planned giving—some decisions already may have been made. For example, the board may have approved the establishment of a gift annuity program. Perhaps legal counsel has been retained or a consultant hired. Regardless of any of these things, the one decision you can count on having been made is the allocation of funds to support the planned giving program. You'll probably think the planned giving budget is too small. Nonetheless, you'll be required to work within it. Don't complain. Use the money wisely for the first year and try to adjust it to a more realistic level for the next year.

For purposes of this discussion, assume no policy decisions have been made. You are it. Sitting at your desk on your first day, you must develop a planned giving program from scratch. To suggest this is a terrifying position to be in would be an understatement. The responsibility is enormous. But, this is probably one of the most exciting and challenging things you will ever do. There is no track record against which you can judge success or failure, no predecessor's trail from which you can get a frame of reference of your own performance. This is your show and a premiere performance at that! Anything you do is more than has ever been done.

Results do not happen overnight. Although your job is to "raise money," it will be several months before you can even begin to think of gifts. In order to keep your sanity, you must think of this as a period of building. Each activity builds on the one before. Your colleagues will not always understand what you are doing nor why it is taking so long to see some gifts. Those who have created a new planned giving program know the first year is surely the toughest because every question must be asked for the first time; every policy and procedure must be created; every battle must be fought for the first time.

This does not pertain only to those who are relatively new to the field. Their credibility will be tested time and time again. But, even those with years of experience will find their judgment and recommendations questioned.

Before you do anything, you must meet with the other directors in your department to understand how the organization's fund raising works. During these early days, listen carefully. Take it all in. Find out if planned giving has been or could be integrated into other activities. The last thing you want to do is present a set of plans without first understanding the level of acceptance for your ideas and the relative sophistication of your colleagues with regard to planned giving. One of the ways to educate your colleagues about planned giving is to hold a staff training session. When you are ready for that, turn to Chapter III–4.

Next, you need to know the makeup of the board. (*Note: You should know this already if you asked the proper questions during your job interview.*) Are the members currently involved in fund raising activities? Do they support the institution? Do they solicit prospects and take on assignments? If you haven't done so, a review of Chapter I-2 about the role of the board may be a good idea now.

Finally, the most important factor on which much of your work will be based is the organization's fund raising history. Has the organization ever run a campaign for capital gifts, endowment gifts, or for a building? How many people have ever contributed $25,000, $100,000, $1 million or more? For what purposes were these larger gifts made? Is there an endowment? How big?

Within the first few weeks, you will begin to get a sense of the kinds of challenges you'll be facing. You'll know whether your business office is capable of assuming the kinds of administrative responsibilities required in a gift annuity program. You'll know whether the director of annual giving is receptive to integrating planned giving into annual giving. You may also realize you have a long, hard year ahead.

It may appear that I'm setting up a recipe for confrontation among your colleagues. Not necessarily. But, I want to prepare you for the fact that some organizations compartmentalize planned giving to such a degree that it operates like an island unto itself. Such a framework will bring frustration for you, especially if you expect complete cooperation and coordination from the start.

Although each organization is different, the program objectives share many of the same elements. Following is a suggestion for a blueprint for program objectives. There are four parts:

- Mission Statement
- Administrative Objectives
- Program Objectives
- Management Objectives

1. Mission Statement: This is where you state the mission of your planned giving program.

   Example:

   - Develop a comprehensive program for long-term support offering the full range of charitable gift options. Provide support to trustees, officers, and other development staff in the area of gift planning. Secure gifts and commitments that utilize the full benefits of tax, income, and other advantages in order to strengthen the institution for the future.

2. Administrative Objectives: This is where you describe the administrative tasks required of the program. These activities will consume considerable amounts of time but have nothing to do with getting the gifts. Yet, they represent collectively the essential backbone and infrastructure of your program.

   Example:

   - Interview and select legal counsel for the planned giving program (See Chapter I–6);
   - Interview and select a fiduciary manager of the life income plans (See Chapter III–9);
   - Establish a gift annuity program (See Chapter II–8);
   - Establish a pooled income fund (See Chapter II-7);
   - Develop procedures and policies for the acceptance, disposition, management, and investment of gifts of securities, life insurance, real estate, charitable gift annuities, pooled income fund gifts, charitable remainder trusts, charitable lead trusts, and revocable trusts (See individual chapters on each gift option.);
   - Develop procedures for recording and tracking planned gifts;
   - Develop appropriate crediting guidelines. (See Chapter III-5).

3. Program Objectives: This is the section where you outline the marketing plan.

   Example:

   - Identify prospects through screenings, research, internal methods, and lead-generating activities;
   - Educate the constituency about the benefits of tax-related gifts through special events, a planned giving newsletter, through articles in the institution's magazine, and through special volunteer training sessions;
   - Develop a plan for cultivation of the donors and prospects through special events, recognition societies, personal communications, phone calls, and visits.
   - Develop a strategic solicitation plan that maximizes the use of available staff and financial resources.
   - Create (or update, revise) a planned giving Internet Site.

4. Management Objectives: This is the most overlooked objective. It involves increasing your professionalism and technical expertise, providing leadership for your staff, maximizing your productivity, acquiring and improving the skills you need to communicate, negotiate, and, most of all, be effective in your job.

Example:

- Maintain appropriate professional affiliations that promote the personal and professional growth of the director of planned giving;

- Subscribe to appropriate publications that provide current tax information, analysis of gift strategies, and that provide expertise about the planned giving field.

- Educate and train support staff in order that they may act independently and confidently in the absence of the director on issues pertaining to gifts, tax-related issues, and procedures.

- Attend one planned giving conference this year.

You may be thinking that the above outline is absolutely basic. Yes, it is. But, this is where you start the very long process of developing your full master plan.

THE DOLLAR AND OTHER GOALS

The planned giving dollar goals are part of the development office's total goal. For this discussion, I'm dealing only with irrevocable gifts (not pledges). One fund raising consultant, Marts & Lundy, suggests that planned gifts should represent 1/3 of the total money raised from individuals. I have never been able to achieve that percentage. Programs that achieve such percentages have two major factors playing into their totals. The first is a healthy stream of bequest distributions. The second is a healthy business in charitable remainder trusts. Unfortunately, if you are just starting a new planned giving program, you will have neither. Not to worry. Everyone had to start somewhere.

At the heart of your process to develop dollar goals is the number of prospects who can be identified at different gift levels. Most experts will tell you it takes three qualified prospects to get one gift. At very high levels, it might take four or five. Thus, you need to look closely at the donor base—a process that demands a considerable degree of volunteer and staff time. Even here, the process is imprecise at best and involves resolving many conflicting opinions about a donor's potential and his or her stage of readiness to make a gift.

For purposes of this discussion, I am assuming that some of the gifts you will receive will be outright gifts, but I am not counting these in the planned giving goals. Don't worry about that for now. Your colleagues will know if you are raising money.

There are two steps to developing your dollar goals. First, review the history of bequest distributions. Nearly every institution receives some money from estates each year. Yours probably does, too. Take the five-year average of bequest distributions and add 5% or 10%. If your organization does not have good records for bequest distributions, you might have to reconstruct information from prior years.

You will have no control over this part of your goal. Nonetheless, the bequest distributions are normally a piece of the planned giving dollar goals. Often, you will know about estates in distribution from a prior year which are not completely paid out to your organization. These known bequests should be considered when you develop your bequest distribution goals.

The second step is to develop a goal for life income gifts (charitable remainder trusts, charitable gift annuities, and pooled income fund gifts). If there are some existing life income gifts under administration, you ought to review the names of the donors toward seeing if any of them have been consistent repeat donors. If someone has been contributing $10,000 per year for a gift annuity, you could expect the same pattern again this year.

Board support can play a major role. But, institutions with a board that is either incapable of or unwilling to make leadership gifts must turn to the general constituency. Unfortunately, without the kind of jump start a board can provide, the range and number of gifts you can expect will be far less than would otherwise be the case.

One of the most useful tools in developing a goal is the gift pyramid.

Following is a gift pyramid for a $500,000 goal.

Prospects needed					Gift needed			Total
3	@	$100,000	+		1	@	$100,000	$100,000
6	@	50,000	to	100,000	2	@	50,000	100,000
12	@	25,000	to	50,000	4	@	25,000	100,000
30	@	10,000	to	25,000	10	@	10,000	100,000
+60	@	5,000	to	10,000	20	@	5,000	+ 100,000
111					37			$500,000

Following is a gift pyramid for a $2 million goal.

Prospects needed					Gift needed			Total
4	@	$500,000	+		1	@	$500,000	$500,000
8	@	250,000	to	500,000	2	@	250,000	500,000
9	@	100,000	to	250,000	3	@	100,000	300,000
18	@	50,000	to	100,000	6	@	50,000	300,000
30	@	25,000	to	50,000	10	@	25,000	250,000
+45	@	10,000	to	25,000	15	@	10,000	+ 150,000
114					37			$2,000,000

A gift pyramid serves a very practical purpose because it allows you realistically to assess your fund raising potential. It forces you to look at the numbers of gifts and the levels of gifts you'll need to succeed. If you cannot identify the prospects needed to support your gift pyramid, you should reexamine your goals. (*Note: The bequest distributions part of the goal count in your gift pyramid.*) The gift pyramid you submit will be integrated into the larger development office gift pyramid.

In the first pyramid above, notice that the lowest gift level is $5,000, whereas, in the second pyramid, the lowest gift level is $10,000. That was arbitrary on my part. You can adjust these pyramids to suit the actual prospect base with which you are working. Some consultants try to get scientific about this, slicing off sections and inserting formulas. You can go nuts making up one of these pyramids if you get too caught up in formulas. However, a rule of thumb is that the lead gift should be at least 20% of the goal.

If you don't have a few prospects for one proper lead gift, then you will have to fill out the bottom of the pyramid a lot more. Doing that adds exponentially to the work at the lower levels. Or, you could lower the goal.

During a fund raising campaign, a gift pyramid can be a motivational tool for donors. The solicitation can be more compelling when the prospect understands the relationship of his or her gift to the gifts of others. Over the years, different ratios have been suggested for the highest level gifts. For example, it was once thought that 10% of the donors give 90% of the money. That ratio has changed. Institutions are finding that the top donors are a smaller percentage of the total number of donors. Instead of the 90%/10% rule, you now have closer to 95%/5% or even 98%/2%. That's scary.

What this really means is that the larger gifts make or break your goals. Although I did not use a formula to create the above sample gift pyramids, I'm sure you get the idea. This is not an exact science. Moreover, depending on the institution, you may have a pyramid with a narrow base (as with the above) or one with a broader base (more $5,000 or $10,000 gifts). There is no magic pyramid. What's right for your institution may be all wrong for another. Nonetheless, the exercise of creating a gift pyramid is a good one for you to understand.

Unfortunately, identifying the prospects for your gift pyramid and actually achieving your goal are two different things. You have to ask people for gifts. Often, the things that impact your goal have nothing to do with the prospects. In fact, most organizations have far more prospects than could ever be solicited. The real challenge is to orchestrate a visit with the right prospect, with the right volunteer solicitor, at the right time. In order to do that, you must have the staff and resources to make the visits and solicitations happen.

Here are several considerations to which you must address yourself if you are to set realistic goals:

- *The number of professional staff devoted to the program.* Remember, fund raising is a people business. If you are a full-time planned giving director, you will be able to establish relationships with more prospects than if you are an executive director who is doing planned giving in your spare time. Be realistic or you will be leaving the office with a big knot in your stomach after a short time.

- *Whether you have a secretary.* A director of planned giving without a full-time secretary is already in an uphill battle.

- *The commitment of the Board.* If you have Board support, the average gift should be higher and the number of prospects from whom a major gift is received should be higher.

- *The funds available for travel, cultivation activities, and other necessary expenses.* In order to conduct your visits and solicitations, you must be able to travel and to entertain prospects.

- *The funds available for legal consultation.* When you encounter a complex situation, your ability to call legal counsel is essential in getting the gift. Without the very minimum of $3,000 to $5,000 for legal fees, many of the biggest gifts will never materialize. You cannot get complex gifts using a volunteer on the Board as legal counsel. (There is more about this issue in Chapter I-6.)

- *The stability of the organization.* If you are employed by a small social service agency that is subject to state budget swings and to other chronic fiscal problems, you'll be perceived as unstable. Thus, you'll have a hard time attracting planned gifts.

- *The organization's fund raising history.* Be realistic with your expectations. If you can count the number of four-figure gifts from past years on one hand, don't expect results in the six-figures range in your first year.

- *The size and age of your constituency.* This factor will determine significantly how you approach your program. For example, the planned giving officer at a large university probably will never be able to handle the responses from a mailing targeted to those age 70 or older. On the other hand, an organization that serves the general public has very little knowledge about whom its donors are and how old they are. Targeting a mailing to the right group will be much more difficult.

- *The use of volunteers.* You can increase the number of solicitations made this year with the help of volunteers. But, even the best volunteer will be lucky to make as many as 10 quality visits in a year.

Many factors affect the development of your goal. For existing planned giving programs, setting a goal is often a matter of tacking on a percentage increase over last year's total. That would be a program running on automatic pilot. It would be better to create a gift pyramid and see where that leads you, perhaps to a higher goal than you would have thought possible.

THE BUDGET

When you are hired, you will be told how much money has been budgeted for the planned giving program. As I said in the beginning of this chapter, this amount is usually not negotiable. Year to year, if you are lucky, you will receive a small percentage increase over the prior year. Equally likely, your budget will stay the same for two or more years—even though expectations for results will be greater with each passing year. New planned giving officers transferring from the profit sector will find this amusing. Whatever your opinion about this policy, you must live within your budget year to year.

Some institutions include in a manager's budget all expenses attributable to that budget area—salaries, benefits, overhead, capital equipment, maintenance contracts on equipment, legal fees, bank administration fees, postage, telephone, mainframe time, office supplies, subscriptions, *etc*. Others separate certain items for inclusion in an overall department budget or in a larger division budget.

For example, your department may have a general supply cabinet for the development department. If so, you don't need to account for yellow lined pads, pens, scissors, tape, photocopy paper, manila folders, letterheads and envelopes, or any of the other general office supplies the department uses daily. Or, you may be required to order these items individually through the purchasing department and pay for them from the planned giving budget.

Having worked in four nonprofit organizations, I have seen a wide variety of practices. In one situation, my planned giving budget included overhead and occupancy charges (by the square foot) for my office and for my secretary's space. In another organization, I was charged by the minute for computer time to order donor lists, labels for a mailing, or reports. In two organizations, the photocopy machine required a key-card to track copies by department. In two others, the photocopies were covered by the division budget. In three organizations, the telephone bills were charged to planned giving. At Boston College, telephone charges are covered by the division budget and not covered by planned giving. As far as I can tell, there is no consistency to how these policies originate. Therefore, you need to photocopy the following check list and ask some questions.

Following is a check list you can use to identify those expenses which will be charged to your planned giving budget:

Included In Planned Giving Budget

Budget Item	Yes	No
Salaries	___	___
Overhead	___	___
Occupancy (charge for square footage)	___	___
Capital equipment (computers, printers, calculators, office furniture)	___	___
Software	___	___
Maintenance contracts on office equipment	___	___
Office supplies (pens, paper, envelopes, letterheads, tape)	___	___
Postage (general correspondence)	___	___
Legal fees for planned giving	___	___
Bank administration fees	___	___
Subscriptions	___	___
Professional memberships	___	___
Consultant fees	___	___
Computer time (for ordering reports, lists, labels)	___	___

Budget Item (continued)	Yes	No
Design fees (for using in-house designers and graphics staff)	——	——
Writers' fees (for using in-house writers and editors)	——	——
Facilities usage (rental charge for using in-house conference rooms, function rooms, or other spaces)	——	——
Conferences/seminars	——	——
Travel expenses/entertainment	——	——
Telephone—general	——	——
Telephone—Toll-Free Number	——	——
Fax	——	——
Telephone—cellular	——	——
Web pages (design, maintenance)	——	——
Photocopying	——	——

Once you have completed the above exercise, you can begin the budget process. Over the years, I have developed my own method for approaching this task. It involves two steps:

Step 1: Identify those expenses you consider to be fixed. Fixed expenses in this sense means, while they are subject to some shifting, they are reasonably certain to show up on your budget printout before the end of the year.

For example, my budget at Boston College had the following annual expenses for the year ending May 31, 2000 (Note that these prices are now out of date.):

- office supplies not covered by the general supply cabinet ($2,000);
- annual service agreements for four licenses of PG Calc—planned giving software (1 @ $575 plus 3 @ $125, total $950);
- luncheon event for 525 member deferred giving recognition society expecting 100 people to attend—invitations, postage, food, liquor, flowers, wait staff, shuttle bus, coat check, *etc.* ($5,012);
- subscriptions and books—*Wall Street Journal* $175, *Charitable Giving and Solicitation* $495, *Taxwise Giving* $195, *The Tidd Letter* $85, and *Giving U.S.A.* $49;
- membership in Planned Giving Group of New England ($250);
- membership in American Council on Gift Annuities ($75);
- postage for general correspondence ($1,000);
- annual fee for American Express card ($45);
- three five-day trips to Florida—taxi, air fare, hotel, entertainment, rental car, gas, house gifts ($6,000);
- Stelter estate planning newsletter mailed to 15,000 people twice per year—production of the newsletter, 300 companion booklets, reply cards, outside envelopes, business reply envelopes, nonprofit bulk-rate postage, and mailing house charges ($19,000);
- toll-free telephone line ($20/mo.)

The planned giving operating budget at Boston College did not include salaries, benefits, overhead, occupancy charges, telephone (except cellular and toll-free line), photocopying, legal fees, computer equipment, bank administration fees for the life income plans, computer time, design or editors fees or general office supplies. My budget did include the cost of furniture, special office supplies, postage, subscriptions, memberships, travel, printing, and planned giving software.

Step 2: Allocate the balance of the budget to all other activities. This is the hard part.

There is no easy way to develop a budget, but the above two-step process works for me. Every year, the process gets easier because you know certain things you are always going to do, and you have the detailed records from the prior year from which to start.

After you have completed Step 1, take the rest of the money and stretch it as far as possible. I cannot tell you the dollar amount you are going to spend this year. However, I can provide a framework which you can use to develop your budget. At the end of this chapter is a form that breaks down your potential expenses into the smallest components. It can be photocopied and used as a helpful tool as you perform this exercise.

Whatever the size of your budget, put money first into personal contact—the essential ingredient in all major gift solicitations. Do the best you can with the rest.

Bear in mind that no two planned giving programs are alike. The nature and size of the constituency, the location and size of the institution, the number of years it has existed, the strength of the leadership, the role the institution plays in the community, the public perceptions about the institution, and its financial status all play a role in shaping the kinds of activities you'll deem appropriate. One thing is surely true: it takes money to raise money. Small institutions never have enough. Ironically, neither do large ones. Some institutions have more than one planned giving officer each of whom has a personal secretary. Others have an executive director who does everything from public relations, to developing programs, to annual giving, to corporate and foundation solicitations, to planned giving. Whoever you are, the budgeting process is not fun because your ideas will always cost more than the money available.

To properly plan your budget, you must start the budget process far in advance of the new fiscal year. This is because many of your activities overlap with other departments and because you are dependent on other people for cost estimates. Take printing, for example. You'll have to discuss each brochure, mailing, or other piece with your designers to get estimated costs on these items. More often than not, your whole budget process will come to a grinding halt while you wait for price quotes. Designers are fabulous on design; they are often very slow on price quotes. To facilitate the process, you must do your homework in advance.

For example, let's assume you want to print a new brochure and have scheduled a meeting with your designer to discuss the project. Within the first five minutes of your conversation with a designer, you'll be asked about size and quantity; whether you want one color, two colors, or more; whether you want coated or uncoated stock; if you need photography; how many words; whether you want graphics, and many other questions. The designer cannot be expected to secure price quotes for unlimited numbers of variables. Therefore, you must come to the meeting with a good idea of what you have in mind.

One way to speed the process is to bring with you a sample brochure along the lines of what you want. The designer must then consult with a printer to secure cost estimates for you. Leave plenty of time for those who must track down your project's costs. Otherwise, you'll find yourself scrambling at the last minute to complete your budget perhaps without the cost estimates so essential to the process.

Estimating the cost of donor events is less difficult provided, of course, you know how many people to expect for your event. Still, the considerations in planning a modest, medium, or extravagant event are important. A working lunch for the planned giving committee can be tastefully done with sandwiches, coffee, tea, or sodas, and brownies. A cultivation lunch for leadership donors demands a more refined dining experience possibly with a full open bar or wine during the meal.

I've always had what I consider to be an inadequate budget, and, as a result, I've had to learn how to be resourceful, and, if possible, get things for free. Here are a few examples of things that have worked for me.

- When I was trying to develop an upgrading incentive program at WGBH, I needed an attractive item to send donors, but I had no money to pay for it. I successfully solicited a donation of 2,000 pewter goblets (including engraving) from a local jeweler in exchange for a promotional credit on my leadership donor brochure. I had to show the jeweler that the demographics of the PBS audience were similar to those of his ideal client and that his company would gain valuable exposure through association with my leadership donor program. I projected over three years the number of donors who would see his company's name within a given radius of his store. I also used statistics from a survey done on the PBS audience to illustrate how closely our constituency matched his.

- One year, when tax reform was a hot item, I received a brochure on tax reform from the bank that managed my institution's deferred giving assets. The brochure would be an excellent offering in my year-end mailing, so I approached the bank with the following offer: If the bank could supply sufficient brochures to handle inquiries from my mailing, I would offer its "Free Brochure on Tax Reform" thus affording the bank additional visibility with the right client profile. I got 400 free brochures.

- A trust company in a neighboring state sent a promotional letter outlining the bank's services in estate planning. It appeared that the bank was in a new business mode and potentially might be willing to collaborate on a joint event. I called the vice president whose signature had been preprinted on the cover letter and asked if I could meet him for lunch to discuss a mutually beneficial proposition. Over lunch, I explained that there were many potential prospects within the area his bank served and that I proposed to join with the bank in producing an estate planning luncheon. As I explained to him, the bank was seeking new trust business and I was seeking life income gifts from these prospects. My problem was simply a lack of money to run an event. I suggested that we work together to create a mutually beneficial event in which I would get the prospects and the bank would pay for everything including printing, postage, and food. The plan was accepted immediately.

There are other ways to cut costs. For example, if your organization sends regular communications to its constituency, you can produce a lead-generating insert that can be included from time to time. (See Chapter III–1 for some ideas on the kinds of inserts you can produce.) In this way, you can get your planned giving message out without the additional cost of postage or envelopes. (*Author's Note: If the weight of your insert pushes the mailing piece into the next postage bracket, your planned giving budget will be expected to pay for the extra postage the insert caused.*)

You can also piggyback on cultivation events planned by the annual giving program. For example, perhaps your annual giving society has a special annual event. Ask if the planned giving donors could be invited at the expense of the planned giving department. If any of them attend, you pay the cost per person from your planned giving budget. In this way, the most important donors in the planned giving program can be cultivated regularly within the context of an ongoing institutional event. The donors receive the attention and recognition they deserve while the numbers are still small enough not to be a problem. All you pay for is the food/beverage cost per person. This works very well for new programs that don't have the numbers of donors or the money to hold lavish events.

You must learn to be very resourceful and imaginative when it comes to planning and monitoring a budget. Be creative and do the best you can. Most fund raisers are working with budgets they think are too small.

Once you have your program objectives outlined, the dollar goals established, and the budget itemized, you can then develop a calendar of activities for the year. Clearly, you have much to do. Many of the activities must be accomplished simultaneously, and, as you get deeper and deeper into the plan, you'll find it increasingly difficult to stay on track.

THE CALENDAR OF ACTIVITIES

This calendar of activities runs from January to December. However, you can substitute any 12-month period, making adjustments whenever necessary, taking into account your organization's fiscal year, year-end giving, or other cyclical activities unique to your organization.

Much of the work during the initial months of starting a new program involves planning and laying the groundwork for the year's activities. The board will need to approve some broad and some specific recommendations. Therefore, your initial two months will be consumed with getting ready for a meeting of the board.

Find out when the next meeting is scheduled and get yourself on the agenda. The board probably meets quarterly. If the length of time before the next board meeting is too short, the chairman may call a special meeting of the executive committee to address only the planned giving agenda items. Or, you may simply wait until the next quarterly meeting.

A few words must be said about the calendar of activities. If you are just starting your program, you need to do several things:

- Select legal counsel.
- Create a bequest or deferred giving society.
- Select a bank manager for the deferred giving assets.
- Create a gift annuity program.
- Evaluate your need for your own pooled income fund or utilize a Common Pooled Income Fund run by a community foundation.
- Identify prospects.
- Plan and implement mailings.
- Develop an estate planning newsletter.
- Create a planned giving committee.
- Cultivate, solicit, and steward prospects.

No two programs are alike. Therefore, the following suggestions should be modified to suit your individual circumstances. A few words of advice are in order before I continue.

The charitable giving landscape has changed since the first edition of this book in 1988. Back in the 1970s, few organizations had heard of a pooled income fund. In the 1980s, the pooled income fund was a very popular vehicle because the rates of return in the 1980s were in the double digits. I can remember when the pooled income fund I was running at public television yielded 14%! At that time, the rates for charitable gift annuities were substantially lower than they are today, except for the very oldest donors. As we move into the 2000s, things are very, very different.

Interest rates are so significantly reduced from their double digit days that a pooled income fund plays a much reduced role in many planned giving programs today. Also, the stakes are higher than they were 10 or 20 years ago. You need to focus your planned giving program on the top donors. That means mastering knowledge about charitable remainder trusts where the practical minimum is $100,000, and even that level is low by today's standards. It would seem that $250,000 is much more appropriate for the entry level of a charitable trust. To a large degree, the increased minimum has to do with the tremendous explosion of planned giving in recent years and the increased fees that fiduciaries are charging for small accounts. The minimum fees will devastate the performance of a small charitable remainder trust if you don't have enough assets to get a consolidated fee schedule. Therefore, the following calendar of activities supports an emphasis on the larger gifts, those that will truly make a difference for your success. The smaller gifts will take care of themselves.

JANUARY

- Interview other planned giving professionals to gather comparison data on the operation, policies, and results of their planned giving programs. (See Chapter I–2)

- Interview candidates for legal counsel for your planned giving program. (See Chapter I–6)

- Send requests for proposals (RFPs) to the top five candidates for management of your deferred giving assets. Give them 30 days to respond. (See Chapter III-9)

  (Author's note: At this early stage, you don't need a manager for your gift annuity program. You can manage the gift annuities in-house in the beginning. Also, you may elect to use a Common Community Foundation Pooled Income Fund instead of starting your own in the beginning. See Chapter II-7 for information about your options.)

- Begin to identify prospects for leadership gift solicitations. (See Chapter I–5 for a discussion about prospecting and research.) Also, during your review of current donors, start to develop a list of those who have the potential to become the core of a planned giving committee. You will begin to cultivate these people so that they will be receptive to helping you when you approach them in July and August. (See Chapter III–2 for a discussion about setting up a volunteer committee.)

- Meet with the chairman of the board to review the board members for gift potential and gift solicitation strategies. The chairman of the board must be willing to make a financial commitment and also solicit the board. Identify leadership potential of board members. (*Author's Note: Unfortunately, not all boards are comprised of people with leadership potential. Do not let this deter you from asking for 100% participation. Even a token gift from a board member of modest means will make a difference. You want to be able to say, "Every board member has made a financial commitment to the program." Outright gifts count. Do not pursue a board member for a deferred gift if he or she has already made a significant outright gift.*)

FEBRUARY

- Set up individual meetings with candidates for administration of your deferred giving assets following responses to your letter in January. Coordinate with your Treasurer's Office.

- Work with director of development to finalize recommendations regarding the gift options you intend to offer as well as gift crediting guidelines. (*Author's Note: In many cases, the comparison data and information secured through interviews with other planned giving professionals in January will support your recommendations.*)

- Meet with the records department to develop methods for recording and tracking planned gifts. Establish codes for various gift arrangements. Develop procedures for communicating accurate information on incoming gifts to the proper source for data entry purposes. Gifts that need to be tracked include: Pooled Income Fund, Charitable Remainder Trust, Charitable Lead Trust, Charitable Gift Annuity, Bequest Distribution, Life Insurance Distribution from a death, Outright gift of Life Insurance , Life Insurance Premium, and Gift of Real Estate with Life Tenancy.

- Prepare and mail a report to board of trustees for review in advance of March board meeting. This report should be sent with a cover letter from the chairman of the board endorsing the planned giving program, and outlining the role the trustees will be required to play. This includes making a financial commitment, assisting with prospect screenings, and assisting with solicitations. Your report includes a summary of your interviews with other planned giving professionals, recommendations on the type of gift options you propose to offer, a summary of your interviews with candidates for legal counsel with your recommendations, a summary of your interviews with trustee candidates for your life income plans with your recommendations, and a summary of your recommended crediting guidelines.

- Work with director of development and chairman of the board to develop appropriate solicitation strategies for each board member. One or two other senior board members may be asked to assist with this work.

- Begin to develop concept for planned giving brochures. (See Chapter III–1)

MARCH

- Board meets to endorse the establishment of a planned giving program, approve the gift options, select legal counsel, designate a manager for the life income gifts, and approve crediting guidelines. Chairman of the board outlines the importance of board involvement in the program especially for leadership gifts phase. Chairman of the board suggests that 100% participation is expected and alerts them that a formal request for support is forthcoming. Chairman of the board also informs the board that there will be a planned giving training session in May. If possible, a date is announced at this time.

- Solicitation letters are mailed to the board with a suggestion of a personal visit by the Chairman.

- Following approval by the board, confirm selection of manager for the deferred giving assets. Meet with asset manager to review procedures for drafting documents, coordinating asset transfers, and administering charitable remainder trusts.

- Following approval by the board, engage legal counsel to prepare sample charitable remainder trust documents for your organization. These can be complete and legally correct except for the percentage payout, the payout schedule, the name of the donor and the sequence of beneficiaries, and other optional provisions.

- Begin to develop internal procedures for administering charitable gift annuities. (See Chapter II-8)

- Complete first draft of planned giving brochure.

- Chairman of the board begins following up with board members to secure gifts and pledges. You will work closely with the chairman at this time to assist whenever possible. Some board members will require a personal visit; others will require a phone call and follow-up proposal. Once the chairman has secured a commitment, it is your job to finalize the details of the gift.

- Develop plans for prospect screenings. Identify and recruit volunteers for first prospect screening in April. (See Chapter I–5)

- Begin developing plans for board training session. (*Author's Note: You can run the training session yourself or hire one of the consultants listed in Appendix IV. If there is resistance to fund raising among the board members, it may be advisable to use a planned giving consultant.*)

- Schedule a planned giving training seminar for staff in April. (See Chapter III–4)

APRIL

- All board members should have been approached for a financial commitment to the planned giving program. (Note: Major outright gifts are the best planned gift—don't forget that.)

- Finalize internal procedures for administering the gift annuities, if appropriate.

- Hold first prospect screening. Begin to compile list of leadership prospects. Isolate top prospects for research if you have a research department. Continue to develop your list of potential members of your future planned giving committee.

- Hold planned giving training seminar for staff.

- Continue developing the planned giving training seminar for the board in May.

- Identify and recruit volunteers for second prospect screening in May.

MAY

- Hold second prospect screening. Pull out top prospects for research; continue identifying potential planned giving committee members.

- Hold planned giving training seminar for board.

- Meet with director of development and chairman of the board to review prospect names to be passed out at June board meeting. Each member receives five prospect assignments. (*Author's Note:*

You will spend considerable time on this process. It includes many different activities from running screenings, having meetings, researching the prospects, determining the proper strategy, making the proper assignments, putting together prospect kits, etc. In this plan, the board members receive their assignments at their June meeting. However, if you can manage it, you can distribute the prospect assignments as part of the planned giving training seminar in May. Moving this process back one month also means moving your printing schedule back one month.)

- Complete final draft of planned giving brochure. Work with communications department on design, color, quantity, size, *etc.* Print brochures, pledge cards, crediting guidelines, and reply envelopes.

- Identify volunteers for third prospect screening in June.

JUNE

- Board meeting. Chairman of the board reports on the progress of the first five months. Legal counsel has been hired, fiduciary manager for deferred giving assets has been hired, administrative procedures have been established for all of the gift options the institution intends to offer. New planned giving brochures and other materials have been produced, and, a list of leadership prospects has been developed. The chairman announces progress of Board commitments. The chairman reinforces the importance of the board's role in the leadership gift phase and passes out five prospect kits to each board member. Each prospect kit contains:

  For the board member: Research profile on the prospect, suggested solicitation strategy, suggested gift size, contact form for reporting results of meeting, phone call, *etc.*, reply envelope. Also include copies of your organization's letterhead. (*Author's Note: Some solicitors will have access to typing resources and will generate their own letters; others will send a draft to you for typing or have their own secretary type the letters.*)

  For the prospect: A pocket folder containing planned giving brochure, gift crediting guidelines, pledge card, reply envelope, a large mailing envelope pre-addressed to the prospect. (*Author's Note: You cannot easily determine how much postage each packet will need. Thus, it will be necessary for each board member to pay the postage individually and then, if desired, ask for reimbursement. Also, providing a pre-addressed envelope does not mean the solicitation kits are supposed to be mailed to the prospects—personal visits must be attempted first. Then, and only as a last resort, the packet can be mailed.*)

  Another way to handle the prospect assignments is to pass out a list of prospects for review by the Board so that prospects can be picked. Then, the prospect kit for each prospect can be given to the appropriate Board member.

- Board members begin solicitations. The timing of these solicitations falls just prior to summer months when vacation schedules can make visits difficult. Still, most of the prospects will be available at some point during this period. Do the best you can and finish the work in September or October, if necessary. Most important is to get leadership solicitations underway. You will want to announce the program to the entire constituency in the September issue of your organization's magazine or newsletter, or in a general communication.

- Begin writing an article that will appear in the September issue of your organization's regular newsletter, magazine, or other publication. Launching the program in September is important in order for you to capitalize on year-end giving. If you do not have a mechanism for communicating to your constituency, you'll have to create a direct mail piece at least this one time. If cost is a consideration, identify the most important members of your constituency who should be informed about your new program. For organizations with a large constituency, you may have to start with the top 10% to 20% of the constituency.

This article sets the tone for the future. It outlines the organization's long-term objectives, instills confidence and faith in the constituency, and generates a new kind of energy and momentum. Many organizations begin building a permanent endowment fund as a result of establishing a planned giving program. Thus, specific dollar goals should be outlined. Foremost, the article should emphasize the institutional objectives followed by a discussion of the gift options that are now available to help supporters participate in building a strong future for the organization. If possible, include donor testimonials (with pictures) of some of the leadership donors speaking in their own words about how they participated and benefited from tax savings, a new income flow, or in other ways with their commitments. Remember to include in your article that you have received support from "100% of the board." Include a response mechanism in order to generate leads.

- Identify potential candidates for chair of your first planned giving committee. (See Chapter III–2)

- Hold third prospect screening. Continue research activities on top prospects. Continue to identify potential planned giving committee members.

- Identify volunteers for fourth prospect screening in July.

JULY

- Finalize article for September communication and submit to newsletter or magazine editor or to the design department for production. (*Author's Note: It will be very useful to create 100 to 200 reprints of this article for use in prospect kits and solicitations throughout the next six-month period. Many people will not have seen it or will have passed over it quickly the first time.*)

- Continue working with the board on solicitation assignments. Follow-up calls by the chairman of the board will be required in many cases. Adjust prospect assignments as necessary. (*Author's Note: Some board members will not contact their prospects. If you are convinced that a member of the group is not going to do the job, reconcile yourself to reassigning some prospects. Do not try to force a square peg into a round hole. It will only make you crazy. Simply take back the prospects and move on.*)

- Recruit the chair of your planned giving committee using a letter from the chairman of the board and a follow-up call from the chairman. Begin to work with the planned giving chair to review the list of potential planned giving committee members you've been collecting since January. Identify other potential candidates with the assistance of the chair and others.

- Chair of planned giving committee sends letters (that you ghost write) to top 10 potential candidates. Chair makes follow up calls to potential members.

- Hold fourth prospect screening. Continue research on top prospects.

- Identify volunteers for fifth prospect screening in August. Or, if you have held enough prospect screening sessions for now, don't do another one just yet.

AUGUST

- Continue working with board members on solicitation assignments. By this time you may want to turn to the beginning of this chapter to reread the short description of a typical day in the life of a planned giving officer which probably describes how you are feeling right now—totally overwhelmed by the pace of your job. Welcome to planned giving!

- Chair of the planned giving committee continues recruiting committee members. By the end of August, all members should be recruited and an orientation day in September is scheduled.

- Hold fifth prospect screening if desired. Continue research on top prospects.

- Begin putting together prospect kits for planned giving committee members who have reviewed prospect lists and have selected five prospects each. Each member gets the prospects at September orientation session.

- Identify volunteers for sixth prospect screening in September, if needed.

- Begin developing agenda for planned giving committee orientation in September. Work with chair of planned giving committee to develop solicitation strategies for committee members.

- Begin development of year-end mailing to go out in November.

- Begin plans for your first planned giving seminar for donors in October.

SEPTEMBER

- General announcement of the establishment of your planned giving program in the organization's regular publication or in a separate mailing.

- Hold orientation meeting for planned giving committee members. Distribute prospect lists created through the past many months of screenings.

- Board members complete all solicitation assignments. (*Author's Note: Equally likely, some are complete, others are still in progress, and still others may never be done.*) Prepare report for September board meeting.

- Continue developing plans for October planned giving donor seminar. Mail invitations four to six weeks in advance.

- Hold sixth prospect screening. Continue research activities on top prospects.

- Begin to assist planned giving committee members with their prospect assignments.

- Identify volunteers and schedule seventh prospect screening for October.

- Meet with director of development to review the year's activities and begin to develop a master plan for next year. Imagine, planning for year two already??? Absolutely!!!

OCTOBER

- Hold planned giving donor event.

- Chair of planned giving committee follows up with committee members on prospect assignments.

- Continue working with planned giving committee on prospect assignments.

- Follow up inquiries generated from September mailing.

- Finalize year-end mailing and deliver to design department for production and mailing in November (day after Thanksgiving).

- Hold seventh prospect screening. Continue to research top prospects.

NOVEMBER

- Meeting of planned giving committee. Review progress. Reassign prospects if necessary. Discuss problems encountered by committee members. Share successes. Deliver hard-hitting message about year-end giving. Identify the most important prospects who must be seen or contacted by mid-December. Leave the rest for next year. You will not have time to finish all assignments that are still remaining now. Don't worry about it. They will still be there in January.

- Mail year-end tax-related mailing (day after Thanksgiving).

- Continue to follow up as necessary with prospects in progress.

- Continue to follow up inquiries from September mailing.

- Continue to work with members of planned giving committee on their solicitation assignments.

- Follow up as necessary with prospects resulting from October planned giving donor seminar.

- Special letter from chairman of the board to board members for repeat gifts.

- Finalize Master Plan for next year, including new operational objectives, calendar of activities, dollar and other goals, and budget.

DECEMBER

- Follow up all solicitations in progress. Contact earlier donors for cultivation visits and possibly additional gift solicitation. Chair of planned giving committee follows up with committee members on prospect assignments.

- Prepare report for December board meeting.

- Identify volunteers and schedule eighth prospect screening for January, if needed.

- Do not under any circumstances take a vacation in December!!! Sorry. This is when lots of action should be taking place.

If you follow the kind of plan I have outlined here, you will create a planned giving program that will be the envy of your peers. If you develop a program that even remotely resembles this plan, you'll be doing far better than most people. This is a blueprint for success—success that is due in large measure to the involvement and commitment of the board and to the proper use of volunteers. Take this blueprint and adapt it to your own institution's cycles.

Recognize, however, that the success of this planned giving program depends not on mailings but on personal contact. And what about cultivation? Yes, you will do all of the things you know are essential to cultivate your prospects or donors. For a wealth of ideas, turn to Chapter III-3. Still, the most important cultivation activity is already running like a thread through your entire program—getting people involved. Planned giving is people giving to people. If you have that, you cannot fail.

SUMMARY

As you have seen through the development of this chapter, running a planned giving program involves a complex set of considerations all of which are related. The objectives, calendar of activities, dollar goals, and the budget become one master plan. You cannot develop one without thinking of the other three. At first, you may feel quite overwhelmed wondering where to start. Perhaps you can take some comfort in knowing it does get easier after you've been through one or more fiscal years. Just between you and me, however, I always got very restless during budget planning because it prevented me from doing the real work (and fun) of the job— visiting donors or prospects. Finding those prospects is the subject of the next chapter.

Worksheet For Developing Planned Giving Budget

Salaries

Director of Planned Giving $_____
Secretary to Director $_____
Assistant Director of Planned Giving $_____
Other _____ $_____
Other _____ $_____ $_____
Benefits @ _____% of total salaries $_____

Occupancy

_____square feet @ occupancy rate of $_____/sq. ft. $_____

Professional Affiliations/Memberships

A. _____ $_____
B. _____ $_____
C. _____ $_____
D. _____ $_____ $_____

Mileage for travel to _____ meetings @ $_____/mile $_____
Parking for _____ meetings @ $_____/meeting $_____
Food charge for _____ meetings @ $_____/meeting $_____

Subscriptions and books

A. *Wall Street Journal* $_____
B. Loose-leaf tax service $_____
C. Monthly tax newsletter $_____
D. Other _____ $_____ $_____

Professional Fees

A. Management of deferred giving assets $_____
B. Legal Counsel $_____
C. Fund Raising Consultant $_____
D. Other _____ $_____ $_____

Office Equipment

A. Computer $_____
B. Printer $_____
C. Planned giving software $_____
D. Other software $_____
E. Maintenance contract for PG software $_____
F. Service contracts for Personal computer/printer $_____
G. Desks, chairs, tables, computer furniture,
   lamps, file cabinets, book cases $_____
H. Calculator $_____
I. Other _____ $_____ $_____

Telephone/Communications

A. General $_____/month $_____
B. Toll Free Number $_____

C. Fax $\underline{\hspace{3cm}}$
D. Cellular Phone $\underline{\hspace{3cm}}$
E. Other $\underline{\hspace{5cm}}$ $\underline{\hspace{3cm}}$ $\underline{\hspace{3cm}}$

Photocopying

_____ copies/month @ $____/copy $\underline{\hspace{3cm}}$

General Office Supplies $\underline{\hspace{3cm}}$

Travel and Entertainment

Includes mileage, hotels, air fare, rental cars, meals,
house gifts, tips, taxis, *etc.* $\underline{\hspace{3cm}}$

Postage

A. General correspondence
_____ pieces/month @ first class rate $\underline{\hspace{3cm}}$
B. Postage for Mailing #1
_____ pieces @ _____ first class _____ bulk $\underline{\hspace{3cm}}$
C. Postage for Mailing #2
_____ pieces @ _____ first class _____ bulk $\underline{\hspace{3cm}}$
D. Postage for Mailing #3
_____ pieces @ _____ first class _____ bulk $\underline{\hspace{3cm}}$
E. Postage for invitations to Donor event #1
_____ pieces @ _____ first class _____ bulk $\underline{\hspace{3cm}}$
F. Postage for invitations to Donor event #2
_____ pieces @ _____ first class _____ bulk $\underline{\hspace{3cm}}$
G. Postage for invitations to Donor event #3
_____ pieces @ _____ first class _____ bulk $\underline{\hspace{3cm}}$
H. Postage for quarterly (semi-annual) newsletter
_____ pieces @ _____ first class _____ bulk $\underline{\hspace{3cm}}$
I. Postage for year-end mailing
_____ pieces @ _____ first class _____ bulk $\underline{\hspace{3cm}}$ $\underline{\hspace{3cm}}$

Volunteer Reimbursed Expenses

Includes mileage, hotels, air fare, rental cars, meals,
house gifts, tips, taxis, telephone, postage, *etc.* $\underline{\hspace{3cm}}$

Print Materials

A. Brochure #1 $\underline{\hspace{4cm}}$
Design (___ hours @ $___/hour) $\underline{\hspace{3cm}}$
Photography $\underline{\hspace{3cm}}$
Printing $\underline{\hspace{3cm}}$
Shipping $\underline{\hspace{3cm}}$ $\underline{\hspace{3cm}}$

B. Brochure #2 $\underline{\hspace{4cm}}$
Design (___ hours @ $___/hour) $\underline{\hspace{3cm}}$
Photography $\underline{\hspace{3cm}}$
Printing $\underline{\hspace{3cm}}$
Shipping $\underline{\hspace{3cm}}$ $\underline{\hspace{3cm}}$

C. Brochure #3 _____
    Design (___ hours @ $___/hour) $_____
    Photography $_____
    Printing $_____
    Shipping $_____ $_____

D. Planned Giving Stationery/Envelopes: Printing $_____

E. Gift Crediting Guidelines: Printing $_____

F. Year-end mailing (pamphlet, outside envelope,
    return envelope, reply card)
    Design (___ hours @ $___/hour) $_____
    Printing $_____
    Mailing house handling fees
    (affix labels, fold, stuff, seal, affix postage, bundle, mail) $_____ $_____

G. Quarterly/Semi-Annual Donor Newsletter

    Purchased from consultant ____ copies @ $_____/copy $_____

    Produced in-house
    Design (___ hours @ $___/hour) $_____
    Photography $_____
    Printing $_____ $_____

H. Pledge Forms
    Design (___ hours @ $___/hour) $_____
    Printing $_____ $_____

I. Invitations

    Donor event #1 _____
    Design (___ hours @ $___/hour) $_____
    Printing $_____ $_____

    Donor event #2 _____
    Design (___ hours @ $___/hour) $_____
    Printing $_____ $_____

    Donor event #3 _____
    Design (___ hours @ $___/hour) $_____
    Printing $_____ $_____

J. Recognition certificates $_____

K. Pooled Income Fund Disclosure Statement
    Design (___ hours @ $___/hour) $_____
    Printing $_____ $_____

L. Instruments of Transfer for Pooled Income Fund
    Printing $_____

M. Generic Brochures purchased from consultant

    Brochure #1 _____

_____copies @ $ ____/copy $_____

Brochure #2 _____
_____copies @ $ ____/copy $_____

Brochure #3 _____
_____copies @ $ ____/copy $_____

N. Direct response mailings

Mailing #1 _____
Design (___ hours @ $___/hour) $_____
Printing $_____
Mailing house handling fees $_____
(affix labels, fold, stuff, seal, affix postage, bundle, mail) $_____ $_____

Mailing #2 _____
Design (___ hours @ $___/hour) $_____
Printing $_____
Mailing house handling fees $_____
(affix labels, fold, stuff, seal, affix postage, bundle, mail) $_____ $_____

Mailing #3 _____
Design (___ hours @ $___/hour) $_____
Printing $_____
Mailing house handling fees $_____
(affix labels, fold, stuff, seal, affix postage, bundle, mail) $_____ $_____

Donor Events

A. Donor event #1 _____
Room rental $_____
Food @ $_____/person $_____
Liquor @ $_____/person $_____
Gratuity @ _____% $_____
Tax @ _____ % $_____
Service staff $_____
Flowers for ____ tables @ $_____/table $_____
Audio/visual equipment $_____
Photography $_____
Pre-paid parking for guests $_____
Coat check $_____
Speaker fee or honorarium $_____
Other _____ $_____ $_____

B. Donor event #2 _____
Room rental $_____
Food @ $_____/person $_____
Liquor @ $_____/person $_____
Gratuity @ _____% $_____
Tax @ _____ % $_____
Service staff $_____
Flowers for ____ tables @ $_____/table $_____
Audio/visual equipment $_____
Photography $_____
Pre-paid parking for guests $_____

Coat check $_____

Speaker fee or honorarium $_____

Other _____ $_____ $_____

C. Donor event #3 _____

Room rental $_____

Food @ $_____/person $_____

Liquor @ $_____/person $_____

Gratuity @ _____% $_____

Tax @ _____% $_____

Service staff $_____

Flowers for _____ tables @ $_____/table $_____

Audio/visual equipment $_____

Photography $_____

Pre-paid parking for guests $_____

Coat check $_____

Speaker fee or honorarium $_____

Other _____ $_____ $_____

Books on Fund Raising, Taxation, Estate Planning

A. _____ $_____

B. _____ $_____

C. _____ $_____

D. _____ $_____ $_____

Miscellaneous House Gifts for Donors

_____ @ $_____ $_____

Special Thank-You Gifts for Donors

_____ @ $_____ $_____

Print Advertising

$_____

Conferences/Seminars

Air fare $_____

Hotel $_____

Conference registration $_____

Taxi/ground transportation $_____

Meals $_____ $_____

Flowers for funerals or wakes

$_____

Miscellaneous

A. Annual fee for business credit card $_____

B. Production of audio/visual aids $_____

C. Membership fee for local "Club" $_____

D. Television or radio advertising $_____

E. Other_____ $_____

F. Other_____ $_____

G. Other_____ $_____

TOTAL:

$_____

Chapter I–5

HOW TO IDENTIFY PLANNED GIVING PROSPECTS

Your position as Director of Planned Giving requires you to raise money. Depending on where you work, the process will be very different. If you are running a new program, you will be starting from scratch. Or, if you arrive at an institution with a mature program, things will be in motion already. In that case, there will be lots of people in various stages of considering gifts, and there will be some gifts already in progress, waiting for you to tidy up the loose ends. In the latter case, you will have to jump on a moving train without losing a beat.

Some very lucky planned giving officers will work in a planned giving department where time will be consumed with incoming calls or incoming letters from people who want to make gifts. I have never experienced such a program, but I know that they do exist. To be fair, I have had the occasional large gift out of the blue, but only rarely and not as a steady pattern. I have also worked with colleagues (major gifts officers) who transferred from an organization where the gifts just rolled in, and I am convinced that they have no clue how to find, cultivate, and solicit prospects. If you have turned to this book as a guide, chances are you are going to put together your own program. If you read and follow the advice in this chapter, you will be able to do a lot more fund raising than some of your more experienced colleagues. My recommendations will not always be easy to pull off. You will become frustrated and impatient. But, just remember, if you lay the right groundwork, you will build a strong program that will be successful.

Prospects and donors come from several places:

- Repeat gifts from existing donors (solicited or unsolicited);
- Inquiries from direct mail and other marketing initiatives;
- Blind inquiries driven by the donor's timing;
- Referrals from other development staff (major gifts officers, annual giving officers, principal gifts officers, *etc.*);
- People you identify, cultivate, and solicit on your own.

A healthy program receives gifts from all of these categories. This chapter deals only with the last group—people you identify. So, where do you start?

Fortunately for you, many kinds of people can be planned giving prospects—young, old, male, female, single, married, very wealthy, living on a fixed income. With such a diverse market, you must understand who your planned giving prospects might be and why so that you can set priorities for your program. First, let me discuss several common myths about planned giving donors.

MYTH I: PEOPLE WHO MAKE OUTRIGHT GIFTS ARE NOT PLANNED GIVING DONORS

Wrong.

> Example: You identify a gift annuity prospect, talk with her several times, prepare a formal proposal, and, finally receive the phone call you've been waiting for. Well, almost. After speaking with her advisor, she decides to make an outright gift instead of establishing a gift annuity. She really doesn't need the income. Instead, she needs the largest charitable deduction.

Is this a planned gift? Of course! This prospect made a gift that best suits her unique financial circumstances. But, if you are new to planned giving, you may feel disappointed because you really wanted to build your gift annuity pool. Don't be disappointed. It is common for donors to make outright gifts as a result of solicitations for all sorts of deferred gift vehicles. It is always better to get an outright gift that your organization can use immediately.

In many, many cases, the planned giving officer is so focused on a life income plan that he or she ignores the outright gift as a possibility. Always remember that the best gift is the straight outright gift. You will be a hero if you come home with an outright gift instead of a gift annuity, pooled income fund gift, or charitable trust.

MYTH 2: PLANNED GIVING APPLIES ONLY TO OLDER PEOPLE

Wrong.

Certainly, there are reasons to target older (70 plus) prospects for deferred gift options—bequests and life income gifts are excellent for older people not only because they can help the donor generate a new income or unlock a highly appreciated, low-yielding asset but also because your institution will receive the funds in a reasonable period of time. Nevertheless, young and middle-aged prospects can also benefit from participation in deferred gifts. This younger group includes individuals who own inherited assets, closely-held stock, real estate, or who are newly wealthy from a dot.com enterprise. As the baby boomers age, they also have millions of dollars in retirement plan assets. Such assets were not a factor in fund raising 20 years ago.

An important category of younger donors who may benefit from a charitable trust or deferred payment gift annuity are those in peak earning years who already have substantial pension plans, retirement assets or IRAs. By establishing a life income gift, a younger person (age 45-60) can continue to build additional funds for income in retirement. I have worked with a number of donors who were nervous about making outright gifts at a young age. In these cases, a charitable trust or deferred gift annuity was the perfect solution. The donor was able to make the gift, receive an income tax deduction, avoid immediate capital gain taxes, and take the plunge to be charitable. At a later date, after becoming comfortable with their financial situation, these younger donors could relinquish their income interests, close out the arrangement, receive a charitable deduction for the relinquished income stream, and let the charity use the funds.

MYTH 3: PLANNED GIVING PROSPECTS ARE USUALLY VERY WEALTHY

Wrong.

This is simply not true. In fact, planned giving works best for a person who is trying to get the most mileage out of fairly limited assets. In such a case, the transfer of very low-yielding securities that are highly appreciated has a positive impact because the donor's income is doubled or tripled, because there is no immediate loss to capital gain taxes, and because the charitable deduction helps to reduce income taxes. In most life income programs, there are many people who would never show up on a list of wealthy individuals.

MYTH 4: YOU CANNOT ASK A SMALL DONOR FOR A LARGE GIFT

Wrong.

Just one example of a gift annuity prospect illustrates this point. I visited a retired postal worker in the class of 1931 who had been contributing $5,000 outright per year. He was a widower, attended every event we held, was incredibly loyal, and had a bequest of an unknown amount. Nobody had ever asked him for a specific gift and nobody had ever visited with him. His annual contributions just showed up each year.

A colleague and I visited him and presented a proposal for a $50,000 charitable gift annuity. He thought about it for a few months and, before the end of that tax year, he said yes. He revealed that he had included the institution in his will for $100,000 and that he would be willing to give half of the bequest early because the gift annuity paid much higher than his money market account. He was very happy with the annuity payment and with the charitable deduction he received. The next year, he gave the other $50,000 for another gift annuity. During this time, he also continued to make his regular annual fund gift of $5,000.

MYTH 5: SMALL DONORS AT THE $5 OR $10 LEVEL ARE NOT PLANNED GIVING PROSPECTS

Wrong.

Many people make tiny gifts to your organization while participating as leadership donors for other institutions. Why? Because they have never been asked by you. Later in this chapter, I discuss how to conduct a screening session to uncover these people. Once identified, it is up to you and your organization to provide these donors opportunities for quality interaction with your president, trustees, and other key individuals using some of the cultivation activities discussed in Chapter III–3.

MYTH 6: PLANNED GIVING HURTS ANNUAL GIVING

Wrong.

As a result of the increase in personalized attention resulting from a planned gift experience with your organization, the majority of planned giving donors will increase their annual gifts in the future. At the very least, they will continue their regular annual gift.

> Example: Think about the elderly widow who has supported your organization for 20 years. She is living on a fixed income which is why her annual gift is only $50 per year. But, she also owns stock (currently yielding, say, 2%) with a low cost basis. This woman is typical of many overlooked prospects who could easily give $5,000, $10,000 or more to one of your life income plans, significantly increase her income, avoid a capital gain tax, and receive a generous income tax deduction in the year of the gift.

In planned giving, the following gift history is not uncommon:

Year 1	$50	annual gift
Year 2	$50	annual gift
Year 3	$50	annual gift
Year 4	$50	annual gift
Year 5	$20,000	Charitable Gift Annuity
Year 6	$100	annual gift
Year 7	$100	annual gift
Year 8	$100	annual gift
Year 9	$25,000	Charitable Gift Annuity
Year 10	$100	annual gift

Or, how about this one that I had:

Year 1	$1,000	annual gift
Year 2	$1,000	annual gift
Year 3	$1,000	annual gift
Year 4	$1,000	annual gift
Year 5	$1,000	annual gift
Year 6	$1,000	annual gift

Year 7	$1,000,000	Charitable Remainder Trust
Year 8	$1,000	annual gift
Year 9	$1,000	annual gift
Year 10	$1,000	annual gift

Furthermore, don't underestimate the possibility of securing a major portion of the prospect's estate through a bequest. Even if the major (or only asset) is a home, just think what your organization would receive with 20%, 30%, or 50% of her estate!

Finally, your mid-range donors are probably not being cultivated by anybody else. Thus the door is open for your organization to make a difference in their lives, bring them closer, and attract a large commitment.

A FEW GROUND RULES FOR PROSPECTING ACTIVITY

First, prospecting is an ongoing process. The work you start today with one prospect may not turn into a gift for several months or several years. Accordingly, you must balance your time between the present and the future.

Second, do not try to uncover more prospects than you, your volunteers, or your staff can follow up in a reasonable time. Each inquiry generated from one of your marketing initiatives deserves prompt attention. That is not always possible, and it is really quite difficult to get to everybody, but you need to strive for quickest and most prompt follow-up possible to the people requesting information.

Once, I did a planned giving mailing to 10,000 people and received 500 reply cards requesting information. While this may sound like fund raising heaven, I can tell you that it was a disaster. It bogged down the office and produced a feeling of helplessness and frustration for me and my staff. There was no way we could follow up such a large number of inquiries in a personalized and timely way (pre-computer age). Even today, it would be difficult.

Has this happened to you? If so, there is an easy solution for the future. Stagger the drop date for a mailing over several weeks. Instead of mailing 10,000 all at once, mail 2,000 per week for five weeks, or 1,000 per week for ten weeks. The mailing house can easily accommodate a staggered mailing schedule. And, this strategy will result in a comfortable pace of inquiries without overwhelming you.

Third, spend most of your money to move existing donors to higher levels rather than mailing to people who have never contributed. This comment is for those charities that do not have a built-in constituency like a school or college. The task of acquiring new donors and bringing them through a structured upgrading cycle rests with the annual giving function. Then, only after interest has been established can your efforts in planned giving be effective.

Your planned giving program will not be successful if you market gift options to people who are not already involved either as donors or as current or past users of your organization's services. Your planned giving program will be successful if you introduce emotionally committed individuals to creative ways to give.

I suppose there might be exceptions to this rule (and even some success stories) from organizations with universal appeal like the Salvation Army, the Jewish Appeal, the Cardinal's Appeal, or the Baptist Foundation where mailings to vast numbers of anonymous people from purchased lists will produce bequests way down the road. On the other hand, most planned giving officers reading this book are just starting out and need to set priorities for the first few years of activity. The best prospects you have in the immediate future are already donors.

An example of my disastrous attempt to acquire new donors through a planned giving mailing illustrates this point:

> When I was employed by public television, I bought from a mailing house 5,000 names, each of which had a very high household income for the time. I mailed what I thought was a very

attractive brochure explaining the benefits of contributing to the WGBH Pooled Income Fund with a reply card that could be returned for more information. I thought I could attract new pooled income fund donors because the tax benefits and other advantages of the pooled income fund were so compelling. *Not one person responded.*

My mistake was clear. Although the people on the list were capable of making what was then the minimum entry level gift of $5,000, they had no prior history of involvement with or interest in public television and thus were not inspired even to inquire about our pooled income fund.

PLANNED GIVING SHOULD NOT BE OPERATED IN A VACUUM

Often a conflict develops between planned giving and other fund raising efforts (annual giving, major gifts, principal gifts, or the campaign). This unfortunate situation can be due to a general lack of understanding of what planned giving is. It can also occur when the director of planned giving is isolated from other fund raising activities and exhibits a protective attitude about planned giving donors.

There is no such thing as a planned giving prospect or donor. The entire development office and, for that matter, the entire organization, has a limited universe of prospects from which to draw financial support, expertise to help run services, and volunteer assistance. Your planned giving program can't have its own set of prospects. The success of the annual giving program will give you a base from which to draw your prospects, and, in turn, your success in planned giving will enhance the annual giving program. Everyone is working for the same purpose—to raise money for operating expenses, to secure capital gifts to expand or improve services, and to build long-term security in the form of permanent endowment.

To be successful and happy as the director of planned giving, you must not become territorial about your program or about your donors. You must continue to promote the overall needs of the institution—annual needs, capital needs, and endowment needs.

As director of planned giving, you will get to know your prospects on a very personal level. Thus, you have the power to influence the prospect's support of your organization's capital needs and also the annual giving program. In addition, you will be able to look for other ways in which an individual can serve the organization. If you already approach your job in a way that promotes the total welfare of your organization, then you are on the right track. You probably maintain a good working relationship with your colleagues, and you should have relatively little trouble running a well-integrated planned giving program. If, on the other hand, you protect your donors from interaction with others, you don't promote the annual giving program during prospect visits, and you feel "nobody understands what I do anyway," then it is time for a change.

Identifying prospects should always include four key questions:

1. What is the donor's potential for supporting our annual giving program?
2. What is the donor's potential for supporting our capital needs?
3. What is the donor's potential for an ultimate gift? (See Chapter III-8)
4. In what other beneficial ways can this individual become involved in our organization?

ACTIVE VS. PASSIVE PROSPECTING

There are many ways to conduct your prospecting work, but they break down into only two categories: 1) Active Prospecting, and 2) Passive Prospecting.

1) *Passive Prospecting: Prospects find you.*

Sending a direct mail piece or an estate planning newsletter with a reply card, or placing check-off blocks on pledge forms are typical methods of passive prospecting. These activities produce inquiries at the initiative of the prospect. Prospects who are identified in these ways expect you to contact them. This part of prospecting is not addressed here. It will be covered in Chapter III–1 within the discussion of print materials.

2) *Active Prospecting: You find prospects.*

Active prospecting involves reviewing lists of individuals to identify those with whom you should be spending more time. It also involves using the many electronic searchable databases available today. Let's start with the most common type of activity, the screening session.

ORGANIZING A SCREENING SESSION

A seasoned fund raiser knows the most successful solicitations happen when the right solicitor asks the right prospect for the right gift at the right time. You and I know it is not always possible to infuse all four key ingredients into each solicitation. Nonetheless, experience tells us we must strive for this ideal.

You may ask yourself how other organizations secure major commitments from people who are currently on your list of $50 donors. Close examination of their strategy will probably reveal a relentless pursuit of information about the prospect and a strategic cultivation plan based on that information.

Every institution has three kinds of prospects worthy of attention. In the first group are those people known to be major philanthropists elsewhere. The second group consists of wealthy individuals unknown to you. And the third group consists of every-day people like the elderly widow with no children. All of them are mixed together on your donor or constituent list.

The major-philanthropist-type prospect has probably been on your major gift list for years. Most likely, you know more about this person than you do about your closest relatives, and, while everyone knows his or her potential, no one knows what it will take to get this person interested. There are many resources, which I'll discuss later, to which you can turn for information about affiliations, interests, and net worth, but there are no books or directories to tell you about personalities and motivations.

Fortunately, you can uncover important information about the elusive major prospect as well as identify others deserving of your attention through the help and guidance of the prospect's peers in a screening session.

A screening session is a meeting in which individuals come together confidentially to discuss a select group of prospects. More often than not, the individuals called upon to participate are themselves major prospects. Thus, the results of a successful screening session are three-fold:

1) unknown individuals of significant gift potential are identified and appropriate cultivation strategies developed for them,

2) more information is learned about elusive major prospects that were already known to you, and

3) those involved in the screening session experience a heightened awareness about the expectations for their own role in the fund raising effort.

There are numerous ways to conduct a screening session. I have selected a sequence of activities to show you how one process can develop systematically.

The rest of this chapter is organized as follows:

- Prepare a Prospecting Form.
- Identify a universe of donors to be screened.
- Identify a group of individuals who will be effective in screening your select universe of donors.
- Recruit the individuals you have identified as screeners.
- Conduct your screening session.

- Process the information from your screening session.
- Electronic screenings.

Prepare A Prospecting Form

In order to plan an appropriate strategy for each prospect, you need to know as much as possible about the prospect's family and personal considerations, business and professional affiliations, financial situation, hobbies, memberships, and other interests. You need to know if the prospect has supported other organizations like yours and at what levels. You need to be sensitive to the prospect's stage of life. For example, does he or she have several children or grandchildren in college who may drain resources for the next few years or is he or she retired and looking to sell the big house to move to Florida or Palm Springs?

If you are employed by a college or university, you may be able to get detailed information through your alumni office which usually performs surveys of graduates regularly, at least in five year intervals or before major reunions like the 25th or 50th.

For purposes of this chapter, assume you work for an organization that does not have readily available information on its constituency or donors. Therefore, you must develop a form that will be used to compile the information from your screening sessions. At the end of this chapter is a form you can copy directly from this book.

Compiling the information on a prospect form takes a lot of time. The information comes from many sources and can take days to complete. The work is tedious. Some development offices have a department that does nothing but research prospects. Without a research department, you will depend even more on the screening session to learn information about who ought to be on your top priority list.

If you cannot afford to hire a researcher, you may be able to create a volunteer research position. I have seen this work very successfully at an organization where I was employed.

A research volunteer should be willing to commit 10-20 hours each week for a minimum of three months. After the three months is up, you can evaluate the performance of the volunteer, and, if you are satisfied with the results, ask the volunteer to stay on. If you are not satisfied with the performance, the three-month limit is your safeguard.

Here are some ideas on where to find a research volunteer:

- Members of the community (possibly retired) who have already expressed an interest in your organization through previous volunteer work;

- Donors or constituents who do not work during the day;

- Women who are re-entering the work force after their children are grown.

Building a research file and keeping it up to date should be an ongoing development office activity. If you are starting from scratch, it will take you several years to establish a solid database of information on key prospects. But, month by month, through personal visits, phone calls, screening sessions and through relentless use of resource directories, and the internet, you can compile the kind of information about your prospects that is absolutely essential to the development of a successful cultivation and solicitation strategy. Because the research activity is extraordinarily time consuming, it should be used only on those prospects who are identified for major gift potential—whatever your organization considers that to be. The names of prospects to be researched will be generated in part from your screening session.

Identify A Universe Of Donors Who Need To Be Screened

One of the first questions you'll have as you attempt to conceive your first screening session is where to start. Looking at this from the standpoint of manpower, you'll realize there is no way you can review every member of your constituency. Nor should you want to. The purpose of your research efforts is to identify individuals at the top of your donor base.

There are many ways to segment your constituency for this important work:

- *By geographic region:* individuals living within one community may know one another from attending the same social club, being involved in local politics, business, or within the context of other nonprofit organizations.

- *By type of business:* You will find networks and professional associations for doctors, lawyers, architects, and for many other trades, businesses, or professions.

- *By membership in a social club:* This is really a further division of the geographic segmentation, but there may be reasons to look at an individual within the context of a club in addition to reviewing the name along with others in a larger geographic region. For example, if your organization serves an area within which there is a yacht club, you can check the yacht club's membership list against your own donor base to see whether there is sufficient overlap to justify a separate screening of just the yacht club membership. These members may not live in the same geographic region and would not necessarily show up together on a list sorted by zip code, especially because of seasonal addresses.

- *By affiliation within your organization:* A hospital has doctors, a college has faculty, *etc.*, and all organizations have a board of directors or board of trustees. Consider the kinds of subgroups within your own organization.

- *By graduating class:* For educational institutions, segmentation by class can be very effective.

- *By type of gift:* For example, you might include every person who has made a gift of securities.

If your constituency is large, you may wish to limit your first review to those already contributing at a minimum gift level. For example, at public television, we had approximately 130,000 donors. To keep the screening sessions to a manageable level, we generated lists within select zip codes of only those donors contributing above a certain dollar level, say $500. Some lists were still so large we arranged two sessions to get through one list. Or, we increased the dollar level cut off for the zip codes with high concentrations of people.

Identify A Group Of Individuals Who Will Be Effective In Screening Your Select Universe Of Prospects

Let's assume you are interested in screening the names of all donors in one zip code giving $500 or more each year. (*Author's Note: If the numbers are small, find a range that will produce approximately 200 to 300 prospects.*)

Your next step is to identify individuals who would be effective screeners. Here are some things to consider in identifying your group:

- Individuals who have already contributed at leadership levels are the best choice for this work. Their personal commitment to your organization has already been demonstrated, and many are eager to help bring others on board. Important for the screeners is their ability to think big (you define big).

- Individuals who are leaders among their peers and who are well connected to the social, political, religious, cultural, or professional network within which you are working. I remember working with one woman who was a big contributor but who knew few people on the list. The session was a total waste of time.

- Individuals already identified for leadership gifts may also be recruited. Involving these prospects in a process that allows them to interact with other highly committed individuals can be an effective method of cultivation. In one case, I solicited a woman for a $50,000 pooled income fund gift. When following up to see whether she would make the gift, I realized her initial enthusiasm had waned and that there was a real question whether she would do anything. I encouraged her to continue considering the gift, but, in the meantime, asked if she would help review some of the people in her area for major gift potential. She and I worked approximately one hour at her home reviewing and rating prospects in her zip code, many of whom she rated higher than the $50,000 I had asked of her. The next week, she contributed $25,000. There is no question that her involvement in the screening process was key to her own commitment.

- Individuals who have already worked in a volunteer capacity for another nonprofit organization are also excellent screeners. They understand the framework in which major gifts are solicited and need very little coaching to deliver the kind of information you need.

With the above thoughts in mind, you are ready to select your screeners. By now, you may be asking yourself how many screeners are appropriate. First, let me say this is not an exact science. You can work with five or more, three, or even just one. If you already have a campaign committee or a development committee, you might have a group screening session at the end of one of your regularly scheduled meetings. The larger the group, the greater the chance more names will be known by someone. On the other hand it is difficult to keep things moving with five or more people talking about the same prospect. I prefer to work with three good people who already know each other.

If you have more than 3-5 people, you cannot discuss each prospect as efficiently. Instead, for larger groups, you should provide information sheets to be completed by the screeners silently. Then, after the information is processed, you can call the screeners individually to discuss in greater depth prospects whom they identified.

Recruit The Individuals You Have Identified As Screeners

Before recruiting a screener, you need to define what you'll be asking of them. Ideally, you want three things from your screeners:

1. A commitment of time to attend a screening session;
2. A willingness to assist in solicitations either by accompanying you on a visit or by opening a door to the prospect through a phone call or letter;
3. A financial commitment.

Realistically, you cannot expect all screeners to agree to your three requests right away. Just getting a major prospect to attend a screening session may be a breakthrough in your cultivation strategy. As a result of the group's dynamics, the prospect may offer to help with one or more solicitations. And, after successfully working with you, learning more about your organization, and receiving progress reports on your work, he or she may become more committed.

Using the right person to recruit the screeners can make an enormous difference. Each potential screener must be reviewed separately to determine the best approach in recruiting. Here are several different approaches to consider:

1. If you know the individual well, you can call without sending a lead letter. Building on an existing relationship, you should have no problem picking up the phone.

2. If the individual requires a peer approach, draft a letter for the signature of the appropriate person. (Recruiting the peer to send the letter is another step requiring all of the same considerations.)

Ideally, the peer will make the follow up phone call to recruit the screener. Or, the letter can end by saying, "I've asked Debra Ashton from XYZ Charity to call you next week in order to explain more about these plans and to learn which dates will be most convenient for you. Your help in this special way will make an enormous difference to the success of our. . . . ."

3. If a screener is recommended by a peer, but the peer doesn't want to get involved, the approach can still be effective if the peer allows you to use his or her name in a letter sent by you. For example, "I am writing to you at the suggestion of _____, who felt you would be an excellent resource to our institution. . . ."

You will not always get the screeners you want. Some people are uncomfortable with the process. For instance, I can remember one man who, in refusing to participate in a screening, gave me a lecture about how the whole idea was tasteless, immoral, and an invasion of privacy. Oh, well. On to the next one.

Other people will caution at the outset not to expect a gift from them, or they may go as far as saying, "I'll help you only if you promise not to solicit me." If this happens, you might say, "We need the broadest possible support to achieve our goal, and we would ask for your support even if you do not help with the screening. If you really feel you cannot support the effort financially, at least now, your help with the screening can still be of enormous value to us." In a case like this, it is possible that the individual will develop a stronger commitment to the cause over time. One way to build that commitment is to report results of your solicitations for prospects identified in the screening, thus making the individual feel very much a part of the success. After six to nine months of this, you might approach the subject again saying, "When you first agreed to help earlier in the year, you told us you could not make a contribution. Still, our success is due in large measure to the information you provided. We are very grateful. With only $_____ remaining, our goal is in sight. It is our sincere hope that you will reconsider supporting this effort now. . . ." Or, whatever. . . .

Still others may be heavily involved with volunteer activities for another organization and may not want to take on another commitment. In this case, put the person's name on a tickler for a follow-up call in six months to a year.

Conduct Your Screening Session

The location and timing of the screening session depends on the screeners. Retired individuals may like to meet during the day, either in the morning or in the afternoon. Working individuals may find an evening session to be better. I prefer to conduct the sessions either at my organization or in the home of one of the screeners. Although I have met several people individually at their own offices, I find the atmosphere there much less relaxed with many more potential distractions for the screener. There is often a feeling that the screener would rather be doing something else.

There is definitely a limit to the amount of time one can spend reviewing names. Your minimum time should be one hour; your maximum two hours. Anything longer and people get restless. As I mentioned earlier, the process moves more slowly as the number of screeners increases.

Before calling the group together, you must decide whether to hold a silent or an oral session. In a silent screening, each person receives a set of prospect forms to complete. Then, the research staff back at the office consolidates the information for each prospect. With this kind of session, you can invite more people without worrying about slowing down the process. There is relatively little discussion. However, the amount of paper generated by a silent screening is overwhelming especially if each person gets his or her own set of pages.

In an oral session, the most important participant is the group leader who runs the meeting. Running the oral screening session takes great skill on the part of the group leader. It is easy to miss information or to forget to ask the right questions. The leader must also know when and how to cut off a discussion that becomes unproductive or goes off track. You can use a key volunteer, a trustee, or any other person such as yourself or another member of the development office staff in this role—a researcher would be good, too.

The key purpose of the screening session is to identify prospects at the top 5% to 10% of your donor base. Thus, you must develop a rating system based on the potential of your constituency. The ratings indicate the maximum gift potential of the prospect and not necessarily what would be expected if the prospect were asked for that amount today. At Wheaton College we used the following ratings:

W	$50,000	to	$100,000	K	Child of a "W"
X	$100,000	to	$500,000	L	Child of an "X"
Y	$500,000	to	$1,000,000	M	Child of a "Y"
Z	$1,000,000		and over	N	Child of a "Z"

At Boston College, we used the following two-part ratings:

4	Up	to	$50,000	A	Ready to be asked for the rated level
3	$50,000	to	$100,000	B	Needs more cultivation for the rated level
2	$100,000	to	$1,000,000	C	No cultivation yet
1	$1,000,000		and over	X	Not viable

Notice that at Wheaton College, we had a separate rating system for children of the wealthy. Over time, we wanted to involve people who one day may inherit the family wealth. At that point, the rating would be changed from the childrens' rating, K, L, M, or N to the final rating, W, X, Y, or Z. Meanwhile, we were able to target these younger people for work on admission committees, reunion committees, alumni board, or as volunteers on the Annual Fund. This was a very farsighted program and one that recognized the importance of continuing involvement over many years, way before the person had wealth of his or her own.

Bear in mind that any rating system is imprecise and should be used only as a broad guide. You'll also find wide discrepancies in the ratings from screener to screener.

Starting from the beginning, here's how one screening session might go:

Sample Screening Session

Location:

Home of Jane Smith, committed supporter and long standing member of her community. Previously worked on local library campaign. Jane was recruited by you, director of planned giving.

Other screeners:

Jane's husband. Local attorney. He agreed to do this but has not previously been involved with your organization. Jane is the primary supporter at this time. His first love is his college. Jane has been trying to get him more involved with your organization but without success.

Jane's friend, Mary. Mary and Jane belong to the local "Friends of the Library." Mary contributes $500 per year to your annual giving program and gave $5,000 several years ago. She has not been cultivated. Jane knows Mary could make a substantial contribution if she got involved. Jane recruited Mary at your suggestion.

Jane's friends, Martha and Bill. They just named the wing of a local hospital and are giving $10,000 per year to your organization.

Staff: You.

Time: 7:00 p.m. to 9:30 p.m.

Introductions are made, and the group of six convenes around the dining room table.

- You thank everyone for participating and give an overview of the process. Several points should be stressed:

  1. The information generated during the screening is strictly confidential and will never be attributed to the screeners without their consent;

  2. The screening is one of many your organization is holding throughout the region (country, city) to both broaden the base of supporters and to involve more people in the work of the organization;

  3. You fully realize that the information gathered on each prospect is taken out of context and may not accurately reflect the current situation of the prospect. Nonetheless, you are trying to identify those individuals who could make a meaningful difference to your organization if they were properly involved;

  4. You intend to spend a minimum of one hour but not more than two hours reviewing the names. At the end of two hours, you will stop whether or not all names have been reviewed.

- At this point, you should pass out the rating chart. Remember to stress that the rating represents the maximum gift potential of the prospect and not necessarily the level of interest today. Ask the screeners to use the letter code rather than the dollar amount. For some reason, people seem to feel more comfortable using a code rather than a dollar amount. Sometimes the rating represents what the prospect could do over a five-year period. You will need to define your parameters.

- Next, distribute a list of names to each screener. The list should include name, address, business, and any other information pertinent to identification within the context of the organization but *not gift history*. Knowing how much a prospect is already contributing may bias or confuse the screeners. Also, don't include business title because knowing the title may make people think there is gift capacity because of the title. Let the screeners volunteer their own information.

- During the screening, one person (the group leader) reads the names and keeps the discussion moving. The screeners ask the leader to stop when they hear a familiar name. Either the leader or another person (usually on staff) writes down the information.

In this screening, you are leader and the one writing down the information. Your personal list includes everything on the screeners' list *plus* a summary of gift histories. You have a set of large index cards (one for each prospect) or one sheet of paper for each prospect. (*Author's Note: Instead of asking a volunteer or intern to type the name of each prospect on the working cards or sheets, try to get your computer department to assist you. You may be able to run the names directly on index cards or, as an alternative, order a set of gummed mailing labels that can quickly be affixed to the cards or forms.*) Your computer department may also be able to program a form to be printed directly from the computer on individual sheets, downloading the select information onto the forms.

You cannot expect to use your multi-page research form during these screenings. There is not enough time for you to search for the correct line on the form flipping back and forth from page to page. In fact, you'll have great difficulty just getting down single words or phrases such as widow, no children, loves music, rating X, inherited wealth, or owns securities on your prospect card or form. Back at the office, however, you'll decide which prospects should move to the next level of research.

Depending on the nature of your organization, you may be able to skip certain questions. For example, a college or university already maintains files that contain age, class year, marital status, children, occupation, affiliations, and many other bits of information secured through regular alumni surveys. On the other hand, an organization like a museum, hospital, religious organization, or public television will be hard-pressed to acquire such information without conducting screenings.

When the screeners know the prospects well, you may spend several minutes discussing one person. You'll find yourself writing at a heated pace barely able to keep up with the flow of information. Don't be afraid to say, "Hold it!" The last thing you want is to come back with illegible or incomplete material. Your scribbles are going to mean nothing to you tomorrow. To ensure you don't forget something, bring with you a list of key data you would like to collect. Refer to it often.

During the session, you may identify prospects for whom one of the screeners is clearly the best solicitor. Don't let an opportunity pass without saying, "Jane, would you be willing to help arrange an appointment with Mr. Jones?" Once the commitment is made, explain that you will call again later to work out the details. Otherwise, you may not finish reviewing the lists.

The screening process can be very exciting both for you and your staff and for the participants. As important names are uncovered, there is a sense of great accomplishment on both sides. The screeners take pride in the depth of their own knowledge about the prospects and in assisting in the strategic plan to draw the prospect closer to a meaningful commitment. Throughout the process, however, the staff must be careful to maintain the highest sense of trust, integrity, and confidentiality. These are real human beings you are discussing. Always be sensitive and respectful with your comments.

As you move from screening to screening, you must also prepare for the inevitable disaster session—the one in which either of two things can happen:

1) The screeners, while knowledgeable about the prospects, feel so uncomfortable with the process they simply can't produce helpful information, or

2) The screeners, while eager and willing to help, know relatively few people on your lists.

If you find yourself in one of these sessions, the only thing you can do is bear with it until it's over. In the first case, the screeners will appear to be in anguish—delivering enough information to feel useful but nothing you can really sink your teeth into. They'll say things like, "Well, yes, I've known Mr. Smith for 20 years, although I've never discussed such personal finances with him. It would be impossible for me to give him a rating." At the end, the screeners know as well as you do that the whole thing was a waste of time. With as much appreciation as you can muster, thank them for their help and end the session.

In the second case, everyone will feel equally frustrated. The most valuable thing you can do now is to review with the screeners the criteria you used to select the names. If possible, try to find the right match for a new set of names and reschedule another session if everyone is willing. You might also say, "Well, it's clear our lists did not pick up the names we might have expected. We've cut this list off at the $500 gift level but perhaps some of those we're missing will show up if we go deeper into our donor base. Can you think of individuals you expected to see?" Often, the screeners will give you new names with comments like, "You really should be talking with Martin Silver. He really knows this area." Don't miss your chance here to ask the screener to make a phone call on your behalf. Another possible comment might be, "I'm very surprised not to see Sarah Goodwin on your list of contributors in this zip code. She is a great fan of your museum, and if you could just get her involved . . ." Here again, ask if the screener can make an introduction. These are the kinds of connections you want. Add the new names to a list that will be reviewed back at the office to see if any of them are already donors even at low levels, or possibly listed from a different seasonal address.

There is no question that the blind geographic screening is the toughest. You hope your screeners will know the people on your lists, but the most you can expect is to gather useful information on a small percentage of the list. At public television, we screened one zip code a minimum of three times with different sets of screeners in order to verify and corroborate information. Only after one prospect was rated at our target level in three different sessions did we move the person to the Research Department for a complete work-up.

After reading this chapter, you may be wondering how much of this activity is necessary. That depends. The life of a fund raiser is one big juggling act—balancing current solicitations against long-term cultivation, against writing publications, against holding events, against generating new prospects, and so on and so on. If you run a one-person shop, the work in organizing, running, and processing the information from just one screening session can immobilize you and your support staff for a disproportionate share of your time. You should, however, run enough screening sessions to keep you busy cultivating and soliciting the prospects at the top giving potential of your constituency.

Processing The Information From The Screening Sessions

Now, here you are, back in the office carrying 200 index cards with hastily scribbled notations. Or, perhaps back from a silent screening, you have 100 prospect forms completed by five screeners in their own sometimes illegible handwriting. What are you going to do now?

The next phase breaks down into two parts:

1. Update master computer records with changes of address, name, or marital status for prospects. This should be done immediately. While it may be days, weeks, or months before an individual is actually moved into cultivation, you want to ensure that your computer records are as up to date as possible. Your data entry staff will flip through the cards or forms and perform whatever immediate maintenance is required and then give the information back to you.

2. Separate the highest-rated prospects for special research.

The research staff transfers all information to the prospect form at the end of this chapter, and an alphabetical listing is kept of all prospects who have progressed to this stage. Then the real work begins. Using a variety of resource directories, the researchers attempt to complete all of the information called for on the research form. Such resources include traditional books that most research departments have from prior years before the internet:

The Social Register
Who's Who in America
Martindale-Hubbell Law Directory (lawyers.martindale.com)
Standard & Poor's Register of Corporations, Directors, and Executives
Telephone books
Dun & Bradstreet Reference Book of Corporate Managements
Directory of Medical Specialists
Encyclopedia of Associations
Quantus (stock holdings for top executives)
National Directory of Certified Public Accountants
Directory of Directors
Who's Who in Real Estate
Who's Who in the East
The Foundation Directory (http://Inp.fdncenter.org/finder.html)
Taft Foundation Directory
America's Wealthiest People
America's Hidden Philanthropic Wealth
Fund Raiser's Guide to Private Fortunes
Online Databases and Services (see below)

Often, you will request that the researchers work on a few key people as top priorities. At other times, the researchers will simply make their way through the group starting with the highest rated prospects.

Once the research on a prospect is as complete as possible, the completed prospect form will be returned to you for assignment of the prospect to a solicitor.

In other cases, a solicitor may be working on a prospect already. Thus, the new research information should be sent to the solicitor immediately.

No doubt, you already realize the burden such screening sessions will place on your research, records, or data entry department. This is no small problem. Being able to record the information in a timely fashion is important because it becomes dated very quickly.

How can one ensure this will happen? First, an analysis of the back-up capacity of the research department must be made. How many people, terminals, *etc.* are there to handle all the new information? What other concurrent demands are being made on those same people for other ongoing research functions? How much more can they each handle?

Hold meetings on a programmed basis, moving gradually from area to area—but only as fast as the research department can remain current in assimilating the information. If necessary, slow down. Don't overwhelm your people—they will feel swamped and even helpless. In this case, everyone will lose, and a lot of time and effort may have been wasted.

Unless you establish the in-house mechanism to handle the information from your screenings, you will undoubtedly collect nothing more than dust from the piles and piles of print-outs, index cards, or prospect forms.

Much of the work in the preparation stage of your program happens simultaneously. You may already feel that prospecting, by itself, is a full-time activity. It can be, but you are the one to judge how much or how little is appropriate.

ELECTRONIC SCREENINGS

Many companies offer electronic screening services that may help you sort through the thousands and thousands of names on your donor or constituent list. One such company is Marts & Lundy which performed an electronic screening on our entire alumni and parent population at Boston College. There were over 125,000 names to put through the process. This took a lot of coordinating by our UIS staff member in the development office. The company you hire will advise you about how your names will be transferred, the format, *etc.* We had to create new fields in the donor database in order to receive the new data that would be appended to our donor records.

ONLINE DATABASES AND SERVICES

There are scores and scores of ways to conduct prospect research on the internet. Some services require an annual fee, which many research departments consider well worth the price. Others are free. Following is a short list of some of the resources you can use. Some of these sites have large listings of resources by category, so I will let you search them all out on your own. The web sites available for research are quite extensive.

DataQuick (Real estate searches)	www.dataquick.com
Edgar Online (searches SEC Filings by name or displays people associated with a company name)	www.edgar-online.com/people
Federal Election Commission (Polital Giving)	www.tray.com
Forbes.com (net worth)	www.forbes.com
Foundations.org (service of Northern California Community Foundation, Inc.)	www.foundations.org
GuideStar (National Database of Nonprofit Organizations)	www.guidestar.org

Hoovers Online (Corporate affiliations, SEC documents, compensation, IPO's)	www.hoovers.com
Insider Trader	www.insidertrader.com
Internet Movie Database	www.imdb.com
JobStar Central (Find salary information on different positions from salary surveys)	http://jobstar.org
KnowX.com (public record information on a wealth of categories)	www.knowx.com
LexisNexis	www.lexisnexis.com
Portico (A collection of web sites with publicly available information, very extensive)	http://indorgs.virginia.edu/portico/home.html
Power Reporting (Extensive list of links by category and well organized)	http://powerreporting.com
Property Assessment Databases	http://adelphia.net/%Ejavaughan/index.html
RootsWeb (Oldest and largest free genealogy site)	http://resources.rootsweb.com
Search Systems, Pacific Information Resources, Inc., DBA (Over 6,315 free searchable public record databases)	www.pac-info.com
Telephone Directories on the Web	www.teldir.com
10K Wizard (Search on SEC Filings)	www.tenkwizard.com
ThomasRegister (Extensive searchable database providing product information, catalogs, *etc.*)	www.thomasregister.com
The Ultimates (Searchable White Pages, Yellow Pages, e-mail directory)	www.theultimates.com
Wall Street Executive Library	www.executivelibrary.com
Wealthy Zip Codes of the U.S.	www.usc.edu/dept/source/sipcode/index.htm
Where to do Research (an unbelievable listing of links by category with hundreds of links imbedded)	www.wheretodoresearch.com

SUMMARY

Sometimes you work in a large development office that has a full department of researchers. If they are doing their work properly, they ought to be proactively identifying worthy prospects to turn over to development officers like you. But, if you are in a small shop, you will have to fit in some of the screening activity yourself. By putting your whole database through an electronic screening, you will be able to narrow down the list. Still, this part of fund raising is very time consuming.

The final chapter in Part I deals with a most important task—that of selecting legal counsel for your program.

PROSPECT FORM

Date Last Updated   _____

Name   _____   Date of Birth   _____
Home Address   _____   Home Phone   _____
     _____   E-mail   _____
     _____

Occupation   _____   Business Phone   _____
Title   _____   Fax   _____
Business Address   _____   Work E-mail   _____
     _____   Cell phone   _____
     _____

Description of Business

Seasonal Address   _____   Seasonal Phone   _____
     _____   Fax   _____
     _____
     _____
     _____

Dates for Seasonal   _____

College and Year   _____
     _____
     _____
     _____

Religious Affiliation   _____

Prefers to be contacted at ___ home ___ business ___ seasonal address

Marital Status   _____
Spouse   _____   Date of Birth   _____
Spouse's Occupation   _____
Spouse's Title   _____
Spouse's Business   _____   Business Phone   _____
     _____   Fax   _____
     _____   Work E-mail   _____
     _____   Cell phone   _____

Description of Spouse's Business

College and Year   _____
     _____
     _____

Religious Affiliation   _____

Children	Date of Birth	College/Year
_____	_____	_____
_____	_____	_____
_____	_____	_____

Professional Affiliations

Prospect   Spouse

_____   _____
_____   _____
_____   _____
_____   _____
_____   _____
_____   _____
_____   _____
_____   _____

Hobbies

_____   _____
_____   _____
_____   _____
_____   _____
_____   _____

Other Charitable Interests

_____   _____
_____   _____
_____   _____
_____   _____

Other information

_____ Has a will   _____ Does not have a will   _____ Owns residence
_____ Owns land   _____ Owns securities   _____ Owns closely-held stock
_____ In or near retirement _____ Living on fixed income   _____ Children provided for
_____ Grandchildren/tuition _____ Art or antiques   _____ Inherited family wealth
_____ Other _____

Income range: _____over $100,000   _____over $250,000   _____ over $500,000
                     _____over $1,000,000   _____over $5,000,000

What volunteers in order of priority would be effective helping with this prospect?

_____
_____
_____

What staff members in order of priority would be effective in working with this prospect?

_____
_____
_____

Other comments

Chapter I–6

SELECTING LEGAL COUNSEL

An important decision you'll make in the early stages of a planned giving program is the selection of legal counsel. Your ability to respond quickly and accurately to gift situations depends in large measure on the backup provided by an attorney experienced in charitable giving tax law.

Some organizations just launching a program will wonder if they can afford the expense of legal counsel and may be tempted to use a member of the Board who volunteers his or her time. But, an experienced planned giving professional knows that the expense of proper legal counsel is money well spent. A volunteer cannot be your legal counsel.

WHAT YOUR LEGAL COUNSEL DOES FOR YOU

Following are just a few of the tasks your legal counsel will do for you:

- Draft your organization's pooled income fund governing instrument;
- Advise you on state regulations related to charitable gift annuities;
- Guide you through the steps necessary to accept and dispose of a gift of real property;
- Prepare sample trust documents for use with donors or prospects;
- Meet with donors when necessary;
- Unravel tough gift situations when something has gone wrong;
- Calculate the tax consequences of gift plans when you are in over your head;
- Prepare sample language for bequests;
- Advise what to do with closely held or restricted stock;
- Act as your agent in probate proceedings when there is a problem with a bequest;
- Work directly with the donor's advisor to help negotiate a gift;
- Advise you on tax law changes;
- Review drafts of new brochures for accuracy and content;
- Provide general or specific advice whenever you need it.

Considerable care must be taken in selecting a law firm or attorney to handle the tax-related and legal issues you'll encounter in running your planned giving program.

Planned giving is the most difficult and technical area of fund raising. As a planned giving professional, you'll be involved in situations that can get you into big trouble. Often, you will know more about the operation and benefits of the gift plan you're proposing than does the donor's attorney. However, as an employee of a charity, you are a fund raiser and not an advisor. You cannot possibly know everything relevant to the donor's gift decision. In such instances when the donor discloses what you believe to be "everything," the suggestions you make must be framed in such a way that you are not perceived as giving legal advice. Regardless of your expertise—and it may be considerable—you need someone whose careful eye and expert knowledge will keep you out of trouble.

If you are new to planned giving, you may not know when you should call your attorney. My rule is simply this: if you have the slightest doubt about something, call. Here are just a few of the reasons I have sought advice in the past:

- to get referrals for one of my donors who needed an attorney in a particular town;

- to request a legal opinion about registration in states that regulate gift annuities;

- to have many charitable remainder trusts drafted;

- to request that my attorney call a donor's attorney to discuss a gift of land to a flip unitrust;

- to request that a sample will be written;

- to have the draft of a new brochure checked for content and accuracy;

- to get a summary of the tax consequences of a mortgaged piece of real estate proposed as a gift annuity;

- to have the cost basis of a stock traced back 20 years through several stock splits and mergers;

- to learn how the lifetime capital gain exemption for a primary residence affects such property being used for a gift annuity;

- to get advice about a gift of a partial interest in a race horse;

- to request a review of the text of a year-end tax mailing.

Often, you will have questions that can be answered with a five-minute phone call. At other times, you will need substantial services or help. Without question, the success of a planned giving program is due in large measure to your ability to call someone with experience beyond your own to help you do your job. Unless you have a formal affiliation with a firm that can respond to the full range of questions you will encounter—however large or small—you'll miss gift opportunities, or, worse, you'll find yourself at the wrong end of a law suit.

One thing that can't be underestimated is the responsiveness of your attorney. When you have a donor or prospect in need of answers, there is no time to waste. You need a quick and accurate response from your tax counsel. You need someone with sufficient experience in charitable giving tax law so that you don't have to wait for days to get an answer. Preferably, you need someone who knows the answers without looking them up. Otherwise, you will find yourself waiting for a return call, and becoming very frustrated.

What you want from your tax counsel can be summed up by the statement made by the late David M. Donaldson, Esq. when I approached him with a complex gift situation that I thought looked hopeless. He said, "If there is any way to make this gift work, Ropes & Gray will find it."

SHOULD I USE THE LAW FIRM ALREADY RETAINED BY THE CHARITY FOR OTHER LEGAL MATTERS?

Not necessarily. Organizations engage law firms for many routine legal matters. However, your organization's choice for advice on union negotiations, employee benefits plans, or musicians' contracts may not be the best choice for charitable giving tax law. Still, existing relationships may be hard to sever.

When I arrived at WGBH to start its planned giving program, everyone assumed its then legal counsel would serve the planned giving program. Unfortunately, the one person at this law firm who specialized in charitable giving was not only unfriendly but simply didn't have the experience I needed. This was an awkward situation. Eventually, after interviewing five firms, including the counsel already retained by the institution, I wrote a report for the Board. In my report, I recommended a different firm. Fortunately, the board approved the new firm. But, I felt like a real trouble maker.

If you find yourself in a situation requiring a change in law firms, here are some questions you can use to conduct interviews of several prospective firms or attorneys:

- Who will be the primary person assigned to our account?
- How many charitable accounts or other clients are assigned to this person?
- How many years has he/she been practicing law?
- Who else in the firm will be available if the primary attorney is absent?
- Please provide references of several other charitable clients.
- Does the firm have a real estate attorney?
- Does the firm have expertise in closely held corporations?
- What is the hourly rate for the attorneys being assigned to our account?
- Does the firm have specialists in estate planning?
- Can the firm act as trustee, executor, or guardian?
- How many attorneys are employed by the firm?

A simple chart showing the answers to the above questions will give you good comparison data. Perhaps your search will provide sufficient reason to select the current legal counsel retained by your organization. If so, great. But don't take for granted that the firm your institution uses for its routine legal matters can serve you in the complex area of charitable giving tax law.

Some organizations have an internal legal department with an attorney who monitors use of outside counsel. I have worked in two organizations with such a structure. Under these circumstances, you may be expected to consult the internal person before calling the outside counsel. Sometimes, the internal counsel knows the answers to your questions. Sometimes, your questions are so specific to planned giving that you require the expertise of your outside counsel. You'll always be allowed to use outside counsel when you need it.

If you transfer from one organization to another and have been accustomed to unsupervised access to your outside counsel, you'll feel annoyed if you must get clearance from an internal person before calling the outside counsel. Don't be. This is a reasonable procedure. It saves lots of money. Remember, each time you call your outside counsel, the billable hours are running. It is a courtesy to your in-house counsel to alert him or her if you are going to be spending money.

WHERE DO YOU FIND GOOD LEGAL COUNSEL?

You may need to get referrals for legal counsel from some of your planned giving colleagues. I would suggest contacting the most prominent nonprofit organizations in your area—those known for their success in planned giving—to ask which firms they use.

Your ideal choice is a firm that employs specialists in areas of law beyond charitable giving. In the course of your work, you may need expertise in one or more of the following areas:

- charitable giving tax law,
- real estate law,
- securities law,
- estate planning,
- probate law,
- closely held stock or corporations,
- restricted stock,
- retirement plans or IRAs.

If you select an attorney with a private practice to serve your program, you may find his or her experience inadequate when a gift plan impacts other areas of the donor's situation. This is why I prefer to work with a firm that employs specialists in different areas of law.

Though the diversity of skills at a large firm is an advantage, you'll most likely pay more per hour with a large firm. Also, I don't want to rule out some of the fine attorneys working in a smaller firm from consideration. I can think of any number of them, even in other states, that I would love to hire.

Sometimes, even when you have a firm that you use most of the time, you might need a specialist from another firm periodically. I can remember one fairly complicated real estate situation in New York City. We had to hire a real estate specialist in New York due to some unique local tax issues that could only be known by an attorney practicing in that state.

HOW ARE LEGAL FEES CHARGED?

When you hire a law firm for your planned giving program, you have two choices with regard to how fees are charged:

- Pay by retainer: One lump sum (supposedly) covers all activity for the year; or
- Pay as you go.

Retainer arrangements don't work well. We tried this at Wheaton College unsuccessfully one year. In our case, we paid $7,000, an amount we thought would cover our needs for the year. During the year, a number of complex situations arose requiring additional time and expense. As a result, our needs far exceeded our projections, and we were billed for the excess at the end of the year. We were not happy.

The most practical way to handle fees is to pay as you go. This means you'll be charged for the following:

- telephone costs of the firm to call you;
- telephone costs of the firm to call other people on your behalf;
- costs of photocopying done for you;
- cost/hour for attorney's time either on the phone, in person, or working on your situation;
- charge for mileage when the attorney travels on your behalf;
- cost/hour of travel time to go to meetings;
- court costs or other filing fees incurred on your behalf;
- costs of sending a FAX to you;
- costs for anything that is done for you.

At the end of each quarter, you can expect a bill. The bill might look like this:

Bill for Services Rendered	Jan. 1 - March 30
Advice with regard to Lloyd Williams unitrust preparation	$ 300
Review of real estate documents for Marjorie Stone	500
Other miscellaneous advice, phone calls, and photocopying	+ 200
Total:	$1,000

Or, you might receive a bill that itemizes every detail including postage. Some bills include the hours (full or fractional) charged by each attorney who billed time to your account. If you receive a bill that appears too high, you can request the detail. Attorneys must complete time-cards for the time spent on each account so don't be shy about asking.

At the end of each billing cycle, one thing will be true. You'll be shocked at what has been charged, and you'll have forgotten precisely how many times you called. If you are new to planned giving, you'll save yourself some anxiety by keeping a record of the dates, times, and duration of your calls so that you can attribute charges on the bill to actual conversations you have long forgotten. It is probably human nature for you to think the firm is charging too much. However, the cost *per* hour for the best attorneys can easily exceed $250 to $300. Sometimes the fee for a given activity is disproportionate to the amount of the gift. In such cases, the firm may charge you less than it actually deserves for its services. For example, once I retained the counsel for WGBH to resolve a conflict relating to a $5,000 bequest. Eventually, the time spent on the problem easily exceeded the size of the bequest. We were charged only $1,000. On reflection, I should have evaluated the projected expense and perhaps not engaged the firm at all.

Occasionally, a complex issue will produce a bill larger than you expected. Here's how. You call your attorney with a question. This attorney walks down the hall into the office of another attorney. They talk for 20 minutes. The second attorney makes a call about the issue and writes a memo. The first attorney receives the memo and discusses it with the one who wrote it. Your bill will include the time for both attorneys working on your single issue. Sometimes three or four of them will bill you for the same question. Outrageous, you say! That's the way it works.

The best way to monitor the charges you're accumulating is to ask for an estimate of the costs in advance. And remember, this is not an exact science.

DON'T PROMISE YOUR DONORS SOMETHING YOUR TAX COUNSEL CAN'T DELIVER

When you are working with a prospect, you will want to follow up immediately. Nonetheless, you must allow a reasonable turn-around time from your attorney for complex requests. You are just one of many clients and you cannot expect answers in 24 hours all of the time. Yes, there will be times when you do need immediate service and when your tax counsel will drop everything else to help you. But don't place urgent demands constantly. You must strike a balance between serving the donor promptly and respecting the amount of lead time your tax counsel needs. Often, donors want the information right away and then sit on it for months.

You can spare yourself a lot of anxiety by telling your prospect the time frame for responding to his or her request.

Even better, sit down with your tax counsel at the very beginning and discuss the lead time he or she will need for various gift plans or situations. Another way to handle a gift situation with a donor is to call your attorney in advance to say something like, "I have a prospect interested in a unitrust, and I'd like to try and arrange a meeting with him for next Friday. If I am able to give you by phone the information you need, let's say, by the end of today, would you be able to prepare a sample unitrust by next Friday?"

If you legitimately feel you're not receiving adequate service, arrange an appointment to discuss the problem. In the worst case, you may simply need to change firms.

SHOULD I ACCEPT THE LEGAL SERVICES OF A BOARD MEMBER WHO HAS VOLUNTEERED HIS OR HER TIME?

Absolutely not. A volunteer cannot possibly serve you well. The arrangement will place you in an awkward position, because you will feel limited in the amount of help you can request. More important, there is liability at stake.

WHAT IF I WORK IN A REMOTE LOCATION?

Try to get an attorney who is inside your own state. The local laws are important and they are different in every state.

WE DON'T HAVE SEVERAL THOUSAND DOLLARS TO SPEND ON LEGAL FEES.

I hesitate to say this, but you must seriously rethink your priorities. It takes money to make money. You cannot run a planned giving program without tax counsel.

If you really don't have the money, solicit a donor for $5,000 to cover your legal fees for the year. Or, ask each of the board members to contribute $500 each toward a legal reserve fund. Or, establish a legal reserve fund by allocating an unexpected bequest distribution toward legal fees.

Surely you can be resourceful enough to get some money set aside. There is no excuse not to have the best tax counsel possible because the money you spend will be returned many times over. You'll never be successful in planned giving unless you resolve this issue early in the process.

SUMMARY

Having read through the first six chapters, you have a good idea of what it will take to create a successful planned giving program. Several chapters in Part III provide additional information about the strategies and suggestions in Part I. Use them as you need them. Up until now, however, there was no real need to discuss gift options or tax consequences. Now, it is time to shift gears and turn to the core of what planned giving is all about—structuring gifts.

PART II

UNDERSTANDING THE GIFT OPTIONS

INTRODUCTION

Many people think of planned giving as life income gifts and bequests. These gifts comprise only part of the body of information you must understand to be successful in planned giving.

In the course of creating and running a planned giving program, you will need four separate kinds of knowledge:

1. an understanding of basic tax considerations;

2. the ramifications of a particular gift plan to the donor, the donor's heirs, or to the donor's beneficiaries;

3. the ramifications of a particular gift plan to your institution; and

4. the considerations necessary to accept, manage, administer and dispose of different kinds of gift property.

The information you need to do most of this is in this part of the book. Others in the institution can also utilize this section. Among them are the following:

- *Executive directors and presidents.* Yours is the toughest job of all—that of juggling multiple tasks and priorities, establishing and monitoring programs and services, soliciting foundation, corporate, or government support, and, at the same time, soliciting individual prospects for major capital gifts. All alone, you cannot run a full planned giving program, but, even by yourself, you can benefit enormously from expanding two areas of support—gifts of appreciated securities (Chapter II–4) and bequests (Chapter II–10).

  As executive director or president, you should also read Chapter II–9 about charitable remainder trusts. Unlike pooled income funds and gift annuities, the charity does not need to manage CRTs in house. Therefore, you ought to be able to discuss the concept of a CRT with your highest-level donors, those on whom you should focus most of your time anyway.

- *Directors of development.* In many organizations, your role involves both managing the development effort and soliciting major gift prospects. This part of the book can help you increase your effectiveness in prospect situations by giving you the tools you need to discuss life income plans, gifts of real estate, or other forms of charitable giving.

- *Major gifts officers.* Your universe of prospects represents the mid to top range of givers. Many will be candidates for deferred gifts. Thus, it is most important for you to be able to articulate the benefits of life income plans and to recognize situations for which another form of gift may be appropriate. Most likely, you work with a director of planned giving who can prepare a proposal for you when necessary. Nonetheless, you should familiarize yourself with the wide range of gift possibilities that are available to your prospects.

- *Support staff.* A properly run planned giving program requires knowledgeable support staff. Administrative procedures must be established and maintained with efficiency and accuracy.

Several of the following chapters include step-by-step instructions for accepting and processing gifts. The chapters that will be most valuable to support staff are Chapter II–4 on securities, Chapter II–5 on life insurance, Chapter II–7 on pooled income funds, and Chapter II–8 on gift annuities.

Beyond administrative duties, support staff should be able to discuss the institution's gift plans with confidence. Often, the support staff member handles preliminary donor inquiries and processes gifts in the absence of the director of planned giving. By reading this section, support staff can begin to understand the complexity of planned giving and become more skilled in assisting the donors.

This part of the book is intended to give you sufficient knowledge about tax laws and gift options such that you can explain general tax consequences to a donor, prepare a proposal, calculate the tax consequences of almost any gift arrangement, and avoid mistakes along the way. Where this book leaves off, there are many resources listed in Appendix III that will provide additional information on a particular gift plan or a specific area of tax law. Your tax counsel is also a vital resource and should be used as often as is necessary to ensure that you are providing both accurate and appropriate proposals for donors.

Keep in mind that tax laws change frequently. This book is as accurate as possible when it was printed, but you must be diligent about keeping up with current laws on your own. I recommend that you subscribe to two kinds of other resources. The first is a loose-leaf tax service that will provide periodic updates of tax changes. I use *Charitable Giving and Solicitation* by Warren, Gorham, and Lamont and *Charitable Giving Tax Service* by R&R Newkirk. The second kind of resource you need is a monthly tax newsletter that provides breaking news and analysis for quick study and condensed information. I use *Taxwise Giving* by Conrad Teitell and *Charitable Gift Planning News* by JAS Destiny, Inc. There is a listing of books, periodicals, tax services, and newsletters in Appendix III.

Chapter II–1

CREATING AN EFFECTIVE PROPOSAL

Once you have identified a prospect (Chapter I–5) and built a relationship (Chapter III-3), you should address yourself to three critical questions. Does your approach meet the donor's emotional needs, personal objectives, and financial planning objectives? The first two of these questions are discussed here; the third is really the subject of the entire rest of Part II.

DOES YOUR APPROACH MEET THE PROSPECT'S EMOTIONAL NEEDS?

Everyone has emotional needs, but it is not always easy to identify precisely which factors will inspire a donor to provide leadership support to one organization while maintaining relatively small gift levels to another. If you have done a thorough job with your research, you probably have a clue about the key motivating factors for your prospect. For example, if you know that your prospect contributed to name a building elsewhere, you might conclude that recognition is important. If the prospect enjoys being part of the top echelon of power, he or she will respond better to a proposal signed by your president or chairman of the board than a proposal signed by you.

One theory of motivational behavior developed by the late Dr. David C. McClelland while at Harvard University involves three kinds of needs.

Following is a summary excerpted from an article by The Forum Corporation of North America. Dr. McClelland identified three types of psychological motivation:

- need for achievement,
- need for affiliation, and
- need for power.

Many other behavioral models exist. Dr. McClelland's is very simple.

Need For Achievement

A prospect motivated by the need for achievement likes to undertake activities that can provide measurable personal accomplishment. Winning and wanting to do better than someone else are primary concerns. Concerns are for:

- outperforming someone else;
- meeting or surpassing a self-imposed standard of excellence;
- striving to make a unique contribution;
- setting long-term goals;
- planning to overcome personal and environmental (business or other) obstacles.

Here are several ways you can satisfy this prospect's needs:

1. Discuss the dollar goals of the fund raising campaign in relation to prior campaigns to show an increase in the expectations.

2. Emphasize how the prospect's participation can help you achieve your goal.

3.   Emphasize how the prospect's leadership gift can inspire others by example.

4.   Reinforce the fact that the success of the campaign is dependent on the leadership support of a select few.

5.   Show how the prospect's support can put your campaign over the top.

6.   Show how the prospect's support can help you achieve your goal ahead of schedule.

Need For Affiliation

A prospect motivated by the need for affiliation enjoys being with someone else and enjoying mutual friendship. Concerns are for:

- being part of a group or team;
- being liked and accepted;
- maintaining positive interpersonal relationships;
- being involved with people in the work situation;
- minimizing conflict.

Here are several ways you can fulfill this prospect's needs:

1.   Show how the prospect's support will make him a part of an important group.

2.   Emphasize the special bond that he will have with the institution after making the proposed major commitment.

3.   Emphasize the fact that the prospect's name will be included with all others for special recognition in your publications.

4.   Inspire the donor with thoughts of the victory dinner when the team will be gathered to celebrate the fund raising success.

5.   Offer the donor a special recognition certificate or plaque that can be displayed prominently in his or her home or office.

Need For Power

A prospect motivated by the need for power is concerned about influencing and controlling others. Concerns are for:

- influencing through powerful actions;
- arousing strong positive or negative emotions in others;
- acquiring a reputation or position;
- having control of situations.

Here are some suggestions on how to motivate this prospect:

1.   Emphasize the importance of the prospect's leadership gift toward the campaign's success.

2.   Use a solicitor who is perceived by the prospect to be in a position of power and leadership—the president, a prominent trustee, or chairman of the board, for example.

3. Invite the prospect to be part of an elite circle of insiders which has regular contact with your institution's leadership.

4. Invite the prospect to chair a committee or fund raising event where involvement can be a source of control.

5. Suggest publicizing the prospect's commitment in a highly visible way in order to elevate the prospect above others as a leader.

You will have the greatest chance for success if you tailor your approach with as much attention to the prospect's emotional needs as possible. Often, the desire for recognition, to be part of a team, or to achieve goals is more important to the prospect than the desire for tax savings. Remember, the primary motivation for giving is the satisfaction of helping your institution—not a tax deduction, not increased income, not avoiding capital gain taxes. Those latter things dictate the type of gift, but will not be the primary reason for acting.

DOES THE PROPOSAL MEET THE PROSPECT'S PERSONAL OBJECTIVES?

During your conversation with a prospect, you should be able to paraphrase what you perceive the prospect's needs to be. For example, you might say, "Let me see if I understand your concerns. Your primary objective, Mrs. Jones, is to make certain that your husband will be provided for after your death." Or, "It looks as though your foremost concern is to cover the fixed expenses necessary to move to a retirement community."

If you can state the needs of your prospects and address them in your proposal, you will be one step ahead of other fund raisers who simply state the organization's needs without concern for the welfare of the donor. Show how you can help solve problems or provide solutions.

STREAMLINIING YOUR PROPOSAL PROCESS

If you are like me, you have probably agonized over writing a proposal. Each one needs a personalized approach reflecting the communications that you have exchanged with the prospect. Often, when I was preparing a proposal, I found myself reinventing the wheel. You may be doing that, too. But, there is a better way if your organization is large enough to justify a new position. Let me explain.

At Boston College, we had a proposal writer on the staff of the development office. I had never seen this type of position before, but I am convinced that it is an essential position for any mature development office. The proposal writer, who was very skilled as a professional writer (unlike the rest of us), spent her time writing the case for different funding priorities at the institution. By the time I arrived on the scene, she had about 50 different topics on a menu. When a fund raiser needed a proposal, he or she could order one by completing a request form that provided to the proposal writer all necessary details for the proposal.

The Proposal Request Form included the following kinds of information:

- Who is requesting the proposal? Is the solicitation date set? When? How soon do you need this?
- Name and address of the prospect
- Amount of the request
- Purpose/funding priority (*e.g.*, general endowment, scholarship, athletics, library, *etc.*)
- Suggested pledge period, if appropriate
- Prospect's current or past involvement (*e.g.*, history of giving, current or former trustee, volunteer activities, *etc.*)
- Special considerations for this prospect
- Other significant information that would help personalize the proposal (*e.g.*, this would be a gift in honor of the 50th college reunion)
- Type of gift to suggest (*e.g.*, outright, charitable remainder trust, charitable gift annuity, *etc.*, or a combination such as $50,000 outright in year one and $50,000 over five years as a gift annuity)
- Reply date for the donor to respond to the proposal

For proposals requesting an outright gift, the proposal writer prepared the whole thing. For proposals requesting a component of planned giving, a member of the planned giving office created that section. The completed proposal had a maximum of four modules.

1. A one page summary of the institution;
2. The complete case for the program area being discussed;
3. The specific request to Mr. and Mrs. Prospect;
4. How the gift could be structured (the planned giving section).

This system worked extremely well. The completed proposal was put in a thin leather loose-leaf binder embossed with the institution's logo. (Note: For low level proposals, say, under $100,000, she used faux leather.) Basically, the case to be made to each donor had the following flow: Here's who we are, here's the project description, here's what we want from you, and here's how you can structure your commitment. The individual fund raiser would bring the proposal on the next personal visit, or, if that were not possible, he or she would mail the proposal with a personalized cover letter.

Compared to how you may be creating proposals, you can see how this system has many benefits, not the least of which is that the proposals are not only well written but also highly personalized. I realize that small development shops cannot possibly afford this kind of staff position. However, you could make your own set of modules in order to save yourself the trouble of starting from scratch each time. First, write a one-page summary of your institution and its mission. Then, the next time you sit down to write about a particular project or program area, make it generic and save it. As you prepare proposals for different purposes, you will build a file of documents that can be used over and over again without recreating them each time.

KEEP YOUR PLANNED GIVING ILLUSTRATIONS SIMPLE

Unless your prospect is a CPA, physician, or engineer, you should avoid the temptation to provide too much information about the planned gift you are suggesting. The average donor will become confused if you produce the kinds of multiple charts, diagrams, and illustrations available from your planned giving software. You can provide more detailed information later. But, keep the initial planned giving narrative simple and concise. Keep the charts and graphs to a minimum. Also, you should prepare your proposals in duplicate so that the donor can give one to his or her attorney or financial advisor.

DOES THE PROPOSAL MEET THE PROSPECT'S FINANCIAL OBJECTIVES?

Finally, your proposal must address the prospect's unique financial considerations. Whether this means achieving the maximum income tax deduction in the current year, deferring income until retirement because there is no current need for more income, avoiding capital gain taxes on appreciated property, or generating as much tax-free income as possible, your proposal should state clearly and concisely the beneficial tax consequences of your plan. There are 11 more chapters in Part II that will help you with these considerations.

Chapter II–2

GENERAL TAX CONSIDERATIONS

INTRODUCTION

A vast body of tax law has been built around the subject of charitable giving. The amount that a donor can claim as an income, gift, or estate tax deduction depends on the type of charity, the nature of the property, the length of time the donor has held the property, the use to which the property will be put, the specific gift vehicle, and the year of the transfer. Donors should always consult their own financial advisor to determine the tax consequences of a particular contribution. But, often, they talk to you first.

As a planned giving officer, you must be well informed about how a particular type of gift will be treated for tax purposes. You are not supposed to be practicing law, but your position requires expertise beyond that of a general fund raiser. In this chapter you will learn some of the basic rules of charitable giving tax law.

For purposes of this discussion, I am assuming that your organization is classified as a "publicly supported" charity under section 509(a) of the Internal Revenue Code. Many readers are employed by an institution commonly known as a 501(c)(3) institution. Every 501(c)(3) is further classified under 509(a) into one of three kinds of public charities. If it isn't a public charity under these three categories, it is a private foundation. To confirm the tax classification, get a copy of your organization's tax status letter from your business office. It is a good idea to keep copies of this document in your files because executors and grant-making foundations will ask you for it before they make a distribution to your organization. Usually, the document is very old, faded, and poorly copied. Sometimes, it is nearly illegible. Don't worry about how badly the document appears. They all seem to be in very poor condition.

While I was working on this book, the President signed two new tax bills into law: The Economic Growth and Tax Relief Reconciliation Act of 2001 (EGTRRA) and the Jobs and Grow Tax Relief Reconciliation Act of 2003 (JGTRRA). This is a real mess.

By itself, EGTRRA is a difficult tax bill to incorporate into a book attempting to present an accurate snapshot of current tax law. Most provisions are phased in over many years. Thus, the impact on charitable giving will change between now and the end of this decade. Further complicating the situation is the fact that the bill expires on December 31, 2010. At that point, unless Congress passes a law to extend the bill's provisions, the law reverts to what we had in 2001 before the bill was enacted. Planning under these circumstances is very difficult.

On top of all that uncertainty, JGTRRA changes the rules again with many phase-ins, phase-outs, and sunsets.

The charitable community will evolve new approaches to gift planning depending on whether one or more of the provisions in these two bills are 1) retained, 2) changed, or 3) allowed to expire. Chances are, there will be new laws in the next edition of this book.

When commenting on EGTRRA shortly after it passed in 2001, Jerry J. McCoy, a charitable tax planning specialist in Washington, DC, and long a leader in the planned giving community said, ". . . the answer probably is that we should continue largely to do what we are now doing. The biggest changes are nearly 10 years off, and even then will not take permanent effect unless and until some future Congress decides that should happen." However, we have a whole new ball game two years later. While JGTRRA didn't address gift or estate taxes, it changed the income tax rates, the long-term capital gain rules, and also changed the way certain dividends are taxed.

As you go forward into this decade, the most important thing you can do is maintain close personal relationships with your donors. Regardless of the tax law, which will always change, donors will make charitable gifts to your organization if you give them a reason to put your organization first on their list of charitable priorities.

In the next series of chapters, you will find comments about the new tax bills, where appropriate. However, I have not included every provision because many do not impact our work.

To get you started, I have included in this chapter the following topics:

- the income tax;
- factors affecting the income tax charitable deduction for gifts of property;
- the capital gain tax;
- the alternative minimum tax;
- floating I.R.S. discount rates;
- tangible personal property for an unrelated use;
- gifts made "for the use of" instead of "to" your organization;
- bargain sales;
- income in respect of a decedent (IRD);
- substantiation requirements of noncash gifts.

THE INCOME TAX

A donor who makes a gift to a public charity generally is entitled to a federal income tax deduction in the year of the gift as long as he or she itemizes deductions using Form 1040, Schedule A. By claiming an income tax deduction, the donor reduces the amount of income subject to the income tax. This means real money in the donor's pocket.

Under EGTRRA, rates were set to phase in through 2010 as shown below:

2001	n/a	15%	27.5%	30.5%	35.5%	39.1%
Prior to July 1, 2001	n/a	15%	28%	31%	36%	39.6%
July 1, 2001 to 2003	10%	15%	27%	30%	35%	38.6%
2004-2005	10%	15%	26%	29%	34%	37.6%
2006-2010	10%	15%	25%	28%	33%	35%

In general, the dollar break point for the above rates is different depending on the taxpayer's filing status, *i.e.*, single, married, *etc.*

Under JGTRRA, the rate reductions due to phase in by 2006 have been accelerated to 2003. Therefore the new rates are now those shown in the 2006 row above. However, all of the income tax rates in JGTRRA are subject to the sunset provisions in EGTRRA. If EGTRRA is not made permanent, then the tax rates in the year 2011 will revert back to the 2001 rates (15%, 28%, 31%, 36%, and 39.6%)

Did I say that this was a mess?

If you know the donor's tax bracket, you can show the donor the estimated amount of tax savings from a gift. Simply *multiply the deductible amount by the donor's tax bracket*. Often, you will not know the donor's tax bracket. In such a case, it would be appropriate to use a hypothetical example. Since your fund raising efforts really should be targeted at the wealthiest individuals, you would be fairly safe to use the top rate for your examples, at least to start. At the same time, you'll find some donors, especially elderly ones with portfolios invested heavily in tax-exempt bonds. Thus, while they may own hundreds of thousands of dollars in tax-exempt securities, their taxable income may be very low, placing them in the lowest tax bracket. When you present the wrong tax rate in an example, you will generally be corrected by the donor, and, of course, you can proceed from there with a new example using the correct rate. In my experience, donors seem to feel quite strongly about telling you where your proposal went astray.

Following is a chart showing the tax savings for donors at different marginal rates. The term marginal refers to the highest bracket. Donors don't pay their whole tax at the marginal rate since the tax structure is graduated. But, most people illustrating the tax savings from a gift use the highest marginal rate to show the tax savings. This is not exactly precise, but it would be way too much trouble to figure the associated tax savings for a gift at the different break points.

Also, the tax savings illustrated below may not be available in one year, or may not be completely available, especially for donors in the lower brackets. Some states also allow a deduction at the state level for charitable gifts. And, sometimes, a state has an alternative minimum tax (discussed later) that could also affect the outcome. Later in this chapter, I discuss the contribution ceiling.

Income Tax Savings for Gifts by Donors at the Top Marginal Rates for 2003

Gift Amount	10%	15%	25%	33%	35%
$100,000	$10,000	$15,000	$25,000	$33,000	$35,000
50,000	5,000	7,500	12,500	16,500	17,500
25,000	2,500	3,750	6,250	8,250	8,750
10,000	1,000	1,500	2,500	3,300	3,500
5,000	500	750	1,750	1,650	1,750

Referring to the above chart, you can see that a donor who contributes $100,000 at a top rate 35% saves $35,000.

3% Floor On Itemized Deductions

Before getting into a full discussion of the income tax deduction, there is one thing that may indirectly affect the charitable deduction. For taxpayers with adjusted gross income (AGI) above a certain amount, personal itemized deductions are reduced by 3% of AGI that exceeds the base figure. This rule started in 1990 with a base level for single taxpayers of $100,000 and is indexed for inflation. The figure is $139,500 for the year 2003.

This limitation is being phased out between 2006 and 2009 and is completely repealed in 2010. Meanwhile, for the intervening years, following is a general explanation of how the 3% floor on itemized deductions works.

Itemized deductions included in this rule are home mortgage interest, state and local income taxes, real estate taxes, personal property taxes, *charitable contributions*, and miscellaneous deductions. Not included under in this rule are medical expenses, investment interest, gambling losses and casualty losses. The reduction cannot be more than 80% of the taxpayer's total itemized deductions.

Example:

A donor has adjusted gross income of $200,000, mortgage interest of $12,000, state taxes of $10,000, and real estate taxes of $3,000. Total deductions are $25,000 for 2003.

AGI	$ 200,000	
Base for 2003	− 139,500	
	$ 60,500	Amount subject to the 3% reduction
	x 3%	3% applied to AGI above $139,500
	$ 1,815	Amount by which itemized deductions must be reduced
Total Itemized Deductions	$ 25,000	
Reduction amount	− 1,815	
Allowable deductions	$ 23,185	

In this case, there is no adverse effect for the addition of a charitable gift because the 3% reduction of $1,815 is used up first on other existing deductions.

What if the donor instead had an AGI of $500,000?

AGI	$ 500,000	
Base for 2003	− 139,500	
	$ 360,500	Amount subject to the 3% reduction
	x 3%	3% applied to AGI above $139,500
	$ 10,815	Amount by which itemized deductions must be reduced

Total Itemized	
Deductions	$ 25,000
Reduction amount	− 10,815
Allowable deductions	$ 14,185

Here, again, there would be no adverse effect of a charitable gift because the $14,185 reduction is being used first on deductions that already exist.

This rule would come into play for your donor if the reduction amount exceeded the donor's existing deductions before adding a charitable gift.

Once in a while, you will have a donor who brings up this problem as a reason not to make a gift. I usually think that a donor raising this objection doesn't want to make a gift anyway. But, is not something that should impact your fund raising much, if at all. Even if the donor's charitable deduction is affected by this problem, he or she still gets the benefit of a deduction for 97% of the gift. Be aware of this rule, but don't worry about it.

No Charitable Deduction For Nonitemizers

Individuals who do not itemize deductions cannot claim a federal income tax charitable deduction for gifts made to charities. For small donors, the tax deduction probably is not a big consideration. For donors making gifts large enough to matter, they probably would elect to itemize deductions in order to take advantage of the tax savings afforded by the gift. Remember, a charitable gift alone may be large enough to justify the taxpayer to become an itemizer and then also deduct additional smaller items. The donor would become an itemizer when his or her itemized deductions exceeded the standard personal deduction. The standard deduction for a single person for the year 2003 is $4,750, for joint filers, $9,500. There is a separate increased figure for blind taxpayers and those over age 65.

So, joint filers would elect to itemize if they made a deductible gift greater than their standard deduction of $9,500. Otherwise, there is no income tax saving from a charitable gift. Some taxpayers bunch their deductions into one year in order to be able to itemize. Then, they take the standard deduction the next year when they don't intend to have as many deductions.

Note: A proposal to allow limited charitable deductions for nonitemizers has been in various tax bills but has not made it to law as of this printing.

FACTORS AFFECTING THE INCOME TAX CHARITABLE DEDUCTION FOR GIFTS OF PROPERTY

There are basically two considerations for the donor with regard to the gift property:

* the actual dollar amount that is eligible to be deducted, and

* the limitations on how much of that amount can be deducted in any one year.

One factor that affects both of the above considerations is the holding period.

The Holding Period

For gifts of capital assets (such as securities, real estate, art or antiques), the amount a donor can claim as an income tax deduction depends on whether the property is considered short-term or long-term capital gain property.

The long-term holding period is 12 months plus a day. Short-term property is that which is held for 12 months or less.

Long-term Capital Gain Property

For gifts of long-term capital gain property the donor generally can claim a federal income tax deduction for the fair market value of the property.

Example:

If long-term securities valued at $10,000 with a cost basis of $1,000 are contributed to your institution, the donor can claim a deduction for $10,000 (subject to the limitations discussed below).

Short-term Capital Gain Property

For short-term capital gain property, the value of the donor's deduction is limited to the cost basis. Thus, it is generally advisable to delay the contribution of appreciated property held less than the required long-term holding period until the holding period has been met.

Example:

If short-term securities valued at $10,000 with a cost basis of $1,000 are contributed to your institution, the donor can claim a federal income tax charitable deduction for $1,000. If the donor defers the gift until the holding period has been met (and if the securities maintain their value), the deduction would be the full $10,000.

Note: Under certain circumstances, the donor may choose to make a gift of short-term property, especially if the market value is lower than the cost basis. For example, if the donor funds a gift annuity with short-term property that is slightly below market value, his or her charitable deduction will have a higher contribution ceiling (see below) and the tax treatment of the annuity payment will be more beneficial without a capital gain tier. For a complete discussion of gift annuities, go to Chapter II-8.

Charitable Contribution Ceilings

Building on the discussion of long- *vs.* short-term property, let's move to the contribution ceilings. There are limitations on the amount an individual can claim as an income tax deduction in any tax year. The limitations apply *only* to the income tax deduction and *not* to the gift or estate tax deduction and are stated as a percentage of the donor's adjusted gross income (AGI).

Long-term capital gain property: Deduction is limited to 30% of AGI with a five-year carry-over period for the excess.

Example:

A donor with AGI of $100,000 can contribute 30% of AGI or $30,000 of long-term property and claim the entire amount as a deduction in the year of the gift. Adding the five-year carry-over period, the donor can contribute $180,000 in the current year, and eventually deduct the entire amount in installments using the current year and five additional years assuming no change in the donor's adjusted gross income. The donor must, however, use up the deduction in the six-year period as quickly as his or her income can absorb it. The donor cannot spread out the deduction in an arbitrary way. The deduction is for the fair market value.

Short-term capital gain property or cash: Deduction is limited to 50% of adjusted gross income with a five-year carry-over period for the excess.

Example:

The same donor with an AGI of $100,000 can claim $50,000 of short-term property or cash all in the current year. Or, if there is a compelling reason to contribute beyond the current year's ceiling, he or she can give as much as $300,000 in the current year taking advantage of the five-year carry-over period to deduct the entire amount until it is exhausted. The deduction is limited to the cost basis (or to the value of the cash).

If you encounter a prospect who has contributed up to his or her contribution ceiling for the current year, you have two options:

1. Remind the donor that any excess over the contribution ceiling can be carried forward and deducted for up to five more years until it is exhausted. This argument does not work with some donors. Many enjoy the fun of making gift decisions year by year rather than overextending in one year. Also, if a donor makes contributions to more than one charity, he or she already will have used up some of the contribution limit before you show up.

2. Lock in a pledge that can be fulfilled in a later tax year. Often, an urgent reason such as the end of a fund raising period or matching challenge grant deadline can be compelling enough to inspire a donor to make a multi-year pledge.

There is some interplay between the 30% and 50% ceiling. If a donor makes some gifts under the 50% ceiling and some under the 30% ceiling, he or she will follow guidelines as to which categories to report first, how carry-overs are handled, *etc.*

Making A Special Election To Use The 50% Ceiling

It is possible for a donor who has made a contribution of long-term appreciated capital gain property to make a special election that will allow a deduction for up to 50% of adjusted gross income instead of the 30% limit usually applied for such gifts. However, the donor must also reduce the value of the contribution amount by 100% of the property's appreciation.

Example:

Adjusted gross income:	$100,000
Cost basis of gift property:	98,000
Market value of gift property:	$100,000

Amounts claimed as an income tax charitable deduction based on the 30% or 50% ceiling

	Year 1	Year 2	Year 3	Year 4	Total
30% Ceiling	$30,000	$30,000	$30,000	$10,000	$100,000
50% Ceiling*	$50,000	$48,000	———	———	$98,000

*Contribution amount reduced by 100% of appreciation (100% x $2,000 = $2,000).

In the above example, by making the special election to use the 50% ceiling for this $100,000 gift, the donor is able to deduct $98,000 over two years instead of $100,000 over four years. Since the appreciation is relatively low, this donor can benefit from taking larger deductions in years 1 and 2.

When a donor makes the election to use the 50% ceiling for one gift of appreciated long-term capital gain property, he or she must do the same for all other similar gifts in the same tax year. Plus, any carry-over must be treated the same way. So, for example, if the donor above made one gift valued at $100,000 with a cost basis of $98,000 and a second gift valued at $100,000 with a cost basis of $20,000, the following two options are available:

1. claim both gifts at fair market value up to the 30% contribution ceiling. The total contribution deduction would be $200,000 ($100,000 + $100,000); or

2. claim both gifts at cost basis up to the 50% contribution ceiling. The total contribution deduction would be $118,000 ($98,000 + $20,000).

Ordinary Income Property

Ordinary income property is another category of property that must be looked at separately. It is property that would produce ordinary income (as opposed to capital gain income) if sold by the donor.

For gifts of such property, the donor must reduce the value claimed as an income tax deduction by the amount of ordinary income that would have been generated by a sale of the property in the donor's hands. Often, the net effect is that the donor's deduction is limited to the cost basis.

The holding period for purposes of this discussion is irrelevant because a different set of rules dictates how much a donor can deduct. In all cases, the contribution ceiling is 50% of adjusted gross income.

Here are five situations when the ordinary income reduction rule applies:

- inventory;
- artistic property created by the taxpayer or received by lifetime gift from the artist;
- property subject to depreciation recapture (not straight-line depreciation on real estate);
- Section 306 stock;
- life insurance (covered in Chapter II-5).

Inventory

In general, inventory is property held for sale in the donor's trade or business. If a donor contributes inventory to your organization, he or she can claim an income tax deduction for the fair market value reduced by the amount of ordinary income that would have been recognized if the donor sold the property. Practically, this means that the deduction is limited to the cost basis.

Sometimes, you will find individuals who could make a gift of property from their trade or business. It is important not to mislead the potential donor into thinking the gift can be deducted at fair market value. Even so, there are often situations that make a gift of inventory advisable. For example, when I worked for public television, we received a gift of a wide-screen video beam unit which we put to immediate use in our main board room. This gift came from the owner of an electronics corporation and it represented a gift of inventory. Although we tried unsuccessfully to solicit a gift of cash or stock, we had no trouble securing this major piece of equipment valued at approximately $3,500. You, too, may find hidden potential in your donor base in the form of inventory gifts. It is not uncommon for charitable organizations to receive gifts of computers, office equipment, furniture, or any other items necessary to carry out their charitable purposes.

Almost anything can be considered inventory. For example, on one occasion, a donor ran a business breeding and racing horses. After much discussion, we determined that the best approach would be to ask for one of the horses. We presented two different scenarios: one for securing a gift of a breeding animal (which could be a long- or short-term capital asset or tangible personal property with an adjusted cost basis), and a separate suggestion for a gift of one of the offspring (inventory). The proposal was not accepted because the animals were held in a partnership. In this case, to secure this particular gift, it would have been necessary for every partner to participate in the gift. But, this is just one example when a single asset—a horse—can be considered a capital asset in one situation and inventory in another. In each case, the value of the donor's income tax deduction and the contribution ceiling would be totally different.

Artistic Property Created by the Taxpayer or Received by Lifetime Gift by the Artist

If an artist contributes a piece of art that he or she has created, the value of the income tax deduction will be limited to the cost basis of the item. For a painting, that would be the cost of materials used to create it (canvass, paint). This is because the sale of the painting by the artist would produce ordinary income for the artist. (Note: provisions in the CARE Act reported out of the Senate Finance Committee early in 2003 would change this rule under certain circumstances, but the bill has not been passed into law as of this writing.)

Can the artist make a lifetime gift of his own artwork to another person who will then contribute the item to your organization? Yes, but the contribution rules still apply. Artistic property owned by the person who created it or by a person to whom it was given the by the artist who created it is treated as ordinary income property, and accordingly, would produce a tax deduction limited to the cost basis.

> Example:
>
> Mary's paintings sell for $10,000 each. She would like to give one to your museum, but she realizes that her tax deduction will be limited to the $50 she spent on paint and materials. Mary gives the painting to her brother, Mark. Mark, in turn, donates the painting to the museum. What is Mark's income tax deduction? $50 because he received the artistic work as a gift from the artist who created it. If he were to sell the painting, he would incur ordinary income to the extent that the sale price exceeds the cost basis of $50. His deduction is, therefore, limited to the cost basis.

This rule does not apply to property received through a bequest. Of course, if an individual purchases a piece of artwork from the artist, he acquires an item that falls under the general rules for capital assets.

Property Subject To Depreciation Recapture

What does this mean and why is it important to planned giving officers? To start, you should know that your life as a planned giving officer will not revolve around this subject. Nevertheless, it is a subject with which you must familiarize yourself early on.

Over the years, Congress has developed a complex set of rules to deal with property that has been depreciated for tax purposes. How property is treated under these rules depends on the nature of the property (tangible personal property *vs.* real property) and the date on which it was put into service.

In this connection, you may hear the terms "straight-line depreciation" and "accelerated depreciation." In straight-line depreciation the cost of the property is deducted evenly over a given number of years, determined in law by the type of property. The accelerated method allows larger amounts to be deducted in the early years of depreciation such that the donor recovers the cost in fewer years than under the straight-line method. The donor does not always have a choice with regard to the method of depreciation used; in some cases, he or she is prohibited from using an accelerated method.

When a donor claims depreciation deductions, his or her cost basis for the property is reduced by the amount of that deduction.

> Example:
>
> Donor purchases a car for $30,000 for use in his trade or business. He can deduct the $30,000 in equal amounts of $6,000 over five years, except that I.R.S. assumes the property is put into service on June 30, so the first year's deduction is half of the annual amount otherwise allowed. (*Note: For property placed in service after December 31, 1986, the law makes a distinction between different types of property and has established a set number of years for each category. Automobiles are in the 5-year category, but other items could be 3, 5, 7, 10, 15, or 20 years. For residential rental real property, the recovery period is 27.5 years; for nonresidential rental real property, the period is 31.5 years. For property placed in service prior to December 31, 1986, shorter recovery periods may apply.*) After the first year's deduction of $3,000, the cost basis becomes $27,000 ($30,000 - $3,000 = $27,000). After the second year's depreciation deduction of $6,000, the cost basis is reduced to $21,000, and so on until the total cost is recovered. As you can see, the spread between the cost basis and the market value widens each year. For an appreciating asset, like real estate, the spread between the cost basis and the market value would be much greater— each year the market value presumably increases while the cost basis decreases after the depreciation deduction.

By setting up such a system, Congress has provided an economic benefit to the individual who puts property into service in a trade or business—the taxes saved by the depreciation deduction. If at some future date, the donor sells the property he may have to repay the tax savings he received as a result of the depreciation deductions. This is *depreciation recapture*. Depending on the circumstances, the recaptured amount may be ordinary income or capital gain.

The amount of income recaptured depends on the following factors:

- when the property was put into service;
- whether the donor used straight-line or accelerated depreciation;
- whether the property is tangible personal property, residential real property, or nonresidential real property.

Therefore, if a donor contributes such property to your organization, he or she may have to reduce the value of his or her income tax deduction by the amount of ordinary income that would have been recaptured if he or she sold the property. Bottom line: A taxpayer cannot take a deduction for the same property twice.

When the income recaptured in the gift transaction is categorized as capital gain income (and not ordinary income), and if the property has been held for the required long term capital gain holding period, the donor does not have to reduce the value of the charitable deduction. He or she can claim the full fair market value.

If you encounter a situation involving property subject to depreciation recapture, your tax counsel can help you sort out the various regulations that impact the donor. It still may be attractive for the donor to contribute the property. However, you need someone to help you who understands the full body of tax law surrounding this situation. Real estate may be the most common asset on which the donor has claimed depreciation deductions. The person with the most knowledge of the actual situation is the donor's accountant. The donor must consult his or her own advisor on the tax consequences here. This is way beyond your ability to help in most cases.

The *ordinary income reduction rule* applies only to the income tax charitable deduction and not to the gift or estate tax deduction.

Section 306 Stock

Section 306 stock is preferred stock that has been issued as a stock dividend on common stock. Under Section 306 of the Internal Revenue Code (hence the name, "Section 306 stock"), any gain on the sale of such stock is taxable as ordinary income. Consequently, under the *ordinary income reduction rule*, a deduction for a gift of "Section 306 stock" is limited to the cost basis. You won't run into Section 306 stock often, but whenever a donor suggests giving you preferred stock, check it out.

THE CAPITAL GAIN TAX

In general, individuals who sell appreciated capital assets are required to report for income tax purposes the full amount of the gain regardless of whether the gain is short- or long-term.

The maximum capital gain tax for most property (other than artistic property at 28% and depreciable real estate at 25%) was 20% prior to JGTRRA of 2003. There formerly was an 18% rate for property held for 5 years when purchased after December 31, 2000 and a rate of 10% for taxpayers in the 15% tax bracket.

The new laws under JGTRRA create lower capital gain rates as follows for sales after May 5, 2003. It is scheduled to expire after December 31, 2008.

The new laws vary depending on the year of the sale and the tax bracket of the taxpayer. The following rules now apply. It is a mess.

Capital Gain Rate	Applies to
28%	Sales of collectables (no change from prior law)
25%	Depreciable real property (no change from prior law)
20%	Sold before May 6, 2003, with marginal rate greater than 15%
18%	Held more than 5 years and sold after 2009
15%	Taxpayers above 15% marginal rate
10%	Held less than 5 years, sold before May 6, 2003, marginal rate of 10% or 15%
8%	Held longer than 5 years, sold before May 6, 2003. Repealed for sales after May 5 and before January 1, 2009
5%	Marginal rate of 10% or 15%. In 2008, goes to zero

Practically, most of the donors with whom you'll be working will have a 15% capital gain rate on their long-term capital gain assets. Therefore, for purposes of the examples in this book, I'm going to assume a 15% capital gain rate for most gift examples. The hypothetical scenarios based on the above rule are too varied to manage. Plus, the point of the examples is to show you how the concepts work. If you need to substitute a lower capital gain rate for your own donor examples, you'll know when to do it.

The capital gain tax is a devastating tax for an individual who sells appreciated property especially if the property's value is highly appreciated:

Example:

Securities valued at:	$ 200,000
Cost basis:	− 50,000
Capital gain if sold:	$ 150,000
Capital gain tax rate:	x 15%
Capital gain tax:	$ 22,500

When a donor contributes appreciated long-term capital gain property, he or she is entitled to an income tax deduction for the full fair market value *and* avoids the capital gain tax that would have applied if he or she sold the asset. This is a significant benefit for donors wishing to make charitable contributions. When you add the tax savings from the income tax deduction to the tax avoided on the gain, you can show the donor significant savings from a gift.

As mentioned earlier, if the donor contributes property held less than the required long-term holding period, he can deduct only the cost basis. Those rules have not changed. Plus, when a donor sells short-term property, any gain must be reported as ordinary income and taxed at the donor's income tax bracket.

THE ALTERNATIVE MINIMUM TAX

There was a time when a taxpayer could manipulate his or her tax situation to avoid tax liability completely. Congress eventually put a stop to this by establishing the Alternative Minimum Tax (AMT) which is a parallel system of computing tax liability that ensures everyone will pay a minimum level of tax.

In general, a taxpayer must calculate tax liability two ways, first under the regular tax, and second, under the Alternative Minimum Tax and pay whichever tax is higher. Charitable gifts are deductible for both the regular tax and the AMT.

You will hear of *tax preference items* in connection with the AMT. These are items isolated for special treatment that must be added to the tax base when a taxpayer computes AMT liability. The more preference items the taxpayer has, the greater the AMT liability will be and the greater the chances of being subject to the AMT Following is a list of tax preference items for the year 2003 taken from I.R.S.' own tax instructions. The donor must use Form 6521 if he or she claimed or received any of the following items.

LIST OF TAX PREFERENCE ITEMS FOR AMT

- Accelerated depreciation.

- The spread on exercising an incentive stock option and you did not dispose of the stock in the same year.

- Tax-exempt interest from private activity bonds.

- Intangible drilling, circulation, research, experimental, or mining costs.

- Amortization of pollution-control facilities or depletion.

- Income or (loss) from tax-shelter farm activities or passive activities.

- Percentage-of-completion income from long-term contracts.

- Interest paid on a home mortgage not used to buy, build, or substantially improve your home.

- Investment interest expense reported on Form 4952.

- Net operating loss deduction.

- Alternative minimum tax adjustments from an estate, trust, electing large partnership, or a cooperative.

- Section 1202 exclusion.

The above listed items probably are strange and confusing to new planned giving officers—and even to many experienced ones. I do not expect you to understand what they are, and I don't understand them all myself. The only people who would understand fully what these items represent would be accountants or CPAs. So, don't despair. Just read them over a few times and remember a few of the key words.

There is nothing wrong with engaging in these activities. You should simply know that if the donor is subject to the AMT, then the tax savings from a charitable deduction will be at the AMT rate and not at the regular tax rate. If the AMT rate is lower than the donor's regular tax rate, then the tax savings from a charitable deduction will also be at the lower AMT rate.

FLOATING I.R.S. DISCOUNT RATES

As a planned giving officer, you'll be creating proposals for donors who are considering all kinds of gifts, some outright and some deferred, during life and after death. Determining the charitable deduction for an outright gift for purposes of the income tax, gift tax, or estate tax is fairly simple once you know the fair market value.

When a donor makes a gift that the charity cannot use right away (*i.e.*, a gift of a future interest in most cases), he or she cannot claim a deduction for the full fair market value. This is because a gift the charity cannot use for five, ten, twenty years or more is not worth the same as it is today. It is worth less. The charitable deduction for such a gift takes into account how much a dollar today will be worth at some future date. By discounting the value of the gift, the I.R.S. entitles the donor to a charitable deduction for the *present value* of the future charitable portion of the gift.

Examples of gifts where this rule applies include:

- charitable gift annuities (Chapter II-8);
- charitable remainder trusts (Chapter II-9);
- charitable lead trusts (Chapter II-11);
- pooled income funds in existence for less than three years (Chapter II-7);
- retained life estates in personal residences or farms (Chapter II-6).

The I.R.S. Discount Rate is factored into a numerous collection of tables used to calculate the following kinds of interests:

- a remainder interest: Donor places property in a trust retaining income for life with the remainder to the charity. The amount passing to the charity is the remainder interest.

- a life income interest: Donor places property in a trust retaining income for life with the remainder to the charity. The income passing to the donor during his lifetime is the life estate, sometimes called the life income interest.

- a life estate: Donor contributes his or her personal residence or farm to a charity and retains a life estate (tenancy for life). The tables allow you to calculate the value of the life estate and the present value of the remainder interest in the property following the donor's death.

Beginning with gifts made after April 30, 1989, you must use a floating discount rate determined as follows:

120% of the mid-term Annual Applicable Federal Interest Rate (AFR) rounded to the nearest two-tenths of 1%

On or about the 20th of each month, the I.R.S. publishes Applicable Federal Rates for the following month. The rates represent the average yield on U.S. obligations that fluctuate monthly. The AFR rates have fluctuated widely since the floating rate was instituted in 1989. If you do an Internet search on "AFR," you will find numerous web sites showing the AFR since its inception. In 2003, when this book will be going to print, the AFR rates are the lowest in history. That makes some gifts less attractive or even impossible because the charitable deduction doesn't meet minimum percentage amounts required for different gift vehicles. A low discount rate also makes other kinds of gifts more attractive than ever. I will discuss these considerations in the appropriate chapters.

In calculating the charitable deduction, a donor is allowed to use the rate for the month in which the gift is made or the rate for either of the two months preceding the month of the gift. This allows the donor to select the rate that will provide the highest charitable deduction. Moreover, if the donor is making a gift after the 20th of the month, he or she will also know the rate for the following month, and, if it is a more attractive rate, can delay the gift until the next month.

If you were doing the calculation manually (not that you would), you would need a copy of two I.R.S. publications where most of its tables are reproduced. The I.R.S. formerly sold these two very large volumes, but they are now free to download at www.irs.gov.

> I.R.S. Publication 1457
> *Actuarial Values: Aleph Volume (formerly Alpha)*
> Remainder, Income, and Annuity Factors for One Life, Two Lives, and Term Certains. Interest Rates from 2.2 Percent to 22.0 Percent. For Use in Income, Estate, and Gift Tax Purposes including Valuation of Pooled Income Fund Remainder Interests

> I.R.S. Publication 1458
> *Actuarial Values: Beth Volume (formerly Beta)*
> Unitrust Remainder Factors for One Life, Two Lives, and Term Certains. Adjusted Payout Rates from 2.2 Percent to 22.0 Percent. For Use in Income, Estate, and Gift Tax Purposes.

There is no reason for you to be doing tax calculations by hand when there are many excellent planned giving software programs (See Appendix II). But, you do need to know what to expect when you start working with real cases.

The software programs available to our industry incorporate the I.R.S. discount rate or Applicable Federal Rate into the calculations you prepare. Most likely the software automatically selects the most beneficial rate for the gift scenario you are developing (the current month or the rate for either of the prior two months). Bear in mind that the donor must file an election if he or she uses a rate other than the one for the current month.

Type of Gift	Discount Rate That Produces Largest Charitable Deduction
charitable remainder trust	highest
charitable gift annuity	highest
charitable lead trust	lowest
personal residence or farm with retained life estate	lowest

Throughout the rest of this book, when you read about how to calculate the charitable deduction for various gifts, you'll be referred back here for an explanation of the discount rate. This will make a whole lot more sense when you get into the discussion of a particular type of gift in subsequent chapters. If this is the first time you are reading about this, and if the information just doesn't sink in, come back later when you have familiarized yourself with the gift vehicles. It will get easier especially when you begin working with planned giving software since you will be able to see where the discount rate fits in.

There is a subtle and often missed point about the AFR and the gift annuity. A lower AFR produces a lower tax deduction, but it produces a higher tax-free portion of the annuity payment.

Pooled Income Funds Treated Differently: You do not use the floating discount rate for a pooled income fund in existence more than three years. You use the actual performance figures for the fund itself. These figures are computed annually by the pooled income fund's manager after the close of the calendar year. This is explained further in the chapter on pooled income funds. For pooled income funds in existence less than three years, the I.R.S. prescribes the discount rate for use until after your fund has three years of actual performance. That, too, is covered in the pooled income fund chapter.

TANGIBLE PERSONAL PROPERTY FOR AN UNRELATED USE

Tangible personal property is personal property you can touch. It includes furniture, books, automobiles, paintings, antiques, clothes, coins, stamps, boats, *etc.* It does not include real estate and it does not include stocks and bonds.

A gift of tangible personal property that cannot be put to a use related to your organization's charitable exempt purpose entitles the donor to an income tax deduction limited to the cost basis. Even when it is related, but you plan to sell it rather than use it, the deduction is limited to the property's cost basis, and the contribution ceiling is 50% of adjusted gross income.

The important concept to understand about the related-use rule is that is turns on whether the donor could reasonably have the expectation that the charity would put the gift to a related use on the date of the gift.

Some examples of a related use include:

- a painting to an art museum,
- an antique car to an automobile museum,
- clothes to a social service agency, or
- books to a library.

These examples are obvious, but, it is not always easy to determine whether an item of tangible personal property can be used for a purpose related to the organization's charitable purposes. For museums, there is a special rule that presumes the expectation of a related use for a gift of art unless the donor knows in fact that the gift will not be put to a related use.

Sometimes, when a gift enhances the environment of the charitable organization, it is considered to be made for a related use. For example, the I.R.S. ruled that donating porcelain art objects to a nonprofit retirement center met the related-use test because the Center's purpose was to create a living environment for its residents and the art directly enhanced that environment. Another example of property put to a related use might be office furniture which helps the charity conduct its affairs in a proper business environment. Or, a car which is donated to a university for the purpose of transporting students on and off campus for an academic purpose.

Gifts to an auction are never for a related use. Consequently, the donor's income tax deduction is limited to the cost basis and subject to the 50% deductibility ceiling. This fact may surprise some people—both donors and fund raisers alike—because many organizations conduct auctions to raise valuable operating dollars. But, beware. A gift of tangible personal property to an auction is not considered to be made for a related use because the organization doesn't use it. In addition, a gift of tangible property to a charitable remainder trust is never a related use.

You should inform the donor of the special treatment of tangible personal property so that he or she can make an informed decision about the gift. Even if the item fails the related-use test, it may have special value to your organization. Perhaps the donor will consider giving it to you anyway. Or, the cost basis may be close to the market value in which case the loss in tax savings from a deduction limited to the cost basis may be small.

The related-use rules apply only for purposes of the income tax deduction; there are no related-use rules with regard to bequests.

During the last month of the tax year, donors frequently offer oddball items to charity attempting to secure a charitable deduction before time runs out. In my opinion, these kinds of offers are a total waste of your time. Planned giving officers spend way too much time trying not to insult a donor by turning down a gift item. My advice is to dismiss these worthless offers quickly and don't spend a lot of time on them. The most common year-end offering is artwork, even for organizations that don't have a museum. If you intend to hang a piece of artwork on your premises, it probably would qualify for a related use. However, these items are usually more trouble than they are worth. Don't waste your time.

The I.R.S. requires special reporting for noncash gifts. These are discussed later in this chapter.

GIFTS MADE "FOR THE USE OF" INSTEAD OF "TO" YOUR ORGANIZATION

In addition to the various limitations discussed above, the I.R.S. also places a limitation on the donor's income tax deduction depending on how the property is given. There is a difference in the I.R.S.'s eyes between making a gift *"to"* your organization and making a gift *"for the use of"* your organization. For example, if a donor contributes securities outright, he or she is obviously making a gift to your organization. You have total control of the gift property and you can sell or retain it as an investment as you choose. On the other hand, if a donor sets up a charitable remainder trust that eventually distributes to a perpetual charitable trust for the benefit of the charity, the gift is *for the use of*. A charitable lead trust is also deemed to be *"for the use of."*

My tax guide, *Charitable Giving and Solicitation*, says that the case of a donor paying life insurance premiums directly to the insurance company is not clear cut. Apparently, some commentators feel this scenario is *for the use of*, but there seems to be some uncertainty among members of the legal community. Your donors should check with their own attorney on this issue. However, if the donor makes a gift directly to the charity, and, in turn, the charity uses it to pay the premium on a life insurance policy, the gift is *to* the institution.

Gifts to a public charity of appreciated long-term capital gain property *for the use of* entitle the donor to an income tax deduction up to 20% of adjusted gross income with a five-year carry-over period for the excess. Gifts of cash and ordinary income property *for the use of* are limited to 30% of the donor's adjusted gross income with the same five-year carry-over period for any amount exceeding the 30% ceiling.

It would get rather complicated to determine how the various contribution ceilings interact when the donor has made many different kinds of gifts in the same tax year. For example, if the donor makes outright gifts of cash and long-term appreciated securities plus gifts of cash *for the use of* plus gifts of long term appreciated property *for the use of*, an accountant would need to be consulted on which gifts get reported first, which get carried over, *etc*. But, regardless of how many categories there are, the overall percentage limitation of 50% of adjusted gross income applies on all gifts combined.

BARGAIN SALES

Income plans that provide payments over a period of years may not be right for the donor who needs cash up front. Thus, if your organization neither runs a pooled income fund nor a gift annuity program, you may feel you have no option for the donor who needs income. The bargain sale is an ideal compromise.

Example:

Mr. Donor owns a painting having a fair market value of $200,000 and a cost basis of $30,000. It has been held the required holding period to be considered a long-term capital asset. You would like to acquire the painting for your art collection. Although the donor is interested in contributing the painting, he cannot afford to relinquish it as an outright gift.

Solution: He sells the painting to your organization for $30,000 in a bargain sale. The transaction is considered part sale and part gift. The donor can claim an income tax deduction for $170,000, the difference between the sale price and the market value. You acquire a magnificent new addition to your art collection at a fraction of its value. And, the donor receives $30,000 in cash.

Almost anything can be sold or exchanged in a bargain sale. As long as your organization has the necessary cash to purchase the property, you can offer the donor an attractive gift option that other nonprofit organizations may not have suggested. Real estate also lends itself very well to the bargain sale option.

Capital Gain Tax Implications Of The Sale

In the above example, the donor has some tax liability on this transaction. Even though the donor sold the property for the amount he originally paid, he is liable for a tax as if the property were split into two pieces—

part gift and part sale. To calculate how much capital gain the donor must report, you allocate the cost basis between the sale portion and the gift portion using the following formula:

$$(\text{Market Value - Cost Basis}) \quad x \quad \frac{\text{Selling Price}}{\text{Market Value}} \quad = \quad \text{Reportable Gain}$$

$$(\$200{,}000 - \$30{,}000) \quad x \quad \frac{\$30{,}000}{\$200{,}000} \quad = \quad \$25{,}500$$

In the above example, the donor must report long-term capital gain income of $25,500 on the $30,000 sale portion. But, he simultaneously claims a federal income tax charitable deduction of $170,000 on the gift portion. Overall, this is a nice compromise that suits the donor and the charity equally well.

The bargain sale rules apply under these circumstances:

- when a donor sells property for less than it is worth (above example),
- exchanges property for something else of lesser value,
- contributes property subject to debt.

Let me review the last situation for you, the case of a person contributing property subject to debt. For tax purposes, the amount of the donor's debt which is eliminated by the gift is considered to be received by the donor as if it were cash in his hand. You use the same formula to determine the donor's reportable gain except that the "sale price" is the amount of "debt" on the property. Note, in the case of a gift of debt-financed property, it is irrelevant that the donor never actually gets the cash benefit. The mere fact that he is relieved of an obligation is sufficient to trigger the bargain sale rules.

Example:

Mr. Donor has land valued at $200,000, a cost basis of $100,000, and a remaining mortgage of $30,000. When he contributes the land to your organization, his liability to pay the mortgage is eliminated and the $30,000 is considered to be realized by him. It doesn't matter whether you choose to assume the mortgage or not; the property was still subject to it. Following is the same formula used above except that the "sale price" is not actually from a sale but rather from the forgiveness of the debt.

$$(\text{Market Value - Cost Basis}) \quad x \quad \frac{\text{Selling Price (debt)}}{\text{Market Value}} \quad = \quad \text{Reportable Gain}$$

$$(\$200{,}000 - \$100{,}000) \quad x \quad \frac{\$30{,}000}{\$200{,}000} \quad = \quad \$15{,}000$$

The net result here can still be attractive to the donor. First, he is able to claim an income tax deduction for the net equity $170,000 ($200,000 - $30,000 = $170,000). Second, he must report the capital gain income of $15,000. The result is a tax saving from a net income tax deduction of $155,000. He has also eliminated the burden of the mortgage payments, insurance costs, taxes, and maintenance expenses.

Taking this discussion of bargain sales one step further, let's say you pay the donor $10,000 for property valued at $200,000 having a cost basis of $100,000 and which has a remaining mortgage of $30,000. You can use the same formula to compute the reportable gain. Here, the "sale price" in the numerator of the fraction (sale price divided by market value) is the sum of 1) the debt forgiven, and 2) the cash received ($30,000 + $10,000 = $40,000). Continue with the equation to arrive at a reportable gain of $20,000 offset by an income tax deduction of $160,000 ($200,000 - $30,000 mortgage - $10,000 cash received = $160,000) or a net benefit from a tax deduction of $140,000 ($160,000 deduction - $20,000 reportable gain = $140,000 net deduction).

The planned giving software I am using (PG Calc) does this in a breeze. Other software programs also offer this calculation, so you may never have to do this manually. Still, you ought to know how the figures are computed.

Bargain Sales With Ordinary-Income Property

When a donor sells ordinary-income property (such as inventory) to you in a bargain sale, another complication arises. In addition to allocating the cost basis between the sale and gift portion (to determine the reportable gain as outlined above), the donor must also allocate between the sale and gift portion the ordinary income that would have been generated by a straight sale. Thus, the gift portion (and consequently the tax deduction) is reduced by the ordinary income attributable to the gift portion. (If you are not following this, go back to the earlier section about inventory and reread it. Then come back here again. Don't give up!)

If you still find this confusing, you are probably not alone. The most important thing when you are considering a bargain sale is to get as much information about the gift property as you can in order that your tax counsel can advise you how to proceed.

Other Considerations

Throughout this discussion of bargain sales, I have assumed that the gift is made on an outright basis. You should also know that a donor falls under the bargain sale rules when he makes a gift in exchange for a charitable gift annuity. (See Chapter II–8 for a discussion of gift annuities.)

When In Doubt, Seek Legal Advice

There is much more to this subject than I intend to cover in this chapter. For example, special care must be taken in the case of a gift of a limited partnership where there is non-recourse debt (debt which is a liability to the partnership but not to the individual partners). Different complications arise when tangible personal property that cannot be put to a related use is the subject of a bargain sale. Further, you will need legal advice if you are considering accepting debt-financed property into a charitable remainder trust because that creates unfavorable consequences.

While the basic concept of the bargain sale is simple, you should seek legal guidance before proceeding with a proposal. But, I hope you'll be able successfully to call up this option in your fund raising travels.

INCOME IN RESPECT OF A DECEDENT (IRD)

Some assets cannot be given to a charity during lifetime without triggering ordinary income for the donor. These assets are better for bequests to charity, because if arranged properly, the asset escapes both the income tax on the donor's last tax return, and the estate tax that would have applied if the donor exceeded his or her lifetime exemption for taxable transfers. Income in respect of a decedent is income that would have been ordinary income if received by the decedent while alive.

There are all kinds of income categories that would be reportable on the recipient's income tax return, or on the decedent's last tax return. The ones that are the most common to a planned giving officer are:

- retirement plan assets;
- IRAs;
- deferred compensation;
- accrued interest on U.S. Savings Bonds.

In all of these cases, a donor is trapped with these assets. In order to make a gift from a retirement plan or from an IRA, the donor must first withdraw the money, report the income, and then make the gift. In most cases, this will be a wash. So, for example, if a donor withdraws $25,000 from an IRA, and then gives the cash to the charity, he will report the withdrawal and claim the deduction on the same tax return. As long as the donor does not exceed his or her contribution ceiling (50% of adjusted gross income for all categories of gifts), then this truly is a wash. But for extremely large withdrawals, the donor may not have enough income to support a deduction for the full amount of the gift. There is still a five-year carry over period, but, frankly, people simply don't choose to make gifts of IRD assets during lifetime.

For deferred compensation, you have the same problem. And, with a U.S. Savings Bond, any attempt to transfer the bond during lifetime triggers the accrued interest which could be 100% reportable as ordinary income to the donor. There is nothing you can do about this.

The only charitable solution for IRD assets under current law is for the donor to leave them to charity at death either outright or in a life income plan such as a charitable remainder trust or a gift annuity. (Note: When a donor funds at death a gift annuity with an IRD asset, 100% of the annuitant's payments will be ordinary income. There is no capital gain tier.) There is a more detailed discussion on Income in Respect of a Decedent in Chapter II-12 so you should turn there if you are interested in reading more about these particular assets and what can be done with them.

SUBSTANTIATION REQUIREMENTS FOR NONCASH GIFTS

The I.R.S. prescribes strict reporting requirements for noncash gifts. They impact both the donor and the charity. If the donor fails to follow the rules, he or she will not receive an income tax deduction for the gift. If the charity fails to follow the rules, it will be fined $50 for each failure.

At the end of this chapter are the two forms (with instructions) that you will need to comply with I.R.S. rules. Basically, a donor must report gifts of noncash property exceeding $500 on Form 8283. If the property exceeds $5,000 ($10,000 for non-publicly traded securities) a qualified appraisal is also required, and the donee charity must file Form 8282 if it disposes of the property within two years. Following is a summary of what you need to know about these forms and reporting requirements. The rest of the detail is fairly well laid out in the instructions.

Warning: Form 8283 and 8282 have been revised many times since February, 1985, when the rules were created. The most up-to-date version as of this printing is October, 1998. You'll find the date in the upper left hand corner of the form. Often, a development office forgets to throw away old forms or to get new, updated ones from the I.R.S. To avoid sending an out-of-date form to a donor, make a special point of checking with your tax counsel periodically for the latest version or simply go to the I.R.S. web site and get your own (www.irs.gov).

Form 8283
Noncash Charitable Contributions

Section A, Part I and Part II:

Publicly traded securities are listed in Section A, Part I, regardless of their value. The donor must show the following for each publicly traded stock:

- Date of the contribution,
- Date acquired by donor,
- How acquired by donor,
- Donor's cost or adjusted basis,
- Fair market value,
- Method used to determine fair market value.

The form provides a section for donors who "contributed less than an entire interest in the property," (Part II, 2). But, the form is inadequate because there are spaces for the detail of only one deferred gift. If your donor has made more than one deferred gift during the year, and many have, he or she should attach separate sheets for the other gifts. Most donors would attach the acknowledgment letter from the charity as well as the detailed tax calculations provided by the charity's planned giving officer. To be safe, the donor's attorney or accountant should prepare the tax calculation figures. In practice, I would be surprised if many donors had their own accountant redo the calculations. If you are aware that the donor has an accountant, you should prepare a duplicate set of documents for the accountant to review, prior to attaching the documents to Form 8283.

For tangible personal property exceeding $500 and less than $5,000, the donor would also list these items in Part I. In determining the value of an item of tangible personal property, the donor must treat similar items as one item. For example, a set of ten books is one item and not ten items (even if the donor gives one book to each of ten charities). An Appraisal Summary (Section B) need not be completed for items listed in Section A. However, the donor should have sufficient information (an appraisal is desirable but not necessary) to verify the amounts claimed on the form should the I.R.S. challenge the deduction.

Your organization is not required to sign the form if the donor's gifts are reported only in Section A. Having said that, I can tell you with absolute certainty that donors and accountants will request your charity to sign Form 8283. Sometimes you can successfully explain to the donor that your organization's signature is not necessary. At other times, you will find yourself arguing with your donor who persists in requesting your signature. In these cases, it is more trouble than it is worth to deny the donor a signature. Get the signature and don't make a big deal out of it. This is a real annoyance, but you must do what the donor wants, especially if there is no harm done.

Section B, Part I, Part II, Part III, Part IV

Section B must be completed if the value of one item or a group of similar items exceeds $5,000 ($10,000 for non-publicly traded, or, in other words, closely-held securities). Publicly-traded securities are reported in Section A regardless of their value.

Part I: The donor describes the property including date of acquisition, form of acquisition, cost basis, and market value. Although this section will normally be used to list items valued over $5,000, you may find items valued at less than $5,000 in this section. This is because the donor has contributed part of a group of items or collection to more than one organization. Your share of the property is less than $5,000 but the total given to all charities is greater than $5,000.

Part II: If the donor signs here indicating that one or more of the items listed in Part II is worth less than $500, your organization is not required to file Form 8282 if it sells the item within two years.

Part III: A qualified written appraisal is required for property exceeding $5,000, or $10,000 for non-publicly traded securities.

The appraisal must be dated no more than 60 days prior to the date of gift and not later than the due date of the tax return on which it is being claimed. The donor does not need to include a copy of the appraisal with the income tax return except for gifts of art where the deduction is greater than $20,000 for all art contributions combined. The donor is responsible for getting the appraisal because he or she—not you—is the one who must verify to the I.R.S. the value of the charitable contribution deduction. For taxpayers who itemize, the appraisal fee is deductible as an expense to determine tax liability subject to the floor of 2% of adjusted gross income on the total of "miscellaneous itemized deductions."

Beginning January 16, 1996, if a person donates an item of art that has been appraised at $50,000 or more, he or she can request a Statement of Value for that item from the I.R.S. This must be done before filing the tax return that reports the donation. The request must include the following:

1. A copy of a qualified appraisal of the item (see Qualified Appraisal, later.)
2. A $2,500 check or money order payable to the Internal Revenue Service for the user fee that applies to the request regarding one, two, or three items of art (add $250 for each item in excess of three).
3. A completed appraisal summary (Section B of Form 8283, Noncash Charitable Contributions.)
4. The location of the I.R.S. District Office that has examination responsibility for the donor's area.

Part IV: (Completed last) Your organization signs the form and in doing so agrees to file Form 8282 (Donee Information Return) if within two years it disposes of all or part of the property being reported here. When the donor presents the form for your signature, he or she must give you a copy of the appraisal. Signing this form does not imply you agree with the appraisal. It simply verifies you received the listed property.

Form 8282
Donee Information Return

By creating Form 8282 and imposing reporting requirements on the charitable donee with regard to certain types of property gifts, the I.R.S. has reduced the potential for fraud as it relates to charitable contributions of noncash property.

Whenever your organization signs Form 8283, your business office must monitor the disposition of the property listed on the form. If you sell, exchange, or dispose of all or part of this property within two years, you must file Form 8282 with the I.R.S. within 125 days of the sale or disposal and also send a copy to the donor. If you give the property to another charity and that charity sells or disposes of the property before the original two years is up, it also must file Form 8282.

If, as sometimes happens, you take in a piece of property that has been appraised by the donor, and you sell it shortly thereafter for much less than the appraisal, your disclosure of the sale price on Form 8282 may subject the donor's tax return to I.R.S. inspection or audit. To avoid this unfortunate and damaging situation, it is important for the donor's appraisal to be as accurate as is feasibly possible. Often, however, there is no way to predict the market price. If special circumstances caused the lower price, you should attach an explanation to Form 8282.

Who Is A Qualified Appraiser?

A qualified appraiser is one who holds himself out to the public as an appraiser and who is qualified to make a determination of the value of the property in question. In general, the appraiser *cannot* be

- the donor;
- your organization;
- a party to the transaction in which the donor acquired the property;
- employed by or related to any of the parties,
- married to any of the parties, or
- any person whose interest in the transaction could be questioned.

Also, the appraiser's fee cannot be based on a percentage of the appraised value. A bizarre consequence of these rules is that an insurance company that issued a life insurance policy cannot appraise it for gift purposes.

Ethical Dilemmas With Form 8283 or 8282

Occasionally, you will come across a situation that involves a bit of tact and some ethical considerations. A donor may offer to give you property, like real estate, on the condition that you do not sell it for two years. Or, the item may be art work or other kinds of tangibles that your organization may choose to sell before the two years are up. While the charity should do nothing to conspire with the donor to defraud the I.R.S., there may be legitimate reasons why the charity may choose to hold an asset of noncash property for two years or more. For example, the donor may know that zoning changes in the town where the real estate is located will cause an increase in value within a couple of years. Perhaps the charity will decide to hold the property for a while rather than sell it immediately. However, if there is some kind of binding agreement that prevents the charity from disposing of the property for a period of years, then that fact alone may affect the value of the donor's qualified appraisal.

SUMMARY

This chapter is a good start as you begin to talk to donors about charitable gifts. But, please, don't get so caught up in the laws that you lose sight of the foremost reason donor's will be making gifts—because they want to help your charity. If you find that after reading this chapter, you want more information about a very specific area of tax law that I did not cover in detail, you should look next for any of the excellent tax guides listed among other resources in Appendix III.

The next chapter explains the very complex generation-skipping transfer tax which needed its own chapter. This is really very advanced for new planned giving officers, but if you can understand this tax, you'll be able to use this knowledge to help donors make major gifts that greatly reduce or possibly eliminate this tax.

Form **8283**
(Rev. October 1998)

Department of the Treasury
Internal Revenue Service

Noncash Charitable Contributions

▶ Attach to your tax return if you claimed a total deduction
of over $500 for all contributed property.

▶ See separate instructions.

OMB No. 1545-0908

Attachment
Sequence No. **55**

Name(s) shown on your income tax return

Identifying number

Note: Figure the amount of your contribution deduction before completing this form. See your tax return instructions.

Section A—List in this section only items (or groups of similar items) for which you claimed a deduction of $5,000 or less. Also, list certain publicly traded securities even if the deduction is over $5,000 (see instructions).

Part I   Information on Donated Property—If you need more space, attach a statement.

1	(a) Name and address of the donee organization	(b) Description of donated property
A		
B		
C		
D		
E		

Note: If the amount you claimed as a deduction for an item is $500 or less, you do not have to complete columns (d), (e), and (f).

	(c) Date of the contribution	(d) Date acquired by donor (mo., yr.)	(e) How acquired by donor	(f) Donor's cost or adjusted basis	(g) Fair market value	(h) Method used to determine the fair market value
A						
B						
C						
D						
E						

Part II   Other Information—Complete line 2 if you gave less than an entire interest in property listed in Part I. Complete line 3 if conditions were attached to a contribution listed in Part I.

2   If, during the year, you contributed less than the entire interest in the property, complete lines a–e.

a   Enter the letter from Part I that identifies the property ▶ _____ . If Part II applies to more than one property, attach a separate statement.

b   Total amount claimed as a deduction for the property listed in Part I: (1)   For this tax year   ▶ _____ .
                                            (2)   For any prior tax years   ▶ _____ .

c   Name and address of each organization to which any such contribution was made in a prior year (complete only if differ from the donee organization above):

Name of charitable organization (donee)

Address (number, street, and room or suite no.)

City or town, state, and ZIP code

d   For tangible property, enter the place where the property is located or kept ▶ _____

e   Name of any person, other than the donee organization, having actual possession of the property ▶ _____

3   If conditions were attached to any contribution listed in Part I, answer questions a – c and attach the required statement (see instructions).

		Yes	No
a	Is there a restriction, either temporary or permanent, on the donee's right to use or dispose of the donated property?		
b	Did you give to anyone (other than the donee organization or another organization participating with the donee organization in cooperative fundraising) the right to the income from the donated property or to the possession of the property, including the right to vote donated securities, to acquire the property by purchase or otherwise, or to designate the person having such income, possession, or right to acquire?		
c	Is there a restriction limiting the donated property for a particular use?		

For Paperwork Reduction Act Notice, see page 4 of separate instructions.   Cat. No. 62299J   Form **8283** (Rev. 10-98)

Name(s) shown on your income tax return	Identifying number

Section B—Appraisal Summary—List in this section only items (or groups of similar items) for which you claimed a deduction of more than $5,000 per item or group. Exception. Report contributions of certain publicly traded securities only in Section A.

If you donated art, you may have to attach the complete appraisal. See the Note in Part I below.

Part I   Information on Donated Property—To be completed by the taxpayer and/or appraiser.

4   Check type of property:

- ☐ Art* (contribution of $20,000 or more)
- ☐ Art* (contribution of less than $20,000)
- ☐ Real Estate
- ☐ Coin Collections
- ☐ Gems/Jewelry
- ☐ Books
- ☐ Stamp Collections
- ☐ Other

*Art includes paintings, sculptures, watercolors, prints, drawings, ceramics, antique furniture, decorative arts, textiles, carpets, silver, rare manuscripts, historical memorabilia, and other similar objects.

Note: If your total art contribution deduction was $20,000 or more, you must attach a complete copy of the signed appraisal. See instructions.

5	(a) Description of donated property (if you need more space, attach a separate statement)	(b) If tangible property was donated, give a brief summary of the overall physical condition at the time of the gift	(c) Appraised fair market value
A			
B			
C			
D			

	(d) Date acquired by donor (mo., yr.)	(e) How acquired by donor	(f) Donor's cost or adjusted basis	(g) For bargain sales, enter amount received	See instructions	
					(h) Amount claimed as a deduction	(i) Average trading price of securities
A						
B						
C						
D						

Part II   Taxpayer (Donor) Statement—List each item included in Part I above that the appraisal identifies as having a value of $500 or less. See instructions.

I declare that the following item(s) included in Part I above has to the best of my knowledge and belief an appraised value of not more than $500 (per item). Enter identifying letter from Part I and describe the specific item. See instructions. ▶ _____

Signature of taxpayer (donor) ▶ _____   Date ▶ _____

Part III   Declaration of Appraiser

I declare that I am not the donor, the donee, a party to the transaction in which the donor acquired the property, employed by, or related to any of the foregoing persons, or married to any person who is related to any of the foregoing persons. And, if regularly used by the donor, donee, or party to the transaction, I performed the majority of my appraisals during my tax year for other persons.

Also, I declare that I hold myself out to the public as an appraiser or perform appraisals on a regular basis; and that because of my qualifications as described in the appraisal, I am qualified to make appraisals of the type of property being valued. I certify that the appraisal fees were not based on a percentage of the appraised property value. Furthermore, I understand that a false or fraudulent overstatement of the property value as described in the qualified appraisal or this appraisal summary may subject me to the penalty under section 6701(a) (aiding and abetting the understatement of tax liability). I affirm that I have not been barred from presenting evidence or testimony by the Director of Practice.

Sign Here

Signature ▶ _____   Title ▶ _____   Date of appraisal ▶ _____

Business address (including room or suite no.)   Identifying number

City or town, state, and ZIP code

Part IV   Donee Acknowledgment—To be completed by the charitable organization.

This charitable organization acknowledges that it is a qualified organization under section 170(c) and that it received t   ated property as described in Section B, Part I, above on ▶ _____

(Date)

Furthermore, this organization affirms that in the event it sells, exchanges, or otherwise disposes of the property describe n Section B, Part I (or any portion thereof) within 2 years after the date of receipt, it will file Form 8282, Donee Information Return, with the IRS and give the donor a copy of that form. This acknowledgment does not represent agreement with the claimed fair m   .

Does the organization intend to use the property for an unrelated use? . . . . ▶ ☐ Yes   ☐ No

Name of charitable organization (donee)	Employer identification number
Address (number, street, and room or suite no.)	City or town, state, and ZIP code
Authorized signature	Title	Date

Instructions for Form 8283

(Revised October 1998)

Noncash Charitable Contributions

Department of the Treasury
Internal Revenue Service

Section references are to the Internal Revenue Code unless otherwise noted.

General Instructions

Purpose of Form

Use Form 8283 to report information about noncash charitable contributions.

Do not use Form 8283 to report out-of-pocket expenses for volunteer work or amounts you gave by check or credit card. Treat these items as cash contributions. Also, **do not** use Form 8283 to figure your charitable contribution deduction. For details on how to figure the amount of the deduction, see your tax return instructions.

Additional Information

You may want to see **Pub. 526,** Charitable Contributions (for individuals), and **Pub. 561,** Determining the Value of Donated Property. If you contributed depreciable property, see **Pub. 544,** Sales and Other Dispositions of Assets.

Who Must File

You must file Form 8283 if the amount of your deduction for all noncash gifts is more than $500. For this purpose, "amount of your deduction" means your deduction **before** applying any income limits that could result in a carryover. The carryover rules are explained in Pub. 526. Make any required reductions to fair market value (FMV) before you determine if you must file Form 8283. See **Fair Market Value (FMV)** on page 2.

Form 8283 is filed by individuals, partnerships, and corporations.

Note: *C corporations, other than personal service corporations and closely held corporations, must file Form 8283 only if the amount claimed as a deduction is over $5,000.*

Partnerships and S corporations. A partnership or S corporation that claims a deduction for noncash gifts over $500 must file Form 8283 with Form 1065, 1065-B, or 1120S. If the total deduction of any item or group of similar items exceeds $5,000, the partnership or S corporation must complete Section B of Form 8283 even if the amount allocated to each partner or shareholder does not exceed $5,000.

The partnership or S corporation must give a completed copy of Form 8283 to each partner or shareholder receiving an allocation of the contribution deduction shown in Section B of the partnership's or S corporation's Form 8283.

Partners and shareholders. The partnership or S corporation will provide information about your share of the contribution on your Schedule K-1 (Form 1065 or 1120S).

In some cases, the partnership or S corporation must give you a copy of its Form 8283. If you received a copy of Form 8283 from the partnership or S corporation, attach a copy to your tax return. Deduct the amount shown on your Schedule K-1, not the amount shown on the Form 8283.

If the partnership or S corporation is not required to give you a copy of its Form 8283, combine the amount of noncash contributions shown on your Schedule K-1 with your other noncash contributions to see if you must file Form 8283. If you need to file Form 8283, you do not have to complete all the information requested in Section A for your share of the partnership's or S corporation's contributions. Complete only column (g) of line 1 with your share of the contribution and enter "From Schedule K-1 (Form 1065 or 1120S)" across columns (c)–(f).

When To File

File Form 8283 with your tax return for the year you contribute the property and first claim a deduction.

Which Sections To Complete

If you must file Form 8283, you may need to complete Section A, Section B, or both, depending on the type of property donated and the amount claimed as a deduction.

Section A. Include in Section A only items (or groups of similar items as defined on this page) for which you claimed a deduction of $5,000 or less per item (or group of similar items). Also, include the following publicly traded securities even if the deduction is more than $5,000.

- Securities listed on an exchange in which quotations are published daily,
- Securities regularly traded in national or regional over-the-counter markets for which published quotations are available, or
- Securities that are shares of a mutual fund for which quotations are published on a daily basis in a newspaper of general circulation throughout the United States.

Section B. Include in Section B only items (or groups of similar items) for which you claimed a deduction of more than $5,000 (omit publicly traded securities reportable in Section A). With certain exceptions, items reported in Section B will require information based on a written appraisal by a qualified appraiser.

Similar Items of Property

Similar items of property are items of the same generic category or type, such as stamp collections, coin collections, lithographs, paintings, books, nonpublicly traded stock, land, or buildings.

Example. You claimed a deduction of $400 for clothing, $7,000 for publicly traded securities (quotations published daily), and $6,000 for a collection of 15 books ($400 each). Report the clothing and securities in Section A and the books (a group of similar items) in Section B.

Special Rule for Certain C Corporations

A special rule applies for deductions taken by certain C corporations under section 170(e)(3) or (4) for contributions of inventory or scientific equipment.

To determine if you must file Form 8283 or which section to complete, use the difference between the amount you claimed as a deduction and the amount you would have claimed as cost of goods sold (COGS) had you sold the property instead. This rule is **only** for purposes of Form 8283. It does not change the amount or method of figuring your contribution deduction.

If you do not have to file Form 8283 because of this rule, you must attach a statement to your tax return (similar to the one in the example below). Also, attach a statement if you must complete Section A, instead of Section B, because of this rule.

Example. You donated clothing from your inventory for the care of the needy. The clothing cost you $5,000 and your claimed charitable deduction is $8,000. Complete Section A instead of Section B because the difference between the amount you claimed as a charitable deduction and the amount that would have been your COGS deduction is $3,000 ($8,000 – $5,000). Attach a statement to Form 8283 similar to the following:

Form 8283—Inventory

Contribution deduction	$8,000
COGS (if sold, not donated)	– 5,000
For Form 8283 filing purposes	=$3,000

Fair Market Value (FMV)

Although the **amount** of your deduction determines if you have to file Form 8283, you also need to have information about the **value** of your contribution to complete the form.

FMV is the price a willing, knowledgeable buyer would pay a willing, knowledgeable seller when neither has to buy or sell.

You may not always be able to deduct the FMV of your contribution. Depending on the type of property donated, you may have to reduce the FMV to get to the deductible amount, as explained next.

Reductions to FMV. The amount of the reduction (if any) depends on whether the property is ordinary income property or capital gain property. Attach a statement to your tax return showing how you figured the reduction.

Ordinary income property is property that would result in ordinary income or short-term capital gain if it were sold at its FMV on the date it was contributed. Examples of ordinary income property are inventory, works of art created by the donor, and capital assets held for 1 year or less. The deduction for a gift of ordinary income property is limited to the FMV minus the amount that would be ordinary income or short-term capital gain if the property were sold.

Capital gain property is property that would result in long-term capital gain if it were sold at its FMV on the date it was contributed. It includes certain real property and depreciable property used in your trade or business, and generally held for more than 1 year. You usually may deduct gifts of capital gain property at their FMV. However, you must reduce the FMV by the amount of any appreciation if any of the following apply.

● The capital gain property is contributed to certain private nonoperating foundations. This rule does not apply to qualified appreciated stock.

● You choose the 50% limit instead of the special 30% limit.

● The contributed property is tangible personal property that is put to an **unrelated use** (as defined in Pub. 526) by the charity.

Qualified conservation contribution. If your donation qualifies as a "qualified conservation contribution" under section 170(h), attach a statement showing the FMV of the underlying property before and after the gift and the conservation purpose furthered by the gift. See Pub. 561 for more details.

Specific Instructions

Identifying number. Individuals must enter their social security number or individual taxpayer identification number. All other filers should enter their employer identification number.

Section A

Part I, Information on Donated Property

Line 1

Column (b). Describe the property in sufficient detail. The greater the value, the more detail you need. For example, a car should be described in more detail than pots and pans.

For securities, include the following:
● Name of the issuer,
● Kind of security,
● Whether a share of a mutual fund, and
● Whether regularly traded on a stock exchange or in an over-the-counter market.

Note: *If the amount you claimed as a deduction for the item is $500 or less, you do not have to complete columns (d), (e), and (f).*

Column (d). Enter the approximate date you acquired the property. If it was created, produced, or manufactured by or for you, enter the date it was substantially completed.

Column (e). State how you acquired the property (i.e., by purchase, gift, inheritance, or exchange).

Column (f). **Do not** complete this column for publicly traded securities or property held 12 months or more. Keep records on cost or other basis.

Note: *If you have reasonable cause for not providing the information in columns (d) and (f), attach an explanation.*

Column (g). Enter the FMV of the property on the date you donated it. If you were required to reduce the FMV of your deduction or you gave a qualified conservation contribution, you must attach a statement. See **Fair Market Value (FMV)** on this page for the type of statement to attach.

Column (h). Enter the method(s) you used to determine the FMV. The FMV of used household goods and clothing is usually much lower than when new. A good measure of value might be the price that buyers of these used items actually pay in consignment or thrift shops.

Examples of entries to make include "Appraisal," "Thrift shop value" (for clothing or household goods), "Catalog" (for stamp or coin collections), or "Comparable sales" (for real estate and other kinds of assets). See Pub. 561.

Part II, Other Information

If Part II applies to more than one property, attach a separate statement. Give the required information for each property separately. Identify which property listed in Part I the information relates to.

Lines 2a Through 2e

Complete lines 2a–2e only if you contributed less than the entire interest in the donated property during the tax year. On line 2b, enter the amount claimed as a deduction for this tax year and in any prior tax years for gifts of a partial interest in the same property.

Lines 3a Through 3c

Complete lines 3a–3c only if you attached restrictions to the right to the income, use, or disposition of the donated property. An example of a "restricted use" is furniture that you gave only to be used in the reading room of an organization's library. Attach a statement explaining **(1)** the terms of any agreement or understanding regarding the restriction, and **(2)** whether the property is designated for a particular use.

Section B

Part I, Information on Donated Property

You must have a written appraisal from a qualified appraiser that supports the information in Part I. However, see the **Exceptions** below.

Use Part I to summarize your appraisal(s). Generally, you do not need to attach the appraisals but you should keep them for your records. But see **Art valued at $20,000 or more** below.

Exceptions. You do not need a written appraisal if the property is:

• Nonpublicly traded stock of $10,000 or less,

• Certain securities considered to have market quotations readily available (see Regulations section 1.170A-13(c)(7)(xi)(B)),

• A donation by a C corporation (other than a closely held corporation or personal service corporation), or

• Inventory and other property donated by a closely held corporation or a personal service corporation that are "qualified contributions" for the care of the ill, the needy, or infants, within the meaning of section 170(e)(3)(A).

Although a written appraisal is not required for the types of property listed above, you must provide certain information in Part I of Section B (see Regulations section 1.170A-13(c)(4)(iv)) and have the donee organization complete Part IV.

Art valued at $20,000 or more. If your total deduction for art is $20,000 or more, you must attach a complete copy of the signed appraisal. For individual objects valued at $20,000 or more, a photograph must be provided upon request. The photograph must be of sufficient quality and size (preferably an 8 x 10 inch color photograph or a color transparency no smaller than 4 x 5 inches) to fully show the object.

Appraisal Requirements

The appraisal must be made not earlier than 60 days before the date you contribute the property. You must receive the appraisal before the due date (including extensions) of the return on which you first claim a deduction for the property. For a deduction first claimed on an amended return, the appraisal must be received before the date the amended return was filed.

A separate qualified appraisal and a separate Form 8283 are required for each item of property except for an item that is part of a group of similar items. Only one appraisal is required for a group of similar items contributed in the same tax year, if it includes all the required information for each item. The appraiser may group similar items with a collective value appraised at $100 or less.

If you gave similar items to more than one donee for which you claimed a total deduction of more than $5,000, you must attach a separate form for each donee.

Example. You claimed a deduction of $2,000 for books given to College A, $2,500 for books given to College B, and $900 for books given to a public library. You must attach a separate Form 8283 for each donee.

See Regulations section 1.170A-13(c)(3)(i)–(ii) for the definition of a "qualified appraisal" and information to be included in the appraisal.

Line 5

Note: *You **must** complete at least column (a) of line 5 (and column (b) if applicable) before submitting Form 8283 to the donee. You may then complete the remaining columns.*

Column (a). Provide enough detail so a person unfamiliar with the property could identify it in the appraisal.

Column (c). Include the FMV from the appraisal. If you were not required to get an appraisal, include the FMV you determine to be correct.

Columns (d)–(f). If you have reasonable cause for not providing the information in columns (d), (e), or (f), attach an explanation so your deduction will not automatically be disallowed.

Column (g). A bargain sale is a transfer of property that is in part a sale or exchange and in part a contribution. Enter the amount received for bargain sales.

Column (h). Complete column (h) only if you were not required to get an appraisal, as explained earlier.

Column (i). Complete column (i) only if you donated securities for which market quotations are considered to be readily available because the issue satisfies the five requirements described in Regulations section 1.170A-13(c)(7)(xi)(B).

Part II, Taxpayer (Donor) Statement

Complete Part II for each item included in Part I that has an appraised value of $500 or less. Because you do not have to show the value of these items in Part I of the donee's copy of Form 8283, clearly identify them for the donee in Part II. Then, the donee does not have to file **Form 8282,** Donee Information Return, for items valued at $500 or less. See the **Note** on page 4 for more details about filing Form 8282.

The amount of information you give in Part II depends on the description of the donated property you enter in Part I. If you show a single item as "Property A" in Part I and that item is appraised at $500 or less, then the entry "Property A" in Part II is enough. However, if "Property A" consists of several items and the total appraised value is over $500, list in Part II any item(s) you gave that is valued at $500 or less.

All shares of nonpublicly traded stock or items in a set are considered one item. For example, a book collection by the same author, components of a stereo system, or six place settings of a pattern of silverware are one item for the $500 test.

Example. You donated books valued at $6,000. The appraisal states that one of the items, a collection of books by author "X," is worth $400. On the Form 8283 that you are required to give the donee, you decide not to show the appraised value of all of the books. But you also do not want the donee to have to file Form 8282 if the collection of books is sold. If your description of Property A on line 5 includes all the books, then specify in Part II the "collection of books by X included in Property A." But if your Property A description is "collection of books by X," the only required entry in Part II is "Property A."

In the above example, you may have chosen instead to give a completed copy of Form 8283 to the donee. The donee would then be aware of the value. If you include all the books as Property A on line 5, and enter $6,000 in column (c), you may still want to describe the specific collection in Part II so the donee can sell it without filing Form 8282.

Part III, Declaration of Appraiser

If you had to get an appraisal, the appraiser **must** complete Part III to be considered qualified. See Regulations section 1.170A-13(c)(5) for a definition of a qualified appraiser.

Persons who cannot be qualified appraisers are listed in the Declaration of Appraiser. Usually, a party to the transaction will not qualify to sign the declaration. But a person who sold, exchanged, or gave the property to you may sign the declaration if the property was donated within 2 months of the date you acquired it and the property's appraised value did not exceed its acquisition price.

An appraiser may not be considered qualified if you had knowledge of facts that would cause a reasonable person to expect the appraiser to falsely overstate the value of the property. An example of this is an agreement between you and the appraiser about the property value when you know that the appraised amount exceeds the actual FMV.

Usually, appraisal fees cannot be based on a percentage of the appraised value unless the fees were paid to certain not-for-profit associations. See Regulations section 1.170A-13(c)(6)(ii).

Part IV, Donee Acknowledgment

The donee organization that received the property described in Part I of Section B must complete Part IV. Before submitting page 2 of Form 8283 to the donee for acknowledgment, complete at least your name, identifying number, and description of the donated property (line 5, column (a)). If tangible property is donated, also describe its physical condition (line 5, column (b)) at the time of the gift. Complete Part II, if applicable, before submitting the form to the donee. See the instructions for Part II.

The person acknowledging the gift must be an official authorized to sign the tax returns of the organization, or a person specifically designated to sign Form 8283. After completing Part IV, the organization must return Form 8283 to you, the donor. You must give a copy of Section B of this form to the donee organization. You may then complete any remaining information required in Part I. Also, Part III may be completed at this time by the qualified appraiser.

In some cases, it may be impossible to get the donee's signature on the Appraisal Summary. The deduction will not be disallowed for that reason if you attach a detailed explanation why it was impossible.

Note: *If the donee (or a successor donee) organization disposes of the property within 2 years after the date the original donee received it, the organization must file **Form 8282,** Donee Information Return, with the IRS and send a copy to the donor. An exception applies to items having a value of $500 or less if the donor identified the items and signed the statement in Part II (Section B) of Form 8283. See the instructions for Part II.*

Failure To File Form 8283, Section B

If you fail to attach Form 8283 to your return for donated property that is required to be reported in Section B, your deduction will be disallowed unless your failure was due to a good-faith omission. If the IRS asks you to submit the form, you have 90 days to send a completed Section B of Form 8283 before your deduction is disallowed.

Form **8282**
(Rev. September 1998)
Department of the Treasury
Internal Revenue Service

Donee Information Return

(Sale, Exchange, or Other Disposition of Donated Property)

▶ See instructions on back.

OMB No. 1545-0908

Give a Copy to Donor

Please Print or Type	Name of charitable organization (donee)	Employer identification number
	Address (number, street, and room or suite no.)	
	City or town, state, and ZIP code	

Part I — Information on ORIGINAL DONOR and DONEE Receiving the Property

1a Name(s) of the original donor of the property	1b Identifying number

Note: Complete lines 2a–2d only if you gave this property to another charitable organization (successor donee).

2a Name of charitable organization	2b Employer identification number

2c Address (number, street, and room or suite no.)

2d City or town, state, and ZIP code

Note: If you are the original donee, skip Part II and go to Part III now.

Part II — Information on PREVIOUS DONEES—Complete this part only if you were not the first donee to receive the property. If you were the second donee, leave lines 4a–4d blank. If you were a third or later donee, complete lines 3a–4d. On lines 4a–4d, give information on the preceding donee (the one who gave you the property).

3a Name of original donee	3b Employer identification number

3c Address (number, street, and room or suite no.)

3d City or town, state, and ZIP code

4a Name of preceding donee	4b Employer identification number

4c Address (number, street, and room or suite no.)

4d City or town, state, and ZIP code

Part III — Information on DONATED PROPERTY—If you are the original donee, leave column (c) blank.

(a) Description of donated property sold, exchanged, or otherwise disposed of (if you need more space, attach a separate statement)	(b) Date you received the item(s)	(c) Date the first donee received the item(s)	(d) Date item(s) sold, exchanged, or otherwise disposed of	(e) Amount received upon disposition

For Paperwork Reduction Act Notice, see back of form.   Cat. No. 62307Y   Form **8282** (Rev. 9-98)

General Instructions

Section references are to the Internal Revenue Code.

Purpose of Form

Donee organizations use Form 8282 to report information to the IRS about dispositions of certain charitable deduction property made within 2 years after the donor contributed the property.

Definitions

Note: For Form 8282 and these instructions, the term "donee" includes all donees, unless specific reference is made to "original" or "successor" donees.

Original donee. The first donee to or for which the donor gave the property. The original donee is required to sign an Appraisal Summary presented by the donor for charitable deduction property.

Successor donee. Any donee of property other than the original donee.

Appraisal summary. Section B of Form 8283, Noncash Charitable Contributions.

Charitable deduction property. Property (other than money or certain publicly traded securities) for which the original donee signed, or was presented with for signature, the Appraisal Summary (Form 8283, Section B).

Generally, only items or groups of similar items for which the donor claimed a deduction of more than $5,000 are included on the Appraisal Summary. There is an exception if a donor gives similar items to more than one donee organization and the total deducted for these similar items exceeds $5,000. For example, if a donor deducts $2,000 for books given to a donee organization and $4,000 for books to another donee organization, the donor must present a separate Appraisal Summary to each organization. For more information, see the Instructions for Form 8283.

Who Must File

Original and successor donee organizations must file Form 8282 if they sell, exchange, consume, or otherwise dispose of (with or without consideration) charitable deduction property within 2 years after the date the original donee received the property. See Charitable deduction property earlier.

Exceptions. There are two situations where Form 8282 does not have to be filed.

1. Items valued at $500 or less. You do not have to file Form 8282 if, at the time the original donee signed the Appraisal Summary, the donor had signed a statement on Form 8283 that the appraised value of the specific item was not more than $500. If Form 8283 contains more than one similar item, this exception applies only to those items that are clearly identified as having a value of $500 or less. However, for purposes of the donor's

determination of whether the appraised value of the item exceeds $500, all shares of nonpublicly traded stock, or items that form a set, are considered one item. For example, a collection of books written by the same author, components of a stereo system, or six place settings of a pattern of silverware are considered one item.

2. Items consumed or distributed for charitable purpose. You do not have to file Form 8282 if an item is consumed or distributed, without consideration, in fulfilling your purpose or function as a tax-exempt organization. For example, no reporting is required for medical supplies consumed or distributed by a tax-exempt relief organization in aiding disaster victims.

When To File

If you dispose of charitable deduction property within 2 years of the date the original donee received it and you do not meet exception 1 or 2 above, you must file Form 8282 within 125 days after the date of disposition.

Exception. If you did not file because you had no reason to believe the substantiation requirements applied to the donor, but you later become aware that they did apply, file Form 8282 within 60 days after the date you become aware you are liable. For example, this exception would apply where an Appraisal Summary is furnished to a successor donee after the date that donee disposes of the charitable deduction property.

Missing Information

If Form 8282 is filed by the due date, you must enter your organization's name, address, and EIN and complete at least Part III, column (a). You do not have to complete the remaining items if the information is not available. For example, you may not have the information necessary to complete all entries if the donor's Appraisal Summary is not available to you.

Where To File

Send Form 8282 to the Internal Revenue Service, Ogden, UT 84201-0027.

Penalty

You may be subject to a penalty if you fail to file this form by the due date, fail to include all of the information required to be shown on this form, or fail to include correct information on this form (see Missing Information above). The penalty is generally $50. For more details, see section 6721.

Other Requirements

Information you must give a successor donee. If the property is transferred to another charitable organization within the 2-year period discussed earlier, you must give your successor donee all of the following information.

1. The name, address, and EIN of your organization.

2. A copy of the Appraisal Summary (the Form 8283 that you received from the donor or a preceding donee).

3. A copy of this Form 8282, within 15 days after you file it.

You must furnish items 1 and 2 above within 15 days after the latest of the date:

- You transferred the property,
- The original donee signed the Appraisal Summary, or
- You received a copy of the Appraisal Summary from the preceding donee if you are also a successor donee.

Information the successor donee must give you. The successor donee organization to whom you transferred this property is required to give you their organization's name, address, and EIN within 15 days after the later of:

- The date you transferred the property, or
- The date they received a copy of the Appraisal Summary.

Information you must give the donor. You must give a copy of your Form 8282 to the original donor of the property.

Recordkeeping. You must keep a copy of the Appraisal Summary in your records.

Paperwork Reduction Act Notice. We ask for the information on this form to carry out the Internal Revenue laws of the United States. You are required to give us the information. We need it to ensure that you are complying with these laws and to allow us to figure and collect the right amount of tax.

You are not required to provide the information requested on a form that is subject to the Paperwork Reduction Act unless the form displays a valid OMB control number. Books or records relating to a form or its instructions must be retained as long as their contents may become material in the administration of any Internal Revenue law. Generally, tax returns and return information are confidential, as required by section 6103.

The time needed to complete this form will vary depending on individual circumstances. The estimated average time is:

Recordkeeping . . . . . 3 hr., 7 min.

Learning about the law or the form . . . . 35 min.

Preparing and sending the form to the IRS . . . . . 41 min.

If you have comments concerning the accuracy of these time estimates or suggestions for making this form simpler, we would be happy to hear from you. You can write to the Tax Forms Committee, Western Area Distribution Center, Rancho Cordova, CA 95743-0001. DO NOT send the form to this address. Instead, see Where To File on this page.

Chapter II–3

GENERATION-SKIPPING TRANSFER TAX

When you think about the taxes imposed on Americans, the situation really is quite devastating. We have a tax on our income through the income tax. We have a tax on the realized appreciation of our capital assets through the capital gain tax. And, we have a tax on the right to transfer property through the gift and estate tax. As if this weren't enough, we have an additional tax on the transfer of property that skips a generation through the generation-skipping transfer tax (GST tax). Here's a monster!

Yet, where there is a tax, there is a donor problem. And, where there is a donor problem, there is a charitable giving solution. Yeah for us! The GST tax is no exception. This chapter will help you understand the GST tax, probably one of the more complicated taxes. Once you understand it, you can add it to your bank of planned giving knowledge to be used when that unique gift situation presents itself. If you do not understand the GST tax, you will be unable to recognize donor situations where a charitable gift would make sense.

Ordinarily, in discussing other tax laws, I have resisted the temptation to give you a history of the laws that preceded the current ones. That could get confusing and would add too much irrelevant information that you simply don't need. My premise is that you will be using this book to get current gifts under current tax laws. If you need historical information, you can get it from many sources on the Internet. Here, though, a little history will be helpful.

Some taxes sprang up out of a perceived abuse. This is true, for example, of the alternative minimum tax. Taxpayers had become so crafty at claiming income tax deductions that they actually were able to reduce their tax liability to zero. Eventually, I.R.S. created the alternative minimum tax. Problem solved.

The generation-skipping transfer tax also sprang up to stop something I.R.S. considered abusive. Here's a short history of the birth of the GST tax.

Before 1977: A person could place property in trust and provide income for life to children, income for life to grandchildren, and remainder to the great grandchildren. In the plan, the enjoyment of the property skipped from one generation to the next without being taxed along the way. The I.R.S. decided that this was too good to be true.

After 1976: The Tax Reform Act of 1976 created the generation-skipping transfer tax to attack the above situation for such transfers exceeding a $250,000 exemption. It did this by imposing a tax each time (and as often as) the beneficial interest dropped from one generation to the next. In general, the tax was computed using the gift and estate tax table as if the property were owned by the person whose beneficial interest had just ended. This law was cumbersome and difficult to enforce. Then, the tax did not apply to the most popular kind of lead trusts (qualified nongrantor lead trusts, see Chapter II-11). The nongrantor lead trust provides income to charity and remainder to grandchildren. It was popular back then because the income tax rate was so high. But, now the GST tax does apply—very much so, notwithstanding changes in the law under the Economic Growth and Tax Relief Reconciliation Act of 2001, to be discussed later.

The Tax Reform Act of 1986: The Tax Reform Act of 1986 repealed the generation-skipping transfer tax back to its inception and created a new, more inclusive, generation-skipping transfer tax. In doing so, the I.R.S. changed three key things: it changed the conditions under which property becomes subject to the tax, it changed the way the tax is computed, and it changed the exemption.

HOW THE GST TAX WORKS

When a transfer of property is made from a parent to a child, it is subject to the gift or estate tax if the transfer exceeds the annual gift tax exclusion ($11,000 for 2003) and the applicable gift or estate tax exemption. (See Chapter II-10 for a more complete discussion about the gift and estate and tax.) Then, when the child transfers the property to his or her children, he or she is hit with another gift or estate tax. Wouldn't it be wiser, then, to have grandma transfer the assets directly to the grandchildren, skipping over mom and dad, especially if mom and dad don't need the money? Formerly, this strategy would have incurred only one gift or estate tax instead of two.

However, the lawmakers saw through this simple device in a flash and decided that if they couldn't get a tax on two transfers, then they would get two taxes on one transfer. And there you have it—the birth of the generation-skipping transfer tax.

It doesn't matter whether the transfer is made directly (outright) or in trust. When it skips a generation, a generation-skipping transfer (GST) tax could apply—and at a hefty rate. In fact, rather than set up new tables for this tax, Congress simply said, apply the highest gift and estate tax rate then in effect—no graduated rates allowed. Essentially, it is a flat tax at a very high rate, currently 49% for gifts that exceed $1.06 million in 2003 ($2.12 million for couples). The GST tax exemption started at $1 million and is indexed for inflation.

When Is The Exemption Taken?

For lifetime transfers, the exemption automatically will be allocated first against lifetime direct skips in chronological order unless the transferor elects out of this order on a gift tax return. The transferor does not have to use the exemption when the transfer subject to the tax is made. The property will be valued whenever the exemption is allocated to the property.

Thus, some strategic thinking is involved at the time of the gift as to how much of the exemption to use. If the full exemption is used for a gift to one grandchild, there would be no exemption left to offset the GST tax on gifts to others.

The transferor can elect to use all or part of the exemption at any time, but once it is used, it is irrevocable. The effect of using the exemption on a GST is to lock in the percentage of the property subject to the tax. For certain transfers, 100% of the property (and its future appreciation) can be sheltered from the tax. This will become clearer to you when you review the formula below.

When the transferor decides to use the exemption, various figures are plugged into a formula to determine something called an inclusion ratio. The inclusion ratio determines the amount included in the taxable base for this tax, to which the tax rate will be applied, resulting in the tax due.

When Is The GST Tax Due?

- Outright gift or bequest: The tax is due out of the gift property at the time of the gift.

- Charitable remainder trust, pooled income fund, charitable gift annuity: The tax is due from the beneficiary's payments (and is also deductible for income tax purposes).

- Non charitable trust which provides income to a child with principal to the grandchildren: The tax is due on the death of the child.

- Charitable lead trust: The tax is due at the end of the trust term when the principal distributes to the grandchild or great grandchild, grandniece/nephew.

What may occur to you immediately from looking at the above list is that the donor could be subject to the GST tax by setting up a charitable remainder trust where the grandchild is beneficiary. Yes, that is precisely what can happen and it will happen for any life income gift if the beneficiary's income interest is paid currently, is large enough, and/or if the donor already has used up his or her GST tax exemption on other transfers. Most simply stated, if a donor makes an outright gift of his or her exemption amount to a grandchild and uses his full exemption on that gift, he or she is done. Any other gift of any kind to a person two or more generations below the donor (above the $11,000 annual gift tax exclusion) will be subject to the GST tax. The only exception is if the exemption increases in a future year as a result of the inflation adjustment.

What Is A Skip Person?

There are three types of generation-skipping transfers. They are subject to tax when a beneficial interest vests in a skip person. A skip person is a person two or more generations below the generation of the donor. Ordinarily this definition is what you would expect it to be—grandchildren, grand nieces or nephews, great grandchildren. When the connection is by blood or marriage, the generation of the lineal descendants is easy to determine. When there is no relationship between the transferor and the transferee, the laws sets up rules as to which generation the transferee is in.

A person is in:	If he or she was born:
The same generation as the transferor	not more than 12 1/2 years after the transferor
One generation below the transferor	more than 12 ½ but not more than 37 ½ years after the transferor
Two generations below the transferor	25 years thereafter
Three generations below the transferor	25 years thereafter

For purposes of this tax, a "person" can be an individual, trust, estate, partnership, association, company, or corporation. Whether or not a payment or distribution to an entity is subject to the GST tax depends on whether any person having a beneficial interest in the entity is in a generation two or more below the transferor. So, for instance, if a donor makes a transfer to a trust that has beneficiaries two or more generations below his or her generation, the GST tax might apply.

TYPES OF GENERATION-SKIPPING TRANSFERS

- *Taxable termination*: A beneficiary's current interest terminates so that the current interests are in one or more skip persons. No non skip persons have a present interest.

  Example:

  Trust established by donor to pay income to son for life, then income to grandson until age 25, and then trust distributes to grandson. When son dies, a taxable termination occurs (*i.e.*, a beneficiary's current interest terminates) so that the current interest is in a skip person (the grandchild). The trust is valued on the son's death and the GST tax is paid from the trust.

- *Taxable distribution*: A distribution of income or principal is made from a trust to a skip person (other than through a taxable termination or direct skip).

Example:

Donor establishes a trust and gives the trustee discretion to pay income or principal to the grand-daughter until she is 25. Then the trust distributes income or principal outright to her. Whenever the trustee makes a payment, it is a taxable distribution. She pays the GST tax on the amount received. When the trust distributes at age 25, it is a taxable termination. The trust property is valued, the tax is paid, and the balance is paid to the granddaughter.

- *Direct skip*: A transfer to a skip person where the donor is subject to the gift or estate tax on the property (outright gift, bequest).

Example:

Donor gives property to grandson. The property is valued, the tax is computed, the property is distributed to the grandson, and the donor or the donor's estate pays the GST tax out of its own funds.

	Taxable Termination	Taxable Distribution	Direct Skip
What property is subject to the GST tax?	Value of the property as to which the taxable termination has occurred	The value received by the transferee	Amount received by the transferee
Who pays the GST tax?	The taxable amount is determined and the tax is paid out of the property	The transferee	The transferor (or the trustee of a trust)
When is the GST tax paid?	When the current interest in the property vests in a skip person	When the distribution subject to the tax is received by the skip person	When the transfer is made

There is no GST tax when:

- the property is subject to the gift and estate tax in the generation one below the donor;

- the parent of a skip person is deceased;

- the gift falls under the $11,000 per donee annual gift tax exclusion.

If two generations are skipped with one gift, the GST Tax is paid only once.

HOW TO COMPUTER THE GST TAX

To determine the GST tax, multiply the *inclusion ratio* by the *top estate tax rate* when the tax is paid by the *value of the property* subject to tax. (A variation on the formula, discussed later, is used for a charitable lead annuity trust.)

1. Inclusion Ratio = 1 minus $\dfrac{\text{Exemption Allocated to the Transfer}}{\text{Property - death taxes - gift or estate tax charitable deduction}}$

2. Inclusion Ratio x Top Estate Tax Rate x Property Value = GST Tax

Example:

A donor makes an outright gift (*direct skip*) of $1,000,000 to a grandchild in 2003 and elects to use $1,000,000 of his $1,060,000 GST exemption for the gift.

1. Inclusion Ratio   =   1   minus $\dfrac{\$1,000,000 \ \text{(Exemption Allocated to the Transfer)}}{\$1,000,000 - (\text{no death taxes}) - (\text{no charitable deduction})}$

    1   minus   1   =   0

2. Inclusion Ratio   x   Top Estate Tax Rate   x   Property Value   =   GST Tax

    0   x   49%   x $1,000,000   =   0 GST Tax

In the above example, there is no GST tax because the inclusion ratio is zero. Thus, any amount multiplied by the inclusion ratio produces a GST tax of zero.

If the donor had elected to use only $500,000 of the exemption toward the gift, the inclusion ratio would have been .5 as follows:

1. Inclusion Ratio   =   1   minus $\dfrac{\$500,000 \ \text{(exemption allocated to the transfer)}}{\$1,000,000 - (\text{no death taxes}) - (\text{no charitable deduction})}$

    1   minus   .5   =   .5

2. Inclusion Ratio   x   Top Estate Tax Rate   x   Property Value   =   GST Tax

    .5   x   49%   x $1,000,000   = $245,000 GST Tax

In the above situation, the transfer of $1,000,000 to the grandchild is a *direct skip*. Therefore, the donor would be responsible for paying the GST tax of $245,000 at the time the gift is made.

If the donor's estate were larger, let's say, $10,000,000, the combined loss from the federal gift and estate tax and the GST Tax would be devastating.

In a planned giving example, if the donor sets up a charitable remainder unitrust to pay income to a grandchild with remainder to a charity, the unitrust payments to the beneficiary are *taxable distributions*. Once the inclusion ratio is determined, it is applied to each payment as made and the beneficiary pays the GST tax. It is important to remember that the Federal Estate and Gift tax is also payable on the value of the beneficiary's income interest; however, that tax might be based on the full present value of the income interest (minus the annual gift tax exclusion) determined at the time the trust is set up.

The planned giving strategy that can save significant taxes on the transfer of property to grandchildren is the charitable lead trust. Ordinarily, all property over the GST tax exemption will be subject to this tax (other than annual exclusion gifts). However, if the donor places property in a qualified charitable lead unitrust which makes payments to charity for a period of years, remainder to the grandchildren, the charitable deduction allowable on the charity's payments will play a substantial role in the denominator of the fraction used to determine the inclusion ratio.

In the Charitable Lead Trust chapter, there are more detailed examples of the use of a lead trust to help reduce not only the gift or estate tax but also the GST tax.

Here is another example of a direct gift to the grandchildren so you can see the effect of the GST tax when combined with the gift tax.

Example:

A couple has an estate of several million and wishes to pass property to five grandchildren. An outright gift to them above the $1,060,000 exemption ($2,120,000 if the husband and wife split the gift) would fall under the GST tax. Let's say they want to give $1,000,000 to each grandchild. In this example, the husband and wife use their exemptions together for both gift taxes and GST taxes. The transfer of $5,000,000 during lifetime would produce the following result. Assume the example is in 2003.

Gift Tax Example

Taxable gift in 2003		
Total transfer		$5,000,000
($22,000 per person is annual gift tax exclusion)		- 110,000
Taxable transfer		$4,890,000
Tentative Tax		
on 1st $2,000,000	$780,800	
on next $2,890,000 @ 49%	+ 1,416,100	2,196,900
Unified Credit for 2003 x 2 (Assume no prior taxable gifts)		- 691,600
Gift Tax Due		$1,505,300

Generation Skipping Transfer Tax

1. Inclusion Ratio = 1 minus $\dfrac{\$2,120,000 \text{ (exemption allocated to the transfer)}}{\$4,890,000 - (\text{death taxes/none}) - (\text{charitable deduction/none})}$

   1 minus .4335 = .5665

2. Inclusion Ratio x Top Estate Tax Rate x taxable gift = GST Tax

   .5665 x 49% x $4,890,000 = $1,357,391 GST Tax

The loss to transfer taxes in the above situation is $1,505,300 from the gift tax, plus $1,357,391 from the GST tax, for a total transfer tax of $2,862,891 on a transfer of $5,000,000!

Instead of losing so much to taxes, the use of a charitable lead trust could save substantial amounts, but, of course, the grandchildren will have to wait until the lead trust terminates before receiving their gifts. Further, one must assume that the donor has charitable intent.

SPECIAL EXCEPTION FOR CHARITABLE LEAD ANNUITY TRUSTS

If you are beginning to understand the GST tax and the importance of the inclusion ratio, here's one final twist that relates to charitable lead annuity trusts only.

The rules and formula for computing the GST tax with a lead annuity trust are different than for a lead unitrust. Instead of being able to lock in the inclusion ratio when the trust is established, you must wait until the trust's termination. This presents a problem for planners because the effect of the GST tax exemption allocated to the transfer is uncertain.

Congress decided that it was too easy to zero out the GST tax for the annuity lead trust. Annuity lead trusts were being used to shift large amounts of appreciation to younger generations without tax. Therefore, I.R.S. has adopted a wait-and-see approach.

When the trust is set up, the donor must decide how much of the lifetime GST exemption to use on this transfer. He or she cannot change it later. When the trust terminates, however, the exemption is adjusted by the same discount rate used to determine the charitable deduction.

Therefore, if the property appreciates more than the initial discount factor would have predicted, the donor ends up paying a GST tax even though the intent was to create the perfect trust term and to allocate just the right exemption amount to effectively zero out the inclusion ratio. If the trust depreciates, it means that the donor has wasted part of the GST exemption. The formula for lead annuity trusts is below:

1. Inclusion Ratio = 1 minus $\dfrac{\textit{Adjusted} \text{ Exemption Allocated to the Transfer}}{\text{Property - death taxes - gift tax charitable deduction}}$

2. Inclusion Ratio x Top Estate Tax Rate x Property Value = GST Tax

EFFECT OF EGTRRA ON GST

Under the Economic Growth and Tax Relief Reconciliation Act of 2001, the generation-skipping transfer tax tracks along with the top estate tax rate and is scheduled to be repealed for 2010, only to return in 2011 to the rates in effect prior to EGTTRA. Following is a chart of the GST tax rate under current law:

Year	GST Tax Rate
2003	49%
2004	48%
2005	47%
2006	46%
2007-2009	45%
2010	repealed
2011	55%

SUMMARY

This explanation of the generation-skipping transfer tax should be enough to allow you to talk about it intelligently, but don't even think of getting into serious discussions with donors without your tax counsel by your side. This chapter gives you only an overview of the basics.

And, there are many ways to look at the advantages and disadvantages of using a lead trust to help reduce the GST tax. For one thing, a donor may not want the heirs to wait 20 years to get the property. Some planned giving software programs (PG Calc for one), can show you the results side by side of taking an asset and comparing the results of placing property in a revocable trust to benefit the grandchildren, an irrevocable trust to benefit the grandchildren, and a lead trust. With yield and appreciation assumptions, projected fees, income taxes, *etc.*, you can examine scenarios in an unlimited way. When you get down to the bottom line, however, the successful planned giving officer knows that charitable intent—not tax savings—really plays the most significant role in closing one of these complicated gifts.

To get more information on the gift and estate tax, go to Chapter II-10 on Bequests or Chapter II-11 on Charitable Lead Trusts.

Now that you have a general understanding of tax laws that impact your work, you are ready to proceed to the first chapter that deals exclusively with one type of gift property—securities. A comment is in order for the small institution that has not yet been able to manage gifts of securities. This chapter tells you everything you need to know to handle gifts of securities—how to value stock gifts, how to work with brokers, and how to process a gift of stock. If you do nothing more than to integrate the promotion of stock gifts into your annual giving program, you will have recovered the cost of this book one hundred fold.

Chapter II–4

GIFTS OF SECURITIES

Gifts of securities, especially stocks and mutual funds, will play a significant role in your planned giving program, whether on an outright basis or on a deferred basis, for either your annual or capital fund raising programs. They are often highly appreciated over their cost basis, and can be used effectively for any life income plan (pooled income fund, charitable gift annuity, and charitable remainder trust) or charitable lead trust. Bonds are also covered in this chapter as one category of securities, but they are not generally the asset of choice when donors are looking for something highly appreciated to contribute to a charity.

Some organizations solicit gifts of securities only for capital projects or for campaigns when they should be doing the same thing for their annual giving program. A variation on the following message should appear on all Annual Giving reply mechanisms:

> "Make checks payable to XYZ Charity. If you are making a gift of securities, please call [name] at [phone number] for instructions."

One person alone in your development office should to be responsible for handling stock gifts and for coordinating with the business office. Usually, the director of planned giving handles securities gifts in the development office and probably delegates the day-to-day tasks to his or her assistant. The treasurer usually handles securities gifts for the business office, and he or she also delegates the day-to-day tasks to his or her assistant. This means that two assistants or secretaries are in charge of a very important gift category. When you take over your position in planned giving, you should call a meeting of the four of you to work out the details of who does what. This chapter can help you sort out the details. If you inherit a planned giving position that is already running, make sure you become an expert at how to accept and dispose of securities gifts for your organization. Regardless of whether or not your assistant is doing it effortlessly, you must know how to handle this yourself. You are the boss.

Usually, a broker calls to inform your organization that a client would like to make a stock gift. There are other ways of handling this, but the call from a broker is most common. He or she needs quick and efficient action on the part of the charity. The broker receiving instructions from a donor is the donor's agent, and no gift is completed until the broker gets the stock into the charity's hands. The charity should handle a call from a broker as soon as possible. If the person to whom you have delegated this task is out of the office, don't wait for that person to return. Take over yourself.

Donors often wait for the right price before initiating instructions for a gift of securities. Then, they become anxious until the transfer takes place. The broker is always working for many clients at the same time, and, if the donor's broker does not receive a quick response from you, he or she may not call you again for another day. If the price of the stock is moving quickly, you could lose valuable dollars that could have been better used by your organization. Also, any delay could cause the donor to lose part of the value of the federal income tax charitable deduction he or she intended to claim. When you are taking in securities gifts from many donors at the same time, especially at year end, or at the end of your fiscal year, it is easy to lose track of the status of each one. By having all securities transfers go through the director of planned giving, you can ensure that the stock gifts will run smoothly and efficiently. This task adds work to your job description, but the process is necessary and it cannot be avoided.

HOW TO PROCESS A GIFT OF SECURITIES

This section explains the considerations and procedures that you must understand in order to process gifts of securities. For this part of the chapter, I am dealing only with stocks and bonds. Mutual funds are a little different, so I have covered them separately at the end of the chapter.

Donors can transfer securities in certificate form or electronically from their brokerage accounts directly into the charity's account. You must know how to handle both scenarios.

Transfer From the Donor's Brokerage Account

- Donor sends a letter to his or her broker asking that a specific number of shares of a specific stock be transferred to your organization as a gift. Often, but not always, the donor will send a photocopy of the letter to you to alert you that a gift is forthcoming. When a donor does not know to whom to address a letter, he or she usually sends it to your treasurer—no name, just the word treasurer. When the treasurer receives the letter, he or she should immediately give a copy to you.

- The director of planned giving should notify the major gift officer, or other person assigned to the prospect, that a gift is on its way. If you have a system of soliciting prospects through mechanical methods, notify whoever is responsible for this process, too, so that the donor's name can be pulled from planned direct mail solicitation lists. If you have an annual fund volunteer committee, or a campaign committee soliciting gifts, you should notify the staff member who is assigned to the volunteer responsible for soliciting that donor. In general, as soon as you know a gift is coming, stop all other solicitations. Each development office handles the communication process for these incoming gifts differently. If you are responsible for stock gifts, you must understand the overall structure and operation of your development office in order properly to communicate the information about gifts of securities to the rest of your colleagues and volunteers.

- When the donor's broker receives the letter of instructions from the client, he or she calls or writes to your organization to notify you of a stock gift. Most of the time, the broker telephones the charity. The broker will request disposition instructions and may also ask for your tax identification number. You can get this from the treasurer. Keep it handy because you will need it frequently for foundation grants and bequest distributions.

- The person responsible for stock transfers at your institution will issue one of the following instructions to the donor's broker, usually by fax.

Depository Trust Company Transfer

"Transfer the shares through Depository Trust Company into our account at [bank, broker, or trust company]. Our (bank's) DTC number is [account number] at [address]."

Banking or brokerage establishments manage the high volume of securities under their management through an electronic transfer process. Instead of keeping the stock certificates of their clients physically on the premises, they deliver them to Depository Trust Company, a clearing house for securities transactions. Then, when a client wishes to make a stock gift to your organization, the stock is transferred electronically from the donor broker's DTC account directly to the charity broker's DTC account. No physical exchange takes place.

Most important in a DTC transfer is to notify the receiving institution (*i.e.*, your bank or broker) that the shares are being transmitted. Otherwise, when the donor's broker transmits 20 shares of IBM to your bank or broker, the shares may be held in escrow or even refused because the receiving bank or broker does not know to which account they should be credited.

Or, if the shares are allowed to post into the charity's brokerage account, they will sit for as long as it takes for somebody to figure out who sent them. Most charities have a practice of selling shares immediately upon receipt in order to transfer cash to their endowment manger. When the treasurer cannot link the shares to a donor, he or she will let the shares sit in the account until the name of the donor is known. This isn't just an investment problem. The donor will eventually think that you were delinquent in acknowledging the gift in a timely fashion. When the treasurer sees unidentified securities in the charity's account, he or she will call the director of planned giving to get the name of the donor. When the director of planned giving does not know who sent the particular securities, he or she will send an e-mail to all members of the development office with a message along the following lines:

"A donor has transferred 325 shares of Lucent Technologies Common Stock as of [date] with a mean value of [amount] from a brokerage account at [brokerage firm]. Please let me know if any of your donors might have made this gift."

Meet with your treasurer and get the instructions for a DTC transfer to your charity's account. There may be more than one account. Transfers through DTC can go through within 24 hours, but the timing of the gift is ultimately controlled by the donor's broker who must put through the transfer instructions. Sometimes, the donor's broker sits on the order for a couple of days.

Transfer within the Same Brokerage Firm

When the donor has an account at the same firm that handles the charity's brokerage account, the instruction is as follows:

"Transfer the shares to the charity's account [number]."

This is very quick. If the charity keeps its brokerage account at Merrill Lynch, and the donor has an account at Merrill Lynch, the broker simply puts through a simple transfer internally. Such transfers usually post to the charity's account on the same day.

Register the Securities in the Name of the Charity

"Transfer the shares into the name of XYZ Charity, [address]. Our tax I.D. Number is [xx-xxxxxxx]. We wish to retain the shares as an investment. Please send the certificate to [treasurer] at [address]."

This procedure is possible, but it is not a good way to handle a gift of securities. It takes up to two months or more to get your new certificates because the broker must return the certificates to the issuing corporation in order that they can be re-registered in your charity's name. Eventually, if you are patient, the stock certificates will arrive. Deliver them by hand (not through inter-office mail) to your business office. If you have waited more than one month and have still not received them, call the broker to ensure that he or she gave the proper instructions. The real problem with this procedure is that the donor's date of gift is the date when the issuing corporation changes the owner's name on the books of the corporation, not when the donor issues the instructions to his or her broker. The date on the new stock certificate generally is the date of the gift.

- Sometimes, a donor wants the charity to set up a brokerage account with his or her broker so that the shares can be transferred from the donor's account to the charity's account within the same firm. The purpose of this procedure is to give the sale commission to donor's broker. Setting up a new brokerage account doesn't take a lot of time, and most charities accommodate the donor's wishes. Generally, the broker will fax an application for a new account to your treasurer who will complete the form and send it back. The broker will transfer the shares into the charity's new account. The charity will sell the shares, receive a check for the proceeds minus commissions to the donor's broker, and may then close the account.

There are circumstances under which a charity will keep the dormant account open for the one donor who makes a large annual gift of stock every year. At Boston College, we had a donor who would make an annual stock transfer of about $100,000 in December and demanded we go through his broker at Goldman Sachs. No problem. We got a Goldman Sachs account and used it once a year for one donor.

• Sometimes a donor wants a particular value for a stock gift and will not commit to the transfer until his or her stock reaches the magic number. To assist this process along, fax or e-mail to the broker the transfer instructions in advance so that the broker can execute the transfer as quickly as possible. The same problem can occur when the donor has certificates. The solution for that case is described below.

Donor Issues Transfer Instructions on the Charity's Web Site

There is another way to transfer securities, but it is so new that only a few charities know about it. A company called AssetStream in Woburn, Massachusetts, which was incorporated in February of 2000, created a technology that has the potential of revolutionizing the securities transfer process. Their web site is www.AssetStream.com. Other companies may be developing such a technology, too, but I not aware of any.

The concept is simple. AssetStream provides the software and infrastructure through which brokers or financial managers, donors, and charities can complete securities transactions initiated by the donor on his or her own computer. The charity must have the service on its web site. The donor needs access to the Internet to enter the gift information, although it is also possible for the donor to call the charity and have someone there enter the information on his or her behalf.

I walked through the process with the founder of the company, Edward Johnson, who is President and Chief Executive Officer. I opened up the web site of one of his charity clients to find, on page one, an icon for "Donate Stock." After clicking on this button, I was brought to the AssetStream server where the rest of the process takes place. First I verified that my broker was in the program. One click and I see that nearly every major brokerage firm participates. If my broker is not on the list, I can continue as long as my gift is a publicly traded stock (mutual fund gifts can be completed only if my broker participates in the program). I filled out my name, address, phone number, and e-mail address. Then, I selected my broker from a dropdown menu, added my account number, and identified the securities I would like to contribute.

After typing in the stock name, I proceeded to the next page, which shows the current price of the shares. Now, I have an estimate of my total gift. (The price quote is delayed 15 minutes.) Then, in another field, I instructed that 50% of my gift be credited to the Annual Fund and 50% to the Debra Ashton Scholarship Fund. It took less than five minutes to do this, then "Submit." Guess what? I just initiated a stock gift without calling anybody. My trial run was only a demo, but it could have been real. This is amazing.

Immediately, I received a confirmation e-mail that is an authorization letter to the appropriate broker. In a real case, I would print the e-mail, sign it, and fax it to AssetStream. Then, I am done.

Depending on the time of day, the transfer of the securities might happen the same day, or within 24 to 48 hours depending on the donor's broker who must complete the transfer. The client charity receives an e-mail notifying it of the impending gift. And, if the charity logs on to its account at AssetStream's secure web site, it will see a detailed set of reporting and tracking tools with a complete list of gifts pending or completed.

AssetStream does all the work behind the scenes to get the transfer through. Each participating broker establishes a master gift account to receive the gifted securities. I asked Ed if legal counsel had approved this technique and whether the charity really had legal receipt of the shares in the master account on the day they post. "The charity signs a contract with AssetStream so that we are agent for the charity in this process. Therefore, when a security posts to the master gift account, it is a completed gift to the charity."

Once the gift posts in the master account, the donor receives an e-mail acknowledgment. This acknowledgment has been approved by legal counsel as the official I.R.S. gift receipt. The appropriate language is included in the acknowledgment including the mean value of the gift, the name of the charity, and the fact that no goods or services were received in exchange for the gift. The broker immediately sells the asset and wires the proceeds, net of commissions to AssetStream for final distribution to the charity's account.

This process works for stocks, bonds, mutual funds, and even stock options held by the donor in his or her account at the participating brokerage firm. Since I own Vanguard mutual funds directly with Vanguard, I can participate in this method of transfer since Vanguard is on the list. If I had an account at Charles Schwab that held Vanguard mutual funds, I could also utilize this method to make a gift of my mutual fund shares because Charles Schwab is also on the list.

Facts you need to know include:

1) Fees: There are a couple of fee structures involving a one-time fee for the initial set-up, a monthly fee, and a percentage of each gift. The percentage is capped so that you don't pay too much in fees for the larger gifts. They also have another fee structure that charges a flat monthly rate instead of a percentage of gifts. Since the fee structure will probably change in the future, I recommend you talk to Ed Johnson or one of his staff at 781-938-0008 for the most current fee schedule to suit your individual needs, volume, and stock activity patterns.

2) Currently, you can transfer only one gift at a time. AssetStream will be adding the ability to do multiple transfers in the future.

3) The one person who is extricated from the process is the charity's broker. In most cases, there is no longer a need to initiate DTC instructions, moving every gift into the charity's brokerage account before the sale of the gifted assets. I suspect that this is more of a political issue than anything else. A charity should not make a decision about using this new technology based on reducing business from its long-standing broker.

4) Donors whose brokerage firms don't participate, or who still have stock certificates in a safe deposit box can also use the online tool to initiate gifts as long as the stock is publicly traded.

5) The online report that shows the charity the pending and completed gifts does not include the names of the donors matched up to the gifts. But, when you click on the gift I.D. number, you will see all the details including the donor's name, address, telephone, and other information.

6) If the donor receives goods or services in exchange for the gift, the AssetStream acknowledgment letter is not right. You would have to tell the donor to throw away the standard e-mail acknowledgment and send a personalized letter outlining the fair market value of the goods and services that you provided. Mr. Johnson told me that he is working with his development team to create a solution to this concern. For example, perhaps AssetStream will add a control so the charity can suppress the automatic acknowledgment for cases that involve a quid pro quo transaction.

If you access AssetStream's web site, you can see a list of their clients. I suggest that you talk to any of the charities listed there for a discussion about their experiences using this new company and its innovations. This will surely eliminate the painful, arduous, part about taking in stock gifts.

Transfer of Stock or Bond Certificates

Some donors keep securities in a safe deposit box. In this case, transfer instructions are different.

• A stock or bond power must accompany a physical gift of securities. Otherwise, your organization cannot sell the stocks or the bonds. A stock power is a form which, when signed by the donor, represents evidence that he or she intends to sell or transfer ownership of the stock or bond. (Note: I refer to this document as a stock power, but if it were used for the transfer of a bond, it would be called a bond power.)

- The donor should have his or signature on the stock power guaranteed. This means taking the stock power to a local bank (not a savings bank) where the donor presents identification to prove he or she is the person signing the stock power. This can be done at brokerage firms or at a bank with investment departments. (Note: This is not a Notary seal.) When the bank representative is satisfied with the identity of the donor, he or she places on the stock power a rubber stamp that says "signature guaranteed." This procedure is inconvenient for donors, but it is one way to protect securities from theft. When the broker knows the donor, he or she probably will accept a stock power without the "signature guarantee," but somewhere in the transfer process, somebody will affix the words "signature guaranteed."

  In daily practice, when one of your donors shows up at your office with a stock power and a stock certificate in order to make a gift, you do not send the donor away to get a signature guarantee. Under these circumstances, you would call the treasurer and explain that a donor has arrived to make a stock gift and does not have a signature guarantee on the stock power. The treasurer will usually say, "That is fine. We will take care of it." As a matter of policy, you should always include the requirement for a signature guarantee with your standard securities transfer instructions.

- If you do not have stock powers, you can get some from the bank that handles your endowment, from your broker, or from most business office supply stores. Usually stock powers work for both stocks and bonds.

- Instruct the donor to send the *unendorsed* stock certificate(s) to you in one envelope and one stock power for each certificate in the other envelope. The donor should sign the stock power exactly as the name appears on the certificate. If the stock is in joint name, both people must sign. The rest of the stock power should be blank and will be filled in by the broker who is ultimately responsible for disposing of the stock. (Note: Sometimes the bank will deny the signature guarantee unless the donor fills out the entire stock power. That will delay the charity in disposing of the gift, but it will not hinder the donor from making the gift. You should alert the donor about the fact that the bank guaranteeing the signature might request the entire stock power to be filled out. Ask the donor to argue the point because it will be better for you if everything except the signature is blank.)

- While the certificate is traveling through the mail, it is safe from theft because it is not negotiable without the stock power. The stock power is worthless without the certificate. As soon as you receive both the certificate(s) and the stock power(s), you have a negotiable gift. In fact, it is negotiable by anyone, even by your organization's night janitor. Proper attention to security is extremely important. If you have stock certificates in your office at the end of the day, put them in the development department's safe or lock them in a drawer.

- Bring the stock certificate(s) and stock power(s) to your treasurer who will take it from there. The treasurer will need the following information: Name and address of the donor, phone number, date of gift, and restriction on the gift, if any.

- There is an easier method of transferring ownership of a stock certificate, but it is risky. On the back of each stock certificate is a line on which the owner can sign his or her name thus making the certificate immediately negotiable—similar to a check payable to cash and signed by the owner. If the donor signs the back of the certificate, he or she should send it registered mail to ensure that it gets to you safely. A signature guarantee is also required on the back of the certificate.

- When a donor is waiting for the right price before making the gift, he or she might suggest driving to your office to deliver the stock in person on the magic day. A better way is to have the donor send the unendorsed certificate and a signature guaranteed stock power (separate envelope) to you with a letter stating the shares should be kept in safekeeping until the donor either calls, e-mails, or faxes you with instructions to treat the stock as a gift. Your business office or your gift processing department has a safe into which you can place the stock, properly documented with instructions. You might want to keep the stock power in your office separate from the stock certificate, just to ensure that nobody can get hold of it. Eventually, you'll receive a communication from the donor to transfer the gift, whereupon you will extract the stock certificate out of the safe, put it together with the stock power and deliver it to your treasurer. Practically, the donor can never use the magic price because the shares will be valued at the average of the high and low for the day (discussed later). Make sure that your staff knows about the situation and where you have stashed the stock power in case you are away when the donor wants to make the gift.

GIVING PART OF A STOCK CERTIFICATE

A donor has a stock certificate for 100 shares of Phillip Morris Common Stock and wishes to contribute to your organization only 40 shares. This is perfectly reasonable and easy to do. Following is a sample letter the donor would send to you:

> Dear [charity]:
>
> Enclosed is a certificate for 100 shares of Phillip Morris Common Stock, certificate number [xxxx-xxx]. I would like to contribute 40 shares to [charity]. Under separate cover is a stock power signed in blank. My signature has been guaranteed. Please have the certificate split and return 60 shares to me registered as follows:
>
>> Name
>> Street Address
>> City, State, Zip Code
>
> My Social Security Number is xxx-xx-xxxx.
>
>> Sincerely,
>
>
>> Donor

Your treasurer will send the certificate, the stock power, and the letter to the charity's broker. The broker will contact the transfer agent and give instructions for two new certificates to be issued: one for 40 shares in the name of the charity and one for 60 shares in the name of the donor. This will take one to two months or more. The gift is complete when the issuing corporation makes the change on its corporate records. The date on the new certificate reflects the date of the gift.

There are a couple of problems with this method. First, if the donor initiates this procedure in December, the gift will not be complete until January or February of the next tax year. The delay throws off the donor's plan to claim the federal income tax deduction in the prior year. Second, the price may change dramatically over the two months it will take to get the two new certificates back from the transfer agent. There is nothing you can do about this. The donor would be better off using a different asset for the contribution so that there is no delay in the official date of gift.

APPRAISAL GUIDELINES

The I.R.S. requires donors to report all noncash gifts valued over $500 on Form 8283, but no qualified appraisal is necessary for publicly-traded securities. For securities to be considered publicly traded, daily quotes must be available to the public. For gifts over $10,000 of closely held stock, a qualified appraisal is necessary. (See Chapter II-2 for a complete discussion of the substantiation requirements of noncash gifts as well as sample copies of Form 8283.)

RESTRICTED SECURITIES

Under certain conditions, the sale of stock is restricted under the Securities and Exchange Commission Rule 144. This can mean a delay in your ability to convert the stock to cash.

Rule 144 applies in situations where the stock was acquired from the corporation in a nonpublic offering. Stock that is owned by the principals of that corporation may fall under this rule.

If a stock certificate is restricted, it may carry a legend on the back stating that certain requirements must be met before the stock can be sold. The requirements involve a holding period and also limitations on the volume and timing of shares sold. If your organization receives restricted stock, you must comply with the regulations of Rule 144 or face penalties. You will know that you are receiving restricted stock because the donor's broker will tell you. Or you may receive a lengthy letter from the corporation's legal counsel outlining specific conditions under which the stock can be sold.

Some brokers specialize in the laws governing restricted stock. If you find a legend on the back of a stock certificate, don't do anything with it before consulting a securities expert. Don't sell it; don't put it in your pooled income fund; don't put it in a charitable remainder trust; and don't exchange it for a gift annuity until you consult with a securities expert or with your tax counsel. The broker who handles your charity's brokerage account or the trust officer who handles your endowment is probably experienced with the procedures and will know what to do.

Gifts of restricted securities usually don't present a problem even if there is a delay in your ability to sell the stock. You simply keep it for the required holding period (maximum two years). The donor's holding period is usually counted as part of the total holding period. However, be careful about accepting restricted stock for any gift arrangement that requires income to be paid to a beneficiary (pooled income fund, regular unitrust, charitable gift annuity, charitable remainder annuity trust) unless the stock is producing a substantial, regular dividend. Suggest instead that the donor use readily marketable securities which quickly can be converted into income-producing investments.

In terms of valuing a restricted stock for the donor's federal income tax charitable deduction, this can be tricky. Due to the restriction on selling the stock, the fair market value may be less than the average of the high and the low for the date of gift. This can only be judged on a case by case basis, and, even if you credit the donor with the full value as if it were marketable on the date of gift, the donor may want to check with his advisor or a securities expert to verify his or her own federal income tax charitable deduction. (Note: Refer to the end of Chapter II-2 for a discussion of the appraisal requirements for non-publicly traded securities. The donor needs a qualified appraisal for non-publicly traded securities for which he or she is claiming a federal income tax deduction of $10,000 or more.)

VALUING A STOCK

Most donors contribute securities that are traded regularly on national or local stock exchanges or in the Over-The-Counter market (OTC). The value of a gift of stock is the average of the high and the low on the date of gift, called the mean. Stocks can be valued only on regular business days and not on weekends or holidays when the stock market is closed.

For a stock received on a day when the shares are not traded, such as a weekend or holiday, here is what the I.R.S says on its web site (www.irs.gov). Do a search on the I.R.S. web site for Publication 561:

> "If there were no sales on the valuation date, but there were sales within a reasonable period before and after the valuation date, you determine FMV by taking the average price between the highest and lowest sales prices on the nearest date before and on the nearest date after the valuation date. Then you weight these averages in inverse order by the respective number of trading days between the selling dates and the valuation date."

The I.R.S. has also given us an example:

Example

On the day you gave stock to a qualified organization, there were no sales of the stock. Sales of the stock nearest the valuation date took place two trading days before the valuation date at an average selling price of $10 and three trading days after the valuation date at an average selling price of $15. The FMV on the valuation date was $12, figured as follows:

([3 x $10] + [2 x $15]) divided by 5 = $12

Your organization's decision to sell or retain the shares is irrelevant to the gift transaction and to the donor's federal income tax charitable deduction. For this reason, the value of a donor's gift should *never* be stated as the amount of the net proceeds you receive on the sale. Remember that there may be a difference in the legally correct amount the I.R.S. allows a donor to claim for federal income tax deduction purposes and the value the charity uses for gift recognition purposes.

An example of two different situations illustrates why the sale price is irrelevant in determining the value of the gift for tax purposes:

Case 1: Donor gives stock with a mean value of $10,988 to a charity on March 1. The charity considers the stock a good investment and elects to retain the shares in its endowment. What is the value of the gift? $10,988.

Case 2: Donor gives the same stock to another charity. The donor's broker transfers the shares into the charity's account on March 1. It takes the charity a couple of days to match the donor with the stock. This charity has a policy of immediately selling all gifted stock in order to give cash to its endowment manager. The charity's broker finally sells the shares on March 4 when the mean value is $10,249. What is the value of the gift? $10,988.

In *Case 2*, the value of the shares could have plummeted to $5 or doubled in value, but the donor still gave $10,988, and this is the value you should acknowledge as a gift.

When you acknowledge the gift, the easiest way is to acknowledge a gift of X shares of ABC Stock on [date]. However, donors will come back to you to ask for the exact figures used to value the stock. They are eager to know the size of the gift they just made to you. So, practically, it is better in the long run to include in your letter the mean value of the shares on the date of gift. Some organizations take the position that they should not put the value of the stock in the acknowledgment letter because they don't want the liability of giving the donor a figure that he or she may use later. What if the figure is wrong? I suppose you might get it wrong occasionally. But, in the day to day practice of running a development office, you'll find that donors want to know these figures from you. (Note: The I.R.S. does not require a statement of the value of the securities on its official gift receipt.)

In many cases (for which the I.R.S. has defined the way you determine the date of the gift), you can use the sample wording below to create your own acknowledgment letter:

Dear [donor]:

Thank you for your gift of 349 shares of [name of stock] to [charity] on [date]. The shares had a high of $_____ and a low of $_____ which results in a total mean value of $_____ on the date of the gift. We believe these figures to be accurate, but you should check them yourself to ensure that they are correct. According to your instructions, your gift has been credited to [Annual Fund, your endowed fund, whatever].

This is also to verify that you received no goods or services in exchange for this gift.

We greatly appreciate your support.

Sincerely,

Director of Planned Giving

If you provided goods or services, you do not need to inform the donor if the amount is considered insubstantial. This figure is updated annually by the I.R.S.

The acknowledgement letter is not so clear cut for a gift through Depository Trust Company since the I.R.S. has never ruled on this procedure. Many charities take the position that the gift is complete when it posts to the charity's brokerage account. However, while that may seem reasonable, my attorney informs me that such a rule has never been articulated by the I.R.S. Though it seems odd, he advises that the charity provide an acknowledgement that states the facts of the transfer so that the donor can use his or her attorney's counsel as to which date to use for the gift.

For example, "Dear Mr. Donor: On March 21, 2004, your broker at Merrill Lynch executed instructions to transfer 250 shares of Kodak common stock through Depository Trust Company to [charity]. The shares were received in our brokerage account on March 24, 2004. On March 24, the high was $____ and the low was $____ for a total mean value of $_____."

In order to find the value of a stock gift, the best place to go is the Internet. Historically, most people used the *Wall Street Journal* to look up the high and low for a stock. However, the *Wall Street Journal* stopped printing the figures in 2001. Here are a few web sites that provide the figures you need. There are many, many more. Bear in mind that the navigation and structure of these sites may change in the future.

bigcharts.com

After going to the site, you will see a field where you can either enter the stock's ticker symbol or the name of a stock in order to do a "Global Symbol Lookup." I typed in Microsoft, and I get a listing of many international Microsoft entities. I then selected "United States" for "Country" and "Stock" for "Security Type." The next narrower search shows Microsoft Corporation on the NASDAQ exchange with a symbol of MSFT. Then, I clicked "Historical Quotes" in the tool bar menu and entered MSFT and a date of 08/03/2001.

For August 3, 2001, the high is $67.36 and the low is $66.00. To find the mean value, simply take the average:

$67.36 + $66.00 = $133.36 divided by 2 = $66.68

quotes.fool.com

This site is excellent because you can get a chart of quotes for a year. I entered General Electric to look up the ticker symbol. The search finds General Electric Company on the NYSE (New York Stock Exchange) with a ticker symbol of GE. Then, I simply click on "GE" in the left column and a new page opens with a menu bar on which is the option "Historical Quotes." Click there and you can enter a date. I entered 7/4/2001. Message: "GE not traded on Wednesday, July 4, 2001." I changed the date to 7/5/2001 and find the following:

For July 5, 2001, the high is $49.40 and the low is $48.40. The average of the high and the low is $48.90 which I figured myself.

edreyfus.com

Right in the middle of the page is the "Symbol Lookup." I clicked there and then typed Intel. The search found Intel Corp. with a ticker symbol of INTC. Then, I clicked on the INTC and it opened a page with today's quotes and other options on the left including "Hist Pricing." On the next page, I entered INTC and I get a choice for how many days of quotes I want, 5 to 360. Plus, I can choose decimal or fraction. Decimal is easier. To see what happens, I selected "360" and I have a chart of the highs and lows for the whole year. The actual listing goes back more than a year because there are no trades on weekends or holidays.

VALUING A BOND

A bond does not have a high and a low. It has a face value, a coupon rate, and a maturity date. For a bond quote, you cannot use the *Wall Street Journal*, because only a fraction of the bonds in existence are listed. You can use the Internet if you have the CUSIP number of the bond. Practically, only the donor or the donor's broker would have the CUSIP number. If you have the CUSIP number, you can go to the following web site: bondsonline.com

To follow this discussion, get yourself a *Wall Street Journal* and find the U.S. Exchange Bond section so that you can look down the columns to see a typical bond quote. The bond section in the WSJ is very tiny. I called the paper to ask why so few bonds are listed and was told that only those bonds traded on the New York Stock Exchange are listed. Most bonds trade on the Over the Counter Market and their quotes are not made available. The editor with whom I spoke said that the SEC has been encouraging the Over the Counter Market to make the rest of the bond prices available. He could not say if the WSJ will print them, but there is a movement afoot to make these available to the public somehow.

In practice, it would be highly unlikely for you to receive a gift bond and actually find it in the Wall Street Journal. My reference to the U.S. Exchange Bond section is to provide something to look at while you read about bonds.

Notice that some companies have more than one bond with varying yields and maturity dates. For some reason, whenever the yield on the bond is a whole number, there's always an "s" after it such as "6s" which means 6% bonds, or "7s" meaning 7% bonds. The year of maturity is expressed as two digits such as "13" meaning the year 2013 or "20" for 2020.

The quotes are based on what the bond closed for on the prior business day. Further, the price of the bond is quoted in relation to its face value. For example, you might have a bond which is selling for "90." This means that you pay $90 for every $100 of face value and the bond is selling at a *discount*. If the bond is selling at "102," you are paying $102 for every $100 of face value. When you pay more than 100, you are buying the bond at a *premium*. If a bond is selling at "100," it is said to be selling at *par*. I did the following examples in the year 2001, but the principles are the same regardless of the year.

Example:

AT&T bond, 7¾%, due 2007. This means that if you buy the bond at *par*, for $10,000, it will pay 7¾% annually in semiannual payments until the year 2007 when the bond will mature and you'll get your $10,000 back.

In the *Wall Street Journal* for January 23, 2001, (close of business for January 22) there is a listing for this bond: ATT 7¾ 07 Close 103¾. This means it is selling for 103¾. The market value of the bond is $10,375. It is selling at a premium because the 7¾% coupon rate is higher than the prevailing rate at the time. Therefore, in order to buy this bond, you pay a premium which has the effect of evening out the yield. Instead of getting 7¾% on $10,000, you pay $10,375 for an effective yield of 7½% ($10,375 divided by $775 interest = .075 yield).

Another one quoted on this day looks like this: IBM 5⅜ 09 Close 94. Translation: these bonds, which mature in 2009, pay 5⅜% on the face value which is selling at a discount of $94. For a $10,000 bond, you'll pay $94 for every $100 in the bond. In this case, you'll pay $9,400 ($10,000 divided by 100 times $94 per $100 face value = $9,400). The actual yield is 5.7%, not 5⅜%. ($537.50 interest divided by $9,400 investment = 5.7% yield.)

Here's one more: Lucent 7¼ 06 Close 99. Translation: These are Lucent bonds, paying 7¼% on the face value, maturing in 2006, selling at $99 per $100. Total cost of a $10,000 bond is $9,900. If the bond is paying 7¼% on $10,000, that's $725 of interest. With an investment of $9,900, the actual yield on your investment is 7.3% and not 7.25%.

Relating this discussion to a donor's gift, let's say the donor wants to give you a $50,000 New York Telephone bond maturing in 2024 with a yield of 7¼%. In the *Wall Street Journal* for January 23, 2001, you'll find: NYTel 7¼% 24 selling at 97½. The fair market value of the bond is 50,000 divided by 100 times 97.5 = $48,750. (Note: The fact that the bond is selling below par does not have any bearing on whether the bond is appreciated over the donor's cost basis because appreciation is always in relation to what the donor paid. If the bond was purchased at 95, the bond would be appreciated. Or, if the bond was purchased at 102¾, the bond would be depreciated.

Bonds pay interest twice a year in equal installments, for example on April 1 and October 1. With a zero-coupon bond, the interest is paid when the bond matures. When a donor transfers a bond to a charity, it comes with a portion of accrued interest, which for purposes of valuing the bond for the charitable deduction is not factored in. If a person buys a bond, he or she has to pay for the accrued interest. With a gift, the charity could send the donor a 1099 for the interest and, then, an acknowledgment for the amount. The donor would claim the 1099 interest as income and then deduct the amount as a cash gift. In practice, charities don't do this.

Series E, EE, H, and HH Bonds

These bonds are issued by the Federal Government and cannot be transferred to the charity during lifetime. As a planned giving officer, you will get a couple of inquiries *per* year about these bonds as charitable gifts. The war generation era bought them in droves. The bonds pay their interest at maturity and many people still have bonds that have stopped paying interest, but they don't want to cash them out because 100% of the interest will be reportable as ordinary income. An owner can convert the Series E or EE bonds to Series H or HH similar to a roll over and not recognize the income. The H and HH bonds pay interest twice per year, but they still have a lot of deferred interest waiting to be taxed if they are transferred or cashed out.

The problem is that these bonds have income considered to be Income in Respect of a Decedent (just like deferred compensation, retirement plans, or IRAs). To read more about the rules for dealing with Series E, EE, H, or HH bonds, go to web site www.publicdebt.treas.gov which brings you to the Bureau of the Public Debt. You can access the section on savings bonds to read more than you ever wanted to know. At such point as the donor tries to transfer a U.S. Savings Bond, the action triggers the reporting of all accrued interest. Of course, the donor could cash out the bond, report and pay taxes on the income, and contribute the cash to the charity, but few donors will be inclined to do this. If there are other publicly traded, appreciated, long-term, securities in the donor's portfolio, look there first for gift assets and not to these bonds.

If the bonds are left in the donor's estate, the income will most likely end up being taxed on the donor's last tax return. Plus, they comprise part of the gross estate and thus will be subject to the applicable estate tax (if any) if the donor's taxable lifetime and death transfers exceed the lifetime exclusion for the year of death. (See Chapter II-10 for more detail about how the gift and estate tax works and how the tax bill in 2001 changes some of these rules.) The better plan is to have the donor make a bequest of the bonds in kind to a charity. Then, the charity will get the actual certificates, complete the forms for re-registration of the bonds, sell the bonds, report the income (for which there is no tax to the charity), and the donor's estate escapes the income tax problem, as well as receiving an estate tax deduction for 100% of the bond's value (if there is an estate tax in place when the donor dies). A private letter ruling in 1998 sanctions this result.

Another option is to bequeath the bonds as a funding asset to a testamentary charitable remainder trust. The trust receives the bonds, disposes of them, receives the income but does not pay tax immediately. As beneficiary payments are made to the beneficiary, they are taxed along the way as tier one ordinary income. But, meanwhile, the entire accrued interest is invested and presumably growing tax free in the trust.

WHEN IS A GIFT OF SECURITIES COMPLETE?

A gift of a stock or bond is complete:

1. Physical Delivery by the Donor

   On the day you receive hand delivery by the donor of the unendorsed certificate together with a properly signed and guaranteed stock or bond power (or when you receive the endorsed certificate). If the stock power is not guaranteed, you need to ask your treasurer's office or broker if you can accept the certificate without the signature guarantee. I have never had a case when this was a problem. The charity's broker, acting on trust that the charity knows the donor, will affix the "signature guaranteed" stamp. Before you start accepting stock gifts, check with your broker or treasurer about this. Some are very strict and will require the signature guarantee. All of those with whom I have worked would take the stock certificate and stock power without the guarantee, but it is a good practice to ask the donor to get the guarantee as your standard procedure. If you have to turn a donor away or go back to the donor for the guarantee, you'll have some unhappy donors on your hands.

2. Mailing Certificates

   On the day the certificate and stock or bond power are postmarked to your organization or to your agent (broker). Practically, if the stock and the stock power arrive on different days, you would take the postmark of the later one.

3. Certificate Registration by the Issuing Corporation

   On the day when the transfer of ownership is made on the corporate books. If the donor instructs his or her broker or banker to transfer securities into your organization's name, *the gift is complete only when the actual transfer takes place on the corporate books and not when the instructions are given.* Transferring securities this way usually takes several weeks to up to two months and can cause two potential problems: 1) the gift may be pushed into another tax year, and 2) the price of the securities may fluctuate, thus changing the value of the gift. There is no reason for a donor to make a gift this way unless he is giving only part of one stock certificate (discussed earlier).

4. Electronic Transfers

   In Depository Trust Company transfers, there is no clear law on this issue. Therefore, you should state the facts. For example, "On April 29, 2003, your broker issued instructions to transfer 400 shares of Kodak common stock through Depository Trust Company into [Charity's] account at Paine Webber. The shares posted to [Charity's] account on April 30."

5. Donor Issues Transfer Instructions on your Web Site

   On the day that the participating broker receives the asset in its master gift account.

The rules are usually very clear as to when a stock gift is complete. But, sometimes, the charity is placed in an awkward position when it receives a letter from a broker saying something along the following lines:

> "We are holding in our gift account 85 shares of [stock name] which is a gift to [charity] on March 15, 2003, from [donor]. The mean value of the gift on that date is $21,234."

Let's assume that you receive the above letter on March 25. You had no knowledge of the gift on March 15, and the stock is now worth $19,500. What do you do? Most business offices will accommodate the quirky situations that occur in the transfer of securities, but you really need to be careful. The broker (who is not your agent) should not be putting stock in a generic gift account and waiting many days to tell you about it. Brokers do this during a time of high volume when they want to get the stock out of the donor's account as quasi evidence of a transfer, but didn't want to take the time to call you for correct transfer instructions. You can't avoid this scenario. It will happen frequently at the end of the year, so be prepared and have a clear gift acceptance and crediting policy in place. In this kind of mess, your acknowledgement letter should state the facts and let the donor's attorney advise as to the date of the gift. Bear in mind that your internal crediting guidelines may result in your crediting the donor with one value while the donor elects to claim a different value for tax purposes.

A worse thing that happens periodically is the case of a broker selling the stock in the donor's account before you ever knew about a gift. If that happens, the broker has forced a capital gain on his or her client.

CLOSELY-HELD STOCK

A donor who started and runs a company in corporate form can make a gift of closely held stock. Closely held stock is share certificates issued by a corporation where no brokers are involved and it is not publicly traded or registered with securities commissions. Because it is not traded regularly, closely-held stock is difficult to value. A few family members own all of the stock, and they have no interest in selling the stock to the general public because they wish to keep control of the company within the family. Also, registering with securities commissions, both state and federal, is costly and time consuming.

The help of an expert is necessary in valuing stock in a closely-held corporation. When I worked at the Boston Safe Deposit and Trust Company, we had a department devoted solely to the valuation of closely-held corporations. Variables that affect the value of the stock include the strength and economic outlook of the particular industry, the amount of control represented by the block of stock, the company's position in the industry, and the value of stock of companies engaged in a business similar to that of the closely-held corporation. Also relevant in valuing the stock is the company's earning history and ability.

A major problem with valuing a small number of shares in a closely-held corporation is the fact that the small number of shares being contributed to you is not equal in value to shares held by the majority shareholders. For example, if you receive 5% of the shares of a closely-held company, you have no voting power to speak of and you control nothing related to the company's operation. The person with 51% of the ownership controls the company. So, if there are 10,000 outstanding shares and the company is valued at $2 million, presumably each share is worth $200. But, the block of majority shares is worth more than your block of a few shares. In the reverse, if A owns 51% and B owns 49%, and if A gives B 2% of the shares, this 2% is valued exponentially higher because it shifts control of the company. Figuring out the value of closely-held shares being contributed to you is the job of the appraiser hired by the donor. It is very difficult and very costly.

Because closely-held stock is not publicly traded, the only way your organization can convert a gift of such stock to cash is to sell it back either to the corporation or to one of the other shareholders. The donor can get into trouble, however, if your organization is legally bound to sell the shares back to the corporation. If so, he or she may end up paying tax on capital gains even though it is a gift, because it will be considered a step transaction. Accordingly, you should not, prior to the gift, formally or informally enter into an agreement to sell the shares back to the corporation. However, mere anticipation is okay.

A gift of closely held stock can provide benefits to the donor and to your organization similar to the benefits of a gift of publicly traded stock. The donor receives an income tax deduction for the fair market value of the shares (subject to the contribution ceilings discussed in Chapter II-2), avoids a capital gain tax on the appreciation, and your organization, after selling the shares back to the corporation or to another family member, has cash to use for its charitable purposes. It is possible that the cost basis is zero; therefore, the value of avoiding a gain can be quite significant.

Example:

Mary Smith started the ABC Company ten years ago. She owns 90% of the outstanding stock which has a zero cost basis. In 2003, Mary contributes $100,000 of stock in ABC Company to your organization. She is in a 35% tax bracket. Mary enjoys an income tax deduction for the full fair market value of the stock or $100,000 which saves her $35,000 in income taxes in the year of the gift (35% x $100,000 = $35,000). She also has avoided paying capital gain tax of $15,000 on the stock's appreciation ($100,000 appreciation taxed at 15% = $15,000).

Her tax savings can be summarized like this:

Fair Market Value of Property:	$100,000
Taxed at 35%:	x .35
Income Tax Savings:	$35,000
Fair Market Value of Property:	$100,000
Cost Basis:	− 0
Appreciation:	$100,000
Capital Gain Tax at 15%:	x .15
Potential Capital Gain Tax:	$15,000
Savings from Tax Deduction:	$35,000
Capital Gain Taxes Avoided:	+ 15,000
Total Tax Savings from Gift:	$50,000
Amount of Gift:	$100,000
Value of Tax Savings:	− 50,000
Net cost of Gift:	$50,000

For the donor, the gift has produced tax benefits similar to those of any gift of appreciated stock. But, what about the corporation? It is out $100,000 in cash with no tax benefit.

There is one way that the corporation can achieve some tax savings from the transaction. When a company operates a qualified Employee Stock Ownership Plan (ESOP), the company can make deductible contributions to the ESOP. In turn, the ESOP is qualified to buy shares of the company's stock. There are rules restricting the amount a company can put into the ESOP each year so an attorney familiar with these rules needs to be involved.

The new sequence of transactions might go like this:

1. Donor makes gift of $100,000 of ABC Company Stock to your organization.

2. ABC Company makes a qualified deductible contribution of $100,000 to its Employee Stock Ownership Plan.

3. The ESOP uses the $100,000 in cash to redeem the shares of ABC Company Stock given to your organization.

Result: The donor claims an income tax deduction for the $100,000 gift, thus saving income and capital gain taxes as outlined above. The ABC Company claims a tax deduction for the contribution to the ESOP, thus saving income taxes in its own tax bracket. You get the cash when the ESOP buys the stock back from you.

Note: In this case, the donor owns less of the corporate stock and thus has less power in the company than she had before the gift. If she is the sole shareholder, this concern is not a problem.

A qualified appraisal, commissioned by the donor, is necessary for gifts of non-publicly traded securities valued at over $10,000. See Chapter II-2 for a discussion of the substantiation requirements of noncash gifts.

When I worked at Boston University, we received many gifts of closely-held stock valued at between $9,000 and $9,999, according to the donor. The donor did not want to get an appraisal and we did not care what the shares were worth. Usually, we put them on the donor's gift record at the value of $1 and kept them in a separate portfolio for all non-publicly traded gift assets. When we finally sold the shares back to the company, to a family member, or when the stock went public, we credited the donor with a gift for the sale proceeds or for the new publicly traded price. In terms of acknowledging the gift, we would simply say, "Thank you for your gift of 200 shares of [company] on [date]." The donor was responsible for claiming whatever federal income tax charitable deduction he or she could justify.

Many closely-held business owners have S corporations. This is a structure whereby all income flows through the tax returns of the shareholders, rather than being taxed at the corporate level. Beginning in 1998, S corporation stock can be given to a charity without adverse consequences to the S corporation. Prior to the Small Business Job Protection Act of 1996, if a charity owned shares of an S corporation, the ownership by the charity would cause the corporation to lose its S corporation status, forcing it to become a C corporation. While that is no longer the case for direct gifts to a charity, the problem still exists for pooled income funds and charitable remainder trusts. Neither of these vehicles is allowed to be an owner of S corporation stock. Therefore, you should be very careful not to take such stock as a gift to either of these gift vehicles.

Chris Hoyt, professor of law at the University of Missouri School of Law, wrote a terrific article on this topic for *The Journal of Gift Planning*, a quarterly publication of the National Committee on Planned Giving. The article was later published on the Planned Giving Design Center. You can go to www.pgdc.net to register for free and then do a search on "S corporation." Chris says, "If a donor makes a mistake and transfers S corporation stock to a charitable remainder trust or a pooled income fund, it may be possible for the parties to reverse the transaction so that the corporation will be treated as never having lost its S corporation status. The parties should apply to the I.R.S. for permission to ignore the error as an 'inadvertent termination' and have the transaction retroactively undone."

Unfortunately, the charity incurs UBIT (unrelated business income tax) on the appreciation when it sells the stock. Therefore, the charity may lose a significant amount of the fair market value paying the tax due following a sale. Also, the charity pays UBIT on any income or distributions attributable to its ownership. This is basically because by owning S corporation stock, the charity is engaging in a trade or business that has nothing to do with its exempt purpose.

The charity also has to watch out for the case where it owes tax on money it never received, commonly called "phantom income." The charity has to pay tax on its share of the corporation's accounting income, but that amount will often be greater than the amount of cash distributions. Your legal counsel should review any proposed gift of S corporation stock to ensure that you don't take as a gift an asset that will create problems.

Finally, the donor should check with his or her accountant to make sure that the full fair market value of the S corporation stock is deductible as a charitable gift. Sometimes, based on the specific activities of the corporation, the donor must reduce the value of his or her charitable gift by the amount of ordinary income that would have been generated if he or she sold the stock. This does not apply to capital gains and it doesn't apply to bequests.

There is a lot more to this topic than I intend to cover here. If you read the article I cited above, you'll learn many other considerations for accepting S corporation stock so that you stay out of trouble.

THE INCOME TAX DEDUCTION

As long as the donor has held the security (other than S corporation stock) the required holding period for it to be a long-term capital asset (more than 12 months), and if the donor itemizes deductions, the donor is eligible to claim as a federal income tax charitable deduction the full fair market value in the year of the gift. The deduction is limited to 30% of adjusted gross income, with a five-year carry-over period for any amount that exceeds the 30% limitation.

If the donor has held the shares for less than the required holding period, the tax deduction will be limited to the cost basis with a limit of 50% of adjusted gross income and the same five-year carry-over period for any amount that exceeds the 50% ceiling. It is extremely rare to receive a gift of shares held less than 12 months.

When the donor's cost basis is greater than the fair market value, the deduction is always limited to the fair market value. Donors who have securities that have decreased in value over their cost basis should sell the shares first and contribute the proceeds to your organization. This allows them to claim a capital loss on the sale against realized capital gains and receive a deduction for the gift of the cash proceeds.

Mutual Fund Considerations

If the donor contributes mutual funds, a slightly different result occurs. Mutual fund owners recognize short-term and long-term gain in the course of a year even if the donor made no sale of the mutual fund shares. The taxable events inside the mutual fund are passed through to the owners and must be reported on their income tax returns. Therefore, for the small amount of short-term gain attributable to the donor's mutual fund shares, the donor must reduce his or her federal income tax deduction for the amount of ordinary income (the short-term gain) that would have been reportable if the donor sold the shares.

The portion of long-term gain received as a taxable distribution is not taken into account in determining the donor's income tax deduction.

Gifts of mutual funds can be a real problem because donors often don't know their cost basis, especially if they participate in a dividend reinvestment plan. (See the next section.)

See Chapter II-2 for a complete discussion of the income tax deduction and contribution ceilings.

Dividend Reinvestment Plans

With a dividend reinvestment plan, either for a stock or for a mutual fund, the donor elects to have periodic dividends reinvested in fractional shares of the stock or mutual fund. For an asset involved with a dividend reinvestment plan, the cost basis of every fractional purchase must be added up to figure the total cost basis of the asset. This can be extremely difficult if a donor has participated in a dividend reinvestment plan for a long time.

If the donor makes an outright gift of a mutual fund (held 12 months or more) that has participated in a dividend reinvestment plan, then the purchases of fractional shares acquired in the past 12 months are short-term capital gain property, deductible at cost basis up to the 50% contribution ceiling. The rest of the federal income tax charitable deduction is based on the fair market value of the rest of it and is deductible up to the 30% contribution ceiling.

When a donor participates in a dividend reinvestment plan with a stock, the issuing corporation does not issue fractional stock certificates. The record of ownership is kept with the transfer agent for the particular corporation on an account statement for the owner. No stock certificates are ever issued.

If a donor wishes to make a gift of the stock's dividend reinvestment shares, he or she must send a letter with a medallion signature guarantee (a more severe version of the regular signature guarantee) to the transfer agent for the stock. A medallion signature guarantee can only be done by a bank that already knows the donor through an existing account. A donor cannot take a stock power to a bank where he or she has no account and get a medallion guarantee.

When the donor requests a gift of securities accumulated in a stock dividend reinvestment plan, the transfer agent will issue certificates in the charity's name for the maximum number of shares the donor's account can buy at that time. The balance of the account will be paid with a check to the charity. The date on the new certificates issued to the charity is generally the date of the gift. A twist on this gift is the fact that the cash for the fractional amount is deemed to be a sale by the donor incurring capital gain if the asset is appreciated.

If a donor sends instructions to the transfer agent for his or her corporate dividend reinvestment account to be transferred to the charity, the people receiving the information will generally create an account for the charity to which they might credit the appropriate shares and then do nothing. For some reason, known only to them, the people who work at the transfer agent will not inform the charity that the shares are ready to be used to create stock certificates. Sometimes, the only way your charity finds out that a transfer has been made is when the donor calls to ask if you received the gifted shares. At that point, many months after the alleged transfer, you must call the transfer agent, make your way into the voice-mail pyramid until, finally, you talk to a human about the fact that you had a charitable gift months ago, and where is it? If you get into the voice-mail pyramid of one of these transfer agents, try to get to the customer service area. When you get a gift of dividend reinvestment shares from a corporation, the transfer agent must issue the certificate and send it to you. You cannot simply issue a sell order because the corporation is not a broker. You will receive a stock certificate for the full number of shares and a check for cash representing the fractional amount which was not sufficient to purchase a whole share.

For transfers of mutual funds involving a dividend reinvestment plan to either a charitable remainder trust, charitable gift annuity, pooled income fund, or charitable lead trust, the donor must provide the cost basis for purposes of long-term gain and also the portion of the asset that has been held short-term (less than 12 months). That would be any additional purchases made in the dividend reinvestment plan in the 12 months prior to the gift.

STOCK *VS.* CASH AS GIFT PROPERTY

Frequently, donors make gifts of cash when they should be making gifts of appreciated stock. If a donor has any appreciated stock at all, it would nearly always be better for the donor to give the stock.

Let's take an example in 2003.

Arthur has stock valued at $10,000 with a cost basis of $1,000. He is in the 15% bracket for long-term capital gains. What would happen if he sold it? 100% of the gain would be taxed at 15%.

Fair Market Value:	$10,000
Cost:	- 1,000
Gain:	$9,000
100% of Gain:	$9,000
Taxed at 15%:	x .15
Loss to Taxes:	$1,350

Arthur also has $10,000 in cash, and needs to decide whether to contribute the cash or the stock. If he likes the stock, and wants to retain $10,000 worth of this stock as an investment, it doesn't matter whether he keeps the shares he currently owns or whether he buys a different lot valued at $10,000. He will still have $10,000 of the same stock. His objective is to make a $10,000 gift and retain the same investment.

By contributing the stock and repurchasing the same stock using his $10,000 cash, he will have brought the cost basis of the stock up to the current market value. Then, when he decides to sell the shares, he will incur a capital gain tax only on the amount that exceeds his new $10,000 cost basis (instead of the amount exceeding his $1,000 cost basis for the original shares).

Another reason to contribute the stock instead of the cash is the fact that he might have had to earn $15,000 in order to have $10,000 after tax.

If you have the chance to work with a donor like this, I hope you will be able to explain this basic concept of contributing stock and repurchasing the same stock with cash thus bringing the cost basis up to the current market value. Many people in this situation make the cash gift on the premise they like this stock and want to keep it. This is flawed thinking.

TRANSFERRING MUTUAL FUNDS

Mutual funds have become a very popular asset to use in charitable giving. These funds present a bit of a problem in the transfer process. Mutual funds do not have certificates. The only evidence of ownership is an account statement.

Mutual funds require a couple of different approaches to the transfer process.

Many mutual funds are listed in the stock market section of the newspaper. Those which trade daily are easy to value. The price is based on the NAV or net asset value which is quoted daily for many. Others trade less frequently or allow purchases and sales at regular intervals (for example, monthly) and, therefore, do not have a price that changes daily. You may need assistance from your broker in determining the fair market value of such a gift.

If you have a donor who wants to contribute mutual funds for a gift, there are basically four options:

Option #1: Your organization needs to establish an account with the mutual fund company. This involves your treasurer completing a new account application form, faxing it to the company, waiting a day or so for the new account to be ready. Next, the mutual fund manger transfers the shares of the mutual fund from the donor's account to the charity's account. Then, the charity sells the shares, receives the proceeds, and closes the account.

Option #2: There are forms that you can use when taking in a mutual fund account. Your own broker will send you copies. These forms are pretty ridiculous because some of the language is so tiny, you cannot read it without a magnifying glass. I am not kidding. The print is smaller than on an aspirin bottle. However, get the form from your own broker, and send it to the donor. The donor completes the form and sends it back to you. Included on the form is the account number of the donor, the name of the fund, the number of shares being contributed, *etc.* When your charity receives the form completed by the donor, your charity's broker can extract the shares directly from the mutual fund company sort of like a DTC transfer.

Option #3: If the charity already has an account with the donor's brokerage firm, the mutual fund shares inside the donor's account can be moved directly to the charity's account, usually the same day.

Option #4: If the charity and the donor's brokerage firm both participate in the AssetStream transfer service described in the beginning of this chapter, the donor simply accesses a computer, opens the charity's web site, and initiates the transfer online.

SUMMARY

If your organization is not already promoting gifts of securities, you should begin to do so immediately. As an outright gift, appreciated, long-term securities can be deducted by the donor at fair market value for federal income tax purposes. Your organization then can sell the shares without loss to capital gain taxes.

The benefits of contributing securities to life income plans are extremely attractive. The immediate avoidance of capital gain tax liability is a big incentive for many donors, and the income derived from life income plans is often double or triple what the donor was receiving from the stock. Each life income plan is discussed in full detail in later chapters.

The next chapter deals with another form of noncash property—life insurance. No doubt, in the course of running your planned giving program, you will encounter a situation involving a life insurance gift. At the very least, you will inherit a group of life insurance policies that need to be maintained. Or, life insurance can be used as wealth replacement for the value of the asset contributed to your organization. The following chapter explains everything you need to know to accept, administer, and dispose of a gift of life insurance.

Chapter II–5

LIFE INSURANCE

INTRODUCTION

If you owned the first or second edition of this book, you'll find that this chapter hasn't changed very much in content in this third edition. I've done some fine tuning and provided more detail on some topics, but there isn't much more to say on this topic over what I said before. I did try.

Life insurance will not be a big piece of your planned giving program. However, a couple of times a year, you will get a question about it. Also, you may also be managing a handful of existing life insurance policies that need to be maintained. The truth of the matter is life insurance can be a real pain in the neck. I apologize to the life insurance agent reading this section, but in planned giving, life insurance is a high maintenance, unproductive gift in comparison to so many other gift options. My comments stem primarily from the fact that you're constantly chasing down the donor's gift in order to pay the premium. Plus, policies that donors bought in the 1980s in good faith to benefit charities have never performed the way they were presented, thus leaving a sour feeling for charities and donors. That having been said, if you are a planned giving officer, you need this chapter.

Millions of people own life insurance. Billions of dollars of life insurance policies are in force. In many cases, the original purpose for which the insurance was purchased is no longer applicable. For example, a parent may have purchased insurance to cover the cost of a child's college education if he or she were to die prematurely. Or, a husband and wife may have purchased insurance to provide support for minor children who are now married with children of their own. Obsolete policies like this can be given to your institution.

Life insurance is both easy to give and receive—so easy you don't need a formal planned giving program to accept a gift of life insurance. In fact, life insurance is one asset the donor can contribute without (or with minimal) help from you. Simply by naming your organization beneficiary and owner, the donor can make a marvelous gift without disturbing other assets and without loss of income. Life insurance also can be used to replace the value of assets or other property contributed to your organization. Thus, life insurance might play a role in your planned giving program either as an outright gift or as part of a donor's total gift plan.

There are many types of life insurance policies and payment plans. Some policies require a fixed premium for the duration of the insured's life. Others allow a reduced premium payment in early years when presumably the owner's earning power is less, and an increased premium beginning at a later date when the owner's earning power and ability to pay is presumably greater. Another type of insurance allows a limited number of premium payments (commonly called vanishing premiums), for example, eight equal payments (or four or even just one) after which the policy allegedly remains in force without further premium payments. An endowment policy distributes its face value to the beneficiary after a certain number of years or on the insured's death whichever comes first.

Regardless of the type of policy or payment plan, most life insurance policies can be contributed to your institution. This chapter covers life insurance under the following main topics:

- tax consequences to the donor;
- considerations for both your organization and the donor;
- how to set up administrative procedures to pay the premiums;
- loans;
- group term insurance provided by employer;
- considerations for a new policy;
- appraisal guidelines—the ridiculous item of the day;

- crediting guidelines;
- creative ideas on making the most of life insurance in your planned giving program;
- how to get information about life insurance products;
- a word about life insurance agents;
- charitable reverse split dollar plans.

Every state's laws are different. You should be aware that some states, but not many, do not allow a charity to own life insurance on an individual claiming that there is no insurable interest. Be sure to check your own state's laws. Your tax counsel rather than I can advise you on this issue.

TAX CONSEQUENCES TO THE DONOR

Life insurance is considered ordinary income property—property the sale of which generates ordinary income to the donor on the appreciation that exceeds the cost basis.

A donor who irrevocably transfers life insurance to your organization can claim an income tax deduction for the policy's cost basis or cash surrender value, whichever is less. The deduction is limited to 50% of adjusted gross income with a five-year carry-over period for the excess. (Note: The donor can never claim an income tax deduction for the policy's face value.) But, because this is ordinary income property, a donor must reduce the charitable deduction by the amount of the ordinary income that would have been recognized had the donor surrendered the policy for cash.

When you accept a policy, ask the insurance company for Form 712. The company will not send this unless you request it. This form completed by the insurance company, will give you its assessment of the policy's current value, taking into account all aspects of the policy including loans, accrued interest, *etc.*

If no premiums remain to be paid on the policy, the income tax deduction is equal to the cost or replacement value of a new policy with comparable benefits for the same face value for a person the same age as the insured, but not greater than the donor's cost basis.

Simply making the charity beneficiary is not sufficient to generate an income tax deduction for the donor. Why? Because the donor can remove you any time. To be entitled to a deduction, the donor must make your organization both beneficiary and owner of the policy, as well as give up all "incidents of ownership"—the rights associated with the policy. Incidents of ownership include the right to change the beneficiary, borrow against the policy, or have dividends applied against the premiums.

If the donor continues to pay premiums after transferring the policy's ownership to a charity, he or she is entitled to claim an income tax deduction for each payment as made. The donor can pay the premium directly to the insurance company or make a gift to your institution equal to the premium amount so that you can pay the premium.

It is important to note that if the donor makes the premium payment directly to the insurance company, he or she has made a gift "for the use of" instead of "to" the charity. That means the donor has lower contribution ceilings than would otherwise be the case. In Chapter II-2, there is a section on these rules.

CONSIDERATIONS FOR BOTH YOUR ORGANIZATION AND THE DONOR

Life insurance is rather straightforward. Donors can easily grasp the concept of providing major support by naming your organization beneficiary of an existing policy or by purchasing a new policy for your benefit. But, like anything else, there are decisions to be made with regard to life insurance gifts:

- Should your organization keep the policy in force or cash it in?
- Should your organization continue to pay the premiums on an existing policy?
- How should you handle premium payments?

Should Your Organization Keep The Policy In Force Or Cash It In?

Whether or not the policy is paid up (no more premiums need to be paid), you have a choice about whether to:

1) Cash in the policy, put the cash to work, and be done with it; or

2) Keep the policy in force until the death of the insured probably long after you and everyone else currently employed there have moved on.

As with many other decisions in fund raising, you must think about the donor's motivation. For example, let's say you receive a gift of life insurance with a $20,000 cash surrender value and a $100,000 face value. If the donor responded to an appeal seeking funds for a new building project, his or her objective was to give you the $20,000 cash surrender value to spend immediately. On the other hand, if the donor wants to establish a named fund in your endowment, he or she may expect you to keep the policy in force to ensure you will one day have the $100,000 required for a named fund. As director of planned giving, you probably know better than any other staff member what motivated this gift. Make certain you communicate the donor's wishes to the appropriate people (director of development, treasurer, business office) and to the donor's file. Document everything.

Should Your Organization Continue To Pay The Premiums On An Existing Policy?

What do you do if you receive a policy for which premium payments remain to be paid, *and* the donor does not want to pay them? You have four choices:

1. Do nothing.

   Sometimes, there is enough value in the policy such that annual dividends pay the premium each year. This is a good situation because you simply sit back and wait. In other cases, premiums remain to be paid. If you do nothing, the accumulated cash value will be eaten away to keep the policy in force for a certain number of years (different for each policy). As the new owner, you can contact the insurance company to find out how long the policy can sustain itself. The company service representative will have to order a copy of the policy from the records department and then perform an illustration for you. This might take a few weeks.

2. Convert it to a paid-up policy of lesser amount.

   Use the cash value to buy a fully paid-up policy. If you do this, the value of the new fully-paid up policy will be different than the original. Depending on the variables, the new policy's face value may be higher or lower because insurance products have changed over time. When you cash in a policy to take out the cash value or to convert it to another policy, there may be a penalty fee depending on how long the policy has been in force.

3. Cash it in.

   Cashing in the policy is very easy. This gives you immediate cash to spend or invest. But, be careful to check with the donor before you do this.

   I had a case at Boston College of a man who was always delinquent on his premium payments. I would send a letter about four weeks before the premium was due notifying him that it was time for his gift. Nothing. Then a second letter a few weeks later. Nothing.

   If you miss the due date on the invoice, you usually have a grace period to get the payment in. In our case, this was 30 days, after which the automatic feature would kick in and take a loan on the policy from the cash value. The loan also carried interest. I wrote a letter that was friendly, but to the point. I also called him and he always said he would pay. Then, nothing for a long time, and finally, a check would show up.

This happened year after year and it became painful to chase him for the gifts. Eventually, in the middle of one of these cycles, I sent him a letter saying that we were going to cash out the policy rather than have the policy eat into itself to cover the premiums. He went ballistic. He was a raving lunatic on the phone and he said that Boston College should be paying the premiums. NOT! In the end, I told our business office that I wasn't going to chase him any longer and that we should just let the policy self destruct.

4. Pay the premiums

I cannot think of a case under which I would want my charity to pay the premiums if the donor chose not to. I suppose if the insured is very old, your organization might consider paying the premiums so that you will receive a distribution for the full face value on the insured's death. But, on the other hand, if the insured is old enough, the policy won't have time to be eaten away. Bear in mind that when people become terminally ill or sick, they might become delinquent on premium payments or gifts because they have other priorities.

Also, some companies pursue "life settlement" business (not viaticals). People will buy policies from charities if the life expectancy of the insured is less than 10 years. They will often pay considerably more than the cash surrender value. This might be important to a charity's decision about whether to keep or sell a life insurance policy.

My advice to you is not to spend a lot of time on these questions but simply be aware that choices do exist. If you think any one of these choices would create public relations problems with the donor, speak up. Otherwise, let your business office dispose of the gift as it deems advisable and consider it an outright gift, equivalent to cash.

Two Ways To Handle The Premium Payments

If you are named owner and beneficiary of a life insurance policy for which premiums remain to be paid, and the donor wants to continue paying them, you have a good situation. Foremost is the opportunity to get to know the donor and to build a relationship toward a larger commitment later. A visit or phone call on or about the time premium payments are paid can be an effective way of thanking the donor and getting better acquainted.

There are two ways to handle the premium payments:

1. The donor pays the premium directly to the insurance company.

2. The donor makes a gift to your organization equal to the premium amount and you, in turn, pay the premium directly to the insurance company.

1. *The donor pays the premium directly to the insurance company.*

Sounds simple, doesn't it? Why change something that has been working quite well for years? Well, for a couple of reasons.

First, when a donor pays the premium directly to the insurance company, an intangible benefit is lost. Although the donor's premium payment is, in every way, just as deliberate an act of support as is another donor's gift sent directly to you, the gesture cannot possibly generate the kind of emotional satisfaction the donor gets from sending the gift to you. Thus, your work and efforts to cultivate the donor are more difficult, and they do not stem from the usual process of "donor makes gift" and "charity acknowledges it" because you have no direct interaction with the donor as he or she makes the premium payment.

Second, you lose control of the situation. How will you know if a donor is late with a payment, misses a payment or even stops payments? It is awkward to ask the donor if he or she has made the premium payment.

Practically, once your organization is named owner and beneficiary of a life insurance policy, you should be getting the bills.

2. *The donor makes a gift to your organization equal to the premium amount and you, in turn, pay the premium directly to the insurance company.*

Handling the gift this way takes extra effort, but it provides a more satisfying gift experience for the donor, better cultivation possibilities for you, and gives your organization control over the fate of the policy.

You'll be responsible for establishing administrative procedures for handling this arrangement. Before getting to that, let me go back for a moment to discuss points one and two.

When the donor makes a cash gift to your organization for the premium amount (*assuming you are under no legal obligation to apply the gift to the premium payment*), he or she receives all of the benefits both in tax savings and in personal satisfaction of making an outright gift. Accordingly, the cash gift entitles the donor to a deduction up to 50% of adjusted gross income with a five-year carry-over period for any amount that exceeds the 50% ceiling.

Note: If a donor makes a gift of appreciated stock to fund the premium payment, and if you are under no legal obligation to make the premium payment, technically, the gift should be deductible for the full fair market value. However, this gets into a gray area (sort of abusive) and I would suggest that you check with your own tax counsel before accepting such a gift.

Having committed to make the payments directly to you, the donor maintains important contact and can be acknowledged properly as each gift is made.

Because your organization pays the premiums, you maintain total control of the policy. Thus, you ensure that payments are made on time.

HOW TO SET UP ADMINISTRATIVE PROCEDURES TO PAY THE PREMIUMS

This section deals with the administration of a life insurance gift when a donor continues making premium payments on a policy transferred to you. The donor should send you the contract showing your name as the new owner and beneficiary. If not, ask for it.

Following are the steps you need to take to manage your institution's life insurance policies:

- Coordinate your activities with your business office.
- Acknowledge the gift.
- Change the billing information for premiums.
- Mark the appropriate record to ensure gift reminders go out to the donor.

Coordinate Your Activities With Your Business Office

No special expertise is required to administer a life insurance program, but you must coordinate closely with your business office. Paying a premium bill is no different than paying any other invoice. Following are suggested procedures that you can review with your business office.

Sample procedures for gifts of life insurance

1. Upon notification of a gift of life insurance, the director of planned giving secures the following information: Name of donor, name of insured (if different from donor), insured's date of birth, date of gift, face value of policy, type of policy, cash surrender value, timing and amount of premium payments, name and address of insurance company, account number of policy.

2. The director of planned giving secures a copy of the contract. You might get this either from the insurance company or from the donor.

3. The director of planned giving delivers the information in items 1 and 2 to the business office.

4. The business office establishes a separate account number for the insurance account. This account will be credited for gifts received and debited for premiums paid.

5. The director of planned giving communicates with the donor outlining the preferred billing/gift procedure.

6. When you receive the donor's gift, credit it according to previously agreed upon crediting guidelines. The donor's periodic premium amount is usually credited as an annual gift. The cash surrender value would also be credited as an outright gift. Some organizations distinguish between annual and capital gifts. If so, the gift of the cash surrender value is a capital gift while the premium payments are annual gifts.

7. The director of planned giving establishes appropriate reminders to secure a gift from the donor equal to the premium amount each year. This can be done easily on your computer calendar. Add a reminder for four weeks before the premium is due. Or, if you have a prospect tracking system in your organizations main computer system, put a note in the donor's comment field to trigger a reminder on the appropriate date.

8. The director of planned giving writes to the insurance company issuing instructions that future premium bills be forwarded to:

    > Name of your organization
    > c/o Director of Planned Giving
    > Street Address
    > City, State   Zip Code

    Sometimes, your business office will want to get the premium bills. That would be fine, but it presents a bit of a problem because these bills often languish in the business office. Therefore, you must coordinate closely with the person responsible for receiving the bills. Otherwise, your own letter to the donor about the gift may be delayed. You would normally send a copy of the invoice to the donor. If your business office will allow you to get the bills, you'll be better off.

9. Upon receipt of the donor's gift, your business office issues a check to the insurance company for the premium amount. When you receive the gift, photocopy the check or gift transmittal form and give it to the business office with the original invoice. In turn, the business office will pay the bill once evidence of the gift is received.

    (Note: For a while, in different organizations where I worked, the business office would pay the premium on time with the expectation that the gift would be forthcoming. It was not until I was at my fourth charity, Boston College, when I decided with the business office that we would no longer do that. Too many people simply didn't make their gifts, and after years of being hounded by the business office to get the gifts, I decided that the charity should not make the payments until the gift was in.)

10. If the donor becomes negligent with premium payments, the director of planned giving contacts the donor to determine if the oversight is intentional, and, if so, whether the donor intends to continue premium payments in the future. Should the donor decide not to continue premium payments, you and the business office will determine whether to cash out the policy, taking into account the particulars of the donor situation, the status of the policy, *etc.*

Acknowledge The Gift

Following is a sample letter you can use to acknowledge a life insurance gift:

Dear (donor):

This will acknowledge and thank you for transferring ownership to [charity] of insurance policy [account number] issued by [life insurance company], having a face value of $_____. The date of the gift is [date]. We are most grateful for the generosity and foresight of your gift.

As long as our institution has been named both beneficiary and owner and you have relinquished all incidents of ownership in the policy, you will be entitled to an income tax deduction this year as a result of transferring the policy to us. Generally, your deduction is equal to the lesser of the cost basis or the cash surrender value on the date of gift. Your insurance company can provide the exact figures for you on Form 712.

If the amount you are able to claim as an income tax deduction is greater than $5,000, you will be required to secure an independent appraisal of the property's value. This means getting an appraisal from a different life insurance company than the one that issued the policy or from an independent life insurance analyst. We will recognize the amount of the cash surrender value as a capital gift to our institution.

We are also required to inform you that no goods or services have been received in exchange for this gift.

Again, deepest thanks for your generous support of our efforts.

Sincerely,

Director of Planned Giving

LOANS

If there is an outstanding loan on the policy, the donor may also be required to report income under the bargain sale rules. (See Chapter II-2 for a more complete discussion of bargain sales.) The bargain sale rules apply when someone gives property subject to debt to a charity. Also, if there is a loan, your organization's distribution on the death of the donor will be less than the face value.

If your organization takes out a loan on the policy and uses the proceeds to reinvest, the reinvestment income will be taxed as unrelated business income since it is debt-financed income. If the proceeds are used for your charitable purposes, the loan proceeds are not unrelated business income.

GROUP TERM INSURANCE PROVIDED BY EMPLOYER

Many employers (yours, too) may provide free life insurance to their employees. This benefit produces no tax liability unless the value of the insurance is greater than $50,000. If so, the employee must report as taxable income the part of the employer's premium payment attributable to the insurance coverage exceeding $50,000. You may have noticed that little income item on your pay stub.

Just like the other types of insurance discussed earlier, group term insurance can be contributed to your organization. Unfortunately, there is no income tax deduction to the donor. But, for key executives with substantial amounts of life insurance (exceeding $50,000 face value), there is a small benefit. By naming your organization irrevocable beneficiary for an entire taxable year, the donor is relieved of the requirement to report as taxable income that excess premium amount discussed above for that year. The employee can also change the beneficiary back to an individual in which case he or she would be liable again for income taxes on the excess premium.

If the value of the annual premium is greater than $10,000, you should consult your tax counsel regarding whether gift taxes have to be paid and on what amount.

CONSIDERATIONS FOR A NEW POLICY

Two other factors come into play when donors purchase a new policy to benefit your organization.

First, depending on the donor's age and medical history, either a minimal or an extensive physical examination may be required. In most cases, the examination can be done in the privacy of the donor's home or office. It involves little more than answering questions and having blood pressure checked. On the other hand, an individual who has been refused life insurance coverage in the past because of medical problems may have difficulty getting insurance or may have to pay higher than usual rates. Even though the medical exam may involve minimal time or inconvenience, it may present an emotional barrier for the donor sufficient to discourage the establishment of a new policy. If this is the case, there are policies that require no medical exam but they are about four times more expensive than a medically underwritten policy for a preferred health nonsmoker.

Second, if you receive a new policy, you will receive from the insurance company a copy of the contract which may, but not always, include information about the donor's current financial situation. Keep this information in strictest confidence. Your financial vice president must sign the contract accepting the policy. In most organizations, such a contract would first be reviewed by the internal legal counsel.

For a new life insurance policy, check with your tax counsel to make sure there are no state laws prohibiting this kind of gift. Board members are a different story.

The donor's first premium payment to the insurance company to start the policy should be credited as an annual gift. Usually, your gift processing department needs evidence of this payment in order to add a gift to the donor's record. See if you can get a photocopy of the donor's cancelled check, and then attach the copy to the contract and process the gift. If your business office wants the original, you would need to wait until the donor's check clears and have it sent to you as evidence. That would delay the processing of this gift quite a bit. Or, you can ask the insurance company for a letter verifying that the premium was paid.

APPRAISAL GUIDELINES—THE RIDICULOUS ITEM OF THE DAY

Life insurance is noncash property. Thus, a qualified appraisal is required if the donor claims an income tax deduction for $5,000 or more. If your donor does not follow the rules, the deduction will be disallowed.

A qualified appraiser cannot be the donor or your organization, or, in most cases, the party from whom the donor acquired the property, or any person acting as agent for either party in the transaction.

Consequently, even though the donor's insurance company can easily provide the appraisal, a different insurance company must do it. Certain individuals may also be qualified to do such an appraisal, for example, an independent insurance broker or an insurance analyst. If the value being claimed by the donor is less than $5,000, no appraisal is required. However, the donor will still have to file Form 8283.

It would be so much simpler if the donor could use Form 712 from the company that issued the insurance, but the I.R.S. won't allow it.

My friend, J.J. MacNab, a co-author of *The Tools and Techniques of Charitable Planning* ©2001, as well as a leader in the gift planning industry offers a wide range of services, including appraisals of life insurance. She says, "While an independent appraisal really shouldn't be required, I provide an inexpensive valuation for those who would rather not take risks with their charitable deduction." If your donor needs an appraisal, just go to JJ and she will take care of you.

Her web site, www.deathandtaxes.com, has lots of helpful information and articles for free. She also has a complete list of the rules for insurable interests by state.

(See Chapter II-2 for a complete discussion of the substantiation requirements for noncash gifts.)

CREDITING GUIDELINES

A gift of life insurance presents interesting crediting problems. There's the face value, the cash surrender value, the premium amounts, and sometimes a separate amount that the donor can claim as an income tax deduction.

You might reason that the most equitable approach is to credit the donor with an amount equal to the income tax deduction. However, you might be cheating the donor because the cash value in the policy against which you can borrow may be greater than the amount the donor can claim as an income tax deduction. What about giving the donor credit for an annual gift of the premium even though you intend to pay that amount, in turn, to the insurance company? There is no simple answer.

At most organizations, a gift of an existing policy entitles the donor to the following gift credit:

1. Gift credit for the *cash surrender value* of a non-paid up policy.

2. Gift credit for the *cash surrender value* of a fully-paid up policy.

3. Gift credit for the amount of *premiums* paid directly to the charity.

4. Gift credit for *premiums* paid directly to the insurance company if the donor sends evidence of his payment (copy of canceled check).

5. No credit unless the gift is irrevocable.

6. Some organizations in a campaign are crediting the face value of life insurance gifts for donors over a certain age. There is more on this crediting issue in Chapter III-5 on Integrating Planned Giving into a Campaign.

Depending on the amount of recognition and personal attention you provide for your life insurance donors, the amount of gift credit may seem unimportant to the donor.

CREATIVE IDEAS ON MAKING THE MOST OF LIFE INSURANCE IN YOUR PLANNED GIVING PROGRAM

Life insurance is one of many assets that can plan an important role in the right situation. You should be able to recognize a situation in which either a gift of life insurance or a gift plan involving life insurance may be just the right thing. Following are some creative ideas on making the most of life insurance in your planned giving program:

- *Insurance gifts from employees of life insurance companies:* Many insurance companies operate matching gift programs in which premiums paid on charitable life insurance are eligible for matching gifts. Therefore, you can do the following to tap a target market:

    1. Identify the list of insurance companies that match gifts to your institution. The head of your annual giving department should have the most current directory of matching gift companies;

    2. Identify current donors who work for these companies by ordering a report from your main computer;

    3. Suggest that the employee use their annual gifts to purchase a new life insurance policy benefiting your institution;

    4. The employee pays the premium each year;

    5. The company sends you a matching gift.

Result: The donor creates a gift many times larger than would otherwise be the case without changing the amount of his or her annual gift. Your institution continues to get an annual gift in the form of matching funds from the insurance company.

- *Trading in paid-up policies for new ones with larger death benefits:* When you are named owner and beneficiary of a paid-up policy, take the policy to a life insurance agent for review. You may be able to cash in the policy and purchase a new one with a larger face value. This is possible because insurance products have been improved over what was available when your donor bought the policy. Check this out in your spare time.

- *Life insurance as a replacement asset:* When a donor rejects a life income proposal because of the loss of assets that would have been given to potential heirs, suggest to the donor that he or she purchase a new life insurance policy payable to the heirs using all or part of the increased annual income payment from the life income plan.

    Result:

    1. Donor makes a major gift to a life income plan (pooled income fund, charitable gift annuity, or to a charitable remainder trust).

    2. Donor avoids an immediate capital gain tax on the transfer of appreciated long-term property.

    3. Donor receives an income tax deduction for part of the gift based on appropriate I.R.S. tables.

    4. Donor receives a new annual income that may be greater than the income earned on the assets before the gift.

    5. Donor uses some or all of the annual income to make a gift to the children or to a trust. The children or the trust purchase a new life insurance policy with a face value equal to the value of the gift.

    6. The heirs or the trust are owners and beneficiary(ies) of the life insurance proceeds.

    7. When donor dies, the principal represented by the gift is available to your institution. The heirs receive the life insurance proceeds.

    8. If the heirs or trust have all incidents of ownership in the policy, the proceeds from the life insurance will not be taxable to the estate. The property originally intended for the heirs may have been taxable to the estate. Thus, estate taxes are saved.

    9. Everyone benefits.

Note: There is a comprehensive example of this technique later in this chapter.

- *Perpetuation of Gift:* All nonprofit organizations have annual donors. When an annual donor dies, the annual gift stops. The donor can set up a life insurance policy with a face amount from which the interest on the principal can perpetuate the annual gift.

- *Endowing or Perpetuating Lead Trust Income*: The eventual problem with a lead trust (Chapter II-11) is that the income stops at some future date. You can ask the donor's approval to use some of the lead trust income to purchase a life insurance policy that will eventually perpetuate the lead trust income.

- *Provide Cash to the Estate*: By transferring assets to a charitable remainder trust (Chapter II-9), the donor receives an income tax deduction for part of the gift and a new income, too. The tax deduction frees up dollars that would have been used to pay income taxes. Instead, use the tax savings to purchase life insurance to assist the estate with cash needs, to redeem assets, or to loan money to the estate.

HOW TO GET INFORMATION ABOUT LIFE INSURANCE PRODUCTS

One way to learn about life insurance is to look in the Yellow Pages section of your local phone book for a life insurance agent in your area. It may be better to talk to an independent agent rather than an insurance company, because the independent agent will have access to life insurance products offered by many different companies. This broader access can be helpful when a donor interested in establishing a new policy has a preference for a particular company. During your search, look for an agent who is knowledgeable about charitable gifts of life insurance. Many are not.

Life insurance agents usually have one or more of the following designations:

CLU:	Chartered Life Underwriter
ChFC:	Chartered Financial Consultant
CFP:	Certified Financial Planner
LUTCF:	Life Underwriter Training Council Fellow
FFSI:	Fellow, Financial Services Institute

Also, there is a local Association of Life Underwriters in most cities which can help with referrals to life insurance agents who are both knowledgeable and well respected by their peers. The National Association of Life Underwriters can provide a list of local offices. If you are a member of a local planned giving council, you may already know one or more life insurance agents who affiliate with your local council. (Note: Since people in the financial services area can also sell insurance, you aren't necessarily limited to life insurance agents.)

Once you identify an agent with whom you can consult or work, ask for comparison figures for life insurance using several variables. Remember, you cannot sell life insurance and you should not be showing donors the financial analysis sheets provided by life insurance agents. This activity is reserved for licensed agents and these agents will get very nervous if you suggest showing their illustrations to donors. However, you can have at your fingertips a general estimate of how much life insurance costs depending on the age, face value, and type of policy.

When you have a prospect considering a new policy, either to benefit your organization directly or to combine with a life income plan for wealth replacement, the problem is getting a current quote so that you can prepare a proposal.

If you can get someone to do it for you, develop a chart for a few ages like 40, 50, 60, and 70 (separate tables for male and female) for policies having a face value of $100,000, $250,000, $500,000, and $1,000,000. You may also wish to examine policies having vanishing premiums (the premiums stop after a predetermined number of years). The following chart will give you an idea about the cost of purchasing various size policies. It was provided by William J. Sullivan, William J. Sullivan Insurance in Milton, Massachusetts (617-698-3838, www.wjsullivaninsurance.com). Bill wanted to make sure that I told the reader that there are many kinds of policies suited to different needs. The following charts give you an idea of what a male or female could buy based on certain assumptions at the time he did these illustrations in July 2003. For a real example, you should get new quotes of your own.

DEATH BENEFIT - Male Preferred Nonsmoker
Annual Premiums*

Ages	$100,000	$250,000	$500,000	$1,000,000
40	$2,035	$4,867	$9,205	$18,410
50	2,808	6,569	13,138	26,275
60	4,050	9,505	19,010	37,512
70	5,677	13,495	26,785	52,964

DEATH BENEFIT - Female Preferred Nonsmoker
Annual Premiums*

Ages	$100,000	$250,000	$500,000	$1,000,000
40	$1,732	$3,771	$7,315	$14,197
50	2,363	5,342	10,450	20,320
60	3,326	7,549	14,858	28,795
70	4,592	10,396	20,541	39,836

Premiums illustrated are from Transamerica Occidental Life Insurance Company. The policy presented is Universal Life with 4.75% interest rate assumptions with the expectation that premiums will end in 10 years, prepared in July 2003.

It is important to realize that the performance of any life insurance policy is based on the interest rates, dividend rates, and mortality rates actually experienced by the company. Often, insurance agents show examples with much more optimistic projections than would be realistic. This could lead to disaster. Many charities have insurance policies that donors purchased in the 1980s under the premise that premiums were supposed to stop after a fixed number of years. Instead, after paying the premium for the agreed upon time frame, the donor was told that interest rates did not hold up and, therefore, the donor would need to continue paying premiums. These situations existed widely and were very difficult for both the donors and the charities.

In selecting a company, the underlying investments and management of the company are important. Several rating services assist individuals in evaluating life insurance companies. Each has its own rating system. Three of them are listed below. Depending on the service, you might have to register online in order to do a search.

A.M. Best
A.M.Best Worldwide Headquarters
Ambest Road
Oldwick, New Jersey
United States
(908) 439-2200
www.ambest.com

Standard & Poors
55 Water Street
New York, NY 10041, USA
Ratings Information Services:
(212) 438-2400

ratings_request@standardandpoors.com
www.standardpoor.com
(Get up to five ratings per call or up to 10 per e-mail)

Moody's
Managing Director
North America
(212) 553-7118
(212) 553-3822 (Fax)
www.moodysinvestors.com.au/default.asp

LIFE INSURANCE AS WEALTH REPLACEMENT

Now, let's take an example of a charitable remainder trust with life insurance as wealth replacement. This could work equally well with a pooled income fund or a charitable gift annuity.

Example:

A couple, male 70, female 70, with $500,000 of appreciated securities having a cost basis of $100,000 and yielding 2.5% wants to make a gift to your organization. They have held the shares for more than one year. Their main objection to giving away assets is that they had intended to leave an inheritance to their son. They are in the 35% income tax bracket and 15% capital gain tax bracket. I assumed a 6% discount rate.

The couple transfers the securities to a 5% charitable remainder unitrust with quarterly payments. (See Chapter II-9 for a complete discussion of CRTs.) The CRT sells the shares and is able to reinvest the full proceeds unreduced by capital gain taxes ($400,000 x 15% = $60,000 capital gain tax if sold by the couple). The CRT pays an annual amount of $25,000 to start, double what they were receiving from the stock. If the trust grows over the years from prudent investments and a good economy, the payment will increase. (The reverse can also happen.)

They can use a portion of the new income, to purchase a life insurance policy benefiting the son. This couple—non smokers, and presumed to be of normal health for their ages—would pay a premium of about $13,000 *per* year to purchase $500,000 of survivorship life insurance. The insurance premium uses up a good portion of their unitrust payment, but they still have some left for themselves.

The couple is entitled to an income tax deduction of $212,600 saving $74,410 in their 35% bracket ($212,600 x 35% = $74,410). The deduction can be used up to 30% of the couple's adjusted gross income in the year of the gift with a five-year carry-over period for any excess.

Take a look at the illustrations on the next two pages.

Exhibit II-5A: Summary of Benefits

The Summary of Benefits is the simplest chart I can produce with my software. I assumed 3% income and 3% capital appreciation for the trust. Not shown in the "Assumptions" are management fees of .72% of principal with a $500 base fee.

Exhibit II-5B: Wealth Replacement Analysis

The Wealth Replacement Analysis shows the after-tax beneficiary income projected each year taking into account the four-tier system and the donors' income and capital gain tax brackets, the insurance premium amount, and what is left over to spend. The after-tax income will vary in a real case since the four-tier system will play out differently depending on the actual performance of the CRT.

Exhibit II-5A

ASHTON ASSOCIATES

Prepared for:
Male 70, Female 70

Life Income Projections
Summary of Benefits

ASSUMPTIONS:
Projection begins in 2003 and runs for 20 years.
Measuring lives age 70, 70.
Original principal is $500,000. Cost basis is 20%.
Donor income tax bracket is 35%, 15% for capital gains.
Beneficiary income tax bracket is 35% (phase in rate reductions), 15% for capital gains.

	Charitable Unitrust 5%
Gross Principal	$500,000
Charitable Deduction	$212,600
Tax Savings	$74,410
Cost of Gift	$425,590
Income	3%
Capital Appreciation	3%
Sell Asset in First Year	Yes
Total Management Fees	$85,293
Life Insurance Premiums	$273,000
Total Income to Spend	$118,807
Life Insurance Benefit	$500,000
Benefit to CHARITY	**$516,235**
Total Benefit	**$1,135,042**

IRS Discount Rate is 6%

Exhibit II-5B

ASHTON ASSOCIATES

Prepared for:
Male 70, Female 70

Life Income Projections
Wealth Replacement Analysis

ASSUMPTIONS:
Projection begins in 2003 and runs for 20 years.
Measuring lives age 70, 70.
Original principal is $500,000. Cost basis is 20%.
Donor income tax bracket is 35%, 15% for capital gains.
Beneficiary income tax bracket is 35%, 15% for capital gains.
Life insurance policy with $500,000 death benefit.
Insurance premiums paid from beneficiary income.

5% Charitable Unitrust

YR	After-Tax Ben. Inc.	Insurance Premium	Income to Spend
2003		$13,000	$-13,000
2004	$19,200	13,000	6,200
2005	19,230	13,000	6,230
2006	19,368	13,000	6,368
2007	19,399	13,000	6,399
2008	19,430	13,000	6,430
2009	19,460	13,000	6,460
2010	19,491	13,000	6,491
2011	19,522	13,000	6,522
2012	19,553	13,000	6,553
2013	19,584	13,000	6,584
2014	19,615	13,000	6,615
2015	19,647	13,000	6,647
2016	19,678	13,000	6,678
2017	19,709	13,000	6,709
2018	19,741	13,000	6,741
2019	19,772	13,000	6,772
2020	19,804	13,000	6,804
2021	19,836	13,000	6,836
2022	19,868	13,000	6,868
2023	19,899	13,000	6,899
TOT	**$391,807**	**$273,000**	**$118,807**

IRS Discount Rate is 6%

Bottom line: On the death of the last survivor, the CRT assets distribute to the charity and the life insurance proceeds distribute to the son free of estate tax. In the example, the life insurance premium must be paid until the death of both husband and wife who have a life expectancy of 20 years. Individual results will vary.

There are two ways to accomplish the life insurance component:

Option #1: Direct Gift to Beneficiary(ies)

The couple makes an annual tax-free gift of $13,000 to the son who, in turn, purchases the life insurance policy on the life of his parents. There is no gift tax because the couple can give up to $22,000 to a single individual under their combined annual gift tax exclusion. As long as the son is both owner and beneficiary and has all incidents of ownership of the policy, the proceeds will be 100% free of estate tax to the son. Important: The parents would need to trust the son to follow through with the purchase of the insurance and not run off to the Bahamas.

Option #2: Irrevocable Life Insurance Trust

The donors set up a life insurance trust with the son as beneficiary. Each year, the donors transfer $13,000 to the trustee of the trust. The trustee notifies the son, and offers him a reasonable period of time, say 45 days, to withdraw the money. That right to withdraw makes the gift a "present interest" to which the $11,000 annual gift tax exclusion applies. If the son does not withdraw the money (an important matter!), the trustee can use the gift to buy survivorship life insurance on the lives of the donors. When both donors have died, the life insurance company pays the insurance proceeds to the trust. Then, the trust's assets are distributed to the son according to the terms of the trust.

The power of the beneficiary to withdraw the money for a short period of time is called a Crummey Power, named after Clifford Crummey, whom I met when I worked for Boston University. Rev. Crummey was a graduate of the BU School of Theology. When I first met him, I commented that his name was famous in tax circles due to a planning technique called a Crummey Power. He took out of his briefcase a reprint of the I.R.S. case and said, "That was me." He has since died, but he was very proud of the fact his name became part of I.R.S. law.

For the insurance to be excluded from the taxable estate, the donors must give up all ownership and control over the trust and the insurance in the trust. They can write whatever provisions they want in the trust, but as soon as they sign it, the trust becomes irrevocable. Donors can contribute existing life insurance policies to a wealth replacement trust, but the famous "3-year rule" of Section 2035 says that if they die within three years, the insurance will be subject to estate tax anyway. If the trustee makes the decision to buy new insurance, the proceeds should be estate tax free from day one.

Note: If the provisions of The Economic Growth and Tax Relief Reconciliation Act of 2001 remain unchanged, there will be no estate tax in 2010, but it comes back in 2011. There will still be a gift tax for lifetime taxable transfers over $1,000,000, with or without the repeal of the estate tax. Therefore, arranging the annual gifts to the children or grandchildren will still require planning so as to utilize the annual gift tax exemption.

Pitfalls To The Wealth Replacement Scenario

- When both a husband and wife are alive, they can use both annual gift tax exclusions (currently $11,000 *per* person, indexed for inflation) to make tax-free gifts to either the intended heir of the life insurance or to the irrevocable life insurance trust (ILIT). So, if there are three beneficiaries of the ILIT, they can give 2 x $11,000 x 3 = $66,000. Let's say they bought a very large life insurance policy with a premium of $66,000 per year. When one of the couple dies, the surviving spouse can no longer make tax-free gifts of $66,000 per year. The surviving spouse can make only $33,000 in tax-free annual exclusion gifts per year. Therefore, the surviving spouse must use up part of his or her lifetime exemption in order to keep the premiums up to date.

- Although the donor's annual gift tax exclusion is $11,000, when the beneficiary of the trust chooses not to withdraw the money, the beneficiary may be "deemed" to have made a taxable gift, to the extent the withdrawal right exceeded the greater of $5,000 or 5% of the trust property [Section 2041(b)(2)]. So, if a husband and wife create a trust and contribute $22,000 for the benefit of their son, they won't have made a taxable gift, but the son may have made a taxable gift of $17,000 ($22,000 minus $5,000). There are several ways for a lawyer to "draft around" the "5 & 5" problem, but planned giving advisors need to be aware that whenever the annual gift to the trust will exceed $5,000 *per* beneficiary, extra care should be taken to find an attorney intimately familiar with the rules. Although extra care is especially important in planning a wealth replacement trust, the tax benefits are so substantial that it is well worth the effort to make sure it is done right.

Generally, this area of law is not something planned giving officers come across often, and is way beyond the scope of this book. If you start down the wealth replacement road with a donor, get an attorney involved immediately and get a competent life insurance agent.

I am grateful to Mark Moritz, an estate planning attorney experienced with planned giving, for help with this discussion of Crummey Powers. Mark is with Custom Estate Planning, PLLC, in Scottsdale, Arizona.

A WORD ABOUT LIFE INSURANCE AGENTS

Life insurance agents have a pretty bad reputation because they can be awfully pushy and some want to sell the insurance even if the client clearly doesn't need it. I had an agent pursuing me at one point to sell me insurance. I said I didn't need it because I am not married and have no children. He said that I could leverage my estate through life insurance to benefit my heirs and also to pay off my mortgage. I asked him why would I care about paying off my mortgage if I died. He kept me on the phone way past the point when I had indicated I was not interested. I can only imagine this salesman in the home of one of my donors. Sheesh!

As Director of Planned Giving, you will be called periodically by life insurance agents who wish to affiliate themselves with your organization as the primary agent with whom you do business. You want to be careful hooking up with any particular person. I would suggest that you identify two to three people with whom you would feel comfortable working. Even if you were to affiliate with a particular agent, the instances in which you would need a life insurance agent in the course of your work would be only a couple of times a year. Under no circumstances should you give your prospect or donor names to a life insurance agent no matter how much future endowment he or she claims to be able to bring you. Life insurance agents make their money only when they make a sale. Even if that sale results in a gift benefiting your organization, there will be no winners if the donor is pressured into a commitment that is inappropriate, badly timed, or otherwise ill-advised.

On the other hand, there are some really good people in the life insurance business who have made a point of educating themselves about development, fund raising, and planned giving, and who are providing a tremendous service to organizations who simply do not have the staff in-house to go it alone.

If you agree to meet with life insurance agents who contact you for informational interviews, listen to what they have to say, and see if you find any with whom you would feel comfortable working. Because I received so many requests from life insurance agents for meetings, I instituted a policy that I would meet only with people who were alumni of my institution or who were already donors. There is no reason to meet with the others. There are simply too many of them.

Sometimes you need a life insurance quote to prepare a proposal. I had built a great relationship with one of our alumni at Boston College. He was a major contributor as well as serving on our campaign committee. Whenever I needed a quick quote for a wealth replacement proposal, he would fax it to me the same day. No obligation and no hassles. It was great working with him. We had no formal arrangement. He was a volunteer whom I trusted completely.

You can also get life insurance quotes from the Internet. On a Saturday afternoon in July of 2003, I did a test with a web site that I found by doing a search on Yahoo with key words "life insurance quotes." Here are the results:

www.termlife4U.com

Criteria: #1) $500,000 face value, male, nonsmoker, born 1/20/1929, whole life, lifetime payments
        #2) $500,000 face value, survivorship policy, male 72, female 68, nonsmokers, whole life, lifetime payments

I received an e-mail Monday morning from Richard Storms, an independent agent in Pennsylvania (Toll-free 877-365-5433) with the quotes I requested. I called the toll-free number and he answered his own phone for which he gets big points. We talked for about 20 minutes about his quotes and the process for buying life insurance.

For the $500,000 policy, male, nonsmoker, born 1/20/1929, the annual premium for whole life was $52,215 using Columbus Life Insurance Company, Rated A++. Ouch!

For the $500,000 survivorship policy, male 72/female 68, non-smokers, I was quoted a minimum premium of $7,532.76 and a target premium of $12,355, current interest rate of 5.9%, and minimum interest rate guarantee of 4%. He quoted universal life instead of whole life which he explained in our conversation.

"Life insurance products vary widely. It is superficial and inappropriate to make a decision based on a simplistic inquiry on the internet, which is why I would have called you this afternoon to discuss this further, if you hadn't called me first. People think that getting the lowest premium is the goal, but that is not true. Some companies will quote a lower premium, but what you don't realize is that the policy may not perform the way you expect. When family security is at stake, paying a little more gives you a safety net that protects you when the markets under perform. Life insurance agents are not always trying to cheat the customer when they recommend paying a little more."

I asked Rick why he switched my survivorship quote to universal life instead of using whole life and reminded him of the 1980s when companies used double digit performance assumptions for universal life, quoting a particular premium and a particular expected performance. Ten years later, the policies looked nothing like what the customers purchased. Vanishing premiums did not vanish. Cash values did not hold up. Lots of people were very unhappy.

Rick said, "Agents in the 1980s were dealing with a new product and they had no track record to look back on. They overestimated the internal rate of return and it took a period of years for reality to set in. The universal life I've quoted you today has a 3.8% guaranteed rate of return and a projection of 6%. These rates are much more realistic. However, if we can do better than the projected 6%, the client will benefit." He says that he used universal life because it was less expense than the whole life product, and because of the long time-frame for the two-life scenario.

He was in Pennsylvania and I was in Boston. I wondered how he would handle a real case so far away. "Well, depending on the circumstances, I might drive to Boston to meet with you. I could visit other clients at the same time. Or, I might refer you to a colleague in your area. Usually, we have a list of people we trust and make referrals back and forth when it is impractical to visit the prospect ourselves."

Rick's choice for a life insurance company was Columbus Life Insurance Company which was rated A++ (superior). Would he ever recommend a company that was not in the highest ranking? "Yes, I would, and it has to do with the different products available. The thing you need to keep in mind is that the difference between A++ and A+ is not something you worry about."

Finally, I asked why he quoted a minimum ($7,532.76) and a target ($12,355) premium for my survivorship scenario. "You see, the $500,000 face value could be purchased for the lower amount, but the time frame is pretty long. Therefore, the lower figure has more risk. Things might change and the policy might not be able to sustain that premium level, let's say, ten years from now. On the other hand, if you go with the target amount, a few thousand dollars higher, you'll have a much more secure product, there shouldn't be any surprises, and you have peace of mind."

For my first experience using the internet to find a quote and a life insurance salesman, I was extremely pleased with the process and with the professionalism and helpfulness of Mr. Richard Storms.

CHARITABLE REVERSE SPLIT DOLLAR

In the late 1990s, there was wave of activity in what is called the charitable reverse split dollar life insurance plan. There are many variations on the plan but the basic operation is as follows:

Donor purchases a life insurance policy, generally for a large amount, $1 million to $4 million. This might be done by using a closely-held corporation that agrees to pay a portion of the premiums in return for a share of the death benefit pursuant to a split-dollar agreement. Then, at some point, the donor approaches a charity with the plan of assigning the split-dollar agreement to the charity so that it is entitled to a portion of the death benefits but must also pay a portion of the premiums. The donor promises to make annual gifts to the charity, for which the donor presumably will claim an income tax deduction. In turn, the charity will make premium payments to keep its share of the insurance in force. On the death of the insured, the charity receives a share of the proceeds that at least will equal the amount of premiums paid, but generally much less proportionately than it should have received based on its share of the payments. The rest of the proceeds go to the donor's heirs.

At Boston College, I was approached with a fairly straight forward proposal. The donor was going to purchase a life insurance policy with a death benefit of about $4 million. The premiums would be approximately $200,000 *per* year for a period of years. The donor would make annual gifts to Boston College and we would pay all of the premiums (the donor's share was zero). The gift would be made with appreciated long-term securities and the donor would avoid all capital gain on the gift. The donor would claim an income tax deduction for the annual gifts up to his 30% contribution ceiling. On the death of the donor, his heirs would receive $3 million and Boston College would get $1 million. What's wrong with this picture?

A financial planner who voiced his opinion to me about this technique said, "What is your problem? If the charity gets more than it had before, what reason could you have for not wanting to do it?"

The I.R.S. found a lot wrong with this picture and has killed this plan for any participation after February 8, 1999. The donor can no longer claim a deduction for gifts made toward what the I.R.S. calls a "personal benefit contract." A reporting form was created, Form 8870, Information Return for Transfers Associated with Certain Personal Benefit Contracts, the latest version of which is dated September 2000.

Basically, there is no charitable deduction to the donor for gifts made to the charity for such a plan. Further, there is no gift tax deduction to the donor for contributing a partial interest in the policy to the charity. If the charity participates, it will be penalized with a fine of 100% of the amounts paid toward such a plan. In addition, the charity must file Form 8870 disclosing the amount of the premiums paid and the names and tax identification numbers of all beneficiaries.

Erik Dryburgh, who runs a practice in San Francisco, California (415-421-7555 Dryburgh@SilkLaw.com) that specializes in charitable giving had this to say about these plans, "If a planned giving officer is approached for one of these plans, he should decline immediately (frankly, he should run like Hell) and consider contacting the local planned giving council so it can alert other local charities. And, if the charity is currently participating in one of these plans, it would be best to contact competent legal counsel for advice on how to extricate his charity and comply with the new reporting requirements."

SUMMARY

Life insurance is the kind of asset that most everyone owns and which can be contributed very easily. Consider it like a bequest, only better if your charity is the new owner. At the very least, you should be encouraging your donors to contribute obsolete policies as a way of supporting your good work. Or, getting your charity named as beneficiary or even contingent beneficiary is a good start. Further, if you can show the donor how to use life insurance to replace another asset given to you, you have facilitated a major gift while preserving the benefit to the donor's heirs.

The subject of the next chapter—real estate—is quite a different story. Real estate probably demands more attention than any other form of gift and probably brings with it the biggest risk. As with anything else, however, when the risks are great, so too are the potential rewards.

Chapter II-6

GIFTS OF REAL ESTATE

INTRODUCTION

Real estate may be one of the most underutilized forms of charitable gift property. In many parts of the country, real estate values have increased many times faster than the rate of inflation and offer both donors and charities magnificent opportunities for mutually beneficial gift arrangements. Even in areas of the country where the real estate market is depressed, real estate values still may be appreciated above their cost basis, especially for the older donors most likely to be participating in planned giving. Positioning yourself to be able to handle such gifts is possible and, with the help of this chapter, you'll be able to evaluate situations, make good decisions, and protect yourself and your institution from unnecessary liability.

If you do not own a house yet, the thought of managing a gift of real property from start to finish may be very intimidating because you haven't gone through the process of taking title to a property on your own. I felt the same way for the first 10 years of my planned giving career. Then, I, too, bought a house, learned a wealth of information in the process, and I felt much more comfortable after that. If you are a beginner, remember that you have an attorney to help you through every step of the process. If you don't have an attorney who represents your planned giving program, turn to Chapter I-6. You must get an attorney before you start down the road with the prospect, especially one who might contribute real estate.

Depending on the nature of your organization, your geographic location, the type of constituency, and the sophistication of your business office, you may already have experience with real estate gifts. If so, you know that accepting and disposing of real estate is costly and time consuming. Add to these considerations the fact that many of the real estate gifts that come across your desk will never materialize.

When I was working for WGBH, a man called to offer us a fully-occupied apartment building. The property was in Boston within a twenty-minute drive from my office. That afternoon, two of us set out in my car to scout out the property. We found a rather shabby looking, poorly maintained brick building in a deteriorating neighborhood. There were broken windows, the front door showed signs of forced entry, and, had we not known it was fully occupied, we probably would have assumed it had been condemned.

After returning to the office, I called our tax counsel to explain the situation and to ask for advice. He instructed me to get a copy of the income and expense statement for the property. We discovered then why the donor was so anxious to unload the property. The costs of maintaining it exceeded the rental income, and there was also one major problem he neglected to mention—the property was under rent control. Thus, neither he nor any other owner could raise the rents to turn it into a profitable entity. He was losing money every day he continued to own it. I told him we could not accept it. "Well, I've already offered the property to three other nonprofit organizations before coming to WGBH." He said, "I tried for the longest time to sell it without success, so I thought I would give it away."

There have been many disappointing situations since then in my planned giving career. Still, it is hard not to get excited whenever there is a possibility of a real estate gift. As fund raisers, we want to get the gift more than anything. Each of us has heard about success stories at other institutions, and it is our nature to assume that our big gift is just around the corner. This is not always the case. In fact, relatively few potential situations will turn into a gift, unless, of course, you are an organization like the Nature Conservancy. The rest of us will get two to three situations a year, and, after spending enormous amounts of time evaluating these properties, we will book only a scant few.

Nonetheless, many organizations are placing increasing emphasis on soliciting real estate gifts, and you, too, should develop a good working knowledge of the subject.

Real estate is versatile. A donor can contribute real estate in many different ways. The easiest way is the straight outright gift. Or, a donor can transfer it in a bargain sale. He or she can also use it to fund a deferred gift annuity (unless local laws prohibit this use), or to fund a flip unitrust. Finally, a donor can transfer the deed for a personal residence or farm to a charity and continue to live on the property for life while receiving a current tax deduction for the discounted remainder value.

This chapter covers a wide range of topics related to gifts of real estate. To start, let's review some considerations for examining the property.

EXAMINING THE PROPERTY

Before you even begin to consider the form a real estate gift might take, the most important thing you can do is learn about the property. At the end of this chapter is a Real Estate Checklist which was developed by Charles A. Sterling, Senior Real Estate Officer at State Street Global Advisors in Boston. A former version of the checklist was in my Revised Second Edition. Charles has updated the form, adding a lot more detail since 1991. The interview I had with him for the last edition is still relevant.

"Generally, the planned giving officer will be the first person to talk to the donor about a property. This is when the charity needs a preliminary overview of the property and when red flags might go up. If you can get the donor to complete the checklist and sign it, you are able to put the burden of disclosure on the donor. Since there are so many details, it would be almost impossible for you to get the necessary information in a free-form conversation. In reviewing the completed form, you need not be alarmed if the donor answers 'yes' to some of the questions. Many problems are easily taken care of and would not be a reason to kill the gift. Most important, the checklist allows the charity and the donor to really focus on the property and to identify very early precisely those things that need further attention—things that affect marketability of the property.

Donor relations can also be preserved more easily if you require full disclosure up front. The information given by the donor on this checklist protects the charity against all kinds of unforeseen difficulties that the donor may have omitted."

Mr. Sterling also suggests getting the donor to agree, in writing, to pay the charity's costs of holding the property prior to its sale. This might include such things as insurance, taxes, maintenance, groundskeepers, utilities, or other anticipated expenses. At the end of the chapter, there is a great sample letter written by Mr. Sterling for outlining the expectations on both the donor's part and the manager's part so that there are no surprises. There will be some negotiating here. And, of course, you'll encounter the donor who does not want to do this. At that point, your organization will need to consider whether the net proceeds (after all expenses, fees, and commissions) eventually will be sufficient to justify your time and money. The answer very well may be yes. At the very least, you must be as informed as possible about what you are committing to.

Since it may not initially be obvious to you why you need so much information about real estate, here are some reasons and some ramifications:

General description. Is the property a personal residence, vacant lot, commercial building, timberland, farm, etc.? Depending on its nature, it will lend itself to different possibilities in charitable giving.

Ownership. Who is the owner? Your prospect may not be the sole owner. Often, property is held jointly with a spouse, with a sister, brother, or other family member, or with a business associate. The property may be held by a corporation, partnership, or a trust. Ownership laws vary from state to state. Therefore, you must verify early in the negotiations exactly who owns the property. Depending on the type of gift suggested, one co-owner might be advised to give his or her interest to the other co-owner before the gift. For example, when a husband and wife own property jointly and intend to exchange it for a gift annuity benefiting only the husband, it may be advisable to have the wife give her share to the husband before the gift. Otherwise, the gift will be subject to immediate capital gain tax liability. (At the end of Chapter II-8, there is a section that covers the implications of ownership for gift annuities.)

Date of acquisition. This is necessary to determine whether the property is a long- or short-term capital asset. Also, if there is a mortgage on the property, the length of time it has been in the hands of the donor affects whether or not your institution may be subject to unrelated business income tax. For example, the mortgage on donated property is treated as acquisition indebtedness and may subject you to unrelated business income tax unless the mortgage is more than five years old at the time of gift *and* the donor owned the property for more than five years before the gift.

Cost basis. This is necessary to determine the amount of appreciation on the property for any capital gain considerations. Or, when the real estate is held by the donor for sale in his or her trade or business (such as land held for sale by a real estate developer to customers), the income tax deduction for contributing the property is limited to the adjusted cost basis as a gift of inventory.

Most recent appraisal. If the property has been appraised recently, get a copy of the appraisal.

Value of land *vs.* value of building(s). This information is necessary if you intend to propose a gift of a personal residence or farm with a retained life tenancy. The calculation used to determine the value of the donor's income tax deduction requires both values.

Mortgage. If there is a mortgage on the property, the donor may incur some tax liability on the transfer under the bargain sale rules. (See Chapter II-2 for a discussion of bargain sales.) Also, the value of the gift to your organization may be greatly reduced when you take into account the net value after subtracting the amount of the remaining mortgage—so much so that the time and expense in handling the gift are prohibitive. In addition, a mortgage may hinder the use of the property in a charitable remainder trust due to adverse consequences of the debt.

Term of remaining mortgage. If you decide to accept the gift, you need to know the extent of your commitment. Also, if the term of the mortgage is almost over, you might consider delaying the transaction to eliminate some of the complications presented by the mortgage. Or, perhaps the donor could pay off the remaining mortgage.

Is the mortgage assumable? Some lenders allow a new owner to take over the mortgage payments under the same terms. Others require full payment of the remaining balance before transferring title.

Form of acquisition. Depending on how the donor acquired the property, it may be difficult to track down the deed, get a clear title to the property, or determine whether there are any restrictions on the use of the property that would complicate a sale. Also, depending on the way the donor acquired the property, a combination of different tax laws and other regulations will come into play with regard to the donor's income tax deduction and capital gain liability.

Property tax assessment/Annual property taxes. Unless you have convinced the donor to make gifts to your organization to cover the real estate taxes, you could be responsible for thousands of dollars in taxes while you are trying to sell the property. Generally, unless the property will be put to a use related to your organization's tax exempt purposes, the property will be subject to real estate taxes. Even if the property will be put to a use related to your charity's exempt purpose, the property may still be subject to real estate taxes.

Zoning. Understanding how the property is zoned in relation to its location can give you a clue (along with many of the other facts discussed here) about the ease with which you can sell the property either now or in the future or whether you can expect appreciation or depreciation. The property may be zoned as residential, commercial, industrial, agricultural, business, planned residential development, cemetery, automobile parking, or recreational just to name a few. Many categories are further subdivided into related but distinct uses. For example, the residential zoning category may be subdivided into one-family dwelling units, two-family dwelling units, multi-family dwelling units, *etc.*

Is the property subject to depreciation recapture? If so, the value of the donor's income tax deduction must be reduced by the amount of income that would have been "recaptured" if he sold the property. Being subject to depreciation recapture will not necessarily deter the donor from making the gift, but he or she will need to review with an advisor how the transaction will impact his or her tax situation. (For more about depreciation recapture, see Chapter II-2.)

Restrictions, easements, liens, or other encumbrances. Making an informed decision about whether to accept the property depends on knowing whether restrictions apply either as part of the deed (a restriction that prevents the property from being subdivided), or whether there are easements (owners of the adjacent property use your donor's driveway to reach their own parking lot), or whether there are liens (the property was used as collateral on a loan, business venture, or other activity).

Toxic waste or code violations. Do not assume that the property is free of serious problems such as toxic waste or chemicals in the soil, lead paint, asbestos, or that it is free from other violations that may hinder your ability to dispose of it. In the Midwest, for example, there are loads of buried gasoline tanks on small farms. There are specialists who can assist in analyzing the property for any legal and life safety violations.

Tenants. For rental properties, you need to know if income from rent and leases can be expected for the period during which you'll be putting it on the market. In addition, becoming a landlord is a serious consideration for your business office.

Some activities associated with real estate can be quite costly and time consuming. Though it would be ideal if you and I didn't have to concern ourselves with them, the reality is that we must. The following is by no means an exhaustive list, but it includes a few items that will prepare you to handle real estate gifts and to identify problems that could create liability and cost to your organization.

Environmental Testing

The purpose of environmental testing is to determine the presence of toxic waste or hazardous materials. Such things may not be obvious—even to the current owner. Since environmental laws are extremely strict and since any person or entity in the chain of title is subject to them, your diligence in this area is important. This is true even when you are able to accept a gift and sell it 30 seconds later to a buyer whom you have lined up in advance. If your organization is linked in the chain of title, if only for a few seconds, you may become liable for any problems that develop. That's a real problem because the litigators will come after the entity with the deepest pockets—often the charity.

Ordinarily, a red flag should go up when you are dealing with any property that has been used for a purpose that involves toxic liquids or other hazardous substances. This includes such things as gas stations, industrial plants, furniture refinishing, dry cleaning, *etc.* The same red flag should also go up if your gift property borders other properties on which toxic materials are currently being used or have been used. Contaminants may have spread under the ground from a neighboring property onto yours. Such leakage cannot be seen.

To uncover toxic substances, one of two tests is available. Whether you are willing to pay for these tests can be determined only by the individual circumstances. It would be best if the donor picked up these costs. However, this would not be possible for property received through a bequest.

Phase I Audit

A Phase I Audit has three components:

1. **Site Reconnaissance.** This involves someone physically walking the property to identify abutters and to look for visible signs of waste. This might take the form of obvious oil or other substances, gassy material floating on standing water, or indications of digging or disturbance of the vegetation that might indicate "midnight dumping."

---

2. **Town Record Inspection.** This is to uncover events of leaking tanks, accidents, or odor violations that have been recorded on or near the property. For example, let's say an oil truck spilled its tank in the road next to your site 10 years ago. There would be no visible signs currently, yet there would be a record of this incident.

3. **State Record Inspection.** This would be the same kind of research as was done at the town level. The Department of Environmental Management has a list of all known contaminated sites; a list of underground tanks, land fills, *etc.* is also on file.

Following a Phase I Audit, the company you've hired will send you a report indicating whether there is any reason to suspect the site is not clean. The cost of a Phase I Audit could be anywhere from a few hundred dollars to many thousands of dollars depending on the size of the site and might take two to three weeks. In many cases, the Phase I Audit is enough.

You must also be aware that the company doing the Phase I Audit will not guarantee that the property is clean. It will tell you that there "is no evidence found of hazardous substances." What does this mean? Well, it means that if you take the property and you later have a problem, you are stuck, even though you paid for an audit.

Phase II Audit

If there is evidence of toxic waste, a second, more costly set of tests needs to be done. This involves hiring an environmental testing company that will dig holes to required depths in order to bring up water and soil samples at periodic intervals on the property. These samples are sent to a lab for testing. If anything is discovered, it will show in the report. A Phase II Audit can cost thousands of dollars—easily $5,000 to $10,000 depending on the size of the site—and can take about five weeks to complete.

If contaminants are discovered, the soil may have to be removed and replaced. Suffice it to say that these procedures are enormously expensive and that you and I should never need to know about this. Another consideration with Phase II Audits is the fact that if contamination is found, the donor may be forced to pay for the clean-up even if the gift never goes through.

Companies that provide such services are listed in the *Yellow Pages* under "Environmental, Conservation & Ecological Services."

Surveys

The purpose of a survey is to determine the boundaries of a property. If a site has changed hands recently, a survey may already exist. If a site has remained in one family for several generations, there may be no survey or a very imprecise one. This is because the title has been passed from one generation to the next with family members feeling no need to pay for a current survey. Under these circumstances, it also is likely that the original boundaries were set by objects such as "the big oak tree" or "the stone wall" or other major features at the boundary line. Such features may no longer exist. Distances often were measured by walking the property by foot. Needless to say, boundaries sometimes are difficult to determine.

When a property lies in two towns, especially if it is a large parcel, it is more difficult to identify the boundary between towns because the markers for town boundaries are set at much greater distances than would be the case for small lots.

Companies that provide this service are listed under "Surveyors" in the *Yellow Pages*. The company will trace the deeds on the property back as far as they go to find the most complete information relating to the way it originally was marked. If this proves unsuccessful, it will be necessary to review the deeds of neighboring properties in the hope that they have been surveyed. Thus, the subject property is identified by its relationship to the neighboring sites. In the most difficult cases, the neighboring sites lack proper surveys. Subsequently, the only way to lock in the boundary lines is to gather the neighbors and to come to an agreement.

Ordinarily, getting a survey should not be a big production. According to one company with whom I spoke, a survey should take no more than seven or eight days. If a survey cannot be produced from existing records in that time frame, it probably cannot be done without gathering the neighbors. The cost of a survey can range from a few hundred to several thousand dollars.

In your work, you might come across a donor who is willing to give you a piece of real estate, yet the parcel lacks a proper survey which is essential for you to market the property. You and I would hope that this donor would be willing to pay for a survey in order for you to accept the property. But, you just can't assume that. This is one of the items you'll need to take into account when you examine how much it will cost you to complete this gift.

Wetlands

You may have heard property described as "wet." This means that the ground water is very close to the surface. In some cases, there may be visible standing water or even swamps, streams, brooks, rivers or ponds. Laws vary from state to state but, generally, you cannot build on property classified as "wetlands." This is not to say you can't walk on it or have a house close to it. But, you certainly can't develop the property without conforming to EPA regulations. And, neither can the person to whom you hope to sell it. So, here again is another negotiable expense. If you are being offered a gift that might be suspected of having wetlands, your donor or you will have to get a wetlands report. The purpose of a wetlands report is to determine the precise areas that are under protection for environmental reasons, and, therefore, cannot be built. There are three types of reports ranging from very quick and inexpensive to very lengthy and expensive.

1. **Computer Mapping.** Several sources provide information on the nature of property. These are United States Geological Survey maps, State Planning maps, Soil Conservation maps, and Assessors maps. Together these include various pieces of information that relate to the topography, vegetation, soil composition, and elevations. A professional skilled in this service will track down the above maps from their various sources. Then, he or she will put each map on a computer, adjusting the size so that the scale of each map is identical. Then, he or she will print out a new map with all information together. There is a 5% to 10% error ratio for this process; however, it can provide an estimate of the major areas of wetlands.

   I commissioned such a report while at Wheaton College on a wooded parcel of 70 acres. It took one week. The report showed that the parcel being offered to us was 23% wetlands. This information was critical because the donor's appraisal assumed subdividing the 70 acres into a certain number of buildable lots. With 23% wetlands, we could not substantiate the appraisal and turned down the gift.

2. **Physical Walk of the Property.** The next level of report involves hiring a wetlands biologist who physically walks the property. Since the definition of wetlands includes land with certain types of vegetation, the only way to identify the actual wetlands is to hire someone who knows how to recognize wetlands plant species. If the property is hilly, the study can be relatively easy since higher grounds can be eliminated right away. The biologist will be focusing on the lowest points or the flat surfaces. When the land is large and predominantly flat, the process involves examining a larger percentage of the property since it would not immediately be obvious where the wetlands might be. This activity could take two to three weeks depending on the size of the property and could range from several hundred to a few thousand dollars.

3. **Certified Survey Map.** The most comprehensive process involves more precise measuring throughout the property with the objective of producing a certified map. This is where you can spend tens of thousands of dollars. Every little area with wetlands will be marked precisely on a map and it may involve measurements by aircraft, *etc*. This is a big production. You do not want to be getting into this.

The wetlands problem is most likely to affect the appraisal and marketability of undeveloped land and should not ordinarily be a concern for residential property in developed neighborhoods. Though the laws and regulations vary, you can expect building structures to have certain required set backs from the wetlands depending on the type of wetlands category you've found. For example, the set backs for different situations might be 200 feet from a major river, 100 feet from a small river, and 50 feet from plant species. Needless to say, the buildable portion of a property could be severely reduced by the presence of wetlands. In summary, the ramifications of this problem may be minimal if you are taking an outright gift which you'll eventually sell for a net profit. However, if you are placing property into a trust or accepting real estate in exchange for a deferred gift annuity, you'll be in big trouble when you have promised the donor income on a highly-inflated appraisal.

Another thing that might not be obvious is the fact that the state or local organization monitoring wetlands has to approve the building projects undertaken on wetlands properties. Since their own inspectors often are backed up with work, you may not be able to get somebody to help you in a timely fashion. When I inquired about the situation in Rhode Island at one point, I was told that we couldn't get on the list for review for more than six months. Bottom line: if you can't get the local regulatory agency to look at your property, you can't even talk intelligently to a prospective buyer. Be very, very careful. Enough said.

Companies that provide the above services are listed in the *Yellow Pages* under "Engineers-Environmental."

Percolation Testing

The purpose of "perc" testing is to determine whether the property meets local regulations for drainage. This process involves digging holes to specific depths, pouring water into the holes, and timing how long it takes for the water to drain. Such testing is critical for properties intended for building projects or housing developments. Each town has regulations on minimum time limits for the water to be absorbed. If the test hole fails, the land would not be able to handle the drainage requirements for sewage especially when septic systems are the method of waste disposal. An appraisal of undeveloped property should reflect the results of perc tests. If not, there may be something wrong.

Companies that provide the above services are listed in the *Yellow Pages* under "Engineers-Environmental."

There are so many issues related to real property that it would be impossible to cover them all here. The above concerns about hazardous waste, wetlands, surveys, and perc testing could present problems for undeveloped land. For residential properties, such hazards as lead paint, asbestos, formaldehyde insulation, carpenter ants, termites or dry rot might surface. In every case, you'll need the advice of an expert skilled in the particular problem before you can know exactly how the presence of these problems will affect your ability to sell the property once you own it. These things may not kill the gift, but the variables of the gift transaction may change as a result of them.

These potential problems should not completely kill your enthusiasm because many, many organizations across this country have taken in successful real estate gifts. And, once you're satisfied that the property being offered to you can be marketed and sold for a price you and the donor both agree on, the next thing you'll be concerned with is the form the gift might take.

WORKING WITH YOUR BUSINESS OFFICE

When you stumble upon a real estate situation, you are entering a realm that involves lots of people who would not necessarily be involved for gifts of cash, securities, or tangible personal property. Your business office cares greatly about what you are up to now.

I asked a good friend, Peg Ferber, who is currently the Associate Vice President for Finance and Administration of the Rochester Institute of Technology about her concerns when the director of planned giving has a "hot" real estate prospect. Her knee-jerk reaction was "Run the other way!" Then, she provided the insights below.

"The planned giving officer should involve the business office as soon as possible, not because we want to kill the deal. There is a lot of liability at stake. At RIT, a gift of real estate has to be approved by the Finance Committee. Otherwise, the next thing you know, you own an old dry cleaning property." Not all institutions require approval at the board level, but you ought to review the rules at your own institution so you will not spend a lot of time on something the board would never approve.

Peg says that there are several issues of importance that come to her mind immediately. "You have to know if the prospective donor is really the title owner. We had a case in which we sent our planned giving officer to British Columbia—and that is a long way from New York—to check out a property only to learn that it was a leasehold for a period of years, 25 or 30, I think. The donor did not hold title to the property, only the right to live in it for the specified period of time. That kind of property would be very hard to market."

I asked about the appraisal issues. Would RIT pay for an appraisal? "No, that is absolutely the responsibility of the donor." Environmental testing is another matter. "I would prefer that the donor pay for any necessary environmental testing. However, this is not a black and white issue. Depending on the value of the property, we might be willing to undertake the testing ourselves. But, these things need to be considered on a case by case basis. You cannot take gifts of real estate in an assembly-line process. Each has its own considerations that vary greatly from case to case." Regardless of who pays for the environmental audit, the charity must obtain one because the potential liability is so great.

Peg considers herself to be a partner with the planned giving office and is open to reviewing situations as needed, but she wants the planned giving officer to do the proper legwork first. "Don't waste my time with impractical situations that involve hours or days of my time and consultations with the board when the donor is 'charity shopping.' You see this frequently. A donor has a dog property that he cannot sell. So, he decides to give it away. By the time he finds you, he has already been turned down by several other charities."

If you want to get a reading on the donor's situation right away, Peg advises the planned giving officer to ask if the property has been offered to other charities in the past 12 months. If the answer is yes, you probably don't want it either. And, you can probably stop the gift right there—before it ever gets to the business office.

At Boston College, I had a good relationship with our business office. If a person expressed interested in making a gift of real estate, I would write a letter of intent for the signature of the donor. Then, with that letter in hand, I met with the treasurer to start our process of review. I told the donor that we would not engage the time of our legal department, outside law firm, and business office without a letter of intent signed by the donor. That procedure worked pretty well to weed out the people who were charity shopping with a dog property.

Many planned giving officers feel that working with the business office is adversarial. It shouldn't be. "A good Financial Vice President wants to take in valuable gifts and to assist in the process. However, inexperienced planned giving officers who don't do their homework about the gift property before it lands in the lap of the business office really are expecting too much. This is a two-way street," says Peg. "If you bring me a situation that has been thoroughly researched before it gets to me, I will be your greatest advocate."

APPRAISALS

Here is a topic that comes up all the time. If you have a donor wishing to make a gift of a property, who gets the appraisal: the donor or the charity? Answer: The donor gets the appraisal because the donor is responsible for substantiating his or her own tax deduction. Sometimes the donor says, "I'm giving you a valuable property. The least you can do is pay for the appraisal."

There are only a couple of situations under which I would recommend that the charity get its own separate appraisal. The first is if you are considering a piece of real property for a deferred gift annuity. Under those circumstances, you must verify for your own purposes whether the property is worth what the donor's appraisal says. In several cases, Boston College was willing to pay for our own appraisal. In one case, the donor's appraisal was $225,000 and our appraisal was something like $180,000. We told the donor we could not issue the gift annuity based on his appraisal. The gift fell through.

The other situation that justifies the charity getting its own appraisal is for a bargain sale. When your organization is putting up cash in the transaction, you must know if the donor's appraisal is valid.

Time and time again, donors will want the charity to pay for the appraisal, and they will put up quite a fight. I can't make it any plainer. This is not the charity's responsibility.

SIX OPTIONS FOR DONATING REAL PROPERTY

Real property is a big subject. Volumes have been written about it. Individuals spend their entire lives working solely on understanding the laws under which real estate is developed, created, controlled, managed, transferred, bought, sold, taxed, rented, or contributed to an organization like yours.

You cannot expect to know everything about this subject. But you can have a working knowledge of real estate sufficient to get you through a meeting with a prospective donor until you can consult your attorney about a specific situation.

Many of the tax laws and regulations you already understand interact with one another differently when it comes to real estate. Numerous results can be achieved—some more favorable than others—depending on the type of property, the tax treatment it has been given in the donor's hands, the tax treatment it will have in your hands, and the form of gift.

One factor, more than any other, negatively impacts and complicates many of the gift arrangements possible with real estate—a mortgage.

For purposes of this section, it will be easier for me and probably clearer for you if I discuss each of the six gift arrangements in the most straightforward way first, that is, with the assumption there is no mortgage on the property.

Following is a summary of six different ways donors can use real estate in charitable giving. Each offers its own set of benefits to you and to the donor. Note: it is also possible for a donor to put real estate into a regular unitrust or a net income unitrust, but these two vehicles are not as good as the flip unitrust. With a regular unitrust, the donor would need to make additional contributions of cash or marketable securities in order for the trustee to make the required unitrust payments.

- outright gift,
- bargain sale,
- gift annuity (not recommended),
- deferred payment gift annuity (under limited circumstances),
- flip unitrust,
- retained life estate/gift of remainder interest.

Several of these topics are treated elsewhere in the book as individual chapters. Therefore, I will refer you to the appropriate chapter for a more complete discussion of the operation, benefits, and other considerations for each gift vehicle.

Outright Gift

As always, the simplest form of transferring any property (real or otherwise) is the outright gift. If the property has been held the required holding period to be treated as a long-term capital asset, a gift to your organization entitles the donor (itemizers only) to an income tax deduction for the full market value. The deduction is limited to 30% of adjusted gross income with a five-year carry-over period for any excess that exceeds the 30% ceiling.

The potentially high degree of appreciation over the donor's cost basis can produce significant tax liability for the donor who sells such property. Under current law, 100% of the long-term gain is reportable and taxable unless the property is a primary residence in which the owner has lived for two of the past five years. In that case there is a capital gain tax exclusion of $250,000 for a single or $500,000 for a couple. The owner can utilize this exemption once every two years.

By contributing real estate, the donor is relieved of the management, taxes, insurance, and maintenance costs. The donor reduces his or her tax liability as a result of the federal income tax deduction. And, he or she avoids the capital gain tax that would have applied on a sale by the donor.

If, on the other hand, the property has been held for less than the required holding period to be considered a long-term capital asset, the same gift will generate a tax deduction limited to the adjusted cost basis; and the contribution deduction ceiling is increased to 50% of adjusted gross income with the same five-year carry-over period.

One of the interesting features of real property is that it can be given in small segments. This method may be attractive if the donor wishes to spread the tax benefits over a period of years. (The carry-over period for contributions above the annual ceilings would also take care of that.) For example, he or she can contribute a 40% undivided interest this year, receive a tax deduction for the fair market value of this 40% share, subject to a discount, avoid the tax that would have been paid on that portion if sold, and retain the other 60% for gifts in future years until the entire property has been given away.

By passing the property to you in installments, the donor can take full advantage of the tax savings without exceeding his or her charitable deduction ceiling. There are also some cautions to keep in mind for a gift of an undivided fractional interest. First, if you own part of a property, you will be responsible for your share of the expenses, maintenance, taxes, or insurance. Second, if you are the fractional owner of a residence in which the donor resides, you deserve access to material ownership for your share. For example, if you are given a 40% interest in a residence, how are you going to use your 40% share? I do not have an answer to this question. This would be something to ask your legal counsel.

Bargain Sale

The bargain sale is part sale and part gift. A donor, who wishes to make a major contribution to your organization using real property, but, at the same time, would like some immediate cash from the transaction, can sell the property to you in a bargain sale.

> Example:
>
> You pay the donor $30,000 for property worth $200,000. The donor receives a tax deduction for $170,000—the gift portion. When you sell the property, you recover your cost plus the excess. Although the donor may be required to recognize as taxable income some gain as a result of the transaction, nonetheless, he or she will receive a substantial income tax deduction, eliminate the burden of management or other expenses associated with the property, and can participate at a much higher gift level than would otherwise be possible.

There is a more complete treatment of the bargain sale in Chapter II-2 in as much as it can be used not only with real estate but also with almost any other type of property. If you are dealing with a bargain sale of real estate, go to that chapter.

Gift Annuity

Do not take a gift of real estate for an immediate payment gift annuity. This is too risky and it will cause you major headaches because you are responsible for the annuity payment regardless of when you sell the property. Plus, if you are registered in certain states that prohibit taking real estate for a gift annuity, you will get into trouble.

Deferred Gift Annuity

Although it is risky to take a piece of real estate for a deferred gift annuity, you can do it under certain circumstances. First, check with your attorney to make sure that your state gift annuity regulations do not prohibit it. With a deferred gift annuity, the donor exchanges property for an annuity payment that begins more than a year following the gift, for example, in five years, 10 years, or at retirement. This gift option provides the window of time your organization needs to ensure the funds are available to generate the payments when they come due.

Deferred gift annuities are discussed in detail in Chapter II-8. When you have finished reading this small section, you will need to go to the other chapter for a complete treatment of the gift annuity.

Here are a couple of true disasters:

Disaster #1: A donor contributed a condominium for a combination bargain sale and current gift annuity. The donor's appraisal was $625,000. The charity agreed to pay $225,000 in cash (ouch!) and issued a current gift annuity on the remaining $400,000. Two years after the gift, the institution still owned the property, but the value had dropped to $425,000. Meanwhile, the donor had been receiving an annuity payment the whole time. Four years after the gift, the charity still owned the property. This was a terrible situation even though all of the parties believed it would work when they entered into it.

Disaster #2: A donor contributed undeveloped land valued at $85,000. The charity issued a deferred gift annuity, delaying the payment for one year. Four years later, the charity still owned the property.

You cannot be too careful with a real estate gift in exchange for a deferred gift annuity. If you absolutely must pursue a deferred gift annuity with real estate, consider the following procedure:

1) Take the market value of the property;
2) Reduce it by the expected commission of the sale (6% for residential, 10% for undeveloped land);
3) Input the reduced figure into your software to determine the dollar payment amount for an immediate payment gift annuity;
4) Defer the dollar payment for a minimum of one year (longer if the donor will agree).

Let's take an example. (See **Exhibit II-6A** on the next page.)

Donor, age 80, wants to contribute a personal residence (not a primary residence) valued at $250,000 for a deferred gift annuity. The cost basis is $40,000. Assume the discount rate used is 4%. What will you offer for this gift?

Step #1: Reduce the value of the gift by 6%, the estimated commission on the sale. If you have a reason to believe that the commission will be 5% or some other amount, use that. ($250,000 - 6% or $15,000 = $235,000). This is an estimate of the cash you will have after the sale. It is important for you to take into account this very large reduction in the proceeds. Since you are about to provide a fixed payment based on this gift, you must consider the reality of what will be lost with the sale. (Note: There will be other expenses like legal fees, closing costs, *etc.*, and you could try to factor those in, too.)

Step #2: Plug $235,000 into your planned giving software, gift annuity module, to determine the immediate gift annuity payment amount for this gift. For an 80 year old, I get 8% or $18,800 annually. Ignore the cost basis here since the only point is to find the current gift annuity rate for a person age 80 on an amount of $235,000.

Step #3: Go back to your planned giving software and change the amount of the gift back to $250,000 and select deferred gift annuity instead of gift annuity. Defer the payment for one year (or more). Defer it to the end of the quarter that falls at least a year from the date of the gift. So, for a gift on July 13, 2003, your first payment would be on September 30, 2004 with quarterly payments at the end of the payment period. (See **Exhibit II-6A** on the next page.)

Exhibit II-6A

ASHTON ASSOCIATES

Prepared for:
Female 80
July 13, 2003

Deduction Calculations
Summary of Benefits

7.52% Deferred Gift Annuity

ASSUMPTIONS:

Annuitant	80
Age at Date of First Payment	[9/30/2004] 81
Principal Donated	$250,000.00
Cost Basis	$40,000.00
Annuity Rate	7.52%
Payment Schedule	quarterly

====

BENEFITS:

Charitable Deduction	**$141,830.00**
Annuity	**$18,800.00**
Tax-free Portion	$1,967.23
Capital Gain Income	$10,327.97
Ordinary Income	$6,504.80

Total reportable capital gain of $91,944.30 must be reported over 8.8 years, the expected lifetime at the date of first payment of the donor currently age 80.

After 8.8 years from the year the payments begin, the entire annuity becomes ordinary income.

IRS Discount Rate used is 4%

The reason you start the calculation over using the market value of the gift is that the donor's payment must be based on the fair market value of the gift and not the value of the proceeds. Don't allow the software to compute the deferred gift annuity amount for you. (In PG Calc I get a prompt asking whether this calculation should be adjusted for the deferral period. I select no.) Instead, input the dollar value of $18,800 that you computed on the reduced principal in Step #2. Ordinarily, people running deferred gift annuity calculations allow the software to select the correct rate. They rarely have a reason to input the annuity payment manually. In this case you must do that.

Step #4: The software will be forced to recalculate the deferred annuity rate from 8.4% (the actual rate for the scenario) to 7.52% because you are paying $18,800 on a fair market value of $250,000.

The final result is a deferred gift annuity (deferred for one year) in which the annuity payment is the rate for the 80 year old, but based on the market value reduced by the commission.

Instead of paying 8.4% on $250,000, you are paying 7.52% on $250,000 which takes into account the fact that you expect to lose $15,000 at the sale. The charitable deduction for this gift is $141,830.

If you follow the above procedure, you will accomplish two things. You will have at least a year to sell the property before beginning payments, and your payments are tied to the actual cash expected. As a further precaution, you could discount the appraised value of the property by another 10% to 20% to protect yourself against market fluctuations.

This is a reasonable plan. Even so, some donors will object because they don't want to wait a year for their payments to begin. Donors who are really charitable will understand the reasoning. I hope this discussion will help you make smart decisions about taking real estate for a gift annuity.

The donor will probably ask, "Why should I have to wait a year for my payment if you sell the property immediately?" Answer: "The start date of a gift annuity cannot be related to the timing of the disposition of the property." That's just the way it is. Many gifts of real estate cannot be sold right away which brings me back to the bottom line: The charity should try to limit its risk in taking a gift. If the donor rejects your proposal, don't worry about it. Go on to the next one.

Flip Unitrust

If your institution does not offer gift annuities, or if state regulations prohibit the use of real estate in exchange for a gift annuity, you have two other options through which a transfer of real estate can generate cash for the donor. The first is the bargain sale, discussed earlier in this chapter; the second is the flip unitrust which is, by far, the best vehicle for an illiquid asset like real estate.

With a flip unitrust, a donor can:

- Make a gift to your institution;
- Avoid immediate capital gain taxes that would have applied if the donor sold the property;
- Receive an immediate income tax deduction for the value of the remainder interest;
- Generate a new income flow once the property is converted to income-producing investments;
- Reduce probate costs by removing the property from the probate estate;
- Eliminate the burden of property taxes, maintenance, and other administration expenses.

The flip feature is the key to this gift. The CRT pays no income to the beneficiary until it generates income after the sale of the illiquid asset. The beauty of the flip unitrust is that the trust converts to a straight unitrust operation after the flip occurs. This topic is covered completely in Chapter II-9 so you should go there after reviewing this condensed summary.

Here are some considerations you must take into account when suggesting this kind of a plan to the donor:

1. The donor may have an unrealistic opinion of the property's value. If the trust sells the property for less than what the donor expects, the donor may become disgruntled.

2. If there is a long delay (as can easily happen) in disposing of the property, the donor may become disgruntled due to an unrealistic expectation of when income payments would begin;

3. The establishment of the trust may require an additional contribution of cash or securities to cover administration expenses and fees associated with managing or disposing of the property. Many donors do not have or are unwilling to put additional assets into the trust to make this work. These considerations are important. When real estate taxes come due, the trust must have a way to pay.

4. A bank trustee will take a percentage of the sale proceeds as its own commission in addition to the commission paid to the real estate broker. It is in your best interests to call several banks to compare fees before speaking with the donor.

5. There are also legal fees and possibly CPA fees for the donor to review the gift plan with his or her own advisors.

The solution to some of these issues is to have the donor name himself trustee while the property is in the trust. Then, the donor resigns and names your organization successor trustee once the cash is in the account. This puts the burden of the sale in the hands of the donor and takes you out of the picture during this sensitive and possibly difficult time.

If you are dealing with a gift of real estate into a flip unitrust, you will be faced with a lot of complex issues simultaneously. First, you have all of the concerns discussed earlier in this chapter for any gift of real estate. (Note: Even if you are not the trustee, the issues of viability of the property, resale, *etc.*, will be a concern for any professional trustee.) Second, you are dealing with the operation of a complex gift vehicle. If you are diligent and persistent, you can prevail. Take your time, understand the issues, and go one step at a time. Now, go to Chapter II-9 for a much more detailed explanation of the flip unitrust, including a comprehensive example.

There are reasons I did not discuss other kinds of CRTs for a gift of real estate. A charitable remainder annuity trust cannot receive additional contributions after the initial funding, but it must make payments to the beneficiary when they are due. Therefore, the cash flow is a real problem. You could use a net income unitrust or a net income with make-up unitrust, but the flip unitrust is better. You don't want to get trapped with a net income payment for the life of the trust. You could also use a regular unitrust, but the donor would have to make additional gifts to the trust when payments come due or when tax, insurance, or other bills come due.

At the end of this chapter is a Sample Letter of Understanding that you can adapt for your own purposes when discussing a gift of real estate in a CRT. Charles Sterling of State Street Global Advisors in Boston provided this very good letter to me.

Retained Life Estate/Gift Of Remainder Interest

The final use of real estate in charitable giving involves the transfer of a remainder interest in a personal residence or farm with a retained right to a life estate.

More simply put, the donor can contribute a personal residence or farm to your institution and continue to occupy or use the property until death. As a result, the donor can:

- Make an irrevocable commitment to your institution;
- Receive a current income tax deduction for the property's discounted value;
- Continue to enjoy the use of the property as usual.

There are several considerations for this unique use of real estate:

1. The property must be a personal residence or farm. A personal residence need not be the donor's *primary* residence. It can be a second home or a vacation home. To be classified as a farm, the land must meet specific criteria under applicable state law.

2. As with all gifts, this arrangement is irrevocable. Thus, a donor cannot draw on equity in the property in the event of an unexpected need for cash. Once the property is given, there is no turning back.

3. A retained life estate using a primary residence is most appropriate for an older person who reasonably expects to stay there until death. If a second home is used for the gift, age is less of a factor in determining the advisability of the gift.

4. The donor is responsible for the regular expenses of maintaining the property as usual—maintenance fees, insurance, property taxes, fixing the roof, putting in a new hot water heater, *etc.*

5. If the donor wishes to vacate the property, he or she can rent it to generate income. Or, the donor can contribute the remaining life estate to your institution, receive an income tax deduction for doing so, and vacate the property in order that you can sell it. Or, your institution along with the donor can place the property on the market for sale, splitting the proceeds in accordance with the I.R.S. actuarial values for life and remainder interests on the date of sale.

The calculation for the donor's income tax deduction takes into account the value of the land and the value of the building separately. The land is considered to be non-depreciable; the building is considered to be depreciable.

Example:

An 85 year old widow owns a summer home valued at $350,000 with a cost basis of $100,000. The non-depreciable portion (land) is valued at $100,000. The depreciable portion (house) is valued at $250,000 and has an estimated useful life of 45 years, at the end of which the salvage value is $62,500. She has owned this summer home for a long time. Let's assume that the discount rate for the month of the gift is 6%, last month 5.6%, and two months ago 5.4%. The discount rate affording the donor the largest income tax deduction is 5.4% (the lowest rate). Note: If you don't know what the discount rate is, go to Chapter II-2.

The donor contributes this property to your organization reserving a life estate for her life. As a result, she is entitled to an income tax deduction of $242,669.50 in the year of the transfer. She continues to maintain the property as usual paying the costs of repairs, insurance, and all other expenses. On her death, the property is available to your organization. An agreement between you and the donor, drawn up by your attorney, lays out the terms of the arrangement.

The gift has allowed her to make a major commitment, thus gaining the satisfaction of being a benefactor for a charitable organization during her lifetime, and she has received a current tax deduction to alleviate her tax burden. She can claim the deduction up to 30% of her adjusted gross income with five additional years to carry over and deduct any amount exceeding her 30% contribution ceiling.

A gift of a remainder interest with a retained life estate requires a deed, a sample of which is reproduced in Appendix V. This is generally accompanied by a Life Estate Agreement. This agreement outlines the rights and responsibilities of each party for such things as fires, floods, insurance, taxes, major repairs, *etc.* Also, be aware that unforeseen circumstances can occur. For instance, if the donor goes into a nursing home, he or she may expect to go home. But, what if that doesn't happen? You end up with a property that is not being maintained. Such circumstances should be addressed in the agreement.

Exhibit II-6B

ASHTON ASSOCIATES

Prepared for:
Female 85

Deduction Calculations
Actuarial Calculations

Retained Life Estate

ASSUMPTIONS:

[1]	Life Tenant Age	85
	Date of Gift	7/13/2003
[2]	Value of Property	$350,000.00
	Cost Basis of Property	$100,000.00
[3]	Value of Depreciable Portion	$250,000.00
[4]	Estimated Useful Life of Property	45 years
[5]	Salvage Value of Property	$62,500.00
[6]	Discount Rate under IRC Section 7520(a)	5.4%

CALCULATIONS:

[7]	Undepreciable Factor for [1] and [6] (Reg. 1.170A-12(b)(1))	0.73982
[8]	Remainder Value of Net Undepreciable Portion ([7] x ([2] - ([3] - [5])))	$120,220.75
[9]	Depreciable Factor for [1], [4] & [6] (Reg. 1.170A-12(b)(2))	0.65306
[10]	Remainder Value of Net Depreciable Portion ([9] x ([3] - [5]))	$122,448.75
[11]	**CHARITABLE DEDUCTION** ([8] + [10])	**$242,669.50**

Refer to **Exhibit II-6B** on the prior page. The Actuarial Calculations shows the detailed computation that would be given to her accountant. It looks complicated, but your planned giving software will produce these figures very easily.

REAL ESTATE SUBJECT TO A MORTGAGE

When a donor contributes mortgaged real estate to any of the gift vehicles discussed in this chapter, all kinds of new complications arise depending on the type of gift.

In some cases, the donor will incur additional tax liability on the amount of the mortgage. For example, the donor may be required to report and pay income taxes on the amount of the remaining mortgage. Additional complications may arise if mortgaged property is transferred to a charitable remainder trust making the trust fail to qualify or causing penalty taxes to apply. Or, your institution may incur unrelated business income tax in connection with a gift of mortgaged property for a gift annuity.

Your tax counsel rather than I can advise you exactly how a mortgage affects the particular gift plan you are suggesting. Be cautious in all cases, and seek experienced assistance whenever you are working with real estate—especially when there is a mortgage. This is one instance when paying for billable hours is a must.

SUMMARY

One of the most important things to keep in mind with regard to real estate is the fact that progress happens at a snail's pace. Working through the details, arranging a plan, and seeing it through will consume a disproportionate share of your time. If you use the real estate checklist on page 180 to secure the information your tax counsel and internal business office needs, you will have done the most you can do to accelerate the discussions.

No doubt, from reading the past six chapters, you are beginning to realize that planned giving involves many flexible plans that benefit both the donor and the charity. The next chapter explains a life income plan that is an invention of the Tax Reform Act of 1969—the pooled income fund. These are not being marketed as much as they were in the 1980s; however, if you are running a planned giving program, chances are you inherited one that needs attention.

The following letter of understanding between State Street Global Advisors and the charity/client is provided by Charles Sterling at State Street Global Advisors and is printed with permission.

SAMPLE LETTER OF UNDERSTANDING

Dear [Donor]:

We are very pleased that you are considering funding a charitable remainder unitrust (CRT) that will benefit you and [CLIENT/CHARITY].

It is our understanding that the CRT will be funded with your real property located at [address]. It is important to us that you be aware of the following:

1. The income from the CRT will be limited to the lesser of (1) the actual net income earned from the property in the CRT or (2) a fixed percentage of (percent) of the CRT value, revalued annually. Therefore, the income received by you may increase or decrease in direct proportion to the change in the net value of the assets in the CRT as they are valued annually.

2. If in any year the actual net income is greater than the percentage amount, the Trustees would reinvest the excess thereby increasing the value of the CRT.

3. After your lifetime, the property in the CRT will pass to [institution] to [state purpose].

4. Because the CRT is not being funded with liquid assets and there could be difficulty in marketing the real estate, substantial time may pass before the property is sold and income payments may be delayed.

5. Since the net proceeds from the sale of the property may be significantly different from the value now placed on the property, future income payments could vary from current income projections.

6. The Trustee(s) will have the sole legal right and fiduciary responsibility to determine the timing and terms of the sale of the property.

7. From the date the CRT is established to the date the property is sold, you will be responsible for making contributions to the CRT to cover all property expenses including, but not limited to, real estate taxes, insurance costs, repairs and maintenance. These additions will serve to protect your potential income return from the CRT assets, and your ultimate gift.

8. The CRT, and payments from the CRT, are supported only by the net assets in the CRT and are not "guaranteed" by the Trustee(s).

9. Prior to accepting the transfer of the property into the CRT, we require the following:

    a) Title insurance policy or certified abstract of title to guarantee marketable title.
    b) A "qualified" fair market value appraisal by a professional appraiser 60 days or less prior to conveyance to CRT.
    c) An environmental review if the property is currently, or at any time in the past, was used for commercial or industrial purposes, or at our discretion.
    d) A satisfactory site inspection completed by:

        (i)   SSGA Trust Real Estate Officer and/or
        (ii) a professional home inspector or engineer and/or
        (iii) qualified person completing Site Review Checklist

    e) As to vacant land, confirmation that the Highest and Best Use of the land can be realized in conformity with all applicable laws and regulations, such as zoning, environmental restrictions, septic systems and water availability.
    f) All mortgages on the property will be removed.

10. Prior to the gift, you will have reviewed the CRT documents and procedures for this gift transaction with your own attorney, accountant or other advisors.

11. If SSGA provides advisory services in the sale of this property, their fee is one percent (1%) of the gross sale price.

If this letter reflects our mutual understanding of the proposed charitable gift, would you kindly sign, date and return the enclosed copy of this letter.

Sincerely,

[Trustee(s)]

Accepted_____Date_____

State Street Global Advisors
Trust Real Estate Advisory Services
for the Disposition of
Gifts of Real Estate

Phase One: OBJECTIVES

In order to provide for a proper due diligence review of proposed real estate gifts to [CLIENT/CHARITY] and to attempt to achieve the highest net return from the sale of the property, [CLIENT/CHARITY] wishes to retain the services of the Trust Real Estate Department at State Street Global Advisors (SSGA) to provide certain services as fiduciary or agent to properly receive, manage, and convert gifts of real estate to cash for investment.

Phase Two: DUE DILIGENCE

[CLIENT] will provide a completed *Site Review Checklist* to allow SSGA to review the risks and holding costs of the proposed real estate gift. SSGA will be entitled to rely upon the information contained in the Site Review Checklist in performing its services hereunder.

Following the above preliminary due diligence review the following additional reports may be required:

1. *Building Inspection Report.* To further evaluate the condition of buildings and their systems.
2. *Property Management Budget.* To determine the costs to maintain the property during the sale, including hiring an outside property management firm if required.
3. *Title Report.* To ensure that the title is satisfactory prior to gift transfer.
4. *Report by Land Planner.* To evaluate subdivision potential, if appropriate.
5. *Engineering Reports.* To evaluate water, sewer, drainage, geological status.
6. *Environmental Report.* To check for the presence of hazardous waste.
7. *Fair Market Value Appraisal.* To determine donor's tax deduction and to establish that the property can be sold in a reasonable time period and for a price expected by donor and [CLIENT/CHARITY].

SSGA in its sole discretion may accept or reject any fiduciary or agency responsibility for the management and/or sale of a real estate gift.

Phase Three: MARKETING

Depending upon the circumstances of each real estate gift, SSGA will serve as sole trustee, co-trustee, agent for the trustee(s).

SSGA will provide the following services:

1. *Fair Market Value Appraisal.* Review "qualified" appraisal obtained by donor.
2. *Insurance.* Verify proper property and liability coverage after transfer.
3. *Property Management.* Supervise all services from property management agents or contractors hired for maintenance and repairs.
4. *Bill Paying.* Pay expenses from the trust or escrow account at SSGA to maintain the property, subject to receiving funds.
5. *Leasing and Rent Collection.* Enforce lease agreements and collect rent.

6. *Listing.* Obtain two marketing proposals from real estate brokers. Recommend a listing price and an exclusive listing contract with the best real estate broker for the sale.

7. *Sales Advisory.* Monitor the sale process and communicate offers and status to interested parties.

8. *Sales Agreement.* Direct the preparation of documents by outside counsel or escrow company.

9. *Closing.* Obtain and pay final bills and deliver closing documents to closing agent. Book proceeds and remove real estate asset from trust account.

SSGA Fees for Services

The SSGA fee for Sales Advisory and Administrative services is based on a percentage of the gross selling price for all sales and real estate management services following the transfer of the property to the trust, payable after the closing. Minimum fees apply *per* real estate gift. An hourly rate applies for administrative services when SSGA is not a trustee. Fees provided upon request.

The following sample letter printed with permission covers the case in which the donor is trustee of the CRT prior to the sale of the real estate. Charles Sterling at State Street Global Advisors provided it.

A LETTER OF UNDERSTANDING ON RESPONSIBILITIES BETWEEN DONOR/TRUSTEE ("DONOR") AND STATE STREET BANK AND TRUST CO. ("STATE STREET") FOR HOLDING GIFTS OF REAL ESTATE IN AGENCY OR CUSTODY ACCOUNTS

THE DONOR/TRUSTEE AGREES TO THE FOLLOWING:

1. State Street will have no responsibility to sell any trust owned real estate and the Donor will hold harmless and indemnify State Street for any liability resulting from the retention and/or the ultimate sale of the property.

2. Provide State Street with the property purchase price, subsequent capital improvements and other costs to establish tax cost basis for income tax purposes.

3. Obtain a qualified appraisal establishing the fair market value of the gift, not later than 60 days before or after gift to the trust.

4. Submit Form 8283 to I.R.S to support income tax deduction.

5. Provide State Street with certificate of insurance for property and liability coverage commencing from conveyance to the Trust Agency or Custody account.

6. If gift property is income producing either (a) forward to State Street tenant rent payments for deposit and invoices approved for payment by State Street from available funds in the account, or (b) maintain separate trust checking account to deposit rental income and to pay expenses, followed by sending State Street net rent check with detailed operating statement to State Street sufficient for income tax purposes if State Street will prepare income tax returns.

7. If State Street will receive rental payments and/or pay invoices directly, inform tenants and/or municipal tax collector, water department, utilities and all other service providers of new billing address:

   [Name] Trust
   State Street Bank and Trust Co.
   Attn: C. Sterling, MAO3
   Box 351
   Boston, MA 02101.

8. Make additional contributions of cash or publicly traded securities to the CRT in advance of required beneficiary payments (if a CRUT), as well as additional contributions in advance based on a budget approved by State Street to cover periodic taxes, insurance, maintenance, and State Street's fees. State Street will not carry overdrafts in the trust account.

9. Offer trust property for sale directly or through real estate agents at a reasonable price not less than appraised value in order to obtain the highest price consistent with current market conditions. With assistance from an attorney or title company negotiate sale, enter sales agreement and convey property at closing. Terminate all utilities and other property services as of the date of closing. Agree not to accept seller financing arrangements such as installment sale contract, purchase money mortgage or deed of trust without consultation and approval from State Street.

10. Provide State Street with Settlement Statement from real estate sale with delivery of net proceeds from the sale.

11. If sold within two years of contribution submit Form 8282 to I.R.S., stating sale price.

STATE STREET AGREES TO THE FOLLOWING:

1. Set-up account and enter real estate gift in Trust Agency or Custody account records. Remove asset upon sale and receipt of net proceeds.

2. Book all rental payments and pay all invoices in a timely manner after receipt from tenants or service providers or forwarded from Donor with approval for payment, but subject to having in the account sufficient funds.

DONOR/TRUSTEE

_____ DATE _____

STATE STREET BANK AND TRUST COMPANY

_____ DATE _____
By:

The following real estate site review checklist is also the creation of Charles A. Sterling, Principal, State Street Global Advisors, Boston, and is reprinted with permission.

STATE STREET GLOBAL ADVISORS
TRUST REAL ESTATE
SITE REVIEW CHECKLIST

Person completing this report _____ Phone _____

Reason _____

Account Name _____ Account Number _____

Policy. The purpose of completing this questionnaire is to perform a due diligence review of real estate prior to accepting title as fiduciary. Most of the information can be obtained from observations during a visit to the property and from conversations with the current owner. The objective is to discover conditions which may create potential liability, unanticipated expenses, or affect the marketability of the property. Photographs should be taken during the visit to supplement this report.

Owner: Donor/ Legal title holder: _____ Phone _____

Address: _____

_____

Gift Property:

_____

| Street | Unit # | City/Town | County | State | Zip | Country |

Land Area: (acres or sq. ft.) _____

General Description: _____

_____

_____

Tax Cost Basis: _____ **Date of Purchase/Inheritance:** _____

Mortgage Balance: _____ Lender _____ Terms _____

Estimated Fair Market Value: _____ Source _____

Real Estate Taxes:
Estimated $/*per* year _____

Assessed value: Building _____ Land _____

Tax Parcel ID Number _____

Assessed value: Personal property_____ Estimated $/ *per* year _____

Occupancy: State plans for continuing occupancy or removal of personal property: _____

_____

_____

Tenants: Provide a copy of lease(s) or summary of verbal understanding with tenant(s): _____

_____

_____

Accounting of rental payments:

Units	One	Two	Three
Monthly rent	_____	_____	_____
Security Deposit	_____	_____	_____
Last month's rent	_____	_____	_____
Arrears	_____	_____	_____

Property Management Services: State name, address, and phone number of contractors used to maintain the property and an estimate of recurring costs:

Property manager	_____	$ _____
Carpenter/handyman	_____	$ _____
Landscaper	_____	$ _____
Heating/cooling	_____	$ _____
Snow removal	_____	$ _____
Security	_____	$ _____
Pool service	_____	$ _____
	Total estimated monthly costs	$ _____

Title: A title policy, or certified abstract of title sufficient for title insurance, will be required. Describe any known rights of way, easements, restrictions, purchase options, *etc.* giving others rights in the property:

_____

_____

Book/Page:_____Certificate of Title: _____

Is a survey plan available?_____Are the corners of the land staked with markers?_____

Does the land have legal frontage or an easement right to cross adjacent land for access?_____

If the land is undeveloped, what evidence exists to confirm that it can be built on?_____

_____

_____

Building Condition: Circle existing building components and note any unsatisfactory building conditions revealed in conversations with owner and/or visible from your inspection with the following:

<u>Foundation</u>: Poured concrete Concrete block Field stone Sump pump _____

<u>Siding</u>: Shingle Clapboard Brick Stucco Asbestos Vinyl Aluminum _____

<u>Roof</u>: Asbestos/tar Shingle Wood shake Slate Metal Tar & Gravel Rubber _____

<u>Plumbing</u>: Copper Lead; Waste: Iron PVC _____

<u>Electrical</u>: Volts 110 220; Amps 60 100 200; circuit breaker fuse _____

<u>Heating System</u>: Hot water* Hot Air Steam* Solar Electric Space heater Wood stove _____

<u>Heating Fuel</u>: Gas Electric Propane Wood Solar Oil (Important: UST ?_____) _____

<u>Air Conditioning</u>: Window units Central_____

<u>Hot Water*</u>: Oil Gas Electric Propane Solar Tankless_____

<u>Water Source*</u>: Municipal Well _____

<u>Sewage disposal **</u>: Municipal Septic system _____

<u>Swimming pool</u>: In ground Above ground Fenced _____

<u>Fixtures included with house</u>: Stove Refrigerator AC unit Chandelier Other _____

<u>Garage</u>: Separate Attached Cars: 1 2 3 4 Heat: yes no Automatic door_____

<u>Security</u>: Burgular Fire Low heat sensor Access: Code Special key _____

Policy.

*Domestic water and hot water heating systems should be drained during periods of freezing weather.

**In Massachusetts, under Title V, a septic inspection and certification is required upon the transfer to or addition of new interested parties in the title.

Environmental:

Policy: For residential property, the necessity for a Phase I Environmental Audit shall be determined after reviewing the following responses. For property used currently or in the past for any commercial, industrial or other non-residential purpose, a Phase I Environmental Audit by a professional engineer shall be performed.

	No	Yes	Don't Know
• The property has prior or current use for industrial, commercial, agricultural, manufacturing, waste disposal or other non-residential purpose.	_____	_____	_____
• Stressed vegetation, unusual bare spots, oil sheens, unusual odors in standing water	_____	_____	_____
• Underground oil tank(s) or unexplained outside vent pipe or unused pipes in basement walls	_____	_____	_____
• Large electric transformers (PCBs)	_____	_____	_____
• Previous tests indicating radon	_____	_____	_____
• Lead paint (usually present in pre 1980 homes)	_____	_____	_____
• Asbestos insulation	_____	_____	_____
• Termites/carpenter ants/ other pests	_____	_____	_____
• Urea foam formaldehyde insulation (installed in 1970s)	_____	_____	_____
• Flood plain or coastal exposure	_____	_____	_____
• Earthquake potential	_____	_____	_____
• Extensive wetlands or drainage problems	_____	_____	_____
• Endangered plants or wildlife	_____	_____	_____
• Hazardous materials or debris stored on land	_____	_____	_____
• Known chemical or oil spill on land	_____	_____	_____
• Adjacent commercial or contaminated property	_____	_____	_____

COMMENTS: _____

_____

_____

_____

Questions? Contact Charles A. (Chip) Sterling 617-664-3282; Fax 617-664-4799; charles_sterling@ssga.com

_____ Date _____
By:

Review and Approval

_____ Date _____
By: Charles A. Sterling
Principal

Chapter II–7

POOLED INCOME FUNDS

INTRODUCTION

The pooled income fund (PIF) is a creation of the Tax Reform Act of 1969. Its concept is simple—a fund maintained by the charity in which all gifts are "pooled" for investment purposes with income shared proportionately among the participants. On the death of the beneficiaries, the principal is distributed to the charity that runs it. Although you should not confuse pooled income funds with commercial investments, the easiest way to conceptualize it is to think of it as the charity's own mutual fund.

For the donor of modest means, the pooled income fund offers many benefits including the opportunity to make a meaningful gift to your organization, receive income for life, avoid capital gain taxes on appreciated, long-term securities, and receive a partial income tax deduction in the year of the gift.

Pooled income funds were very popular in the late 1970s and the early 1980s which is when most charities started the funds in existence today. Back then, interest rates were at double-digit levels making pooled income funds the most popular life income plan, especially because many organizations were not yet offering charitable gift annuities.

Many organizations have stopped marketing their pooled income funds in favor of gift annuities. When donors compare the annual payment from a pooled income fund (limited to ordinary income earned in the fund) to a gift annuity (fixed percentage rate based on age), they often seek the higher payout from the gift annuity.

Nonetheless, a planned giving officer new to a charity is likely to inherit the management of a pooled income fund. In addition, if interest rates swing up in the future, the pooled income fund may again become popular. Therefore, I am including in this chapter a complete treatment of the pooled income fund, including how to start one, even though you are probably not likely to start one in the near future.

The nature and operation of a pooled income fund makes it difficult to market during a period of low interest rates and low stock yields. Since the payment to the beneficiaries is limited to actual income earned, today the payment would be about 5% to 6% at best, even if the account were invested 100% in fixed-income investments (bonds). For an 80 year old donor, compare that to the 8% recommended by the American Council on Gift Annuities for a charitable gift annuity (as of July 1, 2003).

I talked to Abigail Mason, Director of Investments at Kaspick & Company's Boston Office, about pooled income funds. Kaspick manages over $2 billion in charitable assets. I asked Abby for her insights on the topic of pooled income funds. "Hardly anybody is marketing their pooled income fund and we see virtually no new pooled income funds. The low interest rate environment is one reason. The other is the fact that people are more sophisticated than they used to be about structuring the taxability of their income. A pooled income fund pays 100% ordinary income to the beneficiary. Compare that to the preferential tiered system with charitable remainder trusts or gift annuities. Managed properly, a charitable trust should be able to pay a significant portion of its income as long-term capital gain which is taxed at only 15% for most people. A gift annuity pays partly tax-free income and also has a capital gain tier when the gift is funded with long-term capital assets. So, if you have a choice, you would not choose the pooled income fund."

The only activity Abby sees with pooled income funds is with colleges that actually market their pooled income fund as part of their reunion effort. "These donors keep coming back, again and again, to the pooled income fund. They understand it and they are comfortable with it."

In the following pages, pooled income funds are examined under these main topics:

- General operation;
- Establishing a pooled income fund;
- Drafting considerations of your pooled income fund;
- Pooled income fund fees and considerations;
- Administering your pooled income fund;
- Working with your trustee;
- Tax consequences to the donor;
- Questions and answers about pooled income funds;
- Community pooled income funds;
- Crediting guidelines.

GENERAL OPERATION

A pooled income fund serves as a receptacle for gifts from many donors. Gifts are commingled for investment purposes, and each donor (or a beneficiary designated by the donor) receives a proportionate share of the annual income earned. On the death of the beneficiary(ies), the portion of the fund represented by that gift is severed from the fund and available for use by the charity.

Ownership in the fund is represented by units of participation (including fractional units) which rise and fall with the value of the portfolio. Initially, the trustee will assign a round dollar value such as $100 to each unit. Thus, a $10,000 gift is represented by 100 units, a $5,000 gift by 50 units, and so on. In this way, the trustee determines how much income is attributable to each unit and how much principal to sever from the fund upon the death of a beneficiary.

If you own a mutual fund, you are accustomed to receiving periodic account statements that include the current market value of one share of the fund. The pooled income fund units of participation are like the shares of a mutual fund in that they fluctuate at periodic intervals. When the last beneficiary of a particular gift dies, the trustee determines the unit value at the end of the payment period and severs from the fund the current fair market value of the deceased beneficiary's share.

If your organization has a pooled income fund, get a copy of the statement for the last payment period. This might be called the "Holder's List," or the "Units of Participation Report," or the "Participant List." It will show the following information: Name of donor, name of beneficiary, date of gift, amount of gift, units of participation, value of one unit, and current market value of the gift. If you cannot find this document, get a copy from your trustee. With this document in hand, you know who contributed to your pooled income fund, who is receiving income, and you have the critical information you need to steward these people and to manage the fund.

ESTABLISHING A POOLED INCOME FUND

Your legal counsel must draw up the trust document for you. This is very easy because the I.R.S. publishes a standard document for a pooled income fund. It will recognize a fund as a qualified fund if the fund's document is substantially similar to the I.R.S. version. The document is 15 to 20 pages consisting of four parts:

1) an introduction that includes a brief description of your organization (provided by you);

2) a section that explains the operation of the fund and the tax consequences to the donor in plain English;

3) the trust document itself;

4) the "instrument of transfer" pursuant to which the donors will make transfers to the fund.

In Appendix V, there is a copy of the I.R.S. standard pooled income fund agreement. I talked to Michael J. Puzo, Esq. who is a partner at Hemenway & Barnes in Boston about the process of getting a pooled income fund agreement. Michael is the tax counsel for Boston College. "First of all, you have to consider that attorneys who started practicing law in the last decade probably have not created a pooled income fund agreement. If you hire an attorney who has never worked with a pooled income fund, you're going to pay a lot of money to reinvent the wheel. It would be far better to find someone already experienced with these funds—someone who was practicing charitable giving law when pooled income funds were popular." Michael says that since charities are not setting these up today, even an attorney familiar with these funds will have to spend some time reviewing the issues, requirements, and drafting options. But, this process should be fairly smooth and will take only a few hours.

DRAFTING CONSIDERATIONS OF YOUR POOLED INCOME FUND

While most of the language in the trust document is prescribed by the I.R.S., you have flexibility in choosing some administrative features. If you inherit a fund to manage, you cannot change the existing features:

- the valuation schedule
- acceptance of gifts
- the payment schedule
- the investment objective.

The Valuation Schedule

The trust document establishes regular dates on which the trustee must value the fund's assets and units of participation. A pooled income fund must have valuation dates at least quarterly. Since this process is time consuming and costly for the trustee, most funds use quarterly valuations (as opposed to monthly).

Following the close of the valuation date, units of participation are assigned to all new gifts since the last valuation date. Let's assume your fund has valuation dates on the last day of March, June, September, and December. The unit value changes only on these four dates. Gifts received in the middle of a valuation period (for example, February 15) receive units on the next valuation date following the gift (March 31). After the trustee issues units to the new gifts, he or she then calculates the *pro rata* share of income attributable to the new and old units for the prior quarter.

Acceptance Of Gifts

Your fund's governing instrument probably allows gifts to be accepted at any time. This may seem obvious, yet some funds, created in the late 1970s or early 1980s permit gifts only on valuation dates. So, for example, if your fund is valued four times *per* year, it is entirely possible that your trust document allows gifts on only those four dates. If you inherit a fund with this problem, you will have a difficult time accepting gifts to the fund because all documentation and gift property needs to be finalized on a particular day. My guess is that if your PIF has these restrictions, it has been dormant for a while. Leave it alone, wait until the beneficiaries die off and close it. This kind of fund is not practical.

The Payment Schedule

The payment schedule is stated in the trust document, either monthly or quarterly. Almost all funds have quarterly payments.

Usually, the payment schedule is tied to the valuation schedule. If you have quarterly valuations, it is common to have quarterly payments. Payments are generally made about two to three weeks following the valuation date. It takes this long for the trustee to allocate the *pro rata* share of income to each beneficiary. Unless you direct otherwise, income checks will be mailed by your trustee in its window envelopes.

There are two ways to handle the payments:

- Pay exactly the earned income in the account.

  When you use this method, the beneficiaries receive different amounts of money each time, sometimes higher, sometimes lower than they expect. With this method, all income actually in the account is cleared out for that payment period. For a quarterly payment schedule, you would make payments four times.

- Estimate the payments.

  When you use this method, you estimate the total annual income, divide by four, and reduce the amount slightly so that you don't exceed the anticipated income. If you use this method, your beneficiaries receive the same payment every quarter. Then, an adjustment is made in January to take care of any excess income that wasn't paid in the prior year. With this method, the beneficiaries receive five payments consisting of four equal payments and one small adjustment payment.

As you get to know beneficiaries in your fund, you will encounter a few who are disgruntled because they don't want to wait two to three weeks after the end of the quarter to receive their payments. There is nothing you can do about this. The trustee cannot make payments until he or she figures out the new unit value, issues units to the new participants, and allocates the available income among the beneficiaries. The advent of electronic payments, which are readily available today, helps a little. It eliminates the mail delay. You should encourage the beneficiaries in all of your life income plans, especially those in the pooled income fund, to participate in electronic payments. Your trustee can provide the authorization forms.

Banks that manage pooled income funds are sensitive to this problem and usually try to get the payments out within two weeks after the close of the quarter. The earliest I ever saw PIF payments was on the 9th of the following month. Related to this problem is the mail delay in having payments sent to you first. You must decide whether the trustee should mail the checks directly to the beneficiaries. That will save a day or two. The delayed payment issue is always a big aggravation for at least one person in your pooled income fund. So simply be aware of it.

If the trustee mails the checks to you for forwarding with your own cover letter, it should send the checks by overnight mail, and you should mail the checks on the day you receive them from the trustee. Do not let them sit until you "get around to it." Getting those checks in the mail is the highest priority of the day, even if you have to drive them to the post office yourself because you missed the last mail pick-up in your department. No exceptions. No excuses.

At the end of each quarter, ask your trustee what day the checks will be cut and what day he or she will mail them to you. Do not allow any member of your staff involved with mailing the checks to be on vacation the day the checks arrive in your charity's office. Also, your trustee should use the earliest delivery time in the morning for its overnight mail carrier. If the checks arrive at 3:30 pm, you probably will not have enough time to review them, photocopy them for the donors' files, stuff them in envelopes with cover letters, stamp them, and get them in the mail that day.

To save time when mailing the checks from your office, purchase standard window envelopes with the charity's logo. Before ordering the window envelopes, check whether the mailing address is on the right or the left of the check. Then, you won't have to run your own envelopes through your printer. Specify that you want opaque envelopes. Some are made with light weight paper that you can see through.

For beneficiaries signed up for direct deposit to their checking accounts, there will be a notice of the direct deposit information to mail to the donor. Occasionally, a beneficiary wants you to mail the check to a bank, rather than having an electronic deposit. In this case you should include a cover letter to the donor's bank with instructions to "deposit this check to account [number] in the name of [beneficiary]." Send a copy of your letter to the beneficiary.

The Investment Objective

Each pooled income fund operates under investment guidelines set by the charity. Once established, the investment objective, in theory, never changes. There are three types of pooled income funds:

1. *The growth fund*

   Assets are invested in growth-oriented securities toward achieving maximum appreciation with little emphasis on current income. Growth funds are attractive to younger donors who wish to experience appreciation of the principal but who require little income currently.

2. *The balanced fund*

   Assets are invested in a mix of growth-oriented securities and fixed-income investments (bonds), thus providing reasonable income with some emphasis on capital appreciation.

3. *The income or high-yield fund*

   Assets are invested for maximum income in fixed-income securities with little or no emphasis on capital appreciation. A high-yield fund is more attractive to an older donor seeking higher income, possibly in retirement. The income fund is the worst for the charity since the investment strategy required to produce a high yield would leave little chance for appreciation of the principal.

When pooled income funds were popular, it was not uncommon for an organization to establish more than one pooled income fund. The attorney drafting the document for the first one can easily do three at the same time simply by changing the language for the investment objective. Most banks require minimum levels of gifts within two years to justify administration expenses; therefore, you would not start three funds at once. Practically, when the interest rates go up and it becomes desirable for your charity to start a fund, you can do fine with just one balanced pooled income fund.

Some planned giving officers will inherit a planned giving program with more than one pooled income fund and may wonder why an institution would want more than one fund anyway. As you will see when you read the section on tax consequences, the higher the yield on the fund, the lower the income tax deduction for the donor. Therefore, for a donor seeking a relatively high tax deduction but with little need for current income, the growth fund is the way to go. Conversely, a donor who wants current income will choose the high-yield fund—even though the tax deduction is smaller.

You're attorney can prepare the PIF documents, but you incur no management fees until you accept a gift into the fund. During this dormant period, the fund is simply a series of papers in your file drawer. You can go as far as having account numbers issued for them by your bank. Then, the funds are ready to go as soon as you find a prospective donor.

If you are just beginning a planned giving program for your organization, you should not start a pooled income fund in this economic climate. However, I will provide information about creating one because you may need the details some day.

It is a good idea to select the trustee in advance of drafting the trust document. This allows the trustee to review the terms of your fund in order to ensure that they are consistent with its own preferred drafting provisions, if any. If you know the trustee, the name can be written into the original document. (Otherwise, your organization's name will appear as trustee until such time as you appoint a successor trustee—a bank or other administrator). The trustee may even have its own preferred document that it will supply to you and to your attorney.

POOLED INCOME FUND FEES AND CONSIDERATIONS

All banks are different in the way they structure fees. If you are turning over assets for a group of deferred giving vehicles such as a gift annuity pool, some charitable remainder or lead trusts, and one or more pooled income funds, you can negotiate a consolidated fee for the whole group of assets. However, if you have a pooled income fund by itself, following are some of the items on which a bank may base its fees:

1. A fee based on the income earned;
2. A fee based on the market value of the account;
3. An annual charge for each donor or beneficiary;
4. A fee for each payment made to a beneficiary;
5. A fee for each addition to the fund;
6. A fee for each distribution from the fund;
7. A separate charge for the preparation of fiduciary income tax returns.

One manager might have lower fees on income and principal, but it might charge $100 for each addition or distribution and another charge for every payment made to a beneficiary.

If you need to find a manager for a pooled income fund, go to Chapter III-9 on Managing Your Planned Giving Assets.

There are three ways to pay the management fees of your pooled income fund:

1. *Charge the fees to income and/or principal of the account.* If you charge the fee to income, you will reduce the beneficiaries' payments directly. Some organizations charge the fee to principal which solves that problem. By charging the fees to the account, an institution can operate a pooled income fund at no cost to the institution. Check state laws to see if there are rules about whether fees should come from income or principal.

2. *Pay the fees from your planned giving budget.* This option allows the donors and beneficiaries to benefit from the total income earned in the account and aids in the growth of the principal by not reducing it. Thus, your fund can offer a competitive rate of return relative to other institutions' pooled income funds. The problem with this method is that, as you get more and more gifts, the fees will consume an increasingly larger percentage of your planned giving budget leaving less for other activities. This is not a good system.

3. *Submit the bills to your business office for payment.* This option removes the burden of fees from the planned giving budget and places them in the business office as an administrative expense much the same way as other endowment-related management fees are charged. Some institutions start with Option 2 and shift to Option 3 when the fees begin to drain the planned giving budget.

About half of the charities running pooled income funds charge the fees to the account. This is not from a scientific analysis, but from my own inquiries of audiences during workshops I have run.

When you inherit a pooled income fund in your new planned giving position, get a copy of the Disclosure Statement and find the section about fees. Many Disclosure Statements cite a policy of not charging fees to the account but reserving the right to do so after notifying the beneficiaries. My opinion of this issue has changed over the years. I used to think it was always best to pay the fees separately. In fact, all four charities for which I worked used this policy. Now, I think that the life income plans ought to be able to stand on their own, without the charity paying separately for their management. You must decide for yourself.

ADMINISTERING YOUR POOLED INCOME FUND

Administering a pooled income fund requires understanding the operation of the fund and the procedures required by your trustee.

Starting from the beginning, here's what you need before you can run your pooled income fund:

- the pooled income fund disclosure statement,
- instrument of transfer,
- stock powers,
- business reply envelopes,
- your trustee's Depository Trust Company account number.

The Pooled Income Fund Disclosure Statement

This is an explanation of the fund's operation and the tax consequences to the donor. It includes a copy of the trust document. Think of it as your fund's prospectus. You write the introduction, and your legal counsel provides the rest.

Most organizations print the Disclosure Statement in the form of a brochure or booklet. Cost is obviously a consideration, and, in cases where money is limited, it is perfectly acceptable to photocopy the pages. Add a specially-prepared cover page, and you can get along quite well. Often, an organization uses a photocopied version in the beginning while it works with designers, typesetters, and printers to produce a more formal piece. With desktop publishing and laser jet printers, you may very well not need to print it at all.

Your initial instinct may be to produce an award-winning Disclosure Statement. Don't. Few donors ever have made a gift based on reading the Disclosure Statement, if they have ever read it at all. It is long, technical, and deadly boring. This is not an inspirational marketing piece. It is a legal requirement of the Securities and Exchange Commission. Every donor to a pooled income fund must receive this document prior to making a gift to the fund.

After the pooled income fund has been in existence for more than one year, you will receive from the trustee an Annual Report (usually a one-page summary) of the activities in the fund for the prior year. This includes the beginning and ending balances, the change in the value of one unit, additions during the year, distributions during the year, and the fund's adjusted yearly rate of return. *This one-page summary should be inserted into the back of the Disclosure Statement as an integral part of that document.* Note: You should not print the Annual Report as part of the Disclosure Statement, because it will change every year.

Instrument Of Transfer

The Instrument of Transfer is the contract between the trustee and the donor. At the end of this subsection is a sample Instrument of Transfer. This particular Instrument of Transfer has been designed as a form with blanks to fill in. You will notice, however, that the Instrument of Transfer that is drafted by your attorney is written in sentences. You can use either version as long as all of the information is there.

The Instrument of Transfer is the document on which the donor designates the income recipient(s) with respect to the gift. You can refer to the sample to follow along as I discuss the information on the form.

The Gift Property:

> In this section, the donor describes the property being contributed. For cash gifts, he or she simply writes the amount of cash. For stock gifts, he or she includes the number of shares, the name of the stock, the date of acquisition, and cost basis. (*Note: A gift can be accepted without the date of acquisition and cost basis. However, the trustee will need this information to prepare its fiduciary income tax return. Securing the information in the beginning eliminates the additional step of going back to the donor for it later.*)

> The pooled income fund pays no capital gain tax on the sale of appreciated, long-term capital gain property (unless the gains may be allocated to the fund's income). However, *the full amount of gain*

realized on the sale of short-term capital gain property is taxable to the fund. Depending on the size of gift in relation to the total fund's assets, you may choose not to accept a gift of short-term capital gain property. Remember, all donors share the total income of the fund. Thus, you do not want to accept a gift that severely reduces the income for the other beneficiaries.

Frequently, a donor wishes to make a gift of part stock and part cash equal to your minimum gift level, for example, $10,000. In this case, the donor does not know how much cash is needed to bring the total gift to $10,000 until the stock portion of the gift is accepted and valued. The donor should write only the stock information on the Instrument of Transfer. Then, the trustee will determine the value of the stock portion and inform either you or the donor of the amount of cash necessary to bring the total gift to $10,000. (*Make certain you know who is doing what. Don't assume the trustee will do this.*) The donor then writes a check for the balance, sending it to the trustee to be included as part of the gift. (Note: It is not necessary to complete another Instrument of Transfer for the cash portion; it becomes part of the total gift of $10,000.) The trustee will write the cash amount onto the Instrument of Transfer.

The Income Beneficiaries:

The donor has the option of providing income for himself or herself alone or for one or more other people. Legally, the donor can designate anyone to be the income recipient. In practice, most pooled income fund gifts fall into one of three categories:

1. Donor is sole beneficiary;

2. Donor is primary beneficiary and spouse is secondary beneficiary;

3. Donor and spouse are concurrent and consecutive beneficiaries.

When you are running a planned giving program, you want every gift you can get. Because you are virtually the only person with hands-on responsibility for the fund, you have a lot of control by yourself. Most of the other staff members in your department don't understand the fund's operation; therefore, no one else knows what is going on. It is your responsibility to suggest policies about the age limit and the number of beneficiaries you will accept.

Look back at the section earlier in this chapter about how fees are charged. There could be a fee on the income earned, a fee on the market value, and a fee for each beneficiary. Plus, there may be a fee for each gift, a fee for each distribution, and a fee for each beneficiary payment. Think about how this impacts the real value of a gift to your fund. A 70 year old donor has a life expectancy of about 16 years. The fees applied to that gift over the donor's life expectancy diminish severely the real value of the gift to your institution.

Occasionally, donors suggest naming a child or even a grandchild as a secondary or tertiary beneficiary. For them, this may be a wonderful gesture that affords them the satisfaction of providing a future income to a loved one. From a strictly business sense, the gift will probably cost much more to administer than what you will ever get out of it. And, despite the potential for future gifts from the donor, it is probably better to discourage a gift with beneficiaries younger than a certain age. Your trustee should know your rules so that he or she can catch cases in which the donor has added a young person to the Instrument of Transfer.

For a high-yield fund, presumably with a high percentage of bond investments, there will be little chance for appreciation over the many years you'll be managing a young donor's gift. If you are paying the fees separately, the fees will eat up the ultimate benefit of the gift. In such a case, I would recommend a minimum age of 70. On the other hand, a growth fund that is expected to appreciate and that presumably will keep up with inflation could perform reasonably well with beneficiaries much younger, say 50. A balanced fund with a mix of stocks and bonds might require a minimum age of 60. This is not to say you shouldn't be flexible. The rules can be bent depending on the size of the gift and many other factors related to the circumstances of the donor. One way to discourage gifts from younger people is to target your mailings and promotional materials to specific age groups so that you will eliminate inquiries from those who would not fit your guidelines.

In situations where fees are paid from the pooled income fund account, the age limitations may not be as much of a concern. Still, the time and energy expended on a pooled income fund are sufficiently great that it would be prudent for you to establish guidelines that will make your work as productive as possible.

The Right To Revoke By Will The Income Interest Of Any Succeeding Beneficiary:

When a donor names a secondary beneficiary who will receive income after the donor's death, he or she is making a gift to that person of a *future interest* which may be subject to a current gift tax.

By reserving the right to revoke the succeeding beneficiary's income interest, the donor avoids this problem because there is no completed gift at the time of the transfer to the fund. If the donor dies without revoking the income interest of the secondary beneficiary, only then would the value of the second beneficiary's income interest, as of the date of death, be a taxable gift in the estate.

(Note: For deaths in 2010 and later, if the elimination of the estate tax is made permanent, there would no longer be an estate tax for the secondary beneficiary's income interest. However, there would still be a gift tax making this election important to prevent a current taxable gift.)

The Use Of The Funds By Your Organization:

It is a good idea to provide in the Instrument of Transfer a general statement about the use of the gift by your organization. You may decide, for example, that all gifts to the pooled income fund will be credited to your permanent endowment fund. Or, you may earmark the funds for general purposes.

Many donors like the idea of earmarking their gift toward a specific program or project. In this case, you should encourage the donor to discuss the purpose with you before making the gift in order to ensure that the purpose is consistent with your priorities and needs.

XYZ POOLED INCOME FUND
INSTRUMENT OF TRANSFER*
(Sole Beneficiary or Consecutive Beneficiaries)

I herewith transfer to the (Bank) as Trustee of the XYZ Pooled Income Fund under a certain declaration of Trust dated _____ (the "Fund"), to be held, administered, and disposed of under the provisions of the Fund (as the same may be from time to time amended) the following property:

cash amount/securities   date of acquisition   cost basis

_____

_____

_____

_____

I hereby direct the income interest in respect of said property be paid to:

Name (primary beneficiary)_____

Legal residence_____

Date of birth_____Social security number _____

during (his/her) lifetime* and thereafter to:
(*omit all material following the asterisk if there is only one beneficiary)

Name (secondary beneficiary) _____

Legal residence_____

Date of birth_____Social security number _____

during (his/her) lifetime if the secondary beneficiary survives the primary beneficiary.

I reserve the right, exercisable only by my will, to revoke the income interest of the secondary beneficiary. (Strike out this provision if not applicable.)

The amount payable to XYZ Charity upon final termination of the income interests in said property shall be used by XYZ Charity for its charitable purposes. (If for other purposes, please discuss them first with XYZ Charity and then describe such purposes below.)

_____

_____

I intend this transfer to become effective in (state) on the date of acceptance hereof by the Trustee. I hereby acknowledge that prior to my determination to make this transfer, I received and read the brochure, "Gifts to the XYZ Pooled Income Fund," dated   , which includes a copy of the declaration of trust.

Signed this_____day of _____, 20_____

donor print name_____

donor's signature _____

The Trustee hereby accepts said property on behalf of XYZ Charity under the terms and conditions set forth herein and in the Fund, and based on its mean market value of $_____on   , 20_____, has assigned_____Units of Participation to the income interest in said property as of this_____ day of _____, 20_____.

(The Bank) as Trustee of the XYZ Pooled Income Fund by _____

Caution: This form is not a prototype. Ask your attorney to advise you if you plan to use a form Instrument of Transfer. All instruments of transfer that you use must be the same.

Stock Powers

Many gifts to your pooled income fund will come in the form of securities, mostly publicly traded stocks and hardly ever bonds. In many cases, you will have to provide the donor with stock powers and proper instructions for transferring securities to your trustee. A donor needs one stock power for each stock certificate to be transferred. You can get a supply of stock powers either from your trustee or from most business stationery supply stores. When you instruct your donor to complete the stock power, use language along these lines:

"Please sign one stock power for each certificate being transferred leaving everything else blank."

By leaving the form essentially blank except for the signature, the donor gives the trustee the greatest flexibility in disposing of the asset. (See Chapter II-4 for a full discussion about how to handle gifts of securities.)

Business Reply Envelopes

To facilitate the transfer, your donors should send all materials (Instrument of Transfer, stock certificates, and stock powers) directly to your trustee—not to you. Your trustee can send you a supply of its postage-paid business reply envelopes to expedite this process.

If you cannot get business reply envelopes from your trustee, prepare a supply of your own envelopes addressed to your trustee for use with pooled income fund donors.

Your Trustee's Depository Trust Company (DTC) Number

Most donors keep securities in a brokerage account rather than in a safe deposit box. When such donors wish to make a transfer of stock to your pooled income fund, they generally will issue instructions to their broker to do the following:

"Transfer 200 shares of Kodak Common Stock from my account #_____, to [trustee bank's] DTC number [xxx-xxx-xxx] for credit to [charity's] Pooled Income Fund account number [xxx-xxxxx]."

In Chapter II-4 about gifts of securities, there is a complete discussion of DTC transfers.

Other

Each bank has its own procedures. You should meet with your trustee to learn about specific forms or other information that may be required. For example, the bank may require all beneficiaries to complete a form indicating where income checks should be sent, either to their home, office, or to a bank account for direct deposit. Or, all beneficiaries may be required to sign a signature card.

Following is a sample letter that you might use in responding to pooled income fund donors.

Dear [name]:

We are delighted to learn of your interest in contributing to the XYZ Pooled Income Fund. Enclosed are the following:

- Disclosure Statement
- Instrument of Transfer
- Two stock powers
- Two business reply envelopes

The Disclosure Statement outlines the operation of the fund and the tax benefits to you. Please take a few minutes to read it, and let me know if you have any questions.

Gifts of Cash

Please make check payable to XYZ Pooled Income Fund and send it with the completed Instrument of Transfer in the enclosed business reply envelope to:

> Trust Officer or Manager
> Name of Trustee
> Street Address
> City, State, Zip Code

Gifts of Securities

Mail the unendorsed stock certificate(s) to the (name of trustee) in one of the enclosed business reply envelopes.

In the other envelope mail the completed Instrument of Transfer together with one signature-guaranteed stock power for each certificate being transferred. Please sign the stock power and leave everything else blank.

Delivery of stock through a broker

Complete the Instrument of Transfer and mail it immediately to the (name of trustee) in one of the enclosed envelopes.

Ask your broker to call (name of trust officer) at (phone number) for disposition instructions. Tell your broker NOT to sell the securities or to transfer them into our name.

In all cases, the gift will be complete when the (name of trustee) receives the gift property in marketable form *together with* the Instrument of Transfer. Securities received prior to receipt of the Instrument of Transfer will be held in safekeeping.

After the gift is made, the (name of trustee) will be in touch with information about your income tax deduction, payment schedules, and other details about the fund.

We are most grateful for your generous support.

Sincerely,

Director of Planned Giving

WORKING WITH YOUR TRUSTEE

Nothing could be more important to the success of running any life income plan than having a good working relationship with your trustee. The two of you are a team. Your role is to get the gifts; the trustee's role is to manage them. While this division of responsibilities may seem basic on first glance, the day-to-day working relationship goes far beyond the basics.

Sometimes, things go wrong.

For example, let's take the case of William transferring stock to your pooled income fund. Instead of notifying you or your trustee that a gift is forthcoming, William calls his broker issuing instructions to transfer securities to your organization. He considers a gift complete, because he has made other stock gifts this way. The donor then goes out of town.

This is not good enough. In order to consider a gift complete, the trustee must have a completed "Instrument of Transfer" from the donor as well as control of the gift property. If the donor dies on vacation, you have no instructions under which to administer the gift.

The broker notifies your organization about the gift and is referred to the business office. He never mentions that the gift is for the pooled income fund. Your business office sells the stock and credits the donor with an annual gift. When the donor returns three weeks later, he calls to see if you received his pooled income fund gift. There is a mad scramble to trace the gift.

The above scenario is a real mess, but it can happen to you. Things like this happen all the time. Regardless of how specific your instructions are, donors often don't follow them. Thus, a good working relationship with your trustee is essential.

Other things go wrong because there is a basic misunderstanding between you and the trustee with regard to the division of responsibilities.

Your trustee manager should perform the following tasks for your pooled income fund:

- Accept gifts of cash and securities;

- Value new gifts;

- Issue units of participation for new gifts to the fund;

- Calculate charitable deductions;

- Calculate all periodic income payments and mail them to beneficiaries or to the charity client;

- Calculate state tax withholding when applicable;

- Prepare Schedule K-1 Forms;

- Value each fund on valuation dates;

- Calculate annual rates of return for the fund;

- Compile an Annual Report of the fund for each beneficiary;

- Compile "Holders List" after the close of each valuation date;

- Help establish investment objective (target yield);

- Invest the assets, collect income and dividends;

- Prepare an Annual Accounting;

- Prepare federal and state tax returns.

There should be total communication between the planned giving officer and the trustee. It is important that the bank be notified of a gift immediately, especially when the gift involves securities. In dealing with a donor's broker, the trustee should get involved as early as possible in order to expedite the removal of the securities from the donor's brokerage account.

In other ways, the trustee depends totally on your direction. For example, it is the director of planned giving's responsibility to decide whether income checks are mailed from the bank or are delivered to the institution before being mailed to the beneficiaries. It is also the director of planned giving who decides when to enclose a letter with the income checks.

Many new planned giving officers don't realize it is their job to determine the best way to handle the donors or beneficiaries. Perhaps because they have not worked with a fiduciary in a team approach before, they feel reluctant to request a change in the way checks are mailed. The experienced planned giving officers know that it is their job to make these decisions, and they tell the trustee what to do. The trustee, in turn, should be flexible enough to accommodate their wishes.

Following are some of the situations that create problems.

- *Incomplete documentation on a gift*: This causes a delay in processing the gift and can irritate the donor if the trustee or planned giving officer has to go back to the donor several times for additional information. Incomplete documentation may take one of the following forms: 1) no stock power or one that is incorrectly filled out, or 2) no Instrument of Transfer.

- *Delay in receiving proceeds on a gift of securities*: Sometimes the donor fills in all the blanks on the certificate or the stock power. This causes the trustee to re-register the stock and encounter a delay of several weeks in realizing the proceeds. Delays of this kind become an acute problem when the gift in question is large relative to the size of the fund. The new donor is entitled to his or her *pro rata* share of the fund's income from the date of the gift, but the gift property isn't earning income for several weeks. This means that everybody's income will be diluted for that period.

- *Erroneous information given to the donor by the planned giving officer*: Sometimes the planned giving officer gives the donor a charitable deduction figure that is incorrect. Or, sometimes a planned giving officer accepts a gift of tax-exempt bonds to a pooled income fund. (*Note: The regulations governing pooled income funds strictly prohibit the fund from accepting or investing in tax-exempt securities.*)

If you are already running a pooled income fund, you know how much anxiety such things create both for you and for your donor. The donor expects an efficient and uneventful gift experience. Take the time to meet with your trustee, learn about and understand the mistakes others have made, and you will surely benefit by minimizing the potential problems in your own fund.

Following are some guidelines to keep in mind as you manage your pooled income fund:

- It is your job to provide the donor with proper instructions (outlined earlier) for making a gift to your pooled income fund. The trustee can help you, but you are the one closest to the donor and the best one to get things moving in the right direction.

- If you know that a donor intends to make a gift to your fund, call the trustee immediately to report the name of the donor, the property being used for the gift, the name and phone number of the donor's broker, the donor's telephone number and address, and anything else that will facilitate a smooth transaction.

- A gift to a pooled income fund is considered complete only when the trustee has the gift property (cash or securities) in marketable form (meaning a signed stock power has been received for each separate stock certificate) along with the Instrument of Transfer. It is your job to tell the donor his or her gift will be complete *only* when all of the above pieces have been received. Donors often assume that they have made a gift when they issue instructions to their broker to transfer stock to you. This is not true.

- Tell the donor *not* to send the gift property or the Instrument of Transfer to you but rather to the trustee. Donors are accustomed to sending contributions directly to the charity and will do so unless you instruct them otherwise. Even if the donor sends everything to you, there is *no gift until you send the materials to the trustee (unless the charity is also co-trustee.)* One way to arrange a smoother operation with fewer problems is for the trustee to make the charity the agent of the trustee. Another option is for the charity and the donor to be co-trustees. Then, any gifts delivered inadvertently to the charity will still be considered a gift.

At Boston College, we were co-trustee with our bank which meant that physical receipt of gift property by us constituted a completed gift. That worked very well. Still, we had to get the gift property and paperwork to the bank for deposit and reinvestment as quickly as possible.

- For gifts of stock, the donor's broker should call the trustee directly—not you.

- Don't rely on your own calculations with regard to the value of the gift and the income tax deduction (discussed later in this chapter). Check your figures with those of the trustee before sending an acknowledgment letter. Often donors receive different values from the bank and the planned giving officer. Ugh!

TAX CONSEQUENCES TO THE DONOR

Now that you are familiar with the administrative procedures, it is time for an example:

Example:

Mary, age 75, owns stock with a fair market value of $20,000 and a cost basis of $2,000. The stock yields 3% *per* year or $600. Mary's tax bracket is 35%. She has held the stock more than a year. Your pooled income fund's highest rate of return for the prior three-year period is 6.5%. (*If you don't know why I made that statement, read about the Yield of Your Pooled Income Fund two sections below.*)

Sale and Reinvestment

If Mary sells the stock for reinvestment, she must pay a 15% capital gain tax on the entire $18,000 gain losing $2,700. ($18,000 x 15% = $2,700). The net amount available to reinvest is $17,300 which would generate $1,125 at 6.5%. She will have increased her annual income from $600 to $1,125 which looks pretty good until you see the results from a pooled income fund gift. (Note: I used 6.5% for reinvestment simply to be consistent with the yield of the pooled income fun for comparison.)

Gift to Your Pooled Income Fund

Instead, Mary contributes the $20,000 worth of stock to your pooled income fund which is currently yielding 6.5%. Since the fund pays no tax on long-term capital gains, the entire $20,000 is available to generate income for her (brokerage commissions ignored in both cases). Already, she has increased her income from $600 to $1,300 per year. Plus, Mary will receive an income tax deduction of $10,873 in the year of the gift saving $3,806 in income taxes ($10,873 x 35% = $3,806). On her death, the gift will be available for use by your organization.

Depending on the age of the beneficiary, the yield of the pooled income fund, and the amount of appreciation on the gift property, these results can be even more dramatic. This same example done in the 1980s could have shown pooled income payments in double digits. Also, in this example, I used the highest rate of return of the prior three-year period instead of the I.R.S Discount Rate since that is the rule for PIFs. In practice, the yield of the current year will be different from the highest three-year yield figure.

By contributing to your pooled income fund, the donor has accomplished the following:

- Made a meaningful gift to your organization;
- Avoided a capital gain tax of $2,700;

- Received an income tax deduction of $10,873, saving $3,806 in her 35% bracket;
- Increased her annual income from $600 to $1,300 *per* year;
- Reduced probate costs by removing the property from her probate estate.

Acknowledging A Gift to the Pooled Income Fund

When you set up your pooled income fund, you should coordinate with your trustee to decide who is going to send donors their official acknowledgement letter for tax purposes. It does not matter who does the acknowledgement, as long as you both don't do it. Don't forget that there are two separate letters for this donor. The other letter comes from the trustee and notifies the donor of the number of units of participation assigned to his or her gift on the valuation date next following the gift. Since both that letter and your letter below quote a fair market value for the gift, make sure your two figures are identical.

Here is a standard letter that you can adapt to your needs:

Dear [donor]:

This will acknowledge your gift of $10,000 to the XYZ Pooled Income Fund on [date].

or

This will acknowledge your gift of 49 shares of Kodak Common Stock to the XYZ Pooled Income Fund on [date]. The high was $_____ and the low was $_____ so the total mean value of the gift is $_____. Please check these figures to ensure accuracy before you use them on your income tax return.

You have retained a life income for yourself, naming your spouse, [name] successor beneficiary if [he/she] survives you. On the death of the survivor, the remaining principal will be used to [fill in restricted purposes, if any].

The highest rate of return for the XYZ Pooled Income Fund for the prior three year period is [__%] and I have enclosed an Actuarial Calculation that shows the value of your income tax deduction for the gift is [dollar amount]. You should check these figures with your accountant.

I am required to verify that no goods or services were provided to you in consideration of this gift.

Thank you very much for your generosity to [charity].

Sincerely,

Director of Planned Giving

It is important to note that the calculation you will produce from your planned giving software (see **Exhibit II-7A** on the next page) is supposed to be checked by the donor's accountant. Frequently, donors attach your calculations without checking them with anybody. That normally doesn't cause a problem because most of the time, one hopes, your figures are correct. Nonetheless, be aware that the donor is supposed to be substantiating his or her own deduction, even though very few, if any, could do so on their own.

Exhibit II-7A

ASHTON ASSOCIATES

Prepared for:
Female 75

Deduction Calculations
Actuarial Calculations

Pooled Income Fund

ASSUMPTIONS:

[1]	Beneficiary Age	75
	Date of Gift	1/31/2004
[2]	Principal Donated	$20,000.00
	Cost Basis of Property	$2,000.00
[3]	Rate of Return Used for IRS Valuation (Reg. 1.642(c)-6(e)(2)(ii))	6.5000%

CALCULATIONS:

[4]	Remainder factor for values on [1] and [3] (Table S in IRS Publication 1457 (1999))	0.54364
[5]	**CHARITABLE DEDUCTION** ([2] x [4])	**$10,872.80**

(Notice that the I.R.S. Discount Rate is not used in this calculation because the relevant discount figure is the highest rate of return of the PIF for the prior three-year period.)

Donor *Vs.* Beneficiary

The income tax deduction for a gift to your pooled income fund is based on the age and number of beneficiaries—not on the age of the donor *unless* the donor is also a beneficiary. The sex of the beneficiary(ies) is irrelevant.

In most cases, the donor is the beneficiary. But, occasionally, a donor names someone else to be beneficiary.

Two Examples:

1. Mary, age 80, contributes to your pooled income fund and names herself beneficiary.
2. John, age 50, contributes to your pooled income fund and names his mother, age 80, as beneficiary.

The income tax deduction for both Mary and John is the same because the deduction is based on the age of the beneficiary—not on the age of the donor.

Yield Of Your Pooled Income Fund

In order to calculate the tax deduction for a gift to your pooled income fund, you need to know the highest rate of return for the prior three-year period. Your trustee determines the yield each year and can provide the figures for you. The figures will be available about a month after the close of the calendar year. If you potentially have a gift in January of any year, you cannot prepare a tax calculation for the donor until you know the new adjusted rate of return for the year just closed. If you are in the position of discussing a gift in the early part of the calendar year before the trustee gives you the new figures, you should call and inquire if the calculations for your fund could be moved to the front of the list.

The yield is usually expressed as a five-digit decimal. Following are sample yield figures for a pooled income fund:

Fiscal year 1:	.07002
Fiscal year 2:	.06739
Fiscal year 3:	.06501
Fiscal year 4:	approximately 6.5% (in progress)

If you accept a gift in the current year (year 4), you must calculate the donor's tax deduction based on a yield of .07002—not on the 6.5% current yield figure.

For new funds in operation less than three years, the I.R.S. prescribes a rate for you. Ask your trustee for the current figure when you establish your pooled income fund.

Important: You do not use the floating I.R.S. Discount Rate to calculate the tax consequences of a pooled income fund gift.

Relationship Of The Income Tax Deduction To The Pooled Income Fund's Yield

I mentioned earlier that there are reasons for maintaining pooled income funds with different investment objectives. In the following chart, you can see why this consideration is important.

Following is a chart illustrating how the donor's income tax deduction varies depending on the highest three-year return of the fund. I've assumed a $10,000 gift by a 75 year old donor.

Pooled Income Fund's Adjusted Rate of Return (Highest 3-Year Return)	Current Income Tax Deduction
3%	$7,363
4%	6,714
5%	6,151
6%	5,659
7%	5,228
8%	4,847
9%	4,511

Notice that the amount of the income tax deduction decreases as the rate of return increases.

Relationship Of The Income Tax Deduction To The Age Of The Beneficiary

A similar trend can be seen when one looks at the change in the income tax deduction in relation to the age of the beneficiary. In this comparison, assume a $10,000 gift to a growth fund (2% yield), a balanced fund (4% yield), and an income fund (6.5% yield).

Value of Donor's Income Tax Deduction
for a $10,000 gift to a growth, balanced, or income fund
depending on the age of the beneficiary

Age of Beneficiary	Growth* 2%	Balanced 4%	Income 6.5%
20	$3,421	$ 1,340	$ 518
30	4,089	1,863	821
40	4,878	2,592	1,327
50	5,784	3,573	2,136
60	6,743	4,759	3,265
70	7,677	6,058	4,665
80	8,519	7,360	6,239
90	9,170	8,460	7,710
100	9,534	9,114	8,642

An organization with three pooled income funds can offer its donors a choice. But, if your institution is starting a new planned giving program, do not try to activate three funds at the same time.

*To obtain the charitable deduction advantage of a growth fund (e.g., being able to offer donors a fund, gifts to which will generate a higher income tax deduction), the fund must first live through the three-year grace period during which time the income tax deduction is based on a presumably higher rate prescribed by the I.R.S. The solution to this is to activate a growth fund with two small gifts, such as $5,000 each and wait three years before marketing it to the general public.

How To Calculate The Income Tax Charitable Deduction For A Gift To Your Pooled Income Fund.

Calculating the tax deduction for a pooled income fund gift is very easy using any of the available planned giving software programs listed in Appendix II.

Here are the variables you'll need to know to work with your planned giving software:

1. The date of the gift;

2. The highest rate of return for the prior three-year period (or the applicable discount rate prescribed by the I.R.S. for pooled income funds in their first three fiscal years of operation, discussed above). If you do not know the proper figures for your fund, your trustee will be able to tell you;

3. The date of birth of the beneficiary or beneficiaries. Beneficiaries are considered actuarially to be closest to their next birth date. The software programs that calculate the tax consequences will automatically adjust the age to the closest birth date once you input the actual date of birth.

   Example:

   Beneficiary born March 1 makes a gift November 1. The beneficiary is considered to be closest to the next birth date.

4. Fair market value of the gift;

5. The payment frequency (most pooled income funds pay quarterly, but you should check your disclosure statement to make sure you aren't working with one of the few older funds whose payment schedule is monthly);

6. The donor's tax bracket (10%, 15%, 25%, 28%, 33%, or 35%);

7. The donor's capital gain tax rate (most of your donors will be in the 15% capital gain bracket);

8. The beneficiary's income tax bracket (optional on some programs). Then the software may show you a cash flow projection or another analysis of the donor's income tax situation. See item 6;

9. The beneficiary's capital gain tax rate. See Item 7;

10. Other: Each software program is different and most have training workshops to teach you how to use it.

When you input the above variables into your software, you'll generally be looking for the figure that is the donor's income tax charitable deduction, often called the remainder interest.

As with other gifts, the normal charitable contribution ceilings apply (See Chapter II-2 for an explanation of contribution ceilings).

Most software programs allow you to compare the results from a life income plan like this one to the consequences of keeping the asset in tact, or selling and reinvesting. At each point, you'll be able to create your own illustration or you may be able to compare the specific consequences of the donor's situation with the gift you are proposing.

QUESTIONS AND ANSWERS ABOUT POOLED INCOME FUNDS

Q. Is the income from a pooled income fund taxable to the beneficiaries?

A. Yes. The income is fully taxable as ordinary income. The Jobs and Growth Tax Relief Reconciliation Act of 2003 provides for a tax of 15% (5% for people in the 10% or 15% bracket and zero in 2008) for dividends meeting certain criteria until 2009 when dividends become taxable at the recipient's ordinary income rate. So a beneficiary in the 35% income tax bracket might have some income from the PIF reported at the 15% rate.

Q. Is there any limit to the number of beneficiaries that can be named in a pooled income fund gift?

A. No. Practically, you'll see one or two, and rarely three.

Q. If we start a growth fund, the donors who participate in the first three years will receive a tax deduction based on the I.R.S. prescribed rate which will be much higher than the actual earning in the fund. What can we do?

A. Activate the growth fund with two small gifts, invest them in low-yielding securities, and wait three years to market it to the general public. After the third year, you'll be able to use for purposes of the income tax calculation the highest yield of the prior three year period, which should be very low.

Q. My organization would like to start a pooled income fund, but we are not certain we can achieve the fiduciary's required minimum account size. What can we do?

A. Transfer to the trustee endowment funds as seed money. Thus, the trustee will have enough under management to provide lower fees for the pooled income fund. The trustee will track these funds separately. By jointly investing endowment funds and pooled income fund assets in the early years, you'll be able to justify professional management until the fund is large enough to stand alone.

Under no circumstances should you transfer endowment funds into the pooled income fund. The endowment money and the pooled income fund money are simply jointly invested.

Another option is to put the money with a money manager and use the services of PG Calc (www.pgcalc.com) for the specialized administration you need. There is a summary of their services in Chapter III-9.)

Q. Can a donor make a bequest to a pooled income fund?

A. Yes, legally. Ask your legal counsel for special language that may be necessary. If there is still an estate tax when the donor dies, the donor will receive an estate tax charitable deduction for the value of the remainder interest. The calculation is identical to the one that would be done for a current gift for income tax purposes.

In 25 years of running planned giving programs, I have never had a bequest to a pooled income fund. It would present a bit of a problem in the sense that the beneficiary would presumably be due income from the pooled income fund as of the date of death. However, the pooled income fund would not receive the assets or money to fund the gift until after the period of the estate's settlement, many, many months or years later. Therefore, the beneficiary's share of income would come out of the income earned by other gifts already in the fund, thus diluting the income for everybody until such time as the bequest distribution gets into the fund. This is not a good idea.

Q. What kind of property is most appropriate for a gift to a pooled income fund?

A. Cash and readily marketable securities—not real estate, closely held stock, or any other asset that is not readily liquid. Tax-exempt bonds are prohibited.

Q. Why can't a pooled income fund accept a gift of or invest in tax-exempt securities?

A. Congress did not want to permit donors to make gifts of appreciated property to a pooled income fund, get a charitable deduction, avoid any tax on the gain, and receive tax-free income, too. So, pooled income funds cannot accept or invest in tax-exempt bonds.

Q. A donor in our pooled income fund wants to give up her income payments. Can she do this and what are her tax consequences.

A. Yes, provided your trust instrument permits such a transfer. She is entitled to an income tax deduction for the present value of her income interest computed as of the date she relinquishes her right to receive income. Check your state law to determine the method of relinquishing an income in trust. It may be merely paperwork your donor draws up or it may require court approval.

Over the years, I have had a number of donors relinquish their income interest. For the pooled income funds I was running in Massachusetts, it was simply a question of the donor signing a letter stating his or intent to relinquish all income and rights to the fund.

Example:

Katherine made a $10,000 gift to your pooled income fund 10 years ago. Her gift was assigned 100 units of participation at that time. Today, the value of one unit is $225.346. Katherine is 85 years old to the closest birthday and your fund's highest yield for the prior three year period is 6.4%.

Current Market Value of Katherine's units (100 units @ $225.346/unit)	$22,534.60
Remainder interest computed on your software as if the $22,534.60 were a gift today	- $15,874.72
Present value of income interest	$6,649.88

In this situation, you input the variables for her age, the market value of her units, and the highest yield of the fund's prior three-year period. This gives you the amount which is considered to be the remainder interest (also the charitable deduction). When you subtract that figure from the fair market value of the units, you arrive at the amount considered to be her income interest. Thus, she essentially is giving up $6,649.88 and that is the value she can claim as a charitable deduction.

Q. When a donor relinquishes the income interest in a pooled income fund, is the deduction for doing so limited to the 50% or the 30% contribution ceiling?

A. An income interest is considered to be a capital asset with a zero cost basis and, therefore falls under the 30% contribution ceiling.

Q. Can a donor contribute to our pooled income fund and designate part of the principal for another charity?

A. No. All gifts must accrue to the charity that maintains the fund. A donor who wishes to name more than one charity from a life income gift should use a charitable remainder trust or make two separate gifts.

Q. Does a donor making a repeat gift to our pooled income fund have to complete another Instrument of Transfer?

A. Yes. Every gift is separate.

Q. We've had a pooled income fund for many years, but it is currently dormant and we are not marketing it any longer. What should we do with it?

A. Don't worry about it. When interest rates were 10%-14% back in the 1980s, everybody was marketing their pooled income funds. As interest rates dropped, many organizations stopped marketing their pooled income funds in favor of the popular charitable gift annuity. If the interest rates swing back, you may see a resurgence of interest in the PIF. Meanwhile, just watch it and make sure the beneficiaries receive their payments on time, their tax reporting on time, and their seasonal addresses activated when appropriate.

Some organizations are trying to close dormant pooled income funds by asking beneficiaries to relinquish their income interests. It might be difficult to get all of the people in the fund to do that, but you could try.

Q. If a donor makes a gift and names another person sole beneficiary, has the donor created a gift to the other person reportable for gift tax purposes? How do I calculate the taxable gift?

A. Yes. The taxable gift is the value of the beneficiary's income interest. To determine that, simply subtract the remainder interest (charitable deduction) from the fair market value of the gift. The answer is the value of the taxable gift. For the gift you describe, the donor can exclude the first $11,000 *per* donee under the annual gift tax exclusion ($22,000 for a husband and wife who both consent to the gift on the gift tax return, I.R.S. Form 709).

> Example:
>
> A donor, age 75, names her daughter, age 45, sole income beneficiary of a $10,000 gift. The pooled income fund's highest yield of the prior three-year period is 5.2%. Using your software, you determine the remainder interest (charitable deduction) to be $2,266. You subtract this from the fair market value of the gift ($10,000 - $2,266 = $7,734). In this case, there is no taxable gift because the income interest given to the daughter ($7,734) falls under the $11,000 annual gift tax exclusion. Any amount exceeding $11,000 would be a taxable gift to the daughter.
>
> When using the planned giving software, there will be a category for "non-charitable interest dollars." As you input the gift, you may select either the charitable deduction or the non-charitable interest dollars. You don't have to do this manually.
>
> Caution! If your attorney drafted into the standard form Instrument of Transfer the right to revoke by will the beneficiary's interest, mom's gift to the daughter in this case, would be incomplete for tax purposes and no $11,000 exclusion would be permitted. So watch boilerplate language.

Q. I've solicited several prospects for our pooled income fund but have generated more outright gifts than anything else. What am I doing wrong?

A. It is quite common to receive outright gifts when you start out with a life income gift proposal. Some people really don't need the income. In fact, the gifts you've received are better for your institution any way. Don't ask for a life income gift when you can get the same gift outright.

Q. What minimum gift would you suggest?

A. At first, organizations were using $5,000, but many are now increasing the minimum to $10,000. My personal preference is $10,000. When I arrived at Boston College in 1993, the minimum was $5,000. At the beginning of the next fiscal year, I raised the minimum to $10,000 for both the pooled income fund and the gift annuity and the gifts still kept coming.

For additional gifts, I would suggest $5,000. Anything less is not worth the trouble.

Q. Does the pooled income fund pay taxes?

A. Generally, no. However, the fund does pay taxes on short-term capital gains. Consequently, your trustee should not be incurring short term gains in the portfolio and you should generally try to avoid taking gifts of short-term property.

Q. Can a donor make a gift to the pooled income fund and have the income payments measured by the life of another person?

A. No. The income payments must be based on the life of the beneficiary.

Q. Can a donor reserve the right to terminate another beneficiary's income interest during lifetime?

A. No. A donor can reserve this right only by will.

CREDITING GUIDELINES

There are no hard and fast rules with regard to gift crediting for life income gifts. There is a national debate ongoing, but it's something that each organization really needs to work out for itself. It depends on the purposes for which your fund raising efforts are targeted. It would be unwise to give full credit for a pooled income fund gift to a building campaign. On the other hand, to give full credit for an endowment campaign would be fairly common.

Often, an organization without planned giving finally feels pressure from board members. Then, the director of development, anxious to satisfy the grumbling, speaks to a few outside professionals for advice, appropriates a small budget, and hires you. You realize soon after your arrival that you're operating as a separate satellite, disconnected from other activities. When you try to establish gift crediting procedures, you encounter resistance from the data entry department because "we operate on a cash system here." You wonder how it happened you were hired to do this important work, but the gifts you generate don't seem to count.

If this is your situation, you are not alone. The most valuable thing you can do now is to talk to other organizations to see how they credit and recognize pooled income fund and other deferred gifts. You'll find two types of crediting guidelines:

- Gift credit for the full market value of the gift;

- Gift credit for the value of the remainder interest (the value of the donor's income tax deduction);

There are many opinions about this. It is certainly true that if one person, age 70, gives you $100,000 outright and another, age 70, gives $100,000 to your pooled income fund, the first gift is better. A 70 year old has a life expectancy of about 16 years. That's a long time to wait for the money.

An organization with a long history of capital gift fund raising and a dedicated and involved constituency may be able to sustain a policy of crediting the remainder value. Organizations starting a planned giving program may be better off giving full credit on the theory that their donors simply are not altogether comfortable with large gifts yet.

Whatever you do, be consistent. There is a complete treatment of gift crediting in Chapter III-5 about integrating planned giving into a campaign. The crediting issue for pooled income funds is the same for gift annuities and charitable remainder trusts.

COMMUNITY POOLED INCOME FUNDS

If you don't have the time, staff, or donor base to create your own pooled income fund, there are many community foundations with pooled income funds to which your donors can make gifts that will ultimately benefit your charity. Bear in mind that many of the community foundation pooled income funds require that the remainder interest stay with the community foundation to be managed in perpetuity for the benefit of the charity, sort of like an external endowment. Although the foundation would make periodic payments of income to the charity, it keeps the principal. Some donors might find and use these community pooled income funds on their own.

If you make inquiries to your local community foundation about using its pooled income fund for your donors ask if the foundation keeps the entire principal or returns a portion of it to you. Some will give a percentage back to the charity and keep a minimum amount, such as a minimum of $10,000 as a permanent fund. For the small charity with a one-person development office, the community foundation can help you get PIF gifts and, if you don't have a program of your own, you should consider this option.

SUMMARY

The pooled income fund is a really great concept, except that the interest rate climate has put a damper on the marketing of these funds temporarily. The gift annuity which is discussed in the next chapter is the small donor's gift of choice today. Many organizations that have both a pooled income fund and a gift annuity program are marketing only the gift annuity.

The start-up phase of each plan is very different as you will see. My recommendation is to start with the gift annuity if your organization is just beginning a planned giving program. When interest rates go up at some future time and pooled income funds become popular again, you can start a pooled income fund very quickly with the help of this chapter.

Chapter II–8

CHARITABLE GIFT ANNUITIES

INTRODUCTION

A charitable gift annuity is a contract between the donor and the issuing charity. The donor transfers property in exchange for a fixed dollar payment for life. Usually, donors use cash or appreciated securities. Occasionally, if not prohibited by state law, donors fund gift annuities with real estate. These cases are not common due to the legitimate concerns of the charity in promising a payment in exchange for an illiquid asset. I cover those considerations in detail later in the chapter.

Donors can choose an immediate payment gift annuity or can defer payments for a length of time (deferred gift annuity). The deferral period must be for a minimum of one year. There is a separate section about deferred gift annuities later in the chapter.

Whether current or deferred, most other details are similar for all types of gift annuities. The donor can name himself or herself sole annuitant or designate another annuitant solely, concurrently, or consecutively. (Note: You cannot set up a gift annuity for a term of years and you cannot have more than two people as annuitants.)

From the donor's perspective, the gift annuity offers benefits somewhat similar to those of other life income plans—the opportunity to make an irrevocable commitment to your organization, receive a lifetime payment (or provide support to another person), avoid recognizing immediate capital gain on a gift of appreciated, long-term property, receive a federal income tax charitable deduction for part of the gift, and remove the property from his or her probate estate (if the annuity is for the life of the donor only).

From the charity's perspective, the gift annuity is different in principle from the pooled income fund or from any kind of charitable remainder trust. Beneficiaries of a pooled income fund are entitled only to their share of the actual income earned on the pooled income fund's assets. If the fund's principal is lost through bad investments (heaven forbid), the institution is under no obligation to continue payments to pooled income fund beneficiaries. Likewise, a charitable remainder trust makes payments only from its actual assets. There is no connection to the charity's assets.

In contrast, the gift annuity payment is a legal obligation or debt of the charity. The obligation by the charity to make annuity payments remains regardless of what happens to the gifts in its segregated annuity account. Moreover, even if the charity reinsures its annuities with a commercial insurance company, (as is required by some states), it is liable for the payments if the life insurance company goes bankrupt. If the charity goes bankrupt, it retains the annuitants as creditors.

Gift annuities have been around since 1843 when the American Bible Society issued its first gift annuity. In 1927, the Committee on Gift Annuities (now called the American Council on Gift Annuities) was formed to serve the institutions offering gift annuities. One of the primary tasks for sponsoring organizations in those early days was establishing appropriate annuity rates. Dr. Charles W. Baas, former Chairman of the Committee on Gift Annuities, described how the Committee on Gift Annuities got started.

> *"The Committee itself began to function in 1927 as an ad hoc group to consider what to do about the real problem in the then infant gift annuity field. At that time, institutions using this vehicle kept upping the rates to meet the competition from other similar institutions. By 1927, it had gotten to the point where, I am sure, some gift annuity issuers were actually making a gift to the donor rather than the reverse. The conference-determined solution was for a continuing Committee and periodic conferences to act on maximum gift annuity rates. One side benefit was a considerable saving in*

actuarial expense by having a rate study made for the whole group instead of each organization duplicating the effort and paying their own actuarial costs, as had been the case before."

Almost 90% of the 48 charter sponsors were religious organizations. As of 2003, there were about 1,400 sponsoring organizations including religious, educational, health care, cultural arts and virtually every other type of nonprofit organization.

The board of the American Council on Gift Annuities (ACGA) consists of a maximum of 21 members representing a cross section of the sponsoring organizations and includes professionals such as attorneys, accountants, and actuaries whose expertise is necessary to serve the charities. Most committee members are volunteers. Currently, the staff of the National Committee on Planned Giving in Indianapolis provides administration for the American Council on Gift Annuities (www.acga-web.org). The web site has lots of information for charities offering gift annuities. There is a link to the single-life and two-life tables recommended by the Council as well as a link to the state regulations for all 50 states. These regulations change frequently so it is important to check the latest information periodically. I discuss state regulations later in the chapter. The address for the American Council on Gift Annuities is below.

> American Council on Gift Annuities
> c/o National Committee on Planned Giving
> 233 McCrea Street, Suite 400
> Indianapolis, IN 46225
> 317-269-6274 (Phone)
> 317-269-6276 (Fax)
> www.acga-web.org
> acga@acga-web.org

An organization offering gift annuities should become a sponsor of the American Council on Gift Annuities. The cost is only $75 *per* year. The fee includes the availability of advice and guidance when necessary and updates on legal and other matters as required. The volunteer members, many of whom have a specialty area, will be happy to help you. The Council runs an excellent biennial conference in April or May of even numbered years. You can sign up on their web site for notification of conference information. There is also a newsletter for the sponsors. If your organization is offering gift annuities, the small annual fee that also includes a discount at the conference is well worth the price. The Council will notify you of any legislative changes affecting the gift annuity. If your organization becomes a sponsor of the American Council on Gift Annuities, give a copy of any information you receive from the ACGA to your Financial Vice President or Treasurer.

Even if you are not a sponsor, you can access the ACGA web site free of charge. The charity's affiliation with the American Council on Gift Annuities does not preclude the need for retaining professional tax counsel separately for your gift annuity program or for your planned giving program in general.

The rest of this chapter includes the following main sections:

- gift annuity rates;
- assumptions in the tables;
- the philosophy of the gift annuity;
- the annuity contract;
- payment schedules;
- getting the required information from the donor;
- administering your gift annuity program;
- Disclosure Statements;
- donor's election of the discount rate under Section 7520(a);
- state regulations;
- reinsurance;
- calculating the tax consequences of a gift annuity;
- deferred gift annuities;
- flexible gift annuities;

- commuted payment gift annuities;
- property appropriate for annuities;
- acquisition indebtedness;
- considerations for different combinations of donors/annuitants (annuities starting after 1986);
- crediting guidelines.

GIFT ANNUITY RATES

The American Council on Gift Annuities sets suggested maximum annuity rates to which most sponsoring organizations subscribe. The Council reviews the rates every year and changes them periodically to reflect current interest rates and current mortality tables. The Council generally reviews the rates in April and issues changes, if necessary, to be effective July 1 for that year.

Most organizations follow the rates set by the American Council on Gift Annuities. Some states require you to follow the ACGA rates unless you get your own actuary to justify higher rates. Occasionally, you have a donor who agrees to an annuity rate lower than what the Council suggests. This is great. The donor will receive a higher federal income tax charitable deduction, and the institution will retain more of the original gift on the death of the annuitant. Some charities have capped the highest rate they will pay. The Council rates are suggested *maximum* rates.

A handful of charities use rates higher than the Council's maximum recommended rates. This has created some criticism from those who believe such a practice is unfair to the rest of the organizations using the standard rate table. I recommend staying with the Council's rates. If you go lower, donors who support other charities using the Council's higher rates will inevitably confront you. Truly altruistic donors will make a gift to your organization anyway, maybe after expressing objections, but others will take their gifts elsewhere. Fund raising is hard enough without creating an additional barrier to the process.

While running your program, you may find a donor who comes to you with an offer. For example, an 80 year old may say, "I'll give you $100,000 if you pay me 10%." By referring to the single-life table, you will see that the suggested rate for that age is 8.0%. The first thing to do when you have a situation like this is to input the variables into your planned giving software to see precisely how much of the principal will be remaining after the expected life of the donor. The remainder must be a minimum of more than 10% of the gift or you will incur unrelated business income from the transaction. People who ask for higher rates are treating the transaction more as an investment than as a gift. Since annuity rates offered by commercial insurance companies always will be higher than the suggested Council rates, you may lose a few donors along the way. Do not be too disappointed. The donors you will lose were not interested in a gift anyway. Also, be careful in states where the Insurance Commissioner regulates gift annuities because you may have filed a rate schedule you are required to follow for all donors in that state.

Peter Kimball, Director of Gift Planning for the Faculty of Arts and Sciences at Harvard University, wrote an article about just this topic in the February 2001 issue of *Planned Giving Today*. The thrust of his message was maintaining the integrity of the charity. If you make special deals with some donors, you will probably set yourself up for problems later. Donors talk to each other. People will find out. When you deviate from your approved rate schedule for one donor, there is bound to be trouble. Peter says,

> *"In a comprehensive planned giving program, few initiatives are more important than marketing and advertising in helping to generate a flow of inquiries and new gifts to support our charitable organizations. . . . The damage caused by false advertising or by misrepresentation of the complex interaction of the charity's needs, the donor's goals, and the tax and economic intricacies of a planned gift can be irreparable, or take years to correct. In other cases, disgruntled donors who believe they have been victimized by false advertising or misrepresentation may seek legal recourse, which further exposes the charity to negative publicity."*

However, what if the potential gift is $1 million and not $100,000? How would you decide what to do? Can you turn down such a large gift? This is a tough question. In all of the years I ran a planned giving program,

I had only a handful of cases in which a donor wanted a rate higher than my institution offered. We never agreed to go higher than our standard rate schedule. I cannot tell you how to handle such a case since each one has a unique set of circumstances, but it would be best if you did not deviate from your approved rate table.

Once you determine the rate table you will be using, computing the annuitant's payment is easy. Refer below to the single-life ACGA table effective 7/1/03. You will note that the annuity rate increases with the age of the annuitant from a low of 3.7% for annuitants 0-1 years old to a high of 11.3% for annuitants 90 and over. To determine the annual annuity payment for any gift, multiply the fair market value of the gift by the rate appropriate for the age to the closest birth date of the annuitant. There are also two-life tables, but I did not include them because they are unwieldy. You can print them directly from the ACGA web site. When you are working with your planned giving software, you will be able to get a printout of the basics including the rate, annual dollar amount, quarterly installment, and partial payment for the first short quarter if you wish to use partial payments.

ACGA UNIFORM GIFT ANNUITY RATES
SINGLE LIFE
Effective 7/1/03

Age	Rate	Age	Rate	Age	Rate
0-1	3.7	51-52	5.4	76	7.2
2-5	3.8	53-55	5.5	77	7.4
6-12	3.9	56-57	5.6	78	7.6
13-20	4.0	58-60	5.7	79	7.9
21-25	4.1	61	5.8	80	8.0
26-28	4.2	62-63	5.9	81	8.3
29-31	4.3	64-65	6.0	82	8.5
32-34	4.4	66	6.1	83	8.8
35-36	4.5	67	6.2	84	9.2
37-38	4.6	68	6.3	85	9.5
39-40	4.7	69	6.4	86	9.9
41-42	4.8	70	6.5	87	10.2
43	4.9	71	6.6	88	10.6
44-45	5.0	72	6.7	89	11.0
46	5.1	73	6.8	90+	11.3
47-48	5.2	74	6.9		
49-50	5.3	75	7.1		

You treat each gift annuity separately. Thus, a donor frequently has multiple gift annuities with different annuity rates. Following is an example of the annuity rates for one donor with five annuities made at different ages under the ACGA rates effective 7/1/03. Practically, the tables are subject to change every year so it would be unlikely that the 7/1/03 rates would remain unchanged for five years. However, you get the idea.

Age at time of gift	Value of Gift	Annual Rate	Annual Annuity Payment
80	$ 5,000	8.0%	$ 400
81	13,000	8.3%	1,079
82	10,000	8.5%	850
83	5,000	8.8%	440
90	10,000	11.3%	+1,130

Total Annual Annuity Payments: $3,899

Since gift annuity rates for older annuitants are higher than current interest rates, many administrators or board members will say, "How can we pay 8.8% or 11.3%?" They think that the organization must be able to earn the suggested rate on the gift amount. This is not true, however, the better your investment performance, the greater the amount of principal you will have on the death of the annuitant.

The next section explains the assumptions upon which the Council bases its suggested annuity rates.

ASSUMPTIONS IN THE TABLES

When institutions talk about the risk of offering gift annuities, they cite the likelihood of dipping into institutional funds to make the required annuity payments. This fear arises from the misunderstanding that a gift annuity is not worthwhile unless the charity can earn a total return amount equal to or greater than the annuity rate. An examination of the assumptions inherent in the tables may provide some comfort to administrators still hesitant about whether to offer gift annuities.

The actuaries who developed the annuity rates built in considerable protection for the charity by taking into account many factors. The following assumptions for the 7/1/03 rates are on the ACGA web site:

1. The residuum (percentage of contribution remaining for the charity at the termination of an annuity) will be 50%.

2. Life expectancies are based on the Annuity 2000 Tables, assuming all annuitants are female and are one and one-half years younger than their actual ages.

3. Projections of increased life expectancies since the publication of the Annuity 2000 Tables are factored into rate calculations.

4. Annual expenses for investment of gift annuity reserves and administration of gift annuities are assumed to be 1% of reserves.

5. The total return on gift annuity reserves is 6.0%. However, the total return for single-life annuitants under age 51 and over age 86 is lower than 6.0%, and the total return for two-life annuitants where the younger annuitant is under age 59 is likewise lower than 6.0%. The total return, net of expenses, is 5.0% except for the ages noted where it is lower.

6. The compound interest factor for deferred gift annuities for a deferral period of any length is 5.0%.

The ACGA recommends that you check their web site for special exceptions for New York and New Jersey. Go to the link for the current ACGA rates and you will find a separate link for "DPGA Interest Factors for New York and New Jersey only." When you combine the effect of all of the assumptions, the intent of the Council's rates is to provide a remainder or *residuum* of approximately 50% of the value of the gift at the end of the annuitant's life expectancy, if the charity invests the full value of each annuity gift it receives.

What does this mean for you?

Example:

A male, age 70, contributes $50,000 for a gift annuity. The rate for a single-life annuity at age 70 is 6.5% from the 7/1/03 ACGA single-life table.

In the above example, your organization receives $50,000 for which it agrees to pay an annual annuity of 6.5% or $3,250 ($1,625 in two equal semiannual installments) for the life of a 70-year-old man. (If you make payments quarterly, then you are paying out more money earlier than the tables assume.) You are ahead already with a male annuitant because the tables assume longer female life expectancies minus one and one half years. If you have a female annuitant, then you are slightly ahead because the rates assume females have a longer life expectancy than they actually do. You invest the $50,000 for a total return of 6.0%. (Remember, we are following this example as if all of the assumptions in the rates play out) You deduct 1% for administrative fees.

At the end of about 16 years, the life expectancy of a 70 year old, 50% of the original gift or $25,000 remains for use by your organization. (Note: The $25,000 you will have in 16 years is worth less than $25,000 today.)

The above arrangement may not seem lucrative enough to some, but it has conservative assumptions to protect the charity. If your donor above outlives his life expectancy, you presumably still would have approximately $25,000 starting at that point from which to generate income and make payments. In addition, if during the term of the annuity, you had been able to earn more than a 6.0% total return, you will have greater than $25,000 left over when the donor reaches his life expectancy. Of course, not all people live to their life expectancy. The life expectancy is a median number. Some donors will die sooner and some will live longer.

Depending on the regulations in your state (or in other states where you have annuitants or donors), you might have to follow investment restrictions that limit your ability to invest your annuity pool for growth. I remember years when Boston College achieved double-digit returns in our gift annuity pool. Therefore, we were not worried about depleting the principal of a gift even if we paid 12%, the former rate for a 90-year-old annuitant.

In the middle of 2003, the discount rate dipped to an all-time low of 3%. This means that a gift annuity for a person younger than 57 won't meet the 10% test. (A charity incurs acquisition indebtedness and pays tax on the transaction when it takes a gift annuity having a remainder of 10% or less.) Since the beginning of this decade, charities have lost a lot of value in their endowments and in their annuity reserve funds. Some charities are in trouble because they reserved only the amount required to meet their annuity obligations and spent the rest.

The 7/1/03 annuity rates assume a total return of 6% for the life of the contract; thus, they are more realistic for the immediate future than were the prior assumptions for investment performance. Nonetheless, some charities stopped offering gift annuities in 2003 except for annuitants above a certain age.

If you decide to start a gift annuity program, make sure you understand the assumptions in the tables and the relevant state regulations or registration requirements.

THE PHILOSOPHY OF THE GIFT ANNUITY

A charitable gift annuity is part gift and part sale. Technically, it is a *bargain sale*. The gift portion is the value of the property transferred by the donor after subtracting the present value of the annuity. The sale portion is the present value of the annuity. Think of this as two separate transactions: a gift and the purchase of an annuity. The reason that the gift annuity pays less than a commercial annuity is because a part of it is a straight gift.

Unlike payments from the pooled income fund that represent actual investment income and are 100% ordinary income, gift annuity payments are partly a return of the original principal, which is tax-free. That feature makes the gift annuity very attractive to the donor.

The amount of tax-free principal returned with each payment depends on the age of the beneficiary, the size of the annuity payment, the I.R.S. discount rate, and the type of property used—cash or appreciated long-term property. (*Note: You might become a little confused as you go through this section, but stay with me because the confusion will clear up when you get to the discussion about calculating the tax consequences.*)

Cash Gifts

If the donor contributes cash, the portion of principal returned to the donor in each annuity payment is tax free—it was the donor's money in the first place. Commercial annuities also work like this. For gifts after December 31, 1986, the tax-free portion becomes ordinary income at the end of the annuitant's life expectancy. For gifts made before that date, the tax-free portion continues for as long as the annuitant lives. If you inherited a gift annuity program that received gifts before December 31, 1986, you must track the pre-1987 participants separately for purposes of preparing the annual 1099-Rs (discussed later under administration).

Long-Term Appreciated Property Gifts

If the donor contributes appreciated, long-term property such as stock or real estate (where allowed), the donor is deemed to have sold a portion of the property to the charity. As long as the donor is the sole or first annuitant, he or she can spread the gain on the sale portion over his or her life expectancy. If, on the other hand, the donor is not the primary or sole annuitant, he or she recognizes the gain at the outset and incurs immediate capital gain taxes on all of the reportable gain. This latter scenario would result if a donor made a gift of stock of his own property and named his spouse or someone else as primary beneficiary or sole beneficiary. Try to avoid this disaster. Near the end of this chapter, you will find 14 scenarios that you can use as a quick reference to ensure that no donor inadvertently incurs unnecessary capital gain tax on the gift.

A general summary follows:

- *Gift of cash:* The annuity payment is part tax-free return of principal for the duration of the annuitant's life expectancy, and part ordinary income.

- *Gift of appreciated, long-term property:* The annuity payment is part tax-free return of principal for the duration of the annuitant's life expectancy, part return of capital gain income for the duration of the donor's life expectancy, and part ordinary income.

THE ANNUITY CONTRACT

Every gift annuity requires a contract or agreement that outlines the terms between your organization and the donor. The constantly evolving state regulations make the selection of the correct state's annuity agreement a little uncertain. However, your planned giving software should have the legally correct annuity agreements for all 50 states. Practically, you cannot run an effective gift annuity program without the full version of the vendor's planned giving software. At least 29 states require unique, state mandated disclosure language to be in each gift annuity agreement issued by a charity in those states, or issued to a donor residing in the state. (Go to Appendix II for a list of software vendors.)

Once you have the software, or after your attorney approves your standard contracts for different states, you can create the annuity contract automatically from your software. More difficult than preparing the annuity agreement is determining which state's agreement to use.

Both PG Calc's Planned Giving Manager and Crescendo default to the state of the donor for the preparation of the annuity agreement. However, it may not be that simple.

If your charity resides in a state that regulates gift annuities, you would assume you should use a contract that conforms to your state's regulations. As of July 2003, there are ten states requiring registration: Arkansas, California, Hawaii, Maryland, New Jersey, New York, North Dakota, Oregon, Washington, and Wisconsin.

If the charity is in one of the above ten states, fully registered in its own state, and if either the donor or the annuitant is in one of the other ten states, you should ask your attorney which state agreement is appropriate. California takes the approach that the agreement should go with the annuitant (not the donor). Maryland and New Jersey (and most other regulating states) take the approach that the agreement should go with the donor's state.

If you register in California, you will promise California to use a particular format for the annuity agreement whenever you have a donor or annuitant in California. Let's say your charity is located in New Jersey and registered there. New Jersey takes the position that it is the donor's state, and not the annuitant's state that drives the contract. How do you know what to do? Actually, you do not know.

The development of regulations on a state-by-state basis, independent of each other, presents a great deal of uncertainty for the planned giving community. Charities must rely on advice from their own tax counsel in order to run their programs. As a result, charities are handling these details very differently based on arbitrary interpretations case by case and state by state.

If you are a planned giving officer, you must be aware of these state issues, receive a current legal opinion from your tax counsel on what to do in preparing your gift annuity agreements, and then carry on. Be aware that, one of these days, you might have to justify your patterns with one of the regulating states, when two have conflicting rules. If your counsel's legal opinion on this issue is two to three years old, you should get another.

When you create the annuity agreement, you should use the primary legal residence of the donor and/or annuitant in the gift annuity agreement. Do not use a P.O. Box number, and be careful not to use a seasonal address by accident. When you review the donor files you inherited from your predecessor, you will notice that some donors with seasonal addresses have contracts that list the seasonal address and others that list the primary residence. This happens because the planned giving officer forgets to ask which one is the primary legal address. This mistake also occurs when the planned giving officer simply uses the address from the donor's last agreement without checking. I have been guilty of this oversight myself, and it is very sloppy. In other cases, you might copy the address out of an earlier gift annuity agreement without realizing the donor has moved. Be careful! Gift annuity agreements are contracts and follow the rules of state contract law.

PAYMENT SCHEDULES

Legally, you can establish monthly, quarterly, semiannual, or annual payments. Both the monthly and the annual payment schedules are impractical. The monthly payments are costly to administer, and, unless the gift is large enough, provide payments too small to be useful. For example, a $5,000 gift annuity for a 70-year-old donor generates a monthly payment of only $27.08. This is hardly worth the trouble. Annual payments are very rare and cannot possibly serve the donor's needs. I recommend quarterly payments on the last day of March, June, September, and December. Some organizations pay on the first day of January, April, July, and October. However, annuitants become confused over when to report the January 1 payment.

Once you establish your policy, it is perfectly acceptable to negotiate separately with a donor for a more frequent payment schedule. This might be appropriate for a gift annuity large enough to provide several hundred dollars per month. However, it gets more time consuming to administer the program when you make exceptions. I would not do it for less than a very, very special case because you will have to live with the aberration for a long time.

At Boston University, I inherited a gift annuity program in which annuitants were on all four payment schedules. It was insane. Each month, a different set of people received payments. We spent enormous amounts of time each month reconciling who was supposed to receive a payment. It would not have been so bad if all of the semiannual payments were on June 30 and December 31. However, we had semiannual payments on different six-month schedules. We sent payments to some donors in January and July. Others received payments in March and September. Who let this happen? One of my first executive decisions upon taking over this program was to require all new participants to be on the same quarterly schedule. Some day, after the people on the alternate schedules die, the program will be uniform.

The lesson is clear. If you start a program, be consistent. If you inherit a program with multiple schedules, shift to quarterly payments for all future gifts and let the others die. Otherwise, you will spend excessive time figuring out who is supposed to receive payments month to month. If you have already agreed to a particular payment schedule in a gift annuity agreement, you cannot change it to a more frequent schedule later, but you can change it to a less frequent schedule if the donor agrees.

GETTING THE REQUIRED INFORMATION FROM THE DONOR

To run an efficient gift annuity program, you should get all of the donor's information at the same time, preferably on a form. Otherwise, you will find yourself making multiple calls to the donor to chase down information long after the gift is in. You should standardize the format through which you request the donor and beneficiary information for all of your life income plans. This section deals solely with the gift annuity.

You can design your own format, but here is the information you need for each gift:

1. **Name of donor or donors (if joint property)**

   Sometimes, you assume that the person with whom you have been discussing the gift is the donor, only to learn later that the property transferred is in joint names or in the name of the other spouse. In the first case, you have two donors, not one. In the second case, you have a completely different donor. This is extremely important because there are some donor/annuitant/ownership combinations that have tax problems. (I cover 14 possible combinations at the end of this chapter.)

2. **Legal address of the donor(s)**

   Many people participating in life income plans have a primary residence and a seasonal residence, too. Therefore, when you look up the donor on your organization's computer, you may assume incorrectly that the active address is the primary residence, when it may be the seasonal address. Do not use a P.O. Box for the primary residence.

3. **Name of the annuitant(s)**

   The limit is two people who are alive on the date of the gift. The annuitant(s) need not be the donor(s). Depending on the sequence of payments, the type of property contributed, and the ownership of the property, there may be capital gain and gift tax consequences.

4. **Legal address of the annuitant(s)**

   Same considerations as for the donor(s) in item #2 above.

5. **Date of birth of the annuitant(s)**

   You need the dates of birth in order to prepare the tax calculations, and for some states, you must put the dates of birth into the annuity agreements. You have no way of verifying that the dates of birth are accurate unless you require annuitants to supply you with a photocopy of a driver's license, birth certificate or passport. Some regulating states do an audit of the charity's gift annuity program every five years and will find fault with you if you do not require proof of age.

6. **Social Security Number for each annuitant**

   You need the Social Security number to prepare the tax reporting form, 1099-R. For primary and secondary annuitants, get the SSN for both people in the beginning so that you have the second one handy when it is time to start payments. Do not make annuity payments unless you have an annuitant's Social Security Number. You can be fined for supplying a 1099-R without a SSN.

7. **Sequence of annuity payments**

   If you have two annuitants, A and B, you can pay as follows:

   | Consecutive: | A for life, then B, if B survives A |
   | | B for life, then A, if A survives B |

   Concurrent and Consecutive:

   A and B jointly, then survivor

8. **Cost basis for gifts of long-term appreciated property**

   When you get ready to prepare the tax calculations for the donor, you need the cost basis if the donor contributed appreciated long-term property.

9. Holding period for gifts of capital assets (securities or real estate)

   If the holding period for the asset used to fund the gift annuity is 12 months or less, you use the cost basis rather than the fair market value as the base figure for computing the donor's federal income tax charitable deduction. Ordinarily, donors do not contribute assets they have held for less than 12 months and a day.

10. Payment Instructions

    You can send payments to the annuitant's primary address, to the annuitant's seasonal address, to the trustee of an annuitant's living trust, to a legal guardian or to any other location. You can also mail a check to an annuitant's bank or other account. The best option is to have the annuitant enroll for "EFT" payments, which stands for electronic funds transfer. If your business office administers the gift annuity payments, you should be able to do electronic transfers. If you have an outside fiduciary manager, you definitely will be able to offer this option.

    (Note: When you send the donor the information form or application discussed here, you should also send the approval form for "EFT" transfers so that the donor can complete the form, attach a voided check, and get it back to you in the beginning. You can get this form from your fiduciary manager, if you have one, or from your business office.)

11. Gift Restrictions, if any

    People make gifts to all kinds of restricted purposes. Encourage the donor to discuss any restrictions on the use of the gift with you in advance of completing the gift.

12. Right to revoke secondary annuitant's annuity interest.

    Under current law, the annuity interest a donor creates for another person may be reportable on a gift tax return, using up a portion of the donor's gift tax exclusion. If the donor reserves the right, exercisable by will, to revoke the successor annuitant's interest, then there is no completed gift for gift tax purposes. If the donor dies without revoking the successor's interest, then the donor's estate has a taxable transfer of the annuity interest (depending on whether or not there is an estate tax). In your planned giving software, you will have the option of selecting the revocation language for each gift annuity agreement.

    Note: If spouse A names spouse B successor beneficiary without reserving the right to revoke spouse B's annuity interest, spouse A can be liable for a gift tax because there is no marital deduction and no annual gift tax exclusion.

ADMINISTERING YOUR GIFT ANNUITY PROGRAM

Many organizations that hire a bank as trustee for a pooled income fund or for charitable remainder trusts still manage gift annuities in house. It really is quite easy to do, but you need the help of the business office. While there are many different systems for administering a gift annuity program in house, following is a suggested series of steps that you can review with your business office and adapt as needed. This is a long section, but do not be intimidated by its length. Obviously, the charity just starting a program will be creating a manual system in the beginning. However, if you are serious about marketing your gift annuity program, you will definitely want to get administration software. The one with which I am familiar is GiftWrap by PG Calc which is described after this section.

Manual Gift Annuity Administration

1. Donor transfers property (usually cash or securities or both) to the institution.

Specific I.R.S. rules dictate when a gift of cash is complete. Generally, a gift is complete when the donor hands it to a representative of the charity. If the donor mails a check, he or she can use the postmark on the envelope as the date of the gift, assuming the gift is delivered in the normal course of the delivery of the mail.

For a gift of securities, refer to Chapter II-4 for a complete discussion of taking in and disposing of securities. With a gift annuity, the rules are the same as for any other type of gift. The gift value is the mean value of the shares on the date of the gift. It does not matter if you sell the shares for more or less or if you lose money on commissions. You must issue the gift annuity on the full value as determined according to I.R.S. rules for a gift of securities.

Sometimes, a donor wants to make a gift of a specific dollar amount (perhaps to meet your minimum gift level, let's say $10,000). However, the shares contributed may be slightly lower than the full amount needed. Practically, the way most planned giving officers handle this is to get from the donor a blank check dated the same day as the date of the stock gift. After your organization values the stock, you will fill in the precise amount for the check and process the check as part of the total gift. One option would be to forget about trying to achieve a round dollar amount and accept the gift of stock at its odd value of $9,994.20 by itself, but that is simply not as clean as getting another $6.80 in order to have a $10,000 gift. Sometimes, when working with a gift like this, the donor might drive to your office the day after you valued the stock in order to hand over the tiny check. If the donor is close by, this method works. Alternatively, if the donor wishes to be a little more generous by giving an extra share of stock, he or she can be sure that the value will exceed your minimum gift requirement. Of course, you do not return the excess.

A better way to handle this situation is to wait until the stock market closes at 4:00 pm EST, value the securities, and then get a credit card gift from the donor on the same day for the small amount necessary to bring the total gift to the right amount. You will want to avoid the all too frequent trap of relying on brokers to give you a single number as the value of the gift. Too many times, they will assume you want the closing price rather than the "mean" value (average of the high and the low for the day). Always get the high and the low and do the math yourself. If you blindly accept the broker's value, you will find yourself reprocessing the gift at added expense to yourself and possibly creating an unhappy donor in the process.

2. The treasurer's office values the property as of the date of gift and reports the amount to the planned giving office.

   Institutions handle this function differently. As suggested in the chapter on securities, somebody should have sole responsibility for valuing gifts of securities. In some organizations, it may be the director of planned giving. If it is not you, then whoever it is needs a formal procedure to inform you of the date of the gift, the number of shares, the name of the stock, the mean value of the stock, and the total value of the gift.

3. The planned giving officer completes a gift processing form according to the rules of the development office including the relevant gift information so that the data entry staff can add the value of the gift and the type of gift to the donor's gift record.

4. The gift processor requests from the business office an account number for the new gift annuity.

5. The business office issues an account number in the name of the donor and credits the account with the gift amount.

6. The planned giving office calculates the tax consequences of the annuity for the donor. (*I cover how to do this later in this chapter.*)

   (Note: For partial payments, the administrator of the program, which could be your bank or your own business office, needs time to get the new donor information into the system before the payment date. Therefore, you need a rule that if a donor makes a gift after, let's say, the 15th of the payment month, then he or she will receive the partial payment with the first regular payment for the next quarter. You would include those details in the annuity agreement.

An example would be a gift on March 20. You cannot get the information into the system fast enough to produce and mail a partial payment to get it into the annuitant's hands by March 31. Therefore, the agreement will say, "The first partial payment of [amount] will be combined with the first full quarterly payment on June 30.")

7. The planned giving officer prepares two original annuity contracts and delivers them to the institution's internal general counsel for review and approval.

Each organization handles the oversight of the gift annuity agreements differently. In some organizations, your internal general counsel's office will want to review the agreements. This may seem like a real pain in the neck, but after years of preparing these agreements, I think this practice is a good idea. Periodically, the second pair of eyes finds a mistake. Errors are easy to make especially during busy periods like year end. It is much better to find the mistake before mailing all of the documents to the donor.

One of the problems in letting your general counsel review the gift annuity agreements is the potential delay in completing the acknowledgement letter for the donor. If you have a good working relationship with your internal counsel's office, you should be able to get very quick turn-around time on approval of the agreements. A quick phone call is all you need. Still, you will find yourself calling the general counsel's office periodically when one of your gift annuity agreements seems to be languishing for too long.

8. The planned giving office should send to the donor two original contracts and the disclosure statement (if separate from the contract) requesting that the donor sign and return both copies of the agreement (and a signed disclosure statement if required).

Since you are dealing with older donors, you will need to establish gift administration policies that will ensure that you do not begin payments before you have an agreement in place signed by the donor(s) signifying that they understand and agree to the terms of the gift. Never have the charity sign the agreements before sending them to the donor. And, do not start payments until you have the donor's signature on the agreement.

Many charities do not get the donor's signature at all. However, 29 states now require the donor to sign a statement regarding the "Disclosure Language" mandated by these states. Some states require state-specific disclosure language in the annuity agreement.

Failure to follow this sequence will eventually result in disputes with donors who claim they thought the terms were different, or who really didn't know what they were doing.

9. Send the signed documents from the donor to the officer of the charity authorized to execute documents.

The authorized signature is different at every institution. Sometimes, it is the Vice President for Finance, the Treasurer, or the Vice President for Institutional Relations. In some institutions, the business office affixes the corporate seal to the agreements. Since an annuity agreement is a legal contract, make sure that the person signing the agreement has the authority to sign legal documents on behalf of the charity.

10. Mail one copy of the executed agreement back to the donor together with the tax calculations.

11. The planned giving office delivers a set of the executed contract, signed disclosure statement, and the calculation sheet(s) to the appropriate sources.

When you have all the documents signed and sealed, you should deliver one complete set to the business office, put one complete set in your planned giving donor file, and send one complete set to your department's Central Files, presumably where your organization keeps permanent records for all important donor correspondence. (Note: If you have an outside manager, you should send a copy of everything to your liaison there.)

12. The business office records the payment and beneficiary information so that it can track the gift annuity principal, payments, tax reporting, and gift designation information for the life of the contract.

13. The business office records the taxable character of the income for each payment. Provide this information on Form 1099-R to the annuitants by January 31. Your planned giving software probably has a module to calculate the figures.

    Be sure to arrange to send the government's copy of each 1099-R Form to them by February 28 each year using their cover Form 1096.

14. Approximately one week prior to the scheduled payments, the business office issues a payment list for review by the planned giving office.

    This exercise ensures that you make accurate payments and that you use the latest beneficiary information—new address, seasonal address, prorated first payments, deaths, new participants, *etc.*

15. The business office prepares the annuity checks. Each annuitant gets one check for the total amount of all annuity payments due for that payment.

    Date the checks for the due date of the payment so they may be mailed a few days before the due date and not cashed until the due date.

    Simultaneously, the planned giving office prepares cover letters for forwarding with the checks. The letters are not a legal requirement. Rather, they are an ideal opportunity for the director of planned giving to communicate with the annuitants and to use the payment cycle as a chance for cultivation or stewardship. Letters sent for the last quarter of the year can include the suggestion of another year-end gift annuity and a current example. Another cover letter could be used to remind annuitants that for purposes of determining the annuity rate, they become one year older six months and a day after their last birthday.

    Even if you do not enclose a letter with the annuity payments (and you should), it is important to enclose something with your phone number on it when you send checks. A business card works well. Usually, neither the check stub nor the check itself has a phone number. In the course of experiencing your first few payment cycles, you will notice a flurry of calls as soon as people receive their payments. Therefore, always include a phone number with every payment.

16. The planned giving office photocopies all of the checks and mails the checks approximately three to four business days before the payment due date to ensure that the check will arrive on or before the payment due date. Do not mail the checks on the due date or you will have many unhappy annuitants who depend on their payments arriving on time.

    Let me talk about the photocopying suggestion for a minute. You may think this is wasted energy, and that I am neurotic. However, I cannot tell you how many times I had to look up the date or the amount of a check in the course of running the gift annuity program. If you do not photocopy the checks, you should have at least a payment list for each payment cycle that shows the annuitant's name, mailing address, and the amount of the payment, itemized for each gift. Keep the payment lists for about a year because annuitants will claim to be missing a payment many months after you know you mailed it.

    Most of the annuitants, if you are lucky, will elect direct deposit (called ACH for Automatic Clearing House or EFT for Electronic Funds Transfer). Therefore, you will have two separate stacks for each payment period. The first stack represents the real checks, which are a top priority for you to get into the mail. The second stack represents payment notices of an amount deposited electronically to the annuitant's account. If you get behind schedule for some reason during the period when you must mail the payments, start with the live checks because people are waiting for their money. Then, do the payment notices for the electronic payments.

Occasionally, you will also have a live check that you must mail to a donor's bank. In this case, you should include a letter with the check to ensure that the bank credits the payment properly, and you should send the payment stub to the annuitant separately with a copy of the letter you mailed to the bank.

If you mail a payment to an annuitant who died before the due date, then you must correspond with the executor to get the payment back. Many of the permit issuing states require you to make a real effort (of at least three letters claiming it is a legal claim against the estate) to get the payment returned. If an annuitant dies on the due date, his estate keeps the payment. Most of the time, you learn of a death before the payment goes out.

17. The controller, treasurer, or other person assigned to administer the gift annuities in the business office reduces each gift annuity account by the value of the payment made.

18. At the end of the year, or periodically, the business office credits each annuity account with an amount of income or appreciation attributable to the remaining principal. You would prorate the amount credited to each annuity account based on how long you have had the principal. Thus, you can track the amount of principal remaining in the account year to year. The charity severs the remaining principal from the segregated pool of assets upon the death of the annuitant.

If your organization has an endowment, then it already has a way to unitize its endowment funds. Presumably, you can work out something similar for the gift annuity program.

If you are running the gift annuity program in-house, you will also have to decide whether to deduct any amount from the annuity accounts for administration expenses. That is up to you and to the business office. When organizations use outside fiduciaries, they usually charge expenses to the account, but for internal operations, they may choose to ignore the cost of administration, which would be difficult to determine.

19. By January 31, your business office must mail a 1099-R to each annuitant. By February 28, your business office must send the forms to the I.R.S. using a cover Form 1096. If you have more than 250 1099-Rs for your annuitants and W-2s for your employees combined, you must file the information electronically. Your business office should know how to do this.

The head of your business office should be able to create an appropriate system within the framework of its business operation for tracking annuity gifts. Bear in mind that the administrative procedures for deferred gifts vary widely from institution to institution.

Computerized Administration

There will come a point in running your gift annuity program when you will need a system that tracks not only the people and their gifts, but also their payments and tax reporting, FASB regulations, and other activities automatically. One software program that does this extremely well is GiftWrap by PG Calc (www.pgcalc.com). Another one is Gift Admin by CrescendoInteractive (www.crescendointeractive.com).

The software actually tracks your entire planned giving program, but if you only have gift annuities and bequests, then you can benefit from administration software. You can get a free demo from both PG Calc and Crescendo. This is available only for the PC; there is no Macintosh version.

It stores every type of planned gift, including outright gifts and bequests. In addition, it maintains comprehensive biographical information on donors and beneficiaries, and on other people whom you simply want to track.

One of the things it does for the business office is the calculation of the annual amount required under FASB rules. Without the software, either you or your controller must determine each year the remaining annuity payment liability for all annuitants. Ordinarily, somebody must manually do the calculation each year, one by one. With the software, you simply click on the report and you are done. That one function is worth the price.

Another critical function within the software is the calculation of annuity reserves for states that regulate gift annuities. If you are running a gift annuity program with donors in many states and you have registered your gift annuity program in several states, then you need a way to track each state's requirements for annuity reserves. When you use an outside fiduciary manager, the manager should be able to handle that function for you.

Since I use PG Calc's Planned Giving Manager, I got a copy of the GiftWrap demo and spent some time with the tutorial and the workbook. After two hours, I was ready to use the software. There are training sessions for which you can pay extra, but I was able to learn how to use most of it on my own. Since I never dealt with the annuity reserve issue in my own planned giving program, I found that section of the software confusing. Otherwise, I found the software easy to navigate after I became oriented. The PG Calc clients will want to take a look at GiftWrap while the Crescendo clients should check out Gift Admin.

At Boston University and at Boston College, I created an administration tool using FileMaker® Pro. It was a self-made solution to the problem of tracking and administering the deferred gifts. However, either GiftWrap or Gift Admin is much more complete than what I created and there is no reason to reinvent the wheel if you are interested in tracking all of the information you need to run your program.

The optimum operation of GiftWrap is together with PG Calc's Planned Giving Manager (and the same is true for Gift Admin and Crescendo Lite or Pro). When you create a completed gift illustration in Planned Giving Manager, you can import the information directly into GiftWrap such that all of the relevant donor, gift, payment, and tax information that you will need in the future flows into new screens that are set up for administration. That starts the basis of your database. If you get a second gift from the same donor, simply import the new calculation information into the original donor's record.

From the business office perspective, the software prints checks, sends payments by EFT (electronic funds transfer), and does the 1099-Rs. Multiple users can use it at one time. In addition, it can track gifts for more than one entity. Therefore, if you work in the main office of a national organization with many chapters, you can keep them all separate. Alternatively, if you work for a university with many schools, you can track the gifts by school.

Another feature that would help any planned giving officer is the report package. You can literally get any combination of data by donor, by gift type, by organization, by staff member, *etc*. The program comes with a series of preprogrammed reports, but you can also create your own.

There are too many features for me to cover them all in this short summary. Depending on which basic planned giving software you use, get the demo for the gift administration program and try it out.

DISCLOSURE STATEMENTS

The Philanthropy Protection Act of 1995 (PPA) requires charities to provide a federally mandated disclosure statement to donors who participate in the charity's gift annuity program. This applies to all new participants in the gift annuity program after March 6, 1996. In general, the federal disclosure statement explains to the donor the operation of the gift annuity, describes the governance of the charity, and includes general information about how the charity manages its assets. The donor does not have to sign the federal Disclosure Statement, but the charity needs a paper trail in the donor's file to prove that the charity sent the disclosure statement to the donor before the donor made his or her first gift to the charity's gift annuity program. You can view the sample language for the required disclosure statement on the American Council on Gift Annuities website (www.acga-web.org). To find it quickly, go to the "Site Map" first.

This federal Gift Annuity Disclosure Statement (see below) is different than the state mandated "disclosure statements" required to be signed by donors in at least 29 states. All such state mandated statements may be included in the CGA agreement and must be signed by both the charity and the donor(s). Some states require them to be in the agreement and others allow them to be placed in the agreements. If you use either PG Calc's Planned Giving Manager or Crescendo's Lite or Pro, you'll find that all state mandated language is included so that your gift annuity agreements will pass muster with the various state laws.

After enactment of the PPA in 1995, charities were required to send the disclosure statement to all existing donors. Presumably, your organization did that years ago. It would have been very difficult for anyone in planned giving to miss the national coverage of a lawsuit in Texas that resulted in the enactment of the PPA. Going forward, the charity must provide the disclosure statement to each donor prior to accepting the first gift from that donor. It does not have to be repeated for each subsequent gift.

The following sample language for the federal disclosure statement is adapted with permission from the sample language on the ACGA website:

[Charity]
Sample Gift Annuity Disclosure Statement

The charitable gift annuity is a transfer of the donor's gift property (usually cash or securities), to [charity] in exchange for fixed gift annuity payments for life. Payments may be made to one or two persons, concurrently, or concurrently and consecutively. *Per* the gift annuity agreement, fixed payments of the amount indicated will be made to named annuitants for life. Since this arrangement is an irrevocable charitable gift, the donor may be entitled to a charitable deduction for federal income tax, gift tax, or estate tax purposes.

However, because a charitable gift is involved, the annuity rates offered by [charity] are lower than those available through commercial annuities offered by insurance companies and other financial institutions.

The annuity payments are a general obligation of [charity], and they are backed by all of our assets. At [indicate date] our total invested funds exceeded $ _____ (indicate book or market value), and they are invested [describe the general types of investments held by the organization, such as stocks, bonds money market funds, and federal obligations, but do not list assets by name].

(Note: If you offer gift annuities in states that require maintenance of a segregated reserve fund, you should add the following sentence to this paragraph: We also maintain a gift annuity reserve fund valued at more than $ _____ that is invested in accordance with the laws of the states in which we offer gift annuities.)

The [charity] was established in [date]. Responsibility for governing the organization vests in a Board comprised of persons who are [describe manner of selection].

Common investment funds managed by our organization are exempt from registration requirements of the federal securities laws, pursuant to the exemption for collective investment funds and similar funds maintained by charitable organizations under the Philanthropy Protection Act of 1995 (P.L. 104-62). We have provided this information to you in accordance with the requirements of that Act.

We would be pleased to provide any additional information at your request.

The tax counsel for your planned giving program will be able to provide a sample document for your use.

You should update the disclosure statement as needed. For example, when you move your gift annuity management from internal to external management, you would update the information and include the name of the firm that is managing the gift annuity pool of assets.

The simplest way that I found to ensure that the new donor reads the document is to place it on the back of the institution's annuity application.

DONOR'S ELECTION OF THE DISCOUNT RATE UNDER SECTION 7520(a)

If the rate the donor uses to calculate the federal income tax charitable deduction is not the rate for the month of the gift, then he or she must attach to the tax return on which the deduction is claimed a short statement electing a rate other than the one for the current month. This is also true for charitable remainder trusts and charitable lead trusts (not pooled income funds because they use their own actual rate). To assist the donor, you could complete the information, except for the signature, and forward it to the donor with the rest of the documents related to the gift annuity. Alternatively, you can provide to the donor the form below with instructions for the donor to create his or her own.

Following is a basic format:

Election under Section 7520(a)

Taxpayer ID: xx-xx-xxxx

According to Reg. Sec. 301.9100-8 (a) (1), I, [donor], am making an election as provided under Section 7520(a) of the Internal Revenue Code.

The interest being valued is a charitable gift annuity with [Charity] made on [date].

The rate being used to value the transferred interest is (___%, the discount rate) for [month, year] (120% of the Applicable Mid-Term Federal Interest Rate rounded to the nearest two-tenths of one percent). Absent this election, the rate for [month and year of I.R.S. Discount Rate for month of the gift] for the date of the gift is [rate for current month].

_____   _____
Donor Signature   Date

STATE REGULATIONS

I worked for my entire career in the state of Massachusetts, which does not regulate gift annuities. None of the four organizations for which I worked registered in any state. This is partly because registration was not really a problem except for New York until the mid to late 1990s. More recently, this was based on the opinion of our outside legal counsel that our program was fine as long as we followed the laws of the state in which we issued the gift annuity agreement (Massachusetts). Unfortunately, that philosophy may not be valid any longer, and there are many viewpoints on this issue depending on whom you ask. I do not intend to advise you whether you should register in states other than your own. That is the job of your legal counsel. However, you need to be familiar with the issues.

Many states now regulate gift annuities under the jurisdiction of the state insurance department or the state securities commission. If the charter for your charity is in a state that regulates gift annuities, you absolutely must follow the regulations enacted by that state. In addition, some members of the planned giving community and all state insurance department staffs believe that charities must abide by the rules of any state in which a gift annuity donor lives. That gets tricky because a donor who establishes a gift annuity with a charity might name an annuitant who lives in another regulated state. But, the position of the various state Insurance Departments is that a gift annuity follows state contract law. Therefore, the parties entering into the contract are the charity and the donor(s), the signers of the gift annuity contract.

The quagmire in which we find ourselves hinders organizations from initiating a gift annuity program or from registering an existing program because there now is a myriad set of restrictions, regulations, reporting requirements, investment restrictions, gift annuity reserve requirements and licensing issues, all of which vary from state to state. How should you proceed? If you are operating a gift annuity program in a regulated state, you must register your program in that state. That may involve stopping new gift annuity activity for the period during your approval process (possibly three to six months).

Some charities who operate in unregulated states have taken the position that if they follow the rules of their own state, they will be just fine. Rightly or wrongly, most Massachusetts charities feel this way. However, the situation is not that clear cut according to some of the more experienced leaders of the industry. Some believe you cannot just ignore the registration requirements of states outside your home state. One state has a $1,000 penalty for each contract written when the charity is not in compliance.

The American Council on Gift Annuities provides a state-by-state summary of all regulations on its web site at www.acga-web.org. Jim Potter who has been on the board of the Council since 1974 and is the Chair of the State Regulations Committee manages the link for state regulations. This is a wonderful resource because it has a link for each state and includes charts for easy reference. Jim also has a separate website at www.pgresources.com where he has created a huge resource for charities wishing to offer gift annuities as well as other deferred gifts. If you are new to this site, click on "First Time Visitor." Sign the guest book and Jim will send you timely updates about the changes in the state regulations of gift annuities. He has a lot of free information such as articles and other materials about administration. If you are new to planned giving, you should read the article about gift annuity administration. The article is extremely thorough and it will help novices with many of the issues involved in running a gift annuity program.

I cannot possibly cover the ever-changing state-by-state rules in this book. If you go to the ACGA web site listed above, you can see exactly what each state requires and you can see the date that its regulations became law. You can also go to the link for each state's laws so that you can read the actual text.

The first thing you should do as a new planned giving officer is check the regulations for your own state. If you operate in a state that regulates gift annuities and you are not in compliance, get advice from your legal counsel immediately. Second, check the other states that regulate gift annuities and see if you have any donors or annuitants in those states. Make a list of the participants, dates of gift, and gift amounts for each regulated state in which you have activity. Send this to your legal counsel and ask for advice on what to do.

Here is what Jim Potter advises in terms of state regulations issues:

Statement on State Regulations by Jim Potter

The issuance of Charitable Gift Annuities (CGAs) is a state regulated industry. In recent years, an increasing number of states have passed new laws, regulating both CGA funds and the issuance of CGA agreements to residents of their states, or if the charity has offices in their state.

CGA agreements are contracts, not trusts, and are governed under state contract law, both the laws of the situs state of the charity AND the residence state of the donor(s), the two parties that sign the CGA (contract) agreement.

For those charities who have a legal opinion that they need follow only the regulations of the situs state of the charity, they would be well advised to obtain a second, or even a third opinion. The regulating states do not see it that way and many of their state laws permit the fining of a charity up to $1,000 for each CGA agreement that does not comply with their state law. Such states will issue "cease and desist" orders to a non-complying charity and they have been known to increasingly enforce them.

CGA agreements remain in force for the life of the named annuitants based upon the state law in effect at the time the agreement is issued. These laws mandate that any agreement issued after adoption of their law applies to the charity's CGA Fund and all agreements issued after that date. This growing total of potential fines could become a threat to the careers of planned giving officers when a Board is brought to task by one or more regulating states. Many boards will look to staff to protect them from such problems. And, some states have been known to threaten fines of $10,000.

The numbers of states that regulate CGAs are growing each year. At least ten states issue permits, more than 16 require the charity to notify them they are issuing CGA agreements and 29 states require a state mandated "disclosure statement" in the CGA agreement.

While a few states do not require any regulatory action on the part of the charity, they do expect the charity to meet some minimum requirements before it issues a CGA agreement in that state.

Keep up with this constantly changing regulatory landscape by visiting two websites: www.acga-web.org and www.pgresources.com regularly.

If you would like to start a gift annuity program, you must first find a very good attorney who is experienced with the regulations and restrictions in your state.

The kinds of things regulating states require include one or more of the items listed below:

- Creating a reserve fund of a minimum level before starting a gift annuity program;

- Reinsuring annuity contracts (discussed in the following section);

- Having a minimum dollar amount of unrestricted funds;

- Being in existence for a minimum number of years;

- Filing your gift annuity rate tables;

- Providing financial documents, possibly involving trustees;

- Paying an initial registration fee and/or an annual registration fee;

- Inserting specific state-mandated disclosure language into your annuity contracts for both the state of the donor and the state of the charity;

- Providing donors with a federally mandated disclosure statement;

- Numbering your annuity contracts; and

- Segregating a portion of your annuity pool for restricted investments.

There is an effort by the National Association of Insurance Commissioners to adopt uniform regulations for charitable gift annuities. If you would like to read the current status, go to Jim Potter's web site (www.pgresources.com) and click on "NAIC Draft Laws." See also all four links at the top of his "State Regulations" page.

REINSURANCE

In order to protect themselves from risk or liability in running an annuity program, some charities in the past have chosen to reinsure the annuities. By reinsuring the annuities, the organization accelerates the period in which the remaining principal will be available to spend. The charity purchases from an insurance company a commercial single premium immediate annuity sufficient to cover the annuity payments it has agreed to make. (*The insurance company must be a legal reserve life insurance carrier licensed to conduct business in the state where your organization has been incorporated and the state where each annuitant lives whose annuity agreement you are reinsuring.*) Prevailing interest rates dictate the cost of reinsurance.

In the mid 1980s, during the period of double-digit interest rates, it was possible to reinsure annuities for about half the principal donated. Currently, it would cost about 65% to 85% of the gift amount to reinsure the annuity payments. This leaves you with only a very small portion of the original gift. But, if you invest that gift remainder until the demise of the annuitant, as you would do if you maintained the annuity agreement yourself, you will have a remainder much closer to the goal of 50% of the original gift at the demise of the annuitant, without the mortality risk of the annuitant living too long.

One concern with reinsurance involves the special relationship that develops between the donor and the charity throughout the gift annuity relationship. Enormous potential for cultivation exists when the director of planned giving mails the annuity checks to the annuitants with a cover letter. Since the charity buys and owns the commercial annuity contract, the charity should instruct the insurance company to send the payments to the charity who then sends the payments to the annuitants using its own checks. In this way, the important donor relationship is maintained. The charity does not have to tell the annuitant that it reinsured the annuity contract.

If the insurance company mails the checks directly to the annuitants, it might create a problem for you. This involves the tax reporting to the annuitants. When the insurance company sends annuity checks directly to the annuitants, it will also provide tax information to them. However, your institution also sends tax information. Thus, the annuitants receive two different 1099-R forms—one from you and one from the insurance company. This would not necessarily be so bad if it were not for the fact that the information on these forms will be different, not to mention that the I.R.S. will be looking for tax on twice the taxable amount of the annuity. This is because the insurance company bases its information on the commercial annuity contract—not on a gift annuity. You must write to the insurance company and explain that these are charitable gift annuities and that the insurance company should cancel such reporting so you can handle it.

While reinsurance relieves the charity of all investment responsibilities associated with the program and frees up funds for current use, most charities feel they will derive much greater returns on gift annuities through their own prudent investment management. If the insurance carrier goes bankrupt, the charity still has to pay on its contract with the donors. Moreover, the charity will have to maintain appropriate reserves to satisfy the permit issuing states as well as some of the "notification" states in order to continue to issue new gift annuity agreements. This may be very difficult if you have already paid out 65% or more of each gift to the insurance company that just went bankrupt.

One might argue that the donor wishing to establish a $40,000 gift annuity could consider making an outright gift and purchasing a commercial annuity separately. My friend, Vaughn W. Henry, an estate planning consultant in Springfield, IL, (www.gift-estate.com) ran a couple of sample illustrations for me in July 2003. Since there are many kinds of commercial annuity products, your donor has lots of options. However, to be consistent, Vaughn ran illustrations for a single premium immediate annuity for a female donor, age 75, assuming quarterly payments. You can compare the results to the charitable gift annuity.

Amount	Type of Transaction	Rate	Annual Payment	Tax-free Portion	Charitable Deduction
$40,000	Gift Annuity	7.1%	$2,840	68.1%	$16,025
$20,000	Outright Gift	N/A	N/A	N/A	$20,000
$20,000	Commercial Annuity	9.578%	$1,916	84.2%	N/A
$10,000	Outright Gift	N/A	N/A	N/A	$10,000
$30,000	Commercial Annuity	9.59467%	$2,878	84.1%	N/A

Option #3 puts $10,000 into the charity's hands immediately with no risk. Option #1 puts the money into the hands of the charity in 11 years (on average) and the charity assumes the risk of ongoing payments. If your organization is grappling with state laws that require reinsurance or if your charity is nervous about offering charitable gift annuities, you could consider discussing an outright gift/commercial annuity as an option. If you are going to pay 65% to 85% of the donor's gift to reinsure an annuity, why bother?

CALCULATING THE TAX CONSEQUENCES OF A GIFT ANNUITY

A donor is entitled to a federal income, gift, and estate tax charitable deduction for part of the amount exchanged for a gift annuity. Usually, donors set up gift annuities during their lifetimes. Donors rarely set up gift annuities through a bequest.

Consequently, the donor will expect to receive from you a calculation showing the amount he or she can claim as a federal income tax charitable deduction. Further, the donor needs to know how much of the gift annuity payment is treated as ordinary income, tax-free return of principal, or long-term capital gain income (for gifts of appreciated long-term assets).

Every planned giving software program available includes the calculations you need for charitable gift annuities. The formats will be different, but all will require the following information:

1. Date of gift;

2. Fair market value of gift (for a gift with cash and securities together, add the cash to the fair market value of the securities);

4. Cost basis of gift (for a gift with cash and stock, add the cash to the cost of the stock);

5. Birth dates of annuitant(s) or a specific age if your calculation is only an example (the age is to the closest birth date);

6. I.R.S. discount rate. Your software might decide for you which of the rates available for the current month or the prior two months is most beneficial to the donor. For gift annuities, your donor will receive the highest federal income tax deduction when you use the *highest* discount rate for the current or prior two months. (If you do not know what the discount rate is, there is an explanation in Chapter II-2.) If the donor itemizes deductions, he or she will want to use the highest discount rate to maximize the federal income tax charitable deduction. If the donor does not itemize, he or she will most likely want to use the lowest discount rate to maximize the tax-free payments.;

7. The payment schedule (monthly, quarterly, semiannually, or annually);

8. The timing of the annuity payment, either at the end or at the beginning of the payment period. You can find the options for this item somewhere in the defaults section of your software. Set the default consistent with your payment schedule so that you do not need to worry about this for every gift.

9. For gifts of long-term appreciated securities (or real estate when allowed), how capital gains are to be paid. The most common case is an individual donor transferring his or her own property and being the sole annuitant. Then, the donor can spread the long-term gain in the property over his or her life expectancy. At the end of this chapter, there is a list of 14 different combinations of donors and annuitants. You should refer to that section if you have a donor/annuitant combination that is different from the case where the participant is both donor and annuitant. Some combinations create capital gain tax problems or gift tax problems, or both.

10. For partial payments, the beginning date of the payment period and the ending date of the payment period. You are not legally required to offer partial payments, but if you decide to do so, be consistent. You should set the default in your software to the correct policy. I always offered partial payments when I was a planned giving officer. This is fair to the donor, especially if a donor makes a gift shortly after the regularly scheduled payment date.

In most cases, you will be dealing with gifts of cash or gifts of long-term appreciated securities (held 12 months and a day or more). The calculated federal income tax deduction that the donor is eligible to claim falls under the same contribution ceilings as for an outright gift. For cash gifts, the donor can claim a deduction up to 50%

of his or her adjusted gross income with a five-year period in which to carry over and claim any excess above the 50% ceiling until he or she uses up the deduction. For gifts of long-term appreciated property (like securities or real estate), the deduction can be claimed up to 30% of the donor's adjusted gross income with the same five-year period in which to carry over and use up any amount that exceeds the 30% ceiling.

Be careful mixing different kinds of assets in one tax calculation. If a donor gives mostly stock and a little bit of cash for the purpose of bringing the gift amount to a round number, his or her income tax deduction for the stock portion falls under the 30% ceiling; and the income tax deduction for the cash portion falls under the 50% ceiling. This is a messy situation because you should really do two separate tax calculations. Alternatively, the donor can simply use a ratio to determine what value falls under both contribution ceilings. A donor may not think about this nuance; therefore, you should point it out.

Following is an example. Refer to **Exhibits II-8A, II-8B,** and **II-8C** on the next few pages.

Example:

On August 15, 2003, John Smith, born May 9, 1921, transfers stock having a cost basis of $50,000 and a market value of $100,000. He has held the stock 12 months or more. It is yielding 2.3%. Gift annuity payments are quarterly on the last day of March, June, September, and December. The discount rate is 3.2% for August, 3.0% for July, and 3.6% for June. He names himself sole annuitant.

When you input the variables for this gift into your software, you will see that the federal income tax charitable deduction is the highest when you use the discount rate for June at 3.6%. Using that rate, this gift qualifies the donor for an income tax charitable deduction of $47,334 which can be claimed up to 30% of adjusted gross income for tax year 2003.

Each quarterly annuity payment will be $2,125. The first partial payment for the period August 15 to September 30 (47 days) will be $1,085.60.

Exhibit II-8A: Summary of Benefits

When you want to show a donor the basics of a proposed gift, you can produce a summary that shows the relevant information most people want to know. All software programs have a summary chart. Notice that I used the exact date of birth. The software automatically made the donor 82 because he is closest to his last birthday. Always use the actual date of birth when you prepare an illustration. If the donor tells you he is 79, ask for his date of birth because he might be one year older for the tax calculation. In addition, your calculations in the future will always be accurate.

As you review the chart, notice at the bottom, "Total reportable capital gain of $26,333 must be reported over 8.3 years, the expected lifetime of the donor age 82." In addition, notice that if you divide $26,333 by 8.3 years, you get $3,172.65, which is essentially the "Capital Gain Income" showing directly above it. The pennies are off a little because of the way my software rounds off the decimals in the default.

If this were a cash example, the donor would have no capital gain portion and he would have a larger tax-free portion.

When you summarize the situation for the donor, it is not hard to see why gift annuities are so popular. This donor would have had to pay a capital gain tax of up to 15% on the $50,000 of appreciation if he sold the shares himself. Instead, by contributing the shares for a gift annuity, he accomplished the following:

1. Made a gift of $100,000 to your organization;

2. Received an income tax deduction of $47,334 for use in the current year up to 30% of adjusted gross income with a five-year carry-over period;

3. Increased his income from 2.3% to 8.5% generating a new annual payment of $8,500 for the rest of his life;

4. Avoided an immediate capital gain tax on the property's appreciation;

5. Received part of his annuity payment tax-free for 8.3 years;

6. Eliminated management responsibility.

If you have not worked with gift annuities before, you may have many questions about the above calculation. Not to worry. The planned giving software you will be using is so sophisticated that you should be able to follow the input phase with very little trouble. When you are not certain what to do, there is always a support person at the company from whom you purchased your software who is ready to answer your questions. Your legal counsel is there, too. Do not hesitate to ask for help when you need it. In addition, never guess if you do not know what you are doing. Remember, no question is too basic.

Exhibit II-8B: Actuarial Calculations

The Actuarial Calculations provide the step-by-step process through which the software calculated the federal income tax charitable deduction. If the donor's accountant performed the calculations manually, he or she would use the steps in this chart. You should send this kind of page to the donor so that he or she can give it to an advisor or accountant.

Exhibit II-8C: Taxation of Gift Annuity Payments

The Taxation of Gift Annuity Payments provides the breakdown of how the donor or annuitant will report for tax purposes the gift annuity payments received. You should send a copy of this type of chart to the donor for review with his or her attorney.

In addition, your business office or your gift annuity administrator will use this chart to create the tax form 1099-R for each annuitant. Notice that there are three categories in this particular example: Capital Gain, Tax-Free Portion, and Ordinary Income. Notice what happens in year 2012. The donor received all of the capital gain and tax-free return of principal; therefore, his entire annuity of $8,500 becomes ordinary income at that point. (Note: For annuities received before December 31, 1986, the tax-free portion remains tax-free even if the annuitant lives beyond life expectancy. The next section explains that.)

For gifts of long-term capital assets, the breakdown of the capital gain and tax-free tier will vary depending on the amount of appreciation in the asset. If you were comparing the breakdown of reportable income for an appreciated, long-term stock gift and a cash gift, the ordinary income figure would be the same.

Annuities Written Prior to December 31, 1986

Under current law, the tax-free portion of the payment ends after the donor has lived to the life expectancy he or she had on the date of the gift. Thereafter, the donor treats the entire payment as ordinary income.

Prior to 1987, the donor could exclude from gross income the tax-free portion of each annuity for life. Therefore, if you inherit a mature planned giving program that accepted gift annuities prior to 1987, the annuitants from these earlier contracts can continue to report their tax-free portion for as long as they live. For these lucky annuitants, the tax-free portion never becomes ordinary income.

Exhibit II-8A

ASHTON ASSOCIATES   Prepared for:
                                                          Male 82

Deduction Calculations
Summary of Benefits

8.5% Charitable Gift Annuity

ASSUMPTIONS:

Annuitant	[5/9/1921] 82
Date of Gift	8/15/2003
Principal Donated	$100,000.00
Cost Basis	$50,000.00
Annuity Rate	8.5%
Payment Schedule	quarterly
	at end

BENEFITS:

Charitable Deduction	**$47,334.00**
Annuity	**$8,500.00**
Tax-free Portion	$3,174.75
Capital Gain Income	$3,174.75
Ordinary Income	$2,150.50

Total reportable capital gain of $26,333.00 must be reported over 8.3 years, the expected lifetime of the donor age 82.

After 8.3 years, the entire annuity becomes ordinary income.

IRS Discount Rate for 6/2003 is 3.6%

Exhibit II-8B

ASHTON ASSOCIATES   Prepared for:
                                                         Male 82

Deduction Calculations

Actuarial Calculations

8.5% Charitable Gift Annuity

ASSUMPTIONS:

[1]	Annuitant	[5/9/1921] 82
	Date of Gift	8/15/2003
[2]	Principal Donated	$100,000.00
[3]	Cost Basis	$50,000.00
[4]	Annuity Rate	8.5%
[5]	Payment Schedule	quarterly at end
[6]	Discount Rate under IRC Section 7520(a) for 6/2003	3.6%

CALCULATIONS:

[7]		Annuity ([2] x [4])	$8,500.00
[8]	[a]	Value of $1 for age on [1], rate on [6] (Table S in IRS Publication 1457 (1999))	6.1141
	[b]	Adjustment for schedule on [5], rate on [6] (Table K in IRS Publication 1457 (1999))	1.0134
	[c]	Adj. Value of $1 ([8a] x [8b])	6.1960
[9]		Investment in Contract ([7] x [8c])	$52,666.00
[10]		**CHARITABLE DEDUCTION** ([2] - [9])	**$47,334.00**
[11]	[a]	Expected Return for age on [1] (Table V in Reg. 1.72-9)	8.4
	[b]	Adjustment for payment schedule on [5] (Reg. 1.72-5(a)(2)(i))	-0.1
	[c]	Expected Return per $1 ([11a] + [11b])	8.3
[12]		Expected Return ([7] x [11c])	$70,550.00
[13]		Exclusion Ratio ([9] / [12]) (Regs. 1.72-4, 1.1011-2(c) Example (8))	0.747
[14]		Bargain Sale Ratio ([9] / [2]) (Regs. 1.170A-1(d), 1.1011-2(b))	0.52666
[15]		Total Reportable Gain ([14] x ([2] - [3]))	$26,333.00
[16]		Life Expectancy of Donor Age 82 (Reg. 1.1011-2(a)(4)(ii))	8.3

Exhibit II-8C

ASHTON ASSOCIATES

Prepared for:
Male 82

Deduction Calculations
Taxation of Gift Annuity Payments

8.5% Charitable Gift Annuity

ASSUMPTIONS:

Annuitant	[5/9/1921] 82
Date of Gift	8/15/2003
Principal Donated	$100,000.00
Cost Basis	$50,000.00
Annuity Rate	8.5%
Payment Schedule	quarterly at end

CALCULATIONS:

Charitable Deduction	$47,334.00
Number of Full Payments in First Year	1
Days in Payment Period (7/1/2003 to 9/30/2003)	92
Days in Credit Period (8/15/2003 to 9/30/2003)	47
Annuity	$8,500.00
Quarterly Payment	$2,125.00
First Partial Payment	$1,085.60

BREAKDOWN OF ANNUITY:

	Capital Gain	Tax-free Portion	Ordinary Income	Total Annuity
2003 to 2003	1,199.16	1,199.16	812.28	3,210.60
2004 to 2010	3,174.75	3,174.75	2,150.50	8,500.00
2011 to 2011	2,910.59	2,910.59	2,678.82	8,500.00
2012 onward	0.00	0.00	8,500.00	8,500.00

Total reportable capital gain of $26,333.00 must be reported over 8.3 years, the expected lifetime of the donor age 82.

After 8.3 years, the entire annuity becomes ordinary income.

IRS Discount Rate for 6/2003 is 3.6%

DEFERRED GIFT ANNUITIES

A deferred gift annuity is identical to an immediate payment gift annuity except that the annuity payments begin at a future date determined by the donor at the time of the gift. For a deferred gift annuity, you must defer the payment for a minimum of one year.

The deferred gift annuity is excellent for the donor who:

- Wishes to support your organization;
- Does not need additional current income now;
- Seeks a larger federal income tax deduction in the current year;
- Wishes to create a fixed income for retirement;
- Contributes hard to value or illiquid property;
- Desires to establish an arrangement to support another person later in life.

The Deferred Gift Annuity Rates

As you have already seen, you base the annuity rate for a gift annuity that begins payments currently on the age(s) of the annuitant(s). You simply refer to your charity's approved one-life or two-life annuity rate table. Thus, for example, the annuity rate for a 50 year old electing to receive payments currently is 5.3%. Let's assume the same 50 year old elects to defer payments for 15 years, until age 65. Your organization retains and invests the principal for 15 years. As a result, the original gift compounds. This compounding allows you to pay a higher rate than would otherwise be the case for a different 65 year old who contributes property for a current gift annuity at age 65.

To compute the rate for a deferred gift annuity, you would input into your software the variables for the following, not necessarily in this order:

1. Date of gift;

2. Fair market value of gift;

4. Cost basis of gift;

5. Birth dates of annuitant(s) (or a specific age if you don't know the actual date of birth);

6. The date that payments begin.

7. I.R.S. discount rate. (Your software might decide for you which of the rates available for the current month or the prior two months is most beneficial to the donor. (See Chapter II-2 for an explanation of the I.R.S. Discount rate.)

You can see below how the deferral of payments affects the annuity rate a charity would be willing to pay:

1. If a 50 year old establishes a current
gift annuity, the rate is   5.3%

2. If a 65 year old establishes a current
gift annuity, the rate is   6.0%

3. If a 50 year old establishes a deferred
gift annuity deferring income for 15 years
until age 65, the rate is   12.4%

For illustration purposes, let's take the case of a 65 year old who wants to defer payments for 10 years. She may or may not need the annuity payments at that time, but she wants the option.

1. If a 65 year old establishes a current
   gift annuity, the rate is   6.0%

2. If a 75 year old establishes a current
   gift annuity, the rate is   7.1%

3. If a 65 year old establishes a deferred
   gift annuity deferring income for 10 years
   until age 75, the rate is   11.5%

If you are gasping at the deferred gift annuity rate of 12.4% in the first example and the 11.5% rate in the second example, go back to the beginning of this chapter where I discuss the assumptions in the tables. There are six assumptions in the American Council on Gift Annuities Rates that you need to understand.

After you consider all of the assumptions described earlier, when the dust clears, the above deferred gift annuity rates are legitimate.

The Income Tax Deduction For Deferred Gift Annuities

The rate of return increases the longer the donor defers payments. So, too, does the value of the donor's federal income tax charitable deduction. As with other life income plans, the charitable deduction is the present value of the gift at the end of the annuitant's life expectancy, taking into account the fact that a dollar received in the future is worth less than a dollar today.

The standard contribution ceilings apply for donors who establish deferred gift annuities. Donors using cash can claim up to 50% of adjusted gross income with a five-year carry-over period for any amount exceeding the 50% ceiling. Donors using long-term property like securities (or real estate, if not prohibited by state law) can claim up to 30% of adjusted gross income with the same five-year carry-over period. (Note: People who do not itemize deductions cannot claim a federal income tax charitable deduction.)

Administrative Implications Of The Deferred Gift Annuity

If you offer deferred gift annuities, you must maintain proper records on gifts and payment schedules so that you can begin payments on time. To streamline the process, you should require deferred gift annuity payments to coincide with your regular annuity payment dates.

Since you must defer the payment for a minimum of one year, a donor who makes a gift on April 20 this year would receive the first payment no sooner than June 30 next year. It ends up being a little more than a year.

As with the current gift annuities, you can reinsure deferred gift annuities by purchasing a commercial annuity from a life insurance company. You should check the state regulations on the ACGA web site to see if your state requires reinsurance.

How Do Annuitants Report Deferred Gift Annuity Payments For Income Tax Purposes?

The taxable character of each deferred gift annuity payment is similar to that of the payments from a current gift annuity in that the payment may have up to three components. Part is ordinary income, part is tax-free return of principal, and for gifts of appreciated long-term property, part of the tax-free portion converts to capital gain income. The same kind of rule applies with regard to bargain sale rules and unrelated business income.

Since deferred gift annuities begin payments in the future, tax legislation could change the way the annuitant reports annuity payments. You must keep current on tax law changes and check with your attorney for the most up-to-date information. For example, the Jobs and Growth Tax Relief Reconciliation Act of 2003 lowered the tax rate on long-term capital gains. The maximum capital gain tax for most long-term property is now 15% (formerly 20%). Annuitants who receive payments from a gift of appreciated securities got a raise. Plus, individual tax rates went down, too. To read more about the capital gain rules, go to Chapter II-2.

FLEXIBLE GIFT ANNUITIES

The flexible gift annuity is a variation on the deferred gift annuity. I have never done one. Usually, when a donor establishes a deferred gift annuity, the donor selects the date of the first payment on the date of the gift. The flexible gift annuity allows the donor to pick a range of start dates and decide later.

For example, if a donor makes a gift on September 4, 2004, he or she could say, "I would like to select a range of start dates from September 30, 2009 to September 30, 2014." Note that the range of start dates is always tied to the regular payment quarters. The first start date in the range must be as least one year from the date of the gift, so you would move it to the next closest regular payment date. In this case, I have assumed quarterly payments on the last day of March, June, September, and December. Therefore, a gift on September 4 pushes the first available start date to a minimum of September 30 of the following year. The case above is a deferral for a minimum of five years, but it could be any number of years. In another example, if you had semiannual payments on the last day of June and December, a gift on August 10 would require a first payment date no earlier than December 31 of the following year. Thereafter, each date in the range is one year apart.

When you create the annuity agreement for a flexible gift annuity, you must list the dates and payment amounts in the annuity agreement. In addition, you will add a sentence about when the donor can notify you in writing to start the payments, for example, 90 days prior to the start date.

With a deferred gift annuity, the donor receives a higher federal income tax charitable deduction and a higher annuity rate the longer he or she defers payment. However, with the flexible gift annuity, the donor is entitled to a deduction based on the start date that produces the lowest income tax deduction—the earliest start date in the range. This means that if the donor selects a range of start dates between five and ten years after the date of the gift, his or her income tax deduction is based on the five-year date, even though the donor may wait longer to start receiving payments.

Example:

The donor is age 70. Date of gift is June 3, 2003. The range of start dates is 6/30/2008 to 6/30/2012. My planned giving software has the standard American Council on Gift Annuities rate schedule. The appropriate discount rate is 3.8% for May 2003. Donor contributes $50,000 of appreciated long-term stock with a cost basis of $20,000.

Exhibit II-8D: Summary of Benefits

A Summary of Benefits for the above example is on the next page. Under Assumptions at the top, you can see the first payment start date and the last payment start date in the range. The federal income tax charitable deduction of $23,712.50 is tied to the first start date of 6/30/2008, which produces the lowest charitable deduction of the group. Also, notice what happens if the donor waits longer to start payments. If the donor starts payments at age 75, he or she receives $4,450, but at age 79, the payment is $5,950. If I were following through with all of the paperwork involved in this case, I would include the list of start dates and payment amounts as Schedule B of the annuity agreement. The modules you need are available if you own the full version of your vendor's planned giving software.

While I was writing this chapter, I had dinner with Thomas W. Smith, formerly Director of Gift and Estate Planning at Caltech. Tom is currently Senior Philanthropic Advisor at the Vermont Community Foundation and a planned giving consultant (www.plannedgivingstartup.com). We got talking on the subject of flexible

Exhibit II-8D

ASHTON ASSOCIATES

Prepared for:
Male 70

Deduction Calculations
Summary of Benefits

Flexible Gift Annuity

ASSUMPTIONS:

Annuitant	70
First Payment Start Date in Range	6/30/2008
Last Payment Start Date in Range	6/30/2012
Principal Donated	$50,000.00
Cost Basis	$20,000.00
Payment Schedule	semiannual

BENEFITS:

Charitable Deduction   **$23,712.50**

Annual Payment and Taxation for Elective Payment Start Dates

Elective Start Date	Age at Start Date	Capital Gain	Tax-free Portion	Ordinary Income	Total Annuity
6/30/2008	75	$1,281.60	$854.40	$2,314.00	$4,450.00
6/30/2009	76	$1,348.05	$898.70	$2,503.25	$4,750.00
6/30/2010	77	$1,435.14	$956.76	$2,708.10	$5,100.00
6/30/2011	78	$1,518.00	$1,012.00	$2,970.00	$5,500.00
6/30/2012	79	$1,610.07	$1,073.38	$3,266.55	$5,950.00

The entire annuity will become ordinary income after the life expectancy of the annuitant.

IRS Discount Rate for 5/2003 is 3.8%

---

gift annuities and he told me that he has been using them exclusively when a donor wants a deferred gift annuity. "If the donor wants to defer payments for 10 years, why not keep the option to defer for 10, 12, 15, 20, or 25? The donor gets the same deduction, but preserves more flexibility."

Private letter ruling 9743054 in 1997 sanctioned this variation on the gift annuity. However, only the person who gets the PLR can rely on it (rather ridiculous). If you come across this situation, check with your planned giving counsel before proceeding.

COMMUTED PAYMENT GIFT ANNUITY

The commuted payment gift annuity is another variation on the deferred gift annuity. Donors most commonly use it to pay for college tuition. Another name for this is the Tuition Gift Annuity. This starts out as a regular deferred gift annuity with a child or grandchild as the annuitant. As you learned earlier, the deferred gift annuity must have a start date no sooner than one year following the date of the gift. Since there is no such thing as a "term of years gift annuity," the payments normally last for the duration of the annuitant's life.

However, with a commuted payment gift annuity, you provide in the annuity agreement that the annuitant may commute the present value of the payments to a shorter number of equal payments. Then, at some point before the child goes off to college, he or she commutes the payments to four equal payments that start during freshman year. *Voilá!* The child has four years of tuition payments.

Considerations for this type of gift annuity include the following:

- The donor, presumably a parent or grandparent, will be required to file a gift tax return and report the associated taxable gift to the child. Because this is a gift of a future interest, there is no annual gift tax exclusion. Therefore, the donor must use a portion of his or her lifetime gift tax exemption.

- If the donor uses appreciated, long-term securities to fund the gift, the donor will have to pay the reportable gain up front. Go to the end of this chapter for the considerations involved with different combinations of donors and annuitants.

- The teenage annuitant must report and pay appropriate taxes on the payments received through this arrangement.

- The teenage annuitant could quit school, buy a Mercedes, or run off to Paris.

- To avoid a gift tax problem, the parent or grandparent could be the beneficiary, but what if he or she dies before the child reaches college age?

Several private letter rulings including 9108021 sanction this concept. However, as stated earlier, only the taxpayer who filed for the ruling can rely upon it.

I do not intend to walk through every consideration of this gift because it is very rare. Moreover, when I was reading R&R Newkirk's analysis in its *Charitable Giving Tax Service,* I found so much uncertainty and pitfalls that I can't really provide more than the basics for you. Your planned giving software should have all of the mechanics to create the documentation, tax illustrations, and the gift annuity agreement required. Check with your attorney if you have a donor who wants to explore one of these. R&R Newkirk recommends getting your own private letter ruling.

PROPERTY APPROPRIATE FOR ANNUITIES

Being ever mindful that some states prohibit donors from using real property for a gift annuity, there is considerable opportunity for you to construct a plan to serve the needs of the donor.

- Cash is a common asset used to fund charitable gift annuities, especially in April and October when certificates of deposit commonly come due. As people compare their bank's interest rate for rolling over their CDs or money market funds, they often decide then to use the cash to fund charitable gift annuities instead. In addition, some donors will use credit cards to establish gift annuities because they are building frequent flyer miles with every use of their credit card. Receiving gifts up to $20,000 by credit card is not uncommon, especially at year end when donors wait until the last minute to make their tax-motivated gifts.

- Gifts of appreciated securities are also very attractive as gift property to fund a charitable gift annuity. The benefit of increasing one's income over the lower stock dividend rate makes securities a very beneficial asset to use.

  In addition, avoiding the immediate capital gain on the conversion of a low-income producing asset to a higher paying plan is an added incentive for the stock donor.

- Donors can use real estate to fund a charitable gift annuity only in states that do not prohibit its use for gift annuities. There is a full treatment of using real estate for a deferred gift annuity in Chapter II-6. Be very diligent about evaluating the property before entering such an arrangement. Although it is legal to use real estate for a current gift annuity in most states, I would not recommend it due to the very high risk to the charity.

ACQUISITION INDEBTEDNESS

There are six instances when your institution will incur unrelated business income tax on a gift annuity. This means you will pay tax on the net profit from the sale of the gift property (at corporate rates if the charity is a corporation, at trust rates if the charity is a trust). They are:

1. When you accept mortgaged property;

2. When the value of the annuity is greater than 90% of the gift value;

3. When there are more than two annuitants;

4. When you agree to an annuity for a term of years;

5. When you guarantee a minimum or maximum amount;

6. When there is any adjustment of the amount of the annuity payments by reference to the income received from the transferred property or any other property.

Beware of these situations, and avoid them like the plague. Also, be careful not to inadvertently create a charitable remainder annuity trust by doing #6—deriving income directly from the transferred property. It would be an unqualified trust.

CONSIDERATIONS FOR DIFFERENT COMBINATIONS OF DONORS/ ANNUITANTS (ANNUITIES STARTING AFTER 1986)

In the course of running your gift annuity program, you will encounter 14 possible situations that result in different tax consequences for the donors or annuitants. Some of these situations will result in consequences that the donor did not anticipate, and probably did not want.

The tax implications of a gift annuity change depending on who owns the gift property, whether or not the asset has long-term appreciation, whom the donor names as the annuitant(s), and the sequence of the annuitants. Following is a list of 14 different situations. I have examined each with respect to four tax issues:

- How is the term of the tax-free portion of the annuity payment measured?

- If the donor uses appreciated, long-term property, what are the capital gain implications?

- What is the donor's gift tax liability, if any?

- What happens to the unrecovered portion of the principal (cost basis and/or long-term gain) if the annuitant(s) predecease their life expectancy?

When appropriate, I have noted whether the situation creates a problem and what the donor can do to eliminate it. The 14 situations often have similar consequences; however, I have repeated the complete explanation for each case. Although this is repetitious, it will provide the information you need without confusion. This section was very tedious to write, but it will help you when you need to check a situation.

In general, beware of gift annuities where the donor is not the sole or primary annuitant or when the donor uses joint property.

Case #1 **Ownership of Property:** Donor
               Annuitant: Donor

- *Term of tax-free portion of annuity payment:* Duration of donor's life expectancy. Thereafter, payment is fully taxable.

- *Capital gain liability:* A portion of the otherwise tax-free portion of the payment is characterized as long-term gain and is reported ratably over the donor's life expectancy.

- *Gift tax liability:* Not applicable.

- *Donor predeceases life expectancy:* Donor is entitled to a tax deduction on last income tax return for unrecovered portion of principal (cost basis only). The unrecovered long-term gain is neither reportable nor deductible; it represents a gain that the donor did not realize.

Case #2 **Ownership of property:** Donor
               Annuitant: Spouse

- *Term of tax-free portion of annuity payment:* Duration of spouse's life expectancy. Thereafter, payment is fully taxable. Tax-free portion is calculated on full value of property, not just on cost basis.

- *Capital Gain liability:* Donor must report and pay taxes on full amount of reportable long-term gain in year of gift.

- *Gift tax liability:* Gift of annuity interest to spouse qualifies for marital deduction. No gift tax liability.

- *Spouse predeceases life expectancy:* Spouse is entitled to a tax deduction on last income tax return for unrecovered portion of principal (including unrecovered long-term gain that was taxed to the donor when the annuity was created).

  PROBLEM: Donor incurred immediate capital gain tax on the transfer.

  SOLUTION: Donor makes gift of the property to spouse. There is no gift tax between spouses for federal tax, but check state law for taxation on transfers between spouses. Spouse exchanges property for gift annuity. Tax implications are now similar to Case #1.

Case #3 **Ownership of property:** Donor
               Annuitant: Donor, then spouse

- *Term of tax-free portion of annuity payment:* Duration of joint life expectancy. Thereafter, payment is fully taxable.

- *Capital gain liability:* A portion of the otherwise tax-free portion of the payment is characterized as long-term gain and reported ratably over the donor's life expectancy. If donor predeceases life expectancy and spouse survives, spouse continues to report part of payment as capital gain income until end of donor's life expectancy.

- *Gift tax liability:* Gift of annuity interest to spouse does not qualify for marital deduction and does not qualify for annual gift tax exclusion (gift of a future interest).

- *Donor predeceases life expectancy and spouse survives:* Spouse continues to report part of payment as tax-free return of principal until end of their joint life expectancy. If surviving spouse predeceases joint life expectancy, the unrecovered principal is deductible on spouse's last income tax return. If any portion of the unrecovered principal is capital gain income, it is neither reportable nor deductible.

- *Spouse predeceases donor and donor predeceases joint life expectancy:* Donor is entitled to a tax deduction on last tax return for the unrecovered portion of the principal. If a portion of the unrecovered principal is capital gain income, that portion is neither reportable nor deductible.

PROBLEM: The donor has made a taxable gift to the spouse.

SOLUTION: Donor reserves the right to revoke the surviving spouse's survivorship annuity interest by will. On the donor's death, if he or she does not revoke the surviving spouse's interest, then his or her estate receives a marital deduction for the spouse's interest and a charitable deduction for the remainder interest.

Case #4   **Ownership of property:**   **Donor**
                  Annuitant: **Spouse, then donor**

- *Term of tax free portion of annuity payment:* Duration of joint life expectancy. Thereafter, payment is fully taxable. Tax-free portion is calculated using full value of property, not just cost basis.

- *Capital gain liability:* Donor must report and pay taxes on full amount of reportable gain in year of gift.

- *Gift tax liability:* The present value of the annuity interest given to the spouse qualifies for the marital deduction.

- *Annuitants predecease joint life expectancy:* The unrecovered principal (cost basis plus long-term gain) is deductible on last tax return of the survivor.

PROBLEM: Donor incurs immediate capital gain tax on the transfer.

SOLUTION: Donor makes gift of property to spouse. Spouse exchanges property for gift annuity. Tax implications are now similar to Case #3.

Case #5   **Ownership of property:**   **Donor**
                  Annuitant: **non-spouse**

- *Term of tax-free portion of annuity payment:* Duration of annuitant's life expectancy. Thereafter, annuity payment is fully taxable. Tax-free portion is calculated using full value of property, not just cost basis.

- *Capital gain liability:* Donor must report and pay tax on full amount of reportable gain in year of gift.

- *Gift tax liability:* Donor has made a taxable gift to the annuitant of the present value of the annuity. This may qualify for the $11,000 annual gift tax exclusion. If the donor retains the right exercisable by will to revoke the annuitant's interest, the gift that is reportable (and potentially taxable) is the annual annuity payment received by the non-spouse that exceeds the $11,000 annual gift tax exclusion.

- *Annuitant predeceases life expectancy:* Annuitant is entitled to a tax deduction on last income tax return for the unrecovered portion of principal (cost basis plus long-term gain).

PROBLEM: Donor incurs immediate capital gain tax liability on the transfer. Donor may incur current gift tax liability.

SOLUTION: Donor can use cash to fund the gift annuity, thus eliminating the capital gain tax. No way to avoid the gift tax liability if the donor wishes to provide support for the annuitant.

Case #6   Ownership of property: **Donor**
             Annuitant: **Donor, then non-spouse**

- *Term of tax-free portion of annuity payment:* Duration of joint life expectancy. Thereafter, annuity payment is fully taxable.

- *Capital gain liability:* A portion of the otherwise tax-free portion of the payment is characterized as long-term gain and is reported ratably over donor's life expectancy.

- *Gift tax liability:* Donor has made a gift to the second annuitant of the present value of the annuity interest and is fully taxable on the gift amount. Inasmuch as the gift is of a future interest, it does not qualify for the $11,000 annual gift tax exclusion. If the donor reserves the right exercisable by will to revoke the interest of the second annuitant, the gift will not be complete at the time the annuity is established. Thus, there will be no current gift tax.

- *Donor predeceases life expectancy and second annuitant survives:* Second annuitant continues to report part of each annuity payment as tax-free return of principal until the end of their joint life expectancy. Second annuitant continues to report a part of each payment as capital gain until end of donor's original life expectancy. If second annuitant predeceases joint life expectancy, the unrecovered portion of the principal is deductible on the second annuitant's last income tax return. If any portion of the unrecovered principal is capital gain income, it is neither reportable nor deductible.

- *Second annuitant predeceases donor and donor predeceases life expectancy:* Donor receives a tax deduction on last tax return for unreturned portion of principal. If a portion of the unrecovered principal is long-term gain, it is neither reportable nor deductible.

Case #7   Ownership of property: **Donor**
             Annuitant: **Non-spouse, then donor**

- *Term of tax-free portion of payment:* Duration of joint life expectancy. Thereafter, payment is fully taxable. Tax-free portion is calculated on full value of property, not just on cost basis.

- *Capital gain liability:* Donor must report and pay tax on full amount of reportable gain in year of gift.

- *Gift tax liability:* Donor has made a taxable gift to the annuitant of the present value of the annuity. This amount may qualify for the $11,000 annual gift tax exclusion. If the donor retains the right exercisable by will to revoke the annuitant's interest, the gift that is reportable (and potentially taxable) is the annual annuity payment received by the non-spouse that exceeds the $11,000 annual gift tax exclusion.

- *Annuitants predecease joint life expectancy:* The unrecovered portion of the principal (cost basis plus long-term gain) is deductible on last tax return of the survivor.

PROBLEM: Donor has incurred immediate capital gain tax liability. Donor has made a taxable gift to the annuitant.

SOLUTION: Use cash to fund the annuity to eliminate the capital gain tax. No way to avoid the gift tax liability.

Case #8 **Ownership of property:** Donor and spouse
Annuitant: Donor

- *Term of tax-free portion of payment:* Duration of donor's life expectancy. Thereafter, annuity payment becomes fully taxable.

- *Capital gain liability:* Spouse incurs immediate capital gain tax in year of gift for portion of appreciation attributable to spouse's share of the property. Donor's share of long-term gain is reported ratably over donor's life expectancy. Thus, part of the otherwise tax-free portion of annuity payment is characterized as long-term gain.

- *Gift tax liability:* Gift of the annuity interest by the spouse to the donor qualifies for the marital deduction. No gift tax liability.

- *Donor predeceases life expectancy:* Donor is entitled to a tax deduction on last income tax return for unrecovered portion of donor's cost basis plus unrecovered portion of spouse's cost basis plus long-term gain. Unrecovered share of donor's long-term gain is neither reportable nor deductible.

PROBLEM: Spouse incurs an immediate capital gain tax on the transfer.

SOLUTION: Spouse makes a gift of property to donor. Donor exchanges property for the annuity. Tax implications are now similar to Case #1.

Case #9 **Ownership of property:** Donor and spouse
Annuitant: Donor and spouse—Joint and survivor

- *Term of tax-free portion of payment:* Duration of joint life expectancy. Thereafter, annuity payment becomes fully taxable.

- *Capital gain liability:* A portion of the otherwise tax-free portion of annuity payment is characterized as long-term gain for duration of joint life expectancy.

- *Gift tax liability:* State law might not offer an unlimited marital deduction for gifts of future interests. In order to insure that the gift qualifies for the marital deduction on the federal and state level, it is recommended that both donor and spouse reserve the right to revoke by will each others income interest. No gift tax liability.

- *Annuitants predecease joint life expectancy:* Unrecovered portion of the principal is deductible on survivor's last income tax return. Unrecovered long-term gain is neither reportable nor deductible.

Case #10 **Ownership of property:** Donor and spouse
Annuitant: Someone else

- *Term of tax-free portion of payment:* Duration of annuitant's life expectancy. Thereafter, the annuity payment is fully taxable. Tax-free portion is calculated using full value of property, not just cost basis.

- *Capital gain liability:* Donor and spouse must report and pay tax on full amount of reportable gain in year of gift.

- *Gift tax liability:* Donor and spouse have made a taxable gift of the present value of the annuity interest, reportable for gift tax purposes. The gift may qualify for the $11,000 annual gift tax exclusion. If donor and spouse elect to split the gift, they may be able to give $22,000 before they will be subject to gift tax.

- *Annuitant predeceases life expectancy:* Annuitant is entitled to a tax deduction on last income tax return for portion of unrecovered principal (cost basis plus long-term gain).

PROBLEM: Donor and spouse incur immediate capital gain tax and may be subject to gift tax.

SOLUTION: Consider using cash to fund the gift to avoid the capital gain tax. No way to avoid the potential gift tax.

Case #11   **Ownership of property:**   **Donor and spouse**
                 Annuitant: **Donor, then non-spouse**

- *Term of tax-free portion of payment:* Duration of joint life expectancy of annuitants. Thereafter, the annuity payment becomes fully taxable.

- *Capital gain liability:* Spouse incurs immediate capital gain tax on spouse's share of long-term gain. Donor's share of long-term gain is reported ratably over donor's life expectancy.

- *Gift tax liability:* Donor and spouse will have made a gift to the second annuitant equal to the present value of the future interest. The gift does not qualify for the annual gift tax exclusion and must be reported for gift tax purposes and possibly taxed to the donor and spouse.

  Spouse will have made a gift to the donor of one-half the value of the donor's annuity interest. This gift does not qualify for the marital deduction.

- *Annuitants predecease joint life expectancy:* The survivor is entitled to a tax deduction on last income tax return for the unrecovered portion of the donor's cost basis plus the unrecovered portion of the spouse's principal (cost basis plus long-term gain taxed to the spouse). The unrecovered portion of the donor's long-term gain is neither reportable nor deductible.

PROBLEM: Donor and spouse have made a taxable gift to the non-spouse. Spouse has capital gain liability. Spouse has made a possible taxable gift to the Donor. It's a mess.

SOLUTION: Spouse makes a transfer of the property to the donor under the marital deduction. Donor sets up the annuity and reserves the right to revoke the survivor's annuity interest at death. If the donor does not revoke the survivor's annuity interest, there could be an estate tax for the annuity payments that continue after the donor's death. This Case is now similar to #6.

Case #12   **Ownership of property:**   **Donor and non-spouse**
                 Annuitant: **Donor and non-spouse, joint and survivor**

- *Term of tax-free portion of payment:* Duration of joint life expectancy of annuitants. Thereafter, the annuity payment becomes fully taxable.

- *Capital gain liability:* A portion of the otherwise tax-free portion of annuity payment is characterized as long-term gain for duration of joint life expectancy.

- *Gift tax liability:* Each joint owner has made a gift of a future interest to the other that is reportable on a gift tax return. The respective mirror gifts do not qualify for the annual gift tax exclusion and must be reported for gift tax purposes and possibly taxed accordingly.

- *Annuitants predecease joint life expectancy:* Unrecovered portion of the principal is deductible on survivor's last income tax return. Unrecovered long-term gain is neither reportable nor deductible.

PROBLEM: Each person has made a potentially taxable gift to the other.

SOLUTION: They could split the assets in half, then each make a separate gift. Therefore, A as donor names himself primary annuitant with B as successor annuitant and reserves the right to revoke B's interest by will. In turn, B does the same thing. Or, they make one gift of the joint property and each reserves the right to revoke the other's continuing interest in his or her respective 50% share by will.

Case #13   Ownership of property: Donor and non-spouse
            Annuitant: Donor

- *Term of tax-free portion of payment:* Duration of annuitant's life expectancy. Thereafter, the annuity payment becomes fully taxable.

- *Capital gain liability:* Non-spouse incurs immediate capital gain tax in year of gift for portion of appreciation attributable to non-spouse's share of the property. Donor's share of long-term gain is reported ratably over donor's life expectancy. Thus, part of the otherwise tax-free portion of annuity payment is characterized as long-term gain tax.

- *Gift tax liability:* Non-spouse has made a taxable gift of the present value of the annuity interest to donor. The taxable gift may qualify for the $11,000 annual gift tax exclusion.

- *Donor predeceases life expectancy:* Unrecovered portion of principal attributable to donor's share is deductible on Donor's last income tax return. Unrecovered portion of non-spouse's principal and long-term gain is also deductible on donor's last tax return. Unrecovered portion of donor's long-term gain is neither reportable nor deductible.

PROBLEM: Non-spouse has incurred immediate capital gain tax liability as to his or her share and has made a taxable gift of a present interest to donor.

SOLUTION: Avoid the immediate capital gain tax by having the non-spouse give his or her share of the property to the Donor. By doing so, the non-spouse may have made a taxable gift if the value is greater than the $11,000 annual gift tax exclusion. However, when the donor establishes the gift annuity, there is no immediate capital gain tax.

Case #14   Ownership of property: Donor and non-spouse
            Annuitant: Someone else

- *Term of tax-free portion of payment:* Duration of annuitant's life expectancy. Thereafter, the annuity payment becomes fully taxable.

- *Capital gain liability:* Donor and non-spouse must report and pay tax on full amount of reportable gain in year of gift attributable to each one's share.

- *Gift tax liability:* Each joint owner has made a taxable gift of the present value of the annuity interest. The taxable gift may qualify for the $11,000 annual gift tax exclusion for both donors.

- *Donor predeceases life expectancy:* Unrecovered portion of principal and long-term gain is deductible on annuitant's last income tax return.

PROBLEM: Both people have immediate capital gain tax to pay and both must report a potentially taxable gift.

SOLUTION: Use cash to fund the gift annuity to avoid the capital gain problem. No way to avoid a potential gift tax problem.

It may also be possible to revoke an annuity interest during lifetime since there appears to be no specific mention of revocation "only by will" in the annuity regulations as there is in the pooled income fund and charitable remainder trust regulations.

CREDITING GUIDELINES

The considerations for crediting the gift amount are similar to those for the pooled income fund and other life income arrangements. Some institutions provide gift credit for the value of the donor's income tax deduction. Others provide full credit for the fair market value of the gift. There is a complete discussion of this in Chapter III-5, Integrating Planned Giving into a Capital Campaign.

SUMMARY

If you want a complete book on just charitable gift annuities, Frank Minton has written the definitive guide on this topic, *Charitable Gift Annuities: The Complete Resource Manual,* listed in Appendix III.

Now, you have read about two life income gift arrangements, the pooled income fund and the gift annuity, which provide a variable or fixed payment to the donor. In the next chapter, I discuss charitable remainder trusts, which donors can use to provide a variable or a fixed return while offering greater flexibility to the donor of substantial means or with illiquid assets.

Chapter II–9

CHARITABLE REMAINDER TRUSTS

INTRODUCTION

Thus far, you have read about two life income gift arrangements—the pooled income fund and the charitable gift annuity—both of which require an active role on the part of the charity. A donor cannot fund either of these gift vehicles unless the charity offers them.

Gifts made to either plan benefit only the sponsoring charity; the donor cannot use these plans to benefit multiple organizations at the same time. The only exception is in the case of a national organization operating a gift annuity program or a pooled income fund on behalf of its affiliates.

Pooled income funds and gift annuities cater predominantly to the donor of modest means. Although some donors make six- and even seven-figure gifts to these plans, most donors contribute under $100,000 to pooled income funds or gift annuity programs.

When the size of the gift moves above the six-figure range, the degree to which the gift meets the donor's estate planning objectives becomes increasingly important. Moreover, many other considerations influence the form such a gift will take. Fortunately, the ability to tailor a gift arrangement to the special needs of an individual donor is within your power by using a charitable remainder trust.

Charitable remainder trusts can be intimidating for inexperienced planned giving professionals. Prospects interested in contributing six figures or more simply do not seek you out often enough. Thus, there is really no way for you to get into the swing of things. Each case is unique with different considerations depending on the donor's age, the donor's gift assets, and the donor's tolerance for complexity and need for control.

This chapter should give you both the information and the confidence you need to start talking about charitable remainder trusts or to assist in the development of a proposal that someone else on the staff can take to a donor visit. However, remember that charitable remainder trusts are very complex vehicles. In this book, you will learn enough information to be dangerous. The nuances of drafting and managing CRTs are too numerous for me to cover here. Consider this chapter only a starting point.

This chapter examines charitable remainder trusts under the following topics:

- an overview of charitable remainder trusts;
- types of charitable remainder trusts;
- taxation of payments;
- how to calculate the charitable deduction;
- comparing the charitable deduction—annuity trust *vs.* unitrust;
- cost to establish and run a charitable remainder trust;
- getting a tax I.D. number for a CRT;
- private letter rulings;
- tangible personal property in a CRT;
- options for selecting charitable remaindermen;
- considerations for selecting income beneficiaries;
- considerations for selecting a trustee;
- gift tax consequences;
- crediting guidelines;
- questions and answers about charitable remainder trusts;
- summary.

AN OVERVIEW OF CHARITABLE REMAINDER TRUSTS

When people talk about charitable remainder trusts, they are referring to one of two highly structured plans created by the Tax Reform Act of 1969:

- The Charitable Remainder Annuity Trust, and
- The Charitable Remainder Unitrust (now five variations).

The above trusts are different from each other in three basic ways: 1) the form of the beneficiary's payment, 2) the ability to make further contributions only to the unitrust, and 3) the way in which the donor's tax consequences are calculated. You will find a discussion of each variation later in this chapter. First, here are the ways all charitable remainder trusts are similar.

A charitable remainder trust is a separate trust arrangement between the donor and a trustee chosen by the donor. The trustee could be a bank or trust company, brokerage firm, other fiduciary, an individual, a charity, and, in many cases, the donor. The donor reserves the right to receive payments from the CRT or provides for the payment to others. At the end of the trust term, the remaining principal distributes to the named charity or charities.

Most banks and trust companies or charities that serve as trustee require a minimum of $100,000 or more for a charitable remainder trust; some will go as low as $50,000. The administrative costs for managing charitable trusts are high. Consequently, the minimum fees charged by most fiduciary managers will be prohibitive for small accounts. Charities that serve as trustee for CRTs have a big advantage over those that do not. They can negotiate a lower fee schedule for the management of their consolidated deferred giving assets. Thus, a small CRT gets the benefit of a lower fee as part of a larger institutional account. (Note: CRTs may still incur separate expenses for preparation of tax returns or other reporting.)

For charitable remainder trusts established during the donor's lifetime, the trustee is not required to notify the charity or charities named in the trust. The donor simply walks up to his or her bank, broker, or other fiduciary manager, delivers the gift assets together with a trust document prepared by an attorney, and the donor has a charitable remainder trust.

Therefore, any charitable organization can promote the use of charitable remainder trusts to its constituency. For the charity, there are no internal procedures to create, no payments to make, and no administrative considerations. However, if your organization does not serve as trustee, the hard part is becoming knowledgeable enough to discuss these trusts competently without the day-to-day administrative duties and tasks that would get you up to speed more quickly.

If you retain a professional fiduciary to be trustee for your deferred giving assets, you will go through a process of reviewing and approving some standard specimen trust documents. The fiduciary will have specimen charitable remainder trust documents approved by its internal legal counsel. After receiving the sample documents from your trustee, you should send them to your charity's tax counsel for review and approval. If you are a planned giving officer inheriting a planned giving program with an outside manager, get copies of your manager's documents. But, be careful using any standard documents. Laws vary from state to state. Therefore, if your charity provides a sample trust document to a donor in another state, an attorney in the state that governs the trust should be involved.

Often, the donor's attorney is not familiar with the special drafting requirements of a qualified charitable remainder trust and is, therefore, dependent upon you and your tax counsel in generating a sample trust document. It is helpful to maintain a file of boilerplate documents that you can show to a donor when necessary. However, a donor should not use your documents without first consulting his or her own advisor. Moreover, it would be safer to give the specimen agreement to the donor's attorney directly. Still, if the donor's attorney does not specialize in charitable giving tax law, he or she may be ill equipped to advise the donor. Sometimes, due to the donor attorney's lack of expertise, the gift simply falls through.

Some states are stricter than other states on the issue of "unauthorized practice of law." You should be extremely careful when using planned giving software (like Crescendo) that includes specimen agreements. Attorneys trained in charitable giving tax law know what they are doing when they create a CRT document. You probably know enough to be dangerous. If you can arrange it, have your tax counsel deal directly with the donor's tax counsel.

The I.R.S. mandates certain required provisions in the governing instrument of a charitable remainder trust. However, the I.R.S. documents are a starting point, but they fall short on many administrative and other features. CRTs have many flexible options not included in the I.R.S mandatory provisions. Therefore, do not make the mistake of promoting CRTs in an assembly-line fashion using only the I.R.S. version.

An enormous amount of technical expertise is involved here. An inexperienced attorney cannot possibly have mastered the vast body of tax law and regulations surrounding the planning, drafting, and operation of these trusts. An attorney competent in all sorts of other legal matters might take days to write one of these trusts and still get it wrong. As a precaution, when your donor produces a trust document through his or her own attorney, it is a good idea to have the document reviewed by your tax counsel—someone who presumably is working with charitable remainder trusts regularly. No amount of precaution is too great because the I.R.S. will disallow the donor's tax deduction if the trust does not meet strict drafting requirements. For example, although unitrusts are allowed to receive additional gifts in the future, the CRT will be disqualified if it is silent on the matter of additions. If something goes wrong, there is a procedure that your donor can use, except in the most flagrant violations, for reformation of a defective trust.

In the broadest sense, the concept and benefits of a charitable remainder trust are similar to those of the pooled income fund or the charitable gift annuity.

- There is an irrevocable transfer of property by the donor.

- The donor retains a right to receive income from the trust or creates an income interest for other beneficiaries, or both.

- The donor is entitled to a partial federal income tax charitable deduction in the year he or she funds the trust (or an estate tax charitable deduction for trusts funded at death).

- The donor incurs no immediate capital gain tax on the transfer to and subsequent sale by the trust of highly appreciated, long-term assets.

- At the end of the trust's term, the trust principal distributes to charity.

In other ways, the charitable remainder trust is far more flexible than either the pooled income fund or the gift annuity.

- The donor chooses the trustee and, in most cases, can be the trustee.

- A charity can also be an income beneficiary as long as there is one non-charitable beneficiary.

- The CRT can make distributions to charity from principal if the document permits it.

- The donor chooses the type of payment (fluctuating or fixed).

- The donor chooses the amount of the payment (generally stated as a percentage of the initial gift amount).

- The trust term can be measured by 1) the life or lives of persons living when the trust is created, 2) by a term of years (not to exceed 20), or a combination of the two.

- The trustee can tailor the investment strategy of the trust and the taxable character of the income to meet the unique needs of the donor. (Note: The trustee is under a fiduciary obligation to look out for the interests of both the income beneficiary and the charity.)

- The donor can choose the frequency and the timing of the payments (monthly, quarterly, semiannually, or annually).

- The donor can choose one or more charitable organizations to share in the trust principal upon termination of the trust.

- The donor can reserve the right to change the charity.

By reproducing the above 15 items, you will have a good, one-page summary of the general features of a charitable remainder trust.

While there is considerable flexibility with respect to administrative provisions and investment strategies of charitable remainder trusts, the trust must conform to one of two basic types: a charitable remainder annuity trust or a charitable remainder unitrust, of which there are five variations. The following rules apply to all types of charitable remainder trusts:

- A charitable trust's percentage payout must be a minimum of 5%.

  There is no practical reason for this 5% rule; however, it is one of the original drafting requirements for charitable remainder trusts under the Tax Reform Act of 1969. There is no such rule for charitable lead trusts.

- A charitable trust's percentage payout must be no greater than 50%.

- The remainder interest must be a minimum of 10% of the fair market value of the funding assets.

  This rule can be a problem for older intervivos CRTs. Given the combination of 1) a high payout, and 2) an I.R.S. discount rate much lower today than when the donor created the trust, there is a chance that an additional gift to the trust by the donor will not pass the 10% deduction test. I.R.S. came up with a solution to the problem by providing that the nonqualified addition to the existing CRT will be treated as a separate CRT with a different payout rate. If you have a situation involving a problem with the 10% remainder rule for an existing CRT, you ought to get your attorney involved to assist you with the particulars.

  The 10% rule can also be a problem for testamentary CRTs since the age of the beneficiary and the I.R.S. discount rate will not be known until the death of the donor.

I.R.S. created the 50% rule and the 10% rule for transfers after July 28, 1997, due to abuses surrounding the accelerated CRT. The point of both rules is to end a tax avoidance scheme that was being used by donors who were not very charitable. The accelerated CRT goes something like this:

Jack has $4 million of stock having a zero cost basis. The stock pays no dividends. He transfers the stock in January to an 80% charitable remainder unitrust with a two-year term and an annual payment on 12/31. The trustee receives the stock and does nothing. No sale of any assets. No taxable event. After the close of the calendar year, the trustee has a grace period in the next calendar year to make the required 12/31 payment for the prior year.

The trustee sells $3.2 million of assets and pays the 80% payment of $3.2 million. In the year the payment was due, there was no ordinary income earned, no realized capital gains, and no tax-exempt income. Therefore, the trustee deems that the donor's payment is 100% tax-free return of principal. The donor reports no capital gain. At the end of the next year, the donor receives a second 80% payment using the same strategy. He receives another $640,000 as tax-free return of principal. Again, the donor reports no capital gain because there were no realized gains in the CRT to trigger a capital gain tier. There is about $160,000 left in the trust and that distributes to the charitable remainderman at the end of year two. The trust ends and the donor has received $3,840,000 back, reported no capital gain, and the charity receives $160,000.

You can see why the I.R.S. considered this abusive.

TYPES OF CHARITABLE REMAINDER TRUSTS

There are six types of charitable remainder trusts, one annuity trust and five unitrusts. The six variations provide flexibility for the donor in tailoring the perfect plan. Some variations are more common than others.

Charitable Remainder Annuity Trust (CRAT)

A charitable remainder annuity trust (CRAT) provides a fixed dollar payment no less often than annually. The donor chooses the payment upon creating the trust. Further, the donor can never make an additional gift to a charitable remainder annuity trust. That consideration is extremely important when considering the type of charitable trust a donor should create. (Note: When a CRAT is established at death, it may receive funding on different dates throughout the course of the estate's administration. Multiple funding amounts to a CRAT from an estate are not considered additional gifts.)

The format of the CRAT is similar to the charitable gift annuity. Therefore, when the percentage payout is equal to or less than your organization's approved gift annuity rate table, you could consider a charitable gift annuity instead of a CRAT. The charitable deduction is identical when the percentage payout and the payment schedules are the same. In addition, the cost of administering the gift annuity is much less than for the CRAT. Plus, the donor's payment from a gift annuity will generally include a portion of tax-free return of principal that may not be available in a CRAT. Bear in mind that the charitable gift annuity payment is a legal debt of the charity while the CRAT payment is not.

However, some donors may want to keep control or reserve the right to change the charitable remainderman. If so, the charitable remainder annuity trust provides the flexibility and control the donor needs.

The operation of an annuity trust is simple. When the trust earns more than the required annuity payment, the trustee adds excess income to principal; when the trust earns less, the trustee must invade the principal to make the required payment. However, the payment itself remains the same for the life of the trust.

Example:

Donor transfers $100,000 to an annuity trust and selects an annuity payment of $6,000 or 6% of the initial contribution.

	Market Value of Trust	Annual Income of Trust	Annual Payment to Beneficiary
Year 1	$100,000	$4,500	$6,000
Year 2	95,000	3,800	6,000
Year 3	120,000	7,000	6,000
Year 4	125,000	5,625	6,000
etc.			

Some observations about the above situation may come to mind. Although the donor's payment does not change with fluctuations in the market value, the tax treatment of the distribution may be affected by an increase in the trust's value (e.g., when tier two long-term capital gain is paid out). The taxation of payments is discussed later. As long as the assets are not exhausted, the donor receives a $6,000 payment even if the assets fall below the level of the initial contribution.

The fluctuations in the market have reverse consequences for the charity. The full amount of capital appreciation generated in the trust is the charity's at the end of the trust's term. Conversely, if the assets drop in value or become depleted, the eventual distribution will be far less than what the charity anticipated. If the payout is too high, the trust could self-destruct. And, unlike the gift annuity, the charity owes the donor nothing from its own assets.

Two factors are important in establishing a CRAT: 1) the age of the beneficiaries, and 2) the amount of the annuity payment. For example, it may be perfectly reasonable to establish an 8% annuity trust when the beneficiary is 95 years old. However, can the trust sustain such payments over the life expectancy of a 50-year-old beneficiary? Probably not. In the latter case, the trust may also fall prey to the five percent probability test. (discussed below) or it may not pass the 10% charitable remainder test discussed earlier.

Remember, the donor does not have to consult you to establish a charitable remainder trust. Thus, your influence in directing the donor's actions is minimal in cases where your charity is not trustee. The challenge arises when you initiate the idea and must try to create a balance between the donor's needs and the ultimate benefit to your organization.

When charities serve as trustee, they can make rules about minimum gift size, restrictions on beneficiary ages, and can dictate a minimum percentage of the remainder that will benefit the trustee charity. If the charity does not serve as trustee, then it has no say in what the donor does in the drafting provisions of his or her annuity trust.

If you are a planned giving officer taking over a mature planned giving program, you will find some annuity trusts in the mix, mostly from the 1980s. In July of 2003, I.R.S. claims there are 22,669 CRATs and 84,201 CRUTs.

FIVE PERCENT PROBABILITY TEST—ANNUITY TRUST ONLY

Because payments from an annuity trust are fixed, I.R.S. thinks there is a chance the trust principal will be depleted depending on the age of the beneficiary, the dollar amount of the annuity, and the relevant I.R.S. discount rate. (Beyond I.R.S. concerns, poor market performance of the assets inside the trust contributes to this problem.) Revenue Ruling 77-374 requires an annuity trust to meet the Five Percent Probability Test. The purpose of the ruling is to protect the charity's interest by determining the likelihood that the charity will never receive the trust principal.

If the probability the charity will not receive the remainder is greater than five percent, the trust fails the test and the donor's tax deduction is disallowed. If the probability of depletion is less than five percent, I.R.S. considers the probability of exhaustion "negligible" and allows the deduction.

You should not spend undue time worrying about this, but you should know that it exists. Most planned giving software will alert you with an error message when you use variables for an annuity trust that fail the five percent probability test. Whenever your annuity trust example has a percentage payout higher than the I.R.S. discount rate you are using, a red flag should go up. The Five Percent Probability Test could be a problem for testamentary CRATs because the age of the beneficiary(ies) and the I.R.S. discount rate will not be known until the death of the donor.

This test does not apply for unitrusts.

Regular Charitable Remainder Unitrust (CRUT)

This version is the most common form of unitrust (also called a standard CRUT, SCRUT or Type 1 Unitrust). As with the CRAT, when the trust earns more than the required unitrust payment, the trustee adds excess income to principal; when the trust earns less, the trustee invades principal to make the required payment. The payment is based on a percentage of the valuation of the trust's assets (no less frequently than annually).

Example:

Donor transfers $100,000 to a 6% unitrust.

	Market Value of Trust	Annual Income of Trust	Annual Payment to Beneficiary
Year 1	$100,000	$4,500	$6,000
Year 2	95,000	3,800	5,700
Year 3	120,000	7,000	7,200
Year 4	125,000	5,625	7,500
etc.			

Reviewing the above figures, you can see why the unitrust provides a hedge against inflation. The size of the annual payment is tied to the market value of the trust's assets. Thus, both the charity and the donor/beneficiaries share the risk over the life of the trust. Similar to the annuity trust, the value of the payments is *not* tied to the actual income earned. In Year 1, for example, when the trust is worth $100,000, the annual payment must be $6,000 (6% of the market value) even if the actual income is less than $6,000. The balance is made up by invasion of the principal to the extent necessary. As the value of the trust changes year to year, the payment also changes.

The operation of the regular unitrust is similar to the operation of most charities' endowments. The CRUT makes payments based on a total return concept because the trust (like your endowment) generally pays no tax on the sale of investments.

The assets of the endowment are valued on the last day of the fiscal year (for a charitable trust, the valuation is at least annually). Then, the spending limit approved by the trustees is applied to the endowed funds. Similarly, the percentage payout from a CRT is applied to the market value of the trust assets. Each individual endowment fund's spending amount is then determined for the year. If you understand how your endowment works, you will understand how a regular unitrust works. (Some endowments have more complicated formulas to determine the spending amount, but I hope you get the idea.)

Net Income Unitrust (NICRUT)

This version is sometimes called a Type II Unitrust or a NIOCRUT, for net income only. The donor receives the lesser of the stated percentage payout or the net income earned.

Example:

Donor transfers $100,000 to a 6% net income unitrust.

	Market Value of Trust	Annual Income of Trust	Annual Payment to Beneficiary
Year 1	$100,000	$4,500	$4,500
Year 2	95,000	3,800	3,800
Year 3	120,000	7,000	7,000
Year 4	125,000	5,625	5,625
etc.			

In the above example, the trust never earned 6%. Therefore, the beneficiary received only the net income.

Why would a donor choose this type of unitrust? Well, net income unitrusts were popular in the 1980s when it was possible to earn double-digit returns with no end in sight. However, very few donors would choose such a trust in the current economy.

People also set up net income unitrusts in earlier years because they had real estate or other illiquid, non-income producing property. Prior to the invention of the flip unitrust, there were no other options for efficiently dealing with non-marketable, non-income producing assets. Today, if a donor has illiquid property with which to fund a charitable trust, he or she probably would use one of the two versions of the flip unitrust discussed later.

Finally, some donors established net income unitrusts because they did not need additional income and were willing to accept a payment smaller than the unitrust percentage. Thus, the trustee could place the trust's assets in growth-oriented securities with little emphasis on current income. When the donor retired, the entire portfolio, presumably highly appreciated over the initial contribution, got shifted to high-income producing investments. At this point, the donor received the percentage payout from a larger pool of assets at a stage of life when unearned income represented most of his or her entire livelihood. In addition, the donor was probably in a lower tax bracket after retirement.

If you inherit a mature planned giving program, you may find some net income unitrusts set up in earlier years. There was a period during which the I.R.S. allowed net income unitrusts to be reformed into straight unitrusts, but that period ended. If your predecessor did not get the trusts under your control reformed, then you must run them according to their original trust agreements. That will be very frustrating to the beneficiaries who may have expected a much larger payout than what you are able to generate today.

A major problem with these trusts is that the trustee must invest a disproportionately larger share of the assets in fixed-income investments. Unfortunately, with more fixed-income investments, the trust's chances of appreciation are bleak. Therefore, the beneficiary and the charity find themselves in a non-productive situation as long as the prevailing interest rates are lower than the trust's required payout.

With the creation of the flip unitrust, discussed later, there is no reason to use a net income unitrust for an illiquid asset today.

Net Income Unitrust With Makeup Provision (NIMCRUT)

This next version of the unitrust (Type III) is similar in all respects to the one above except for one very important difference. If the trust earns less than the percentage payout in one year, it pays net income. However, if it earns more than the stated percentage in a later year, the trust will pay as much income as is necessary to bring prior payments up to the maximum amount that should have been paid in those prior years had income been sufficient.

Example:

Donor establishes a 5% net income unitrust with the makeup provision. On the valuation date, the market value of the assets is $100,000. If income is sufficient, the beneficiary's payment will be $5,000. The trust earns only $3,500. Thus, the trust pays only $3,500 and has a deficiency of $1,500.

The next year, the trust is worth $110,000; the 5% payment would be $5,500. The actual income earned is $6,000. Here, the makeup provision kicks in. Accordingly, the beneficiary's payment is as follows:

$5,500	for the current year
+ 500	deficiency from prior year leaving $1,000 as a deficiency.
$6,000	total payment

If the account earns more than 5% next year, it will pay out the excess up to the $1,000 of deficiency payments owed.

Formerly, a net income unitrust with the makeup provision was an excellent vehicle for donors who wished to prevent invasion of the principal or who contributed illiquid property. Moreover, if the illiquid property earned any income at all, it would probably earn the same after the donor put it in the NIMCRUT. The donor received the same income he or she had before the gift, but by using the NIMCRUT, the donor gave the trustee more flexibility by not forcing a sale if the market took a downturn. The makeup provision also allowed the donor to plan present and future income in a strategic way as the following example illustrates.

Example:

Patricia, age 55, establishes a 5% net income unitrust with the makeup provision. She funds the trust with $100,000 of cash. The donor currently enjoys a healthy salary as a partner in a law firm. She has no current need for more income. In ten years, she will retire.

For the first nine years, the trustee invests for growth with little emphasis on current income. As a result, it generates only 2% in income *per* year but it appreciates 10% annually.

Year	Market Value of Trust	Required Payment @ 5% of Market Value	Actual Income Earned @ 2%	Net Income Payment Made To Beneficiary	Annual Deficiency in Payment	Cumulative Deficiency in Payment
1	$100,000	$5,000	$2,000	$2,000	- $3,000	- $3,000
2	110,000	5,500	2,200	2,200	- 3,300	- 6,300
3	121,000	6,050	2,420	2,420	- 3,630	- 9,930
4	133,100	6,655	2,662	2,662	- 3,993	- 13,923
5	146,410	7,321	2,928	2,928	- 4,393	- 18,316
6	161,051	8,053	3,221	3,221	- 4,832	- 23,148
7	177,156	8,858	3,543	3,543	- 5,315	- 28,463
8	194,872	9,744	3,897	3,897	- 5,847	- 34,310
9	214,359	10,718	4,287	4,287	- 6,431	- 40,741

Notice the size of the beneficiary's payments for the first nine years. The trust earned less than the stated percentage payout. Thus, she received only the net income. Over the nine years, the trust accumulates $40,741 in deficiency payments (the difference between the amount she should have received and the amount she actually received). Donor retires. The trustee shifts assets from growth investments to high-income investments yielding 9%. Annual appreciation is now 4%. This kind of example was possible at one time. Obviously, there are few 9% investments today. This example shows how people used the net income with makeup unitrust in the past. The scenario described is unlikely to be achieved in the current economy.

Year	Market Value of Trust	Required Payment @ 5% of Market Value	Actual Income Earned @ 9%	Required Payment Made To Beneficiary		Deficiency Payment		Total Payment	Cumulative Deficiency Paid
10	235,795	11,790	21,222	11,790	plus	9,432	=	21,222	9,432
11	245,227	12,261	22,070	12,261	plus	9,809	=	22,070	19,241
12	255,036	12,751	22,953	12,751	plus	10,202	=	22,953	29,443
13	265,237	13,262	23,871	13,262	plus	10,609	=	23,871	40,052
14	275,846	13,792	24,826	13,792	plus	689	=	14,481	40,741

After the shift in investments in year 10, there is enough income to meet the 5% payout as well as to begin making up for the lean years. Thus, in year 10, the payment is $21,222 representing 5% of the market value or $11,790 plus $9,432 to begin reducing the accumulated $40,741 in deficiency payments.

In year 14, the trust completes all deficiency payments from the first nine years. Thereafter, as long as the trust earns a minimum of 5%, it will pay the donor the required 5% payment each year.

The donor used the following strategies in the above example:

1. The donor selected the minimum payout allowed (5%) because it afforded her the highest income tax deduction possible for this transfer. (The lower the payment, the higher the tax deduction.) Plus, the lower payment allows the trust to grow faster, thus producing more distributable income over time.

2. The donor received a low income from the trust during her peak earning years. During this time, the trustee invested the assets for maximum growth.

3. Upon retirement (or at some future date), the change in investment strategy provided income much greater than the stated percentage payout of 5%, the excess of which was returned to her as makeup payments when she needs it most.

Flip Unitrust

The flip unitrust is a marvelous blend of a net income unitrust and a regular unitrust. It operates on a net income basis in the beginning. Then, on January 1 following the year of what is termed the "flip-triggering event," the trust flips to a regular or Type 1 unitrust. It is perfect for illiquid assets.

Example:

Mark and Julie Spencer, age 75 and 70 (to their closest birth dates), jointly own undeveloped land having a current market value of $550,000 and a cost basis of $68,000. They are in a 35% federal income tax bracket. Property taxes run $7,000 *per* year. There is no mortgage on the property. They are in a 15% capital gain tax bracket.

They receive no income on this property and they would incur a capital gain of $482,000 if they sold it. In their 15% capital gain tax bracket, they would lose $72,300 if they sell the land. While visiting with the director of planned giving of State University, they learned that they could convert the property to a new income with favorable tax benefits using a charitable remainder flip unitrust.

The Spencers transfer the land to a 5% flip unitrust retaining a joint and survivor income interest. The flip triggering event is the sale of the property. The valuation date is January 1, and payments are semiannual at the end of June and December. Assume the I.R.S. discount rate is 6%. On the death of the survivor, the remaining principal distributes to State University.

By transferring the land to a flip unitrust, the Spencers accomplished the following:

- Made an irrevocable commitment to one or more of their favorite charities;
- Avoided an immediate capital gain tax of $72,300;
- Generated a new income as soon as the trustee sold the property (Note: in the year of the sale, the trust pays net income up to 5%. On January 1 of the year following the sale, the trust flips to a regular unitrust, and carries on from there);
- Received an income tax deduction of $254,095 in the year of the transfer saving $88,935 in their 35% federal income tax bracket;
- Reduced probate expenses and potential estate taxes by removing the property from their probate estates.

In this case, the net income feature is critical because it gives the trustee a window of time needed to dispose of the property in order to convert it to income-producing investments. Until the trust earns income, the trustee makes no payment. The beauty of the flip unitrust is that it starts as a net income version but it does not have to exist as a harder-to-manage net income version for the life of the trust. Before the I.R.S. approved the flip unitrust, donors with illiquid assets had to use one of the two net income versions (net income only or net income with makeup) and were trapped with a net income payment for the life of the trust. With the flip version, the trustee does not have to worry about the percentage payout requirement prior to the flip-triggering event (discussed below), and will have greater opportunity for investing in a balanced portfolio following the flip. That benefits both the donor and the remainderman.

The donor must understand a couple of points with respect to an illiquid, non-income producing asset in a CRT. Even though the trustee makes no payment to the beneficiaries until he or she receives income in the CRT, there could be expenses associated with the property while it is in the CRT. For real estate, these could include taxes, maintenance, or insurance premiums. In addition, the trustee charges fees. Therefore, the donor should agree in writing to make additional gifts to the CRT prior to the anticipated bills. (This is one reason a CRAT doesn't work well for an illiquid asset—additions can never be made.) At the end of Chapter II-6 covering real estate, there is a sample letter of understanding between the trustee and the donor. If you don't have an agreement with the donor prior to the trust's funding, you may get into trouble when bills come due without the cash to pay them.

This example is straightforward because there is no mortgage or other encumbrance. In general, when a CRT owns debt financed assets (real property subject to a mortgage), it may create unrelated business income tax in the trust, which will cause the trust to pay tax on its income and gain. It may also be an act of self-dealing. The worst possibility is when the donor is liable on the mortgage and the trust makes mortgage payments—this will cause the trust to fail as a charitable remainder trust entirely. Some of the things that affect the outcome include:

1. how the donor acquired the property;
2. how long the mortgage has been on the property;
3. who put the mortgage on the property;
4. whether the donor is personally liable on the mortgage.

If you get the answers to the above questions, your legal counsel can advise you about whether you'll have a problem with a gift of mortgaged property to a CRT. For a more complete discussion of the considerations involved in accepting real estate, refer to Chapter II–6.

THE FLIP-TRIGGERING EVENT

Flip unitrusts provide great drafting flexibility. In general, many different kinds of events can trigger the flip provided that the event cannot be discretionary by the trustee or by anyone. Examples of flip-triggering events include the following:

- A specific date or a single event;
- Marriage, divorce, death, birth;
- Sale of an unmarketable asset;
- A person attaining a specific age.

Example: Create a flip unitrust and invest for growth while the beneficiary is in peak earning years. Use an age or a specific date for the flip-triggering event. Presumably, the assets will grow over the years and provide a much greater payment at retirement.

Example: Create a flip unitrust with donor's spouse as beneficiary. The flip triggering event is the death of the donor.

Example: Create a flip unitrust with marketable assets and one unmarketable asset (one share of closely-held stock), the sale of which triggers the flip. If something unforeseen happens (you lose your job, you become disabled), sell the unmarketable asset and flip the CRT.

Flip Unitrust with Makeup Provision

A flip unitrust can also have a makeup provision. If you are not familiar with how makeup provisions work, go back in this chapter and read the section about net income unitrusts with makeup provisions (NIMCRUT). They work the same way in the flip unitrust. However, any makeup amount eligible to be paid to the beneficiaries is lost (and remains with the principal) if it is not paid out before the end of the year before the trust flips.

For example, assume the flip triggering event is the death of a spouse. The trust has been earning less than the stated percentage payout and has been accumulating deficiency payments for several years. The spouse dies in June causing the trust to flip to a regular unitrust on the following January 1. Any accumulation in the deficiency amount must be paid by the end of the year in which the spouse dies or else it remains in the trust. Since the flip unitrust must earn more than the stated payout in order to pay makeup amounts, it is unlikely to do so sufficiently before the end of the year for all deficiency payments to be paid out. Thus, having a makeup provision is a nice thought but it probably won't accomplish what you want in practice.

Annuity Trust (CRAT) *vs.* Standard Unitrust (CRUT)

	Annuity Trust	**Unitrust**
Suggested minimum for funding with single lump sum	$150,000 to $200,000	$150,000 to $200,000
Additions allowed	No	Yes, if allowed by the trust document
Type of payment	Fixed dollar amount based on a percent of the initial contribution (minimum 5% and not greater than 50%)	Fixed percentage of market value each year (minimum 5% and not greater than 50%)
Property appropriate for funding	Cash, readily marketable securities	Cash, readily marketable securities. Illiquid property could be used if the donor agrees to make extra contributions to cover fees, payout requirements, or other expenses before the trustee sells the illiquid assets.
Results if assets appreciate	Beneficiary's payments remain fixed. Charity's remainder interest increases.	Beneficiary's payments increase. Charity's remainder interest increases.
Results if assets depreciate	Beneficiary's payments remain fixed. Charity's remainder interest decreases and is subject to depletion.	Beneficiary's payments decrease. Charity's remainder interest decreases.

TAXATION OF PAYMENTS

Charitable remainder trusts can generate up to four categories of income with some subcategories. Compare below the way income could be taxed from the various plans. (Note: Long-term capital gain on the sale of securities or nondepreciable real estate was taxed up to 20% for sales prior to May 6, 2003.)

- Pooled income fund: Payments reportable in one category

  1. Ordinary income.

     Qualifying dividends are taxed at 15%. For taxpayers in 10% or 15% income tax bracket, dividend tax rate is 5% and 0% in 2008. In 2009, dividends go back to being taxed at ordinary income tax rates.

- Charitable gift annuity: Payments reportable in up to three categories

  1. Ordinary income

  2. Long-term capital gain income

     Gain on securities is taxed at 15%. For taxpayers in 10% or 15% income tax bracket, capital gain is 5% and 0% in 2008. In 2009, capital gain rates increase to 20% for everybody.

     Gain on tangible personal property (for a related use) is 28% for everybody.

     Gain on depreciable real property is 25% for everybody.

  3. Tax-free return of principal.

- Charitable remainder trust: Payments reportable in up to four categories taken in the following order:

  1. Ordinary income (This includes short-term gain.)

     Qualifying dividends are taxed at 15%. For taxpayers in 10% or 15% income tax bracket, dividend tax rate is 5% and 0% in 2008. In 2009, dividends go back to being taxed as ordinary income.

  2. Capital gain income

     Gain on securities is taxed at 15%. For taxpayers in 10% or 15% income tax bracket, capital gain is 5% and 0% in 2008. In 2009, capital gain rates increase to 20% for everybody.

     Gain on tangible personal property is 28% for everybody.

     Gain on depreciable real property is 25% for everybody.

  3. Tax-exempt income

  4. Tax-free return of principal

The taxable character of the trust's payments can be tailored to the individual needs of the beneficiary if you have an astute trustee and if the economy cooperates. However, because of the four-tier system of reporting income, the donor cannot transfer highly appreciated assets with the intention that the trustee will convert them to tax-exempt bonds and subsequently receive tax-exempt income. The tax-exempt income would not begin to flow until the beneficiary receives all income in the first two categories. Following is a simplistic example using an annuity trust.

Example:

Donor establishes a 5% annuity trust with $250,000 of appreciated long-term securities having a cost basis of $50,000. The annual payment from the trust will be $12,500 ($250,000 x 5% = $12,500). The trustee sells the shares and reinvests in tax-exempt bonds yielding 6%.

Although the trust earns $15,000 in tax-exempt income, many years will pass before the donor sees one penny of tax-exempt income because the $200,000 of long-term gain realized when the trustee sold the stock must pass through to the beneficiary first. Meanwhile, the trust has little chance for growth with fixed-income investments.

At the end of the first year, the trustee reviews the nature of the trust income and finds the following tiers of income:

1. Ordinary income   -0-
2. Long-term capital gain income $200,000
3. Tax-exempt income   15,000
4. Tax-free return of principal   N/A

First, the trustee looks to see whether there is any ordinary taxable income. In this case, there is none. Then the trustee looks at the long-term capital gain income. The trust has $200,000 of long-term capital gain resulting from the sale of the securities that funded the trust. Thus, the donor's entire $12,500 annuity payment is long-term capital gain income.

The donor's payment will continue to be long-term capital gain income until the entire $200,000 of gain is exhausted. In this case, the beneficiary will receive long-term capital gain income for about 16 years.

Bear in mind that routine sales and reinvestments of the portfolio generate additional gains and losses all of which affect the taxable character of the payments. For example, if the trust incurs a capital gain in exchanging one investment for another, the amount of the gain is new capital gain tier. Thus, it will pass through to the donor before the tax-exempt income.

The only way a donor could receive tax-exempt income is if he or she funds the trust with cash or with property that has little or no appreciation. Consequently, when the trust holds only tax-exempt securities, it will pay only tax-exempt income with very little or no other income category to block the tax-exempt income. If you are working with a professional fiduciary as trustee (a bank, trust company, or other professional manager), you will probably have a problem with the investment strategy of 100% tax-exempt bonds. Such a strategy hurts the remaindermen due to the lack of capital appreciation that would generally result from such an investment plan.

Practically, the four-tier system of tax reporting from a charitable remainder trust benefits the beneficiary significantly. If the trustee is attentive to the trust's investment strategy, he or she can invest a portion of the assets for growth with little emphasis on current income. Then, when a payment is due, the trustee sells an appreciated asset to raise the cash. The sale generates long-term gain that will be passed out to the beneficiary.

The Jobs & Growth Tax Relief Reconciliation Act of 2003 created a new 15% rate for dividends of U.S. corporations and foreign corporations that meet certain requirements. Therefore, the strategy of purposely trying to generate long-term gain may not be as important as it was before JGTRRA. The trustee has more options to structure the investments since most people will pay 15% on both long-term gain and most dividends. Since the provisions of JGTRRA are temporary, there will still be a long-term need to pay close attention to the investment strategy of a CRT.

HOW TO CALCULATE THE CHARITABLE DEDUCTION

The establishment of a charitable remainder trust entitles the donor to a federal income, gift, and estate tax charitable deduction for the present value of the remainder interest calculated using I.R.S. tables. Under current law, the estate tax will be relevant until 2009, eliminated in 2010, and reinstated in 2011, unless Congress passes new laws in the meantime. However, for purposes of this current discussion, assume that there is an estate tax.

For income tax purposes, the charitable deduction ceilings apply as usual. For gifts of appreciated long-term property to public charities, the deductible limit is 30% of adjusted gross income; for gifts of cash and ordinary income property, the limit is 50% of adjusted gross income. In both cases, the donor can carry over the excess for up to five more years.

For estate tax purposes, there are no charitable contribution deduction ceilings.

The charitable deduction for a CRT is calculated the same whether or not the donor creates it during lifetime or at death. (Bear in mind that the type of assets used affects the income tax deductibility.) If the donor creates the trust during lifetime, the associated deduction is an income tax deduction. If he or she creates the trust at death, the associated deduction is an estate tax deduction. In both cases, the donor's deduction is based on the following variables:

1. The date of gift;

2. The type of trust (annuity trust or unitrust);

3. The fair market value of the property transferred to the trust;

4. The date of birth (or age to the closest birth date) of the income beneficiaries or a term of years not to exceed 20, or a combination of lives and a term of years;

5. The percentage payout chosen by the donor;

6. The frequency of the payments (monthly, quarterly, semiannual, annual);

7. The timing of the payments (at the end of the payment period or at the beginning of the payment period);

8. The I.R.S. discount rate. To get the highest charitable deduction, you would use the highest discount rate for the current month or for the prior two months. (See Chapter II-2 for an explanation of the discount rate.)

NOTE: The calculation of the tax deduction for a unitrust is the same regardless of the type of unitrust. The tax deduction for a 6% regular unitrust is the same as for a 6% net income unitrust or a 6% flip unitrust.

As with other life income arrangements, I.R.S. has tables that take into account the different operational features of a trust. These tables reflect the ultimate performance of the trust and how much income the beneficiary will receive over the term of the trust. They also project the present value of the principal available to the charity at the end of the trust. Bear in mind that the calculations provide only a snap shot in time and bear little resemblance to the ultimate performance of the CRT.

Once you input the above variables into your planned giving software, you will be able to select any number of charts and illustrations for your example. Among them is a chart showing the value of the donor's charitable deduction. Remember that the deduction for an intervivos charitable remainder trust is an income tax deduction, and the deduction for a testamentary charitable remainder trust is an estate tax deduction. (Note: we don't know whether the provisions of the Economic Growth and Tax Relief Reconciliation Act of 2001 dealing with the phase out and elimination of the estate tax in 2010 will be made permanent.)

COMPARING THE CHARITABLE DEDUCTION—ANNUITY TRUST *VS.* UNITRUST

Side by side, when you compare an annuity trust and a unitrust with the same percentage payout, the annuity trust will generate a larger charitable deduction as long as the percentage payout is less than the I.R.S. discount rate you are using.

Following is a chart showing how much of the gift is deductible for a charitable remainder trust paying income to a 70-year-old beneficiary in quarterly installments at the end of the payment period. The discount rate used is 6%.

| Stated Percentage | Charitable Deduction | |
Payout	Annuity Trust	Unitrust (all 5 types)
5%	56.6%	53.9%
6%	47.9%	48.3%
7%	39.2%	43.5%
8%	*	39.3%
9%	*	35.6%

*Using a 6% discount rate, the 8% and 9% Annuity Trusts fail the 5% probability test.

Notice that the charitable deduction decreases as the percentage payout increases.

Since the creation of the CRT in the Tax Reform Act of 1969, these trusts have operated through good economic times and through bad. Not all trusts have performed the way the donor expected or the way the planned giving officer originally illustrated. When you create scenarios to illustrate the performance of such a trust over the lifetime of the donor, especially for unitrusts that have fluctuating payments, be extremely careful to incorporate a realistic total return in your examples. The donor will use your figures as promises made when your performance does not measure up. Ask your planned giving manager for a suggestion as to an appropriate rate of return for income and capital appreciation for use in your examples. If you don't have an outside manager, check with your treasurer.

The age of the donor is extremely important when selecting a payout rate. If the payout is too high, the trustee will be forced to use more fixed income investments in the portfolio. Such a strategy hinders growth in the account. Unfortunately, many CRTs created in the 1980s and 1990s are having trouble in the 2000s and are at risk of drilling themselves out of existence.

Although some donors want a high payout, they may eventually regret this choice. When discussing a charitable remainder unitrust with a prospective donor, the planned giving officer must be able to explain why a lower payout could potentially provide a more beneficial outcome for the donor and why a lower payout gives the trustee more flexibility in creating a prudent investment strategy.

The common argument in favor of a lower CRUT payout goes something like this: If the trustee need pay only 5% of the market value each year, he or she can invest a larger percentage of the portfolio in growth-oriented securities. Presumably, the market value of the account will grow each year. As the trust grows, the dollar value of each year's 5% payment will increase. When this plan is plotted along side a similar trust with, let's say, an 8% payout, there will be a point at which the 5% trust's payments catch up and eventually exceed the payments from the 8% trust. For this concept to work the trustee must experience a healthy amount of appreciation each year and the term of the trust must be sufficiently long. Through most of the 1990s, it was easy for trustees of charitable trusts to generate total returns in the double digits. Even trusts with high payouts were able to survive and grow. That is no longer true. If the trust cannot keep up with the payments, it will go into a death spiral during a period of flat growth or market declines.

In addition, the investment strategy for an 8% payout normally would include a larger percentage of fixed-income investments than would the strategy for a 5% payout. Therefore, the appreciation in the 8% trust would typically not be as good as what could be achieved for the 5% trust. That makes the selection of a higher payout very unwise.

Nonetheless, there is an opposing viewpoint from the perspective of the beneficiary. What would happen if you incorporated the present value consideration into the picture? One trust pays 5% and, due to an aggressive investment strategy, grows by 10% each year. The other pays 8% but experiences little if any growth because the trustee must invest more heavily in bonds in order to generate sufficient income for the payment. In year one, the first trust pays $5,000; the second trust pays $8,000.

As the first trust grows, the payments get larger while, at the same time, the other trust still is paying about the same $8,000. At some future date, the 5% trust will surpass the 8% trust in the actual dollar value paid out. However, one must factor inflation into the equation. The extra $3,000 paid up front from the 8% trust is worth more to the donor in purchasing power than the same $3,000 paid five years from now, or ten years from now. Consequently, if a donor really were interested in getting the most purchasing power from the trust payments, he or she would need to see a cash flow computed on a "present value" basis. The argument against this, however, is that the 8% trust will pay a relatively fixed $8,000 for the life of the trust. Years from now, let's say 10 or 20 years, what will the $8,000 be worth? The purchasing power of the $8,000, with no chance for growth, will steadily decline. This debate is also complicated by the taxability of the payments since the 8% CRT probably distributes all ordinary (tier one) income.

In the year 2003, many CRTs are in trouble. Rather than allow their trusts to deplete themselves, some donors have opted to trade their income interest in a CRT for a charitable gift annuity payment. Such a drastic measure would not be necessary if donors had selected lower payouts for their CRTs and had been more conservative with their investment allocations.

COST TO ESTABLISH AND RUN A CHARITABLE REMAINDER TRUST

The costs to create a charitable remainder trust depend on the experience of the tax counsel involved and the complexity of the donor's special requirements. The cost would be at least a few hundred dollars. Many charities provide this service free for their donors. Still, the donor should always review the charity's sample document with his or her own financial advisor. As director of planned giving, you should not engage in the unauthorized practice of law; therefore, any document that you prepare for a donor should be clearly marked "Sample" on every page. You do not want to expose yourself or your charity to the risk of a lawsuit for drafting a trust incorrectly or inadequately for the donor's needs.

The costs of a CRT would be significantly higher if the donor uses real estate or other illiquid assets that are hard to value, require specialized handling, or have other exceptional considerations. Usually, the trustee will charge extra for time or legal expenses incurred in the handling of real estate, closely-held stock, or tangible personal property.

Fee schedules vary widely among managers, but you can expect to pay between .75% to 2% depending on the manager and how much total market value your charity has placed with the particular manager. In Chapter III-9, there is a discussion about managing your planned giving assets, including a sample "Request for Proposal." You will get a better price if you combine all of your deferred giving assets under one roof.

Usually, the trustee takes fees from income or principal of the account, or apportions the fees between the two. There are rules about where different types of fees should be charged. Your trustee will know these rules, and, generally, such things will not be your responsibility. Some organizations that serve as trustee for charitable trusts pay the fees for trust management separately considering them a cost of fund raising. That becomes very expensive for the charity and it diminishes the real value of these accounts to your organization. Many charities charge the relevant fees to the trust accounts. The trust accounts should be able to carry their own fees.

GETTING A TAX I.D. NUMBER FOR A CRT

A charitable remainder trust needs a tax I.D. number because it is a taxpaying entity. If you have a professional trustee manager working with your charity, the trustee will apply for the tax I.D. number for the trust. See I.R.S. Form SS-4, available on the I.R.S. web site at www.irs.gov. There is no charge to get a tax I.D. number for a CRT.

PRIVATE LETTER RULINGS

The variations on drafting charitable remainder trusts extend far beyond the body of tax law governing their creation. Frequently, interpretation of the laws is difficult even for an attorney experienced with these trusts. The I.R.S. sees the trust document when the trustee files the trust's first tax returns (Form 1041 and Form 5227 for federal purposes. Note: Your state may require a filing of some kind, too.) In the worst case, a trust can be defective due to an omission after the donor has already funded it.

For unusual cases that fall outside the historical case law, the donor can request a Private Letter Ruling from the I.R.S. before he or she funds the trust. The I.R.S. makes public its private letter rulings but deems them to be legal only for the taxpayers who requested them.

Even though most trusts can be reformed to fix an error in drafting (called a scrivener's error), this is not something with which you want experience. The best way to avoid a problem is to get an attorney who knows what he or she is doing. And, if your donor wants to do something with a CRT that has not been allowed by statue, he or she should get a private letter ruling first.

TANGIBLE PERSONAL PROPERTY IN A CRT

There are a couple of problems when a donor funds a charitable remainder trust with tangible personal property during lifetime. First, there is no federal income tax charitable deduction until the trustee sells the tangible asset if the donor, donor's spouse, siblings, or lineal ancestors or descendants are beneficiaries, or until the interests of these people expire (they die or the term of their payments end). The second problem is that tangible personal property used as the funding asset for a CRT is considered not for a related use by the charity. Therefore, the value for computing the charitable deduction is the cost basis. (Note: If the cost basis is close to the market value, you wouldn't worry about this issue.)

On the other hand, if the donor names a beneficiary not in the disqualified class, he or she can claim the deduction immediately.

The only reason for funding an intervivos CRT with tangible personal property is that it is a convenient way to convert a non-income producing asset to a new income stream without paying the immediate capital gain tax for a sale by the owner. For such a transfer, the donor would generally use a flip unitrust or a flip unitrust with makeup provision. There is a discussion about both earlier in the chapter.

If a donor funds a CRT with an item of tangible personal property at death, he or she has a different situation. There is no related-use problem for bequests of tangible personal property, so the estate receives a charitable deduction computed on the fair market value of the funding asset (as opposed to the cost basis). Moreover, anyone can be a beneficiary without creating a delay in the estate's ability to claim the deduction.

Remember that a trust funded with an item of tangible personal property still incurs trustees fees. Therefore, the donor should agree in writing to make periodic additions of cash or marketable securities to pay the trustees fees prior to the sale and reinvestment of the asset.

OPTIONS FOR SELECTING CHARITABLE REMAINDERMEN

With a charitable remainder trust, the donor has the opportunity to select one or more qualified charities to share the trust principal at the termination of the trust. From the donor's perspective, a CRT is an efficient vehicle through which to fulfill several charitable objectives with one single gift.

If you are discussing the idea of a charitable remainder trust with a donor, you would be prudent to tell the donor that it can be used to benefit other charities, too. The donor will find out anyway. In fact, the donor may be more inclined to create a CRT if it can serve many charitable interests at the same time.

The donor can also include a provision to change the charitable remaindermen as long as any charity meets the appropriate requirements of the Internal Revenue Code. (Note: If the donor initially chose a public charity, he or she cannot change to a private foundation.) If a donor retains this right, then, for all practical purposes, such as gift credit or donor recognition, he or she has made no gift to a specific charity—yet. Such a gift would have the certainty of a bequest intention. However, the donor has made a gift for federal income and gift tax deduction purposes.

Finally, the donor can give the trustee the power to select the charity provided again that it meets the appropriate tax-exempt requirements. But, be aware that the standard boilerplate language for a CRT creates a trap that donors may not understand. The I.R.S. requires wording to the effect that the charitable remainderman must be a charity described in certain sections of the I.R.S. code. This ensures that the CRT will qualify for the relevant federal income, gift, and estate tax deductions. Many people drafting CRTs cite Code section 170(c). However, this section also includes private foundations. That is a problem for two reasons. First, private foundations have a lower contribution ceiling than do public charities. Second, if the CRT has the potential of distributing to a private foundation, the donor's income tax deduction is computed on the cost basis for any appreciated assets that are not marketable securities.

I.R.S. updated its boilerplate documents in 2003 and provided some alternate provisions to prevent unintended mistakes. For example, Conrad Teitell's August 2003 edition of *Taxwise Giving* recommends that the governing instrument limit the choice of remainderman to an organization "described in IRC §170(b)(1)(A) as well as IRC §§70(c), 2055(a), and 2522(a)." If the donor inadvertently provides for a remainderman under §170(c), then the donor will have a reduced contribution ceiling since there is a chance the remainder could go to a private foundation. Further, depending on the funding assets, he or she may be forced to use the cost basis for computing the tax deduction.

In practice, the planned giving officer is interested in booking a gift. However, you cannot book the gift if the donor reserves the right to replace your charity with another. However, a donor can generally execute a document that relinquishes his or her right to revoke your charity's interest. If the donor executes such a document, he or she has made a gift to your charity on the date he or she signs the document. Then, you can book the gift. If the donor named several charities, he or she can revoke the right to change one of them, but retain the right to change the others.

I had a case at Boston College where a women named five charities as remaindermen in a trust valued at over $1 million. Boston College's share was about $400,000. She said that her advisor pressured her to include a few of his favorite charities. "If he predeceases me, I will remove them all." I asked her if she was likely to remove Boston College's share. "No. I will never remove Boston College." She agreed to sign a document that revoked her right to remove Boston College. We booked the gift for our share based on the market value as of the date she signed the document.

The donor's attorney, looking out for the best interests of his or her client, will usually recommend that the donor reserve the right to change the charitable remainderman by a provision in the will. That makes sense from an advisor's perspective, but donors who are interested in having gift credit in a fund raising campaign cannot get credit if they reserve this right.

CONSIDERATIONS FOR SELECTING INCOME BENEFICIARIES

If a trust is measured by the lives of individuals, the beneficiary(ies) must be living when the trust is created.

For a trust measured by a term of years, the beneficiaries do not need to be living at the creation of the trust. The designation of a class of beneficiaries is sufficient (like, "equally to all my grandchildren"). The donor could also provide in a term of years CRT for payments to "my children living at my death."

For all CRTs, at least one beneficiary must be a non charitable beneficiary. Allowable beneficiaries of a term of years CRT include an individual, trust, estate, partnership, association, company, or corporation.

Generally, a CRT payment can be made to a trust, to a guardian, or to a conservator if the income beneficiary is incompetent, physically disabled, or financially disabled. The I.R.S. deems the intervening trust an administrative tool to serve the beneficiary.

An S-corporation or a partnership can also be the beneficiary of a CRT for a term of years. Any income received by the S-corporation would be taxable to the shareholders or partners under the four-tier system on a *pro rata* basis.

When designating a wife or husband as a secondary life beneficiary, the donor needs to be careful. The secondary beneficiary must be a specific person and not simply any spouse who happens to be the spouse at the time of the donor's death. The beneficiaries have to be known at the time the CRT is created.

Once the donor sets up the order for the beneficiary payments, he or she cannot change it later, even if the change in the payment schedule wouldn't change the donor's original federal income tax charitable deduction. For example, if you set up a CRT to pay income to your sister until her death, then to your brother, you cannot switch the order of payments later.

When making payments to the beneficiaries, the donor cannot arbitrarily make discretionary decisions about how much each beneficiary should receive. He could provide for a 2% payment to one and a 3% payment to another. However, an independent trustee who is not being controlled by the donor could make discretionary payments among the named beneficiaries if the governing instrument provides for this power. The independent trustee must make all required payments on time according to the payment schedule in the CRT and cannot delay payments.

The donor may reserve the right to revoke only by will the income interest of any beneficiary. For successor beneficiaries, this has the effect of preventing a completed gift until the donor dies without revoking the interest. However, if there is a current income beneficiary, the tax consequences change. If the donor reserves the right to revoke a current beneficiary's income interest, then each payment as made is a current gift that may qualify for the annual gift tax exclusion (currently $11,000). Any annual payments exceeding the annual exclusion are taxable gifts to the beneficiary. However, they qualify for the gift tax exemption ($1,000,000). There is a more complete discussion of gift and estate taxes in Chapter II-10 on bequests.

CONSIDERATIONS FOR SELECTING A TRUSTEE

Many banks, trust companies, brokerage houses, and specialty planned giving firms provide services as trustee or manager of charitable remainder trusts. Many charities also serve as trustee. This job should not be taken lightly and should not be assumed by a charity that does not have the expertise to do it right. Some advisors think that charities should not be trustee due to the inherent conflict of interest. They claim that only an independent trustee can impartially balance the interests of the income beneficiaries and the interests of the charity. Nonetheless, many charities who serve as trustee do a fine job and often bend over backwards to cater to the donor's needs, sometimes at their own expense.

When the charity serves as trustee, it will generally hire an asset manager and administrator to handle the day-to-day activities of the account. But, the charity is still responsible for whatever happens with the accounts.

When the charity does not serve as trustee, it must be able to steer the donor to competent managers so that the donor can select his or her own trustee.

Sometimes, the donor wants to be his or her own trustee. This is allowed in most cases, but a donor often underestimates the technical expertise required to run a CRT. I can think of one instance when a donor told me he was his own trustee for a CRT that he funded a few years earlier. He said he didn't need the income so he never took a payment and I believe he had never filed a tax return. Gulp. Some donors want to be their own trustee because they don't want to pay the management fees. This is foolhardy. Since brokerage firms are promoting CRTs to their existing clients, assets get shifted out of a custody account into a CRT account and remain with the same brokerage firm. Unfortunately, not all firms have the expertise to manage a CRT competently. A general stock broker simply does not have the training required.

For assets that are hard to value such as real estate or other illiquid assets, an independent trustee or a separate independent appraiser is required. Otherwise, the charitable deduction would be denied. The donor cannot be his own trustee and be responsible for valuing nonmarketable assets.

What should you do? If your charity does not serve as trustee, you need a list of potential trustees/managers to whom you can refer your donors. That could be difficult if your donors are all over the country. However, for your local donors, you can develop a list of possible trustee/managers by first looking at the membership of your local planned giving council (if you have one in your area). Most likely, representatives from local asset managers are members of the council.

If you are not a member of a local planned giving council, you could call a few charities known to have mature planned giving programs and ask for recommendations. Bear in mind that it is quite difficult to close a CRT if your charity is not trustee. A CRT is complicated enough without the donor being forced to find a manager.

Usually, when the charity can be trustee, it is the sole trustee. However, a few donors want to be co-trustee with the charity. If so, that adds an extra level of consideration for your CRT manager and for the charity. Some managers add a surcharge to the fee schedule if there is an individual trustee because there tends to be a lot more maintenance and hand holding on the account when an individual is involved.

GIFT TAX CONSEQUENCES

One consideration often forgotten by planned giving officers is the implication of the gift tax.

> Example:
>
> Donor creates a $500,000, 6% unitrust. Payments are made quarterly at the end of the payment period to donor's sister, age 72. The discount rate is 4.2%.

Does the donor owe a gift tax?

In this example, the value of the remainder interest is $255,145. By subtracting the remainder interest from the total gift amount, you arrive at the beneficiary's income interest—the amount considered to be given to the sister ($500,000 - $255,145 = $244,855).

The donor has created a taxable gift to the sister of $244,855. Because income is paid currently, the gift may qualify for the $11,000 *per* donee annual gift tax exclusion (or $22,000 if the couple splits the gift). The balance of $233,855 is subject to the gift tax.

Here are some points to keep in mind:

- The income interest created for a spouse (as sole income beneficiary or as the only beneficiary other than the donor) qualifies for the marital deduction and generates no gift tax for the donor. If someone else is a beneficiary (child, friend, sibling), too, the marital deduction is lost.

- The present value of the income interest created for an individual other than a spouse may qualify for the annual gift tax exclusion, but this is not absolutely clear. Therefore, the donor should get advice from his or her attorney on this issue.

- If the donor provides income to the survivor of himself as primary beneficiary and of another person (not a spouse) as successor beneficiary, the successor beneficiary's interest will be subject to a current gift tax unless the donor reserves the right to revoke it by will (see below). In this case, the gift of the future interest does not qualify for the annual gift tax exclusion.

- If a gift tax is due, the donor can use his or her gift tax exemption (for lifetime gifts) or estate tax exemption (for testamentary gifts) to offset the tax. (Go to Chapter II-10 for a detailed explanation of the gift and estate tax.)

Reserving The Right To Revoke A Successor Beneficiary's Interest By Will

The donor can retain the right, exercisable only by will, to revoke the successor beneficiary's income interest. This has the effect of postponing the completed gift and delaying the gift tax due. If the donor revokes the interest at death, the trust distributes to the named charities on the death of the donor, and no taxable gift will have been made.

If the donor does not revoke the interest, the trust will continue for the benefit of the successor beneficiary, and the income interest created on the donor's death is taxable in the donor's estate, unless it is for a spouse. Note: The estate still receives a charitable deduction for the remainder interest.

Determining the amount of the gift to the survivor is very simple:

Annuity Trust Example:

Donor transfers $250,000 to a 7% charitable remainder annuity trust providing $17,500 annuity payments quarterly at the end of the payment period only to himself (age 75) for life and, then to his sister (age 72) if she survives him. The Discount Rate is 4.2%.

Your task is to determine the value of the sister's annuity interest (called the present value of the annuity).

First, calculate the present value of the annuity for the two lives (75 and 72). You do this by inputting the variables for this case into your software.

Date of Gift:	Today's date for an example (or the actual date of gift)
Amount of Gift:	$250,000
Beneficiaries:	75 and 72 (or the exact birthdates if you know them)
Payment Frequency:	Quarterly
Timing of Payments:	End of Period
Discount Rate:	4.2% for this example, or for an actual gift, the highest discount rate for the current month or for the prior two months

The answer will appear in a couple of ways. Either the present value of the annuity for the two lives will be calculated or the value of the charitable deduction will be shown. If your software provides the charitable deduction, then subtract the charitable deduction from the total gift amount. The answer is the present value of the annuity for the two lives together.

Next, do the same calculation for the donor's life alone at age 75. Subtract the income tax deduction for age 75 from the gift value to find the present value of the annuity on the donor's life alone.

Then, subtract the annuity value for the donor's life from the annuity value of the two lives. The answer is the annuity value considered to be contributed to the sister. You have just figured out how much income will be paid to the sister based on her longer life expectancy.

For a unitrust example, the process is the same. You calculate the remainder interest (charitable deduction) for the two lives and subtract that figure from the gift amount to determine the life income interest for the two lives. Next, you calculate the remainder interest for the donor's life alone, and subtract that figure from the gift amount to determine the life income interest for the donor's life. Finally, you subtract the donor's life income interest from the two-life income interest. The answer is what is considered a taxable gift to the sister.

If you read the above explanation quickly, you'll become confused and close the book. Don't give up because the language sounds foreign. Take it slowly; you *can* do this.

CREDITING GUIDELINES

The considerations for gift crediting are similar to those for the pooled income fund and the gift annuity. Some organizations provide full credit for the value of the gift amount. Others recognize only the value of the remainder interest (charitable deduction). Still others offer a compromise depending on the age of the beneficiary(ies) such as full credit for beneficiaries age 70 and older, remainder value credit for beneficiaries younger than 70. There is a detailed discussion of crediting issues in Chapter III-5.

QUESTIONS AND ANSWERS ABOUT CHARITABLE REMAINDER TRUSTS

Q. If a CRT is drafted to conform to all I.R.S. requirements, will it also conform to state laws?
A. Not necessarily. Since each state has its own laws governing trusts, an attorney experienced with the laws of the state where the trust is created, or where it is administered, or where the donor lives should review it.

Q. Is there really a need for a qualified attorney given that the I.R.S. issued standard language for CRTs?
A. The standard language is very limited and cannot possibly be adequate to cover the many, many variations and provisions which become necessary for an individual donor. It is essential that you work with an attorney who really knows charitable giving tax law.

Q. Can a person set up a CRT to fulfill alimony obligations?
A. Yes, if the CRT gets set up during the divorce degree. The grantor would get a marital deduction for the spouse's interest. But, if the ex-spouse sets up the CRT after the divorce, there are gift tax issues (as they are no longer married). Also, a CRT remainder cannot be used to discharge an existing legal obligation (like a legally binding pledge).

Q. Can a CRT be created to fulfill a campaign pledge?
A. No. A CRT remainder cannot be used to discharge a legally binding obligation.

Q. Can a trust make a payment in-kind? If so, what are the tax consequences to the trust and to the beneficiary?
A. Yes. A trust can make its required payment of $10,000 by giving the income beneficiary $10,000 of appreciated securities having a cost basis in the trust of $1,000. The income beneficiary must recognize $9,000 of capital gain, but his new cost basis for the stock is $10,000. Ask your attorney for special language that will be necessary in the trust document.

Q. Can a charitable remainder trust benefit a pet?
A. Technically, a trust can be set up to benefit a pet in some states. But, the donor will not receive an income, gift, and estate tax charitable deduction for a CRT benefiting a pet because the pet does not fit the I.R.S.'s definition of a "person." A "person," according to the I.R.S., can be an individual, trust, estate, partnership, association, company, or corporation, but not an animal.

Q. Can Subchapter S corporation stock be put in a CRT?
A. Legally, yes, but it will have the effect of forcing the S corporation to lose its S corporation election and become a C corporation. S corporation stock can be given outright to a charity without adverse consequences to the S corporation's status. There are also other considerations related to S corporation stock (whether put in a CRT or given outright to a charity) including unrelated business taxable income.

Q. What happens if a charitable remainder trust is created by the donor's will and the beneficiary dies during the period of estate administration before the trust is funded?
A. The trust is deemed to be created on the donor's date of death. Therefore, the donor's estate will receive whatever estate tax deduction would have been generated on the date of death. In addition, the beneficiary's estate will be due a small portion of income for the period from the date of the donor's death to the date of the beneficiary's death.

Q. How much more is there to know about the variations and possibilities for drafting and planning trusts?
A. This chapter covers only the minimum to get you going. There is a wealth of information, rulings, nuances, and variations that you'll find only in a full-service tax guide. I use two: *Charitable Giving and Solicitation* by Warren, Gorham & Lamont and also *Charitable Giving Tax Service* by R&R Newkirk. Appendix III includes these and many other books, periodicals, and resources.

SUMMARY

Charitable remainder trusts require close coordination between you, your donor, your tax counsel, the donor's tax counsel, and the professional trustee. They can require considerable time and effort and can cause you to commit to legal fees in the planning stages without a guarantee that the donor will go through with the gift. If you are new to planned giving, you will spend a lot of money on legal fees getting yourself up to speed. However, if you don't spend the money on billable hours, you are likely to get into trouble.

Up to and including this chapter, I have been discussing the lifetime transfer of property. But, not all donors can or will make lifetime gifts. Moreover, all charities are not ready either to accept or to administer all of the kinds of assets and gift options available. Fortunately, the single most untapped area of charitable giving and the one that holds the most potential for the future is available to everyone—donors and charities alike, the large and small institutions, the big and the small donors. Bequests is the subject of the next chapter.

Chapter II–10

BEQUESTS

INTRODUCTION

Throughout history, the health of America's charities, in fact, the very existence of many, has been due in large measure to the vision of individuals who created a memorial to themselves through a gift, the benefits of which they would never see. Through a bequest, individuals of both great wealth and of modest means can help to preserve, or to create for the enjoyment of future generations, an institution, a way of life, or an ideal that has had special meaning for them.

In this chapter, when I talk about bequests, I am referring to the distribution a charity receives from a document created to handle the distribution at death of assets owned by the donor. This document could either be a will or a trust. Technically, a bequest comes from a will and a trust distribution comes from a trust. Both documents are used to distribute assets at death, but, it would get cumbersome for me to continually qualify my language. Therefore, if I use the words will or bequest, I also mean trust and trust distribution. The effect for you is the same—a gift on the donor's death. I'll talk about some distinctions later.

Of all the deferred gift arrangements, bequests are the most easily understood. If you do nothing else in planned giving, by creating a bequest program you can tap a severely underutilized form of support and create long-term security for your institution. In a one-person shop, you can easily run a bequest program.

This discussion of bequests, however, is related to many of the other sections of this book. You will be most successful in a bequest program if you have a strong base of supporters, a systematic program for identifying prospects, a good system of cultivation, and an effective volunteer network. Plus, you simply have to get the message out.

A 2000 survey done by the National Committee on Planned Giving (available at www.ncpg.org for $30) uncovered some interesting statistics:

- 31% of all planned gift donors have never made a cash contribution to the charity that will benefit from their planned gift;

- 21% of bequest donors and 24% of CRT donors report no affiliation with the charity that will benefit from their planned gift;

- 68% of bequest donors and 50% of CRT donors have not notified the charitable beneficiary of their gift.

When I told the publications director at Boston College that 68% of the people who name a charity in their estate plan never tell the charity, he said, "Debra, that's because you'd jump on them like a tick on a dog." Probably true. Resulting from the above statistics, I came to the conclusion that providing bequest language to as many people as possible would do a lot of good—even if there is no way to quantify the results of a bequest mailing. If you mail correct bequest language, some people will use it, and 68% of them will not tell you. Just do it.

One of the problems you'll have as a planned giving director is how to balance your time between bequests and other parts of your planned giving program. It takes a lot of time to work with a donor to the point of receiving a bequest. Initial discussions with a donor, who has good faith intentions to provide for your organization, may not come to fruition for years. Many people do not have a will or they have a severely outdated one. In so many cases, the process of including a bequest to your organization is hindered by the donor's ability to make decisions about other aspects of a total estate plan. While it is true that a donor can simply execute a codicil, an amendment to an existing will, it is more common for the donor to revamp the whole plan rather than to deal with one provision for your organization. That slows the process considerably. People get around to updating their plans on their own timetable. The charitable institution needs to be positioned in the forefront of the donor's mind when his or her process for revising or making a plan begins.

I remember working with a professor at Boston University who wanted to include a bequest to BU. We had that part worked out, but two years later, after hours and hours of meetings, he had done nothing because he could not make a decision about who would be named guardian of his minor children. That one consideration crippled his ability to do anything. Finally, I put him on the back burner.

Directors of Development and others in the institution love bequests when the institution receives a distribution. In an odd way, they treat it as a windfall having nothing to do with the planned giving office. At the end of the year, your boss will see how much income was generated by realized bequests and will say, "We've got to more of these." But, generally, at the end of a year, the planned giving officer must report what actual gifts he or she received. Unfortunately, the time spent talking to people about new bequests will be discounted, as if this time really doesn't count fully in the final evaluation of your performance. On one hand, you are supposed to be marketing the bequest program; on the other hand, if you don't get current gifts to show the trustees, you'll be working with a big knot in your stomach all of the time.

Unless you stay at one charity for a very long time, you won't see realized bequests from donors who establish bequests during your reign. Building the bequest program is a lifetime project for the institution. Your successor will see your new bequests come in. Whenever I changed institutions, I would receive periodic calls from my successor at the prior institution to tell me that a bequest donor with whom I had worked had died. In the year following my departure from Boston College, many of the people with whom I worked died. And, so it goes.

The people who supervise you must understand that pursuing new bequests is an important part of your work, even if the future income cannot be counted this year. Especially in the early years of building a new planned giving program, bequest income will be sporadic. But, adding new names to your bequest society is extremely important.

Beyond the obvious benefit of securing future gifts, a bequest program has three positive effects:

1. The promotion of bequests encourages the constituency to think long term about the institution;

2. Bequest donors are likely to develop a stronger interest in the current welfare of the institution, and, therefore, can be cultivated toward making current outright or deferred gifts;

3. The average bequest is relatively high in comparison to other fund raising averages so when one comes in it makes a difference.

In the following chapter, bequests are examined under the following topics:

- Why everyone needs a will
- Types of bequests
- What property passes under a will?
- Understanding the gift and estate tax

    - The basics of transfer taxes
    - Capital gain rules for transfers to individuals
    - Gifts within three years of death
    - State death taxes
    - Applications for planned giving
    - Transfers between spouses

- Gift crediting issues
- How to establish a bequest program
- Administering your bequest program

  - Learning about the death
  - The probate notice
  - Communicating with the executor
  - Monitoring the process
  - Bequests of real estate
  - Recording the bequest distribution
  - Receiving distributions
  - Following up with the executor
  - Restricted bequests
  - Bequest Income Processing Software© (BIPS©)

- Summary

WHY EVERYONE NEEDS A WILL

The greatest obstacle to the success of your bequest program has nothing to do with you, your institution, or the compelling mission you serve. The reality is that most people die without a will or, the existing will is rendered invalid by another event in the person's life, such as a marriage or divorce. Most people know that a will is important, but here are some specific reasons why.

With a will:

- You can direct the distribution of your assets to those you care about most;

- You can choose a personal representative (executor) who will oversee the distribution of your assets;

- You avoid unnecessary expenses on the administration of the estate;

- You can provide for family members, friends, or relatives according to their needs;

- You can provide appropriately for minor children by naming a guardian or establishing a trust;

- You can save considerable estate taxes by utilizing proper estate planning techniques;

- You can provide support for charitable causes that have a special meaning for you.

Without a will:

- State intestacy statutes determine the distribution of your property;

- The court appoints an administrator for you;

- Because the administrator is subject to constant court supervision, the cost of administering the estate may be greater;

- Your heirs will benefit equally by class, not necessarily in the proportions you would have intended;

- You cannot provide for minors. The court will appoint a guardian for them, and the guardian will make decisions about a child's care that you should have made;

- Your estate may lose thousands of dollars in needless taxes because you did not take advantage of the tax-saving opportunities available to you;

- You cannot support a charitable cause.

Some of the reasons people use for not having a will include:

1. "I don't have much property."

   Each of us has property worthy of distribution to someone—an automobile, bank account, stereo, home computer, furniture, jewelry, paintings, china, *etc*. Even if everything were sold at an estate auction, it would probably yield several thousand dollars which could be useful to your institution.

2. "My property is in joint names."

   This is a trap into which many people fall. Having property in joint name is no excuse for not having a will. In the event of a common disaster, you will have no distribution plan. Or, the other joint tenant could predecease you. Having everything in joint name is also a bad estate plan because the first spouse to die loses the benefit of his or her lifetime estate tax exemption (discussed later).

3. "My spouse will get everything anyway."

   This is an invalid premise. If you die without a will, your children may share in a major part of the estate. Your spouse may predecease you, or you may get a divorce. Both of you may die in a common disaster with the result that everything will be left up to chance. Did you know that if you die without a will in Massachusetts, your children share in the estate? Do you want your 21 year old college student to receive a percentage of your estate rather than having it all go to your spouse?

4. "I'm young. I have plenty of time."

   A review of the obituaries will show that death is not a state reserved only for the elderly. Many people in their forties and fifties and younger die from all kinds of unexpected accidents and diseases. (The number of court appointed guardians after 9/11/01 should be a reminder that we're surrounded by uncertainty.)

6. "I'm not married so I don't need a will."

   This is all the more reason why you need one. Who knows what haphazard distribution will result from a distribution under state laws in your case.

7. "My wife and I already split out estates into two revocable trusts. Everything worthwhile is in the name of either my trust or my wife's trust and will be distributed according to the terms we have outlined."

   Each of you still needs a pour-over will that simply provides for anything standing in your name alone upon your death to be distributed to your trust. Then, the trust takes over the distribution plan. It is very unlikely not to own something outside the revocable trust at death. Moreover, some people set up living trusts but neglect to fund them.

Many of the consultants listed in Appendix IV supply wills packages that can help bring a donor through the steps necessary to make or revise a will. Most would be happy to send you sample brochures and mailing pieces.

TYPES OF BEQUESTS

Often donors cite the uncertainty of future circumstances as the reason they cannot provide a bequest to your institution. This may speak more to a lack of commitment than anything else. Bequests are the most flexible form of support. If someone really is interested in assisting your institution, there are ways to arrange the bequest to ensure that family obligations are satisfied first. Following is a summary of the different ways bequests can be accomplished, with advantages and disadvantages to the charity where appropriate.

Specific Bequest: A bequest of a specific item which is distinguishable from all other items, for example, "my grandfather clock," "my savings account #12-3347 at Fleet Bank," "my 500 shares of Kodak Common Stock," or "my oriental rug."

> Advantage: During the distribution of the estate, specific bequests are satisfied first. Thus, when the estate is not sufficiently large to cover all bequests, those entitled to specific bequests are more likely to benefit.

> Disadvantage: If the donor disposes of the item during lifetime, but neglects to update the will, the intended legatee receives nothing.

General Bequest: A bequest of property that is similar to all other items of the same kind, usually cash.

> Advantage: General bequests are satisfied second. When there is insufficient cash to meet the general bequests, property passing under the residue will be sold to raise the necessary cash.

> Disadvantage: A general bequest might be smaller than a bequest of all or part of the residue.

Devise: A bequest of real property.

Residual Bequest: A bequest of all or a portion of the rest of the estate after specific and general bequests are distributed.

> Advantage: If the estate increases in size following the execution of the will, the excess property, appreciation, or other assets will be passed under the residue clause. Thus, the residual legatee can see a substantial increase over what was originally intended.

> Disadvantage: The residue is the last portion of the estate to be distributed. Thus, for an estate that is substantially smaller than expected, the residue may be exhausted in order to satisfy the general bequests. Also, taxes may be paid from the residue, which can reduce further the amount of property remaining after specific and general bequests are satisfied.

Contingent Bequest: A bequest to take effect only if the primary intention cannot be met or if the original legatee predeceases the donor.

> Advantage: Perhaps the greatest advantage of being named as a contingent legatee is that you have your foot in the door.

> Disadvantage: There is little hope you will receive anything. Having said that, I can think of several cases in which my institution received a contingent bequest. In one very sad case, Wheaton College was to receive the whole estate if one spouse died and if the other did not survive by 30 days. They were in a car accident. The first was killed, and the second did not survive the 30 days.

Percentage Bequest: A bequest based on a percentage (5%, 10%, 50%) of the residue or of another asset.

> Advantage: Most likely, you are assured something regardless of the size of the estate.

> Disadvantage: There is no way to tell exactly what you will get.

Charitable Remainder Trust: A donor can provide for the funding of a charitable remainder trust in a will, most commonly to support a surviving spouse, after which the remaining principal distributes to one or more charities. (See Chapter II-9 for a complete treatment of this topic.)

Charitable Lead Trust: A donor can provide for the funding of a charitable lead trust in his will, most commonly to provide income to one or more charities for a period of years after which the principal remaining distributes to heirs, usually, children or grandchildren. (See Chapter II-11 for a complete discussion of charitable lead trusts.)

Pooled Income Fund: A donor can legally make a gift through a will to a pooled income fund with income to a surviving heir, but I wouldn't recommend it. He or she would need special language from you to refer to your Fund properly. But, the real problem is that the new beneficiary would technically be due income from your Fund from the date of death and you may not receive the funding assets for one to two years. This could be a real problem for other beneficiaries in the fund whose income will be decreased by sharing with a non-participant. (See Chapter II-7 for a complete treatment of pooled income funds.)

Charitable Gift Annuity: Here again, it is legally possible to fund a gift annuity for a survivor beneficiary at death, but it is extremely rare. In 25 years, I had only one of these at Boston University and we issued a gift annuity, paying an annuity rate based on the age of the surviving spouse as of the date of death. (See Chapter II-8 for a complete treatment of charitable gift annuities.)

Beneficiary Designation: This is for property that passes under contract or by operation of law (not under the will) such as when the donor names the charity beneficiary of a life insurance policy, retirement plan or IRA, commercial annuity, *etc.*

Understanding the different kinds of bequests will be helpful when you discuss the donor's commitment to your institution. Just getting yourself into the will is a major step, and the most productive thing you can do is promote the following two messages:

1. Put us in your will, and

2. Tell us if you do.

Later in this chapter, I will cover conversations and strategies for working with your donors. But, before I get to that, I want to cover more about the probate process. In this next section, you'll see that what appears to be a very nice bequest provision may not necessarily be so nice.

WHAT PROPERTY PASSES UNDER A WILL?

Most people understand what a will does and why it is important. Fewer understand exactly which property passes under a will. Therefore, improper assumptions either on the part of the donor or on the part of the fund raiser can produce disappointing results.

Example:

A donor has these assets:

IRA	$500,000
Life Insurance	100,000
Real estate	300,000
Securities	120,000
Bank accounts and CD's	50,000
Furnishings	+ 20,000
Total estate	$1,090,000

You learn that the above donor has provided a bequest to your institution of 50% of the residue of his will. How much will you receive? The answer to this question depends on whether the assets will pass under the will or by operation of law. Looking further into this situation, you might find the following:

IRA	Spouse is named beneficiary
Life Insurance:	Daughter is named beneficiary
Real Estate:	Held jointly with spouse
Securities:	Held jointly with spouse
Bank accounts and CD's:	Held jointly with daughter who handles the bills
Furnishings:	Passes to the spouse under the will

In this situation, unless the daughter and/or the spouse have predeceased the donor, you get a big fat zero because nothing passes under the will except the furniture, and you don't even get that.

In discussions with donors, you should learn how property is owned (in sole name or in joint name) in order to determine exactly how your institution will benefit.

The following kinds of property will be distributed according to the terms of a will:

- property standing in the donor's name alone (securities, real estate, bank accounts);

- tangible personal property owned by the donor (paintings, furnishings, jewelry, clothes, automobiles, stamp or coin collections);

- property over which the donor exercises a general or limited power of appointment (For example, the donor may receive income and/or principal from a trust during lifetime. At death, a *general* power of appointment allows the donor to designate the distribution of the property to one or more individuals or institutions including his or her own estate. A *limited* power of appointment allows distribution to individuals and institutions other than the decedent's estate.);

- the proceeds of life insurance payable to the decedent's estate.

The following kinds of ownership arrangements distribute by operation of law and are not distributed by the terms of a donor's will or trust:

- joint tenants with right of survivorship (on the death of the first, the other joint tenant becomes 100% owner);

- tenants by the entirety (restricted to joint ownership between spouses, on the death of the first, the other spouse becomes 100% owner);

- charitable remainder trusts, pooled income funds, or charitable gift annuities (These are all controlled by the governing instrument, agreement, or contract. Bear in mind that donors can exercise certain rights related to these gifts through a provision in a will. The donor may reserve the right to revoke the income interest of a survivor beneficiary for these plans. Moreover, the donor may reserve the right to change the remainderman for a CRT);

- the proceeds of a life insurance policy (the beneficiary form signed by the donor controls the distribution of insurance proceeds);

- property held in a revocable or irrevocable trust (the trust's governing instrument controls distribution);

- retirement plans and Individual Retirement Accounts (the beneficiary form signed by the donor dictates the survivorship plan).

UNDERSTANDING THE GIFT AND ESTATE TAX

If you know the donor's income tax bracket, you can show a savings in taxes using a simple example:

> Example:

> A donor in the highest marginal income tax bracket (35%) can give $10,000 to your institution and save up to $3,500 in federal income taxes (Gift amount x income tax bracket = income tax savings).

Also, if you know the donor's estate tax bracket, you can show an estate tax saving:

> Example:

> A donor in the highest marginal estate tax bracket (49% in 2003) can give $10,000 through a bequest and save $4,900 in federal estate taxes (bequest amount x estate tax bracket for year of death = estate tax savings).

In the vast majority of cases, the above examples are sufficient to illustrate the benefits of charitable giving.

As you move into more complex situations, it will benefit you to understand how the U.S. transfer tax system works. This chapter will help. Without knowing any of the following detail, you can still get a lot of bequests. Therefore, if you are running a one-person shop and just want to start your bequest program without a lot of the detail skip this section and go to the last part of this chapter. When you have time to study, come back here.

The Basics of Transfer Taxes

Under current federal law, there is a tax on the right to transfer property to other people either during life or at death. However, under certain conditions, the tax does not apply. Following is a summary of how the transfer tax system works.

If you give property away, you will be treated as having made a taxable gift for which a gift tax (lifetime transfers) or estate tax (death transfers) could be due depending on:

- the category of the transferee,
- the dollar value of the gift,
- the type of gift; and
- the year of the gift.

The transfer tax rules cover transfers like the following:

- outright gifts of cash to a spouse, children, grandchildren, or to any other persons;
- giving your child stock or a new car for graduation;
- buying your child a house or letting him live rent free in a newly purchased house;
- giving your child a house;
- giving your child stock in your closely-held company;
- giving someone an income interest in a life income plan such as a charitable remainder trust, pooled income fund, or charitable gift annuity;
- giving someone a remainder interest in a home;
- giving someone a life estate in a home;
- giving your grandchild your stamp collection; and
- any other transfer you can think of.

The following are exempt from the federal transfer tax:

- Annual Gift Tax Exclusion: $11,000 per year ($22,000 for couples) during lifetime to any person and to unlimited numbers of different persons. This exclusion is indexed for inflation and will be increased in increments of $1,000 to the lowest $1,000 on a year-by-year basis if appropriate.

  When a donor tells you, "My wife and I are giving $22,000 per year to our kids," it might be a tip off that the couple's net worth exceeds the couple's combined estate tax exemption for the current year. Often, they are moving the taxable excess above their combined exemptions to their heirs using the annual gift tax exclusion. By doing so, they reduce their taxable estate with no gift tax due on these transfers.

- Assets passing to a U.S. citizen spouse.

- Assets passing to a charity.

If a donor makes lifetime taxable gifts exceeding the annual gift tax exclusion in any year, he or she is still pays no gift tax as long as the lifetime taxable gifts do not exceed the lifetime gift tax exemption of $1 million.

However, if at the donor's death the decedent's *cumulative* lifetime and death transfers exceed the applicable exemption for the year of death, then he or she will pay an estate tax on the excess. The rates are based on a graduated rate table. The Economic Growth and Tax Relief Reconciliation Act of 2001 (EGTRRA) created the following exemptions and top gift and estate tax rates.

Year of Death	Estate Tax Exemption	Highest Estate and Gift Tax Rates
2001	$ 675,000	55%
2002	1,000,000	50%
2003	1,000,000	49%
2004	1,500,000	48%
2005	1,500,000	47%
2006	2,000,000	46%
2007	2,000,000	45%
2008	2,000,000	45%
2009	3,500,000	45%
2010	estate tax repealed	35% gift tax rate
2011	1,000,000	55%

For many years, the transfer tax system was unified such that the exemption for lifetime gifts and estate gifts was cumulative. The exemption was being phased in over a period of years to a maximum exemption of $1 million. In 2001, EGTRRA threw out the old system and created a temporary transfer tax system that reverts to the pre-EGTRRA rules in 2011.

Starting in 2004, the gift tax and the estate tax have different exemption amounts. The gift tax exemption remains at $1 million. But, the estate exemption increases to $3.5 million by 2009, is repealed in 2010, and returns at $1 million in 2011.

Thus, a person who makes taxable gifts during lifetime up to the $1 million gift tax exemption might be able to leave additional amounts at death up to the relevant exemption for the year of death.

There is a big problem with EGTRRA and that is the uncertainty of planning for a system that has no estate tax in 2010, but which has the tax come back in 2011 (unless Congress makes the repeal permanent). It is a real mess for planning.

Capital Gain Rules For Transfers To Individuals

There are different rules for lifetime and death transfers for gifts to individuals. If a person gives a capital asset (stock, real estate, art, *etc.*) to another person during lifetime, the new owner picks up the donor's cost basis and date of acquisition.

Lifetime Transfer Example:

March 1, Doris buys stock for $1,000 and gives it to John September 5 after it has doubled in price to $2,000. John's holding period for determining long and short-term capital gain starts on March 1 and his cost basis upon selling the shares is $1,000. John must hold the shares 12 months and a day for it to be a long-term capital asset.

Death Transfer Example:

March 1, Doris buys stock for $1,000, dies September 5 after it has doubled in value to $2,000, and leaves it to John in her will. John's new cost basis is $2,000, the date of death value and the asset is deemed to be a long term capital asset even though Doris did not own it for 12 months or more prior to her death. (Note: Executors have an option to use an alternate valuation date for estate assets. The alternate date is six months after the date of death. If the executor uses the alternate valuation date, then the value of the new heir's cost basis is that date. The reason the executor would use the alternate is to save estate taxes if the assets decreased in value following the date of death.)

Under EGTRRA of 2001, these rules change for deaths in the year 2010 only. The rules for lifetime transfers do not change; however, the I.R.S. is creating new reporting requirements to document the date of acquisition and cost basis for lifetime transfers between individuals, all in preparation for 2010. In 2010, the one year during which the federal estate tax and generation-skipping transfer tax are repealed, the I.R.S. wants to recover some revenue using the capital gain tax.

Therefore, if you die in 2010, and if you own appreciated assets, your executor can allocate up to $1.3 million of stepped-up cost basis to those assets. For assets passing to a spouse, the executor can add an additional $3 million of stepped-up cost basis. All other appreciated assets pass to the heirs with the donor's original cost basis and date of acquisition. It may be difficult, cumbersome, costly, and, in some cases, impossible, for an executor to find the cost basis of the decedent's assets. Did I say that EGTRRA is a mess?

Starting again in 2011, the gift, estate, generation-skipping and capital gain rules revert to what they were pre-EGTRRA.

Gifts Within Three Years Of Death

The gift tax paid on a taxable transfer during lifetime is added back to the gross estate at death. This has the effect of inflating the taxable estate at death. However, the decedent gets credit for any gift tax paid during lifetime.

Consequently, there may be some benefit to making a lifetime taxable gift in excess of the $1 million applicable gift tax exemption if the donor survives more than three years. The result is that *the amount of the gift tax paid is excluded from the taxable estate*, but it is still used as a credit against the estate tax due. One would have to compute the merits of such a plan considering the loss of earned income that could have been generated on the gift tax amount during the donor's lifetime. Moreover, most taxpayers simply don't like to pay taxes before they are absolutely due.

State Death Taxes

In general, an estate receives a state death tax credit on the estate tax due for the amount of state death taxes. Prior to EGTRRA, some states had a system whereby the state death tax was not a separate tax, but rather a piece carved out of the federal tax, commonly called a sponge tax. Some other states tacked on a completely separate death tax, above the state death tax credit.

EGTRRA phases out the state death tax credit from 2002 to 2005. In 2005, the state death tax credit is repealed and replaced with a deduction for death taxes actually paid. With the increase in the estate tax exemption, most estates will not owe an estate tax. Therefore, there has been a huge drop in the former revenue states received from the sate death tax credit amount. To make up for the lost state revenue, many states have uncoupled their state death tax from the federal tax and enacted new separate state death taxes.

Every state has its own rules, but the estate planning process will increasingly involve strategies to deal with the new state death taxes. At the very least, you should find out what the state death tax laws are in your state.

Applications For Planned Giving

An estate is allowed an unlimited charitable deduction for a bequest to a qualified charity. No restrictions and no limits. If a donor leaves 100% of his or her estate to charity, there is no federal estate tax. In brochures or mailers, it is perfectly safe to say the following: "If you leave a bequest of any amount to [charity], your estate will receive a federal estate tax deduction for 100% of the amount."

In general, the calculation for the federal estate tax deduction received for the creation of a testamentary life income gift is the same as the federal income tax deduction for the identical gift made during the donor's lifetime.

Example #1:

Intervivos: Donor establishes a $300,000 5% unitrust during lifetime with income to a spouse who is age 75 at the time the trust is created. Discount rate is 6.4%. Quarterly payments at end of the period.

Testamentary: Donor dies and the will sets up a $300,000 5% unitrust to provide income to the surviving spouse who is age 75 on the date of death. Discount rate is 6.4%. Quarterly payments at end of the period.

Results:	Intervivos	Testamentary
Income tax deduction	$183,687	n/a
Estate tax deduction	n/a	$183,687
Tax on income stream to spouse (100% marital deduction)	-0-	-0-

Example #2:

Intervivos: Donor establishes a $500,000 6% unitrust during lifetime with income to his son who is age 50 at the time the trust is created. Discount rate is 5.6%. Quarterly payments at end of the period.

Testamentary: Donor dies and the will sets up a $500,000 6% unitrust to provide income to the son who is age 50 on the date of death. Discount rate is 5.6%. Quarterly payments at end of the period.

Results:	Intervivos	Testamentary
Income tax deduction	$114,000	n/a
Estate tax deduction	n/a	$114,000
Income interest to son	$386,000	$386,000

(Notice that the remainder interest ($114,000) and the income interest ($386,000) add up to the whole $500,000.)

The point of showing these two examples is to illustrate that the charitable deduction (either income tax or estate tax) is computed the same way. The only difference is that the donor may be able to use the annual gift tax exclusion for lifetime transfers but not for death transfers. Of course, other considerations may affect a lifetime gift compared to an estate gift. For example, if tangible personal property is used in a CRT during lifetime, there are complications depending on who is the income beneficiary. Also, for lifetime CRTs funded with tangibles, the donor's deduction is based on the cost basis rather than the fair market value. In general, however, the remainder interest of a life income gift is computed the same regardless of when the donor creates it. (See Chapter II-9 for a complete treatment of CRTs.)

Transfers Between Spouses

There is an unlimited marital deduction for qualifying lifetime and testamentary transfers between U.S. citizen spouses.

In most cases, this means that no federal tax is due for gifts between spouses during lifetime or at death. But, because of the unlimited marital deduction, tax-saving strategies must be directed at the estate of the survivor. Following is an example of what can happen without proper planning:

Example:

Husband's estate:	$1,500,000
Wife's estate:	+800,000
Combined estates:	$2,300,000

When one spouse dies, the property can pass to the other spouse free from federal gift or estate tax under the unlimited marital deduction. However, the estate could incur unnecessary estate taxes on the survivor's death. To be simple, assume the couple had split the assets down the middle. If the husband dies in 2003 with a taxable estate of $1,150,000 there would have been an estate tax only on the amount exceeding $1,000,000. The estate tax would be $61,500. If the wife dies in 2005 with $1,150,000 when the exemption is also $1,500,000, she would pay no estate tax.

However, if the husband dies in 2003 leaving everything outright to the wife and she dies in 2005 with $2,300,000, when the exemption is $1,500,000, her estate tax would be $365,200.

Thus, the marital deduction turned out to be only a deferral or delay of taxes to the survivor's estate. As mentioned above, one way to reduce the tax liability is to equalize the estates and to establish a credit-shelter trust in the estate of the first to die so both spouses use their full lifetime exemptions against estate taxes. In simplified form, here is the process:

1. Husband transfers $350,000 during lifetime to wife resulting in two estates of $1,150,000. There is no tax on the transfer because it qualifies for the marital deduction.

2. The assets of the first to die, up to the lifetime exemption for the year of death, are placed in a credit-shelter trust. The trust provides income and principal in the trustee's discretion to the

surviving spouse with remainder to the heirs (children, grandchildren, others). Arranging the assets this way prevents the trust from being included in the estate of the second to die. The survivor has all of the income from the trust and can get principal for care, maintenance and support in the trustee's discretion.

Result: The property in the first estate escapes federal taxation through the use of the maximum estate tax exemption. When the second spouse dies, there is no tax because the second spouse uses the full estate tax exemption for the year of death on the other half of the estate.

On the death of the survivor, the assets in the credit shelter trust pass to the heirs free from tax because they are not includable in the survivor's taxable estate while the survivor's estate passes free of tax to the heirs because the survivor has also made full use of the estate tax exemption.

No doubt, you can see that there is little reason from a purely tax standpoint to talk to a couple about the tax savings of charitable bequests when they can arrange their respective estates to use their exemptions. As the exemption grows to $3.5 million per person in 2009, very few couples in this country will have an estate tax (until 2011 when it comes back).

However, another option would be to provide a bequest within the credit shelter trust, for example, 50% of the remaining assets to your institution on the death of the survivor. The result is that the surviving spouse has the benefit of the income from the trust during lifetime in addition to principal at the trustee's discretion. The assets are not includable in the survivor's estate because the survivor has no power to access the principal alone or the power to appoint the principal. That part of the trust distributing to the heirs still escapes taxation using the exemption on the death of the first spouse. Your organization receives a share of the trust in the end.

It is important to recognize why this couple does not use a charitable remainder trust in this situation. There are two reasons:

1. The full use of the estate tax exemption in both estates is sufficient to shelter almost all of the assets from federal estate tax, and

2. The couple may want to provide a mechanism through which the surviving spouse can have access to principal if necessary, but, in such a way that the assets are not includable in the second estate.

GIFT CREDITING ISSUES

The considerations in crediting other forms of charitable gifts are usually straightforward in that you know the value of the gift, you are able to determine the actuarial value (remainder interest) for life income gifts, and most important, the gift generally is irrevocable. Remember that there is a difference between the amount the donor legally can claim as a federal income, gift, or estate tax deduction and the amount your charity arbitrarily sets for gift credit and recognition purposes.

With a bequest intention, there is uncertainty because:

1. The commitment is not irrevocable, and

2. The value of the gift is difficult to determine especially for a percentage bequest or the remainder interest of a testamentary trust.

Most, but not all, organizations take the position that bequest intentions do not entitle the donor to current gift credit. Rather, separate recognition is provided through the activities of a bequest society, discussed later.

Other institutions have developed a compromise with respect to crediting bequests. For example, the crediting policy for bequests during Wheaton's Sesquicentennial Campaign was as follows:

- Full credit for the value of a bequest for donors age 70 and older;

- Credit for the equivalent remainder value of a 6% unitrust for donors younger than age 70 (this was rather odd);

- In all cases, credit was contingent on receiving from the donor a signed Standard Bequest Form (reproduced later in this chapter).

Advantages of crediting bequests:

- People who would otherwise not be able to participate in the fund raising effort are included;

- People who would otherwise not divulge the nature or existence of a bequest provision for your institution are encouraged to come forward;

- Highly committed individuals identified through the process can be cultivated for a current gift.

Disadvantages of crediting bequests:

- People who might reasonably be expected to make a current gift are let off the hook;

- People receive gift credit for a gift that can be changed and cannot be guaranteed;

- Bequest commitments provide no spendable dollars to the institution.

The usefulness of allowing bequest credit in Wheaton's campaign is clear to me inasmuch as I entered the picture two years after the policy started. The incentive for gift credit inspired approximately 300 people to disclose previously unknown bequest intentions. Many eventually made current gifts as a result of being cultivated separately within Wheaton's bequest society. More than half of the people who came forth over a three-year period chose not to tell us precisely what they had done; nonetheless, they were inspired to come forth. Thus, many years later, they are being tracked and cultivated toward greater involvement. Many indicated informally the value of their bequests but were unwilling to sign a form.

This policy is not without problems:

1. Some people could not receive credit because the nature of their bequest was too difficult to value;

2. People who left their entire estates to Wheaton technically could no longer receive gift credit for current gifts—we had already given them credit for a gift of everything they own. Any gifts above a nominal annual gift would be quasi pledge payments;

3. Bequest intentions were recorded on our computer as pledges. Thus, pledges will remain on the computer (for 10, 20 or 30 years), long after the rest of the campaign's records are closed. Most computer systems generate pledge reminders periodically; but, any generated for the bequest intentions would need to be pulled manually from the batch before they are inadvertently mailed.

4. Some people within one or two years of turning age 70 waited until turning 70 before signing the Standard Bequest Form.

5. For people who received actuarial credit because they were younger than age 70, we ignored the question of whether or not to add an incremental amount to the donor's gift record for each additional year, or whether to add the full amount to the donor's record once the donor reached age 70. There were a lot of messy details that we never reconciled.

Notwithstanding the above messy problems, following the end of the campaign, visibility for bequests was so high that donors continued to come forth for gift credit for new bequests. We continued the campaign crediting guidelines for one year after the close of the campaign.

Having identified 300 people in three years, we were in a position to continue a bequest program as a real legacy from the campaign.

[CHARITY NAME]
STANDARD BEQUEST FORM

Name _____

Address _____

_____

_____

_____

_____

Date of Birth _____ Phone _____

Type of Provision   Estimated Amount

I have made provision for (Name of Institution) in my estate planning
as follows:

A. Outright bequest in my will. $_____

B. Provision in the will of the survivor of my husband (wife) and myself
    (Spouse's date of birth:_____) $_____

C. Life Insurance Policy $_____

D. Trust under my will with [charity name] the final beneficiary $_____
    (Please include date of birth of income beneficiaries, or describe other
    conditions.): _____

    _____

    _____

    _____

E. Other (please describe): $_____

    _____

    _____

    _____

                                            Total: $_____

(Attachments or letters that further describe the nature of the above provision(s) are welcomed in addition to
that section of the will or trust in which our institution is mentioned.)

In the event of unforeseen circumstances which require any further change in the above estate planning
provision(s), I agree to notify [charity name] of such change.

Date _____ Signature_____

HOW TO ESTABLISH A BEQUEST PROGRAM

A bequest program should be an integral part of your planned giving program. If you are running a one-person development office, you may be able to manage only a bequest program. To start, you need to do the following:

- Determine crediting guidelines, if any, for bequest intentions. (See Chapter III-5 for more discussion about gift crediting in a campaign.)

- Prepare a one- to two-page summary of the wording your institution suggests for a bequest provision. You may wish to consult your attorney if you do not currently have suggested wording readily available for use by donors or their attorneys. It is helpful to provide wording for an unrestricted bequest as well as wording for a restricted (endowment) gift.

- Make a list of the people who have already included your institution in a will, estate plan, life insurance policy, retirement plan or other revocable gift.

- Create a bequest or deferred giving society. To do this, you simply need to select a name and have it approved by your board of trustees in a Board Resolution. Many organizations include all deferred gifts in their planned giving society.

- Develop the incentives you wish to offer to the bequest or deferred giving society. You don't have to spend a lot of money to do this. Here are some ideas for recognition.

  - List the names of members annually in your annual report or in your annual report of gifts;

  - Invite members to an annual event (luncheon, dinner, *etc.*). If you don't have enough money in the budget to start a new cultivation dinner, invite the deferred giving society members to your annual giving recognition dinner as special guests. If the annual giving department has a problem with this, offer to pay from your planned giving budget the cost *per* person for the planned giving donors' meals.

  - Create a recognition certificate, suitable for framing. This is very easy and inexpensive to do especially because you can buy special paper, have them printed with your corporate seal, and run them through your computer printer. Something like the following would be appropriate: "The Trustees of [charity] are pleased to welcome the undersigned to the Heritage Society. This generous expression of support is most deeply appreciated, *etc., etc.*" Your publications department can help you create an appropriate design and format.

  - Put the names on a plaque or engrave them on a wall;

  - Buy a memento for each member (pin, tie clip, something with your logo);

  - Provide gift credit for a campaign (see Crediting Guidelines earlier in this chapter or Chapter III-5 Integrating Planned Giving Into a Campaign).

- Create a Standard Bequest Form for use in documenting bequests. (Note: Not all people will be willing to sign this form. That is fine. You should ask them all at least once.)

- Write to the people on your current bequest or deferred gift list (even if there are only 10), explain that you are creating a bequest society, welcome them as charter members, and ask them if they are willing to complete the Standard Bequest Form. You can also outline for them the activities or incentives you have created especially for them.

- Plan a series of articles or ads in your institution's newsletter or other publication to create visibility for the program.

- Put check-off blocks on every reply mechanism or pledge form. Note: If annual giving pledge forms are already printed for the current year, you will have to wait until they are reprinted. The check-off blocks could say:

  _____ I have included XYZ Charity in my will. Please send me information about the (name of recognition society).

  _____ Please send me information about including XYZ Charity in my will.

- Contact several of the vendors listed in Appendix IV to request sample materials on wills programs. You can start with The Stelter Company, Robert F. Sharpe & Co., The Ford Thompson Company, Longman/R&R Newkirk, Pentera, Conrad Teitell, or Young Preston Associates, all of whom offer wills materials, brochures, booklets and other mailers. Through a review of different kinds of brochures, you can select a program of direct mail appropriate for your institution and also get ideas on the kinds of information you can include in a bequest brochure should you decide to write your own.

- Identify a target group for a bequest mailing. You can use the following criteria to narrow your list:

  - people age 50 and older, especially widows, widowers, and single people, or married without children;

  - people who have been contributing at any level for ten years or more;

  - people who are already participating in one of your life income plans;

  - people who have made stock gifts;

  - people who live in wealthy zip codes. Note: You and your colleagues should know which zip codes in your area hold the most potential.

If you work for an institution which carries information about age, you should target _everyone_ age 50 and older without regard to the other criteria (unless the numbers are so large that the cost of a mailing is prohibitive). In this case, narrow the field by selecting only those above age 50 who fit the other criteria. It is not advisable to target only major donors because often bequests of substantial amounts come from small donors who are unable to contribute large amounts currently. Many other bequests come from people who have never contributed at all.

ADMINISTERING YOUR BEQUEST PROGRAM

When a person with a bequest to your organization dies, certain things will happen. As Director of Planned Giving, you will be responsible for monitoring the process.

Learning About The Death

Planned Giving Officers learn about deaths several ways.

- A family member tells you because you have been close to the donor's family;
- A friend of the donor calls you;
- A member of your department who checks the obituaries alerts you;

- Mail comes back with the words "deceased" written on the address label;
- Your planned giving manager informs you that income checks to a particular beneficiary are not being cashed;
- The executor sends you a letter announcing that the will is about to be probated and that your charity is named as a legatee or has an interest in another part of the estate. Usually, these letters go to the treasurer of the organization because the executor does not know who to inform. If you have a good relationship with the treasurer's office, you should get copies of these probate notices as soon as possible from the treasurer's office.

Your organization should be notified for any death involving a deferred gift, but an official notification may not happen right away. This includes deaths involving beneficiaries of your life income plans, deaths of people who are the insured on a life insurance policy that benefits your institution, or deaths in which your organization is named in a will or revocable trust.

Often, the records department learns of a death because someone wrote "deceased" on a piece of mail and returned it to the institution. However, there is rarely a cross check in the data processing area to see if the deceased is involved in planned giving. To be on top of things, you should set up a mechanism so that you will know when a deferred giving donor or beneficiary dies. (Note: You also have to track successor beneficiaries, but you probably need to depend on the primary beneficiary to inform you about these deaths because the secondary beneficiary generally does not have an individual gift record in your institution's database.) When the primary beneficiary dies, you should set up the secondary beneficiary in your institution's database so that you can now track the new person.

At Boston College, we had over 500 people in the deferred giving society, which included all deferred gift categories. We created a code for the society and entered it into each member's computer record. Then, I ordered a standing monthly report for all people with that code who died in the prior month. That method worked well. Each month, the report would arrive, often with no names on it, but sometimes with one or two names. This procedure guaranteed that the planned giving office received the names of deceased planned giving donors in a timely way.

Most offices have files for people with known bequests. In some cases, the information is valid. In other cases, the files are old and there has been no contact with the individual other than a ten-year-old reply card sitting by itself in a folder. Therefore, you cannot always be sure that you will receive a bequest from those on your list. If you learn that someone has died, and you believe the institution is named for a bequest, do nothing other than to set the file aside as an "Estate in Distribution." Then wait. Within the month, the executor will send you a notice of the probate of the will. If you receive nothing for a couple of months, chances are, you are not in the will. There can be disappointments with this process. Files in your office are old. Your predecessor never verified the bequest information. He or she probably inherited those files from another person who never verified the information.

If you believe you should have been listed in the will and there is no probate notice after several months, the reason may be that the bequest will distribute on the death of the surviving spouse.

The Probate Notice

When you receive a probate notice, you know for sure that somebody died and that you have an interest in the estate. The probate notice tells you that the will is going to be presented to the probate court by an individual claiming to be the executor(trix). Sometimes, there will be a copy of the will with the probate notice. Sometimes not. If your organization had any reason to contest the will, you would need to send an attorney to the court hearing and file a will contest. Such a procedure is extremely rare. Most of the time, you do nothing.

Communicating With the Executor

Once you have the name and address of the executor, you should write a letter along the following lines:

> Dear (executor):
>
> Thank you for informing us about the death of [name] on [date] and for informing us that [charity] is named as a [legatee of the will, beneficiary of a revocable trust, *etc.*]. Could you please provide the following?
>
> - Copy of the will or other document in which [charity] is named;
> - Estimated size of the bequest;
> - Timetable for the distribution;
> - Names of any family members to whom we might send a note.
>
> Future correspondence concerning this matter should be addressed to me at the following address:
>
> [name]
> Director of Planned Giving
> [charity]
> Address
> City, State, Zip Code
>
> Thank you for your help.
>
> Sincerely,
>
>
> Director of Planned Giving

If the executor is on the ball, the answers to this inquiry should be forthcoming in a short time. If not, you will have to call to follow up. You may also wish to make a call before you send the letter.

When your organization's provision is in a will, you should receive a copy of the entire will. Sometimes, if the provision is simple like "I leave $10,000 to [charity]," the executor will send only that provision. Most of the time, this is fine.

When your organization's share is in a revocable trust, you will almost never get a copy of the whole document because a revocable trust is not public. In fact, the executor may simply type the relevant provision for your organization in a letter without showing you the real thing. This can be a problem because you may never really know whether you received the proper amount. It is very awkward if you have to confront the executor to ask for the whole document. Your request will not be well received. If you have a situation in which you feel that viewing the entire document is important, the best way to handle it is to have your tax counsel correspond with the executor on behalf of your institution. State law issues might be involved and your charity may have the legal right to see the whole document.

Monitoring the Process

At some point, the executor should send you an inventory of assets, an account of the estate's income and expenses, and a summary of the distribution plan for the bequests. When your organization is named for a specific amount of money, there is not much that can go wrong with your bequest unless the estate is completely insolvent, which means that all bequests other than specific bequests will be reduced proportionately.

You should review the documents to see if anything unusual strikes you. It is hard to say what might look unusual. Things like executor's fees and attorney's fees will show up. You will also see expenses for the funeral, last illness, hospital fees, utilities, and possibly maintenance fees for a piece of real estate. If anything strikes you as outrageous, you should tactfully ask the executor about it. Sometimes people make mistakes. Sometimes the executor has been negligent. A few things to look out for are listed below:

- an asset that the executor sold for substantially less than what it was worth on the date of death or which has depreciated substantially from the date of death (a portfolio, real estate);
- an asset that you think is in the wrong category. Example: a bank account at Bank of Boston was left to your organization, but prior to the donor's death, Bank of Boston merged with Fleet to become Fleet Boston. Does the Fleet Boston account go to your organization?
- A specific number of shares of stock are bequeathed to you. The shares split several times since the donor executed the will. How many shares do you get?
- A specific stock is bequeathed to you. The company merged with another and changed its name prior to the donor's death. Who gets the stock?

If you think that something looks wrong, ask your attorney to check the accession rules according to your state statues. It is very easy for an executor to make a mistake in the distribution of the assets, especially when things have changed in the structure of a company stock or a corporation before the donor's death.

Bequests of Real Estate

If you receive a bequest of a piece of real property, you should check it out first prior to accepting it. Basically, you should get somebody to inspect the property to ensure that there is no hazardous waste problem or any other code violation that would be an obstacle to selling the property. Review Chapter II-6 on Real Estate for a more complete discussion about liability. Usually, when you receive a piece of real estate, you can elect to have the executor sell the property and give you the proceeds. However, the executor cannot transfer the title to the real estate into the charity's name without its permission. If your organization takes title, it will be responsible for the property's insurance, maintenance, and other expenses until you sell it. A prevailing opinion is that if you sell the property yourself, you will get a higher price than what the executor will get trying to sell it quickly. Also, be wary of executors selling real estate for below market value to family members of the deceased.

Recording the Bequest Distribution

You need a way to track the bequests within your gift-recording system. I found it easiest to record a pledge for the verified bequest amount on the donor's gift record. First, issue a change of name for the donor's record from "John Smith" to "Estate of John Smith."

Before doing this, talk to the head of your gift processing department to see if that procedure will work. As long as you provide a copy of the legal documentation for the bequest, you should have no problem. If the bequest is hard to value because it is a percentage bequest, get an estimate from the executor and record a conservative amount, leaving a little wiggle room in case the bequest comes in low. For example, if a percentage bequest is estimated at $125,000, record $100,000. If you receive more than what you recorded, add the rest to the donor's record after you receive the final distribution.

Frequently, the executor will make partial distributions as the process of settling the estate moves along.

Receiving Distributions

Eventually, you will receive a letter from the executor with a check for your charity's share and an assent form enclosed. Usually the treasurer or another person authorized to sign documents signs and returns the assent form verifying that it received the distribution. But, executors are also using another practice more often. In the latter case, the executor sends a letter with an assent form but no check. The executor asks you to sign the form which says you have received the bequest. The cover letter from the executor states that you will get the money or the asset as soon as he or she receives your signed form. Executors do this because they don't trust the charity to return the form after receiving the bequest. The executor cannot close the estate nor file the final tax return until all of the assent forms come back. If you receive one of these, you may find that your business office will not sign the form without receiving the money. This is not worth the battle. A solution is to write a letter to the executor along the following lines:

> Dear (executor):
>
> We have received your request to sign an assent form for receiving [$_____] from the Estate of [name] with the promise that you will send the funds upon receipt of our assent. Although we have not received the funds, we are forwarding the assent as requested.
>
> Sincerely,
>
> Director of Planned Giving

It is highly unlikely for you not to get the money, so do whatever the executor asks you to do (within reason) and don't fight with the executor about it.

Following Up With the Executor

Sometimes, the executor is extremely professional and will follow through with the administration of the estate efficiently and expeditiously. At other times, you will be dealing with a single practitioner who is very slow and takes what seems like forever to distribute the money or assets due your organization. You should have a tickler file to remind you to follow up about every three months to push things along.

Restricted Bequests

Occasionally, you will receive a bequest that you cannot use. Here are a few examples:

- You receive a bequest of $25,000 to establish a named endowment when your endowed fund minimum is $50,000 or $100,000.

  If the amount is clearly too small, you probably should disclaim the bequest. Hard as it is to do, this may be your best option. Your organization does not want to manage a fund whose income is so low as to be useless for the purpose designated.

  Another option is to put the funds in your endowment and let the fund grow for several years before activating the fund.

  Put the funds in your endowment and let the income accumulate for several years before using the income for the designated purpose. This works for such things as an endowed lecture. If you require a $100,000 endowment for an annual lecture, but you receive $50,000, then do the lecture every other year.

  Under some circumstances, you can ask other family members to add enough money to the bequest to bring it to the desired level.

- You receive a bequest for a purpose that is obsolete.

  Under such situations, you can petition the probate court to suggest an alternate use of the funds consistent with the wishes of the donor.

- You receive a bequest to establish a scholarship to be awarded to descendants of the donor.

    This can never be done. You should ask your tax counsel whether there is a possibility of petitioning the court to broaden the restriction. Otherwise, you cannot use this gift.

Most bequests should be straightforward and easy to use according to the wishes of the donor. Many will be completely unrestricted.

Bequest Income Processing Software© (BIPS©)

If you are running a mature bequest program that has on average 6-10 or more bequests in distribution at any one time, you will want to check into software created by Susan DameGreene. It is called BIPS, short for Bequest Income Processing Software. You can download a free demo that holds up to 10 estates from her web site at www.bipster.com. Or, she will mail you that same demo on a CD. Call her toll free at 888-588-BIPS.

The software has been created with all the tools to allow you to track and monitor your bequest program. It has a letter generator with sample letters. You can input the names of executors, the name of the deceased, other beneficiaries, amounts, types of bequests, *etc.* There is also an automatic reminder feature that will alert you when it is time to follow up. You can also graph your bequest income and create reports immediately.

According to Susan, "The software is designed to be run by an administrative assistant, freeing the Planned Giving Professional for planned giving work." I got a copy of the software to test and found it to be easy to use after a little orientation. There are different versions of the software to suit your needs and level of activity. Check out her web site for the latest costs.

For organizations tracking a large group of estates, this software can save you a lot of time because most development office software for tracking outright gifts is sorely inadequate for planned giving.

SUMMARY

Bequest income is extremely important in a planned giving program. Even though this chapter is rather long, the subject is really very simple. Ask constituents to provide a bequest to your institution and give them the language to do it.

The next chapter of Part II deals with a less common form of gift vehicle—the charitable lead trust. Few planned giving officers have ever secured a charitable lead trust. However, the historically low I.R.S. discount rates make lead trusts more attractive than ever before. Under the right conditions, a lead trust is a perfect way for a donor to provide significant cash flow to your organization and save taxes in a number of ways at the same time.

Chapter II–11

CHARITABLE LEAD TRUSTS

In preceding chapters, you studied life income gifts—pooled income funds, gift annuities, and charitable remainder trusts. While these vehicles are distinctly different from each other in operation and tax consequences, they all share two points:

1. Income stream currently to the donor or to another person or persons;
2. Remainder to charity.

This chapter discusses the charitable lead trust—a gift arrangement that basically is the opposite of a life income gift. It provides:

1. Income stream currently to charity;
2. Remainder to the donor or to another person or persons.

Donors use lead trusts for one of the following purposes:

- to accelerate an income tax charitable deduction for future charitable gifts into the current tax year (qualified grantor trust);

- to pass property to heirs at reduced transfer tax cost (qualified nongrantor trust);

- to make charitable gifts beyond the federal income tax charitable contribution ceilings.

In order to give you the most useful understanding of the lead trust, I have organized this chapter as follows. First, there is an explanation of the types of lead trusts and the special considerations that distinguish one type from another. Second, there is a summary of each type of lead trust including an explanation of the tax consequences. Then, there are other sections involving unique issues with lead trusts. Finally, there is a set of questions and answers to bring in issues not covered in the narrative. Please remember that this chapter is only a beginning.

Lead trusts have a simple premise, but the rules and regulations governing them are complex. Since I.R.S. provides no prototype documents for charitable lead trusts, there are a lot of pitfalls and ways to go astray. Attorneys unfamiliar with their unique regulations and rules should stay away from lead trusts. A novice planner will easily get into trouble because there are many nuances in the drafting, operation, and investment rules.

This chapter is divided into the following main sections:

- general operation;
- types of lead trusts;
- qualified grantor lead trust;
- qualified nongrantor lead trust;
- nonqualified grantor lead trust;
- nonqualified nongrantor lead trust;
- taxation of the lead trust;
- excess business holdings and jeopardy investments;
- questions and answers about charitable lead trusts.

GENERAL OPERATION

A lead trust operates under the terms of its trust instrument drafted by a competent tax lawyer and is usually managed by a professional trustee chosen by the donor. The donor can also be trustee as long as he or she does not retain the power to choose the charitable beneficiaries year to year. A donor transfers property to the trust and provides "income" payments for a period of years to one or more charities. If actual income is insufficient to make a payment, the trustee will dip into principal to the extent required. Any amount exceeding the CLT payout will be returned to principal. Lead unitrusts must be valued at least once annually (the same day each year) during its fiscal year in order to determine the unitrust payout. A lead unitrust can also have multiple valuation dates from which an average fair market value would be taken. At the end of the lead trust's term, the principal either reverts to the donor or distributes to one or more persons designated by the donor.

If the trust term is measured by the life of a person, he or she must be living at the time of the creation of the trust and must be one of the following: the donor, the donor's spouse, a lineal ancestor or the spouse of a lineal ancestor of all the remainder beneficiaries. (Note: A lead trust term cannot be measured by anyone else's life. This rule is to prevent the donor from using the life of a young and sickly unrelated third party who will not be expected to live a normal life expectancy but who is not terminally ill according to I.R.S. standards. By selecting a sickly young person, the donor would receive an inflated federal income tax deduction or an inflated gift or estate tax deduction while the charity's interest would be cut short. This strategy became known as the "Vulture" or "Ghoul" CLT.)

The management fees for the trust (based on a percent of the income earned and/or on a percent of the market value) are usually charged to the trust and would be similar to those for charitable remainder trusts.

TYPES OF LEAD TRUSTS

The characterization of a lead trust takes two things into account:

- whether or not the trust is qualified under I.R.S.'s strict guidelines (qualifed *vs.* nonqualified), and

- whether or not the donor is treated as the "owner" of the trust under the grantor trust rules so as to be taxable on the trust's income (grantor *vs.* nongrantor).

By combining the above considerations, you produce four possible lead trust variations each of which generates different tax consequences. The four variations are as follows:

1. Qualified grantor lead trust
2. Qualified nongrantor lead trust
3. Nonqualified grantor lead trust
4. Nonqualified nongrantor lead trust.

Before discussing the applications of each of the four variations, I would like to describe the difference between a qualified and a nonqualified trust and between a grantor and a nongrantor trust.

Qualified *Vs.* Nonqualified Lead Trusts

Nonqualified trusts *do not* entitle the donor to an income, gift or estate tax charitable deduction. While there may be other reasons for creating a nonqualified trust, the motivation is *not* 1) to receive a current income tax deduction on the creation of the trust, or 2) to reduce transfer taxes. Nonqualified lead trusts are uncommon.

A *qualified* trust, on the other hand, entitles the donor to both a gift and estate tax charitable deduction for the charity's income interest, and an income tax deduction for the charity's interest if the donor is treated as the owner.

Many requirements must be satisfied to produce a qualified trust. Not all of them are discussed here because many are technical drafting requirements about which your attorney rather than you would be concerned. There are three requirements with which you should be familiar.

- The "income" payment to the charity must be in the form of either an annuity interest (fixed dollar payment annually), or a unitrust interest (fixed percentage of the market value determined at least annually). Unlike the CRT, there is no minimum or maximum payout.

- The trust's term must be measured by the life of one or more persons living when the trust is created or by a term of years. If these first two requirements are met, the lead interest can be calculated using the same I.R.S. tables on which tax-related calculations are performed for charitable remainder trusts (Chapter II–9). Although a CRT term cannot exceed lives in being plus 20 years so as not to run afoul of state laws against perpetuities, the lead trust has no such restrictions if state law doesn't restrict such trust terms. Most CLTs have a term measured by a specific number of years because the donor is trying to achieve a particular gift and estate tax deduction based on running the trust out to a specific number of years.

- The charitable beneficiary must be described in the appropriate sections of the I.R.S. Code. [for the income tax deduction, Section 170(c), the estate tax deduction, Section 2055(a), and for the gift tax deduction, Section 2522(a)] Since contributions to different kinds of charities are not always deductible for both income and estate tax purposes, you should consult your attorney to determine your institution's classification with respect to this subject. The gift tax allows a deduction by citizens or residents to foreign charities, but the income tax does not. Gifts to public charities have more favorable tax treatment for tax deductibility than do private foundations. Moreover, CLT payments to private foundations under the donor's control often cause tax problems. These issues are discussed in detail later in the chapter.

As you can see by the above considerations, a key thrust of this issue (qualified *vs.* nonqualified) is whether or not the trust's payments conform to certain measurable standards so that a dollar value can be determined using I.R.S. tables.

Unlike the charitable remainder unitrust, however, a qualified lead trust *cannot* limit its payout to the lesser of net income or the unitrust amount; there is no such thing as a net income lead trust. Therefore, it must pay out the unitrust amount regardless of the income earned. However, lead trust payments *do not* have to be a minimum of 5% of the initial contribution (or the annual fair market value of the trust assets) as is the case with payments from charitable remainder trusts. You can have a 2% payout or a 4% payout. Moreover, you are not limited to a 50% payout as you are with CRTs, though it would be unusual to have a payout that high.

Grantor *Vs.* Nongrantor Lead Trust

Building on the preceding section, another consideration is whether or not the donor is considered to be the "owner" of the trust. The I.R.S. sets forth strict guidelines with regard to this area of income tax law. The operative provisions in the I.R.S. Code are called the grantor trust rules. If the donor is considered to be the owner under the grantor trust rules, the trust is called a "grantor trust." If he or she is not owner, the trust is a "nongrantor trust."

Why is this important?

Unlike the tax-exempt CRT, the CLT is a tax paying irrevocable trust. The donor cannot claim a current federal income tax charitable deduction for establishing a lead trust *unless* he or she is also taxable on the trust's income (grantor trust). In other words, the income in the trust flows through the donor's individual income tax return. And, to be taxable on the trust income, the donor must be considered the "owner" of the trust. Therefore, in drafting a lead trust, special attention must be paid to the conditions under which the donor is treated as the owner.

When the donor is not the owner, he or she is neither taxable on the income in the trust nor is entitled to an income tax deduction on creating the trust.

There is a complex set of guidelines to determine exactly when a donor is treated as the owner of a trust. For lead trusts created after March 1, 1986, the donor is treated as the owner if there is more than a 5% chance that a reversion will take place.

As you read through the following discussion of the four types of trusts, try to keep in mind the distinct features that make a lead trust qualified, nonqualified, grantor, or nongrantor.

SUMMARY OF LEAD TRUST VARIATIONS
If The Trust Is Structured Properly, The Following Results Can Be Achieved:

	Qualified Grantor Trust	Qualified Nongrantor Trust	Nonqualified Grantor Trust	Nonqualified Nongrantor Trust
Donor is entitled to income tax deduction for lead interest at creation of trust	yes	no	no	no
Donor is taxable on trust's income and capital gains	yes	no	yes	no
Donor is entitled to income tax deduction for payments made to charity each year	no	no	yes	no
Trust is entitled to income tax deduction for payments made to charity each year	n/a	yes	n/a	yes
Can help avoid charitable contribution deduction ceilings	no	yes	no	yes
Accelerates deduction for future payments to charity into current year	yes	no	no	no

QUALIFIED GRANTOR LEAD TRUST

The primary purpose of establishing a qualified grantor lead trust is to accelerate a deduction for future charitable gifts into the current year.

However, the income tax charitable contribution ceilings for a gift to a lead trust are different from the rules for outright gifts or for life income gifts. A gift to a lead trust is considered "for the use of" the charity and not "to" the charity. This is similar to the case of a donor making a life insurance premium payment directly to an insurance company to pay for a life insurance policy benefiting a charity. It is "for the use of" and not "to." (Note: There is an explanation of this issue in Chapter II-2.)

Therefore, lower charitable contribution ceilings apply for grantor lead trusts for federal income tax charitable deduction purposes. If the donor uses cash or ordinary income property to fund a grantor lead trust for the benefit of a public charity, his or her deduction is limited to 30% of adjusted gross income (AGI) with a five-year period in which to use up any excess over the 30% ceiling. (Note: gifts of cash to a CRT enjoy a 50% contribution ceiling.) For gifts of long-term capital gain property to a CLT, the contribution ceiling is 20% of AGI. The deduction for cash gifts to CLTs that support a private foundation is limited to 30% of AGI and 20% for gifts of long-term capital gain property.

The usefulness of the qualified grantor lead trust was far greater when tax rates were higher. Before the Tax Reform Act of 1981, the maximum individual tax rate was 70%. Back then, a deduction of $100,000 by a donor in the 70% income tax bracket saved $70,000 in taxes! When the top rate was 50%, he or she still saved a whopping $50,000. Today, the same $100,000 deduction at today's 35% top bracket will generate savings of only $35,000. And, the donor continues to report and pay taxes on the annual income of the trust.

So, where does the qualified grantor lead trust fit in?

When you think about the variables in the equation, not much is subject to strategic maneuvering. The federal income tax rates are fixed; the donor's income, while subject to some shifting, is also known. However, the donor has control over the type of property transferred to the trust. Since the trust income is taxable to the donor, by using tax-exempt bonds to fund the trust, the donor is able to benefit from the current tax deduction without paying tax on the trust income as it is earned each year. However, using municipal bonds in a lead trust hinders the possible appreciation. Nonetheless, if the donor already owns tax exempt bonds, then getting them back is probably what he or she wants anyway. On the other hand, if the donor has tax-exempt bonds, his or her taxable income may not be high enough to absorb the up front income tax deduction generated by setting up the lead trust.

Example:

Mr. Donor is in the 35% tax bracket with an adjusted gross income (AGI) of $400,000 (Note: The starting point for the 35% bracket in 2003 is $311,951 under JGTRRA of 2003). He would like to make a commitment to your organization's capital campaign without completely relinquishing ownership of his capital assets. His charitable contribution ceiling for a gift of appreciated, long-term securities to a CLT benefiting a public charity is limited to 20% of his adjusted gross income with a five-year carry over for any excess exceeding the 20% ceiling. For an AGI of $400,000, his maximum deduction for a gift of long term property for one year is $80,000. ($400,000 AGI x 20% = $80,000.) Assume the I.R.S. discount rate is 4.2%. (Note: The donor may use the discount rate of the current month or the rate of either of the two months preceding the month of the gift. The donor receives the largest tax deduction by using the lowest rate.)

Donor transfers $400,000 in tax-exempt bonds yielding 6% to a grantor lead annuity trust and provides a 5% annuity or $20,000 *per* year to your charity for five years. The payments are to be made quarterly at the end of the payment period. At the end of the five years, the assets revert to the donor. The donor chooses five years because this is the term necessary to generate a deduction close to his $80,000 contribution ceiling. He wishes to claim the whole deduction in one lump sum without being forced to carry over much, if any, of it to a later year.

RESULT:

Assets transferred to trust:	$400,000
Annual payments to your organization:	20,000
Total contribution to your organization over five years:	100,000
Income tax deduction on creation* (Donor can claim $80,000 in year of funding and carry over the excess $9,920 to the next year.)	89,920

Tax savings from deduction in year of transfer @ 35% rate ($80,000 deduction x 35%)	28,000
Additional income from investment of tax savings in 6% tax-exempt bonds ($28,000 @ 6%):	1,680
Tax on income earned in the trust (assuming no redemption, call, or sale of the bonds at a gain):	none
Assets returned to the donor after five years	All

This is the same calculation as for a charitable remainder annuity trust except that you are focusing on the income interest instead of the remainder interest. Your planned giving software will prompt you with appropriate questions about the gift, type of payment (unitrust or annuity payment), term of years or based on lives in being, I.R.S. discount rate of 4.2%, etc.

In this example, the donor has accomplished the following:

- provided $100,000 to your organization, all of which came in during the five-year campaign pledge period;
- received an income tax deduction of $89,920 of which he can claim up to $80,000 saving $28,000 in the current year. He carries over $9,920 for a deduction in the second year;
- generated $1,680 in additional income from investment of the tax savings in more municipal bonds;
- retained ownership of the assets for ultimate distribution to heirs;
- incurred no income tax on the trust's earnings because he used municipal bonds to fund the trust.

For a grantor lead trust to be attractive, the donor must be able to survive without the annual income generated by the trust for the duration of the trust's term. One would have to consider whether there is a greater benefit from the one-time deduction of $80,000 currently than there is for a $20,000 deduction in each of the next five years if the donor had, instead, simply made annual outright gifts. By making outright gifts over five years, the donor would have had a higher contribution ceiling (30% of AGI as opposed to 20% of AGI). And, he would have been able to claim the full $100,000 over five years.

QUALIFIED NONGRANTOR LEAD TRUST

The primary purpose of the qualified nongrantor lead trust is to reduce the gift or estate tax on property passing to heirs, most commonly, children or grandchildren. With a nongrantor trust, the donor is not treated as the owner. Therefore, the donor neither reports income earned in the trust nor receives an income tax deduction for the charity's lead interest. However, the goal of using a qualified nongrantor lead trust is *not* to get an income tax deduction—rather, it is to use the gift or estate tax charitable deduction to offset the otherwise potentially high transfer tax that would apply to a taxable transfer of property that exceeds the gift or estate tax lifetime exemption. (For more about the transfer tax system, see Chapter II-10.)

A qualified nongrantor lead trust can help a donor make a major gift to your organization and, at the same time, save estate or gift taxes and also generation-skipping transfer taxes (for transfers to grandchildren). It should be noted that when a lead trust is compared side by side with a "no trust" option or an irrevocable trust option, the donor's heirs may receive more without the lead trust. However, as the following examples show, the lead trust can do a pretty good job of passing assets to heirs while providing a tremendous amount to charity.

It is important to note the capital gain implications for a qualified nongrantor lead trust. If the trust is set up during lifetime, then the heirs must assume the cost basis from the CLT which were tied to the donor's cost basis upon setting up the CLT. However, if the CLT is set up at death (notwithstanding the terms of EGTRRA of 2001 which changes the step-up cost basis rules for 2010), if the CLT is created at death, all assets funding the CLT get a stepped-up cost basis.

A donor who sets up a nongrantor lead trust must understand that he or she cannot get the assets back. Also, he or she must be comfortable with the fact that the heirs will not receive the assets for many years. When heirs are young, the lead trust serves the donor well by putting the assets into the heirs' hands at a mature age, when presumably, they will handle the inheritance responsibly (Some market these trusts as "deferred inheritance trusts").

Intervivos CLT Example:

The best way to understand a nongrantor lead trust is to compare it to a "no trust" example (where the donor does nothing) and to an irrevocable trust example. (Refer to **Exhibit II-11A** on page 301.) Let's take the case of Sam, a single divorced father who wishes to split $5,000,000 equally among his four children. His total estate is $10,000,000. His life expectancy is 20 years. Assume income of 2%, appreciation of 5% and management fees of .75% of principal each year. The I.R.S. discount rate is 3.2%. Sam has made no prior taxable gifts.

Since there is some gift tax to pay up front on both the lead trust example and on the irrevocable trust example, the amount of the principal needed to start each scenario is $5,000,000 plus $144,855 (gift tax on the lead trust) for a total of $5,144,855. By accounting for the gift tax in the original principal, all three scenarios are compared fairly and totaled up. (Note: I could have run the lead trust out longer or set a higher CLAT payout rate to zero out the gift tax in the lead trust, but I wanted to show a more complex example so that I could discuss aspects of the scenario that would not be addressed if I zeroed out the gift tax.)

Qualified Nongrantor Charitable Lead Annuity Trust

Sam starts out with $5,144,855. He puts $5,000,000 in a 5%, 20-year charitable lead annuity trust entitling him to a federal gift tax deduction of $3,651,500 assuming an I.R.S. discount rate of 3.2%. He files a gift tax return and pays a gift tax of $144,855. Note: if he gave the $5,000,000 outright to the kids, he would have made a taxable transfer of $4,000,000 since the lifetime gift tax exemption is $1,000,000. With the use of the lead trust, his taxable transfer is the amount transferred to the CLAT minus the federal gift tax deduction ($5,000,000 - $3,651,500 = $1,348,500). The gift tax on $1,348,500 is $144,855.

After paying $250,000 *per* year to charity for 20 years, the CLAT is worth $7,281,747 which distributes to the kids without any further tax. The donor paid tax on a taxable transfer of only $1,345,500 but gave the kids $7,281,747, albeit, 20 years in the future.

Over the 20 years, the CLT is subject to federal income tax at trust rates for any income earned, but the CLT receives a tax deduction for any amounts paid to charity. Important for the lead trust option is the fact that it paid no income tax over the 20 years. That is because this particular CLT payout of $250,000 is higher than the 2% ordinary income earned. Therefore, no excess income remained in the trust to be taxed. In practice, things don't turn out as tidy as they do in a hypothetical example. However, with a savvy manager and an experienced attorney advising the donor, a charitably-minded individual should be able to structure a lead trust that achieves the desired objectives.

No Trust

Sam starts out with the same $5,144,855 and invests it for a period of 20 years. He conveniently dies at the end of 20 years, leaving this appreciated pool of assets to the kids. During the 20 years, he pays income taxes on the income earned at his 35% individual income tax rate. (Bear in mind that in 2003, there is a 15% marginal tax rate for most dividends. That provision expires at the end of 2008. For purposes of the comparison, I assumed a constant tax rate of 35% for the 20 years. Realistically, we have never had a period of tax history of 20 years with the same tax rates. However, this illustration is for comparison; therefore, some assumptions are required. All three options have the same assumptions.) At the end of the 20 years, the amount will have grown to $15,853,003. His estate pays $7,133,851 in estate taxes and the kids split $8,719,151. Charity gets nothing. (Note: We don't actually know what the estate tax will be in 20 years. Under EGTRRA of 2001, the estate tax exemption rises to $3,500,000 in 2009. Then, the estate tax and generation-skipping transfer tax is repealed in 2010. In 2011, the estate tax and GST tax exemptions return at $1,000,000. For this example, I assumed 2009 rules carry into the future.)

Regular Irrevocable Trust

Sam starts out with the same $5,144,855. He wants to make a transfer to an Irrevocable Trust that would grow for 20 years and distribute to the kids at the end. By transferring money to an irrevocable trust, he is able to freeze the amount on which a gift tax is due. Appreciation in the trust will pass free of gift tax since the donor has given away all rights to the assets. In order to structure this option so that it is comparable to the others, he has $5,144,855 to work with.

He puts $3,818,695 in an irrevocable trust and pays a gift tax of $1,326,160. (Note: the amount placed in the trust added to the gift tax equals $5,144,855.) Income earned in the trust will be taxed at trust rates. Trust tax rates have the same brackets as individuals, but they hit the maximum tax rate at very low income level. For example, in early 2003, it took only $9,350 of trust income to be taxed at the highest marginal rate. This is a very high tax rate for a very small amount of income. The example shows a tax of $568,494 over the 20 years and is figured on the pre-JGTRRA rules since the latest rules were not available at the time of this writing.

Over 20 years, the irrevocable trust grows to $11,791,332 and distributes to the heirs without any further gift tax. Remember: the donor paid the appropriate gift tax 20 years earlier and no further tax is required upon distribution.

Refer to **Exhibit II-11A**. Notice that the donor gave much more to the kids by using an irrevocable trust than he did with either the lead trust or the "no trust" options. Still, some wealthy individuals don't want to ruin their kids' lives by making them too rich. Also, it is interesting to note the comparison of the "no trust" option to the lead trust option. By doing nothing, the donor gave his heirs $8,719,151. With the lead trust, he gave them $7,281,747 plus he gave $5,000,000 to charity. That's not too bad.

As a caveat, you also need to know that comparing these simplistic options is sorely inadequate to show you the breadth of what individuals could do to structure their assets so as to avoid tax and pass assets to heirs effectively. If a person has significant wealth or complicated assets, there are other ways, beyond the scope of this book, to arrange affairs so as to minimize transfer taxes.

NONQUALIFIED GRANTOR LEAD TRUST

As its name suggests, the nonqualified grantor lead trust does not conform to the required annuity trust or unitrust payout requirement to afford the donor an income, gift, or estate tax charitable deduction for the charity's income interest. Yet, the donor, as owner, must report and pay taxes on the income earned in the trust. However, if the trust is structured properly, the donor can claim an income tax deduction each year that income is paid to charity.

This type of trust serves little useful purpose.

NONQUALIFIED NONGRANTOR LEAD TRUST

A nonqualified nongrantor trust technically can be established during lifetime or at death, but, as its name implies, the donor cannot claim an income, gift, or estate tax charitable deduction for the charity's income interest on its creation. Therefore, one would not create such a trust at death because the entire value of the principal might be subject to the estate tax.

Exhibit II-11A

ASHTON ASSOCIATES

Lead Trust Projections
Benefits and Tax Consequences

ASSUMPTIONS:
Non-grantor Inter Vivos Trusts established for 20 years.
Lead Trust makes annual, end of period payments to CHARITY.
Original Principal of 5,000,000 has a cost basis of 50%.
Donor income tax bracket is 35%, 15% for capital gains.
Beneficiary income tax bracket is 35%, 15% for capital gains.
Value of donor's estate is 10,000,000. Prior taxable gifts are 0.
Transfer tax: Continue 2009 tax rates for future years.
Income is 2%, capital appreciation is 5%.

	Charitable Lead Annuity Trust	5% Regular Irrevocable Trust	No Trust
Gross Principal	$5,144,855	$5,144,855	$5,144,855
Annuity to CHARITY	250,000	0	0
Gift Tax Deduction	3,651,500	0	0
Gift Tax (Paid 2003 by donor)	144,855	1,326,160	0
Net Principal Placed in Plan	5,000,000	3,818,695	5,144,855
Total Management Fees	923,038	1,082,679	1,456,891
Total Income Tax Paid	0	568,494	785,102
Principal after 20 Years	7,281,747	11,791,332	15,853,003
Estate Tax on No Trust (2023)	0	0	7,133,851
Benefit to Family	**7,281,747**	**11,791,332**	**8,719,151**
Total Distributed to CHARITY	**5,000,000**	**0**	**0**

IRS Discount Rate is 3.2%

A nonqualfied nongrantor lead trust ultimately passes assets to the donor's heirs while allowing the donor to make charitable gifts above his charitable contribution ceilings.

> Example:
>
> A donor who wishes to support your institution but who has already exceeded his contribution ceilings transfers property to a nonqualified nongrantor lead trust. He receives no current income tax deduction. After income is earned in the trust, the donor designates income payments to your institution each year. The trust receives a charitable deduction for the amount of the charitable gifts.

There is no contribution ceiling with which to be concerned, but the donor would be subject to a gift tax on its lead interest!

The real problem is that the full value of the trust is subject to gift tax for the amount of the present value of the charity's payments that exceeds the annual gift tax exclusion ($11,000 for 2003). That is a very high price to pay in order to permit the donor to make gifts in excess of the annual income tax deduction limitations.

Thus, as with the nonqualified grantor lead trust, the nonqualified nongrantor lead trust serves little or no useful purpose.

TAXATION OF THE LEAD TRUST

Unlike CRTs which are tax exempt trusts, CLTs are taxable entities. Therefore, structuring the payout and term of years and managing the taxable events in the trust takes skill and expertise. An inexperienced attorney or manager will easily fall into traps if he or she is not intimately familiar with the trust's taxation rules.

There are different issues for grantor and nongrantor CRTs.

Qualified Grantor Lead Trust Tax Considerations

The income earned in a grantor lead trust must be reported by the donor each year as if it was his or her own income. In addition, any long or short term capital gain incurred in the trust must be reported by the donor. When the assets in the grantor lead trust revert to the donor, they carry the cost basis and holding period in the CLT back to the donor. Therefore, the manager of the CLT must pay attention to the way the trust is managed. As I mentioned earlier in this chapter, if the donor funds the CLT with tax exempt bonds, he or she avoids the income tax problem year to year. But, if the donor funds the trust with bonds, the charitable distributions of the CLT must not be higher than the combined income of the bonds plus management fees. If so, the CLT would be forced to sell assets, possibly incurring capital gains that the donor does not want and even drilling the value of the account down.

If the donor sets up a grantor lead trust and dies before the term is over, the trust will be taxed as a complex trust for the rest of its term. This means it will pay federal income tax for any income earned that is above the required payout to charity. The trust is taxed in the highest federal income tax bracket at a very low rate ($9,350 for 2003 pre-JGTRRA of 2003). Thus, you can understand that managing the income after the donor dies is extremely important.

Qualified Nongrantor Lead Trust Tax Considerations

A nongrantor lead trust is a tax paying entity at trust tax rates. The trust has the same tax brackets as individuals, but the income ceiling for the tax rates in a trust (or estate) goes up very quickly. For example, in January of 2003, the individual tax rate for the 38.6% federal income tax bracket starts at $311,951. However, the highest tax rate of 38.6% starts at only $9,350 for trusts. Any amount paid to a charity is a deduction for the lead trust. However, it is important to note that any amount of income exceeding the lead trust payment is taxable at these ridiculous trust rates. Therefore, the payout rate for the lead trust should be at least higher than the income rate earned in the trust.

When the lead trust distributes to the heirs at the end of the trust term, the cost basis and holding period from the lead trust gets transferred to the heirs. Therefore, the heirs have to deal with the capital gain tax on assets distributed to them at a low cost basis. Of course, there is no capital gain tax until the heirs sell the appreciated assets.

GENERATION-SKIPPING TRANSFER TAX ISSUES

Sometimes, people want to benefit grandchildren (or grandnieces/nephews) rather than children. Perhaps the children are financially secure and don't need additional assets that would serve only to inflate their own estates. Instead, they want to leave an inheritance to their grandchildren. As you know, there is a generation-skipping transfer tax imposed on amounts above the applicable lifetime GST tax exemption. For 2003, the GST tax exemption is $1,120,000 ($2,240,000 for couples). See Chapter II-3 for a discussion and explanation of how the GST tax works.

For a large estate, the GST tax (when added to the regular gift or estate tax) will eat up a large amount in taxes. However, charitably motivated donors can use a lead trust to reduce or eliminate the gift or estate tax and the generation-skipping transfer tax while providing significant amounts to charity in the meantime.

Bear in mind that the GST tax and the federal estate tax are repealed for 2010; however, they both return in 2011 unless Congress makes the repeal permanent. These are the terms of the Economic Growth and Tax Relief Reconciliation Act of 2001.

If the GST tax and the estate tax repeal are made permanent, then nongrantor lead trusts would be rendered useless for GST tax and estate tax purposes, but they would still have a role for gift tax purposes. (The gift tax exemption was frozen at $1,000,000 by EGTRRA of 2001.)

When would you want to explore with a donor a charitable lead trust to avoid GST tax? Given the uncertainty of the laws under which we are working in 2003, I would recommend that you check with your attorney. If you own this book for a while, you will be working under completely different laws soon enough.

EXCESS BUSINESS HOLDINGS AND JEOPARDY INVESTMENTS

Charitable lead trusts have restrictions on the kind of assets that can be held in the trust depending on certain conditions. The restrictions come from the I.R.S. code sections dealing with private foundations. The trustee cannot have investments that would be risky such as buying on margin, trading in commodity futures, or investing in oil or gas wells, *etc.* These may be classified as jeopardy investments.

If the charity's income interest in a lead trust is greater than 60% of the original funding amount, then the trust cannot have what I.R.S. calls "excess business holdings." If the trustee is deemed to have excess business holdings, he or she has five years to get rid of them. If not, the trust will be subject to a 5% tax on the value of such holdings. The tax is imposed on the greatest amount of excess holdings at any time during the taxable year; plus, a tax of 200% is imposed if the excess business holdings are not disposed of by the end of the charitable lead trust's tax year.

From the I.R.S. web site:

1. A foundation and its disqualified persons together may not hold more than 20% of the voting stock of a corporation conducting a business that is not substantially related to the exempt purpose of the foundation. If someone else can be shown to have control of the business, the 20% limit is raised to 35%.

2. If disqualified persons hold more than 20% of the voting stock, or 35% where someone else has control, a foundation must also dispose of its nonvoting stock.

And, this, also from the I.R.S web site:

1. A private foundation is not subject to the excess business holdings tax unless it has an equity interest in a business enterprise.
2. The term "business enterprise" includes the active conduct of a trade or business, including any activity regularly carried on for the production of income from the sale of goods or the performance of services and that constitutes an unrelated trade or business under IRC 513. Where an activity carried on for profit constitutes an unrelated trade or business, no part of such trade or business is excluded from the classification of a business enterprise merely because it does not result in a profit.

The part of the I.R.S. Code that covers these issues is quite extensive and you can find it in the Internal Revenue Manual at www.irs.gov/irm/index.html. If your donor is planning on funding a charitable lead trust with anything other than cash or publicly traded securities, bring your tax councel in on the discussions early. Also, if the donor wants to be the trustee, he or she needs an attorney experienced with the laws that govern vehicles as complex as charitable lead trusts.

QUESTIONS AND ANSWERS ABOUT CHARITABLE LEAD TRUSTS

Q. Can a private foundation be the income beneficiary of a charitable lead trust?
A. Yes, but there may be a self-dealing problem if the donor or the donor's family run the foundation. The private foundation could change its by-laws to prohibit any disqualified persons from making decisions about the distribution of income payments received from the CLT.

Q. Can the trustee be empowered to select the charities year to year?
A. Yes. But, the trustee cannot make CLT payments to any entity over which the donor has control over the use of the funds. The trustee, if empowered by the governing instrument, can allocate the income interest among multiple charities and pick them year to year.

Q. For a testamentary CLT, how does the donor know the variables in advance in order state the payout and the term of years to achieve the estate tax savings or the generation-skipping transfer tax savings he or she wants?
A. The I.R.S. allows the donor to use a formula to determine the variables as of the date of death. As long as the payments are determinable when the trust is funded, there is no problem in having the exact terms determined on the date of death.

Q. Is there such a thing as a net income CLT?
A. No.

Q. Can additional contributions be made to a CLT?
A. Yes for both lead unitrusts and lead annuity trusts, but special rules apply for lead annuity trusts. Consult with your attorney doing such a thing.

Q. Can the donor retain the right to select the charities year to year?
A. Yes, legally. However, if the donor has the right to select the charities each year, the value of the lead trust will be included in the donor's estate if he or she dies prior to the trust's termination.

Q. Can a lead trust be set up to fulfill the obligations of a pledge?
A. No. As with a CRT, a donor can't use a CLT to fulfill the obligations of a binding pledge.

SUMMARY

You won't run into many lead trusts, but, in the right situation, the qualified nongrantor lead trust might work. The viability of the lead trust (grantor and nongrantor) is related directly to income tax rates, gift tax rates, estate tax rates, and GST tax rates. Their usefulness will change as the tax laws change.

The last chapter of this section is about assets that could have double taxation at death if not handled strategically. This is a category called income in respect of a decedent of which the most common asset is an IRA or retirement plan.

Chapter II–12

INCOME IN RESPECT OF A DECEDENT (IRD)

INTRODUCTION

In the other tax-related chapters of the book, you learned about types of gift vehicles and how they work or specific tax laws as they relate to donor considerations. This chapter is different because it describes a category of income that the I.R.S. treats differently than all other categories of income. Planned giving officers should take the time to understand the concepts described here or they may miss charitable giving opportunities about which their donors are unaware.

The topic of income in respect of a decedent is covered under the following main headings:

- overview of income in respect of a decedent;
- examples of IRD assets;
- lifetime charitable gifts of IRD assets;
- charitable gifts of IRD assets at death;
- special exception for profit sharing plans;
- summary.

OVERVIEW OF INCOME IN RESPECT OF A DECEDENT

Income in respect of a decedent is a concept of tax law that comes into play at death. It includes any assets, income, or other payments that would have been ordinary income for the donor if he or she received them while living. Most people immediately think of IRAs or retirement plans in this category, but there are many others.

Since the donor would have reported such assets or income as ordinary income if received during lifetime, the donor's estate must treat them as taxable income at death. This has the unfortunate result that the IRD assets may be taxed twice at death (federal income tax and federal estate tax). For purposes of this discussion, let's assume that Congress does not make the repeal of the estate tax permanent after 2010.

For 2004, the highest federal income tax bracket is 35% and the highest federal estate tax bracket is 48%. Although the decedent receives an income tax deduction for the estate tax attributable to the IRD asset, the tax bite of imposing both the estate tax and the income tax on one asset is confiscatory. Donors often don't know about this at all. Therefore, they make heirs beneficiaries of IRD assets, risking unnecessary tax erosion, and select for charitable bequests assets that would have been more appropriate for the heirs.

In general, when an heir of the decedent is named as the recipient of an item of IRD, then the heir would be responsible for the income tax (at his or her own tax rates), and would also receive an income tax deduction for the share of estate tax attributable to that asset.

Sometimes, IRD is ordinary income and sometimes it is long-term capital gain income. For example, installment payments received from the person who bought your vacation home includes both ordinary income (the interest on the note), and capital gain income. If you die with payments still due, your estate will have two-tier IRD. Or, if you sold long-term stock at a gain and died before receiving the proceeds, then any gain attributable to the sale would be long-term capital gain IRD.

Under current tax law (except 2010), an individual who inherits capital assets receives a stepped-up cost basis, either the value on the date of death or the value on the alternate valuation date. (See Chapter II-10 for a complete discussion of the transfer tax system.) In addition, the inherited capital asset is deemed to be a long-term capital asset regardless of how long it was held by the donor. Ordinarily, an individual would have to hold an asset 12 months plus a day for it to be considered long-term capital gain property. Therefore, heirs get more mileage from a bequest of an appreciated long-term capital asset than they would from an item of IRD. Since the item of IRD receives no step-up in basis at death, the heir of an IRD asset picks up whatever the decedent's tax liability would have been.

Therefore, donors who own both capital assets and assets that would be IRD must consider carefully how to structure transfers at death to both heirs and charities so as to minimize the taxes that could be imposed.

EXAMPLES OF IRD ASSETS

As a planned giving officer, you should be able to recognize IRD assets when you are working with your donors. Some IRD assets present particularly attractive options for charitable giving, especially if the donor is already charitably motivated. Here is a list of some things that would be considered IRD in the decedent's estate.

- deferred capital gain as installment sale;
- accrued interest on savings bonds;
- commissions earned but not received at death (real estate, insurance, brokerage);
- remaining payments from lottery winnings;
- unused vacation pay;
- grain in storage, cranberries in a bog, harvested fruit, or bales of hay;
- unpaid fees from people or firms for whom the decedent provided services (doctors, attorneys, *etc.*);
- payments to a survivor annuitant from a joint and survivor commercial annuity;
- IRAs and retirement plans;
- profit sharing plans;
- deferred compensation;
- nonqualified stock options.

The above list gives you an idea of the kinds of items that are IRD. There are others, but you get the idea. In dealing with IRD assets, a donor must consider the consequences of making charitable gifts of such assets either during lifetime or at death. Moreover, there are some very creative charitable giving options for certain situations.

LIFETIME CHARITABLE GIFTS OF IRD ASSETS

Donors periodically ask if they can contribute U.S. savings bonds to charity. A more common question is whether they can make a current charitable gift from an IRA or retirement plan. Or, what about the large pot of deferred compensation? Legally, donors can give you any of these things. But, under current law, there are unfavorable federal income tax consequences.

In general, if an individual withdraws, sells, or otherwise disposes of during lifetime an item that would be IRD at death, he or she must report any amount above the cost basis as ordinary income.

In general, U.S. savings bonds have accrued interest that has never been taxed. If the donor holds the bonds to maturity, he or she will receive the face value of the bond, plus the interest which is fully taxable as ordinary income. The U.S. Government does not allow savings bonds to be given away during lifetime since the rules for such bonds are different than for regular corporate bonds. The donor would have to sell the bond, report and pay income tax on the accrued interest, and contribute cash to the charity. The donor's charitable deduction is diluted by the tax paid on the interest.

The same problem occurs with IRAs or retirement plan assets. In general these assets are mostly ordinary income. Some people may have a small amount of cost basis, but most contributions to retirement accounts are pre-tax dollars. Therefore, neither the contributions to the plan nor the appreciation in the plan has ever been taxed. A donor who makes a transfer from a retirement plan to a charity during lifetime must report the withdrawal as ordinary income, then he or she gives cash to the charity for which he or she receives a federal income tax charitable deduction.

I remember receiving an in-kind transfer of about $25,000 of securities from a donor's TIAA-CREF retirement plan to fund a charitable gift annuity at Boston College. Since the entire value of the stock was ordinary income to the donor, we deemed the gift annuity to be funded with the equivalent amount of cash, even though actual shares of stock were transferred to us. He reported the full amount of the withdrawal and claimed a federal income tax deduction for setting up a gift annuity.

Note: As of this writing in September of 2003, the House of Representatives passed The Charitable Giving Act (H.R. 7), a tax bill that would loosen the rules for lifetime transfers of IRAs to charity. The Senate passed a different version of the bill earlier in 2003 (CARE Act, S.476). Variations on the concept of a charitable "roll-over" of an IRA have been inserted into many different tax bills going back many years. Since final provisions of any tax bill will be hashed out by the House-Senate Conference Committee, check with your attorney to see if the rules for lifetime charitable gifts of IRAs have changed.

CHARITABLE GIFTS OF IRD ASSETS AT DEATH

In general, there are far better results for a donor who makes charitable gifts of IRD assets at death than there are under current law for lifetime gifts of the same assets. Following are some considerations and strategies that can allow a charitably motivated donor to support your organization at death while saving significant taxes that could potentially dilute the value of his or her estate as well as the value accruing to the heirs.

Outright Gifts At Death of IRD Assets

When a donor provides at death for a direct transfer to a public charity, the entire value of the IRD asset distributes to the charity free of both federal income tax and federal estate tax. Since a public charity is tax exempt, it pays no income tax when disposing of the asset. In addition, the estate receives a charitable estate tax deduction for the entire amount of the gift, without the charitable contribution ceilings imposed for federal income tax purposes.

Some IRD assets are specific items that could be identified in the donor's distribution plan. For example, the donor could make a specific bequest to charity of U.S. savings bonds owned at death. Or, the donor could change the beneficiary designation on the relevant contract for a commercial annuity, IRA, or retirement plan. (Note: a donor's spouse must sign a waiver agreeing to the transfer to charity of a qualified retirement plan but not for an IRA.) It is important that the asset go directly to the charity and not through the estate first. Otherwise, the asset may still be taxed in the estate prior to being distributed to the charity.

Even if the donor does not provide for a specific IRD asset to go to charity, many estate planning attorneys recommend standard language in a will or living trust so that, lacking specific reference to an item of IRD, charitable bequests will be satisfied first with assets considered to be IRD. Following is sample language, but donors should get their own language from their attorneys.

> *"I instruct that all charitable gifts, bequests and devises should be made, to the extent possible, from assets that constitute Income in Respect of a Decedent, as that term is defined in the Internal Revenue Code."*

In the case of an IRA, it is important to note that a donor can name charities and heirs as beneficiaries on the same IRA account. When a charity is named together with an heir on the beneficiary form, there is no adverse consequence to the heirs as long as the charity receives its share by December 31 of the year following the year the donor dies. Depending on the class of beneficiary (spouse or non-spouse) and age at death (before or after minimum required distributions), the heirs will be able to exercise their options for dealing with the IRA the same as they would without a charitable beneficiary. (Note: That was not always true.)

To make a charitable gift of an IRA cleaner, the donor could carve off a portion of an IRA account and put it into a separate account with the charity or charities named as beneficiaries upon the death of the owner. When the owner begins required distributions, he or she can select which of the two accounts to use for the mandatory distributions.

Even if the federal estate tax repeal in EGGTRA of 2001 is made permanent, there will still be a value to making charitable gifts of IRD assets at death because such a gift will save any income tax at death.

Since some kinds of retirement plans terminate at death, only the kinds of retirement plans that represent an account can be used as charitable gifts at death, *e.g.*, IRAs, 401(k)s, 403(b)s and defined contribution plans.

An individual can also leave nonstatutory stock options or deferred compensation to charity at death and avoid both the federal income and estate tax.

Life Income Gifts of IRD Assets At Death

While there are many categories of income or assets considered to be IRD at death, the most common one, deserving of special emphasis in this chapter is the IRA. Trillions of dollars are held in retirement plans, including IRAs, in the United States. Often, a retirement plan or IRA is the largest asset in one's estate. Therefore, the possibilities for charitable gifts with these assets are significant. Unfortunately, donors often don't know the severe potential for taxation at death or the options for using them wisely in charitable giving. In addition to providing to charity an outright gift at death with IRD assets, the donor could consider transferring such assets to a life income plan (charitable remainder trust, charitable gift annuity, or pooled income fund.)

As mentioned above, legislation pending at the time of this writing would loosen the rules for lifetime gifts of IRAs. Specifically, pending tax bills would make it possible for individuals who meet age requirements to transfer IRAs outright to charity during lifetime or to life income plans without requiring them to report for income tax purposes the ordinary income otherwise taxable to them. However, there would be no charitable deduction for any amount exceeding the cost basis. If the legislation passes, donors would have options during lifetime to use IRAs for charitable giving.

Meanwhile, under current law the most advantageous time to make charitable gifts of IRAs is at death.

Example:

Tom has an IRA valued at $2 million. He wants to provide for his second wife but also wants to control the ultimate distribution of the principal. Tom names a charitable remainder trust as the beneficiary of his IRA and provides for payments to his wife for life. (See Chapter II-9 on CRTs.) His estate will receive a charitable deduction for the remainder interest going to charity and a marital deduction for the CRT payments to his wife. Thus, the entire value avoids federal estate tax. Moreover, there is no income tax on the IRA at death. The wife will report income from the CRT each year. On her death, the remaining principal will distribute to one or more charities.

The concept of leaving a retirement account to a CRT is fairly simple, especially when a spouse is the beneficiary. However, Chris Hoyt, professor of law at the University of Missouri School of Law, wrote an excellent article on this topic in the April 2002 issue of *Planned Giving Today*. He points out that there are instances where it would be better to make an outright gift of a portion of the IRA to charity and structure the rest of the IRA to pay to a designated beneficiary.

Chris says, "If estate tax will be due, my general recommendation is to ditch the CRT strategy and instead make outright bequests from retirement accounts to charities and then structure 'stretch IRAs' for friends and family."

This is a very complicated topic since you would need to have knowledge of the rules under which IRAs and retirement plans operate depending on the type of retirement plan, age of death of the owner, the age of the designated beneficiary or beneficiaries, and whether the designated beneficiary is a spouse or other person. A complete discussion of these issues is beyond the scope of this book.

Let me quote two paragraphs from the article referenced above.

"By way of background, unlike most inheritances, a distribution from an inherited IRA produces taxable income: 'income in respect of a decedent' (IRD). The person who receives such income can usually claim an income tax deduction for the federal estate tax that was triggered by the IRA's inclusion in the decedent's estate.

If, however, the IRA was first distributed to a CRT and then the CRT makes distributions to a beneficiary, the I.R.S. has ruled that the CRT effectively strips that income tax deduction away. The numbers can be huge. A CRT might deprive the beneficiary of a $40,000 income tax deduction for a $100,000 IRA that was transferred to the CRT."

There are a couple of issues that will affect whether a transfer of a retirement plan to a CRT, PIF, or CGA is a good idea. Under certain instances, the entire amount of the retirement plan must be paid out to the beneficiary within five years of the date of death. That could trigger a large amount of income tax either to the estate or to the beneficiary upon receiving the assets. Such a result could diminish the value of the asset significantly. According to Chris Hoyt, "Many employers have policies that require a deceased employee's entire account balance in a profit-sharing plan or a 401(k) to be distributed shortly after the employee's death, even though much longer payout periods are legally permissible." Instead, by providing a distribution to a CRT, there is no immediate loss to income taxes and the life income plan will retain all of its value to pay income to the beneficiary.

By reviewing the follow sample cases, you can see that there is a lot of uncertainty about what will happen to an IRA depending on the age of the donor's death.

- If the owner dies before 70½ and names a non-spouse beneficiary, the plan will have to be distributed within 5 years unless the beneficiary starts payments based on life expectancy before the end of the year following the owner's death.

- If the owner dies before 70½ and names a charity and a designated beneficiary (spouse or non-spouse), the plan must be distributed within five years unless separate accounts are set up.

- If the owner dies before 70½ and names both a spouse and non-spouse, the payments would be for the life expectancy of the oldest unless separate accounts are set up and they must start payments before the end of the year after the owner's death or have everything distribute within five years.

In general, if the owner dies after 70½, the IRA can be paid over the life expectancy of the single person named or on the life expectancy of the oldest person named (unless they set up separate accounts.) When the account can pay out over the beneficiary's life expectancy, there is no loss up front from the income tax in the donor's estate. But, if the circumstances result in the plan assets being paid out quickly, then the loss to taxes could be confiscatory.

Example:

Jane has a 401(k) with her employer. She is a retired widow with one daughter. Currently, she is taking mandatory withdrawals from her 401(k). Her daughter, Ellen, age 56, is the designated beneficiary upon her death. When Jane dies, the company requires that the entire remaining amount be distributed to the beneficiary. Ellen would not choose to take the whole thing up front, report the amount in her 35% bracket and invest the balance. Plus, there could be additional loss to federal estate taxes (depending on the lifetime exemption for the year of death). Note: The estate tax exemption rises to $3.5 million by 2009 under EGTRRA of 2001, so Jane may not have an estate tax.)

Instead, Jane provides for a distribution of the entire 401(k) to a CRT that will make payments to Jane for life. Jane's estate will receive a charitable estate tax deduction for the remainder interest going to charity, and the CRT, being a tax-exempt entity, will pay no up-front income tax when the trust is funded. Mary will report income each year that she receives payments from the CRT. Meanwhile, it has the potential to grow tax free.

Jane names her church and the hospice program that cared for her deceased husband as remainder beneficiaries of the CRT.

Don't forget that Jane would be taking required minimum distributions from her retirement plan as of April 1 following the year she turns 70½. She won't know exactly how much money will be remaining in her 401(k) at her death. (She could also close it out and take the whole thing, albeit with a heavy income tax under most circumstances.)

When a donor provides for a distribution to a life income plan at death, he or she has to take into account the minimum charitable remainder requirements for CRTs. If the beneficiary is too young, or the payout is too high, the CRT may not meet the 10% remainder test and will be disqualified.

Although there are many things to consider when structuring a gift of an IRA or other retirement plan, under the right circumstances, such a strategy may be perfect.

SPECIAL EXCEPTION FOR PROFIT SHARING PLANS

A profit sharing plan is a type of retirement account run by an employer, for example, a 401(k). According to the Profit Sharing Council of America, there are about 29 million participants with $1.5 trillion in 250,000 employer-sponsored retirement plans in the U.S. Moreover, many have a high percentage of employer stock in the plan. For example, a recent report shows a very high percentage of employer stock in their own plans (Proctor and Gamble with 94.7%, Sherwin Williams with 85.5%, Pfizer with 85.5%, Anheuser Bush with 81.6%, and Coca Cola with 81.5%).

Ordinarily, a withdrawal from a retirement plan is treated as ordinary income by the owner. However, employer stock inside of a profit sharing plan receives different treatment.

Within certain guidelines, employers can set up their own rules and restrictions for the retirement plans offered to employees, but they generally want the participant to remove his or her assets after terminating employment with the company. A common practice for retired or terminated employees is to roll-over the assets into a personal IRA account following termination or retirement. A roll-over of one type of retirement plan into an IRA does not result in recognition of tax to the taxpayer. Following the roll-over, the entire account will continue to grow tax deferred until the owner makes withdrawals, at which time 100% of the withdrawals are ordinary income.

However, if the participant owns shares of the employer's stock in his or her profit sharing plan, he or she can request an in-kind distribution of that stock. In general, the participant would need to meet certain restrictions including being in the plan for 5 years, reaching age 59½, and terminating employment with the company. Becoming disabled is also a condition under which a participant can exercise this option.

Instead of being treated as all ordinary income, any net unrealized appreciation (NUA) in the employer stock will be capital gain and is neither reportable nor taxable until the individual sells the shares. Some companies add their own stock as matching contributions to these plans. That portion of the employer stock may also have net unrealized appreciation. The entire amount of its own stock contributed by the employer also enjoys this benefit.

However, the individual will have to report as ordinary income the amount of cost basis in any shares purchased with deductible contributions. This presents a problem to the individual who receives the in-kind distribution of employer shares, *e.g.*, how to come up with the money to pay income tax on the cost basis without being forced to sell the asset to raise the cash. Short of selling the employer shares to raise the cash, thus triggering the capital gain, too, there are not a lot of options.

In a private letter ruling, PLR 200335017, the I.R.S. ruled that shares of employer stock received from such a distribution can be contributed to a charitable remainder trust. Since the CRT is a tax exempt entity, there is no tax when the CRT sells the entire lot of employer stock in order to diversify its investments.

Example.

John has a 401(k) plan with Proctor and Gamble. He has participated in the plan for more than five years before retiring at age 65. His account is invested 94.7% in P&G stock. He has several options for dealing with his retirement plan following his departure.

1) He can leave it where it is and begin required minimum distributions by April 1 following the year he turns 70½. All payments will be ordinary income.

2) He can roll the entire account over to an IRA with no tax consequence, control the investments himself, and begin required minimum distributions by April 1 following the year he turns 70½. All payments will be ordinary income.

3) He can receive an in-kind distribution of the P&G stock and roll-over the remaining balance to an IRA. He will report and pay income tax on the cost basis of the employer stock. The roll-over to the IRA incurs no tax until such time as he makes a withdrawal. When John sells the P&G stock, he will pay tax at capital gain rates.

4) John puts the P&G stock into a CRT with himself as beneficiary and his spouse as survivor beneficiary. The income tax paid on the cost basis of the stock is offset (wholly or partially, depending on the variables) by the federal income tax deduction received for creating the CRT. When the CRT sells the P&G stock, there is no immediate capital gain tax because the CRT is a tax exempt entity.

In option #4, John solves a problem and accomplishes important goals. He provides an income to himself and to his wife. He offsets the tax on the cost basis of his P&G shares with a charitable deduction. He avoids paying the up-front capital gain tax on a sale of the P&G shares if he sold them himself. Plus, the remainder of the CRT will distribute to one or more charities. This is a great plan.

If you have a prospect who tells you that he or she is retired and has a profit sharing plan with his or her former employer, the chances are good that there will be employer stock in that plan. Get advice from your tax counsel and see if the strategy described here will work. Bear in mind that a private letter ruling is only valid for the taxpayer who received it.

SUMMARY

It would be unusual for a person to read this whole book from the beginning since individual chapters provide detail on specific topics that one might need at a particular time. Nonetheless, you have come to the final chapter in Part II. Some issues or gift assets were not covered simply because the field of tax law is immense. I apologize for leaving out particular topics that might be of interest to you. Where this book leaves off, there are numerous resources listed in Appendix III. I recommend that you subscribe to one monthly tax newsletter and one complete tax service. You should also join your local planned giving council if there is one in your area.

Part III of this book has nine more chapters to round out your knowledge and provide guidance when you need it.

PART III

RUNNING A SUCCESSFUL PLANNED GIVING PROGRAM

INTRODUCTION

There are many components to running a planned giving program. If you have made your way through Part I and Part II, you may be overwhelmed, especially if you are new to planned giving. Or, maybe you already have a mature planned giving program, but are looking for some new ideas. I structured this book so that you can focus on one thing at a time. In this narrative part of the book, there are nine chapters to do just that. Some of the material in these chapters is unchanged from the Revised Second Edition. However, I updated the advice when appropriate to reflect a different kind of fund raising climate than we had in 1991, when the last edition was published. I hope you will find these chapters helpful, whether you are new to the field or a veteran planned giving officer.

Chapter III-1
How To Create Effective Print Materials For Your Planned Giving Program

Prior to the computer, the production of print materials was very cumbersome, time consuming, and costly. Today, your publications department can design and produce brochures in a fraction of the time that it formerly took. You also have a many more choices for flexibility than ever before, but printing brochures is an expensive proposition. In a small shop, you could manage quite well creating a series of documents on your own computer and printing them only as needed. The chapter walks you through the considerations for producing effective planned giving materials to support your program.

Chapter III-2
How To Use Volunteers

As an integral part of developing and running a successful planned giving program, you will have to consider how and when to use volunteers. In Chapter III-2, I have provided the framework for working with one volunteer or with many so that you can tap the full potential of your program without having the volunteers control you.

Chapter III-3
Cultivation And Stewardship

In planned giving, you will have many categories of prospects and donors, each with varying gift potential and different needs. You cannot treat everyone with the same amount of attention. The relationships with some will require more time than others. Unless you make rules and set priorities, you'll find yourself scattered and ineffective, wasting time on low priority donors at the expense of those who have much greater potential. This chapter discusses the considerations for planning and managing a cultivation and stewardship program in an efficient and productive fashion.

Chapter III-4
Working With Your Colleagues

Running a successful planned giving program is more than getting gifts. You don't work in a vacuum, though it may feel that way at times. You must strive to create an environment within the institution such that planned giving is an integral part of the overall development effort. By building good working relationships with your colleagues, you can ensure a happy and productive life as a planned giving officer. Chapter III-4 provides tips and considerations for getting planned giving into the main stream.

Chapter III-5
Integrating Planned Giving Into A Campaign

No matter where you are working, your organization will launch a capital campaign. Depending on the institutional culture, however, one of two things will happen: 1) planned giving will flourish with renewed energy and interest from colleagues, or 2) planned giving will be put on hold. This chapter provides honest advice on what to do when you see a campaign coming.

Chapter III-6
Planned Giving In A One-Person Shop

For the person running a one-person shop, this chapter is for you. Any amount of planned giving is better than none. If you are all by yourself, you may be stretched to your limits. Plus, you may feel ill equipped to add such a complicated, technical, and confusing area of fund raising to your daily activities. You are not alone. However, with the help of this chapter, you can identify certain limited tasks and activities that can make a big difference to your development program.

Chapter III-7
Planned Giving And Major Gifts: Adversaries Or Partners

This chapter is both philosophical and practical. It discusses the working relationship between the planned giving office and the major gifts office. Often, the planned giving staff and major gifts staff work as adversaries instead of partners. In such an environment, the institution loses many gifts. The corporate culture of your development office may not be within your control, but with the help of this chapter, you will have some ideas on how to make it better.

Chapter III-8
The Ultimate Gift

Periodically, we hear about a staggering gift at a peer institution. We are all jealous and wonder if such a windfall will ever happen to us. In reality, these once-in-a-lifetime gifts are not windfalls at all. When the institution reveals the details, it usually cites involvement by the donor in the institution's activities for decades. To be the recipient of one of these transforming gifts, you need to raise the cultivation level several notches above the usual. I know you will be inspired by this chapter, and I hope you can incorporate the strategies described here into your program.

Chapter III-9
Managing Your Planned Giving Assets

Finally, the last chapter of this book discusses issues and considerations for managing your deferred giving assets. If you don't pay close attention to this process, your program will fall apart and you will have angry donors. People will not contribute a second or a third time if they experience delays or other problems with their gift transactions. The individual chapters in Part II provide detailed information about the specific administrative procedures required of different gift vehicles. Chapter III-9 provides an overview of the issues involved in working with your fiduciary manager—your own business office or an outside manager. In addition, I have provided a sample Request for Proposal so that you don't have to reinvent the wheel when it is time to change managers.

Chapter III–1

HOW TO CREATE EFFECTIVE PRINT MATERIALS FOR YOUR PLANNED GIVING PROGRAM

When an institution starts a planned giving program, it is making an institutional statement. Instead of focusing only on current operating needs, the institution is now looking to the future, perhaps for the first time in a public way. Such a shift in philosophy needs to be communicated to the constituency. Beyond the obvious objective of gaining financial security comes the challenge of convincing the constituency that there is a need, a long-term plan, a compelling case. Will the organization be around in 20 years? 50 years? 100 years? Will the purposes for which it currently exists be viable into the next century?

Ann W. Caldwell, President of the Massachusetts General Hospital Institute of Health Professions, says, "People who make major gifts to an organization really are making an investment in its leadership." This simple statement is at the very core of your challenge in planned giving. Does your organization's leadership inspire faith, dedication, and confidence from your constituency such that a program for long-term support can succeed? Is the leadership itself committed enough to set the pace? Does your constituency even know your leadership? If not, regardless of the money you spend on staff, brochures or other planned giving activities, the underlying perception of the institution may undermine all that you are trying to accomplish.

Therefore, the shift from focusing only on current needs toward the creation of long-term stability carries with it the additional challenge of presenting the organization in a completely new light. One way to do this is through print materials. Print materials allow you to get the message out and also serve the following purposes:

1. create an image;
2. provide information to your constituency;
3. save you time by answering questions for which you would otherwise have to prepare a letter;
4. lend credibility to the planned giving program;
5. generate leads;
6. provide reference tools for volunteer solicitors;
7. increase the visibility and reach of your program.

For purposes of this discussion, print materials include:

- a general planned giving brochure;
- one or more companion brochures;
- planned giving ads;
- planned giving inserts;
- planned giving newsletters;
- integration of planned giving into other fund raising materials.

Each of these items is discussed separately.

HOW TO CREATE AN EFFECTIVE WAYS OF GIVING BROCHURE

For the institution starting a planned giving program, it is important to develop a marketing piece that gives credibility to the program and which shows that you are serious about taking a new direction. In the early years, your momentum will build slowly. Thus, the only evidence that you have a planned giving program will be the existence of a brochure that says you do. Through the brochure, you are creating a perception of strength before you actually have it. After several years, your results and successes can be highlighted in a new version of the same brochure.

You need three things to produce a brochure: 1) money to pay for it, 2) time to write it, and 3) knowledge of planned giving. This book provides the knowledge; the other two are not so easily acquired. If you have neither the money nor the time to produce a brochure, you still can do a lot of planned giving. Many of this country's largest donors probably have never seen a planned giving brochure. Their charitable gifts more appropriately have been inspired through personal visits and personalized proposals, or from advice of an advisor. You, too, will find many prospects for whom a brochure is too general, or who require information beyond that which reasonably can be included in a brochure. Do not let the lack of a brochure stop you from contacting, cultivating, and soliciting prospects.

However, you cannot always hop the next plane to visit a prospect. Further, your board of trustees and other volunteer solicitors will need something to bring with them to prospect visits. Equally likely, many prospects do not know what they want. They will say things like, "Just send me information on how I can support the institution." It is almost impossible to respond effectively to these people with anything less than a four- to five-page letter. A planned giving brochure, then, serves multiple purposes, but, remember, it is only as good as you are on the follow-up call (discussed later in this chapter).

If you have a small budget, don't despair. You can purchase a fine generic brochure at minimal cost. Many firms listed in Appendix IV produce planned giving brochures to serve every need. Many of these can be personalized to suit your needs for an additional charge, or you can use the standard version with your institution's name on the front and back covers. The price *per* copy decreases for larger orders. These firms will be happy to send you sample copies for free or for a very minimal cost.

Perhaps, however, you are in a position to produce your own brochure. How should you proceed? Several factors come together to make an effective brochure. They include content, narrative, type face, size, color, contrast, paper stock, photography, and, of course, design. Together, these considerations create an image of the institution.

Bear in mind that a comprehensive "Ways of Giving" brochure is very expensive so you should consider how you are going to use it before jumping to this piece.

Here is a suggestion for what could be in your brochure:

Content

1. A listing of the board of trustees on the front inside cover as well as a listing of the members of a planned giving committee if you have one. Most likely, you will not have a planned giving committee during the early months of your planned giving program when the first brochure is in production.

2. A table of contents on page 1.

3. A message from the chairman of the board on page 2. This message introduces the program, highlights the need for long-term support, and explains briefly what is in the brochure.

4. A summary of your institution's mission on page 3.

5. A summary of ways to give. Following is a list of the kinds of gifts you need to cover:

    *   Gifts of appreciated securities;
    *   Life income plans
        - Pooled income fund (optional because you may not be using your pooled income fund)
        - Gift annuities (requires approval by the Board of Trustees)
        - Charitable remainder trusts;

- Real estate;
- Life insurance;
- Bequests;
- Retirement plans and IRAs
- Lead Trusts;
- Other—art and antiques.

Keep the discussion of each gift plan to one page. Here is a general summary of what you need to include about each gift option:

- Two paragraphs explaining the benefits to the donor and/or the general operation of the gift. Refer to the individual chapters in Part II for language and ideas on how to talk about the gift arrangements.

- A case study (preferably of a real donor) illustrating these benefits. (Note: You must first secure permission to use the donor's name.) Following are guidelines on developing an effective case study:

  - To be able to show savings in capital gain taxes for gifts of appreciated property (securities, real estate, art or antiques), use a ratio of 2:5, for example, property with a cost basis of $4,000 and a market value of $10,000, or property with a cost basis of $40,000 and a market value of $100,000.

  - Assume that the donor is in the highest marginal tax rate.

  - I.R.S. Discount Rate: For any example where the charitable deduction is tied to the fluctuating discount rate, include a statement like, "individual results may differ slightly. Please contact us for a personalized example."

  - When illustrating the results from a life income plan, assume a donor's gift property is earning less than your illustrated gift vehicle.

  - Following are gift amounts appropriate for your examples:

    - Gifts of appreciated securities $10,000 - $25,000
    - Life income plans
      - Pooled income fund $10,000 - $25,000
      - Gift annuity $10,000 - $25,000
      - Charitable remainder trusts $100,000 - $300,000
    - Real estate $200,000 - $400,000
    - Life insurance
      - New policy created $500,000   Face Value
      - Old policy transferred $100,000   Face Value
      -    $25,000   Cash Surrender Value
    - Bequests   Varies   Endowed Fund Gift Level
    - Retirement Plans and IRAs $2,000,000   Size of Retirement Plan
    - Lead trusts $1,000,000

  - For life income examples, use a donor age 70 or older, or a couple, age 70/68.

  - For gifts of real estate, assume there is no mortgage on the property.

- A statement of the gift crediting policy.

- A statement of the minimum gift size and other restrictions if applicable.

6. A summary of naming opportunities, incentives, benefits, or privileges associated with the gift options.

7. A response mechanism on the last page (or an insert in the back flap). Following is a response mechanism that is consistent with the themes presented in the brochure and is action oriented:

XYZ Charity

Please send me information about:

_____	Establishing a named fund.
_____	Making a gift of appreciated securities.
_____	Generating income from my gift.
_____	Converting real estate to a new income.
_____	Making a gift through life insurance.
_____	Transferring a personal residence or farm with life tenancy
_____	Providing for XYZ Charity in my will.
_____	Making a gift of art or antiques.
_____	Using my IRA or Retirement Plan to make a charitable gift.
_____	Transferring income to XYZ and principal to my heirs

Date of birth: _____

Type of property I am considering _____

Cost basis _____ Market value _____

Name _____

Street Address _____

City, State, Zip _____

Phone _____ Date _____

Best time to call _____

Send or Fax to: Name, title, institution, street address, city, state, zip code. (phone) (Fax) (e-mail)

8. The name, title, address, phone number, fax number, and e-mail of the person who can provide additional information about the gift plans discussed in the brochure. This information should be on the back inside cover. (Note: The contact information should be included separately from the response mechanism, because the donor may wish to contact you after using the reply mechanism.)

9. A disclaimer on the inside back cover: "The information contained in this brochure is meant as a guide only. Individual results may differ. Please consult your own financial advisor before entering into any gift arrangement."

10. A business reply envelope to suit the size of the reply mechanism. During mailing, the reply envelope should be inserted between the cover and the last page.

Language

In your explanation of gift arrangements, avoid technical language. Develop the case for each gift arrangement by highlighting the ways in which it can solve a problem. Attorneys or financial advisors who have become planned giving officers will be tempted to write extremely precise legal narratives about the gift vehicles rather than stories about people. Don't take this approach. The most effective brochures talk about real donors who had certain desires, assets, and wanted to help the charity. Through the right kind of charitable gift, a donor is able to help the charity in a special way and solves income, capital gain, gift or estate tax problems.

Type Face

The vast majority of prospects who'll be reading your brochure will be age 65 or older. Do not use a type face that is difficult to read, such as script or other embellished forms of type, italics, or type that is too small. Ask your designer to help you select the type face that is the most readable for an elderly audience.

Size

For ease of handling and to allow for compatibility with other standardized materials, the best size is 8½" x 11" or standard for a #10 size envelope. Don't create an odd shape unless the planned giving brochure has to match an odd-shaped campaign brochure, which would also be a mistake.

Color

You want to create a feeling of permanence, stability, soundness, and strength. Your designer will help you select the right color(s) to achieve these objectives for your institution. If you have certain theme colors, by all means, incorporate them.

Contrast

The most effortless reading takes place when there is the greatest possible contrast between the text and the background. This means black type on white or cream paper. As you decrease the contrast between the text and the background, you increase the amount of effort necessary to read the material, and, thus, the likelihood your brochure will not be read. To use color without decreasing readability, add it in titles, headlines, borders, bullets, and captions leaving the general text black on white. Never use red type. It is extremely difficult to read.

Paper Stock

The considerations in paper stock are partly a function of cost and partly a function of the image you are trying to create. The same considerations listed above with regard to color must be considered in selecting the right texture and weight of the paper. You must rely on your designer to help you identify the best possible choice for paper once you have established a budget.

Photography

We've all heard the saying, "A picture is worth a thousand words." And surely nothing adds more to the effectiveness of a brochure than pictures. They remind the donors exactly why your institution is so special. If possible, you should also include pictures of the people who have been used as case studies with an inspirational quote from the donor as a caption. A great quote can draw the reader into the text.

The full outline of the brochure looks like this:

Page	Content
Inside Cover	Listing of Board of Trustees
	Listing of planned giving committee
1	Table of contents
2	Message from chairman of the board
3	Statement of institution's mission
4	Gifts of appreciated securities
5	Pooled income fund (if you use it)
6	Charitable gift annuity
7	Charitable remainder trusts
8	Gifts of real estate
9	Gifts of life insurance

CREATING COMPANION BROCHURES FOR TARGETED MARKETING EFFORTS

In addition to the general ways of giving brochure discussed above, you will find it helpful to create or buy one or more targeted pamphlets or booklets that can serve the following purposes:

- Expand on the gift arrangements discussed in your general planned giving brochure;
- Allow you to target segments of your constituency with specific gift appeals;
- Provide a follow up to lead-generating activities.

There are multiple ways to isolate or combine gift arrangements to serve different target groups. Here are several ideas for developing companion brochures:

1. **How to make a gift of appreciated securities to XYZ Charity.** Includes a discussion of the tax savings and other benefits derived from making a gift of appreciated securities (generally stock and mutual funds). Provides instructions for transferring securities including whom to contact, how to mail securities, how to complete a stock power, how to split a certificate, when the gift is considered complete, and how the gift will be valued.

   Target group. Donors who have made a gift of securities in the past, donors age 50 and over contributing $500 or more to the annual giving program. This brochure should be mailed with your regular annual giving mailings, especially in the fall leading up to year-end giving.

2. **Receiving income from your gift.** Discusses one or more forms of life income gifts. Includes case studies illustrating the comparative benefits of the plans you are discussing. Outlines the procedures for accomplishing each type of gift including minimum gift levels and any restrictions on the age of beneficiaries. Includes gift crediting guidelines as well as a summary of the kinds of assets appropriate for each plan.

   Target group. Primarily individuals age 70 or over who are presumably in retirement already. Separate target group age 50 to 65 who are interested in creating supplemental retirement income, but who are still working. People who have made stock gifts in the past. People who have contributed $5,000 or more in the past. Widows, widowers, and singles. People without children.

3. **Generating a fixed income from your gift.** Discusses the gift annuity. Includes two case studies—one for cash and another for appreciated stock. Sets forth minimum gift and minimum additional gift levels. Explains how to establish a gift annuity. Tells when payments are made and how they will be taxed. Provides a chart showing the single gift annuity rates and a sample for different two-life combinations. Shows the approximate value of the donor's income tax deduction for gifts made at different ages.

   Target group. Primarily individuals 70 or over. Special focus for individuals 80 and over. People who have made stock gifts in the past. Widows, widowers, and singles. People without children.

4. **The XYZ Pooled Income Fund.** Explains the general operation of your pooled income fund or funds including a case study illustrating how a donor can unlock highly appreciated securities, pay

no capital gain tax, increase his or her annual income, generate a current income tax deduction, and support your institution at the same time. Includes information on the investment objective, who manages the fund, minimum gift and additional gift levels, restrictions on the age of the beneficiary if any. Explains the procedure for making a gift including where to get the necessary documents.

Target group. For an income fund invested primarily in bonds, the target group is 70 and over. For a balanced fund, let's say with 65% equities and 35% bonds, the target group is 55-70. For a growth fund invested primarily in growth-oriented equities, the target group is 45-55.

5. **Endowing your annual gift.** This brochure discusses the concept of making a current or deferred gift or bequest sufficiently large to earn an amount equal to the donor's annual gift each year. The donor makes a commitment to perpetuate his or her annual gift. Most endowments have spending limits. For example, at Boston College, the spending limit was 6% of the June 1 value. At Boston University, it was 5% of the average market value of the prior 20 quarters. So, to endow an annual gift of $1,000 at Boston College, it would take $16,666, and at Boston University, it would take $20,000.

   Target group. Individuals with minimum ten year history of annual giving. Individuals capable of making a commitment at least 20 times the size of their annual gift. Bequest prospects.

6. **Providing for XYZ Charity in your will.** Explains the different ways a bequest can be arranged including specific, general, percentage, contingent, or residual and includes language the donor can use to accomplish each of these. Provides the wording for an unrestricted or a restricted bequest. Identifies areas of support to which the donor can earmark the bequest. Outlines naming opportunities. Includes case studies showing tax savings and other benefits. Outlines the usefulness of charitable remainder trusts in charitable planning to provide support for a surviving spouse at death with the remainder to your institution.

   Target group. People age 50 and older. Primary target group would be age 70 and older, widows, widowers, singles, and people without children. People with at least a ten-year history of support.

7. **Three ways to make a gift of real estate.** Using three case studies, the brochure shows the benefits of making an outright gift of real estate, a transfer of real estate to a Flip unitrust, and a gift of a personal residence or farm with life tenancy.

   Target group. People age 50 and older because they are more likely to have inherited real estate from deceased parents. People who are age 75 and older who may be interested in a retained life estate. People who have seasonal addresses like a second home or vacation property.

8. **How to convert real estate to a new income.** This brochure discusses the Flip unitrust. The objective is to show how the donor can make a magnificent gift to your institution, generate a substantial income tax deduction, and convert real estate to a new income without incurring current capital gain taxes.

   Target group. Same demographics as for brochure #7.

9. **How to reduce the cost of passing property to your heirs.** This brochure outlines the concept and operation of a qualified nongrantor lead trust. It includes a case study comparing the results of transferring assets to heirs in a bequest to the results of transferring the same assets through a lead trust paying income to your institution first.

   Target group. People with known substantial wealth and a concern for transferring assets to family members.

10. **Why you need a will.** A brochure with this title can develop the case for a bequest to your institution in the context of explaining the importance of making a will.

   Target group. People age 50 or older. People with children. People who own real estate. Almost anyone.

11. **Planning a gift that provides for your future.** Discusses the deferred gift annuity. Explains through a case study how a donor can establish a future income stream with your institution using cash, appreciated property, (or real estate except where prohibited by state laws), receive a substantial tax deduction, avoid immediate capital gain taxes, and make a major gift. Includes minimum gift and minimum additional gift. Restrictions if any. Provides a chart showing how the rate of return and the charitable deduction increase the longer income is deferred.

   Target group. Individuals 45 to 55.

12. **Using retirement plan assets for charitable giving.** This piece lays out the double taxation of both income tax and estate tax which can eat up 75% of the retirement plan value. Since there is currently no way to withdraw retirement plan assets during lifetime without paying ordinary income tax on the amount, the main focus is the testamentary transfer of retirement plan assets to the charity either on an outright basis or through a testamentary transfer to a charitable remainder trust.

   Target group. People who are a few years younger than the start date for mandatory withdrawals from their retirement plans. Current law requires withdrawals to begin by April 1 following the year the donor turns 70 ½.

In the first year of your planned giving program, you will have a lot to do. Therefore, don't be overwhelmed by the suggestions for all of the above brochures. Your planned giving program can do very well with a brochure about bequests and one about life income plans. Add others as you can.

Considerations For Size Of Your Companion Brochures

You will find that companion brochures serve you best if they fit into a #10 business envelope. Thus, you avoid the necessity of printing more expensive odd-shaped, separate outside envelopes in which to mail them; your institution's regular business envelopes are probably produced in sufficiently large quantities that the cost *per* thousand is less than what you would pay for a separate order of new outside envelopes. The brochures can also be used in a direct-mail initiative. (Note: If you intend to use a mailing house for a direct mail piece, pay attention to the strict size requirements of automatic insertion machines. To be inserted into a #10 envelope by machine, the brochure must leave 1/4" space on all sides after insertion. Otherwise, the mailing house will have to insert the pieces manually and that will cost you significantly more *per* piece.)

Reply Mechanisms For Companion Brochures

Each companion brochure should have its own reply mechanism that can be 1) a tear-off section of the brochure, or 2) a separate card. Both versions appear to work equally well.

Formerly, I felt it was a good idea to include options for many gift arrangements on all reply mechanisms—the cross fertilization strategy. After years of receiving reply cards with every item checked off, I decided this is not a good idea. People simply check off all categories and have no clue what they are doing. Then, you are faced with follow-up activity that is wasteful and unproductive.

Instead, my new opinion (and you can disagree), is to focus only on the content of the mailing piece that you sent. If you target the population properly, the responses will be more qualified and the replies won't drive you into therapy. Give the recipient the chance to say "yes" or "no" to the specific information you provided. You can always expand your discussion later, if necessary.

PLANNED GIVING ADS

Building an awareness of your planned giving program is an ongoing activity. Through placement of ads in your institution's newsletter, magazine, or in other publications, you can plant seeds for the future and generate not only leads but also gifts.

The first task you must undertake is that of getting a commitment of space in your organization's regular publication or publications. You may think that this is simply a question of asking for the space you need and getting it. But, it does not work this way. Negotiating space is often difficult, and part of the problem relates to the structure of the development office. Some organizations have a director of development or a vice president of development who oversees several areas: development, public relations, and publications (and in higher education, the alumni office). This is the proper structure because these operational areas must be coordinated. Under this structure, the director or vice president sets the vision and can easily ask the publication director to give you space. Be aware that some publications directors consider ads to be crass and do not want to damage the editorial integrity of their publication with ads. This is ridiculous. But, if you are dealing with such a mentality, you could use feature stories about planned giving donors instead of traditional ads.

In any event, if you work for a charity where the key external functions all report to your boss, then you are very lucky, and you should be able to get space in every issue of the publication either for an ad or for an article. You should ask for the inside back cover even though you may not get it. Or, ask for the inside back cover in every other issue. Most likely, you are competing with the annual giving program or the campaign for prime space. Negotiation is common in these dealings so be prepared to share space and to compromise. I tried to get the inside back cover of the alumni magazine at Wheaton College, Boston University, and Boston College. I couldn't get it. This is all very political. Instead, I was able to get a full page somewhere else. That worked for me. Consistency is important, so you ought to try for a spot at the same place in the publication each time.

If you work in a development structure in which your boss does not control the publications, your process should be first to discuss the space issue with your immediate boss who will, in turn, address the issue at the next level. Meanwhile, you can call a few peer institutions to get sample copies of their latest publication and the evidence of how they position the planned giving program.

Moving along, let's assume you have some space (a full page, a half page, something). Go with what you have. Now what?

A while ago, I attended a direct mail seminar and learned an advertising statistic that I found quite compelling. "Consumers need to see the same message an average of seven times over an 18 month period before they decide to buy." This means to me that it is not only okay, but it is probably advisable, to repeat the same ad multiple times. Doesn't this sound boring to you? Don't you feel an inner need to continually change the message? Well, after years of rotating ads at several institutions, I did something completely different at Boston College.

A little history: The planned giving program at Boston College was still in its infancy when I arrived in 1993. There were about 18 donors in the pooled income fund and about the same number in the gift annuity program. We knew of a handful of charitable trusts but were not serving as trustee. In addition, the position of Director of Planned Giving had been vacant for a while. Not much was happening.

Before describing what worked for us, let me say that there is only one purpose for a planned giving ad: to get inquiries. Unlike annual giving initiatives, planned giving ads are not expected to result in money. Your only hope is that interested people will contact you to talk. From there, you can begin a dialog that may last months or years before a gift is closed. For most organizations, two categories comprise the bulk of planned giving. These are bequests and life income gifts. Environmental organizations like The Nature Conservancy attract a high volume in real estate gifts, but let's put that exception aside for now.

At Boston College, I wanted to get a message out and I wanted to keep the message simple. So, we focused on bequests and gift annuities. Why gift annuities and not pooled income fund or charitable trusts? When the pooled income fund was launched, around 1983, interest rates were in double digits. By the mid-1990s, the rates were 7% or so and dropping still. The pooled income fund would not be as attractive to the donors, in my opinion. Second, the charitable trust appeals to a much smaller market because the entry level gift is at least $100,000 to $250,000. Considering the high entry level amount for the CRT and the fact that Boston College did not serve as trustee at that time, the CRT would be much more difficult to promote initially. And, remember that the only goal is to get prospects to contact you. Then, once you are in a dialog with a person who feels a gift annuity is attractive, you can expand the discussion to include any other life income plan that suits the donor's needs better.

There were four issues *per* year of our alumni magazine, divided as follows:

Issue	Month	Topic	Comments
Spring	April	Gift Annuity	Attract gifts before May 31 fiscal year close
Summer	July	Bequest	Alternate bequest message, no timing reasons
Fall	October	Gift Annuity	Tie into year-end tax season, stock gift potential
Winter	January	Bequests	Add names to planned giving society prior to spring luncheon

Other aspects of the ad campaign were coordinated. For example, we were promoting heavily the gift annuity to the 50th reunion class in which the incentive to give was high. Therefore, the example in the gift annuity ad was for a member of the 50th reunion class. Also, in the beginning, the topics for our biannual estate planning newsletter were coordinated with the magazine topics.

This strategy worked. We repeated the same ads over and over again while drawing a healthy number of inquiries and gifts from each successive exposure. It was a simple message. People understood it, and the alumni were passing the message by word of mouth. We also attracted a fair number of gifts far above the minimum gift requirement ($5,000 before 6/1/94, and $10,000 after 6/1/94). There were gifts annuities of $50,000, $100,000, $200,000, $350,000, all from the repeating gift annuity message in the magazine.

Over the years, I've tried many kinds of ads in my institution's publications. Some were traditional ads and some were ads disguised as donor profiles or stories. The only ad feature I can point to that affected our response rate was whether or not there was a reply form to complete and return. Whenever we tried a new approach without the reply form, we received nearly no response. When we put the reply form back, we received a flurry of replies. The donors appeared much less likely to call the phone number listed or to write their own letter of inquiry.

PLANNED GIVING INSERTS

An excellent way to extend the reach and visibility of your program at minimal cost is to produce one or more messages that can be inserted into other regular mailings. For example, you can produce a #10 size rider to insert into direct mail packages, annual giving mailings, pledge reminders, or for inclusion with pledge forms following a telephone campaign.

With this strategy, you are able to spread your message without the necessity of printing additional envelopes or paying additional postage. But, beware of the following pitfall. Sometimes the weight of an insert (as small as it is) pushes the weight of the direct mail piece into the next postage rate. Before printing your inserts, take one complete direct mail package to your mail room to have it weighed with and without the proposed insert. This precaution will protect you from the unfortunate situation in which your planned giving insert increases the postage of someone else's mailing.

If your proposed insert does increase the weight of the mailing piece it is intended to accompany, test different kinds of paper to see if there is a lighter weight you can use, or offer to pay the extra postage and/or handling costs from your planned giving budget. Once I added an insert into an annual giving mailing with exactly this result. It was big mess and I had to pay the extra postage from my planned giving budget.

PLANNED GIVING NEWSLETTERS

Another method of educating your constituency about the benefits of creative gift planning is through the use of a planned giving newsletter. Some organizations write and print their own; others purchase a newsletter from a vendor. There are many vendors in Appendix IV who provide this service.

The cost *per* thousand from a vendor varies depending on the quantity ordered, the paper stock, the number of colors, the frequency of the newsletter, and the number of pages. Most vendors allow your institution's name, logo, and address to be printed on the newsletter free of charge if you provide the art work. When you do not have the resources in house to produce the necessary art work, you will be charged for this service. There is great flexibility in the market with regard to newsletters. Some have a predetermined title. In other cases, you can choose your own title as well as provide your own text for an introduction or for a whole page while using the balance of the boiler-plate language as is.

About two months before the newsletter mailing date, you will receive a list of topics available for that cycle. Most companies offer 25 to 50 topics from which to select your piece. Once you select the topic, you will receive the draft copy for review and editing. You don't have to change the text, but at the very least, you should change generic phrases like "our institution" to the real name of your institution. You can also delete a section and insert your own text, making the piece as personalized as you wish.

When you review the cost of buying or creating a newsletter, don't forget the mailing house. You will need to contact a mailing house for a quote on your job. Start with the one that works with your annual giving program. (Note: In some charities, there is a rule that you must get three bids for any project or cost over a certain dollar amount. At Boston College, the dollar amount for three bids was $1,000.) Before starting this project, talk to your purchasing office to learn the rules of your own charity.

The typical newsletter package from a vendor includes four pieces: 1) the newsletter folded into #10 envelope size, 2) a #9 reply card, 3) a #9 business reply envelope, and 4) companion booklets that will be used to follow up the inquiries. As an example, we got 200 booklets at Boston College for a biannual mailing of 15,000 newsletters *per* mailing.

The reply envelope can be either a postage-paid business reply envelope or one that requests the donor's stamp. You can call the post office to get a postage paid account very easily. You'll get a bar code from the post office and a specific layout for printing it on your envelopes. A designer will have to do a layout for the return envelope, which you will send to the newsletter vendor for printing. When a postage-paid envelope comes back, you get charged. You don't get charged if nothing comes back. Nasty people might put rocks in your postage-paid envelope and mail it. Or, they might save up every direct mail piece they have received from your institution and mail them back to you in your postage-paid envelope. People are so weird. These annoyances don't happen often, but, you pay for whatever postage is required for the items inside the envelopes. I received a postage-paid envelope filled with sand once.

Some organizations print the words "your stamp helps" on the business reply envelope. That's a nice idea. Some donors who have postage stamps handy put their own stamp on the envelope. Most important: don't be cheap about the business reply envelope. You will get more replies if you have a postage-paid envelope.

The final piece of your newsletter package is the outside envelope. You are responsible separately for printing the outside mailing envelope which is usually not included in the package purchased from the vendor. You can buy your own institution's #10 envelopes for much less than you would pay for a specially tailored outside envelope. Therefore, after you get your counts figured out, add the cost of more regular envelopes to your planned giving budget.

The quote from the mailing house includes stuffing 3 pieces into a #10 envelope, affixing labels that you provided according to their requirements, affixing postage, sealing, and sorting for bulk rate postage rates. Ask your mailing house the current U.S. Post Office rules for bulk rate because your labels must be ordered in a certain way.

There are restrictions and rules for bulk rate postage and they change from time to time. Ask your mailing house about the rules to make sure you follow them.

A planned giving newsletter can be an excellent vehicle with which to educate and cultivate a group of prospects or donors and to generate leads. When you decide to do a newsletter, you will need to ask yourself whether to select a fixed target group or whether you will change the target group depending on the topic. There are arguments in favor of the regularity of mailing a recognizable piece to the same people each time. Presumably, the target group would eventually get the idea that the organization is capable of helping them with a complex gift. At Boston College, we sent our newsletter in the spring and fall and changed the target group depending on the topic. I am not aware of any statistics on the merits of either plan; however, I spoke to a couple of people in the newsletter business to see what they had to say.

The Stelter Company, which was founded in 1962 to do mailing pieces for trust companies, branched out into the charitable giving market in 1979 and has served many charities with extremely high-quality publications and newsletters. I used the Stelter Company for a biannual, 100-percent custom planned giving newsletter at Boston College. We were producing 15,000 pieces at a time.

I asked Larry Stelter about the question of whether to pick a target group that would receive a newsletter regularly or whether to target the newsletter to the topic. He offered this advice: "If your consistency is large enough, it definitely pays to segment your list in order to communicate to a group's specific needs. Newsletters to women, age 45 to 70, and adults age 70 or older, have usually generated three to four times the response rate over a generic newsletter that tries to be all things for all people."

Building on new technology, The Stelter Company in late 1999 partnered with an Internet consulting firm to design a Web-based version of Stelter newsletters. Larry says, "You can't just put your print newsletter onto your Web site because the Internet requires a more dynamic exchange of information. Our Web pages are designed so that people have quick and easy access to a huge volume of information. Visitors can read an introductory paragraph about a topic and then "drill down" for more complete coverage if they're interested. What's more, we regularly update the content to bring the most relevant and important news to your potential donors. Some of our clients also use the gift calculation software link that allows potential donors to do their own charitable deductions online."

According to Larry, "This web-based product enables clients to reach their entire universe at a very low cost, eliminate postage and handling, offer additional planned giving information instantly, and link to other sites offering financial, travel and health information."

With two levels of service, the client can create a seamless interface of their own corporate site with the Stelter server. On its Web site (www.stelter.com), you can test-drive a variety of client sites currently using the Stelter Web services. Go to the Stelter Web site and play around to see what others are doing.

Another leader in the planned giving field, Robert F. Sharp, Jr., President of Robert F. Sharpe & Company, Inc., talks about responses to marketing initiatives in an article he wrote for his client newsletter, *Give & Take*, which is available on the Robert Shape website (www.rfsco.com). He says "Over the years we have seen response rates from various gift planning mailing approaches that range from 10% (and more) to one-tenth of 1% or less. Ironically, some of the development executives receiving five responses in 5,000 are the most pleased. They often find that the results are much greater from a few highly interested respondents than from a multitude of 'lookers.'"

Bob makes a good point because I can remember countless times when a mailing produced so many responses that it was crippling to our office. On the matter of selecting the target group for a newsletter mailing, I spoke to Timothy D. Sharpe, Executive Vice President of Robert F. Sharpe & Company. I asked Tim if it is better to pick one group for each mailing or to change the target group based on the topic. Tim says that there are wealth-based plans and age-based plans. To the extent that you can segment your market, you should do so. For example, you would be best to target older folks for a bequest mailing or a gift annuity mailing. On the other hand, you ought to target mailings about charitable lead trusts or short term charitable remainder trusts to high net worth individuals regardless of age. These groups may overlap, of course. Tim also acknowledged that some smaller organizations do not have specific data on their donors that would allow proper segmenting of the database. In these cases, the organization simply has to pick a group. In all cases, the quality and not the quantity of the inquiries is key. The more you can tailor the topic to the group, the better the leads will be.

In addition to the wide selection of brochures and newsletters, Sharpe is also developing planned giving narratives and information that would be linked to the charity's web site and maintained or updated on the Sharpe server so that the content is always current. For charities that do not have the time, expertise, or in-house web staff to create their own planned giving web pages, these services for planned giving web design are excellent. There is no reason for a charity's web site not to have links to planned giving information.

INTEGRATION OF PLANNED GIVING INTO OTHER FUND RAISING MATERIALS

Building visibility for planned giving is an ongoing process. The inquiries you receive will be generated from many sources, and it is incumbent on you to utilize every conceivable method—personal contact, telephone calls, newsletters, brochures, inserts, and ads—to expose your constituency to the program. The use of check-off blocks on other fund raising materials can produce a consistent flow of inquiries at no cost. Here are some ideas on where you can place check-off blocks:

1. annual giving pledge cards, for example, those used for regular renewals or for telephone campaigns;

2. response cards from annual giving mailings, either acquisition mailings or additional gift mailings to current donors;

3. pledge reminders.

You will want to include the kinds of check off items similar to those used in your general planned giving brochure. If you are allowed only one line on one of the above items, you probably should alternate among one of the following messages:

_____ I have included XYZ Charity in my will.

_____ Please send me information about providing a bequest to XYZ Charity.

_____ Please send me information about receiving income from a gift.

You might also consider printing the following message on the bottom of your institution's letterhead: "Put XYZ Charity in your will."

PURCHASING GENERIC BROCHURES

As I mentioned earlier in this chapter, many vendors listed in Appendix IV offer brochures on a wide variety of topics. Some consultants charge a minimal fee for sample copies; others will send free samples. You can also preview the brochures on the company's web page in PDF format in many cases.

Most of the generic brochures can be imprinted with your institution's name, logo, and address on one or more spots in the brochure. There is usually no fee for this personalization if you provide camera-ready art work.

Generic brochures can be used when you:

1. are understaffed and cannot take the time to write a brochure;

2. do not have the in-house expertise to create a brochure;

3. want to test something new in a limited way;

4. wish to target a special group of prospects;

5. do not have the money to produce your own brochures;

6. want to capitalize immediately on a change in the tax law that creates a new marketing opportunity.

GETTING THE MOST MILEAGE FROM YOUR PRINT MATERIALS

Tax reform and changing objectives of the institution often make brochures obsolete sooner than anticipated. Such a situation is costly and unnecessary. To ensure that your message will be up to date and accurate, the shelf life of a planned giving brochure should be no more than two years.

While the cost *per* thousand decreases as you increase the quantity, the problem with overprinting is that large quantities remain in unopened boxes long after their useful shelf life, finally to be thrown away. To utilize just 2,000 follow-up brochures in one year, you need a flow of inquiries at the rate of 39 per week. Do you realize the kind of operation it would take to sustain that level of activity?

Following is a chart showing the pieces of direct-response mail you would need to send to generate a response of 39 *per* week in order to utilize 2,000 brochures in one year?

Percent Response	Number Mailed	Average Responses *Per* Week
1%	202,800	39
2%	101,400	39
3%	67,600	39
4%	50,700	39
5%	40,560	39

Taking the most optimistic case, the mailing of 40,560 pieces generating a response of 5% would cost $15,007.20 in postage alone at 37¢ first-class rate or $6,692.40 at the nonprofit bulk pre-sorted rate of 16.5¢.

There is obviously efficiency to printing large quantities, but my point remains—how much activity can you really expect or handle? In my discussion on volunteer committees (Chapter III–2), I suggest structuring a planned giving committee of 10 including a chair. Each committee member might reasonably solicit 5 prospects each quarter. Thus, for one year, the minimum quantity for committee solicitations is 5 times 11 times 4 or 220. For two years, you'll need 440 prospects. Next, ask yourself whether you have the staff and back-up support to conduct enough screening sessions and other research activities to generate 55 prospects every three months for your committee? Perhaps a more realistic scenario for your program is a committee of five plus a chair each soliciting 10 new prospects every six months. Thus, you'll need 10 times 6 times 2 or 120 for one year, 240 for two years.

As you consider the quantity of brochures you'll need, consider carefully how many are in your target group— that segment most likely to participate in the gift arrangements you're offering. If you work for a university or school, you will know exactly who your constituency is and how many are in it. But, if you work for any other type of organization, you may not know. Therefore, your decision on quantity should be based on how many copies you need for:

- trustees and for solicitations by trustees;
- planned giving committee activity;
- following up inquiries;
- other fund raisers; and
- purposes of visibility or leads—rather than for a personalized solicitation or follow up.

A BROCHURE IS ONLY AS GOOD AS YOUR FOLLOW UP

The most basic principle of fund raising is that people don't give unless they are asked. Sending a brochure to a prospect is not enough.

Here is a sequence of steps you should use in responding to an inquiry:

1. Review the prospect's history of support and involvement with the institution.

    *   Check your standing files, research records, or other sources to determine how or whether the prospect has been involved in the past—as a donor, as a volunteer, or in some other capacity. If the prospect already has a relationship with another member of the staff, you must consult with that person before following up the inquiry. Otherwise, you risk damaging a relationship with your colleague and you will appear to be stealing prospects. It will take more time to coordinate with another person before following up with the prospect, but it is worth the trouble.

2. Call the prospect.

    *   Do not assume the prospect knows why, when, or how to support your institution. On one occasion, I received an inquiry requesting information about life income plans. Before sending a letter, I called to learn something about the motivation for the inquiry. During the conversation, I asked whether the prospect needed more current income. The answer was, "Well, actually, I don't need income, but I really need a tax deduction." I asked, "Why don't you just make an outright gift?" She did!

    *   Determine why the individual requested information. For example, start the conversation with, "We were very pleased to learn of your interest in XYZ Charity. Tell me what prompted you to send this card back to us at this time?" The information provided in answer to this question will help you to evaluate where to take the conversation.

    *   Prompt the prospect to talk about your institution. Let the prospect's own words reinforce the value of the institution.

    *   Ask specific questions about the prospect's situation that will help you identify the form of gift that best suits the prospect. (Note: If asked, most people will answer very personal questions about their situation.) Follow are some questions you might consider:

        –   What is your most important source of income (salary, investment income, retirement income, rental income, *etc.*)?
        –   How do you see your role in providing for a spouse or other family members?
        –   What is the average income you are receiving from your investments/portfolio?
        –   What tax goals are most important to you right now?
        –   Is there a change coming in the near future related to your income needs (retirement, change in career, college tuition, *etc.*)?

    *   Do not try to sell anything. The point of this first conversation is to build a rapport and to figure out what issues are most important to the prospect. Using this information, suggest a method of support that combines the prospect's area of interest with an appropriate gift vehicle.

    *   Ask the prospect about his or her timetable for making a decision about a gift or contribution.

3. Suggest a course of action.

    *   If the conversation is promising, try to arrange an appointment. Often, an appointment can keep things moving in a positive direction. You can say, "Based on our conversation, I'll put a

proposal together, and perhaps I can arrange an appointment to meet you to explain in greater detail how this kind of gift can benefit you. How about next Thursday?" If the prospect does not want a visit right now, don't aggravate the prospect by trying to force your way in. A little persuasive energy is good, but don't overdo it. Many people prefer to review the information privately first.

- Send a proposal. In your letter, end with a sentence like, "I look forward to hearing your thoughts and will call you next week to see whether I can be of further assistance." You absolutely must call when you say you will. I once followed up a person who put me off three months at a time for two years. Finally, he made a gift and he told me that it was only my religious follow up that finally got him to do it.

4. Follow up.

- If after meeting with the prospect or making your follow-up call, you are put off because the prospect wants to "think about it for a while," ask when you may call again. Don't be concerned if the follow-up date is three to six months away or more. Keep track of when you are supposed to call, and, follow up when you are supposed to. Eventually, you will have a full year of calls ahead of you and multiple prospects in different stages of cultivation or solicitation.

In addition to tracking your own prospects, you'll also be responsible for tracking those of your volunteer solicitors or of the board of trustees. As each solicitation is made, the solicitor should send you a report form summarizing the contact and outlining whatever follow-up must be done. It is up to you to keep a record of the follow-up plans. Your volunteers will not do this.

SUMMARY

I want to emphasize again that you do not need brochures to get gifts. Yes, it is very nice to be able to send an attractive brochure to a prospect. But, you can get lots of gifts simply by being out of the office visiting prospects. Nonetheless, brochures and other print materials serve many useful purposes. They save you considerable time in explaining gift options. They can be used to generate leads. And, they provide security for volunteers—the people who are the subject of my next chapter.

Chapter III–2

HOW TO USE VOLUNTEERS IN PLANNED GIVING

INTRODUCTION

You have turned to this chapter for one of three reasons:

1. After reading through the Calendar of Activities in Chapter I–4, you are interested in learning exactly what it will take to create the volunteer committee suggested there.

2. You already have a volunteer committee and may be experiencing some frustration in working with it.

3. You have been running your planned giving program without volunteers, have raised substantial funds on your own, and you are curious about what I have to offer. Is there a better way?

Let me begin by saying that volunteers comprise only a part of the full picture. Many major donors develop a relationship directly with the institution (possibly with you) and already are highly motivated. No doubt, if you are an experienced planned giving officer, you can point to countless examples in which you alone cultivated and solicited major gifts. This is especially true for prospects who respond to ads or other lead-generating activities. When people seek you out, you don't need a third party. However, your totals could have been doubled or tripled during any period you wish to measure if you used volunteers, too, for all of the other prospects.

Volunteers are invaluable for several reasons:

- The number of solicitation visits or cultivation visits you can make by yourself is limited. Use of volunteers multiplies the impact and reach of your planned giving program far beyond what you could ever do alone.

- A volunteer can speak on behalf of the organization in ways you never can. The message is very different coming from someone who is not being paid to deliver it.

- A volunteer can give you access to individuals otherwise out of reach because, hard as it is to believe, some people will not respond to you.

- A volunteer provides continuity and will remain committed to the organization long after you are gone. The average turn over for fund raising staff is two years. That is pathetic.

- A volunteer can inspire others by example.

- By involving prospects as volunteers, you are engaging them in the most effective form of cultivation possible because they are also prospects, too.

Anyone who has worked with volunteers knows that there is another side of the same coin. Volunteers can waste your time. They can make your life miserable by knit-picking you or your programs to death. They demand more attention than you can ever hope to give. You cannot ignore them. And, bad ones don't just go away. Firing a volunteer takes more skill than almost any other form of personnel management.

The only way to survive volunteer management is to cultivate the right mental attitude before you start. This means understanding and accepting three inevitable facts about volunteer management:

1. You will always spend more time managing the volunteers than you will spend on actual solicitations. This is okay. The volunteers are being cultivated in the process.

2. Volunteers will not always do everything they are supposed to do. This is okay. At the end of a year, they still will have contacted and solicited more people than you could have handled alone.

3. Volunteers will not always perform their tasks in the time you've set for them. This is okay. Remember, your primary objectives are still being met: to cultivate the committee members and to extend the reach of your program.

Before you recruit your first volunteer, post the above three items on your wall. You will need to refer to them often. Trust me.

Do you need more convincing? Here are three conclusions from a former study called "The Charitable Behavior of Americans" which was commissioned by the Rockefeller Brothers Fund and produced for the Independent Sector. It is an old study, but it sums up things pretty well.

- When asked to rate the effectiveness of eight different solicitation approaches in terms of their own charitable motivations, 77% of the respondees giving $500 or more to charity . . . cited that being asked by someone they knew was the best approach.

- Volunteering ranked fourth out of 10 possible options as an indicator of giving 2 percent or more of one's income to charitable causes. The four indicators in order of priority are listed below. You have no control over the first three.

  1. attend church weekly;
  2. have a moderate amount or a lot of discretionary income;
  3. no worry about money;
  4. *volunteered past year.*

- "There is a relationship between volunteer time and giving. Giving increases among those who are involved as volunteers and giving generally increases as the amount of volunteer time increases. . . Those who volunteered on average less than three hours per week contributed more than one-third more money to charity than those who did not volunteer at all, while those who volunteered three or more hours per week on average gave twice as much money to charity as those respondents who did not volunteer."

The conclusions drawn from the above study are proven time and time again by our own experience. But, the trick is to be able to use volunteers effectively without having them control you or put you into therapy.

Volunteers can do more than solicitations. This chapter discusses not only how to create a solicitation committee but also how to use volunteers for one-time assignments. Volunteers are discussed in the following pages under six topics:

- How to create a solicitation committee;
- How to create an advisory committee;
- How to use volunteers in planning events;
- How to work with one volunteer on a solicitation;
- Office uses for volunteers;
- How to use volunteers for screening sessions.

HOW TO CREATE A SOLICITATION COMMITTEE

The solicitation or development committee serves exclusively a fund raising purpose. Its membership is comprised of people who are or whom you hope will become major supporters. They must be willing to solicit prospects either alone, in teams, or with you or other staff members.

You cannot have an effective committee unless you are prepared to accept full responsibility for directing its activities. This means time, organization, and purpose. Once you have a committee, you will find yourself engaged in the following activities:

1. motivating the members through letters, phone calls or visits;
2. training the members either in group settings or individually;
3. meeting with the members either in groups or individually;
4. calling the members to follow up on prospect assignments, assist with solicitations, or to help plan strategy for the prospects;
5. receiving calls from the members about the prospects, to explain problems with the prospects, to report on calls or visits, to request proposals, or to schedule meetings;
6. preparing solicitation assignments for the members;
7. preparing progress reports;
8. reassigning prospects.

Here are the steps you need to take to develop a planned giving solicitation committee:

- Determine the job description of the chair;
- Determine the job description of the committee members;
- Identify candidates for the position of chair;
- Recruit the chair;
- Identify potential committee members;
- Recruit the committee members;
- Prepare prospect lists;
- Hold an orientation day;
- Prepare solicitation kits.

Determine The Job Description Of The Chair

The chair is the most important member of the committee. He or she provides the leadership for the committee and will work closely with you in planning strategy, motivating the members, and overseeing the work of the committee. The chair must be highly motivated, have strong leadership abilities, and must be willing to make a personal gift large enough to set an example for others. The chair must also be a real worker—not simply a highly visible person willing to lend a name to the cause. Following is a sample job description for the Planned Giving Committee Chair:

Planned Giving Committee Chair
Job Description

- Reports to the Director of Planned Giving and works in cooperation with the Office of Planned Giving. (For more complex structures, the head of the planned giving committee can report to the Chair of the Trustee Committee on Development with you as staff liaison.)

- Is responsible for overall direction and scope of the Planned Giving Committee.

- Recruits the Planned Giving Committee members.

- Acts as a resource for the Planned Giving Committee members.

- Assists staff and volunteers in identifying, educating, and soliciting planned giving prospects.

- With the assistance of the Planned Giving Office, provides updates to the members on pertinent tax changes affecting Planned Giving Committee efforts.

- Attends and chairs all meetings of the Committee.

- Monitors the progress of solicitation assignments by members of the Planned Giving Committee.

- Acts as a general advocate to promote imaginative and creative gift arrangements from the constituency.

- Is a member of the Campaign Steering Committee and attends regular meetings of the Campaign Steering Committee (optional for institutions in a campaign);

- The term of the Chair is two years.

Determine The Job Description Of The Committee Members

One of the most important things you must do to ensure a successful experience with the committee is to determine what it will be expected to do. For example, how many solicitation assignments will each member have? What is the time frame within which they will be expected to accomplish their assignments? How often will they be required to meet?

Following is a sample job description for a planned giving committee member:

Planned Giving Committee Member
Job Description

- Attends regular meetings of the Committee (*not more frequently than quarterly*).

- Acts as a general advocate to promote imaginative and creative gift arrangements from the constituency.

- Assists staff and other volunteers in identifying and screening prospects.

- Assists staff and other volunteers with solicitations including phone calls, letters, and personal visits.

- Is responsible for the solicitation of not more than five prospects for each three-month period. (*Note: My last edition of this book suggested 10 prospects per quarter which I have now decided is impossible.*)

- Reports to the Chair and works in consultation with the Office of Planned Giving.

- Is responsible for increasing the visibility and reach of the planned giving program by drafting or signing periodic letters for reproduction and mailing by the Office of Planned Giving.

- The term of the Committee member is two years.

Identify Candidates For The Position Of Chair

The ideal chair should have the following qualifications:

1. highly visible and well respected within your constituency;
2. ability to articulate the needs of the organization;
3. effective at running meetings. Able to keep control and provide direction and leadership;
4. ability to motivate others;
5. willingness to make a leadership gift;
6. willingness to solicit others;
7. willingness to make a commitment of time;
8. ability to articulate the general benefits of the gift options you intend to offer;
9. has even-keeled personality and will not be high maintenance or knit-pick you to death.

Where do you find this person?

For mature planned giving programs, you can start by reviewing the people currently participating in one of your life income plans or your bequest program. Also, you can consider people who have made major outright gifts. An ideal person may already be a member of your board of trustees. If possible, your ideal candidate will also live within two hours driving time from your organization. The closer the better. That is not to say you shouldn't recruit a person in another state if he or she is the obvious choice. Sometimes, you don't have a local person who fills the bill. Still, the daily dealings will be easier if you can find a local person to be the chair.

For new planned giving programs, you'll be looking for someone who already has good leadership skills and the potential to make a substantial gift. Sometimes, the best candidate for chair is a major prospect who needs the kind of serious cultivation that can only be accomplished by getting the person involved. Rarely does anyone remain in such a capacity without making his or her own commitment.

As you undertake your search, you cannot assume the biggest donors will necessarily have the kind of personality to take on a fund raising role. Narrowing down the field will be difficult because you'll find few if any candidates with all of the qualifications. Leadership potential is more important than geographic location. Enthusiasm and commitment far outweigh technical expertise. You can teach a good person anything.

Try to identify at least three strong candidates because two will say no.

Recruit The Chair

Anyone being asked to serve in a volunteer capacity wants to know *exactly* what will be expected. Thus, before recruiting the chair, you must have most of your preliminary planning done. This means having the following things already in place:

- a list of potential committee members for the chair to recruit;
- a set of goals, objectives, a calendar of activities and a budget (Chapter I–4);
- a method and a plan for identifying and researching prospects (Chapter I–5);
- a board-approved list of the gift arrangements you intend to offer;
- a board-approved set of gift crediting guidelines;
- appropriate brochures for use in solicitations (Chapter III–1).

This is not to say that the chair has no role in developing the plans. But, it is your responsibility to provide guidance, direction, and structure to the committee's activities. Do your organizing and planning before you start recruiting volunteers.

When all of the above items are in good order, your next task is to select the best person to recruit the chair. It may be the president, vice president, chairman of the board, or executive director. Don't be alarmed if it is not you. Remember, this entire business revolves around orchestrating the right connections. If you have a great relationship with the perfect candidate, you may want to have a discreet conversation with the candidate to discuss the idea of his or her nomination for the position. During this conversation, it is extremely important that you not actually do the recruiting. Separate yourself from the process and use this opportunity to feel out the candidate in advance.

Even though you are not doing the recruiting yourself, you are the one responsible for preparing the information that will be sent to the candidate. This packet should include:

1. a letter to go out over the signature of the person selected to do the recruiting. This letter outlines the institution's goals and objectives, the purpose of establishing such a committee, and the staff responsible for it (you);

2. a job description of the chair;

3. a job description of the committee members;

4. a copy of your ways of giving brochure. (If you do not have a brochure yet, don't worry about it.)

In the best of all worlds, the person who signs the recruitment letter should follow up personally to get the commitment. If that is not possible, then you will have to follow up yourself. In the latter case, the recruitment letter should state that you will be calling.

Don't even think of beginning this process until you have fully thought through how you intend to proceed.

Identify Potential Committee Members

The best committee members have many of the same qualifications as the chair—highly visible, highly motivated, willingness to make a commitment of time, not afraid to ask for money, willingness to make a financial commitment, ability to articulate the general concepts about gift options, and the ability to discuss the needs of the institution.

For organizations serving a local community or region, the committee should represent a good cross section of the constituency. You can attempt to cover the North, South, East, and West providing additional members in areas where there may be a larger critical mass of good prospects. If you are working for a college or university, the strongest connections evolve from the class structure rather than on a geographic basis; therefore, your committee will be more effective if you identify potential members from the classes with the greatest fund raising potential, for example, those having major reunions within the next two years.

In the Calendar of Activities (Chapter I-4), you begin identifying possible members in January, but the committee is not set up until July. Thus, you will have plenty of time to identify and cultivate a strong group of candidates throughout the start-up phase.

Not everyone on your list will agree to serve in this capacity. You will need at least twice as many potential candidates as you want on the committee.

Recruit The Committee Members

The dynamics of a volunteer committee can be powerful if the committee is set up properly. One hopes to create a sense of obligation and commitment to the institution—not necessarily through you but through the chair. In order to engender the right kind of commitment, the committee members must be recruited by the chair. The chair is the one whose direction and leadership will be key to the success of the committee. When people agree to serve, you want them to be making a commitment to the chair and to the institution—not necessarily to you. As we all know, people like us may be offered another job and leave the institution.

To begin, you should review with the chair your list of potential committee members. In some cases, you and your colleagues will have selected the candidates. In other cases, the chair will have picked them from lists of names you have provided. In new planned giving programs, for example, you may wish to run a computer list of all people giving $5,000 or more. For mature programs, you may find good candidates in your life income plans and bequest program. The process depends very much on the nature of the constituency. Within a local community or metropolitan area, many of the city's best volunteers know one another because they share volunteer duties for other charities. For a national constituency, the chair will depend on you to identify the best possible people.

Let's assume you have identified 20 people, hoping for a committee of 10. First, divide the list into two parts. The top ten will now receive a letter from the chair. The letter sets the stage for the follow-up phone call from the chair. It should include information about the institution's objectives, the challenges it faces, the context within which the committee will be working (for example, in a capital campaign), what will be expected of the members, the long- and short-term goals and objectives of the committee, a job description of the committee member, and when the chair will be calling to follow up.

The chair must schedule time to telephone the top ten candidates within a week following the letter. The chair will need from you the following information about each person: full name and address, business affiliation, business address, home and business phone numbers, and any other information about the candidates that may assist the chair in this work, for example, past involvement with the institution, number of years as a contributor, history of giving, special interests, *etc*. Make sure that you stress the importance of discretion with the information about the candidates.

Depending on the outcome of the chair's calls, you must be ready to generate one or more of the following letters:

1. Acceptances: People who accept receive a confirming letter from the chair outlining the schedule of activities (meetings) for the next year (if you know them) and a time frame within which they will hear from you again. You will send this letter and forge the chair's signature.

2. Refusals: People who decline receive a letter expressing regret that the individual cannot participate. Maybe they can participate in the future.

3. Back up list: After each refusal, a letter is sent to one of the people on the back up list.

When the entire committee is recruited, the chair should write a final letter to everyone welcoming them to the committee and listing all of the members, their affiliation with the institution, and business affiliations if appropriate. This letter should also include a list of the scheduled meetings and an invitation to an orientation session.

Also, you should draft a letter to the committee from the president, chairman of the board, or from another prominent person in order to reinforce the importance of the committee's work and to thank each one for his or her commitment to the institution.

Prepare Prospect Lists

Each committee member will select five prospect assignments at the orientation session. Presumably, you have been identifying prospects from screening sessions (Chapter I-5). Here is the meeting when you are able to show the names to the committee members for the purpose of designating prospect assignments. You need to know who knows who.

Hold An Orientation Day

There is more to running a successful fund raising committee than simply passing out solicitation assignments. From day one, you must make the committee members a part of your institution's inner circle. You want to provide an insider's view of the people and programs that make your organization so special. You want to build enthusiasm for the exciting plans that lie ahead. And, you want to put the work they'll be doing in the broadest institutional context.

The first step in expanding their knowledge of the institution is to provide an orientation day. There are many ways to handle a session like this, and you'll have to determine how best to educate your own committee. Here is a sample agenda for a full-day orientation session. Take this idea and adjust it to suit your own situation.

SAMPLE SCHEDULE FOR ORIENTATION SESSION

8:00 am - 9:30 am	**Breakfast With The Chief Executive Officer.** Members meet for the first time and receive their inspirational words from your organization's president, executive director, or another person associated with the leadership of the organization. The speaker should announce that every member of the board of trustees has made a financial commitment to the program. (See Chapter I–2 for a discussion of the board's role.)
9:30 am - 10:30 am	**Tour Of Your Organization's Facilities.** The tour should end in a room where the Committee can stay for the next two hours.
10:30 am - 11:45 am	**Panel Discussion.** In this session, your institution's top managers present an overview of their specific area of responsibility. For example, you should include the vice president for finance and operations or treasurer, the director of communications, the vice president for resources, and the heads of other important departments.
11:45 am - 12:00 pm	Break
12:00 pm to 1:30 pm	**Lunch With the Development Professionals.** This is a chance for the new committee members to learn about the other development activities within which their work will be conducted. Participants at this lunch include the director of development, director of major gifts, director of the campaign, director of research, director of the annual fund, *etc.* Each person should prepare a 10-minute presentation explaining the workings and purpose of his or her office, the goals and objectives, and the ways in which each area will overlap or be enhanced by the work of the planned giving committee.
1:30 pm to 2:30 pm	**Planned Giving Presentation.** This is your session. You must educate the members about the various gift options with which they need to be familiar. Stick to concepts; don't get technical. More than anything else, you want to make them aware of possibilities.
2:30 pm to 3:30 pm	**Discussion of Committee Assignments.** The chair will pass out a list of prospects. Each list has the committee member's name at the top. The members should review the names and identify people they feel comfortable contacting. There will be names that don't get picked and also names that are picked by more than one person. Instruct the members to select at least five names, and more if they really know the names. Also, the members should write in names that are missing. The lists will be collected at the end of the meeting so that selections can be coordinated back at the office. After reviewing each member's list, assign prospects first who are selected by one person only. Then, review the names selected by more than one member, discuss each one with the members, and make a decision about the assignment. For write-ins, do some research to verify, if possible, that these are legitimate prospects.
	During this part of the meeting, you can provide advice on how to get an appointment, how to counter objections, and you can offer assistance in preparing proposals, traveling with the solicitors, or providing any other back-up support that may be necessary.

It is the chair's responsibility to emphasize the importance of each member's own financial commitment. The chair should state that each member who is not already a donor will be asked to consider a gift and that he or she will be following up for a personal appointment. (Note: This will make some people squirm, but don't worry about it.)

3:30 pm to 4:00 pm   **Refreshments.** By now, everyone (including you) will be exhausted. You may wish to unveil a selection of refreshments (cocktails?) in order that the group can unwind, think about what they have heard and seen today, and talk to one another about the months that lie ahead. The chair should make a toast to a successful year.

The orientation session discussed above is just the beginning of the kind of effort to which you and your chair must commit yourselves in order to ensure your committee activities will be successful. By introducing the committee to management and to other development professionals, you will gain their confidence and trust. You will also help your colleagues to understand the importance of the committee's work. Such a session promotes good will throughout the organization and will get the committee off to a strong start with enthusiasm, commitment, and the feeling that they truly play a key role in ensuring the success and financial stability of the institution. After a day like this, each one surely will be impressed with the quality of the leadership, and with the strength of the resources that are committed to help them.

Prepare Prospect Solicitation Kits

Once you determine the committee assignments, you must prepare a solicitation kit for each prospect. The prospect kit includes the following items:

For the solicitor:

- research profile on the prospect, including suggested strategy and proposed gift amount or a gift range.

- contact sheet for each prospect and return envelope addressed to you. On this form, the solicitor records details of a conversation, meeting, or other pertinent facts about contact with the prospect.

- volunteer expense report.

For the prospect:

- pledge form and return envelope;

- gift crediting guidelines;

- planned giving brochure;

- envelope (addressed to the prospect) sufficient to hold the pledge form, return envelope, crediting guidelines, and brochure).

Questions And Answers About Working With A Volunteer Solicitation Committee

Q. How do I determine the size of my planned giving committee?

A. The size of the committee is determined by the number of staff responsible for directing its activities. By reading through the above process, you can see that considerable amounts of time are spent working with a committee of 10. Each solicitor (plus the chair) receives five solicitation assignments each quarter. This means you must prepare 55 solicitation packets containing 55 brochures, pledge forms, reply envelopes, contact sheets, research profiles, crediting guidelines *etc.* <u>each quarter</u>. Who is going to coordinate this work? If you intend to use the committee in quality solicitations, you'll be hard-pressed to work with more than 10, in other words, no more than 10 committee members *per* professional staff person.

If you cannot handle ten, try five, or even just three. Start slowly and add members as your experience or staff increases. Two good solicitors working with you on even five solicitations for a whole year can be very productive if you choose your prospects well.

Q. How often should a committee like this be required to meet?

A. At least quarterly. You'll realize that volunteers work more slowly than you might hope. Even five solicitation assignments will take as much as 90 days to complete because prospects are not always available, it takes time to get meetings set up, you'll need turn-around time to have proposals prepared and forwarded to committee members, and any of the players will go on vacation. Three months is probably about right to be able to show progress and to provide a necessary check-point. Also, you may find it harder to recruit good people if you require them to meet more often. If three months between meetings seems too long for you, try having meetings every two months. However, I think you will find it difficult to prepare for so many meetings. Remember, both you and the chair will be in touch with the members by telephone throughout the three-month period.

Q. How do I handle volunteer expenses?

A. Some organizations pay the expenses for their volunteers to attend meetings, including airfare and hotels. That can be extremely expensive. However, I have worked in enough charities to know that you don't need to do this. For the National Campaign Committee at Boston College, we sent a list of hotels where we had negotiated a reduced group rate, but we did not pay for the airfare or hotel. If you get the right people on the committee, you will not receive a request for reimbursement. During the recruitment process, tell the volunteers that they are expected to pay their own way. Do not make the mistake of omitting this part of the recruitment discussion.

Some volunteers will submit telephone expenses. If that happens, just pay the bill from the planned giving budget.

Some volunteers will expect to be reimbursed for catering or bar services arranged by them for an event at their homes. This can be very embarrassing if you assumed the volunteer was paying for the event. When you ask the member to host an event, make sure you specify that you are asking for a donation of the expenses. In turn, some volunteers will submit the expenses of a large event for gift credit. This is fine. You would book the amount as a gift-in-kind and send the donor a gift receipt for tax purposes.

Q. Exactly what does the chair do?

A. The chair becomes as close to staff as you can get without being paid. Often, you will consult with the chair on motivation problems with the solicitors or strategies for keeping the momentum going. You will work closely with the chair to plan the agenda for meetings, set reasonable objectives and goals, review progress, and make decisions about future assignments. The chair monitors the solicitors by telephoning them periodically about their solicitation assignments. This means that the chair must be willing to commit not only the time to perform his or her solicitation assignments but also the time to monitor everyone else's work. The chair runs the meetings.

Q. Beyond solicitations, what else might the committee members be asked to do?

A. Depending on the constituency, either the chair or the individual members can be asked to write a letter that you will reproduce over his or her signature and send to a target group. This activity is in addition to their specific prospect assignments. For target groups of 100 or less, it is not uncommon for the committee member to write special notes on the letters especially to those prospects known to the member.

Or, if you are speaking with a prospect about the gift annuity program, you might say: "May I suggest that you talk with Sarah White. She's a member of our planned giving committee and is also a participant in our gift annuity program."

Committee members may also be asked to host a breakfast, lunch, cocktail party, dinner, or other gathering or to assist with the planning and logistics of an event.

Finally, the members may be asked to assist with prospect screening sessions. (Chapter I–5)

Q. What is an appropriate term for the chair and for the committee members?

A. Volunteers, just like staff, burn out. Between two to five years is probably the length of time a volunteer may be willing to serve. One year is too short because the investment of time in training will eat up some of the first year. If you are starting a capital campaign, your committee's term should run parallel to that of the Campaign Steering Committee, which is probably set for the entire duration of the campaign. Some volunteers will continue to be active almost indefinitely. If they are good, keep them. Others prefer a limited commitment and will move on to something else.

Q. How much do the volunteers really need to know about planned giving?

A. They need to understand general concepts. For example, they should know that it is possible to make a gift, receive income, avoid capital gain taxes, and receive a partial income tax deduction. They do not need to know the technical details of every form of life income gift. Rather, they should know that there are a variety of ways to arrange a gift to receive a fixed or fluctuating return and that you (the director of planned giving) can provide an example based on the needs of the donor.

Although there will be people who can speak articulately about the benefits of life income gifts, especially when they themselves have participated in a life income plan, it is unrealistic to think these volunteers will develop anything other a general knowledge of how gifts can be structured. What they do best is present concepts to their prospects.

Volunteer solicitors need to know how to recognize situations that have potential. For example, they need to know that it is possible to convert real estate to a new income, or to arrange a gift of closely held stock.

The volunteer should be able to point out possibilities without knowing the whole story, for example, "You know, John, I don't pretend to understand everything about this, but I do know that XYZ Charity can work with you to convert that land into a new income. Why don't I ask (your name) to prepare an example for you?"

These volunteers provide more in the way of peer to peer encouragement than anything else. They get things moving. They help you get appointments. They ask for the gift and then steer the prospect to you for a discussion about how to do it.

Q. Day to day, how much support do I have to provide to the planned giving committee?

A. You must provide support in many areas. This includes meeting individually with the members to review prospect assignments, preparing a draft letter for a committee member to send to a prospect, checking further into a prospect's background, or telephoning a prospect after the solicitor has opened the door for you. Much time is spent checking up on the solicitors to ensure that they are doing their work. In some cases, one of the volunteers is simply wrong for the job—either too timid to ask for the money, too busy to get the work done, consumed by a family crisis such as a death in the family, or simply is a procrastinator. In this situation you may have to take back and reassign some prospects or solicit them yourself.

Q. What do I do about a volunteer who is not doing his or her job?

A. Discuss the problem with the chair. The chair should be able to talk to the volunteer as a peer about the importance of the committee's work and the volunteer's role. Perhaps the volunteer is uncomfortable about specific prospect assignments, and, as a result, has been procrastinating. By reassigning prospects, the problem may be solved. Or, the volunteer may have an unusually high level of anxiety about possible rejection. Again, the chair can be supportive and encouraging to try to move the volunteer past whatever fears may be present. In the worst case, the chair should ask the volunteer to resign. This kind of situation is tough on everyone, but it must be confronted if the proper work is to continue as planned. If the term is almost up, you can let the term expire.

Q. How far can a volunteer be expected to travel on behalf of the organization?

A. Volunteers can be asked and are willing to do almost anything as long as you treat them properly and give them the support, recognition, and appreciation they deserve.

For example, the chair of my planned giving committee drove three hours to meet me at a prospect's home for a $50,000 gift annuity solicitation. Another volunteer drove three hours to make a presentation at a planned giving luncheon. Still another drove three hours with me for lunch with a prospect and three hours back in the same day. It is inspiring how much a volunteer will do.

Some volunteers think nothing of driving an hour by themselves to visit a prospect alone. As the trips get longer and the stakes get higher, you should include either yourself or another person as a traveling companion. For example, if the two of you can go together in one car, and you offer to drive, you can expand the length and scope of your trip far beyond what you could expect the volunteer to do alone. Working in teams works extremely well.

When it comes to putting a volunteer on a plane with perhaps an overnight stay in another city, the volunteer needs a travel companion (either you or someone else best suited to make this visit).

HOW TO CREATE AN ADVISORY COMMITTEE

Some organizations have a committee of professionals that serves as an advisory board to the planned giving program. Such a committee can be helpful to an institution serving a local community and can help increase visibility for the institution. The committee would consist of the following types of people:

- life insurance agent
- stock broker
- real estate broker
- probate attorney
- trust officer
- accountant
- tax lawyer
- estate planner

There are three uses for such a committee. First, by recruiting key individuals from the local community, the charity gains visibility and exposure for its work. Second, the collective expertise of the committee can be called upon when needed with regard to specific gift situations. Third, the committee members may be used to screen donor lists, identify major prospects, and, in rare cases, help in fund raising.

Another way the committee can help is in providing articles about various gift arrangements for inclusion in your institution's magazine or newsletter. You can quickly see how mutually beneficial such an arrangement can be. For example, the trust officer can write an article about the use of charitable trusts in estate planning. This saves you time, gains valuable exposure for the bank, and may trigger support for your organization.

The composition of the advisory committee also provides a built-in panel for an estate planning seminar with donors.

When it comes to legal matters, however, there is a limit to the amount of work they can or will be able to do for you. You cannot expect a volunteer committee member to help you devise an estate plan, draft a charitable remainder trust, or prepare a draft will for a prospect. Your institution's own legal counsel should handle specific donor-related matters.

The one thing you cannot really expect from your advisory committee is fund raising. Generally, the people you recruit will not be major prospects or donors. My own experience in inheriting an advisory committee at Boston College was that it had outlived its useful life. It had been created long, long ago during the period when the planned giving program was new. When I entered the picture, I had to figure out what to do with it. After two years, I disbanded the committee, deciding instead to focus on working only with fund raising volunteers. That was a good decision for me.

I suspect there may be planned giving officers, especially in the health care field, who have a vigorous advisory committee that is active and productive. If I were employed by an organization that did not have a built-in constituency, I would probably explore such a committee myself.

HOW TO USE VOLUNTEERS IN PLANNING EVENTS

A volunteer contact in another city can be an invaluable resource in helping to make arrangements for a donor event.

Here are just a few of the things a volunteer can do for you:

- Help locate an appropriate location for an event. The volunteer can telephone local hotels, restaurants, or clubs to research prices, facilities, menus and other details. Often, a donor is a member of a local club and can reserve facilities for you, act as the local contact with the facility, and handle the logistics for you by arriving in advance of the other guests to ensure that the proper arrangements have been made. Such tasks as laying out name tags on a reception table, arranging place cards, checking equipment like microphones, projectors, or other audio-visual aids can be done for you.

- Host an event at his or her home. The event can be a small luncheon of two to three people or a buffet dinner for 50.

- Be the local contact for RSVPs. This simply means putting the volunteer's name, address, and phone number on the reply card and having all responses directed there. A local contact also will be able to provide directions more easily than you can.

- Provide overnight accommodations for you or other staff.

- Pick up and drop off elderly guests who might not otherwise be able to attend.

- Call people on the invitation list to encourage them to attend.

HOW TO WORK WITH ONE VOLUNTEER ON A SOLICITATION

You do not need a formal committee to use volunteers in solicitations. But, if you have not worked with volunteers in the past, you might be a little apprehensive about where to start. Let me walk you through one situation so that you can see how easily you can work with a volunteer.

First, review your list of donors. Who has participated in one of your life income plans at a fairly high level? Realizing that each organization has different levels for major gifts, you could be thinking of someone with a $10,000 gift annuity or a $500,000 charitable remainder trust. After a while on the job, you'll have relationships with some very good and loyal people, most of whom have probably never played a role as a volunteer. Still, you can probably identify one or two whom you like, and whose commitment to the organization through a deferred gift has clearly been a good experience. Pick one.

How do you approach the subject of recruiting your volunteer to go on a visit with you? It starts with a frank conversation during which you acknowledge the donor's support, loyalty, and dedication to the institution.

"Hello, [name of donor]. This is [you] from XYZ Charity. Is this a good time to talk? As you know, we've been working very hard to [fill in your own message]. Your support has meant a lot. Over the past few months, we've been trying to do a couple of things. The first is to identify potential supporters from reviewing our donor lists with friends like you in order to see who ought to be in our sights. The second is to identify current donors who know these individuals and who would be willing to help us approach them."

The donor may not have volunteered in a fund raising capacity before. He or she may be hesitant. Or, he or she may not want to do this at all. You need to ask for two things.

"Today, I want to talk to you about helping us in one or both of these two activities. Would you be willing to review a list to help us identify people who could be involved to a greater degree? And, would you be willing to help with one or more of them?"

Usually, people are willing to review lists for you. If you have already been conducting screening sessions, you may have a set of names already identified. Then, you will go through the following process.

1. After reviewing a screening list with the donor, you'll know if there are prospects known to the donor.

2. Ask if the donor feels comfortable helping with any of these people.

3. Get an appointment. There are many ways to do this, but the one that seems to work best for me is to write a letter to the prospect for the donor's signature. You can get the basics on paper and allow the donor to fine tune it to suit the individual circumstances of the relationship.

4. Following up on the letter. The best approach is for the donor to call the prospect with a couple of mutually convenient dates to meet. If your donor does not want to make the call, then the letter should say, "My liaison at XYZ Charity will be calling you to see if either of these dates is convenient for you."

5. If, as does happen, the donor simply feels uncomfortable about being involved, you can still discuss a strategy for the prospect that you would carry out on your own.

If you get an appointment, you must determine the purpose of the visit and the role each of you will play.

- Who is going to say what?
- Is the prospect ready to be solicited or should this be a cultivation visit?
- How much are you going to ask for?

- What type of gift arrangement will you suggest?
- How will you counter objections?
- What special incentives can be used?

Make a list of things you intend to cover during the meeting and review them with your volunteer in advance. Also, prepare a formal proposal summarizing those things and reinforcing the request you intend to make. The proposal can be left with the prospect at the end. If you have the time, you can prepare more than one proposal with different gift amounts. That way, depending on the discussion, you can leave the prospect the one that makes sense.

During the visit, don't beat around the bush. Get to the point. The prospect knows the purpose of the meeting. If the prospect were not interested in your organization, he or she probably would not have allowed the visit in the first place.

The volunteer—not you—should ask for the gift. Practice in advance with the volunteer. Encourage the volunteer to look the prospect straight in the eyes without blinking and say, "Joe, it is our hope you will consider a commitment of $_____ to this cause." Or, "Joe, we're counting on you to provide the leadership support so vital during these initial stages and hope you can join us with a commitment of $_____."

Sometimes it is helpful to use a gift range. "Joe, we're talking to people like you in the hope of attracting gifts in the rage of $50,000 to $100,000."

After *the* question has been asked, there may be a tendency for everyone to become anxious. This is the worst thing that can happen. As a result of getting nervous, there is a good chance either you or the volunteer will speak without giving the prospect the time needed to think and to respond. Don't make a peep until the prospect says something. Let the prospect fill the awkward silence first.

There are times when such a visit will require a detailed discussion of the gift arrangement. The volunteer can be an excellent advocate if he or she already has participated in the form of gift you are suggesting.

In other cases, it will be more appropriate to leave the proposal behind and follow up personally to discuss the details of the proposal. Most important, the volunteer reinforces the importance of the cause while deferring to you any complex discussion of the form the gift might take.

You will rarely receive a direct answer during the visit. The prospect will need to think it over, or consult with a financial advisor, spouse, or other person. If you're soliciting a campaign gift, most experts advise against leaving a pledge card behind because you may never see it again. A better approach is to schedule another visit when you can return to continue the discussion and perhaps close the gift. Some prospects will not let you do this. As a result, you must use your skill and sensitivity in delivering the urgency of the message without going overboard.

Throughout this encounter, the volunteer needs your full support and encouragement. He or she will be just as anxious as you are about the outcome and may feel unduly pressured to perform. The fear of rejection is ever present. Whatever happens, you must reinforce the value of the volunteer's role.

Your chances of success are good provided that you have orchestrated the right meeting at the right time with the right person. As soon as you get the gift (or pledge), notify the volunteer immediately. Make sure your volunteer gets plenty of credit. The volunteer should telephone the prospect to say thank you.

After a successful solicitation, it is not hard to see how quickly you can develop a lasting relationship with the volunteer. Whether the volunteer is a trustee, a donor, a program director, a faculty member, a doctor, or any other person, with this success behind you, the two of you will share a new camaraderie.

OFFICE USES FOR VOLUNTEERS

If your office is like most, you never have enough hands. And, while some donors would never volunteer for fund raising duties, they may be eager and willing to do other things. Following are some tasks that volunteers can do:

- address invitations or holiday greeting cards;
- stuff envelopes;
- affix postage to a mailing;
- conduct research activities on prospects (See Chapter I–5);
- compile information packets or solicitation kits;
- type and file;
- collate.

HOW TO USE VOLUNTEERS FOR SCREENING SESSIONS

In this activity, a volunteer is recruited to help identify leadership potential in your donor base, and will, one hopes, join the team in helping to solicit one or more of those key prospects. Refer to Chapter I–5 for a full discussion of the screening process.

SUMMARY

Without volunteers, many nonprofit organizations would not exist. But, managing volunteers requires patience, sensitivity, and, most of all, time. Select your volunteers carefully and keep their activities to a level that you can manage. Otherwise, you will find yourself spending a disproportionate amount of time managing them.

As I mentioned at the beginning of this chapter, involving prospects as volunteers is an important technique in cultivating them for future gifts. Because only a select few can work directly with you in a volunteer capacity, you must use other methods to ensure that the rest of your donors or prospects are being cultivated on a regular basis. The next chapter examines cultivation—an essential ingredient in all successful fund raising programs.

Chapter III–3

CULTIVATION AND STEWARDSHIP

Cultivation is important in any successful fund raising program. Planned giving is no exception. Cultivation involves many levels of activity, some that are very time consuming, some that are costly, and some that can be done on a mass scale for minimal cost. Not everyone needs the same level of cultivation or stewardship. As a planned giving officer, you must develop a method of setting priorities. Then, you must be able to carry on many activities simultaneously and track them religiously.

In the 12-month Calendar of Activities in Chapter I-4, cultivation is being accomplished on many levels:

1. Members of the board are being cultivated through their involvement in the leadership gifts phase of the program. They are gaining knowledge of planned gift options by attending a training seminar. They are screening lists of potential donors. They are soliciting prospects or helping you with calls or visits. And, they are receiving progress reports at their quarterly meetings. All of this will result in a greater understanding of their role, a renewed pride in and a commitment to the institution, and, one hopes, financial support.

2. The members of the planned giving committee are being cultivated within the context of their work. They undergo an orientation day during which they meet your institution's leadership; they attend a training session about planned gift options; they make visits and solicitations, and some may be involved as hosts for an event.

3. Other prospects and donors are assisting with screening sessions. In the process, they are learning first hand about your institution's plans, needs, and long-term goals and are gaining a heightened awareness of their own role.

4. Some individuals may be profiled in case studies in your planned giving brochure. Thus, they are receiving public recognition as leaders in the program and will be more inclined to remain involved.

5. Other prospects and donors may have been recruited as office volunteers. Their time spent helping out, even in the most tedious ways, will make their commitment to the institution stronger.

Notwithstanding that many activities in building your program fit into the category of cultivation, there are decisions to be made about who gets attention and how much attention each will get. Let me start with a discussion of those prospects assigned to you.

CREATING AND MANAGING YOUR PROSPECT PORTFOLIO

If you had the title of Major Gift Officer, you probably would have 250 to 300 prospects in your prospect portfolio. Presumably, your organization has a way to track prospect assignments by computer. Some organizations have a computer field for a staff name assigned to a prospect. In other organizations, there may be more than one slot for staff assignments (a primary and secondary contact). Still in others, you will find spaces for volunteer assignments as well.

Usually, major gifts officers receive prospect assignments based on a minimum expected gift level. At Boston College, for example, a major gift prospect was determined to be $50,000 to $100,000, and a leadership gift prospect would be capable of $100,000 to $1 million in gift potential. Principal gift prospects had a potential gift level of $1 million and over. Some organizations have levels above $5 million or $10 million.

Each gift range assumed a five-year pledge of the required amount. Because our development office was fairly large, the major gifts prospects were assigned to the annual giving department, thus affording the annual fund an element of a capital-type or multi-year fund raising operation. The annual giving staff would attempt to get pledges of $10,000 per year for five years for a $50,000 pledge where each $10,000 was a repeatable annual fund gift.

Some smaller organizations will be surprised that gifts or prospects of this size would be solicited by the annual giving program. If you can manage it within the culture of your development office, prospects for $5,000 or $10,000 should be steered into the annual giving department, even if the expected gifts from some of the people would be in the pooled income fund or in the gift annuity program. Training the annual giving staff in the basics of the gift annuity or the pooled income fund is not difficult. Of course, your organization would also need a gift-crediting policy such that gifts to life-income plans count in the annual giving program. Not all organizations are willing to do this.

In contrast to the major gift or leadership gift officers whose prospects are assigned primarily by gift level, the planned giving officer's assignments are quite varied. This is a big problem because planned giving officers spend way too much time on small prospects that ought to be assigned to annual giving. Most likely, the planned giving officer will be assigned not only large planned giving prospects but also $5,000 gift annuity prospects, as well as bequest prospects. Plus, the planned giving officer may also be assigned other miscellaneous prospects who have returned reply cards but who are yet unrated or unverified as legitimate.

If you inherit a planned giving program, you will most likely inherit the following categories of prospects:

- Donors in the pooled income fund and the gift annuity program including those who made one gift of $5,000 years ago and never intend to give again;

- Donors who have a charitable remainder trust;

- Donors who have charitable lead trusts;

- Donors who contributed a primary residence or a farm with retained life tenancy;

- Donors who have named your organization beneficiary and/or owner of a life insurance policy;

- Donors who have a known bequest or other estate gift;

- Donors who have contributed odd assets or tangible personal property;

- People who have made inquiries from your marketing activities, ads or other promotions;

- People who live in a region where there is critical mass of retired people.

Dealing with this diverse group is difficult so you must divide the group into categories and set priorities.

Group 1   Identify the top 100 people with the greatest capacity to give from all of the above categories. At first, you will be making some guesses as well as taking the advice of your colleagues. Your first pass on this process will give you a working group with which to start. As you learn about the prospects, you will adjust the group continually, removing some people who should not be in the top 100, and adding others who are uncovered or reevaluated later. Some of the people in this group have already made large gifts and need to be stewarded, some of the people are already in a cultivation process that should lead to a gift as the process unfolds, and some of the people on your list have no involvement yet but are known to have high gift potential.

Group 2   The next group is comprised of lower level donors already in the pooled income fund or the gift annuity program. Some may be giving $5,000 or $10,000 *per* year as repeat donors to their favorite life income plans. Others are one or two-time donors to these plans, but they haven't made a repeat gift for a number of years.

Group 3   The next group is comprised of the known bequest intentions (or revocable life insurance donors) who are not already identified separately for Group 1 or Group 2.

Group 4   The final is comprised of miscellaneous prospects identified through your marketing activities (ads, mailings, *etc.*).

Focus on Your Top 100 Prospects

There are many ways to cultivate prospects. Still, the most important thing you must do is visit with your prospects. Visits are costly and time consuming, and they take a lot of planning, effort, and initiative. Obviously, you should spend the most time on the people with the biggest potential. This happens to be your top 100. If you are running a mature planned giving program, you might have as many as 200 or 300 on your official list. However, always keep a separate priority list of the top 100. To do this, your organization should have two ways to tag prospects in its computer system. You need a staff assignment and also a dollar rating. Then, you can sort your prospects by dollar potential so that you can keep the top 100 in your sights.

Invite Prospects To A Cultivation Event

Every contact with a donor should not be a solicitation. Unfortunately, this is exactly what happens in too many cases. The result is that a donor contributes once, maybe even twice, but soon feels taken for granted. There has to be something more between solicitations.

An excellent way to educate prospects or donors about your institution's work is to hold a series of group events. For example, invite prospects to a breakfast, lunch, cocktail party, or dinner. If you do not have facilities in house for a proper event, hold it somewhere else. The objective is to introduce the prospects to your president, executive director, or to any other prominent person(s) connected to the institution. Give your donors an insider's view of your current activities or plans. In some cases, especially during a campaign, these events are quasi group solicitations with the expectation that you will follow up with the attendees after the event for a private discussion about a contribution. In other cases, the event is an educational experience for the attendees.

Once you determine the format, you can repeat the same event for different groups. Here are some tips to make the most of these events:

- Invite about 50 people to get a group of 10 to 12 (five or six couples).

- To increase attendance, recruit a donor to call the others to encourage attendance.

- Select one of the guests to be the honorary host or hostess for the event. Then, let the host pick the guests from a larger list of prospects. In this way, the invitation can come from a peer and will generate a higher response rate. The host or hostess should make a brief introduction before introducing your president or the featured speaker or speakers.

    Here is a sample breakfast introduction: "I have long been interested in the important work of this institution, and I'm delighted to be part of this gathering today. Our purpose is to share with you some of the exciting programs this institution is running. We realize everyone is on a tight schedule; therefore, we have allowed 45 minutes for breakfast, 20 minutes for the presentation and 10 minutes for questions. As promised, the program will end at 8:45 am, but you are welcome to stay longer if your schedule permits."

- Stick to the schedule. Here are suggested times for various events:

  Breakfast: 7:00 am or 7:30 am to 9:00 am
  Lunch: 12:00 pm to 1:30 pm or 2:00 pm
  Cocktails: 5:30 pm or 6:00 pm to 7:00 pm or 7:30 pm
  Dinner: 7:30 pm to 9:30 pm

- If you are planning several similar events, find good caterers and stick with them. Eventually, they'll know exactly what you want, and you can get the whole thing running like clockwork—from introduction to coffee.

- Identify one or more of the participants from one event who might be willing to be host or hostess of a future event.

Create A Recognition Society

One of the greatest challenges for many institutions is creating a bond or an affiliation where none exists. Colleges, universities, religious organizations and perhaps hospitals are the kinds of institutions that already have a constituency. The others draw from the general public a varied group of supporters. A recognition society can build an important bond between you and your constituency.

One of the most obvious groups for such a society is your universe of bequest donors. (See Chapter II-10 for a discussion of incentives for a bequest society.)

Most organizations have a society for donors who have made any kind of deferred gift or commitment. This includes donors with bequest intentions, life income plans, real estate with retained life tenancy, life insurance, and charitable lead trusts. It is often appropriate to have a recognition society that covers both irrevocable gifts (such as life income plans) and revocable gifts (such as bequest intentions). You will have a larger critical mass, especially if you are running a new planned giving program.

Recruit Donors Or Prospects To Conduct Screening Sessions

During a screening session, individuals develop a heightened awareness of their own role from talking about the potential role of others. When a prospect is reluctant to support the fund raising effort, involving him or her in a screening session may provide the necessary inspiration. For a discussion of how to run a screening session, refer to Chapter I–5.

Recruit Donors Or Prospects To Accompany You On Visits

Probably the best way to cultivate a prospect or donor is to involve the person in visiting or soliciting someone else. Chapter III–2 tells you how to create and work with a volunteer solicitation committee or how to work with just one volunteer.

Ask Donors Or Prospects To Submit An Article For Your Organization's Newsletter Or Magazine

Many people enjoy being the center of attention. Highlight the accomplishments of members of your constituency by asking them to submit an article for general consumption. For example, a Red Cross volunteer can write about a success story. A doctor can explain a new medical breakthrough. An attorney can discuss how to select the best legal counsel. A heart attack victim in a hospital can write about the experience. Within your constituency, regardless of who you are—the Red Cross, a hospital, a law school—there are people with a story to tell.

Write A Feature Story About A Donor

Recognition for major support can be very important both to the donor and to others. You can illustrate the benefits of a specific gift vehicle by explaining how the gift worked for one donor. By providing a real life example of a planned gift, you both cultivate the donor and educate your constituency at the same time.

Call Donors Just To See How They're Doing

When was the last time you called a donor just to talk? A ten minute phone conversation creates an enormous amount of good will and friendship.

When I was at Wheaton College, we had a database that included the date of birth for all deferred giving donors. I am making a distinction between "deferred gifts" and "outright gifts" because usually we learned the date of birth for a donor in the context of processing a deferred gift (pooled income fund, gift annuity, charitable remainder trust, life insurance, or bequest intention). At the time, there were about 425 people on our list. Each month, I produced a list of upcoming birthdays and routed it to our president, vice president, director of development and director of annual giving so that every staff member working in a solicitation capacity had a chance to select one or more donors for "Happy Birthday" calls. It did not matter who called the donor as long as the staff member with the most important relationship made the call.

The birthday calls served several purposes:

- Every person was called at least once per year.

- People liked being called on their birthdays.

- Within the context of a birthday call, it was possible to maneuver the conversation toward a discussion of life income gifts, especially for those donors already participating in a life income plan.

It may take some persuasive tactics on your part to get the chief executive officer to make some of these phone calls. To introduce the idea, start with one donor whom you know has a good relationship with the CEO—perhaps someone who was solicited within the year. To make this as easy as possible, you should prepare for the CEO a summary of the donor's involvement including a history of contributions. Include the phone number and a blank "memo for the file." After the call, the CEO writes a brief summary of the conversation on the memo and returns it to you. The whole thing takes 10 minutes. This approach may not work in every organization because some executives will not want to do this. Don't worry about it. If you suggest an activity and it doesn't go over well, drop it and move on.

Those donors who do not warrant a phone call can receive a birthday card instead. Most important, this activity affords you the opportunity to make a determination about each donor's cultivation needs at least annually. Some donors will be passed over because they don't need this phone call. For example, a person who would otherwise receive a call may have sat next to you at last week's bequest luncheon. Enough is enough. Use your time on the person who may be geographically distant and who rarely visits the institution.

Send Greeting Cards For Holidays And Special Occasions

Building on the discussion above, those people who cannot be called can receive a birthday card instead. Again, you may wish to select several who deserve a card (which you prepare, of course) from your CEO. The CEO (or someone else assigned to do this) absolutely must sign these cards. A preprinted signature is no good. You should also suggest appropriate comments like:

- "Thank you again for your gift last month."
- "I'm glad to hear you're coming to our luncheon next week."
- "I'm sorry I was out of town when you visited recently."
- "Debra tells me you're considering another gift annuity. That's wonderful."

The CEO probably doesn't have daily knowledge of the above items; therefore, your suggestions can be very helpful.

The same activity can be undertaken during the holiday season except that a holiday greeting card list usually encompasses a more general group of donors. Before you send holiday cards, you should review the list and remove the ones that need a handwritten message from you, from the CEO, director of development, or from one of your other colleagues.

Sometimes, the organization plans a holiday greeting card list for the president whose signature is preprinted on the card and then mailed to a cast of thousands. If that approach is taken in your organization, you should still do your own set of cards to allow more personal notes to your donors. This activity takes a lot of time. Luckily for me, I worked 15 years for higher education and there was always a work-study student to write envelopes for me or, more recently, to feed envelopes into a printer for a couple of hours. You would never use mailing labels on a greeting card.

Usually, you'll receive some kind of marketing piece in late summer from a greeting card vendor who found your name. You should order your holiday cards early and plan the logistics in the fall before you get busy with year-end giving.

Send Special Thank-You Gifts During The Holiday Season

Everyone likes a surprise. Each year, select a group of special donors for a token holiday gift. For example, when I was at WGBH, we sent chocolates made into the shape of our logo. Another year we sent a WGBH Calendar, a Julia Child cookbook, or a WGBH umbrella. Route the list of names to the CEO and to other development professionals so that each donor receives the item from the best possible contact within the institution. At Boston College, we had logo chocolates one year. If you don't have an item specific to your organization, you can simply go to a store and select something for between $5 and $10. Don't get bogged down in what to send. You could wrap up a jar of apricot jam or gourmet mustard and ship it off knowing that the donor would be delighted upon receiving it together with a personal note from you. This doesn't have to be a big, time-consuming and costly activity at all.

Ask Donors To Loan You Something

An excellent way to cultivate prospects or to steward donors is to ask them to loan you something. The most obvious thing people can loan you is space. Donors can loan you a home or a country club for an event. At Wheaton, we did not have a telemarketing or phonathon room and, therefore, asked donors or trustees to let us use their centrally-located offices in different cities for group calling nights with alumni callers. We also asked brokers, attorneys, or bankers if we could use space in a corporate conference room for volunteer meetings in other cities or states.

How many of your donors own airplanes? Borrow a donor's plane to take your president somewhere. Borrow a painting for an exhibit. Borrow a Rolls Royce for a special procession. Borrow expertise. Whenever you ask for help, you will involve the prospect in a process that builds a stronger relationship.

Invite Major Donors Or Prospects To Become A Member of Your Board of Trustees

As board members turn over or come to the end of their terms, replace non supportive members with others who have already demonstrated the financial commitment necessary for a board member. There is no magic dollar amount for a board member's gift. For some very small organizations, the level might be $10,000. For others, the level will be $1 million. I am not suggesting that you let people buy their way onto the board. I am suggesting that you look closely at your current donor or prospect list to see if there are prospects who could be invited to be on the board as a way to cultivate or steward them further.

Invite Donors Or Prospects To Become Featured Speakers At An Event

Sometimes there is no gracious way to start a relationship with a prospect who is not close to the institution. Perhaps you have already tried approaches that involve your trustees or president, all unsuccessfully. When all else fails, an invitation to speak may be perfect. There are opportunities for such an approach all around you, but you must be creative.

Whatever the nature of your organization, you ought to be thinking about these kinds of opportunities constantly. Whenever your institution is planning an event, try to make some kind of a match between the purpose of the event and the list of your top 100 prospects or donors.

At Wheaton, we invited major prospects for things like the following:

- For a volunteer training day, the wife of the governor of Pennsylvania was asked to make a keynote address;

- On a career planning day for students, four major prospects were asked to participate in a panel on the subject;

- At an estate planning seminar, a probate attorney was invited to discuss the importance of having a properly drafted will;

- During a reunion weekend, the wife of the former U.S. Ambassador to Russia and her husband were asked to do a lecture on international diplomacy.

At Boston College, we invited major prospects to participate in all kinds of speaking roles from keynote speeches at Commencement to panel discussions in front of a room of other prospects, to guest lectures in classrooms.

You, too, can add this strategy to your list of cultivation activities.

Naming Opportunities

Leaving one's mark on the world is an important desire for many people. Your institution has the unique power to give a donor immortality through one of the following ways:

- Honor a donor by associating his/her name with a building, floor, wing, conference room, classroom, office, or smaller division of your building. You can also broaden the list of naming opportunities to include equipment, walls, stairs, handicapped-access ramps, atriums, patios, bridges, roads, elevators, lockers, pews, floors, skylights, trees, pools, saunas, studios, galleries, automobiles, and ponds. The list of naming opportunities is unlimited.

- Create ways to link someone's name to an important aspect of your operation. For example,

A Scholarship Fund	college or school
A Lecture Series	art museum
A Program Fund for Feeding the Homeless	social service agency
A Library Fund	library, college, school
A Research Fund	hospital, university
A Fund for Classical Programming	National Public Radio
An Endowed Fund for Vehicles	Meals on Wheels

For organizations just starting an endowment program, you may not have a structure to allow for a named endowed fund concept. Therefore, you need to create one. For higher education, the culture for such funds is well in place. Other organizations may be reluctant to create restricted endowed fund programs for the simple reasons that they don't want restricted gifts or they don't have the infrastructure to manage them.

The fact of the matter is you need an endowed fund strategy because many donors want to tie their large gifts to something specific with their name on it. So how do you do this?

First, you must identify restricted purposes for endowment income use. Organizations have varied needs, but surely each one can create a method to do this. Consider the overall objectives of the organization. What activities do you perform? Can you isolate expenses for a particular program or activity and create an endowed fund opportunity to support it? Of course, you can!

What is the appropriate minimum gift size for a named endowed fund? When I posed this question to a group of nonprofit organizations, the response was very broad. Organizations allow endowed funds to be set up from $5,000 to $100,000.

Here is an unscientific sample list of endowed fund minimums around the country:

Boston College	$100,000. Spending limit is 6%. Fund is activated in first fiscal year following the year it is completely funded.
Vassar College	$100,000.
Yale University	$100,000.
Santa Clara University	$50,000. Three-year pledge okay.
Memorial Medical Center Foundation	$50,000. Considering $100,000.
Smithsonian National Air and Space Museum	$50,000. Considering $100,000.
Marietta College	$25,000. Spending limit is 5.5%.
Lifespan Foundations	$25,000. Fund must exist three years before using payout of 4%.
Baylor Healthcare System	$25,000.
Children's Hospital of the Kings Daughters	$25,000. Can be paid over five years. For funds established with gift annuities, minimum is $50,000.
University of Scranton	$25,000.
Iowa Health Foundation	$25,000.
Lake Forest College	$25,000. (book fund). $50,000. (scholarship). $1.5 million (professorship)
Children's Hospital of Wisconsin	$25,000.
St. Louis Children's Hospital	$25,000.
SUNY New Paltz	$20,000 (usually scholarships). Can start with $5,000 and pay over five years.
Middlesex College County Fdn.	$20,000. Can pay over several years.
Ball State University	$20,000. (general endowment). $25,000. (scholarship).
Keuka College	$15,000.
The Seton Fund	$10,000.
Webster University	$10,000. Going to $25,000 in 2002.
Madison Community Foundation	$10,000. Can build in increments of $1,000.
Creighton University	$10,000. (book fund). $25,000. (scholarship). $50,000. (annual lecture, graduate scholarship).
University of Alaska Foundation	$10,000. Probably going to $20,000.
San Francisco Performances	$10,000.
Christopher Newport University	$10,000.
Elkhart County Community Fdn.	$5,000. Would like to move it to $10,000.
Merrimack College	$5,000. (book fund). $20,000. (scholarship).
Rockhurst University	$5,000.

Some of the organizations allowing $5,000, $10,000 or $25,000 gift minimums for endowed funds consider the lower minimums important in getting people in the door. In many cases, the programs are relatively young so that there is not yet an administrative problem. My guess is that there will eventually be a huge administrative burden for institutions with low endowed fund minimums. No doubt, this pressure will drive the minimum gift levels up in the future.

To manage an endowed fund program, the trustees of a nonprofit organization establish a spending limit for endowed funds based on a percentage of the fund's value, usually on the first day of the fiscal year. This spending limit changes over time, but it is tied to the concept of investing for a total return on the assets. There is no tax on short-term or long-term capital gain for a nonprofit organization. Therefore, while the endowment investment objective is for total return including income and capital appreciation, a separate spending rate allows for reasonable use of the donors' funds while allowing excess income or appreciation to stay in the fund so that the principal can keep up with inflation.

When I was working for Boston University, the spending limit for endowed funds was 5% of the average market value for the prior 20 quarters. That strategy evened out the ups and downs of the market and provided a spending limit that took into account a historical perspective on the asset value. At Boston College, the spending limit was 6% of the June 1 value of each account. The percentage spending limit is agreed upon annually at a trustees' meeting. Most organizations currently have a spending rule of between 4% and 6%.

For a $10,000 endowed fund at the 5% spending limit, the annual spendable income is only $500. For a $100,000 fund, the spending amount is $5,000. My recommendation is that you consider endowed fund opportunities for no less than $50,000. Otherwise, you are managing very small funds for restricted purposes, and that is very, very costly to do. However, there are still unique situations that justify smaller funds. For example, one person I spoke with commented that the tuition at a state school is only $6,000, so $500 makes a difference to a student. Even this person said that his organization wanted to get to a point where it is awarding no less than $1,000 at a time.

One final comment on this topic: In 1993, the endowed fund minimum at Boston College was $25,000. By mid-1994, the minimum was raised to $50,000. A couple of years later, the minimum was raised to $100,000. Each time we raised the bar, there was an uneasiness among the staff because certain donors would be left by the roadside. In reality, while that was true, the increased levels were quickly and easily incorporated into the plans such that the fund raisers increasingly focused on larger prospects. The entire program was ratcheted up very effectively. Looking back, I remember strongly opposing the increase from $50,000 to $100,000, but, the higher levels forced all of the fund raisers to work on larger prospects. And, the money still kept coming in. A consequence of increasing your endowed fund minimum is that you immediately relegate a group of your prospects to a lower priority list all at once. You will feel badly about this when it happens. For a while, you can still keep relationships with some of the lower-level donors, but for all practical purposes, you must move on and spend your time on the larger prospects.

Print Lists of Supporters

A quick look at the institutions that raise the most money will show a highly structured plan for recognition of contributions. Printing the names of your supporters has two beneficial results: 1) it creates an elite affiliation, and 2) it serves as an example and inspiration for others. Donors check the list and want to see who else has contributed at each level. Frequently, they will also tell you who is missing from the higher levels. Cultivation in this way goes beyond planned giving and really starts with the annual giving program.

If you have a deferred giving society, you ought to print a list of the members annually. Before doing so, you must ask the members if they wish their names included. There are a couple of ways to approach this. You could send a letter and ask the donor to return a card if he or she wishes to be included. That approach will work poorly because people who simply don't return the card will be excluded. If that happens, as it did to me once, you will have a significantly smaller list. On the other hand, if you send a letter that says you are planning to list the names of the members but would be happy to exclude anyone who returns the card, you will receive back hardly any cards. Give the members plenty of time to respond if you take the latter approach.

Once you list a donor's name the first time, you probably don't have to ask again in future years. Just worry about the new ones.

Involve Donors Or Prospects In Non-Fund Raising Activities

Your institution probably offers programs or services that lend themselves to new or increased volunteer involvement. Remember, whenever a donor or prospect does anything for your institution, he or she is being cultivated. Don't limit your cultivation or stewardship activities to fund raising.

TURNING CULTIVATION INTO SUPPORT

There are a lot of activities listed earlier in this chapter with regard to cultivation and stewardship. You can, no doubt, think of others. Most of them are not unique to planned giving. They apply to most fund raising positions where relationships and involvement are critical to getting a gift. Regardless of the amount of planned giving you think you are doing, there are some universal reasons why you are not closing as many gifts as you would like. These reasons have nothing to do with your technical expertise in planned giving. The next time you are feeling frustrated by the fact that you are not getting gifts, return to this section and read it again. It can give you the impetus to change a few things that can make a real difference.

You Are Cultivating Prospects Too Long

Sometimes donors or prospects remain in a cultivation stage too long. You must not forget the ultimate objective of the entire process—bringing the prospect to the point where asking for a gift makes sense.

I remember speaking with one of my professional colleagues about cultivation. She had developed many close personal relationships with donors but was not generating gifts. Finally, I asked whether she had actually asked anyone for a gift. Bingo! She admitted that she didn't know when to ask, and that she felt uncomfortable bringing up the subject.

To get control of this problem right now, review the list of people who have been in cultivation for a long time. Focus on the top ten. Decide on a timetable that makes sense for approaching them. The date might be in the next one to six months. Each will be different, but most important is to have a plan that will get each prospect solicited in the near future. Some will say yes and some will say no, not yet, or maybe. Don't worry about the results. Just do it.

You Have Become The Prospect's Friend

Do you have any prospects who feel like friends to you? After the hours and hours of visits, you know them so very well. You know their kids. They know your spouse. You know them so well that it is now awkward to solicit them. How can you make the transition from being the donor's friend to asking for a gift without feeling you have betrayed or tricked the donor? The problem is very common.

You must remember that the donors know what is going on. They know you have a job to do. They expect you to ask for a gift eventually. At the same time, many of your older donors like the personal attention and will continue to enjoy your company month after month, year after year, without ever making a substantial gift. I don't count token gifts. I'm talking about the kind of gift that put the donor in your sights in the first place.

If you find yourself in this situation, here are some suggested ideas for broaching the subject of a gift on your next visit:

- "Mrs. Smith, in the past year, I've come to appreciate how much you care about this institution. When I visited you last, we talked about how important your affiliation has been to you, and few people understand better than you do the challenges we face to continue the quality of our programs.

As you know, we must look to the future and place greater emphasis on building our permanent endowment fund. Today, I want to talk to you about several ways others have helped and to learn whether you would be interested in considering how you, too, can become involved. . . ."

- "Mrs. Jones, when I met you for the first time last year to thank you for including XYZ charity in your will, I realized how much satisfaction you derived from making a commitment like that. Since then, you have visited the institution and have seen first hand how great an impact XYZ has had on this community. The kind of commitment you have made indicates a deep understanding of the value of the institution as well as the depth of your interest. I want to explore with you today a way you can convert your bequest into a current gift while retaining income for your lifetime as well as enjoying other economic benefits. . . ."

- "Mr. Maxwell, when you helped us in March with our screening session, I realized how much your knowledge of our constituency would mean to the success of the campaign. Your help has been invaluable, and I'm pleased to tell you the results of our solicitation efforts. We've since met with many of the prospects and have secured commitments from three on our major gift list. Our success is due in large measure to the information you provided. In order to reach our goal, we will need the broadest possible participation from our constituency, and, as you can surely guess, we're counting on you, too. Your leadership can make a meaningful difference, and I'd like to present one plan that will allow you to participate at our leadership level while generating the income you need. . . ."

- "Gary, your 50th reunion is coming up next year. Your long affiliation with this college demonstrates a strong dedication and commitment. As you consider how best to mark your milestone reunion, what would you say to the idea of permanently linking your name to. . . ."

Take some time to formulate a conversation in advance for the people on your list of donor friends. Practice what you are going to say, and say it on the next visit.

You Talk Too Much

Fund raisers like you have a lot to say. But, sometimes you talk too much, especially in the early stages of a relationship. By doing that, you prevent the prospects from telling you what is important to them. You can turn your visits into important discussions by getting the prospects to do the talking. Don't be concerned if you don't have a chance to describe the latest hot program at the institution. At this stage, you still don't know what the donor feels is important. During your discussion, ask questions that the donor cannot answer with a yes or no. Try some of these openings and see how much more productive your conversations become.

- Tell me about . . . .
- Describe . . . .
- How do you . . . .
- When do you . . . .
- How is it that you . . . .

You Don't Have A Strategy For The Prospect

It is not good enough to be able to chat with a person in a friendly way. Most fund raisers can do that very well. People like us can meet a new person, engage in conversation, and never let a pregnant pause occur. But, at the end of the visit, what have we done to move the prospect along? In many cases, not much.

Before you meet someone, whether it is the first time or the fifth time, determine what you want out of that visit. Perhaps you are still trying to determine how family obligations will affect a charitable decision. Perhaps you need to know if the prospect uses an advisor. Maybe you need to convince the prospect to agree to a meeting with someone at the institution. Or, perhaps you want to find out whom the prospect respects the most on your board of trustees.

Before you meet with your next prospect, review the history of the relationship. Write down two or three things that are important to discuss on this visit. If you do that, you will always move a prospect along during the visit instead of simply treading water.

You Don't Bring A Proposal With You On The Visit

How often have you solicited a prospect and promised to put something in writing just as soon as possible? How many times after saying that did you find days and weeks passing before you were able to write the proposal? Your intentions are honest, but the reality of the work on your desk thwarts your best plans. Sometimes, you wait so long before sending the proposal that it becomes embarrassing. Don't let this happen again.

Instead of waiting until after the visit, prepare a proposal to bring with you. No doubt, by the time you are ready to discuss a particular kind of gift for a particular purpose, you are ready to put it on paper before the visit. If you don't know exactly what gift amount to suggest and want some flexibility during the visit, bring several different proposals. You'll know during the conversation which one to leave behind.

There Are No Defined Institutional Goals

If your organization's president and board members are doing the job, there will be a set of long-term goals. It is much easier for a fund raiser to perform his or her job when there is a clear direction and a clear set of funding priorities. The priorities and goals should have timetables and specific dollar amounts for each category, even if you are not in a campaign. Otherwise, you cannot possibly focus the message for your donors.

If your organization doesn't have clearly defined goals, you cannot create them yourself. On the other hand, if you are either the executive director or president, and sometimes the director of development, you have the power to take charge of this task.

Having properly defined goals includes a structure for naming opportunities which was discussed earlier in this chapter. If you are working in a small development office, you could possibly put together a suggested list and move it up the food chain for action by those with the power to make decisions. However, if you are working in an organization that has not defined its needs, you are working without a full deck. Do the best you can.

You Procrastinate On Making The Appointment

You have eight hours each day, probably more, to perform your job. But, there are lots of distractions. Plus, menial tasks that you could delegate are still consuming your time. If you analyzed your tasks during a week and rated them on a priority list of one to ten, how many would be tens? My guess is that you are wasting at least half of your day.

Meanwhile, you are avoiding the one task that can bring you success: picking up the phone to get an appointment. Of course, I know that there are tasks you must do in so many categories. Still, if you are honest and were to evaluate precisely how you are spending your time, you would realize that instead of making the important appointments that will allow you to be truly successful, you are wasting time on all kinds of tasks that don't matter.

Here is a simple plan. As long as your schedule allows, begin every day by making one appointment. That includes either calling the prospect directly or writing a letter requesting an appointment or discussing with a volunteer an appointment that he or she could set up. If you tackled this one prime directive each day, you would have attempted five appointments each week and successfully scheduled two or three. As you progress through the month, your schedule will be packed with appointments, and you will be a very happy director of planned giving.

When you have a series of visits continually, you won't be worrying any longer about the other tasks that used to seem so important.

You Are The Wrong Person To Ask For The Gift

If you are like me, you are confident about your ability to build a relationship, establish a bond with a donor, and solicit the gift. Each one of us wants the satisfaction of actually closing the gift. In fact, closing the gift ultimately validates our existence. Still, sometimes the best thing to do is step aside. This is very hard to do, but knowing when to do it and being willing to do it is important. You cannot let your ego interfere with what is right in terms of getting the biggest gift. As good as you are, you cannot always be the right person.

As a planned giving officer, you will develop relationships with some donors whom you can solicit by yourself. Other donors need a more complex strategy if they are to respond with their largest possible gift. Sometimes, after you have developed the relationship, you will lose the prospect to someone else. This could occur under a number of circumstances. For example, a prospect might be reassigned during a prospect review meeting. Or, a member of the board may select a prospect for a personal visit without regard to any prior relationship with you. Also, you may hear at the water cooler about situations or plans related to prospects who are assigned to you.

When this happens, you will feel angry and frustrated because something that was yours has been taken away. In these situations, you may be able to contact the person to whom your prospect is now being linked in order to provide background information about the prospect and to suggest how you can be helpful to the process. Depending on who is involved, you may or may not be allowed to participate. One hopes that the new solicitor will consider your prior relationship before moving ahead with a plan. If not, you must put your ego aside.

For all kinds of reasons, you may be out of the loop completely. Most often, you are out of the loop because you are not a peer of the donor. You are an employee of the institution. If possible, teaming up with a volunteer, with a trustee, or with the president would be excellent. But, always making the solicitation alone is a big mistake. Take this advice to heart. The situation I describe will arise periodically as you negotiate your way as director of planned giving. When you lose control of a prospect who is important to you, let it go. There are plenty of other donors to work on.

On the other hand, you will find that people in your organization are soliciting prospects for deferred gifts without your input. This is a completely different problem. The only way to engage yourself is to build the trust of your colleagues so that they feel comfortable bringing you along or consulting you in the background. If you are new to planned giving, you do not deserve this trust. It will be difficult for you to understand why colleagues exclude you from prospect strategy sessions when you, alone, can deliver the most complex and compelling gift proposal for the prospect. I know how you feel. Being excluded from critical strategy sessions is extremely common for planned giving officers. I have been excluded from so many strategic discussions in my various positions that I could have resigned my positions many times out of frustration. Just know that if this happens to you, it is also happening to many of your peers. Over time, you must build trust among your colleagues so that your input will be sought.

As you gain experience, have some successes, and demonstrate your competence, things will change. Meanwhile, pursue your planned giving objectives, go out and visit people, and close gifts. Don't obsess about the ones you could have had.

You Don't Give The Donor A Date To Respond

When you solicit a gift, do you attempt to close the gift within a certain time frame? Probably. But, do you give the prospect a suggested date to respond to your proposal? Maybe not.

Sometimes, a prospect approaches you with questions about a particular kind of gift. You cannot gracefully give this person a date to respond because the inquiry is driven by the donor, not by you. In other cases, you initiate the gift discussion. Even if you are not in a campaign, you could increase your success rate with these latter cases if you suggest a date to respond.

Each organization has its own timetables and rhythms that make it easy to construct a deadline. For example, there may be a deadline around the following dates:

- the end of the fiscal year;
- the end of the calendar year;
- the end of a challenge grant period;
- the end of a campaign year;
- the end of a reunion cycle; or
- the next trustees' meeting.

If you have a legitimate deadline that you can incorporate into the proposal, you will have a much better chance at getting a decision by that date.

You Solicited The Wrong Person

Who is the donor? Do you really know? Is the donor a male, a female, or a couple? Is there a third party, such as a child or a parent, who ought to be included? You cannot possibly know who the donor is unless you have done your research properly or have inquired about this issue with the prospects themselves. At Wheaton College, the alumnae were women. However, the male spouses of the Wheaton women were critical to the decision making. At Boston College, the older alumni were men. However, the female spouses were often critical to the gift decision.

If you are dealing with only one spouse, don't make the mistake of assuming this person makes the gift decisions alone. You must find out who is the decision maker. Soliciting one half of a couple when both are involved in the gift decisions will doom your plan from the start.

This is an issue for any fund raiser soliciting any prospect, but the problem is magnified if your organization has a single-sex constituency. At Wheaton College, we started a methodical interviewing process for our largest prospects using a strategy developed by Marts & Lundy, our consultants at the time. During the interviews, we moved through a series of questions designed to give us the information we needed to create a proper strategy. The people being interviewed knew that the visit was not a solicitation. Nearly everyone we asked to participate agreed to the interviews. The project was extremely successful at uncovering critical information about prospects who were not close to us. We called our project the W.I.T.S. program standing for Wheaton Interest Test for Support.

We asked questions like the following:

- Whom do you respect most at Wheaton College? [looking for some indication of a current trustee, faculty member, the president or someone else who could be important to the relationship]
- Who were your roommates during your college years? [looking for names who could be connected in a more complex cultivation strategy]
- With whom from your college years do you still remain in touch?
- When was the last reunion you attended?
- Do you read the alumni magazine and what do you think of it?
- What is Wheaton's greatest strength?
- What is Wheaton's greatest challenge?
- What are your top three charitable interests?
- Which of your charitable interests is number one?

- [If Wheaton was not number one] What would it take to make Wheaton number one? [people would describe precisely what was important to them]
- Who makes gift decisions in your household? Is it you, your spouse, or do you do it together or is there someone else involved?

Develop your own questionnaire that elicits the kinds of information described above. Then, you will determine not only who your donors are (the husband, the wife, the couple, *etc.*), but also how to create a long-term strategy for their cultivation and solicitation.

You Talk About What You Need

If you talk about what you need before you know what the donor needs, you are dead in the water. Practically, the donor may very well need income tax savings, capital gain tax savings, or estate tax savings. But, the donor's emotional needs often drive how the donor resolves the others. Beyond the issues of financial or tax planning, the donor may need recognition through a named opportunity. He or she may need an association with a cause that has meaning. He or she may need to control something.

Try to resist the temptation to talk about what you need until you absolutely know what the donor needs. In the end, the donor will drive the gift. Determine what is important to the donor before you offer a lot of information you think is important.

Do your homework first. Figure out the pulse points of the donor before you provide information. Otherwise, you are wasting your time.

You Don't Ask For The Gift

Although you will receive some gifts over the transom, you cannot rely solely on such gifts if you are to be a successful director of planned giving. On average, one third of the people whom you actively solicit for a gift will say yes. The more prospects you solicit, the more gifts you will get. There is nothing more complex about it.

The most flagrant violation of our fund raising culture is the case where the fund raiser does not ask for a gift. You might be able to cite all kinds of excuses for your own poor performance. Complaints such as the following may be familiar to you:

- I have too much work.
- I don't have a secretary.
- I have a terrible list of prospects.
- I have to get out the gift annuity payments this week.
- There is too much administration bogging me down.
- Not only am I doing planned giving, but I am also assigned to other non fund raising tasks.

Let's assume that all of the above complaints are true. So now what? It looks like you will always have excuses not to be soliciting gifts. To get beyond this problem, restructure your priorities so that solicitations move to the top of your to-do list. Instead of avoiding your most important function, do that first, and let something else fall to the bottom.

If you are not asking for gifts, you are not doing your job. As a result, you are nervous all the time. You should figure out who is ready to be asked and go ask them. Enough said.

You Are Afraid Of Rejection

The most intimidating aspect of fund raising is the fear of rejection. We all experience it. New fund raisers experience it. Veteran fund raisers experience it. I never could avoid the heart palpitations of picking up the phone to set up an appointment or the anxiety during an actual solicitation. We all want success. Rejection is not an option for us. It is a failure. We hate to admit our approach didn't work. Our competence depends on getting the gift.

The problem with this anxiety is that it is simply there all the time. You cannot get rid of it. This is true even though the donor is not necessarily rejecting you. Your role is as an agent for the charity. If you believe in the cause, you ought to be able to discuss gifts or appointments without being personally hurt by the result.

One seminar I attended about sales had an interesting approach to rejection. After the first unsuccessful call, you feel a degree of rejection. After the second unsuccessful call, you have an increased degree of rejection. But, on the third call, you should be extremely optimistic. Why? Because, statistically, one out of three people will give you an appointment. So, after two rejections, the third is likely to succeed. Be happy as you approach your third call.

When you are in sales, it is a game of numbers like anything else. If you call enough people, you will get appointments from one third of your calls. If you solicit enough people, you will get gifts from one third of them.

THE FAILED SOLICITATION

If you do everything right, and still get turned down, you must determine whether to keep the prospect on your active cultivation list, reduce the level of cultivation to a lower priority, turn the prospect over to someone else, or eliminate the prospect altogether. The following questions should help:

- Was the prospect solicited by the right person?
- Is there something the prospect is not telling you?
- Did you offer the appropriate gift vehicle?
- Do you have a chance for resubmitting your proposal in the future?
- Was your request too high?
- Should you continue to invite the prospect to events?
- Is there a better way to involve the prospect in your institution's activities?
- How can you move your institution higher up on the prospect's list of priorities?
- Was the refusal due to a temporary state of the donor's affairs?
- Have you left the door open for consideration later?

SUMMARY

My very first performance review at WGBH in 1979 included the following remark: "tries to get blood out of a stone." I always felt that I could turn around the tough prospect if given enough time. Unfortunately, the vast majority of names on our lists will never give. Therefore, be smarter than I was. Drop those people from your list who continue to enjoy your company, your time, and your efforts, but who will never deliver the support you seek. There are too many other promising visits to be made. I didn't understand this in my first planned giving position, so I wasted a lot of time.

The money spent on cultivation is an investment in the future. Also, you should note that there was little talk about planned giving within this discussion of cultivation and stewardship. Let me restate the point I made at the beginning of this book. People don't give to pooled income funds; they don't give to institutions; they give to people.

Up until now, I've been discussing how to cultivate your donors and prospects. It is equally important to cultivate a good working relationship with your colleagues. In the following chapter, I discuss the considerations of working with your colleagues in a complex development office.

Chapter III–4

WORKING WITH YOUR COLLEAGUES

Whether you are creating a program from scratch, continuing a program you've been running for years, or taking over an existing program, planned giving impacts many other departments in the organization. However, it is not uncommon to find that your colleagues know very little about what you do.

To run a well-integrated program, your colleagues must understand how planned giving fits into the larger picture. Otherwise, you will encounter a situation common in many organizations in which planned giving runs as a satellite program, forever circling the edges of the development effort but never becoming fully integrated. One way to facilitate proper integration is to hold a planned giving presentation for staff on a periodic basis.

HOLDING A PLANNED GIVING SEMINAR

Here are just a few of the reasons this makes good sense:

- Annual giving staff who are out visiting prospects ought to know how to recognize planned giving prospects. In addition, they should be comfortable discussing bequests with long-time annual giving donors. Often, there is a perception that planned giving will hurt annual giving when exactly the opposite is true. Building trust and a comfort level about planned giving with the annual giving staff is very important because these staff interact with a critical mass of loyal donors, many of whom could be doing more.

  Another benefit is that the annual giving staff, often oriented to cash gifts, will gain greater understanding of the role of appreciated stock in the annual giving program. Most likely, you are responsible for coordinating gifts of securities with the business office anyway.

- Running a planned giving workshop will help staff in the records department understand the nature of the gifts they will be recording. Prior to starting a planned giving program, the function of recording gifts probably was limited to receiving cash, checks, or stock physically, or the occasional credit card gift. If you have a fiduciary manager for your life income plans, the assets (cash, securities, real estate) will not be processed through your data-entry department at all. Instead, they will go directly to the fiduciary manager. Therefore, people recording gifts must learn new procedures and understand deferred giving documents that represent evidence of a gift.

  Another source of confusion will be the fact that deferred gifts may be recorded on an actuarial basis rather than at face value, depending on your crediting guidelines.

- It will help your writers and editors to serve you better through the production of effective print materials. Your in-house writers and editors assist every other department with the writing and editing of publications. You, too, should use their expertise to ensure that your planned giving brochures are clear, concise, and understandable. Providing a general understanding of planned giving concepts through a staff presentation will enhance their ability to work with you.

- The initiation of a planned giving program will bring to the business office a whole range of new responsibilities. An institution without a history of capital gift fund raising will need to establish new procedures. In some very small organizations, gifts of securities may be a new subject. Beyond that, the business office will have a role in the administration of gift annuities, charitable remainder trusts, gifts of life insurance, *etc.* Therefore, a planned giving presentation will educate members of the business office about the kinds of gifts it is responsible for processing and managing.

- Major gifts officers are visiting some very serious prospects yet many major gift officers ask for an outright gift nearly all the time. It is important for the major gift staff to be able discuss more complex gifts.

- It will educate campaign staff about the role planned giving can play in the campaign, especially for prospects incapable of making an outright gift.

- It will promote good will and team effort within the development department and will establish you as the in-house expert on creative gift planning.

The degree of sophistication in your presentation will depend on your audience. Most important is your ability to generate an understanding of, enthusiasm for, and support for the kind of exciting work you and I know planned giving to be. Don't wait for someone else to suggest this idea. Just do it.

Following is a suggested agenda and a brief summary of the kinds of things you might cover in a staff presentation. You can adapt this to your own skills and to the unique circumstances of your existing planned giving program.

Planned Giving Presentation for Staff

9:00 a.m. - 9:15 a.m.	An Overview of Philanthropy
	(Get a copy of the recent issue of *Giving USA*, listed in Appendix IV, for a discussion of the latest trends, statistics on giving, and climate of philanthropy.)
9:15 a.m. - 9:30 a.m.	Myths about Planned Giving
	(See Chapter I-5 for a discussion of six myths at the beginning of the chapter.)
9:30 a.m. - 9:45 a.m.	Appreciated, Long-Term Securities
	(Show the impact of the capital gain tax on the sale of appreciated stock and the taxes saved from contributing such stock to your institution. Sometimes, other fund raisers don't understand why they should discuss securities gifts instead of cash. Also, discuss transfer instructions for gifts in certificate form or from brokerage accounts. You can find a wealth of information on this topic in Chapter II-4 on Securities.)
9:45 a.m. - 10:45 a.m.	Overview of Life Income Gifts
	(Summarize the benefits)
	Make a gift For appreciated long-term assets, avoid immediate capital gain taxes

Receive a partial income tax deduction
Receive new income, often higher than before the gift

A. Pooled Income Fund

(If you are using your pooled income fund, you can do a basic example of how it works, what income donors can expect, and why the pooled income fund works well for gifts of appreciated securities.)

B. Charitable Gift Annuity

(For this section, you can pass out a chart of the one-life and two-life gift annuity rates and show how to compute the payout based on age. You should discuss the different tax consequences for gifts of cash *vs.* gifts of securities. Show an example so that the attendees can see the approximate charitable deduction. Include a sample gift annuity agreement. You can include a brief summary of the deferred gift annuity.)

C. Charitable Remainder Trusts

(Charitable trusts are complicated. There are lots of options and many variations. You do not need to explain all of the nuances and details. Near the beginning of the Charitable Trust Chapter is a list of features that will be helpful. You should focus on the fact that the CRT is the only life income plan that can be tailored to the donor's needs. It is also the one most appropriate for non-marketable assets.)

10:45 a.m. - 11:45 a.m.	Overview of Real Estate

Outright
Bargain sale
Flip unitrust
Deferred gift annuity
Retained life estate

11:45 a.m. - 12:00 a.m.	Break
12:00 p.m. - 1:00 p.m.	Lunch
1:00 p.m. - 2:00 p.m.	Bequests

(Focus on the fact that this is the one kind of gift all members of the organization should be able to discuss. Provide sample bequest language. Emphasize that there is an unlimited estate tax charitable deduction for charitable bequests, as long as we have an estate tax. Describe the flexibility of bequests.)

2:00 p.m. - 2:30 p.m.	Charitable Lead Trusts

(You won't have a big business in charitable lead trusts. Therefore, don't spend a lot of time on this. However, you should explain the lead trust as the reverse of a charitable remainder trust. Don't worry about complex examples.

Get across the message that this vehicle can be useful for very wealthy individuals who wish to transfer assets to heirs and save estate taxes or generation-skipping transfer taxes while giving an income stream to your charity first.)

2:30 p.m. - 3:00 p.m.   Wrap Up. Questions and Answers.

Here are a few points to keep in mind:

- Don't get technical—focus on concepts.
- Use hand-outs.
- Don't just talk at your audience. Encourage participation. Ask questions. Let others show their familiarity with the subjects.
- Don't be condescending.
- Be enthusiastic and enjoy yourself.

You should plan a staff seminar at least annually and especially after a tax reform bill. You could plan one all-day seminar once *per* year and periodic shorter sessions (one hour) when time permits.

The primary purpose of this session is to help your colleagues understand what planned giving is and to show them how their own programs can be enhanced, too. If your organization is new to planned giving, some people will be intimidated, but that has a lot to do with you. If you present concepts rather than technical jargon, you will be successful. Focus on how planned giving can solve donor problems.

CONSIDERATIONS FOR A DECENTRALIZED DEVELOPMENT OFFICE

Sometimes, an organization has different departments, units, regional field offices, or branches, each with its own dedicated fund raising staff while planned giving runs out of the central office on behalf of everybody. This structure is common in a university setting. In addition, if you work for a national organization with lots of field offices or branches, the planned giving function generally is centralized while the branches operate independently. Your job as Director of Planned Giving takes more coordination and negotiation under this model. Such a development structure can make you feel very overwhelmed because many different people need your help in different ways.

When I ran the planned giving program for Boston University, I had 15 schools and colleges requiring activities, but each had both an alumni representative and a fund raiser based in the school. The difficulty for a centrally-located planned giving officer is lack of control. In my case, the alumni population for each school was controlled by the Dean. Therefore, in order to do a bequest mailing, for example, I had to negotiate with 15 different organizations, many of whom wanted approval for both the marketing initiative and the population to which the initiative would be targeted. The larger problem was that nobody told me the internal politics until after I had sent my first mailing. I was in big trouble very early.

At Boston College, I ran a planned giving program for 11 schools and colleges in a centralized development office, except for the Law School. That was a much easier development culture within which to work.

If you find yourself in a central development office with no authority to make decisions about the planned giving program without first negotiating with each separate unit or division, you will learn quickly that you cannot have an assembly-line planned giving program. It will take a while, but you must determine the kind of activities appropriate for each population. Considerations include the following:

- Some units or regions have more potential than others. For example, at Boston University, the School of Management, Engineering, or Medicine had an alumni population with more gift potential than the School for Social Work, School of Education, or School for the Arts.

- Some fund raisers have more major gift experience than others and will be more amenable in a working partnership with the planned giving office. Some are oriented to small annual gifts usually through direct mail while other fund raisers have a broader range of experience and are comfortable operating at higher levels involving individual donor visits, long-term cultivation strategies, and more complex gift activities.

- Some fund raisers will be capable of incorporating planned giving into their own donor discussions while others will be very ineffective or uncomfortable doing so. Strangely enough, some people in fund raising positions will claim it is not their job to discuss bequests or deferred gifts.

- Some units will have stronger leadership than others, making it easier for you to establish a marketing plan that builds on existing strengths and goals.

- Some people in field offices or in independent units will want more control over collaborative efforts and marketing initiatives. They will be nervous if you visit members of the constituency alone because they will be afraid you will steal donors for generic institutional programs at the expense of the local unit's needs. They will also be worried when reply cards for planned giving return to you, even though these fund raisers have no experience to deal effectively with such inquiries. I remember an absurd situation when I forgot to ask permission to visit a prospect from the BU School of Medicine during a trip to Florida. Although I got a gift annuity from the individual, I was reprimanded for visiting him.

For all of the above reasons, running a centralized planned giving office in the midst of a decentralized development office will give you lots of stress. At first, you will treat all field offices or units equally, expecting to develop a set of uniform activities that could be used across the board. Eventually, you will realize that you cannot force planned giving into every unit, field office, or other independent program at the same pace. In some cases, you will find that it is advisable to focus on those with whom you can work easily and productively.

At Boston University, I tried for a year to run 15 planned giving programs simultaneously. People told me at the beginning that such a strategy would fail. I didn't believe it. However, after many frustrating meetings, battles, and territorial squabbles, I cut back my activities to five schools. It was not worth the aggravation to deal with people who were not ready to deal with me. If you have this kind of experience, you are not alone. You need to figure out which "units" will be productive and which ones will not. Don't despair about the ones that you need to abandon. Make an informed decision about which "units" can handle planned giving and don't worry about the others.

COORDINATING PLANNED GIVING ACTIVITIES WITH YOUR COLLEAGUES

Every development office is different in terms of how marketing, direct mail, or other fund raising activities are coordinated. You need to know the rules prior to developing a plan for your program. If you are in a fairly organized development operation, you will have regular staff meetings with other members of the development department so that each of you knows what the others are doing. Possibly, you will have a retreat in the summer during which each director reveals his or her plan for the next year so that others have an opportunity to make comments, suggest alternate plans, and coordinate activities.

The kinds of things you'll need to consider include the following:

- Who must approve mailings or other marketing initiatives? Do you have authority to select any prospect population for your initiatives, or are some prospects off limits?

- What initiatives or mailings are planned by other development office fund staff (annual giving appeals, campaign-related information, newsletters, annual reports, telethons, year-end appeals)? How will you coordinate planned giving with other activities?

- Should the existing planned giving donors receive mailings from other fund raising departments? What rules exist for excluding certain people from receiving mailings? For example, would a donor who set up a $500,000 charitable remainder trust receive the next Annual Giving mailing that asks him to renew his $1,000 annual gift?

- When you receive inquiries from donors or prospects who are assigned to another member of the development office, what is the protocol for following up? Are you free to call these prospects yourself or should the individual who already has a relationship with the prospect make the call?

- Who is the arbiter of prospect squabbles when they occur?

There are many different answers to the above questions depending on the culture of the development office. For you, understanding the rules will keep you out of trouble.

SUMMARY

Cultivating a good working relationship with your colleagues is essential if you are to maximize the results of your program. Nowhere is this more important than within the context of a capital campaign. Unfortunately, some institutions stop planned giving during a campaign or consider deferred gifts to be separate from and not counted in the campaign's totals. If you find yourself in this situation, the following chapter is for you.

Chapter III-5

INTEGRATING PLANNED GIVING INTO A CAMPAIGN

Working within the context of a campaign is the most exciting and rewarding experience for a planned giving officer. At no other time is the need for support so compelling, so specific, and so urgent. Everyone on the team has a reason to be out soliciting in full force. It is a time when:

- The entire institution is mobilized for a common purpose, and there is a feeling of excitement and energy all around.

- The board (usually) becomes fully involved in the fund raising effort, providing the true leadership so essential to fund raising success.

- Additional budget dollars are added with the result that many more cultivation activities and events can be undertaken.

- The institution allocates extra dollars for new print materials so that you can produce a higher-quality planned giving brochure than would otherwise be possible, or perhaps there will be a "Ways of Giving" section in the campaign case statement.

- Research efforts are initiated or expanded in order to provide better information about prospects for staff and volunteer solicitors.

- Out-of-state offices may be created to serve as a home base in key cities with the result that planned giving prospects can be visited by the field office on a much more regular basis than would be possible on your own planned giving budget.

In addition, several other benefits that seemed out of reach may accrue to you:

- Additional staff members are added to the existing team, and, finally, you get a full-time assistant.

- A campaign newsletter is created to report progress and to highlight major campaign commitments so that, finally, you have a regular planned giving column going out to your constituency.

- The long-awaited computer upgrade becomes a reality to accommodate the increased volume of gifts and to provide better recording and tracking of campaign gifts and pledges with the result that, finally, you can have a system that can handle planned gifts.

- Office equipment such as personal computers and printers are upgraded to handle the increased volume of external communications with the result that, finally, you and your staff are equipped to handle the demands of your office.

- The office space dedicated to the development department is expanded so that, finally, you can have your planned giving donor files close to your office instead of around the corner and down the hall.

- A campaign consultant is hired, and the board is convinced that planned giving must be an integral part of the campaign with the result that, finally, you begin to be pulled in to work on prospects who were formerly off limits to you.

- All of a sudden, everyone cares very much about charitable remainder trusts.

"Wait a minute!" you say. "That's not what happened to me when my institution launched a campaign." I hear you. For you, it was a time when:

- The board gave its collective stamp of approval, one or two board members made token gifts, then, they disappeared.

- Your planned giving budget was cut.

- You became responsible for the entire foundation or corporate effort.

- The life income donors became second-class citizens.

- You were told, "Deferred gifts don't count."

- The ad space in your institution's newsletter (for which you fought long and hard) was taken away, because there was not enough space for the campaign's message and planned giving, too.

- You had to share your secretary with new campaign staff.

- Planned giving was put on hold.

Unfortunately, the latter situation is all too real for many planned giving officers. If you are one of these planned giving officers, ask yourself the following questions:

1. Why am I here? Do I really want to be practicing planned giving, or can I be equally happy soliciting foundations and corporations for a few years? If I have to be doing something for eight hours each day, will this new situation be just as fulfilling? Let's be realistic. You'll probably receive the same annual percentage increase in your salary soliciting foundations as you would receive soliciting gift annuities. Maybe you are the kind of person who excels at almost any task. Maybe it doesn't matter what you do as long as your work is needed and appreciated. No problem.

   On the other hand, you may be miserable. You have grudgingly assumed new campaign responsibilities, but you're holding on to the idealistic and ever-hopeful view that you can sustain the same planned giving activities you were doing before. Soon, however, you discover you cannot do it all. This is a no-win situation. It produces anger and resentment on your part, and irritation and discontentment aimed at your boss. In order to survive a campaign under these circumstances, you simply must cultivate the right mental attitude. Stop doing planned giving!

2. Is there something I can do to change the situation? Perhaps there is. Most likely, management's attitude filtered down from the board level. The discussion in Chapter I–2 on board commitment will be of use to you now. You may be able to mount a counterattack—not with whining or complaining but with facts, figures, and comparison data from the experience of others.

   Also, don't forget that certain kinds of planned gifts work well in a campaign that needs cash. Charitable lead trusts provide immediate income and are more attractive then ever before given the low discount rate. Also, you can promote charitable remainder trusts with a term of years. If you allow a five-year period for outright gifts, why not promote five-year term CRTs? By the end of a pledge period you afford to others, the CRTs assets will distribute to you.

3. Do I want to stay? After many years of sharing experiences with fellow planned giving officers, I have concluded that we are cut from a different mold than are other fund raisers. We really do have a passion for what we do! The rewards of our work come from building solid relationships with our donors and from creating mutually beneficial gift plans that serve both our institution and the donor equally well. We recognize potential gift situations that others don't see. We are facilitators—using all of the laws and regulations created by the I.R.S. to find just the right match between the institution's needs and the donor's needs. To tell us to stop doing planned giving is to

take away the essential ingredients of our work that drew us to planned giving in the first place. So, my advice to you is this: If you have done everything possible to make your best case for integrating deferred giving into the campaign, but nobody is listening, don't hang around and complain. Start looking for another job.

Few topics stir up as much controversy as this one. Organizations that promote the full range of gift options during a campaign can point to successes far greater than would otherwise be the case. In fact, campaigns with fully-integrated planned giving programs receive 20% to 30% or more of their individual gift totals through deferred gift arrangements.

Why then do so many institutions reduce or stop deferred giving during a campaign? The problem probably is deeply rooted in the board's lack of knowledge about the proper role and potential of planned giving. The most common objection to crediting deferred gifts is, of course, that deferred gifts cannot be spent today. Fine. I cannot argue with that. But let's look at this issue from a number of different angles:

The Campaign Goals. Does an organization expect to spend all of the money from a campaign shortly thereafter? Is there no place for an endowment portion in the campaign? Even when the primary purpose of the campaign is to raise funds for a new building, you still must raise additional endowment dollars to cover your new maintenance expenses. Planned giving is perfect for building critical endowment which you are going to need anyway down the road.

The Campaign Prospects. The successful campaign taps all three sources of support—foundations, corporations and individuals. The foundations and corporations will supply spendable cash for the pressing current needs. Most of the individual donors also will make outright gifts. Thus, there should be plenty of cash to spend.

The Needs of the Donor. If you limit gift options, you'll be limiting the size of the gifts. A donor who could otherwise contribute $25,000 to your gift annuity program may be willing to give only $2,000 to $3,000 outright, if that. Or, the prospect capable of creating a $500,000 charitable remainder trust may be willing to give only $50,000 outright.

Institutional Message. The emphasis on "cash now" creates a perception that the institution really is not looking to the future. Therefore, your job after the campaign will be that much harder. If you need cash now and are not looking to the future, do you create the impression that this is a hand-to-mouth operation?

Harvard University concluded a six-year campaign in December of 2000, raising over $2.6 billion. I talked to Peter Kimball, Director of Gift Planning for the Faculty of Arts and Sciences about the campaign totals. Here are some figures on the role planned giving played in the Harvard campaign. There were 393 gifts of $1 million or over from individuals and private foundations totaling $1.5 billion. Almost 54% of the gifts made by this group of donors contained at least one planned giving component. Overall, planned gifts accounted for about 35% of Harvard's totals.

Gift Range	Percentage of Gifts Having a Deferred Gift Component
Over $10 million	50%
$5 million to $10 million	25%
$1 million to $5 million	31%

The question is not whether to integrate deferred giving into the campaign, but how to integrate it most effectively.

The introduction of a campaign affects every department. Most simply, there is more work—more prospects to screen, more research to be done, more visits to make, more donor events to plan, more gifts to process, *etc.* For the planned giving office, several things are going to happen:

- The fees for the fiduciary management of the deferred gifts will increase as a result of receiving more and larger gifts. If the management fees prior to the campaign were paid from the planned giving budget, there will come a point during the campaign when one of two things will have to occur: 1) the planned giving budget must be increased to accommodate the increased fees, or 2) payment of the fees must be shifted to the business office or to the deferred assets themselves. If you are already charging fees to the assets, you don't have this problem.

- The fees for legal expenses will increase. As you solicit more and more prospects, you will find increased incidence of gift situations that require expert legal counsel. At the same time, you'll be generating more complex gift proposals at the higher gift levels. Thus, you may need to shift the legal fees to the business office if you are currently paying them from your planned giving budget.

- The institution will need a full-time director of planned giving and a full-time assistant for the director. Regardless of what you had before, the institution must commit itself to two full-time staff now.

- You must purchase planned giving computer software in order to be able to manage the increased volume of life income gift and other complex proposals. Otherwise, you will be unable to function. There is a chapter in the Appendix with a list of companies offering planned giving software.

CONSIDERATIONS FOR CREDITING GUIDELINES

When you are not in a campaign, your donors usually are not concerned about how you credit their gifts. There may be internal designations or gift restrictions (such as a minimum gift level for naming opportunities), but, otherwise, there is no public measure of one donor's support in relation to the gifts of others.

During a campaign, donors care very much about gift credit. As director of planned giving, you will confront five basic questions:

1. Should we credit life income gifts at fair market value or remainder value?

2. Should bequest intentions be credited, and, if so, under what conditions?

3. How should we credit the income stream from charitable lead trusts?

4. How should we credit gifts of life insurance?

5. What do we do about IRAs and retirement plans?

General Guidelines

The Council for Advancement and Support of Education (CASE), publishes two guides for campaign reporting.

- *Management and Reporting Standards*: This is targeted to educational institutions (K-12 plus higher education).

- *Fund-Raising Standards for Annual Giving and Campaign Reports: For Not-for-Profit Organizations Other than Colleges, Universities, and Schools*: This guide is similar to the education version (without the unique issues of education).

A new edition of the *Management and Reporting Standards* is coming out in the fall of 2003, too late to incorporate into this book. However, you can get it through the CASE web site at www.case.org for $46.95 (CASE member price).

While writing this section, I spoke to John Taylor who is Vice President of Research and Data Services at CASE (formerly of Duke University). He is rewriting the reporting standards. The purpose of the *Management and Reporting Standards* is to provide institutions uniform gift reporting policies so that data collected from educational institutions will be consistent. How an educational institution reports its gifts for CASE purposes may be very different than how it credits them for campaign purposes internally.

John has seen a drastic change in how educational institutions credit planned gifts in a campaign. "You would be surprised at how many institutions are using remainder value and not face value." That's an interesting commentary on our charitable industry. The trustees of charities are becoming keenly aware that deferred gifts are not worth the same as outright gifts.

That said, if you are planning a campaign, you should buy one of the above guides. By having it, you will save a lot of time when developing your campaign crediting guidelines. CASE has thought through many things that you wouldn't think of on your own.

In the 1996 version of the *Management and Reporting Standards*, there was a reporting form that required both face value and remainder value. The new version of the guide asks only for remainder value since so many institutions don't track face value any longer. In addition, CASE no longer counts gifts that are revocable. That means no bequests, IRA designations, and no revocable life insurance designations.

Here are some items from the 1996 version of the CASE guide with commentary from yours truly in italics. Even though CASE has revised its rules, this section is still valuable since it will help you think about crediting issues. You may choose to do something else, but at least you have a place to start the process.

1. Campaigns should not exceed seven years in duration including the advance-gifts phase.

   Any campaign that lasts longer than seven years is destined to run out of steam. Even seven years is extremely long for staff and volunteers to sustain the urgency and keep their energy levels high. If you can't do what you want to do in seven years, reduce your goal.

2. Pledge-payment period should not exceed five years regardless of when the pledge is made.

   Sounds reasonable to me. Get the money in as soon as possible so that you can move on to the next campaign probably starting five years or so from the official end date of the current campaign.

3. Count only gifts and pledges actually received or committed during the specific period of time for the campaign including the advance-gifts period.

   I suspect this is necessary because some organizations will be inclined to add large gifts that don't fit the campaign's time-frame. Be honest here.

4. Gifts and pledges may be counted in only one campaign.

   Duh! Why would such a thing need to be stated? Somebody has been cheating. Not you!

5. The value of canceled or unfulfilled pledges must be subtracted from campaign totals.

   This means that you should not stop removing bogus annual fund pledges during a campaign so as to inflate your totals. As soon as you know that a donor will not fulfill a pledge, get rid of it and adjust your totals along the way.

6. Advance-gifts phase should be limited to a set period of time and may be defined in one of two ways:

   - As a pre-public announcement period during which only commitments for featured objectives are counted, or

- As a pre-public announcement period during which all gifts and pledges are counted.

  If the latter option is chosen, campaign managers need to explain to (institution's) personnel and campaign volunteers that the reported results will inflate somewhat the true impact of the campaign effort.

  This means that if you receive gifts during the advance-gifts phase (commonly called the nucleus phase) for purposes not included in the campaign, you should identify those separately. Practically, such a situation is inevitable especially when you pick a start date for counting gifts at an institution that already has a complex and mature development operation. There will always be many gifts not targeted to campaign purposes. These gifts technically do not count in the campaign. Therefore, you must consider early on how you intend to report such gifts. As a practical matter, I worked at four charities, all of which ran campaigns when I was there, and nobody concerned themselves with this issue. There was always a miscellaneous campaign category to catch the gifts targeted for non-campaign objectives.

Reporting Guidelines

Here are some additional suggestions from the 1996 CASE guide. In this version of the guide, CASE suggested a five-column report that includes columns for both face value and remainder value. Since their new policy is to require only remainder values for irrevocable deferred gifts, the new book coming out in the fall of 2003 doesn't include the form. However, for internal reporting within the institution, the practice of tracking both the face value and the remainder value in separate columns is a good idea. By doing so, you can see the public campaign totals in the face value column and the real value to the institution in the remainder column. Here are the kinds of things you can track separately.

1. The total of outright gifts and pledges received and payable within the campaign period and post-campaign period, reported at face value.

2. The total of deferred (future) commitments that will be received at an undetermined time in the future, reported at face value.

3. The total of deferred (future) commitments that will be received at an undetermined time in the future, discounted to present value.

4. The grand total of 1 and 2 above.

5. The grand total of 1 and 3 above.

Additionally, totals for featured *vs.* other campaign objectives would also be appropriate, if you choose to separate them.

The calculation to determine the present value of a deferred gift is defined by the I.R.S. for income tax purposes as it relates to the charitable deduction. According to CASE, credit for deferred gifts to a campaign should be the same as the amount allowable as a tax deduction by the I.R.S. That value may not represent the true value to the institution, but it is all we have to keep the reporting uniform for all charities.

For gifts from Canadian citizens, CASE recommends using the U.S. rules because the charitable deduction for Canadians is different than in the U.S.

What Should Not Be Counted In A Campaign?

1. Oral pledges

2. Gifts or pledges counted in a previous campaign even if realized during the campaign reporting period.

3. Investment earnings on gifts, even if accrued during the campaign, and if required within the terms specified by the donor. (The only exception here would be interest accumulations counted in guaranteed investment instruments that mature within the time frame of the campaign, such as zero coupon bonds.)

4. Earned income transfer payments from medical or analogous practice plans.

5. Surplus income transfer from ticket-based operations, except the amount permitted as a charitable deduction by the I.R.S. or Revenue Canada.

6. Contract revenues.

7. Contributed services, except those permitted by I.R.S or Revenue Canada as a charitable deduction.

8. Governmental funds

Crediting Closely-Held Stock

Often, charities receive shares of non-publicly traded securities that are hard to value. For gifts of such shares valued at over $10,000, the donor's qualified appraisal, necessary for the donor to claim an income tax deduction, should be used. For gifts of closely-held stock valued at under $10,000, you can use either a qualified appraisal from the donor, if there is one, or the *per* share price of the most recent trade. If the corporation buys the stock from your institution, the price used for the sale would be appropriate.

These guidelines from CASE don't cover all situations since there may be instances when the charity cannot sell the shares for a period of time. If you have no way of valuing the shares, you should record the gift at $1 and then adjust the value at the time you actually sell the shares. At Boston University, we had a segregated portfolio for closely-held or non publicly traded securities. If there was no donor appraisal, frequently the case, we simply used $1. Some companies went public eventually and we recorded on the donor's gift record the sale price. Other gifts of closely-held stock were eventually bought by the company. Since donors frequently didn't want to pay for an appraisal, they made gifts that they claimed were worth under $10,000. Ha! Don't worry if your donors do this. Simply acknowledge a gift of X number of shares of Y Corporation on a particular date and wait it out. But, don't take such a gift into any life income plan unless it is a flip unitrust. You can go to the CRT chapter and learn more about that.

Crediting Real And Personal Property

Following are rules for non cash gifts other than securities:

1. Gifts in kind, *e.g.*, equipment, books, software, *etc.*, that qualify as a charitable deduction should be reported at their (institutional) discount value which, for these purposes, is deemed to be fair market value.

2. Gifts of noncash property exceeding $5,000 value, report at the fair market value placed on it by a qualified independent appraiser.

3. Gifts of noncash property valued under $5,000, report at value declared by donor or a qualified expert at the institution.

   Practically, for any item of noncash property, you really need a qualified appraisal, preferably from the donor. Also, for real property having a mortgage, you should count only the net equity value. Expenses incurred in selling an asset should not be deducted from the gift value.

If you receive a noncash asset that has not been appraised, you should give the donor's appraiser access to the asset, but you should not pay for the appraisal. The only case in which a charity would pay for its own appraisal is the case of an item that the charity must add to its insurance policy. In this situation, you don't necessarily want to tell the donor since the donor should not use your appraisal anyway.

Irrevocable Charitable Remainder Trusts And Pooled Income Funds

1. Should be credited as a future commitment at the discounted present value of the remainder interest allowable as a deduction by the I.R.S. and at face value in the face value column.

Charitable Gift Annuities

1. Report only the excess of the gifted value over the cost to the donee of producing the annuity.

2. Report the face amount transferred under the section for the face value of gifts.

3. Report the amount allowable as a deduction by the I.R.S. in the deferred gifts section.

Charitable Lead Trusts

1. If terms extend five years or less, report face value in current gifts and pledges section.

   This means the total dollars expected from the income stream, not the principal of the trust.

2. If more than five years, report amounts beyond the first five-year gift and pledges value both at remaining face value of the income stream in the face value section, and at the discounted present value of the remaining income stream in the deferred gifts section.

   This could get a little tricky because the gift is being split into two pieces. However, if you have a five year-campaign with a charitable lead trust that runs for 10 years, you'll be able to count the first five years of payments at face value (similar to an outright five-year pledge), and you should be able to count the remaining lead trust payments using the present value.

   A very real problem here is the issue of what dollar amount should be put into the donor's gift records in your database. If you add up the five-year income stream (not an exact dollar amount if you have a lead unitrust), and then add the present value of the future payments for any payments that extend beyond the five years, you have a blended amount that will be shown on the donor's gift record. That is not exactly workable, in my opinion. Usually, a donor's gift record reflects the exact amount that the donor contributes. At Boston College, the computer system couldn't handle a pledge for longer than five years. We had one charitable lead annuity trust for a 20-year term. The way I handled this was to submit a five-year pledge and then enter the same thing again at the end of each five years.

Bequest Intentions

Institutions debate widely the concept of including bequest intentions in a campaign. Some argue that bequest intentions should never be counted because they are not irrevocable. Others count them under a variety of rules that vary by institution. When you plan a campaign, you must address this issue because, if you don't, you'll hear about it from the trustees anyway. Inevitably, a trustee whom you hope will make a major gift will instead offer the fact that he or she has a huge bequest. And, there you have the problem. What are you going to do?

The CASE Guidelines suggest it can be appropriate to count bequest intentions if you separate them from the irrevocable gift totals and include them only in the deferred or "future commitments" totals. Following are some specific guidelines from the 1996 CASE guidelines:

1. A specified amount or percentage of the estate must be stated in the will based on a credible estimate of the future value of the estate.

2. Commitment verification should be in one of three forms:

   - Affirmation letter from donor or donor's attorney stating institution will be informed of any changes.

   - Commitment should be accompanied by a charitable or deferred pledge agreement, or

   - Commitment should be accompanied by a contract to make a will.

3. The amount specified or estimated must be reported at both the discounted present value and at face value.

4. Bequests realized during the defined duration of the campaign should be counted at full value so long as they were not reported in a previous campaign.

   You need to consider item #4 carefully. It may seem like a good idea now to credit bequest intentions for your current campaign, but things can get very messy down the road. Let's assume you credited bequest intentions in a campaign that ended five years ago. Now, you are beginning a new campaign. But, when the donors for whom you documented those prior bequests die, the cash will come in during the current campaign. You counted them before, so you cannot count them again. Only those amounts that exceed the amounts credited in an earlier campaign can be counted this time. Plus, you would need to know precisely which bequest intentions you counted in the prior campaign. Further, if a donor decided to make an early gift of a bequest amount, this gift would not be counted in a later campaign. Such a gift would be fulfilling a "bequest pledge" recorded earlier. It's a real mess.

   Assuming you decide to count bequests in your campaign, you must make the rules very thoughtfully. Most organizations do this by age. For example, if the donor is age 70 or older, the documented value of a bequest intention will count at face value. If the donor is between 50 and 69, the campaign value will be 50% of the documented value. Some organizations use a graded set of percentages that start at one age and cover a 20 to 30 year range. I wish I could give you a commonly agreed upon set of rules, but there aren't any. You have to make these rules up based on your own needs and objectives.

Crediting Life Insurance

Life insurance gifts may be revocable or irrevocable. To be eligible to be credited in a campaign, the life insurance policy must be given to the charity as owner and beneficiary (unless you put them in the bequest category with the same rules as you use for bequests). The donor must also relinquish all rights in the policy (called incidents of ownership). Then, according to CASE, here's how you may credit the policy:

1. Paid-up Policies

   - Count the cash surrender value as a current outright gift, or

   - The death benefit value, at both the face value and the discounted present value in their respective categories.

2. Existing Policies Not Fully Paid Up

   - Count the existing cash surrender value as a current outright gift.

- Also, if premium payments are pledged over a five-year period, count the incremental increase of the cash value in the current outright gifts and pledges section.

Practically, if you try to credit the incremental increase in cash value every time the donor makes a premium payment, you will be adding insignificant amounts, and you will spend way more time figuring out what to credit than it is worth. I wouldn't bother with this rule at all, even though it makes sense technically. (Note: According to John Taylor who is writing the new guidelines, CASE's new suggestion is to count the annual premium amount. That makes sense to me.)

3. New Policies

- Count as current gifts and pledges the value of premiums paid or pledged over a five-year period.

Don't forget that you must be both owner and beneficiary.

4. Realized Death Benefits

- Policy does not need to be owned by the institution.

- Count the company's settlement amount realized during the campaign period provided no gift amount was previously credited.

If you credited the cash surrender value at the time the donor made your organization owner, you cannot then credit the proceeds if they distribute during the campaign. Once credited, the asset is on the books of the institution, and that's the end of it. You can't count these things twice, once when the donor puts the asset in your institution's name and once when the policy pays off.

Crediting IRAs And Retirement Plan Assets

In the 1996 book, CASE provides no guidelines on how to credit retirement plan assets in a campaign. Primarily, this is because these assets present unique problems due to mandatory withdrawals that will reduce the value of the account over time. These assets are particularly difficult because the donor cannot currently transfer ownership during lifetime without being deemed to have made a taxable withdrawal. For a full discussion about these assets, go to Chapter II-12.

Meanwhile, for purposes of the crediting issue, let me explain the problem using an example.

Mr. Donor has a $3 million IRA. He is 66 years old. He names your organization sole beneficiary upon his death. He wants credit for the $3 million in your campaign. "Like a bequest," he says. Sounds good. He sends you a copy of his account statement showing $3 million. Is this like a bequest? Absolutely not.

When he passes age 70 ½, he must withdraw a mandatory amount starting on the next April 1st. If he does not withdraw the prescribed amount, he will pay a 50% penalty on the amount. So, each year that he lives, he must take out a prescribed amount. That reduces the value of the account and reduces the potential gift to your institution.

When Mr. Donor dies, his account will distribute to you whatever is left. How do you know what will be left? I called about 25 universities to inquire how they handled this issue. Most had no policy. Others treated retirement plan assets like bequests even though that is not valid.

Here are two suggestions for a crediting policy. This works only if you also credit bequest intentions:

Option 1: The full value of an IRA or retirement plan account will be credited in the campaign under the same rules stated for bequest intentions provided that the donor contributes to [charity] any amount withdrawn from the plan, without reduction for any tax occasioned by the withdrawal, until such time as the full amount credited in the campaign is received by [charity]. The donor will provide for the full payment of the pledge through a provision in his or her will to ensure that any deficiency from the retirement plan account is covered at death.

Option II. The full value of an IRA or retirement plan account will be credited in the campaign under the same rules stated for bequest intentions provided the donor establishes a provision in his or her will that covers any underpayment of the pledge from the retirement plan account at death.

To properly account for such a pledge, add the full pledge amount to the deferred giving categories of your report, for both face value and discounted value.

Special Circumstances

If you credit a deferred gift as a future commitment and if the donor dies within the five year reporting period for the campaign resulting in the institution receiving the gift in full, you may revise the crediting of the gift to show it has been paid in full.

INTEGRATING PLANNED GIVING INTO CAMPAIGN SOLICITATIONS

As a planned giving officer, you will be responsible for helping the institution integrate planned giving into the campaign. In general, this means providing information to the rest of the team that can be used by those who know much less about the techniques of giving than you do. By creating solicitation tools, such as the one below, you can assist the team, the volunteers, and the staff. You can adapt this format to suit your own situation.

14 WAYS TO MAKE A $100,000 COMMITMENT TO THE XYZ CAMPAIGN

1. **An outright gift of cash or securities.** For gifts of cash, itemizers are entitled to an income tax deduction up to 50% of adjusted gross income with a five-year carry-over period for the excess. For gifts of long-term, appreciated securities or real estate, the limit is 30% of adjusted gross income with the same five-year carry-over period. In addition, you will be able to avoid the capital gain tax that would have applied had you sold the appreciated property yourself.

2. **A two-year pledge of $50,000 per year.** The full value of your pledge will be credited in the year of your commitment.

3. **A five-year pledge of $20,000 per year.** We want to accommodate your unique circumstances and are happy to allow installment gifts of up to five years.

4. **A gift to the XYZ Pooled Income Fund.** You will receive a lifetime income (currently ___%); there is no capital gain tax on the transfer and subsequent sale by the fund of appreciated, long-term securities; you will be entitled to an income tax deduction for part of the gift subject to the same contribution ceilings mentioned above; and it is possible to experience an increase in your annual income as a result of the gift. On the death of the beneficiary (you or another person), XYZ will have use of the funds.

5. **A gift to the XYZ Charitable Gift Annuity Program.** In exchange for a gift of cash or securities, you will receive a fixed annual annuity for the rest of your life. The rate of the annuity is based on the age of the annuitant or annuitants (maximum of two). You will incur no immediate capital gain tax on the transfer; part of the annuity payment will be tax-free for the duration of your life expectancy; and you will receive an income tax deduction for part of the gift.

6. **A gift in trust.** We are happy to work with you and your financial advisor to create an income arrangement that suits your unique circumstances. For example, you may choose a fixed or fluctuating payment, the rate of such payment, as well as many other features to suit your needs. You will incur no capital gain tax on the transfer of appreciated, long-term securities or real estate to the trust and you will receive an income tax deduction for part of the gift. As with all of XYZ's life income plans, the funds will be available to us on the death of the beneficiaries.

7. **An outright gift of real estate.** Most real estate has appreciated faster than the rate of inflation and offers great potential in charitable gift planning. We would be happy to explore with you a gift of a home, vacation property, condominium, undeveloped land, or other real estate in support of the XYZ Campaign.

8. **A gift of a personal residence or farm with retained life tenancy.** It is possible to transfer ownership of your personal residence or farm to XYZ while retaining the enjoyment of the property during your lifetime. This may be an excellent way to support the Campaign, receive a current income tax deduction for the property's discounted value, and continue to use the property for as long as you live.

9. **The purchase of a new life insurance policy benefiting XYZ.** You can make a magnificent commitment to XYZ through a life insurance gift. Through relatively modest annual gifts, you can create a major gift. Plus, your annual premiums will be deductible for income tax purposes. To receive credit for a $100,000 gift, you would need to make premium payments totaling $100,000 over a five-year period. Thus the face value would be significantly larger.

10. **A gift of an existing life insurance policy.** Many people own insurance policies that are no longer needed for their original purposes. Such policies can be given to XYZ. In general, you will be entitled to an income tax deduction for the cash surrender value, and can also deduct the amount of future premiums paid on an annual basis.

11. **A gift of art or antiques.** Over the years, the beauty and charm of XYZ has been enhanced by the generosity of our supporters through gifts of art or antiques. We are pleased to consider a gift of tangible personal property as an addition to our _____ Collection.

12. **A gift of an income stream.** You can provide annual payments to XYZ from a pool of assets that later distributes to your heirs or returns to you. One plan allows you to transfer assets to family members at a reduced transfer tax while providing meaningful support to our institution for a period of years, for example, $20,000 per year for five years. Or, the same fund may return to you at the end of the five years. The latter option entitles you to an immediate income tax deduction for the present value of the income stream.

13. **A bequest.** If you are 70 years of age or older, you will receive full gift credit for the documented value of a bequest to XYZ.

14. **Creative combinations.** You can make a commitment of $100,000 to XYZ Campaign through any one of the above gift arrangements, or you can combine them in creative ways to suit your unique circumstances.

For more information, please call or write: Name, Title, Institution, Street Address, City, State, Zip Code (phone, fax, e-mail, web site.)

The above summary gives you some ideas on how to create this tool. Adapt it as you see fit to suit your institution. It will be useful to create similar summaries for gift levels of $50,000, $100,000, $500,000 or for a $1,000,000 or more.

DONOR PRESENTATIONS

Planned giving officers run all kinds of seminars to educate donors and prospects about the multiple ways they can arrange support for a charity. Some hold wills clinics in which a group of prospects is shown why a will is necessary and how to approach the task of writing a will. One hopes these people will include a bequest to the institution in the process. Considering the high percentage of people who die without a will, getting them started on a process might eventually work.

Others hold estate planning seminars with a panel of professionals such as trust officers, estate planners, or attorneys in order to show donors how smart charitable gifts can play a role in estate planning. Consultants offer seminars tailored to trustee groups or donor prospects. Most of these presentations focus on educating donors with the hope that some of the attendees actually will make a gift. Unfortunately, most of these seminars are focused on general information, but not on immediate methods to make gifts. The hidden message for charitable giving is always there, but I'm not sure it is effective unless you have the right people in the audience.

During a campaign, you might consider holding one or more of the above kinds of sessions, but unless you focus the event toward the campaign's objectives, you may find the seminar produces nothing more than an educational experience for the donors. Equally important is how you follow up. If you run a seminar, you should have a plan to follow up each person after the seminar. That can be difficult when you don't know the interest level of your attendees and when you have so many other viable prospects already assigned to you. It's a mess.

In Appendix IV, there is a list of consultants, many of whom can be hired to do a planned giving or estate planning seminars for your donors. Many of you reading this book could be the presenter yourself, but it is often better to have an outsider do the seminar. The presence of an outsider might make the experience less threatening to squeamish donors.

Others may disagree and may be able to point to very successful results from group donor seminars. I tried many kinds of seminars, but most required way more work and time than they were worth primarily because the mailing list was not qualified enough. Simply getting old people in the room is not good enough. The problem is that old people attend free seminars especially if there is food, but they are not necessarily inclined to be charitable. My dad was the worst nightmare of every brokerage firm and life insurance agent. He was constantly reporting to me about attending this or that seminar. I always got a report on what he got to eat.

The most successful planned giving educational events I held were at Boston College. The difference was that we had a multi-millionaire trustee host, over whose name the invitation went to an elite group of his very rich peers. There was no hiding the fact why we were there. The charitable giving emphasis was out in front. Our message, delivered by the host trustee was something along the following lines: "Boston College is trying to raise $400 million for the following reasons. (A summary of the campaign's goals were outlined.) These funds are extremely important to the future of this university. Therefore, we brought you together tonight, insiders and good friends, to show you creative charitable giving strategies that could help solve problems in your estate while you support Boston College." The audience was hand picked. They were motivated, and they were already well cultivated so that they cared deeply about Boston College. It was incredible. We went on to close extremely large commitments to our campaign from many of those attendees.

CAMPAIGN STEERING COMMITTEE

No doubt, your campaign will have a campaign steering committee composed of trustees and major prospects or donors. Most likely, this committee's staff liaison will be the campaign director. If you have both a campaign steering committee and a planned giving committee, the chair of the planned giving committee should sit on the campaign steering committee.

When there is a campaign consultant, the consultant may assume the responsibility of volunteer training. Or, you may have to do this through a separate planned giving expert. If you are sufficiently knowledgeable about planned giving yourself, you can help to plan the training, or possibly do it alone.

Chapter III–2 covers many more considerations with respect to volunteer management. In fact, the planned giving committee discussed in that chapter can be a campaign steering committee.

SUMMARY

Deferred giving will flourish during a properly-run campaign. But, don't forget that the most important type of planned gift is the straight, outright gift. Every other gift vehicle comes after you realize you cannot get the outright gift you want.

The next chapter is an important one for many nonprofit professionals. It is for the executive director, president, or director of development running a one-person office. If you find yourself with limited time and limited resources, you may feel hopeless and frustrated. What can you do all by yourself? Actually, there is much you can do to strengthen your organization through planned giving if you know how to set priorities and manage your time. If you follow the advice in the next chapter, you'll be surprised at how easy it really is.

Chapter III–6

PLANNED GIVING IN A ONE-PERSON SHOP

If you are reading this chapter, you probably are not a director-of-planned-giving-turned-administrator. In that situation, you already would know how to run a pooled income fund, how to process a gift annuity, or how to show the merits of a charitable remainder trust. And, you would not have to spend time studying what these gift vehicles are, how they work, or whether they are right for your institution. Most likely, you are an administrator or director of development who wants to enhance the fund raising of your organization, but you, alone, are it. There is only one problem. You know very little about planned giving.

Before going any further, you should read Chapter I–1. Throughout this book, I have been telling you that planned giving is a full-time job and that the director of planned giving must have a full-time secretary. That's easy for me to say, isn't it? I was a full-time director of planned giving, and I had a full-time secretary most of the time. Even for two full-time people, however, the job is more than 9:00 a.m. to 5:00 p.m.

The problem with fund raising of any kind is that fund raisers make our own work. Short of bringing a sleeping bag into the office, you must find a balance between what you want to accomplish, what you reasonably can accomplish, and when to go home. If you send a mailing, you create inquiries that you must follow up. If you hold a screening session to identify prospects, you add more names to your list. The job never will be done.

Running a one-person shop is even tougher. It is taking four or five full-time jobs and making them into one job. Annual giving is a full-time job. So is soliciting corporations or foundations. Add to that whatever administrative duties you have, and you'll find yourself cutting corners on everything just to keep your head above water. You feel as though you are on a treadmill.

If there is any chance you can convince the board to let you hire a full-time director of planned giving, you should try that route first. Don't assume you will fail. Give yourself six months to get this one thing accomplished. If you do everything I suggest in Chapter I–1 and you still cannot get the approval and the resources you need to hire a director of planned giving, then, come back here . . .

. . . Okay, it didn't work. Depending on the institution, some or all of the following will be true:

- You are responsible for corporate solicitations.

- You are responsible for foundation solicitations; you have been known to mail a preprinted letter to dozens of foundations listed in *The Foundation Directory*, but rarely do you have time to follow up.

- You run the annual giving program primarily through direct mail (*i.e.*, little or no personal contact with leadership donors); perhaps, you are doing two appeals *per* year.

- Your average annual gift is under $50.

- Rarely, if ever, does anybody make a stock gift. Perhaps you don't have a brokerage account to deal with stock transfers at all.

- The board generally is uninvolved in fund raising; some members make modest annual gifts, or one or two "champions" of the cause bail you out of a deficit each year.

- You do not use volunteers for fund raising.

- You never have held a screening session to rate prospects.

- You do not have a researcher to do the necessary investigative work on prospects so that you can make a proper approach.

- The last capital campaign came in under goal; it was a long and grueling experience for everyone.

- You have little or no endowment.

- The business office consists of a treasurer and a couple of other people who pay bills and do the payroll.

- You have fewer than 5,000 donors.

- You raise an extra $1,000 to $10,000 *per* year from auctions, craft shows, concession stands at community events, bake sales, holiday sales, and other events.

- You receive one or two surprise bequests each year.

- The fund raising strategy has been pretty much the same for a very long time.

The reason you cannot get a full-time director of planned giving is because your development effort needs a complete overhaul from the bottom up before you ever can think of hiring a director of planned giving. While the plan for a full development program is beyond the scope of this book, at the very least, you should have:

- financial support from every member of the board;

- a structured upgrading system to bring donors from $500, to $1,000, to $2,500, to $5,000, to $10,000 in your annual giving program, including an annual dinner for the top-level supporters with your chief executive officer;

- personalized letters for annual gift appeals that include the amount of the donor's prior support and a specific dollar request for this year's support; abandon your "dear friend" approach.

- volunteer solicitors for the higher levels of annual giving and especially for major gifts;

- a comprehensive approach to "program" or "project" funding such that the budget includes not only the obvious new cost to the institution but also a proportionate share of salaries, space costs, equipment, travel, utilities, heat, telephone, and promotion, all of which usually are considered "operating" expenses;

- a five-year plan;

- a full-time director of annual giving to free you up to work only on major gift prospects—corporations, foundations, and individuals.

This message is not what you expected nor is it what you wanted to hear. If you hired me as director of development, I would spend considerable time reworking the entire development effort.

But, let's assume things are going reasonably well in most areas of development, and you are ready to do some planned giving. By yourself, you cannot run a comprehensive program. You simply don't have the time. Given this situation, and assuming you are not a former director of planned giving, you must set some priorities. Before discussing some of the things you can do, let me suggest a few reasons you may be dragging your feet.

1. *You don't have the time.* If you are the executive director, director of development, or other administrator, you have lots to do. Making time for a new venture is almost impossible. So let's start with

only four hours per week—four continuous hours. How about Tuesdays from 9:00 a.m. to 1:00 p.m.? Sit down with your calendar right now and block out this time for several weeks. Alert your staff that this time simply will not be scheduled for other things. Week to week, the occasional emergency may force you to move your four hours to another day of the week. But most things can wait four hours. Block out this time now.

2. *You're afraid of what you don't know.* Sign up for a planned giving workshop or seminar at an introductory level. Concentrate on the general concepts, not on the details. For example, don't try to memorize every little detail about the operation and tax aspects of pooled income funds, gift annuities, and charitable remainder trusts. You'll drive yourself crazy, become frustrated again, and go back to your old ways. To start talking to donors, here's all you need to know about life income plans:

People can transfer assets to charitable organizations while retaining the right to receive the income for life. There are different plans for different needs. In general, the donor incurs no capital gain tax when transferring highly appreciated long-term capital assets to one of these plans. In addition, the donor will receive a charitable deduction for part of the gift. The combined effect of avoiding capital gain taxes, receiving a new, often higher annual income, and receiving a charitable deduction make this a wonderful way for the donor to help you.

This is not hard, is it? If you can get that much of a paragraph out of your mouth while visiting with a donor, you're doing planned giving. What then? Be honest. "I don't pretend to be an expert on such things but if these concepts sound beneficial to you, perhaps I could bring our tax expert with me next time to explore some ideas." Remember, it is not your job to be a tax expert and no one expects that of you.

3. *You're afraid of rejection.* This is probably the biggest obstacle to successful fund raising—even for the most experienced professionals. No matter how many times I've done it before, I have anxiety before picking up the phone to call a prospect, before arriving at the prospect's home, before getting to the real purpose of my visit. It's part of the territory because you and I want to be liked. The emotional pain of rejection is very powerful. Therefore, you must cultivate the right mental attitude. Your organization is important to those you serve. People want to help you. You are offering them the opportunity to do something they want to do and that makes them feel good.

4. *You're unwilling to build relationships.* People will not contribute to your organization if they feel uninvolved or that their gift doesn't matter. Why should they? The kind of major gifts worthy of your time evolve from long-term relationships that require time and patience to build. By yourself, you can develop relationships with a limited number of people. If you try to take on too many at one time, you'll become overwhelmed and unproductive—and none of the prospects will get the quality time that will make a difference.

Set a goal for this year of creating or building relationships with 20 people—the people most capable of making the biggest difference for your organization. Visit someone every other week using your four-hour planned giving period for these visits. Learn about these 20 people; identify their interests, family priorities, needs. Why do they support your organization? Use the first visit to gather information. Then develop a 12-month strategy that leads to a solicitation for each one.

If you can overcome these four reasons for not starting planned giving, you're on your way to success. Perhaps you're asking yourself where the mystery is. This sounds too easy. Precisely. Now, if you're ready to start working, here are several activities you can include in your four-hour weekly planned giving sessions.

1. Retain legal counsel. Though you are undertaking only a minimal level of activity, you need an attorney experienced in charitable giving tax law who is prepared to help you with gift transactions and with questions. You will pay only when you use his or her services. To select a competent attorney in your area, ask several charitable organizations in your city whom they use. (See Chapter I-6 for a full discussion about legal counsel.) Visit several firms yourself and select one. The

individual or the firm you have chosen will be your right hand in the coming year. To help pay for the legal fees, solicit each member of the board for $500 for a total legal reserve fund of, let's say, $5,000 for the first year. Or $3,000, or whatever you can get.

2. Begin a concerted effort to promote gifts of appreciated stock in the annual giving program. Chapter II–4 covers how to accept and dispose of stock gifts. If your annual giving pledge forms are already printed for the coming year, create a small insert to be sent with annual giving appeals to highlight the benefits of contributing appreciated securities. You must establish a brokerage account to handle gifts of securities when you receive them. You will find many brokers listed in your local Yellow Pages. Your treasurer should be able to help you set up an account.

3. Begin a visibility campaign for bequests. (See Chapter II–10) As I suggest in the bequest chapter, "Get the message out!" Many companies in Appendix IV have brochures on wills and bequests so that you do not have to write your own.

4. Study Chapter II–9 on charitable remainder trusts. Contact several of the companies listed in Appendix IV for sample copies of brochures on charitable remainder trusts. With a minimum amount of coaching from your tax counsel, you should feel completely comfortable talking about these life income plans with major prospects. Do not be concerned with pooled income funds and gift annuities at this point. By yourself, you will be hard pressed to set up the procedures and to become the expert you need to be to make these programs work. If you are feeling ambitious, however, go back to Chapter II-7 on Pooled Income Funds and Chapter II-8 on Charitable Gift Annuities for a complete explanation of these plans and how they work.

5. Redesign the reply mechanisms for your annual giving program so that they include such things as:

   Please send me information about:

   ____ Establishing an endowed fund.
   ____ Making a gift of appreciated securities.
   ____ Making a gift of life insurance.
   ____ Providing a bequest to XYZ Charity.
   ____ Receiving income from my gift.
   ____ Making a gift of art or antiques.

   ____ I have included XYZ Charity in my will.

6. Purchase planned giving software. (See Appendix II) If you intend to solicit charitable remainder trusts or other life income gifts, you will be much more successful and confident if you have a computer program to do the tax calculations. If you do not have the budget to pay for planned giving software, find one board member or one prospect willing to contribute the cost of buying the initial license.

7. Place appropriate lead-generating ads in your newsletter or publication.

8. Recruit the chairman of the board, the president, and one or two trustees to work with you on your top prospects. Establish regular meetings to review the status of each prospect. Otherwise, months will slip by with no progress or results. Read Chapter III-3 on Cultivation and Stewardship.

Remember, outright gifts are the best and most useful "planned gift." Many people on your list probably can make major outright gifts. After meeting with 20 people this year, you should have at least six capital gifts that you did not have last year. If you can do more, great! But, be realistic with your time. If this sounds too simple, just wait until the end of a year when your plate is very full.

Nonetheless, if you are promoting stock gifts, increasing the visibility of bequests, personalizing annual fund solicitations, holding an annual cultivation event for leadership donors, and soliciting a limited number of high-level prospects with the chairman of the board, you should see some of the following results before too long:

- increased revenue from the annual giving program such that there is more money to pay for a full-time director of annual giving, thus, freeing you up to do more major gift work;

- more possible prospects for capital gift solicitations because you have a larger number of $1,000 donors to the annual giving program;

- more involvement and support from the board because they can sense the change in momentum and real progress in other areas of development;

- the beginning of an endowment fund;

- a small but growing number of known bequest intentions.

This is planned giving in a one-person shop. It is as much as you reasonably can be expected to do given the fact that you also have substantial responsibilities in other areas already. Do not dwell on the fact that you cannot do everything. You are only one person. Rome was not built in a day. Neither is a program for long-term support.

SUMMARY

Regardless of who you are, the success of your planned giving activities will be due not from knowing tax law, but from meeting with people. If you involve your constituency in the activities of the institution, you are sure to succeed in generating support. Do not dwell on the gift vehicles and the tax consequences so much that you lose sight of the real reason people give to a charitable cause—it makes them feel good. The next chapter describes the critical relationship between the planned giving officer and the major gifts officer. Often, they work as adversaries in the same development office when they really should be working as a team. If you are a planned giving officer or a major gifts officer, you may find this chapter helpful.

Chapter III–7

PLANNED GIVING AND MAJOR GIFTS: ADVERSARIES OR PARTNERS

Up until now, I have been addressing the creation of your planned giving program. Some chapters give practical advice about why you need legal counsel or how to develop a budget. Some explain tax laws and provide technical information. Some offer marketing tips and advice on how to attract donors. This chapter is different. It is about setting priorities and making every minute count. It is also about the working relationship you'll develop with members of your organization who solicit major gifts, leadership gifts, or principal gifts, whatever levels you create.

This chapter is important even if your office currently does not have a staff member whose title is Major Gifts Officer. Most likely, someone is soliciting the top prospects. It may be the director of development, the president, or a trustee. Very likely, it may not be you. Unfortunately, if your shop is typical of many shops, you are missing many opportunities. This is due in large measure to wasteful daily routines into which you can slip so easily. Often there is an adversarial relationship between the planned giving officer and the people who solicit the largest gifts.

To fully understand the problem, you need a brief history of our industry.

If you surveyed the nation's nonprofit organizations in 1980, you would find that a relatively small minority of charities employed planned giving officers. In those days, planned giving was reserved for a few highly prestigious institutions and a smattering of others fortunate enough to attract bequests. Although planned giving exploded in the 1980s, it was still an up-hill battle for an institution to convince its board that it should enter planned giving. Not any more.

Anyone who has watched the evolution of fund raising for the past two decades knows that planned giving was the hot topic of the 1980s. One example is the growth of the Planned Giving Group of New England. When it was formed in 1978, there were 25 members compared to about 450 in 2003.

Planned giving has had a lot to do with the increase in charitable giving in the past two decades. This is partly due to the fact that planned giving officers as well as financial professionals are giving donors access to philanthropy in new and creative ways. It is also due to the fact that the personalized attention surrounding the stewardship and cultivation of planned giving prospects simply makes them feel quite good about the institution. Planned giving officers are spending more time developing quality relationships. And, it is paying off. It's as simple as that.

Enter the major gifts officer, leadership gifts officer or the principal gifts officer. Some organizations have enough prospects to create several levels of high-end solicitors.

When I wrote the first edition of this book in 1987, there weren't very many major gifts officers. Principal gifts officers were unheard of. In fact, I never used the words "major gift officer" at all in the first book. In those days, the people who really were soliciting the largest gifts were called campaign directors.

Campaign directors aren't the same as today's major gift or principal gift officers because, in addition to soliciting big gifts, they managed the strategy and the plan for the entire campaign. Equally likely, the campaign director collected his or her last check and was on to the next campaign before anyone could consider how to steward the campaign's major donors. Often, an institution ran a campaign, perhaps the first in its history, and focused primarily on outright gifts. Then, after raising more money than ever before, it hired a director of planned giving to launch a planned giving program on the heels of the campaign. As short-term campaigns came and went, planned giving officers began to spring up as permanent fixtures within nonprofit America. Often the planned giving officer picked up the large campaign donors and carried on from there. Remember, the traditional structure involved hiring a campaign director who picked off the large donors but who left at the end of the campaign.

The major gifts officer is now a permanent addition to many development offices. The principal gifts officer is also common. With the addition of these new positions, we see the evolution of personalized donor stewardship taken to a whole new level.

Depending on the institution, the responsibilities of the major gift, leadership gift or principal gift officers vary, but one thing is true—they focus on the top of the donor pyramid.

Major gift officers and principal gift officers came into being because organizations understand the importance of cultivating the biggest prospects separately from the masses. Those large gifts at the top of the donor pyramid mean the success or failure of everything you'll do. They set the pace, they inspire others, and they challenge peers. They make or break your institution's goals. Spending time on the largest prospects is precisely what we all should be doing.

And, now the problem.

The planned giving officer used to be the only person working with the biggest gifts. Now, the elevated status of major or principal gifts has siphoned off the top of the donor pyramid for special attention. Usually, the major gifts director is a peer of the planned giving director, both reporting to the same person. Unfortunately, in far too many institutions, the planned giving officer is being squeezed out of the game. This is a serious state of affairs and one that institutions must address if they are to meet their own highly ambitious goals.

In the first place, major gift or principal gift officers don't necessarily have a background in planned giving or charitable giving tax law. There are exceptions, but the sad truth is that many major gift or principal gift positions have been filled with people who don't understand the complexities and opportunities for fashioning a proposal that meets the donor's unique financial circumstances. They are operating in large measure at half capacity doing a disservice to their institutions as well as to their donors. This problem is compounded by the fact that few, if any, of these major or principal gift solicitors seek help regularly from the planned giving staff.

Meanwhile, the planned giving officer, who should be helping the major or principal gift officer explore creative gift solutions for the biggest prospects, is spending disproportionate amounts of time with $5,000 to $10,000 life income donors. That is because $5,000 to $10,000 is the most common gift size for the pooled income funds and gift annuity programs started in the 1980s. It was fine twenty years ago for the planned giving officer to focus on entry level gifts to the life income plans. Twenty years ago, $5,000 was a lot of money. Today, $5,000 is an annual giving level.

The fund raising climate is more competitive than it has ever been. As a result, there must be a more cooperative model for how planned giving and major or principal gift officers do their jobs. To understand the magnitude of the problem, we need to look at the traditional role of the planned giving officer.

The planned giving officer is the one person at the institution who has mastered the body of tax law related to charitable giving. There may be others at the institution who know bits and pieces of planned giving, but the planned giving officer is required as part of his or her job description to know the full range of options available, to be the expert.

Let's look at a typical job description for a planned giving officer.

Planned Giving Officer
Job Description

1. Responsible for educating the constituency about creative ways to give. Plans and implements mailings, ads, and other promotional print materials to generate leads. Follows up leads.

2. Educates and trains volunteers, donors, and staff through seminars and other estate planning presentations or events.

3. Writes or acquires brochures on creative gift planning.

4. Monitors the administration of the pooled income fund. Is responsible for working with the fiduciary manager or business office. Establishes procedures for accepting and managing pooled income fund gifts. Works with donors on the transfer of assets. Periodically reviews pooled income fund accountings. Oversees year-end tax reporting to beneficiaries.

5. Monitors the administration of the gift annuities. Establishes procedures. Prepares annuity contracts and tax calculations for the completed gift annuities. Oversees annuity payments and tax reporting to annuitants.

6. Works with donors on the establishment of charitable remainder trusts. Secures trust documents from tax counsel. Monitors the transfer of assets. Periodically reviews trust accountings. Stewards the trust donors. Oversees tax reporting to the beneficiaries.

7. Promotes bequests. Provides appropriate bequest wording to donors and attorneys. Stewards bequest donors. Monitors and tracks estates in distribution.

8. Promotes real estate gifts. Works with the business office to ensure smooth and efficient transfer of the property.

All of this sounds quite reasonable and important. But, if we examine what is really happening day to day, we will see that a lot of valuable time is being wasted. Perhaps you, too, are guilty of some of the things that follow.

Let's take direct mail, for example. In an effort to produce inquiries, you, the planned giving officer will develop mailings. This is an important activity because it identifies interested prospects who, one hopes, ultimately will make a gift. However, the only way you can get gifts from a mailing is by following up each and every lead personally. Unfortunately, the successful mailing rarely produces the gifts it should. The problem? You mailed too many pieces at the same time resulting in more reply cards than you can reasonably follow up in a timely fashion.

For example, if you send 10,000 letters and get a 1% response, that's 100 reply cards requiring attention. There is no way you or I could handle such volume with the kind of personal attention necessary to convert these inquiries into gifts. Day after day, as you receive more reply cards, you will develop a feeling of panic and frustration. Bear in mind that your work day already is quite full with all sorts of other activities. If you take the time to review the prospect's history of support before telephoning, and add to that the 15 to 20 minutes you'll spend on the phone, plus the time to write a letter, plus the time to follow up again in a few days, plus a possible visit, a successful mailing will render you immobilized in only a few days.

Eventually, you will have reply cards from your mailing stacked in neat little piles on your desk until the guilt over not following up forces you to take swift and quick action. That swift action involves writing a form letter to everyone. Ordinarily, you would end such a letter with, "I'll call you next week to answer any questions" or some such proactive closing. Instead, your work is so backed up that you end with, "Please let me know if there is any way I can be of further assistance." Whew! Now, you don't have to think about them any more.

If you are smiling, it is because this has happened to you. And, it has happened to many planned giving officers. This is one very good example of how planned giving officers waste time and money when a very simple solution can eliminate this unproductive cycle. Instead of mailing 10,000 letters at once, send 1,000 pieces every other week for ten weeks. Your mailing house is perfectly capable of staggering the drop date such that you'll have a manageable flow of inquiries on a regular basis. The result is obvious. You'll be able to spend time with each prospect in a timely fashion. And, you will get more gifts.

Planned giving officers also waste time cultivating the small, life-income donors who will never make more than a $5,000 repeat gift annuity each year. They really should be spending their time on higher-level prospects. All planned giving officers have these small donors in their planned giving programs—the nice little old ladies. You know the ones I mean. Listen to me here. You cannot afford to visit nice little old ladies any more, that is, unless they are also on your institution's list of major gift prospects. Do you hear me? Stop visiting people who are not highly rated. If you have small life income donors whom you feel have the capacity to do something really big, by all means keep seeing them. There is more about managing your prospect portfolio in Chapter III-2 on Cultivation and Stewardship.

While you are trying to digest this seemingly cold-hearted suggestion, get a list of all life income donors and a red marking pencil. Now, rate these people as follows:

- people who have the capacity to make a nice gift ($50,000, $100,000, you decide based on your organization's standards),

- people who are in the $5,000 to $10,000 gift range, and

- people who need further research to determine future potential.

With this newly-classified list of your planned giving universe, you can set priorities properly. This is not to say you should ignore the existing small donors. There are many ways to steward them in ways that appear highly personalized but that take very little time. For example, the next time your organization gets good media coverage, ask your secretary to send the article and your business card to everyone. Or, instead of visiting these people, telephone them instead. At least you'll be saving time over what you used to do—time that can be better spent on the larger prospects.

Other ways that planned giving officers waste time include:

- compiling reports that can easily be prepared by your assistant;

- personally delivering stock certificates or other gift documentation to your business office when your assistant can do it for you;

- photocopying, filing, and other routine tasks;

- writing routine letters when your secretary could be handling such things;

- creating comparisons or examples from your planned giving software program when your secretary or assistant can do it;

- following up estates yourself when your secretary can easily create a follow-up and tracking system and write letters for your signature;

- processing gift annuities and pooled income fund gifts when your assistant could be doing all of this.

In general, whenever you are not talking to a prospect, writing to a prospect, or strategizing about a prospect, you are wasting time. Consider for a moment how many people you could contact if you eliminated those things from your daily routine that are in a category I call safe and efficient. Stop doing things that are safe and efficient and do more things that are risky and uncertain, like calling higher-level prospects.

Meanwhile, as all of this unproductive and wasteful work is going on in the planned giving office, the major gifts officer or principal gifts officer has a completely different and basically simpler agenda. Here is a typical job description of a major or principal gift officer.

Major/Principal Gift Officer
Job Description

1. Identifies, cultivates, and solicits top prospects. (Gift levels considered "major gifts" or "principal gifts" vary by institution.)

2. Works with trustees, high-level volunteers, or the president to orchestrate the cultivation and solicitation plan for the top prospects.

3. Is responsible for and is assigned to a specific number of prospects.

4. May be assigned to a regional territory.

5. May be assigned to a project-based or program-based campaign.

You'll note that this job description is considerably simpler than the one for planned giving officers. That is not to say this is an easy job. In fact, it is highly stressful. For one thing, everyone at the institution is watching what's happening here. Everyone knows when a gift comes in. The problem with many major gift or principal gift officers is that they take this all very seriously. Planned giving officers better not get caught talking to someone assigned to a major or principal gift officer. Right? The planned giving officer might actually pull in a gift because he or she actually knows what to talk about. Then what? Who gets credit for this gift?

Major or principal gift officers have meetings with important people at the institution. The purpose is to talk about the top prospects. Then, major or principal gift officers, trustees, volunteers, or other leaders go on a solicitation call. What types of gifts are they suggesting? Who knows? What creative gift options are they presenting to these prospects? Who knows? In the vast majority of cases, the major or principal gift officers and all of the other people concerning themselves with these top-level prospects would never dream of calling in the planned giving officer for help. There are exceptions, and if you are one of them, bravo! But, too often, what I am describing happens day in and day out in many, many organizations.

So, if you consider the kinds of things the planned giving officer is doing and the kinds of things the major or principal gifts officer is doing, gifts are being lost for two reasons:

1. The planned giving officer is being wasted on the stewardship of $5,000 to $10,000 life income donors, and

2. The major or principal gifts officer is too territorial about his or her prospects to ask for help on developing a strategy from the one person qualified to give it.....you.

Planned giving blossomed out of a basic realization that if an organization caters to the donors' gift planning needs, more and larger gifts would result. Taking this one step further to the major or principal gift position, we see a whole science surrounding the art of managing the relationship between the prospect and the institution. Now, we must go one step further and combine the tax knowledge of the planned giving officer with the interpersonal strategies employed by the major or principal gift officer to complete the picture. Otherwise, they are both working in a vacuum.

This requires a greater level of tax expertise on the part of the planned giving officer. No major or principal gifts officer will draw you into the discussions unless you can demonstrate a credible, mature, and professional approach to planned giving on one hand and interpersonal relationships on the other. You must earn the right to be part of this team, especially if you are new to planned giving. You have to pay your dues first and get some experience. However, the major or principal gifts officer must take the initiative to learn about planned giving, too. A working knowledge of the basic concepts is essential.

Developing a major gift team instead of operating planned giving, major gifts, and principal gifts separately will necessitate an institutional philosophy quite different from what may exist today at your organization. Such a change will cause anxiety and uncertainty across the department. For example, up until now, the planned giving officer could point to certain types of gifts as resulting from planned giving activity. If the major or principal gift officer were working hand-in-hand with the planned giving officer, he or she might be bringing in some deferred gifts that will also end up in the planned giving reports. On the other hand, the planned giving officer might also be attracting some large outright gifts that would not ordinarily show on the planned giving reports.

Initially, the number of gifts will go down because the planned giving officer would be spending less time pursuing the $5,000 to $10,000 life income gifts. Eventually, the gift size will increase as the team members plan better strategies for the people already identified for larger gifts.

In order to nurture the staff partnership so essential to major gift success, here is a list of the changes that need to take place for planned giving, major gift or principal gift officers.

Planned Giving Officer
Suggested Changes

1. Stop paying disproportionate attention to the small, life income donors. Develop more efficient and streamlined methods of providing personal stewardship that require less of the director's personal time.

2. In general, pay less attention to anyone not identified as a top prospect.

3. Streamline proposals used to follow up general inquiries so that time is not spent on people whose gift potential is only $5,000 or $10,000. See if you can turn over these small donors to the annual giving staff. Annual giving staff ought to be able to handle a discussion about a gift annuity. If not, it is time for you to run the planned giving staff presentation described in Chapter III-4.

4. Continue educating the general constituency about creative ways to give (articles, ads, and mailings) with emphasis on larger gift examples to screen out the $5,000 to $10,000 donors. For mailings, stagger the drop date to spread the flow of inquiries over a longer period. Please do not think that this is unfair. People who give your organization $5,000 are giving much larger gifts elsewhere.

5. Stop doing estate planning seminars or wills clinics for the general public because, generally, you're not attracting the right people. Better: Hold a targeted seminar for a hand-picked group of major gift prospects and concentrate on how to get the highly-rated people to attend.

6. Stop focusing on the growth of the pooled income fund, the gift annuity program, or, for that matter, any particular type of gift. Focus instead on getting the right gift from the top prospects, whatever form the gift might take.

Major Gift Officer
Suggested Changes

1. Become familiar with the concepts of planned giving so that meetings with significant prospects can take on a whole new dimension and all new possibilities when the donor says no to the outright gift. Don't let that "no" be the end of the discussion.

2. Never orchestrate a major gift solicitation without involving the planned giving officer. This doesn't mean taking the planned giving officer on every visit. It means getting advice back in the office.

3. Involve the planned giving officer at the very initial stages of developing a strategy so that he or she can offer questions to ask the donor—questions that will lead to a more successful proposal when the time is right.

4. Recruit the planned giving officer to prepare gift proposals for use in solicitations or invite the planned giving officer to go on the visit.

5. Stop thinking that he or she alone is the only person to be in contact with the major gift or principal gift prospect.

SUMMARY

It sounds like I am suggesting that the small donor is not important. That is not really the point. Often, a $5,000 gift from one person is a real stretch while $500,000 from another person is a drop in the bucket. Still, consider the challenges your organization faces in the next decade. Many campaigns now being conducted are in the $1 billion or over range. Harvard finished a campaign for $2 billion and exceeded the goal. In 2002, Dartmouth College launched a $2 billion campaign. Whatever your goals may be, surely they are ambitious. Your success will be based on getting the top 5% of your donors to give at very high levels. If everyone focuses on the top of the donor pyramid, you will succeed. And, you'll continue to get the $5,000s and $10,000s anyway—not by working for them as hard as you used to but because those people giving $5,000 will simply be there. Working as adversaries, planned giving and major or principal gift officers do themselves and their institutions a great disservice. Together in a partnership, the team will flourish and so will the institution.

If you reached this chapter, you have come a very long way in your education about planned giving. If you have digested the advice in this chapter on the working relationship between planned giving and major or principal gift officers, you are ready for a chapter that will bring you to a new level of understanding about the kind of commitment it will take for your organization to receive what David Dunlop, formerly of Cornell University, calls "The Ultimate Gift."

Chapter III–8

THE ULTIMATE GIFT

This chapter will give you enormous insight about major gift fund raising. It will provide a framework for you in attracting that once-in-a-lifetime gift that we all hear about from our peers.

I didn't write this chapter. It is an article from CURRENTS magazine (May 1987) and is reprinted in this book with permission. The Council for Advancement and Support of Education, an international association of education advancement professionals, publishes CURRENTS and retains the copyright and reserves all rights to the article. CURRENTS is published ten times a year for CASE members worldwide. For more information, visit www.case.org.

The article was written by then CURRENTS editor Robin Goldman Netherton (now a freelance editor based in St. Louis) and is based on an interview with David R. Dunlop, former Director of Capital Projects for Cornell University of Ithaca, New York. David has since retired from Cornell after a career that spanned over three decades at one institution. It doesn't get any better than that.

When I first heard David Dunlop give a speech called "The Ultimate Gift" at a CASE conference in Washington, DC, in May of 1989, I knew that his visionary concept had to be a chapter of my second book in 1991. I subsequently read the article that follows, and asked for permission to print it in its entirely.

So, I invite you to savor every word of this chapter. If you follow the advice here, you will change your institution. Even after all these years, the words still ring true. I have not changed one word from the last edition of my book even though some of the details related to the program at Cornell have changed.

Since the article was written for higher education, it has an orientation to campus activities and to a university setting. Many people reading this book represent other kinds of organizations. If you are one of them, don't get hung up on the article's orientation to higher education. The principles apply across the board.

THE BIGGEST GIFTS OF ALL TAKE A SPECIAL KIND OF FUND RAISING

Two of our givers, whom I'll call the Smiths, never went to college here. Mr. Smith planned as a youth to follow his family's Cornell tradition, but he became ill with tuberculosis and went instead to the Adirondack Mountains to recover. Smith eventually bought a farm in the Adirondacks and settled there.

Decades later, Cornell approached the Smiths to ask if they'd sell part of their farm. It seems their land was particularly suitable for a proposed agricultural research project. The Smiths declined to sell the land—and then surprised us all by making a gift of it.

As they watched the work being done on the land they'd donated, the Smiths became more and more interested in the project. They became friends with the researchers working there and shared their pride in the results. When the project grew, the Smiths gave more land, and they loaned other property for other projects. And when the need for a laboratory arose, the Smiths provided that as well.

Twenty-five years later, when the faculty member who'd begun this research project approached retirement, the Smiths made a suggestion of their own. They realized that this researcher's use of their gifts had produced far-reaching benefits for humanity. To preserve what they'd given in the past and to ensure continued leadership for the future, they decided to endow a professorship for the direction of the project.

The Smiths didn't give that gift because a fund raiser asked them to, or even because the need was immediate or pressing. They gave because over the years, they'd grown close to and involved with Cornell and its programs. So when they reached the point where they wanted to make one of the largest commitments of their lives, they thought of Cornell. And they chose the project that meant so much to them as their means of making that commitment.

Every fund raiser dreams of getting gifts of this magnitude. But a program of fund raising calls, however carefully arranged, or a well-presented case, however persuasive, won't in themselves convince a person to make the gift of his or her lifetime.

Still, that doesn't mean you have to wait and hope that an unexpected multi-million-dollar bequest will appear out of nowhere. You *can* pave the way for the truly big gift. But you must first understand why people give these gifts—and tailor your own fund raising behavior accordingly.

A DIFFERENT KIND OF GIFT

Many fund raisers class gifts as one of two types: annual or capital. I prefer to see giving as a spectrum that includes an infinite variety of types of gifts. And on that spectrum, we can identify not two, but three major points.

The first is *annual* giving. Almost every giver makes annual gifts every year to one or more causes. These gifts are small and easy to give, and they usually require little decision making on the giver's part. I know one man who supports 87 causes annually.

The middle point on the spectrum is what I call *special* gifts. These are the gifts people make for a specific purpose or campaign—say, when their church needs a new roof. Special gifts often run five to ten times larger than the same person's annual gifts. Givers may take several years to pay off a special gift; meanwhile, they'll still support their annual causes.

These two kinds of giving are basic to philanthropy. But there's a third type of giving that fund raisers often ignore and that requires a different kind of fund raising than the first two. That's the gift that someone probably can give only once because it represents such a substantial portion of his or her resources—perhaps 1,000 to 2,000 times the size of an annual gift. (Depending on individual circumstances and personal obligations, this might account for a small part of the giver's total wealth—or nearly all of it.)

These I call *ultimate* gifts. Although these commitments are often arranged as trusts or bequests, note that I don't call them "planned gifts" or "deferred gifts." Those terms focus on technique. What's different here is not the *method* a person uses to give the gift, but rather the magnitude of and motivation for the gift.

People give these truly major gifts because they want to express a deeply felt commitment, not just because someone happens to ask them for money. And they give *when* they want to—because it's the right time in their own lives, not necessarily because it's the right time for the institution.

Thus, to raise these gifts, we need to position our institution in these people's lives so that when the time comes for them to make their ultimate philanthropic commitment, they'll feel that ours is the right cause. Ultimate gift fund raising, then, depends on our ability to build and develop long-term relationships with a few special givers.

A DIFFERENT APPROACH

The fund raising methods that work for annual and special gifts are seldom sufficient to prepare people to make their ultimate gift to an institution. Ironically, the fund raising approach that paves the way for an ultimate gift will almost always guarantee other giving as well.

Before we discuss how the process works, let's look quickly at two basic points that make this kind of fund raising different.

For annual and special gifts, our standard fund raising behavior is largely speculative. We do a lot of asking, knowing that only a certain percentage of people will actually respond. We run phonathons, send out direct mail appeals, organize committees, and pass out pledge cards—all on the speculation that a fair percentage of our efforts will pay off.

Ultimate gift fund raising, however, is costly—not simply in financial resources, but in the time and talent of the volunteers, staff, and faculty it involves. It requires a great deal of personal attention, often over a period of many years.

Since you can't afford to commit this intense an effort to any but your best prospects, this means you have to choose your prospects carefully. More often than not, your choices will be obvious. Nearly every development office can identify which prospects have both the financial capacity to make large gifts and a philanthropic nature. Very likely, they're the friends on your board and among your volunteers. And they're probably already giving at lower levels.

A second major difference concerns the role of solicitation. Many fund raisers see solicitation as their primary activity—getting the right person to ask for the right amount at the right time. Concentrating your efforts on making or arranging fund raising calls is in fact appropriate for annual or special giving, where the emphasis should be on the asking.

But that philosophy doesn't hold true for the ultimate gift. For this type of fund raising, the actual closing of the gift accounts for maybe five percent of the work. The other 95 percent comes earlier, in building the attitudes that bring people to want to make these gifts.

That doesn't mean you eliminate solicitation. Rather, solicitation takes on a different form. Instead of concentrating on the "ask," you concentrate on bringing prospects to a point where they virtually solicit themselves.

PROSPECTS AND PROCESS

G.T. (Buck) Smith, a nationally recognized fund raiser (former president of Chapman College), once pointed out that the heart of our business is changing people's views of the institution from "they" and "them" to "we" and "us." Once that change occurs, you'll get not only financial commitments, but personal, moral, and spiritual support as well.

So how do we change the "them" perspective to an "us" perspective?

As I look at people who have made ultimate gifts, here and elsewhere, I've noticed that the specific experiences they've had leading up to those commitments vary widely. But the *types* of experiences are identical. All these givers had experiences with the institution and with the projects they've supported that developed their:

- awareness,
- knowledge,
- interest,
- involvement,
- sense of commitment, and
- expressions of commitment.

If this process is common to all past givers of major gifts, then it's obvious that we should try to duplicate these sorts of experiences for prospective givers. Thus, major gift fund raising comes down to the business of enhancing the prospect's relationship with the institution. Ideally, we'll encourage a series of experiences that will lead prospects through these various stages to the point of feeling, and expressing commitment.

Let's look more closely at the idea of tracking the progress of a relationship. The typical way fund raisers measure progress is to count up the number of dollars and donors they've acquired in a given year. At the top giving levels, though, that's not an accurate measure. These gifts are based not on what you did last year, but on what's happened over the last 25 or 30 years.

So if you measure the dollars that happen to flow in during, say, last year, you're not looking at the process. You're just totaling the cash register tape at the end of the process. Likewise, if you count the numbers of givers based on when they happened to become givers, as opposed to looking at those who are developing relationships, you're not measuring the thing that really matters.

Our object, then, is to track not dollars but involvement. Our means of measurement is the number and type of contacts each of our top prospects has with the institution. If we can monitor their experiences—and initiate additional experiences of the right sort at the right time, we can deepen that person's relationship with the institution. And, the deeper that relationship, the more likely that person will eventually consider our institution for an ultimate gift.

(One point worth noting: Like all models, this one is less complex on paper than it is in life. Ideally, we'd be able to work systematically to develop awareness first, then knowledge, and so on. In reality, an individual giver's development can be unpredictable. Different experiences—many of which you'll never know about—can bounce a prospect among these different stages. And you may not even identify a prospect until he or she is well into the process.

THE PLAYERS

Here's a scenario common at many institutions: The major gifts committee—sometimes staff members, sometimes volunteers—will sit around a table and talk about the top prospects. And as each name comes up, someone will say, "Oh, I'll take Harry," or "I'll take Cynthia."

These people are full of good will and the right motives. And this is appropriate at annual or special gift levels. But for the top gifts, these people might not be the best ones to coordinate and develop the relationship. For this, you must identify the prospect's *natural partners* at the institution.

What individuals on campus (or at your institution) are in touch with the prospect? Perhaps the prospect still corresponds with an old professor (or a former minister). Perhaps a relative or friend of the prospect is enrolled as a student (or is now being cared for by the hospital). Anyone might end up being a link. For example, one of our leading benefactors became friends with a campus gardener because he tended a garden that was named in her honor.

These natural partners are in the best position to tell you what kind of contact would be most significant to that prospect and, in some cases, to help you make that contact.

From among these people, consider who might be willing to help you with building the relationship. You won't ask them to solicit; you won't send them any formal progress reports or computer printouts. Their role is simply to help you involve the prospect more deeply with the institution. It's important that you don't interfere with the natural friendship, and under no circumstances should the partner feel manipulated. Most often, you'll find these people happy to help their friends receive the attention and recognition you want to provide.

Once you've identified the prospect's campus (or institutional) connections, your contacts with the prospect will involve people in three different roles:

- *The Primary Player.* This is the natural partner in the best position to monitor the prospect's relationship with the institution. He or she keeps a hand on the pulse of that relationship.

- *Secondary Players.* These natural partners help guide and carry out contacts with the Prospective giver. They provide ideas and feedback about the prospect's interest and concerns.

- *The Moves Manager.* This person—you or a member of your staff—works with the primary and secondary players, tracks the prospect's progress, and makes sure the institution maintains sufficient and appropriate contact with the prospect.

On occasion—for example, if the prospect is also a volunteer for the development office—the moves manager will actually come into direct contact with the prospective giver. More likely, the moves manager simply guides and assists the people who already have natural connections with the prospect.

Bear in mind that these prospects tend to be most interested in dealing with the people who work on the projects they support. Rarely will they consider a fund raiser their first or most important link with the institution. If you impose yourself artificially into the giver's relationship with the institution, you may hamper that relationship. Instead, let your own involvement grow naturally.

TAKING INITIATIVES

Individual contacts made at random won't in themselves move a person toward commitment. Your efforts much have:

- quality,
- quantity,
- frequency, and
- continuity.

Without these four characteristics, your ultimate gift fund raising may be ineffective and inefficient—perhaps even a costly distraction. In other words, your institution must enter the life of your prospect in some substantive way every few weeks over a long period of time. If your contacts are inappropriate or sporadic, your prospect's ultimate gift will probably go to a cause with which he or she is more closely involved.

We can class the contacts you initiate in two categories.

1. *Foreground initiatives* are activities planned with a specific prospect in mind. For example, you might:

    - Arrange a visit from the president.
    - Plan a private lunch with faculty members (or other leaders at the institution).
    - Hold a testimonial dinner.
    - Report to the prospect on the impact of his or her last gift.
    - Send a card to congratulate the prospect on a business success.
    - Use the prospect's home for a reception.
    - Borrow art for a campus showing (or borrow something that would be appropriate for your institution's mission).
    - Get a student to write to express thanks for a scholarship.
    - Ask for advice in the prospect's area of expertise.
    - Borrow the prospect's private plane to bring a VIP to campus.
    - Give the prospect an award for distinguished service.
    - Name a room for the prospect.
    - Offer special seating for events or activities

2. *Background initiatives* are activities or services planned for groups of people that may include one or more prospects. For example:

    - visiting committees,
    - advisory councils,
    - alumni clubs,
    - class reunions,
    - student recruitment interviewing,

- annual reports, alumni periodicals, brochures, and other publications,
- films, videos, and slide shows,
- receptions and dinners, or
- institutional tours.

Sometimes the same event can serve as both a foreground initiative for one person and a background initiative for another. For example, when we dedicated the Smiths' laboratory, we invited 200 people out to the farm in the Adirondacks. We pitched a circus tent, served meals, and expressed thanks. That event was a foreground initiative for the Smiths—one action in a long string of contacts that had gone on for many years.

The event also served as a background initiative for the guests who attended. As it happened, one of those guests—a neighbor of the Smiths and a Cornell alumnus—struck up an acquaintance there with the dean of our College of Agriculture and Life Science, who was the son of one of the guest's classmates. The resulting friendship led within a year to the guest's gift of his own Adirondack farm. After eight years and many meaningful contacts, this man left Cornell an eight-figure bequest, the largest in the University's history.

MANAGING THE MOVES

You've identified prospective givers and their natural partners. You understand what sort of initiatives you might make. How do you put all these things together into a coherent program of regular contacts, or, as we call them, "moves?"

- *Review* the prospect's relationship with the institution regularly.
- *Plan*, in consultation with your primary and secondary players, what sort of contact would be most appropriate next.
- *Coordinate* that plan with the players involved.
- *Execute* the plan.
- *Evaluate* its impact.
- *Record* and *report* the move to the appropriate staff or players.

Although I'd recommend reviewing each prospect's status monthly, the time it takes to complete a move can vary widely. If the right move is simply to write a letter or make a phone call, those six steps can happen very quickly. But sometimes the right move is to pitch a circus tent and invite 200 people to dinner—and take six months planning it.

When you start thinking about the numbers of contacts that you need and the numbers of people involved in making these contacts, the sheer volume of activity starts to look impossible. And, it would be, except for the saving grace that many of these experiences happen spontaneously.

Obviously, background initiatives require much less of the manager's time than do foreground initiatives. A skilled moves manager can handle perhaps 400 foreground initiatives per year. Since most prospects will experience as many background moves as they do foreground moves, we can assume that one ultimate gift fund raiser can be responsible for about 70 prospects. In an ideal world, one staff person would handle half that many prospects—about 35.

At Cornell, which started its major gift program in 1973, we have seven staff members serving as moves managers, at both major and special gift levels. Among them, they manage moves for about 1,180 top prospects and track some 1,200 givers at lower levels of involvement.

For a program of this size, we've found a computer essential for tracking prospects. When we began the program, and we were tracking fewer than 200 prospects, we did all our work on an office word processor. Now, we use the university mainframe, and Cornell's programmers have developed a tracking system to suit our special approach.

The computer allows us to store contact information for each prospect and automatically distributes information to the appropriate staff members and those key players who should receive reports. Most important, though, it provides a tangible record of what led up to each major gift. These records provide the perfect education for new staff members and faculty who are unfamiliar with the fund raising process.

THE HEART OF THE MATTER

Even if you have a small staff, don't think you can't apply these concepts to cultivate your top prospects. In fact, an institution with a small donor base or a small fund raising program needs this approach more than a larger institution does, simply because you must make the most of every potential giver.

To begin, start small. Identify five or ten of your best prospects. Then identify their natural partners and think of those people in terms of primary and secondary. And with utter faithfulness, review every one of those prospects every month. Plan contacts if necessary and keep records by hand.

Remember, just because an ultimate gift may be 30 years in the making, that doesn't mean you'll have to wait 30 years to see results. Even if you haven't been actively managing prospects' moves, some moves are still going on. Your prospects' relationships are with the institution, and your institution does all manner of things to build relationships whether a fund raiser is there to watch it or not.

In fact, that last point is vital. If we want to go beyond the annual and special gifts to the gifts that are of the greatest importance to the giver, we need to look beyond our own particular needs and campaigns and causes. We must look instead at the needs and interests of the giver and respond to those needs—even as we go about the business of serving our institution.

At base, the heart of our business isn't charitable lead trusts and bequests and gifts of real estate. And it isn't even moves and initiatives. It's human values and human purposes. Those are the things people will commit themselves to. And it's those values and purposes that make our givers friends for life.

SUMMARY

When you and your colleagues share the wisdom of this chapter, you may need to step back from your pressing priorities to consider what it would take to create an ultimate gift culture within the organization. No doubt, the collaboration, coordination, and diligence necessary are daunting. You also need to evaluate how to measure your success in this long-term approach. Instead of measuring gifts, you measure moves. It will take strong leadership from the Vice President of Development to foster a culture that allows the process described by David Dunlop to flourish. If you are the one in charge, the onus is on you. This is the sort of thing that ought to be discussed at a staff retreat so that each member of the team understands his or her role in the big picture. I suppose the challenge for any development office is to ensure continuity of staff in the midst of an industry marked by staff turnover every two years on average.

No doubt, some gifts that fit into the ultimate gift category, and many smaller ones, will need to be managed by a fiduciary manager. While some institutions use their own in-house resources to administer, invest, and manage deferred giving or general endowment assets, other institutions retain a professional fiduciary for these responsibilities. The next and last chapter discusses issues and considerations for the management of your planned giving assets.

Chapter III–9

MANAGING YOUR PLANNED GIVING ASSETS

If you made it this far to the last chapter of this book, congratulations. I guess you have some gifts that need managing. This chapter will help you with that process. If you need specific information about how to administer individual gift plans, you should turn to the relevant chapters in Part II.

Although the most enjoyable part of your work will be building relationships with donors and assisting them through their gift decisions, life as a planned giving officer also means working with somebody who administers the gifts. The functions of the administrator include most, if not all, of the following tasks, and could include others depending on the complexity of the gift assets or the gift vehicles:

- Accepting, valuing, and disposing of assets;
- Making investment decisions or following investment guidelines provided by your organization's investment committee;
- Keeping track of the donors and beneficiaries, including seasonal addresses in many cases;
- Making payments to beneficiaries in an accurate and timely way;
- Preparing tax returns for appropriate accounts;
- Preparing tax forms for beneficiaries including K-1s for pooled income fund and charitable remainder trust beneficiaries and 1099-Rs for charitable gift annuitants;
- Calculating charitable gift annuity reserves as mandated by certain regulating states;
- Preparing legal documents and agreements in some cases;
- Meeting with or interacting with donors or beneficiaries;
- Periodically performing valuations of accounts, depending on the type of deferred vehicle and governing instrument;
- Providing periodic reports to the donors, beneficiaries, and to the charity.

The administrator might be a bank, trust company, brokerage firm, specialized deferred giving manager, or it could be your charity's own business office. In some cases, your planned giving assets might be spread among several managers.

Some organizations manage deferred giving assets in house until the responsibilities become too unwieldy for their own business office. Some manage one type of deferred gift in house while farming out others.

As director of planned giving, your job is to oversee all of the managers and to make sure that each kind of deferred giving asset is being handled properly. You'll find that the administrative tasks take up a lot of time especially because things go wrong frequently.

Close coordination with each of the managers is extremely important. If you are new to your position, you should begin by arranging a meeting with the people who manage your institution's deferred gift assets. If the assets are managed outside your institution, you'll usually find a trust officer and an investment officer assigned to your account. The trust officer will generally be your primary liaison.

I cannot stress strongly enough the importance of focusing on the smallest details, almost to an obsessive degree. But, even in the most efficiently run shop, things go wrong all the time. Undoing or fixing a problem will take up double or triple the time it would have taken to get it right in the beginning. However, even if you follow strict procedures, some things are out of your control. The following are all real examples of things that happened when I was a director of planned giving.

- A donor mailed a stock certificate but neglected to send a signed stock power which is essential for the gift to be complete. The next day, he had a stroke and went into a coma for three months. He finally came out of the coma and signed a stock power. However, the date of gift was now three months later than he intended. In this case, the donor's stock doubled in value over the three months but it could just as easily have gone the other way.

- A donor received from me instructions for making a gift to our pooled income fund. He told his broker to transfer stock through Depository Trust Company directly to the DTC account of our pooled income fund's manager. However, he neglected to send the Instrument of Transfer pursuant to which the gift would be administered. He promptly went on vacation for a couple of weeks. We could not deem this to be a gift until he returned from vacation and sent the Instrument of Transfer. He was extremely upset because the price of the stock had declined.

- A donor sent a check to establish a charitable gift annuity, but he never told us he was making a gift. That would not normally be a problem except for the fact that he put the check in a postage-paid envelope he had saved from an Annual Fund mailing. The envelope was addressed to a Post Office Box at our lock box service. If you haven't worked in an organization that uses a lock box, let me explain. This is an external vendor who receives checks from direct mail activity and is most commonly used when there is high volume such as we had at Boston University or WGBH. The lock box service opens the mail, tallies the checks, batches them for deposit into the institution's account, and eventually sends the batches of data to the institution for input into the donor records. Even though the donor wrote "gift annuity" in the memo field of the check, the notation meant nothing to the lock box service. The check was put into the Annual Fund. A few weeks later, the donor called to ask why he had not received his new gift annuity agreement. We found the money, but this episode consumed an enormous amount of time.

It would have been difficult to prevent the above situations because certain things are out of your control. However, you can prevent most problems by coordinating the following kinds of items with your account manager or managers.

- Instructions on transferring securities electronically to the manager of your accounts.
- Rules on minimum gift size for various gift vehicles and rules on age restrictions.
- Procedures for updating donor records or addresses.
- Guidelines for investment decisions for various gift vehicles.
- Procedures for providing tax information to the beneficiaries. Who prepares the documents? Who needs copies? Who mails them to the beneficiaries?
- Timetables for account statements or reporting. How frequent? Who gets them?
- Procedures for getting payments to the beneficiaries. Does the manager mail them directly or does the manager mail them to you for forwarding to the beneficiaries?
- Procedures for setting up automatic deposits.
- Who is in charge when your account manager is away?
- Who would your account manager call if you are away?
- Who prepares the documents for the different gift vehicles?
- Who prepares the tax calculations for the donors?

If you work with multiple managers, you'll have to keep the rules for each manager straight. That will make your administrative tasks more time consuming than if you worked with one manager. I talked to Jan Adams in the Charitable Asset Management group at State Street Global Advisors here in Boston about the difficulties encountered most often with her clients. She said that planned giving officers often neglect to get all of the essential information from donors up front. For example, when taking in any kind of life income gift, you need the date of birth, the social security number of the beneficiary or beneficiaries, the primary address and a seasonal address if appropriate. But, she says that the piece of information that seems to be the hardest to get is the cost basis for gifts of securities. "Without the cost basis, a manager cannot do the proper tax reporting. For a CRT, you can't track the four tiers without the cost basis."

Jan stressed the importance of the planned giving officer notifying the manager as soon as possible when he or she is expecting a gift. "What kind of asset is coming? Where is it coming from? Since securities coming through Depository Trust Company often don't have a donor name attached, knowing in advance the name of the donor and the exact securities being transferred will prevent the asset from sitting in escrow or even being rejected."

If you are just starting a planned giving program, you will be distressed with the landscape for planned giving managers. Most fiduciaries require minimum size accounts, a state of affairs that leaves the newcomer to planned giving out in the cold. In the beginning, you don't have the minimum account levels to make your account attractive to the mainstream managers. This forces you to assume the responsibilities in house when your own business office may not have the expertise necessary to manage planned giving assets.

SELECTING A MANAGER

Whether or not you already have one or more outside managers, eventually you may reach a point when you will need to change managers or consolidate assets under one manager. This means preparing a Request for Proposal (RFP). Sometimes, you already know that you would like to select a particular manager, but you still must go through the RFP process in order to justify the decision. Sometimes, you simply know that you would like to remove a manager. Very likely, members of your board of trustees have affiliations with various financial institutions. Therefore, it is important to establish an impartial process so as to avoid the politics that will inevitably be involved in selecting a new manager or removing assets from another manager. Be prepared to spend a lot of time on the whole process.

When I first started in planned giving in the mid-1970s, only a handful of trust companies had expertise in planned giving administration. Today, the choices for planned giving administration are extremely broad including banks, trust companies, and most brokerage firms. There are even companies that specialize solely in planned giving administration. Depending on the geographic region in which your charity is located, you'll probably be aware of the institutions that have the highest profile in the planned giving field. However, if you need suggestions, simply call another director of planned giving in your area.

In the early part of my career, I thought that it was important to have a manager located in my city so as to facilitate the smooth running of the account. In those days, there was no overnight mail delivery, no such thing as a fax machine, voice-mail, or e-mail. Today, I don't feel it is necessary to have a manager in the same city. And, due to the fact that there are extremely experienced planned giving managers all over the country, you should not limit the list to those that are local. However, you might start the process by talking to your treasurer to see if he or she has any preferences for which institutions should be on the list. Make sure that you find out if there are any trustee connections that would dictate putting those institutions on the list. To be thorough, I would have a list of five.

To begin your process, call the prospective managers on your list and inquire as to whether they would consider taking on a new institutional planned giving account. Ask about the minimum account level for planned giving assets. Right away, you may have to eliminate one or more in the group simply because your organization doesn't meet the minimum account size. Most managers are looking for accounts above $3 million to $5 million. As a result, sometimes the only solution is to include all or part of your general endowment in the deal. That solution could present political problems of its own since your institution may have a long standing relationship with its endowment manager.

The process of developing your RFP will vary from institution to institution, but you don't have to reinvent the wheel. Charities that have gone through the process would probably be willing to share their proposal with you. In addition, financial institutions accustomed to responding to RFPs may already have a guide that you could use to develop your own model.

I talked to a friend of mine, Charles Gordy, who formerly ran the planned giving program at Yale University and is now the Managing Director of Planned Giving Services at the Bank of New York. He sent the following sample of a Request for Proposal. You will, no doubt, realize quickly that responding to an RFP is no small task.

Request for Proposal Planned Giving Services (Sample from Bank of New York)

1. Describe how your bank (firm) is structured to provide investment management, administration, tax preparations, and custody services for planned giving assets. Highlight those units responsible for the specialized services required by planned giving clients. Describe the staffing (professionals and others) in the investment management, administration, and custody areas. Please include an organizational chart of those responsible for planned giving.

2. Complete the following summary as of (date):

	Investment Management	Custody	Administration
A. Charitable Gift Annuities # of CGA Accounts	$ _____ _____	$ _____ _____	$ _____ _____
B. Charitable Remainder Trusts (all) # of CRT Accounts	$ _____ _____	$ _____ _____	$ _____ _____
C. Pooled Income Funds # of PIF Accounts	$ _____ _____	$ _____ _____	$ _____ _____
D. Charitable Lead Trusts # of CLT Accounts	$ _____ _____	$ _____ _____	$ _____ _____
E. Donor Advised Funds # of DAF Accounts	$ _____ _____	$ _____ _____	$ _____ _____
Total Assets	$ _____	$ _____	$ _____
Total # of Accounts	_____	_____	_____

3. How many years have you provided investment management, administrative, and custody services for each of the indicated charitable asset categories (CGA, CRT, PIF, CLT)?

4. Please describe your investment strategy for different kinds of deferred gifts.

5. If you are chosen as the manager, would we be required to use any specific managers or mutual funds?

6. Please describe how your planned giving staffing has changed over the past three years. Include head counts for key functional areas.

7. Please list any planned giving clients that have left your institution in the last three years.

8. Identify the person (including back-up personnel) who will be responsible for day-to-day administration of the account. Detail each individual's qualifications to provide the required service. How will your firm assure staff continuity in case of turnover on the account? How many other relationships would the primary contact also manage?

9. Please describe your procedures and time schedule for distribution of payments to beneficiaries.

10. Please note if you are restrained from meeting any required tax reporting dates throughout the year, and describe your timing for performing necessary tax work.

11. Do you have in-house counsel to advise on tax and legal matters pertaining to planned giving? If not, do you retain outside counsel?

12. May donors contact your financial institution directly with appropriate questions?

13. What is the expected turn around time of questions posed to your staff either by telephone or e-mail, particularly with respect to donor payments?

14. Are all planned giving accounts accessible *via* the Internet? Can our donors have Internet access to their accounts?

15. Do you report at calendar year end the estimated or fixed amount of unitrust income for the subsequent calendar year, and applicable deficiencies of income?

16. Will the (firm) send check registers and how timely? How quickly will we be notified of ACH rejections and returned checks? How quickly will a payment be made after the bank learns of a failed payment?

17. Does the bank (company) print checks with the charity's logo?

18. What types of reports, if any, are sent directly to donors and how often?

19. What type of software product does the bank use to process gift annuities (off the shelf product, such as PG Calc, Crescendo, or PhilanthroCalc, or a proprietary system)?

20. Will the bank perform gift annuity filings to state insurance agencies and does the (firm) assist with state regulations?

21. Please provide samples of reports for CRTs, CGAs, PIFs, tax reporting statements and returns, ACH statements and checks, as well as samples of investment reports and any other information you will regularly convey to us or to our donors.

22. Please explain briefly why the client should select your organization to provide the needed services. How do you compare to your competitors? What are your competitive advantages?

23. Please list all non-profit institutions for which you provide planned giving services, including the names and phone numbers of three that can be contacted as references.

24. In what cities do you have branches?

Charlie suggests giving the prospective managers five to six weeks to prepare their proposals. Jan Adams at State Street Global Advisors suggests at least three to four weeks. As a courtesy to the prospective managers, ask each one what timetable would be acceptable and then set a reasonable time limit that satisfies everybody. In addition to coordinating the timetable with the managers, check with your treasurer or financial vice president about getting the selection process on the agenda for an appropriate board of trustees meeting. Perhaps this process can be done with only the members of your investment committee, or perhaps the full board will need to be involved.

As you can see from the above sample RFP, the amount of information to be evaluated is extensive. For each response, you will receive about an inch of information. But, that is not all. You also need to ask for investment performance figures, an extremely important criterion for selection of your manager. This section of the RFP should be done in consultation with your treasurer, but here is a suggestion of what you need, again provided by Charles Gordy at Bank of New York.

"Ask the provider for Investment performance numbers for the mutual funds and individual managers that will be available to you if you select that provider, and for a comparison of those funds and managers to appropriate indices and peers (*e.g.*, the S&P 500, Russell, Wilshire, MSCI EAFE (international), Lipper (mutual funds), NAREIT (real estate investment trusts), Lehman Brothers (bonds). Make sure to ask if you are limited to the provider's family of mutual funds and managers or whether you will have access to outside mutual funds and managers. Make sure to ask if the performance numbers are net of fees and the total fees associated with different investment options."

Also important for the potential manager are the figures for your planned giving assets currently. You should provide a grid that shows the following:

- Type of deferred gift by category,
- Number of contracts or agreements for each category,
- Market value of each category,
- Payment schedules. For CRTs, you should report how many have payments annually, semiannually, quarterly, or monthly because some fee schedules are based on a *per*-transaction cost;
- Number of beneficiaries for each category. Practically, this applies to your PIF and your CGA program. The potential manager needs to know how many beneficiaries you have in your gift annuity pool or pooled income fund.

If you are digesting this chapter properly, you have already figured out that doing an RFP means a lot of work on your part, too.

When we did an RFP at Boston College to five planned giving administrators, we received reams and reams of information. Some institutions put their information in a ringed binder with tabs. Others provided a narrative with multiple exhibits. There was no consistency in the formats; therefore, sorting it all out is difficult.

Although each prospective manager wanted to meet with us, our treasurer wanted no part in having a stream of managers coming through with a presentation to the board of trustees. The entire selection process was done based on a grid that I prepared from the responses. Basically, it came down to the fee structure.

At the time, we managed gift annuities in house. We had an outside manager for our pooled income fund, and, prior to the RFP, we did not serve as trustee of CRTs. The investment performance was fairly uniform among the five managers we selected, but the fee structure was extremely varied. Two of the institutions on the list due to trustee connections were not equipped to manage planned giving assets. In the end, were able to select an extremely strong candidate with full approval of the entire board. The process was very political, but we got through it by having an impartial process.

After you select a manager, phase II begins. In order to transfer the gift annuity pool, for example, the charity has to photocopy every tax calculation and annuity contract in the program, including providing current addresses that are different from the addresses in the original contract, dates of birth, and social security numbers. Be mindful also of two-life agreements where one annuitant is now deceased. The beneficiaries who were signed up for automatic deposits will need to sign up again with the new manager. To move methodically through the transfer process, you must have a very tight system for keeping track of the donors and beneficiaries.

During the transfer of your information to the new manager, you will feel crippled from getting new gifts. Your secretary, your assistant, or you will be spending time taking out files one by one in order to photocopy the information your new manager needs to set up the administration. It is a grueling process.

KEEPING YOURSELF ORGANIZED

In order to keep track of your donors, their documents, and the history of the gifts, it makes sense to institute procedures that will allow you to find essential information easily and quickly. Most planned giving officers keep donor information in a manila folder, possibly slipped into a Pendaflex file. Over time, the file will be filled with documents, agreements, tax calculations, correspondence, post cards, proposals, and contact reports. Thus, it becomes difficult for you to find gift detail or beneficiary information easily with so much else cluttering up the file.

When a donor or beneficiary calls to inquire about a missed or a lost payment, to get copies of his or her tax calculations, or for any other question, you should be able to find the information instantly. Therefore, you should keep gift documentation separate from the rest of the information in the file.

For example, the documents involved in processing a charitable gift annuity include the following:

1. An acknowledgement letter stating the type of gift, date of gift, asset contributed, value of the gift, payment schedule, *etc*;
2. A signed copy of the gift annuity agreement; and
3. A copy of the tax calculation illustrating the gift detail.

Perhaps there is also a fact sheet or application that the donor completed with essential information like social security number, date of birth, beneficiary name and address, cost basis, or direct deposit authorization. Thus, there are at least four essential documents relevant to one charitable gift annuity at the final stage of processing it. Not only must the four pages stay together, they must be in a place that allows you to access them immediately. As you probably know already, donors to the life income programs make repeat gifts. I had one donor with 12 gift annuities.

There are, no doubt, many methods to keeping your files organized, but mine is simple and it works well. We affixed gift documentation chronologically to the left side of the donor's manila file with metal binder clips, using green paper between each set of documents. Thereafter, it was very easy to answer donor questions. If you inherit a planned giving program where the files are not organized this way, you should immediately review each donor file one by one, separating gift documentation from everything else.

INVESTMENT TRUSTEE CONSIDERATIONS

The investment strategy appropriate for different kinds of deferred gifts is beyond the scope of this book. I am not an investment expert. But, I would like to make a couple of points on this topic. Periodically, someone asks about co-mingling the assets of charitable remainder trusts with the assets in a charity's endowment. This is a terrible idea. Don't even think about doing this. Each charitable trust has different beneficiaries of different ages, different payout rates, different provisions, and different tax considerations. The general investment guidelines for running an endowment have no relevance to the tax sensitivity of a charitable remainder trust or to the beneficiary's needs. Every charitable remainder trust should be managed individually.

For split interest gifts, there is always a balance to be met. The trustee must look out for the income beneficiary's interests as well as for the charity's remainder interests. This became a big problem for pooled income funds that started up in the 1980s. Donors signed on in large numbers when pooled income funds could pay double digit income while still maintaining a healthy mix of both equities and fixed income investments. As interest rates came down, many charities shifted more assets into fixed income investments in order to maintain the yield. When I arrived at Boston College in 1993, the pooled income fund was 100% bonds, but it started as a balanced fund in 1984. The result? Zero chance of appreciation in that account. It is a costly disaster for the institution because fees are paid separately by the business office so as not to dilute the beneficiaries' income any further.

The pooled income fund must be maintained by the sponsoring charity, but what about charitable remainder trusts? Some people feel that a charity should not be the trustee of a charitable remainder trust because there is a conflict of interest. In addition, while there are competent charities serving as trustees all over the country, there are also some charities that don't know what they are doing. I heard of a case in which a charity merged its charitable remainder annuity trusts with its gift annuity pool because the annuity payouts were drilling the accounts out of existence. The charity needed a way to keep the annuity trust payments going. Why not use the gift annuity reserves? Gulp. In another case, the individual in the charity's business office missed the Tax Reform Act of 1969. For 23 years, he prepared incorrect K-1s and did not track the four tiers of income in the CRTs.

Sometimes, donors want to be their own trustee even if your charity can serve that role. However, they rarely have the expertise to manage the complexity of a CRT. I had one donor who disclosed to me that he established and funded a $1 million charitable remainder trust about six years earlier. "I don't need the income so I've never taken a payment. I figure I'll let it keep growing tax free until I need the money." The I.R.S. has already ruled on a case like this saying that if the account is not run like a CRT, then it does not entitle the donor to a charitable deduction. Further, many donors get into trouble by taking the advice of financial planners selling CRTs as tax avoidance schemes, then selling an inappropriate type of investment inside the CRT. A strong advocate for keeping the donor's or client's interests in front is my friend, Vaughn W. Henry, of Henry & Associates in Springfield, Illinois. He is strongly against having a charity serve as the trustee of a CRT, and he has a monster web site (www.gift-estate.com) filled with articles and cases of gifts gone wrong. Included as well are numerous case studies of innovatively crafted estate plans done the right way. It is worth a look, especially because it is much better to learn from the mistakes and horror stories of others than to be the subject of one of Vaughn's malpractice series of articles.

Setting aside the issue of whether or not a charity should be the trustee of a CRT, there are certainly advantages for both the donor and the institution. First, the fee schedules for the management of a charity's deferred giving assets will nearly always be lower than what the donor would have to pay alone. That is not an insignificant consideration for either, especially over the life of a CRT. For example, when Boston College became trustee of a $1 million charitable remainder trust, the fee on the account was 72 basis points. (1% = 100 basis points.) On his own, not under the umbrella of the Boston College account, he would have paid 115 basis points for a $1 million account.

Also, when the charity is trustee of its own CRTs, the planned giving officer has a set of procedures, sample documents, and a system that allows a smooth process step by step along the way.

SUMMARY

If your institution's planned giving assets are spread around, my recommendation is to consolidate them under one manager. Dealing with the details of each gift is hard enough when you have one manager, but with several managers, you'll waste a lot of time that simply could have been spent more productively. Plus, you'll get a better fee schedule by consolidating your assets.

Staying on top of the administration is difficult, especially if you are running a mature planned giving program with lots of activity. Unfortunately, many people in planned giving positions haven't been trained properly in any of this. Often, they rely too much on their asset manager for advice or help and muddle along, one hopes, without doing to much damage.

With the help of this book, you will be better equipped to raise more money than you did before, assist more donors in structuring smarter gifts, and oversee the administration of those gifts competently. I wish you much success.

CONCLUSION

Except for a few isolated cases, major gifts don't just happen. They are the result of prolonged cultivation activities, diligent follow up, relentless attention to stewardship, and, of course, donors who feel inspired by your charity's good work. The commitment to start planned giving is critical to your success. The fact that you are reading this book is a wonderful start.

Often, you will be fighting an institutional battle that will wear you down. Don't let it. Often you'll doubt whether your time, efforts, and money will pay off. They will. But, bear in mind that planned giving will not bring immediate gratification because many of the gift vehicles and plans distribute to the charity at the donor's death. But, don't forget that the best planned gift is the straight outright gift. Fortunately for you, some people don't need complicated gift plans. They simply need the largest income tax deduction and that results in an outright gift.

It is unlikely that you will be able to do everything suggested in this book. For small agencies, you may be happy to add gifts of securities to your fund raising program. Or, you may simply be ready to promote bequests. Congratulate yourself for doing something more with your development program than you ever did before.

Keep this book on your shelf and use it when donors approach you with deferred gift suggestions that are unfamiliar to you. You need to be ready to handle many kinds of gift plans. Donors are learning about techniques from seminars and from the Internet. If your charity is unable to deal with planned giving, you will lose out on important gifts.

With this book, you can compete with every other nonprofit organization. The principles for every charity are the same. Build a relationship first and the gift type is merely a detail.

I wish you much success in your mission.

This book reflects the tax laws as of its publication date and is believed to be accurate. Toward this end, I am indebted to my attorney, Jonathan Tidd. However, tax laws change frequently and it is essential that you consult with your own tax counsel to ensure that you have the most up-to-date information. No book can cover every situation you will encounter. This guide is an overview of most things you will encounter running a planned giving program. Where this book leaves off, go to Appendix III for resources that you need.

Thank you very much for buying this book. I predict it will be tattered and dog-eared in the coming year.

Debra Ashton

PART IV

Essential Resources

INTRODUCTION

The last section of the book has five appendices that should be helpful to you. The information here was correct at the time I compiled the information.

Appendix I
Associations And Networking

It is a good idea to be connected to other people who do what you do. Sharing ideas, strategies, techniques, and also war stories will help you enormously. In this section, I have listed a number of membership organizations or Internet networks. Some are free and some require membership dues.

Appendix II
Planned Giving Software

In order to run a comprehensive planned giving program, you need planned giving software. There are many options depending on whether you want a basic charitable deduction calculation or a full estate planning analysis. The listing of software vendors in Appendix II provides a wide range of options to suit your ever need, including administrative functions for your planned giving assets.

Appendix III
Bibliography

Listed in Appendix III are numerous books, periodicals, loose-leaf services and newsletters for gift planning professionals. I recommend that you subscribe to at least one loose-leaf tax service and one monthly newsletter which provides up-to-date tax analysis on current issues on a monthly basis.

Appendix IV
Planned Giving/Fund Raising Consultants

There are so many consultants serving the charitable industry that this section is very long. I added as many as I could, but I know I didn't get everybody. The list of possible consultants is endless. My list will give you a start, but you should read Chapter I-3 about whether you need a fund raising consultant.

Appendix V
Specimen Agreements

Many people trying to start planned giving programs have never seen a CRT document or the trust document for a pooled income fund, or charitable lead trust. This Appendix includes a sampling of specimen agreements. However, these documents, provided by Emil Kallina of Kallina & Associates, LLC, Baltimore, MD, are not meant to be used out of the book. They are samples only. If you need to provide a legal document to your client or donor, hire a competent attorney experienced in charitable giving tax law. Do not use these documents. They are only specimen agreements. Each case is unique and requires legal counsel in the state where the documents will be executed. Don't forget that state law and federal law diverge and require special provisions that vary from state to state.

Appendix I

ASSOCIATIONS AND NETWORKING

There are many professional associations and listservs that provide educational programs for fund raisers, planned giving officers, estate planners, and others involved in gift planning or advice to the wealthy as well as online networks. Here is a summary of the ones I know about.

ABA-PTL Listserv

The Probate Division of the Real Property, Probate & Trust Law Section of the American Bar Association first opened its own Internet listserv, called "ABA-PTL" (stands for Probate & Trust Law) on July 31, 1995. This list, which now has more than 1345 subscribers, is intended primarily for the use of Section members and related professionals so they can discuss estate planning and administration issues by e-mail. This is free and you don't need to be a member of the ABA to participate.

To join, send an e-mail message to listserv@mail.abanet.org. Do not put anything on the Subject line in the Header unless you have to (AOL users). In the message part, put the text: subscribe aba-ptl (Your Real Name).

American Association of Fund Raising Counsel	317-816-1613
10293 N. Meridian Street, Suite 175	800-462-2372
Indianapolis, IN 46290	317-816-1633
	info@aafrc.org
	www.aafrc.org

AAFRC was founded in 1935 to promote the need for professional and ethical standards of practice, and to influence the creation of laws governing philanthropy. It publishes *Giving USA*, an annual publication reporting philanthropic trends (See Appendix III). Fund raising consultants who are members subscribe to a professional code of ethics. Standards of membership in AAFRC are rigorous and include the completion of a letter of intent and a subsequent formal application including sponsorship by two Member Firms of the AAFRC. There is a lengthy member directory of fund raising consultants on their web site as well as a section with advice on how to choose fund raising counsel. You can download for free the 88-page Member Directory which has text summaries of the services of every Member Firm.

American Association of Grant Professionals	913-788-5310
8541 Waverly Avenue	913-788-3398 (Fax)
Kansas City, KS 66109	GrantServicesInc@aol.com
	www.grantprofessionals.org

AAGP is a nonprofit membership association that builds and supports an international community of grant professionals committed to serving the greater public good by practicing the highest ethical and professional standards. AAGP serves as a leading authority and resource for the practice of grantsmanship in all sectors of the field, advances the field by promoting professional growth and development, enhances the public image and recognition of the profession within the greater philanthropic, public, and private funding communities, and promotes positive relationships between grant professionals and their stakeholders. Membership $75 annually.

Founded in 1997, AAGP holds an annual conference. Membership benefits include an online listserv (AAGP Forum), member directory, Consultants Directory, e-mail newsletter, and biannual *Journal*.

American Council on Gift Annuities
233 McCrea Street, Suite 400
Indianapolis, IN 46225

317-269-6271
317-269-6276 (Fax)
acga@acga-web.org
www.acga-web.org

ACGA is a qualified nonprofit organization formed in 1927 as the Committee on Gift Annuities for the purpose of providing educational and other services to American charities regarding gift annuities and other forms of planned gifts. The annual cost for sponsoring charities is $75 which also gets you a discounted registration for their conferences.

One of the primary activities of the Council is the publication of suggested charitable gift annuity rates for use by charities and their donors. The Council retains the services of an actuarial firm to advise and consult on matters pertaining to life expectancies and related matters. The Council has a long and distinguished record in this area (since 1927), and its suggested rates have long been recognized, not only by charities and donors, but also by state insurance departments and the I.R.S. as being actuarially sound and in the best interests of all parties involved.

The Council's volunteer board of directors is comprised of professionals active in the field of planned giving with some of America's most well-respected charities. These individuals give unselfishly of their time and energy to assist others in their gift annuity programs. The annual fee is $75 to receive updates on CGA regulations, tax changes and a discounted registration for their biannual conference.

(Note: The ACGA web site has the complete list of state regulations.)

Association of Fundraising Professionals
1101 King Street, #700
Alexandria, VA 22314

800-666-3863
703-684-0540
sfoster@afpnet.org
www.afpnet.org

Founded in 1960 as the National Society of Fund Raising Executives (NSFRE), AFP represents 26,000 members in 174 chapters in the United States, Canada, Mexico, and China working to advance philanthropy through advocacy, research, education, and certification programs. Active member $200 plus Chapter dues. Introductory member $75 plus Chapter dues.

Association for Healthcare Philanthropy
313 Park Avenue, Suite 400
Falls Church, VA 22046

703-532-6243
703-532-7170 (Fax)
ahp@ahp.org
www.ahp.org

AHP is an international professional organization dedicated exclusively to developing the men and women who encourage charity in North America's health care systems. Established in 1967, AHP is the complete source for education, networking, information and research opportunities in health care philanthropy today. AHP is a not-for-profit organization with more than 3,400 members (more than 1,900 are from the largest health care facilities in the United States and Canada). Its international headquarters is located outside Washington, D.C. in Falls Church, Va.

Regional districts include Canada, Mid-Atlantic, Midwest, New England, Pacific, Rockies & Southwest, and Southeast. Regional and annual conferences, audioconferences, online courses, Annual International Madison Institute for Healthcare Philanthropy (5-day intensive curriculum). There is also an AHP Long-term Care Network. Nonprofit membership for individuals $395. For-profit membership $675. Other rate schedules also apply.

Association of Professional Researchers
for Advancement
40 Shuman Blvd., Suite 325
Naperville, IL 60563

630-717-8160
630-717-8354 (Fax)
info@APRAhome.org
www.aprahome.org

APRA represents over 2,100 development professionals around the world who are dedicated to meeting the data and information needs of the nonprofit community. Advancement researchers are the development officers on the front line of data management, uniquely positioned—and qualified—to gather, interpret, analyze, and disseminate the information critical to securing support for nonprofit organizations. APRA offers a wide variety of opportunities and services intended to enable our members to more effectively meet the needs of their institutions while maintaining the highest ethical standards.

There is a network of regional chapters, regional conferences, newsletters, publications, professional development grants, and conference tape lending libraries. Each APRA chapter has an executive committee that determines dues, recruits members, organizes chapter activities, and communicates with APRA International about chapter events and membership. Individual or institutional membership $150.

Canadian Association of Gift Planners   888-430-9494
10665 109 Street   780-421-7781
Edmonton, AB T5H 3Bf   780-438-4837 (Fax)
Canada   glyn@cagp-acpdp.org
                                                  www.cagp-acpdp.org

The purpose of CAGP is to support Philanthropy by fostering the development and growth of gift planning. The Association creates awareness, provides education and is an advocate of charitable giving. CAGP brings together professionals from various disciplines to ensure that the gift planning process achieves a fair and proper balance between the interests of donors and the aims and objectives of registered charitable organizations in Canada in accordance with the Association's Standards of Professional and Ethical Practice. All CAGP members are also members of a local or regional RoundTable of their choice.

Membership benefits include networking opportunities, membership to a local or regional RoundTable, mentoring, education, seminars and workshops with local RoundTables, periodic communications including the CAGP/ACPDP Planner Newsletter, updates on legislation, advocacy and lobbying with the Federal government on tax implications, reduced rate for annual conference and educational activities, priority registration for educational activities, educational credits from annual conference credited to other professional designations, CFRE certification exam at annual conference, national annual awards program, members-only section of web site for resources, articles, research, current and past copies of the Planner, and membership directory. Also job postings. All information in English or French. Membership $240 (includes GST). Student membership $80 (includes GST).

CharityChannel, LLC   949-589-5938
30021 Tomas Street, Suite 300   949-589-4399
Rancho Santa Margarita, CA 92688   subscriber-payment@charitychannel.com
                                                  www.charitychannel.com

CharityChannel was established in February 1992 as an online discussion community of nonprofit-sector professionals. It quickly grew into the largest nonprofit-sector online community in the world, serving more than 100,000 professionals as of March 2002. Go to the home page and click on the "Tour." Subscriber fee $18 for 6 months. $24 for 1 year.

(Note: This is a monster charitable community involving articles, newsletters, more than 30 listservs for any nonprofit, charitable giving, fund raising, or tax law topic you can think of. There are articles, links to helpful resources, book reviews, job postings, consultants directory, audio and video interviews and so much more that you'll have to check it out for yourself.)

Council for Advancement and Support of   202-328-2273
Education   202-387-4973 (Fax)
1307 New York Avenue, NW, Suite 1000   MemberServiceCenter@case.org
Washington, DC 20005   www.case.org

CASE Europe
Entrance A

Travistock House North
London
WC1H 9HX UK

+44 (0)20 7387 4404
+44 (0)20 7387 4408 (Fax)

CASE is a membership organization serving educational institutions. The Council advances and supports educational institutions by enhancing the effectiveness of the alumni relations, communications, and fund-raising professionals who serve them. It runs many conferences annually on all areas of fund raising or institutional advancement. There is a large list of publications on their web site for any topic you could possibly need.

Council on Foundations
1828 L Street, NW
Washington, DC 20036

202-466-6512
202-785-3926 (Fax)
info@cof.org
www.cof.org

Council on Foundations is a membership organization of foundations and corporate giving programs that make grants. Our mission is to serve the public good by promoting and enhancing responsible and effective philanthropy. Council members adhere to the Principles and Practices for Effective Grant Making. Council membership also provides a variety of networking and professional opportunities to keep your foundation staff in the know. Offers conferences, publications, newsletters, and numerous services for foundations and corporate giving programs. Membership minimum $400 and a sliding scale based on the size of the foundation and dollar level of grants made annually.

The Council sponsors ten listservs for community foundation members, affiliates and supporting organizations including development staff, community foundation affiliates, communications and marketing professionals, CEOs, CFOs, program and grant making staff, among others.

(Note: Their web site has a massive amount of helpful information for grant makers. The web site also lists 24 other associations both locally and internationally. Click on the "Networking" link.)

European Association for Planned Giving
c/o Brakeley, LTD
162-170 Wardour Street
London W1V 4AB

44-0-20-7734-0777
44-0-1622-850771 (Fax)
info@plannedgiving.org.uk
www.plannedgiving.org.uk

EAPG aims to be the premier source of information on planned giving in Europe, play a leading role in promoting planned giving and in advocating supporting fiscal policies, be a dynamic network for sharing information and experience on planned giving in Europe.

EAPG brings together non-profits, professional advisers, financial intermediaries and other consultants through its series of interactive roundtables, seminars, publications and other media, promotes education and awareness about major gift fundraising, tax efficient giving and cross-border tax and legal issues affecting charitable gift planning. The Association explores planned giving techniques and solutions that can be used in a European context

EAPG is linked to the North American planned giving community through its affiliation (the International Gift Planning Alliance) with the (US) National Committee on Planned Giving and the Canadian Association of Gift Planners.

EAPG Membership benefits you and your organization by giving you access to its roundtable programs and publications, according discounts at seminars and allowing access to its members-only secure area archive of reference materials as developed by EAPG members.

Membership quoted in Sterling, Euros, and US dollars. $750 sustaining member, $300 for-profit organizations, $165 not-for-profit organizations.

Financial Planning Association™
5775 Glenridge Drive, NE, Suite B-300
Atlanta, GA 30328

Other offices: Denver, CO., and Washington, DC

800-322-4237
404-845-0011
404-845-3660 (Fax)
info@fpanet.org
www.panet.org

FPA is the membership organization for the financial planning community. FPA's strategy to accomplish its objectives involves welcoming all those who advance the financial planning process and promoting the CFP marks as the cornerstone of the financial planning profession.

FPA was created on the basic foundation that the CFP marks best represent the promise and the future of the financial planning profession. CFP® certification offers the public a consistent and credible symbol of professional competence in financial planning. And FPA benefits the public by helping to ensure that financial planning is delivered through competent, ethical financial planners. There are different membership benefits for individual CFPs, broker/dealers, or corporations. Provides conferences, training, audio conferences, *Journal of Financial Planning* (monthly), *Solutions* (bimonthly practice publication), online communities, membership directory, and other services for the financial planning profession.

Forum of Regional Associations of Grantmakers
Suite 650
1111 19th Street, NW
Washington, DC 20036

202-467-1120
202-467-0055 (Fax)
info@givingforum.org
www.GivngForum.org

The Forum of Regional Associations of Grantmakers is a learning community and network composed of and supporting geographically focused associations of grantmakers. The Forum helps leverage our collective knowledge and resources to serve the public good and enhance, expand, and explain philanthropy in our regions. We provide member services that enhance the capacity and effectiveness of regional grantmaker associations through professional development and training for regional associations of grantmaker staff and volunteer leadership; collection, management, and dissemination of knowledge useful to grantmaker associations and their members; and development and management of communications and technology links that support sharing of knowledge and collective action.

The Forum of Regional Associations of Grantmakers is a national network of local leaders and organizations across the United States that support effective charitable giving. The Forum's network focuses on the philanthropy of the city, state, and multi-state areas of the U.S. and encompasses 29 regional associations of grant makers. These regional associations collectively represent more than 5,000 grant makers and others interested in philanthropy.

Through our national office in Washington, DC, and through our network of member associations and other regional coalitions that cover all 50 states, the Forum works to expand philanthropy, enhance philanthropy and explain philanthropy.

The Grantsmanship Center
P.O. Box 17220
Los Angeles, CA 90017

213-482-9860
213-482-9863 (Fax)
info@tgci.com
www.tgci.com

Founded in 1972, TGCI offers grantsmanship training and low-cost publications to nonprofit organizations and government agencies. TGCI conducts some 200 workshops annually in grantsmanship and proposal writing. The workshops are held all over the country. They also publish *The Grantsmanship Center Magazine* (free to staff of nonprofit organizations and government agencies), the best of federal funded grant proposals on CD-ROM, and also a proposal writing guide. Membership benefits include one proposal review annually, discounts on TGCI publications and CDs, searchable database of federal grant opportunities, network of links to state funding sources for all 50 states, searchable database of staffed foundations and corporate giving programs, and downloadable updates for the TGCI training manual. $250 renewing members. $375 TGCI alumni becoming first-time members.

Institute for Private Investors
74 Trinity Place
New York, NY 10006

212-693-1300
212-693-2797 (Fax)
ipi@memberlink.net
www.memberlink.net

Founded in 1991, the Institute for Private Investors has provided innovative educational and networking resources to families with substantial assets and their advisors. Our primary goal is to change the way investors work with advisors and advisors work with investors, for the benefit of both. The Institute sells no investment products or consulting services, and the non-commercialism is a carefully guarded tradition. Membership dues are the sole revenue source of the Institute. Also runs a listserv for members. Membership in two categories (private investor and advisor). Membership requires a rigorous review process and recommendation by a current member.

National Association of Independent Schools
1620 L Street, NW, Suite 1100
Washington, DC 20036

202-973-9700
202-973-9790 (Fax)
info@nais.org
www.nais.org

This is a membership organization of about 1,200 day schools, boarding schools, and combination boarding and day schools. They provide support in all areas of operations and fund raising. Membership costs depend on the number of students. NAIS runs many conferences or workshops annually and has a massive web site with resources, free articles, and links for every conceivable need of an independent school.

National Association of Philanthropic Planners
Attn: Amanda Simmons-Myers
754 111th Avenue North
Naples, FL 34108

800-342-6215
888-471-8475 (Fax)
napp@napp.net
www.napp.net

This is a nonprofit group of 150 to 200 independent financial professionals who advance donor advocacy by bringing the heart of philanthropy to the business of philanthropy. Through annual educational conferences and our unique Conference Philanthropy℠, we build America's philanthropic capacity and unite financial advisors, charitable planners, financial services firms, family wealth counselors, and nonprofit planned giving officers and executives in a non-biased, collaborative environment. Membership $250.

National Association of Family Wealth Counselors
P.O. Box 298
Morgantown, IN 46160

888-597-6575
812-597-4251 (Fax)
dtinkler@nafwc.org
www.nafwc.org

NAFWC is a non-profit member-run association that provides its member firms with opportunities for ongoing education and networking in the Family Wealth Counseling field. Family Wealth Counseling addresses the financial, social, spiritual and emotional aspects of a family's life and wealth within a broader context of life planning instead of the more traditional and less effective context of estate planning.

Membership benefits include an annual fall conference, monthly educational teleconferences (many with CFP CE credit), use of a teleconference line for business and personal use, networking, access to other members and their resources, synergistic alliances with two sister organizations (National Network of Estate Planning Attorneys/Esperti Peterson Institute and National Association of Philanthropic Planners), a monthly e-mail to keep you abreast of Association activities, a members-only web site, and *Thinking Beyond* quarterly newsletter which you can customize and mail to clients and advisors. Membership is selective and requires sponsorship by two current members. An initiation fee of $500 will be assessed with annual dues to follow January 1.

National Center for Family Philanthropy
1818 N Street, NW, Suite 300
Washington, DC 20036

202-293-3424
202-293-3395 (Fax)
ncfr@ncfp.org
www.ncfp.org

The National Center for Family Philanthropy was founded to encourage families and individuals to create and sustain their philanthropic missions. The National Center, a nonprofit, 501(c)(3) organization, was established in 1997 by a group of family philanthropists. It is the only national resource center that focuses solely on matters of importance to families engaged in philanthropy and their effective giving.

The National Center maintains referrals to a nationwide network of resources and philanthropic service organizations and can bring families together with advisors and experts across the full range of donor interests; regional associations of grant makers—membership groups that operate in specific areas of the country; affinity groups—organizations that explore common grant maker interests; other philanthropic organizations that support family donors; and media, policymakers and other avenues of access and information. Also, the Center runs workshops and seminars for philanthropists, advisors to the wealthy, trust officers, and other groups.

Also, provides research, books on philanthropy, workbooks for trustees, staff and advisors to family foundations, and a newsletter, *Passages*, (bimonthly) that explores key topics in family giving research and practices.

(Note: There is a wealth of helpful information and resources for philanthropists and for families who want to set up their philanthropic goals and structure.)

National Committee on Planned Giving	317-269-6274
233 McCrea Street, Suite 400	317-269-6276
Indianapolis, IN 46225	ncpg@ncpg.org
	www.ncpg.org

NCPG is the national organization for people whose work involves charitable gift planning. Our network includes more than 100 local planned giving councils working close to home to provide education and professional community. Currently, NCPG has about 8,000 members nation wide. Membership includes a quarterly publication, *The Journal of Gift Planning*, Gift Planner Update (e-newsletter), Workbook for Gift Planners, annual National Conference on Planned Giving (discounted registration for NCPG members), web-based Virtual Seminars (discounted registration for NCPG members), and pals™, online search service for gift planning jobs. Also, online Directory of Council members, *Gift-pl*, (an online listserv), articles, Gift Planner Profile (survey data on salaries and demographics of the profession), and Research Links (studies related to gift planning conducted by NCPG and other related groups.

Educational videos, LEAVE A LEGACY®, European Association of Gift Planning, and Online Speakers Bureau. $90 if you are a member of a local affiliated planned giving council. $130 for all others.

National Network of Estate Planning Attorneys	888-337-4090, ext. 3868
One Valmont Plaza, 4th Floor	402-964-3700, ext. 3868
Omaha, NE 68154	866-549-6827 (Fax)
	info@nnepa.com
	www.netplanning.com

A membership organization of about 600 attorneys nationwide who spend most of their time in estate and business planning. Our vision is to become the leading single-source provider of education and information services, products, and practical tools which empower Estate Planning professionals to provide superior client service while building prosperous and satisfying professional careers. The members are available to clients through a searchable database.

Attorneys pay an initial fee, and a monthly fee to receive educational courses, practice development and practice management tools, document creation systems, *etc.*

New England Development Research Association	781-397-8870
389 Main Street, Suite 202	781-397-8887 (Fax)
Malden, MA 02148	NEDRA@guildassoc.com
	www.nedra.org

NEDRA is a non-profit association for professionals with an interest in development research. Our membership includes experienced information professionals, novice researchers, fundraisers, and managers of fundraising research departments. NEDRA promotes the professional status of researchers in the development community and provides educational, training, mentoring and networking opportunities to its members. Membership $65.

Philanthropic Advisors Network
c/o Council on Foundations
1828 L Street, NW
Washington, DC 20036

202-466-6512
202-785-3926 (Fax)
PAN@cof.org
www.cof.org

PAN is a network of legal and financial advisors and provides opportunities to discuss charitable issues, assist your clients and learn from one another. PAN focuses on the complex areas of foundation and giving program creation and growth, tax issues and governance. Members are professionals who advise foundations and donors interested in creating foundations, giving programs or special funds from their wealth. PAN members include accountants, attorneys, bank trust officers, financial advisors and investment managers. Membership $150. Firm rate $400.

The Philanthropy Roundtable
1150 17th Street, NW, Suite 503
Washington, DC 20036

202-822-8333
202-822-8325 (Fax)
main@philanthropyroundtable.org
http://philanthropyroundtable.org

Founded in the late 1970s as an informal network of grantmakers, The Philanthropy Roundtable today is a national association of more than 600 individual donors, corporate giving representatives, foundation staff and trustees, and trust and estate officers. Its Associates include donors who are involved in philanthropy on a professional basis, as well as individual donors for whom giving is a serious avocation. As an organization dedicated to serving donors' needs, the Roundtable represents a unique resource for those who want to make the most of their giving. Provides regional and national conferences, publications, and *Philanthropy* magazine.

Planned Giving listserv on Yahoo

Founded January 4, 2002, this is an open forum of 770 planned giving professionals. No fee and no membership of any kind required. To join, send a blank message to: plannedgiving-subscribe@yahoogroups.com.

Society For Nonprofit Organizations
5820 Canton Center Road, Suite 165
Canton, MI 48187

734-451-3582
734-451-5935 (Fax)
info@snpo.org
www.snpo.org

The Society For Nonprofit Organizations was founded in 1983 as a 501(c)(3) national membership organization, and it serves as the premiere provider of products and services for all those involved in the nonprofit sector. The Society encourages networking, alliances, collaborations, and sharing among nonprofit organizations and their leaders. It promotes excellence in leadership, management, and governance practices. It conducts research to identify emerging trends, issues, and opportunities for nonprofit organizations. And, of course, it facilitates and provides wide-ranging education, training, and support services through its Learning Institute. *Nonprofit World* (bimonthly magazine), *Nonprofit World Funding Alert* (monthly) electronic newsletter. Electronic membership $29. Individual membership $59. Organization membership $99.

Women in Development of Greater Boston
93 Concord Avenue, Suite 8
Belmont, MA 02478

617-489-6777
617-489-7799 (Fax)
widgb@widgb.org
www.widgb.org

WID of Greater Boston offers a variety of programs, services and opportunities for volunteer involvement. Members help one another develop and improve professional skills, share information about employment opportunities, and foster a climate which promotes professional achievement. Since its founding in 1980 by a small group of development professionals, WID has matured into a vital organization of over 850 members. Today it is one of the largest organizations of advancement professionals in Massachusetts. Nonprofit organization member $110. Affiliate member $175.

Appendix II

PLANNED GIVING SOFTWARE

There are many software programs available to compute the tax consequences of deferred gifts. Many software vendors have not only the full version but also a "lite" version, as well as various administration programs. Although many of the vendors listed below offer other services, too, this listing is just for software so that you don't have to wade through a lot of other details if you're simply looking for software.

It would be difficult to run a fully comprehensive planned giving program without planned giving software. You might be able pay a software vendor on a case-by-case basis for charts, illustrations, or proposal language, but you'll find it difficult to get into the full swing of planned giving without having the software yourself.

The cost for planned giving software generally includes a fee for the initial license and then the annual cost of updates. If you go to the web site for the various programs listed below, you can read about the full range of options and fees.

For small charities or those just starting planned giving, you may not have the money to buy planned giving software. My recommendation for you is to solicit a restricted gift from a board member to pay for the initial license. Then, add the cost of the annual updates to your planned giving budget or development office budget. The price is very reasonable considering the potential that the software gives you in dealing with your donors. Most of the vendors offering software provide training sessions for additional cost several times a year. This is well worth the time and expense. The training sessions are often planned the day before a major planned giving conference you may already be attending.

In addition, many web sites have a gift calculator that you can use for free to get the charitable deduction figure for various split interest gifts. These include financial professionals, many charities or others engaged in gift or estate planning.

<u>ATTENTION MAC USERS</u>: As far as I know, there is only one planned giving software program for the Mac and that is PG Calc's *Planned Giving Manager*.

PLANNED GIVING SOFTWARE VENDORS

The following companies provide software for planned giving, estate planning, financial planning or gift administration. All descriptions are derived from the vendor's own marketing materials or web sites in their own words. Each vendor has much more detail, illustrations, graphics, and samples of their products or displays on the web site. I pulled enough information for the reader to have a head start, but I did not include everything I found on the vendors' web sites. If a vendor thinks I have omitted something essential to understanding the products, send me a note and I will add it for the next edition (although by then, everything will be different.)

The list may not be complete since it is difficult to know all of the vendors or companies who make software for gift planners or financial planners. Some of the products are targeted to commercial advisors, managers, or administrators. If I have omitted software that should have been included, please send me an e-mail so that I can include it in the next edition of this book (debra@debraashton.com). The listings do not indicate an endorsement since I have not used most of these programs. Also, bear in mind that software does not guarantee competence. In fact, if you don't know the underlying principles about the scenarios you're modeling, you can be dangerous.

BIPSTER, LLC
P.O. Box 3022
Salem, MA 01970

888-588-2477
978-744-3198
978-744-0319 (Fax)
www.bipster.com
info@bipster.com

BIPS© is software that helps you keep track of your bequest program. It includes the ability to 1) time your communications with estate professionals so that you are proactive rather than reactive (*e.g.*; *BIPS©* makes it easy to request early distribution rather than relying on the distribution timing of executors), 2) communicate almost automatically with executors, attorneys, trust officers, using built-in form letters, 3) make it easier to send condolence and thank you letters to surviving family members (who are an often underutilized source of future bequests), 4) maintain a database of estate professionals for future communication and development correspondence, 5) produce reports totaling bequest income expected over various timelines, and 6) compute present values of future income to meet the new FASB and AICPA rules on reporting requirements.

Brentmark Software
3505 Lake Lynda Drive, Suite 212
Orlando, FL 32817

800-879-6665
407-306-6160
407-306-6107 (Fax)
www.brentmark.com
sales@brentmark.com

Charitable Financial Planner handles split-interest charitable transfers (term, one to five lives): charitable remainder and lead unitrusts and annuity trusts, farm/residence remainders, pooled income funds and gift annuities (immediate and deferred). Charitable remainder annuity trust life cases include 5% probability test of Rev. Rul. 77-374 with year-by-year report. Exhaustion test of §7520 regs included in various models. Program also handles GRITs, GRATs, GRUTs, and interrelated charitable and estate tax calculations. Presentation graphs may be used to show the effect of varying payouts on the charitable deduction or to compare different charitable models.

Estate Planning Tools. Cutting-edge estate planning tools and techniques and financial planning models! 99 different calculation models in 15 areas: *Trusts* (includes our most comprehensive coverage of GRATs with calcs under example 5 of the Regs and Rev. Rul. 77-454 calcs with year-by-year report, GRITs/QPRTs, GRUTs, Dynasty Trusts; *Tools of Estate Planning* (private annuities, SCINs); *Charitable* (charitable remainder unitrusts and annuity trusts), *Estate Planning Techniques* (§6166, §303, installment sales, group term cost); *Retirement, Taxes, Present/Future Value Calcs, Valuation, Investment, Inflation, Real Estate, Insurance, Net Worth, Financial Goals,* and *Budgeting.* Most of the models include presentation graphics. Calculation reports may be sent to a printer, text file, or spreadsheet file. One of Brentmark's most popular programs.

Estate Planning QuickView. By presenting a comparison of eight major disposition plans for each spouse, QuickView finds in seconds which estate planning strategy provides the most for a client and their family. Use this program to significantly reduce the time needed to analyze multiple disposition plans. Customizable flow-charts, graphs, and summaries are all presented for the client.

IRS Factors Calculator calculates the value of annuities, life estates and remainders (term, one or two lives). Completely replaces I.R.S.' Beth and Aleph volumes including all the examples in the front. Also includes GRITs, GRATs, GRUTs, and various tables: H, K, 80CNSMT, 90CM, V, and VI. The program to use for many estate valuation issues.

PFP Notebook™ takes a real world approach to profitable personal financial planning. It uses a step-by-step modular notebook approach which incorporates the philosophy of Jim Wilson, a pioneer in the field of personal financial planning. He developed *PFP Notebook* in order to make the process more efficient and easier. You'll like it for the same reasons. *PFP Notebook* is practice-oriented. It not only handles the calculations, but handles the otherwise time-consuming paperwork.

PFP Notebook consists of a number of modular areas including: Client Section, Financial Data, Risk Management, Investments, Retirement Planning, Estate Planning, Education Funding, and Income Tax. These areas are designed to allow you flexibility of use. The program offers optional links between modular areas so that you can use them all as part of one seamless whole or use them separately, choosing only what's appropriate for individual clients.

PFP Notebook not only generates calculation reports and spectacular 3-D color graphs, it also includes explanatory text. All of the text is completely customizable by you. Over 800 inputs and calculation variables are available to be automatically merged into the text.

PFP Notebook offers you and your client an alternative to the traditional initial forms packet—the Financial Planning Data Gatherer. You can distribute this separate program on a disk to your clients. When the client first loads the program at home, your firm's name is shown on the screen. After your client returns the disk to you, *PFP Notebook* can import the information.

Retirement Income Navigator™. Too often, the focus of financial retirement planning is on the allocation of assets for growth based solely upon personal risk tolerance. However, to achieve success, goals must be set according to the true objective—providing income. Capital must be strategically balanced to meet both short-term and long-term income needs. The *ISG™* technology underlying the *Retirement Income Navigator* was developed to calculate the optimum balance between fixed-rate investments for income and investments in stocks for growth. The unique *ISG* methodology results in a mathematically precise and individualized approach to retirement planning. Comprehensive plans can be developed that show how to achieve the desired income with retirement plan assets. Detailed information on the *ISG* methodology may be found at the authors' web site (http://www.isgplanning.com).

(Note: Generally, the same software is offered by Leimberg.com below.)

CCH INCORPORATED
4025 West Peterson Avenue
Chicago, IL 60646

888-879-5515
773-866-3095 (Fax)
http://tax.cchgroup.com
cust_serv@cch.com

CCH ViewPlan software, used in thousands of estate planners' offices around the country, provides practitioners like you with a powerful, yet easy way to present visually appealing and understandable estate planning and generation-skipping transfer planning proposals.

ViewPlan allows you to view virtually unlimited number of plans, and compare up to three alternative plans at one time to facilitate the client presentation of the optimal planning technique. Each scenario has built-in explanatory text and allows you to append your own notes. In addition, *ViewPlan* performs federal estate calculations quickly, and also calculates for all 50 states and the District of Columbia.

ViewPlan also allows you to show your clients where there may be additional liquidity needs. Colorful graphs, flowcharts, spreadsheet-like calculation reports, and easy-to-understand explanatory text can be arranged in customizable presentations, adaptable by you to virtually all planning options. To improve your workflow, data input is organized to reflect how you work with a specific part of a plan. To help avoid possible costly errors, we've even included a "calculations log" which creates an audit trail and allows you to actually see how the calculator arrived at given results and to more quickly identify possible input errors.

CCH ViewPlan Advanced is a powerful and versatile estate planning software program that transforms your PC into a creative estate-planning laboratory and development studio. With fast, easy data input and manipulation, you can view virtually an unlimited number of plans, and compare up to three plans at one time to facilitate the presentation of optimal planning techniques to clients. And, with *CCH ViewPlan Advanced*, you can generate professional, customizable and easy-to-read flowcharts, graphs, and reports that visually guide your clients through your planning scenarios—motivating them to take action. *CCH ViewPlan Advanced* includes the most popular charitable and intra-family wealth transfer techniques.

CCH Enteract helps you explore alternate financial planning routes quickly and easily. Discover a whole new way of developing personal financial plans for your clients. *CCH Enteract* is an easy-to-use software program that is 100% integrated (no separate modules) and provides comprehensive coverage of the pertinent financial planning issues you need to effectively advise your clients.

Cowles Legal Systems, Inc.	800-366-1730
3410 Sky Park Blvd.	715-835-7792 (Fax)
Eau Claire, WI 54701	www.cowleslegal.com
	cowls@cowleslegal.com

Cowles Legal Systems, Inc. provides estate planning and postmortem software, substantive legal resources, and practice development and practice management tools and techniques to professional advisors for operation of the streamlined, client-centered, profitable professional practice.

The Trust Plus estate planning system includes document assembly software modules to generate revocable trusts, wills, and irrevocable trusts. Each module includes supporting documents as appropriate (*e.g.*, state-specific powers of attorney for health and financial), funding documents (*e.g.*, instruction letters to third parties to fund revocable trusts, state-specific deeds to transfer real estate to trusts, and various assignments), correspondence, invoicing, custom covers and envelopes, and various other documents for one-time data entry to create comprehensive estate plans. Modules are integrated so client data may be shared. Substantive legal help including drafting guidance, legal citations, and discussion is available on a phrase-by-phrase basis with the click of a mouse. Extensive customization features are included for software users to edit our language or create their own documents with point and click drop-down menus to insert necessary code. *Cowles Customizer™* also allows subscribers to add any documents of their choice and to program merge and formatting codes by simply clicking on drop-down menus.

The TrusTerminator system generates correspondence and documents required to terminate a revocable trust at the time of the client's death. This system allows for immediate, personal response to the trustee and beneficiaries, beginning with initial notification of a death through all details needing to be considered (correspondence to ensure that insurance is in place on assets, change of address, notification to social security, *etc.*), correspondence and tracking tools to obtain asset information and create the inventory of assets showing date of death values and types of assets, through final accounting and distribution of assets. The system even creates state-specific deeds to convey real estate to beneficiaries! *TrusTerminator* takes the mystery and the overwhelm out of postmortem services—which can otherwise be incredibly paper and labor intensive.

CrescendoInteractive	800-858-9154
110 Camino Ruiz	805-388-2483 (Fax)
Camarillo, CA 93012	www.crescendointeractive.com
	crescendo@cresmail.com

Included in *Crescendo Pro*'s 50 programs are calculations and marketing proposals for planned gifts such as Current, Flexible and Deferred Gift Annuities, Unitrusts and FLIP Unitrust, Annuity Trusts, Transfer of IRA into Testamentary Unitrust, Home Buy-Down, Bargain Sale, College Annuity, Education and Retirement Unitrusts, Lead Trusts, Estate Models, Electronic Tax & Gift Planning Library, Unitrust Documents, 50-state Gift Annuity Documents and more. *Crescendo Pro*'s main strength is simple graphics and flow charts that communicate effectively with senior persons. Crescendo's one-on-one presentations with high quality print and full color graphics are both powerful and persuasive. There are full unitrust, annuity trust and lead trust documents and also a full and regularly updated tax library called the "Gift Advisor." *Crescendo Pro* now includes *GiftLaw Pro*, a complete charitable giving and tax information service inside the Software. With one click on the *GiftLaw Pro* button, you have access to a user-friendly and very comprehensive source for answering any of your planned giving questions. *GiftLaw Pro* is a planned giving electronic library with over 5,000 links. Select a link and you can view any topic and take a quiz, look at related information and view the actual regulations, private letter rulings or cases.

With *Crescendo Plus Software* for PowerPoint you'll create dynamic seminar presentations that will hold your donors' attention. Strengthen your message with high-powered visual illustrations of "Why Planned Giving?" and motivate your audience to take immediate action. It's easy to customize each *Crescendo Plus* slide, brochure or flyer with your logo. Your presentations instantly become more professional and personalized with successful results. In addition, the literature section of *Crescendo Plus* includes brochures, ads and articles for gift annuities, unitrusts, wills, IRAs, DAFs, and many other gift concepts. It is a "stand alone" program. It does not require other Crescendo Software to operate and it is compatible with any other planned giving software in the marketplace.

Crescendo Presents Software is a breakthrough in allowing donors to run their own presentations. In using the Crescendo Presents, a donor or gift planner enters the basic age, property value and other information for the donor. After selecting the view option, the donor merely presses the space bar to view a full color presentation with audio on a notebook computer. *Crescendo Presents* is a stand alone program designed to engage and inform donors quickly, easily and professionally without lengthy tax calculations.

Crescendo Lite contains the features of *Crescendo Pro*, such as *GiftLaw Pro*. It also includes the supreme graphic capabilities of *Crescendo Pro* and a detailed electronic operations manual, CD, update services and the renowned Crescendo customer support services. A thoughtfully prepared package, *Crescendo Lite* software is designed for the individual or organization whose planned giving needs are less extensive than the comprehensive gift plan options of *Crescendo Pro* or *Crescendo Estate*.

Crescendo Estate includes hallmark features of *Crescendo Pro*: *GiftLaw Pro*, *Calculator*, integrated graph/chart illustrations, comprehensive tax planning library... and much more. *Crescendo Estate* focuses on the charitable tax planning concerns of the advisor, *i.e.* Attorney, CPA, Financial Planner or Underwriter. There are 23 planning and presentation programs that cover most of anything a gift planner might need to model.

Crescendo Admin is a program for administering charitable gift annuities. Records are easily imported from *Crescendo Lite* and *Pro* simplifying data entry. Easily input annuitant records into customizable data entry windows. Maintain a comprehensive database on all donors and annuitants. Track annuity balances based on reserve account earnings. Easily track annuities for one charity or multiple charities. Print checks and automatically inform user of upcoming payments. Electronic fund transfer capability. Create reports for donors, annuitants, payments schedules & more. Create state present value reports for regulated states. RCV Calculator for calculating CA RCVs. Actuary services available for state reporting. Four security access levels. Assign each user a user name and password for authorized access.

HWA International, Inc.	800-328-8661
8363 Wolf Lake Drive, Suite 101	901-388-6120
Memphis, TN 38133	901-338-5574 (Fax)
	www.hwainternational.com
	sales@hwainternational.com

TrustNet is a comprehensive, time-tested Trust Accounting System. It separates principal from income, and tracks tax lots in multiple portfolios. The product was first developed in 1977 for IBM desktop computers, and has been enhanced every year from suggestions of trust departments across the country.

There is an enormous list of this software's functions and features on HWA's web site.

InsMark, Inc.	888-467-6275
2274 Camino Ramon	925-543-0500
San Ramon, CA 94583	925-543-0501 (Fax)
	www.insmark.com
	sales@insmark.com

InsGift is a sophisticated estate planning program that factors in the client's specific cash flow needs as well as individual asset yield and growth assumptions. Unless a client's desired cash flow from available assets is measured, it is impossible to tell if an estate will grow, remain flat, or diminish. Unfortunately, this issue is usually not addressed in estate plans, but is a critical component since most people fear running out of money far more than they fear estate taxes. It is only after a "comfort zone" of net worth has been established with a satisfactory cash flow (for, say, retirement income) that most clients are willing to consider suggesting gifting strategies. The *InsGift* approach allows clients to make *informed* gifting decisions in the context of their overall net worth. *InsGift* allows numerous comparison illustrations such as Term versus Permanent Life Insurance; Variable Annuities versus Mutual Funds; and Tax Deferred Accounts versus Taxable, Tax Exempt, or Equity Accounts, and much, much more. Includes graphs, bar charts, and pie charts to compare the impact of different strategies on net worth, transfer taxes, wealth to heirs, and wealth to charity

Documents On A Disk® (DOD) and *Documents On The Net* (DON) contains 620 specimen documents organized in 147 document sets. In addition, the system contains 34 Flow Charts. This includes noncharitable agreements and documents as well as charitable trust documents for every scenario your client might need.

Kettley Publishing Company	800-777-3162
20271 SW Birch Street, Suite 200	www.kettley.com
Newport Beach, CA 92660	sales@kettley.com

Back Room Technician. Explain complex financial subjects simply and easily. Nearly 500 illustrations of today's most popular financial topics and strategies in colorful graphic, text and numeric formats. Each illustration is written in everyday language clients can understand. Find what you're looking for quickly with our "key word" search feature. Group favorite reports into proposals that can be recalled with the push of a button. *Back Room Technician* meets current NASD compliance guidelines, and special disclosure features are designed to comply with NAIC model Illustration guidelines.

Financial Planning Solutions. Provide key needs analysis and planning services to your clients. Includes modular analyses for retirement and survivor needs planning along with education funding and other accumulation planning. Powerful, simple to use, and fully integrated with other Kettley software modules. Lots of calculating power with minimal input, *Financial Planning Solutions* can be as comprehensive or as specific as your clients' needs.

Advanced Planning Solutions.
Business Quick-Plan - Everything you need to provide business valuation, business continuation and key employee proposals that your clients will understand...and act on!

Estate Cost Estimator - Thorough analysis capability, informative reports, and eye-catching illustrations enable you to provide motivating and understandable estate planning solutions...with less time and effort.

Estate Quick-Plan - Easily prepare personalized presentations that quickly qualify prospects for estate planning. Complete estate planning proposals in 10 minutes or less!!

Charitable Quick-Plan - Compare charitable gifting strategies with other options for saving income and capital gains taxes while improving cash flow.

Leimberg Associates, Inc.	610-924-0515
and Leimbert & LeClair, Inc.	610-924-0514 (Fax)
144 West Eagle Road	www.leimberg.com
Havertown, PA 19083	info@leimberg.com

Charitable Financial Planner. Even if you are a computer novice, you'll be up and running Steve Leimberg's *Charitable Financial Planner* in less than five minutes. *CFP* works on any Windows based laptop or desktop computer and requires less than 2 MBs of drive space. Absolutely minimal data entry. This intuitively easy-to-use tool requires practically no learning curve. New users will be astounded by how quickly *Charitable Financial Planner* can be mastered, how many creative tasks it performs, and how amazingly fast you have your answers.

Steve Leimberg's *Charitable Financial Planner* is a software package that takes charitable planning significantly beyond where we go in *NumberCruncher*, yet is as easy to learn and use as *NumberCruncher*, and is quite comprehensive. It even compares various charitable plans so you can quickly see which is best in your situation. Aside from Charitable Lead Annuity and UniTrusts, *Charitable Gift Planner* will instantly do calcs for pooled income funds, gift annuities, remainders in residences, remainders in farms, Charitable Remainder Trusts, and much more. You'll also be able to "eyeball" the client's specific income tax advantage to implimenting the suggested concept. The *Charitable Financial Planner* has built in warnings regarding I.R.S. exhaustion and other (*e.g.* 5%/10%/50%) tests and will automatically optimize many calcs. It also has an "age" calculator and contains copies of Rev. Rul. 77-374, I.R.S. Notices 89-24 and 89-60.

Steve Leimberg's *Charitable Financial Planner* is loaded with powerful graphs, easy-to-follow numbers, and will streamline and quicken decision making.

NumberCruncher is Steve Leimberg's authoritative estate planning decision-maker and "electronic survival tool." It performs about 100 different kinds of calculations and is the essential "instant answers" solution for estate, business, and financial planners. This intuitively easy-to-use tool requires practically no learning curve. New users will be astounded by how quickly *NumberCruncher* can be mastered, how many creative tasks it performs, and how amazingly fast you have your answers. *NumberCruncher* couples numbers, Windows graphics, and client-ready explanatory text for each of its many programs. This makes it possible for planners to use *NumberCruncher* on a stand-alone basis or "cut and paste" any calculation, graph, or report into a Word, WordPerfect, or other client presentation format. The *NumberCruncher* Manual is built into the program for instant assistance and extensive help.

LMNOP
Seminars Software Publications
701 Palomar Airport Road
Carlsbad, CA 92009

760-804-8058
lsm@lmnopstuff.com
www.lmnopstuff.com

Docs in a Box is truly easy Windows software for drafting charitable gift vehicles, including Charitable Remainder Trusts, Lead Trusts, Charitable Gift Annuities, Pooled Income Funds, Life Estate Contracts and Deeds of Gift, covering almost every drafting situation you will come across, with help screens, impressive on-screen library of codes, regulations, rulings, announcements, legislation, cover letters and other resources.

PG Calc Incorporated
129 Mount Auburn Street
Cambridge, MA 02138

617-497-4970
617-497-4974 (Fax)
info@pgcalc.com
www.pgcalc.com

Planned Giving Manager is powerful, flexible, easy to use, accurate, and comprehensive. It is the ideal tool for planned gift calculations and proposals. With the right combination of user-friendly features and authoritative planned giving expertise, *Planned Giving Manager* is trusted by top charities and allied professionals in the nation. Vary investment assumptions and use different assumptions for each gift option, do build-up illustrations, distribute realized capital gain as income, wealth replacement, model any combination of gift plans for up to ten lives, estate plans for married, single, or surviving spouse, testamentary gift of retirement plan assets, elect part sell/part gift, show gift and estate tax and much more. Model your gift in *Planed Giving Manager*, then one click of our mouse sends everything to Word, WordPerfect or Excel. Three clicks and it's in PowerPoint.

Mini Manager and *Gift Annuity Manager* are smaller versions of the software, perfect for smaller shops or programs that focus on gift annuities. *Mini Manager* offers deduction calculations and gift benefits for all types of planned gifts. *Gift Annuity Manager* performs calculations only for gift annuities. All versions produce proposals and gift annuity agreements.

GiftWrap is a Windows database for the administration of all types of planned gifts and bequests. *GiftWrap* produces extensive reports for your gift officers, board of directors, and accountants, such as FASB liabilities, CGA reserves for all sates, and cash flow expectancies; tracks planned gift donors, beneficiaries, and prospects; and accepts address uploads from other systems. Check writing, EFT, and 1099-Rs are an optional component. *GiftWrap* stores data for more than one organization, making it suitable for banks, financial service providers, and consultants. A link with PG Calc's *Planned Giving Manager, Mini Manager* and *Gift Annuity Manager* streamlines entry of new gifts.

Pooled Fund Organizer is available as stand-alone software or as a module of *GiftWrap*. *PFORZ* stores complete beneficiary and gift information, precisely determines fund units for each beneficiary, distributes units for each beneficiary, distributes fund income among beneficiaries, and produces payment checks and yearly K-1 tax reporting letters. *PFORZ* handles pooled funds of any size and offers reports in a wide range of formats.

GiftCalcs is a planned gift calculator that makes deduction calculations available right on your web site. Donors and advisors calculate their own deductions while visiting your planned giving page. Set the gift options to match your policies and choose from three levels of customization options.

Universal Sub-Account Organizer performs unitized sub-accounting tasks for pooled investments, such as endowment accounts, community foundation funds, and charitable trusts that invest in a single equity or bond fund. *USA* accommodates any number of separate investment pools and up to ten levels of accounts. Reports present the full detail or focus on net income and distributions.

PhilanthroTec, Inc.   800-332-7832
10800-D Independence Point Parkway   704-845-5528 (Fax)
Matthews, NC 28105   info@ptec.com
                                            www.ptec.com

PhilanthroCalc for Windows and *PhilanthroCalc DC for Windows*, PhilanthroTec's new planned giving software, has been designed to save planned giving professionals time, increase their productivity, enhance the image of their organization and increase completed planned gifts. Based on Microsoft Excel®, *PhilanthroCalc for Windows* contains a fast, simple user interface and the legendary computational power of PhilanthroCalc's software predecessor, *The Charitable Scenario*. While *PhilanthroCalc for Windows* and *PhilanthroCalc DC* require Microsoft Excel, no previous experience with Excel is necessary. The program functions in much the same way as any stand-alone Windows program and is very easy to operate.

PhilanthroCalc for Windows currently contains the following gift planning techniques: Charitable Remainder Unitrust, Charitable Remainder Annuity Trust, Pooled Income Fund, Charitable Gift Annuity (immediate and deferred), Charitable Lead Unitrust, Charitable Lead Annuity Trust, Life Estate Agreement. Two variations of these techniques are currently available, Deductions and Presentations. Deductions allow the user to quickly create, preview, print or export detailed deduction reports that qualify under IRC 7520. Presentations provide elaborate presentation reports from a customized title page to text explaining the technique, diagrams illustrating the process and reports and graphs that explain the numbers.

PhilanthroCalc DC for Windows is a subset of *PhilanthroCalc for Windows* and allows the user to quickly create, preview, print or export detailed deduction reports that qualify under IRC 7520.

Additional Features:

- One to eight non-charitable beneficiaries or remaindermen
- Calculates lives, term of years, the shorter of lives or term, the longer of lives or term, lives or term following other lives for most techniques
- Automatically selects the best AFR for the calculation or allows the user to override
- Will calculate the optimum payout rate to achieve a defined remainder interest such as 10% for the 10% remainder interest test
- Automatically calculates and reports on 10% remainder interest test, 5% probability test, Clay Brown rule for gift annuities and others
- Easily export all text, numbers and graphs to Excel for enhancement. Change colors on graphs, add text boxes with explanations and more
- Unprotect reports and simply copy and paste and report or graph to another Windows program such as Word or PowerPoint
- Database to store all donor and charitable technique inputs. Individual donor data with all attached cases can be emailed to anyone that is using *PhilanthroCalc* as well

- Customize your reports with your organization's name and information in the header or footer of every report
- Customize reports with your organization's logo
- Complete help system on the operation of the software and all inputs for all techniques

PhilanthroCalc for the Web is connected to your website *via* a link to your customized URL provided to you when you register. The calculations are run and delivered to the Internet through our powerful Sun servers. Our clients require no expensive computer equipment or fast Internet lines. The only requirement to use, administer or customize your *PhilanthroCalc for the Web* web site is a standard Internet connection and browser such as Netscape or Internet Explorer.

PhilanthroTec's web site allows you to do unlimited calculations for free.

Tiger Tables Software	314-552-6187
4529 Pershing Place	314-367-4193 (Fax)
St. Louis, MO 63108	info@tigertables.com
	www.tigertables.com

TIGER TABLES FOR WINDOWS

QUALIFIED PERSONAL RESIDENCE TRUST. Qualified Personal Residence Trust calculator allows direct input of dollar amounts for the value of the residence and produces printouts suitable for client conferences.

GRANTOR RETAINED ANNUITY TRUSTS (GRATs). Grantor Retained Annuity Trust (GRAT) calculator allows the user to calculate the GRAT gift taking into account mortality or ignoring mortality, and taking into account trust exhaustion per Revenue Ruling 77-454 or ignoring trust exhaustion. GRATs can also be calculated on a graduated basis as permitted by the regulations. The GRAT calculator permits input of an assumed rate of growth so you can see how your trust would perform at various assumed growth rates. The GRAT calculator alone will be worth the cost of the new program for many users.

CHARITABLE FACTORS. The charitable factors calculator allows direct input of dollar amounts for calculation of the remainder interests in an annuity trust, unitrust, pooled income fund, personal residence with reserved life estate and so forth. Most of these factors can be calculated for up to 10 lives. The gift annuity calculator will calculate both current and deferred gift annuities, including the charitable deduction, the excluded portion of each annuity payment and, if appreciated property is used to purchase the annuity, the capital gain reportable each year over the life of the annuitant.

Tiger Tables has 32 different calculations to cover nearly every need of your clients.

WealthTech LLC	443-535-8675
5919 Perfect Calm Ct.	443-535-8676 (Fax)
Clarksville, MD 21029	howard@wealthtec.com
	www.wealthtec.com

WEALTHMASTER™. A suite of advanced planning models that enables you to create powerful illustrations in the areas of tax planning, financial planning, retirement distribution planning, planned charitable giving and estate planning. In addition, *WEALTHMASTER*'s Cash Flow & Estate Planner helps you produce integrated cash flow and estate planning illustrations, taking into account many variables other software programs don't. The *WEALTHMASTER* system can help you discover new ways of examining popular advanced planning techniques. In some cases, its analyses can actually debunk a myth or two... Includes stock options, qualified plan distributions and Monte Carlo simulations. In addition, WealthTec's unique sensitivity analyses are available for all models covering specific planning techniques and scenarios.

FOUNDATIONS™. The ultimate planning suite for integrated lifetime cash flows, insurance and estate planning. *FinancePro* covers lifetime cash flows and insurance planning, while the *EstatePro-DesignPro* tandem clearly represents WealthTec's finest achievement in estate planning.

What-if scenario modeling is at the heart of *FOUNDATIONS*. In *FinancePro*, you can model the impact on projected lifetime cash flows of premature death, long-term disability and long-term care events. Each scenario can be subject to Monte Carlo Simulations.

EstatePro is the tool to use for creating integrated estate planning illustrations. It incorporates basic and advanced planning techniques into a single model, which includes an integrated lifetime cash flow capability as well. *DesignPro* then compares up to three *EstatePro* cases side by side.

COUNSELOR™. A suite of client-friendly PowerPoint® presentations covering a variety of estate and charitable topics. Everything from an in-depth overview of estate planning to split-interest charitable trusts to planning for distributions from qualified plans and IRAs is included. Presentations covering specific advanced planning techniques are organized in a standard fashion. Each presents an overview of the technique, its advantages and potential drawbacks, requirements, tax treatment, suitability, enhancers and even one or more quantitative/graphic examples highlighting the tax and projected financial consequences of implementing the technique. You can customize the design layout of *COUNSELOR*'s presentations by applying your own template, and the presentations can be printed for delivery to your clients.

zCalc, LLC
574 North 550 East
Lindon, UT 84042

801-785-1300
801-785-1328 (Fax)
sales@zcalc.com
www.zcalc.com

The zCalc Tool Box is a set of spreadsheet models that analyze various estate planning strategies. These models were built using the *zCalc Function Library* and run inside a customized Excel environment that allows for, among other things, easy navigation and the separation and storage of client data from the templates themselves. These models are also available in regular spreadsheet format so that you can customize them further with the use of the *zCalc Function Library*.

Appendix III

BIBLIOGRAPHY

Many books, periodicals, newsletters, tapes, and other resources are available to help you where this book leaves off. I have listed as many as I could find, but new ones are coming out every day. To save you time, I organized this listing by category. The prices listed were current at the time of this printing. They do not include shipping and handling.

Since many of the vendors offer other products or services for planned giving or gift planning professionals, vendors may also be listed separately in Appendix II or Appendix IV. There are so many publications related to charitable giving today that I simply had to stop at some point. You will find many, many other resources on every topic related to this industry by searching on the Internet. This listing is a start.

LOOSE-LEAF TAX SERVICES

Charitable Giving and Solicitation. (monthly updates) Richard L. Fox, LL.M, Author. Sue Stern Stewart, Jon L. Schumacher, and Patrick D. Martin, Editors. Warren, Gorham and Lamont, Research Institute of America (RIA), 395 Hudson Street, New York, NY 10014. 800-950-1216. Initial purchase $640. Annual update service $640. www.riahome.com.

Charitable Giving Tax Service. (quarterly updates) R&R Newkirk, 8695 South Archer, Suite #10, Willow Springs, Illinois 60480. 800-342-2375. 708-839-9207 (Fax). inquiries@rrnewkirk.com. Initial purchase includes 4 volumes for $250 plus $186 for a year of updates (total initial purchase $436). Annual updates $186. www.rrnewkirk.com.

Charitable Lead Trusts: Explanation, Specimen Agreements, Forms. Taxwise Giving, 13 Arcadia Road, Old Greenwich, CT 06870. Annual subscription $175. www.taxwisegiving.com. 800-243-9122 or 203-637-4553.

Deferred Giving: Explanation, Specimen Agreements, Forms. Taxwise Giving, 13 Arcadia Road, Old Greenwich, CT 06870. 800-243-9122 or 203-637-4553. Two volume set. Annual subscription $295. www.taxwisegiving.com.

Outright Charitable Gifts: Explanation, Substantiating, Forms. Taxwise Giving, 13 Arcadia Road, Old Greenwich, CT 06870. 800-243-9122 or 203-637-4553. Annual subscription $175. www.taxwisegiving.com.

Planned Giving: Starting, Marketing, Administering. Taxwise Giving, 13 Arcadia Road, Old Greenwich, CT 06870. 800-243-9122 or 203-637-4553. Annual subscription $175. www.taxwisegiving.com.

NEWSLETTERS

Charitable Gift Planning News. (ten times annually) Jerry J. McCoy, LL.B, LL.M., Terry L. Simmons, J.D., LL.M., Eric Dryburgh, J.D., Katelyn Quynn, J.D., and Reynolds Cafferata, J.D. JAS Destiny, Inc., P.O. Box 551606, Dallas, TX 75355. 214-349-2209. contactgpn@aol.com. Annual subscription $168 for hard copy, $148 for e-mail version, or $195 for both.

Directions in Development. (periodically) Barnes & Roche, Inc., Rosemont Business Campus, Building Three, Suite 302, 919 Conestoga Road, Rosemont, PA 19010. **Free.** 610-527-3244. www.barnesroche.com.

Gift Planning in Canada™. (monthly) 100 Second Avenue South, Suite 180, Edmonds, WA 98020. 800-525-5748. 425-744-3837. $175 USD. $230 CDN. www.pgtoday.com.

FRM Weekly Newsletter. (50 issues *per* year, electronic version) Hoke Communications, Inc., 224 Seventh Street, Garden City, NY 11530. $125. 516-746-6700.

Give & Take. (monthly) Robert F. Sharpe & Company, Inc., 6410 Poplar Avenue, Suite 700, Memphis, TN 38119. 800-2383253. 901-680-5300. **Free** on e-mail or $89 by U.S. mail. Free to clients. www.rfsco.com.

Planned Giving MENTOR™. (monthly) 100 Second Avenue South, Suite 180, Edmonds, WA 98020. 800-525-5748. 425-744-3837. $99. ($75 if subscribed to **Planned Giving Today**®) Other pricing structures for different categories. www.pgtoday.com.

Planned Giving Today®. (monthly) 100 Second Avenue South, Suite 180, Edmonds, WA 98020. 800-525-5748. 425-744-3837. $195. Discounts for multiple year subscriptions. www.pgtoday.com *(Also, many books of compiled articles and other resources are available.)*

Taxwise Giving. (monthly) Conrad Teitell, LL.B., LL.M., Editor. Taxwise Giving, 13 Arcadia Road, Old Greenwich, CT 06870. 800-243-9122 or 203-637-4553. Annual subscription $195. www.taxwisegiving.com.

The Tidd Letter. (monthly) Jonathan G. Tidd, 9 Beaverbrook Road, West Simsbury, CT 06092. 203-651-8937.

MAGAZINES AND JOURNALS

The Chronicle of Philanthropy. (biweekly) 1255 23rd Street, NW, Suite 700, Washington, DC 20037 help@philanthropy.com. 202-466-1200. $69.50 *per* year. www.philanthropy.com.

Contributions. (bimonthly) P.O. Box 338, Medfield, MA 01052. 508-359-0019. $40. *(Note: There are many books for sale on every area of fund raising topics on their web site.)* www.contributionsmagazine.com.

Currents. (monthly) CASE, 1307 New York Avenue, NW, Suite 1000, Washington, DC 20005. $100 non-members. Included in CASE membership.

Estates, Gifts and Trusts Journal. (bimonthly) BNA, 1231 25th Street, NW, Washington, DC 20037. 800-372-1033. www.bna.com.

Estate Planning. (monthly) Charis Emley, LL.M., Editor. Warren, Gorham and Lamont, Research Institute of America (RIA), 395 Hudson Street, New York, NY 10014. 800-950-1216. Annual subscription $295. www.riahome.com.

Estate Planning Review. (monthly) CCH INC., 4025 W. Peterson Avenue, Chicago, IL 60646. $288 Internet subscription. $268 print. 800-TELL-CCH. http://tax.cchgroup.com.

Fund Raising Management. (monthly) Hoke Communications, Inc., 224 Seventh Street, Garden City, NY 11530. $90. 516-746-6700.

The Grantsmanship Center Magazine. (3 times *per* year). The Grantsmanship Center, P.O. Box 17220, Los Angeles, CA 90017. 213-482-9860. **Free** to staff of nonprofit organizations and government agencies. www.tgci.com.

Grassroots Fundraising Journal. (bimonthly) 3781 Broadway, Oakland, CA 94611. 510-596-8160. 888-458-8588. $32. www.grassrootsfundraising.org.

The Journal of Gift Planning. (quarterly) National Committee on Planned Giving, 233 McCrea, Suite 400, Indianapolis, IN 46225. 317-269-6274. Free to members, $45 nonmembers. www.ncpg.org.

Journal of Practical Estate Planning. (bimonthly) CCH INC., 4025 W. Peterson Avenue, Chicago, IL 60646. $245 Internet subscription. $225 Journal. 800-TELL-CCH. Also available through CCH are Journal of Passthrough Entities, Journal of Tax Practice and Procedure, TAXES THE TAX MAGAZINE®, Journal of Retirement Planning, and Journal of Taxation of Financial Products.

The NonProfit Times. (biweekly) 120 Littleton Road, Suite 120, Parsippany, NJ 07054. Free to full-time U.S. nonprofit executives. $65 all others. 973-394-1800. www.nptimes.com.

Nonprofit World. (bimonthly) Society For Nonprofit Organizations, 5820 Canton Center Road, Suite 165, Canton, MI 48187. 734-451-3582. Free to Society For Nonprofit Organizations members. $79 nonmembers. www.snpo.org.

Philanthropy. (bimonthly) The Philanthropy Roundtable, 1150 7th Street, NW, Suite 503, Washington, DC 20036. 202-822-8333. $55. http://philanthropyroundtable.org.

Trusts & Estates. (monthly) 249 W. 17th Street, New York, NY 10011. 212-462-3300. $149. www.trustandestates.com.

BOOKS

The Art of Planned Giving: Understanding Donors and the Culture of Giving. 1998. Douglas E. White. John Wiley & Sons, Inc., 10475 Crosspoint Blvd., Indianapolis, IN 46256. 362 pages. $27.95. 877-72-2974. www.wiley.com.

Asking: A 59-Minute Guide to Everything Board Members, Volunteers and Staff Must Know to Secure the Gift. Jerold Panas. Bonus Books, Inc., 875 N. Michigan Ave., Suite 1416, Chicago, IL 60611. 112 pages. 800-225-3775. $24.95. www.bonus-books.com.

Boardroom Verities: A Celebration of Trusteeship with Guides and Techniques to Govern. Jerold Panas. Bonus Books, Inc., 875 N. Michigan Ave., Suite 1416, Chicago, IL 60611. 238 pages. 800-225-3775. $32. www.bonus-books.com.

Born to Raise: What Makes a Great Fundraiser, What Makes a Fundraiser Great. Jerold Panas. Bonus Books, Inc., 875 N. Michigan Ave., Suite 1416, Chicago, IL 60611. 228 pages. 800-225-3775. $32. www.bonus-books.com.

Charitable Gift Annuities: The Complete Resource Manual. (updated periodically) Frank Minton. Planned Giving Services, 1910 Fairview Avenue East, Suite 102, Seattle, WA 98102. $325. $250 for owners of PG Calc Software. 206-329-8144. www.plannedgivingservices.com.

Conducting a Successful Fund Raising Program: A Comprehensive Guide and Resource. 2001. Kent E. Dove. John Wiley & Sons, Inc., 10475 Crosspoint Blvd., Indianapolis, IN 46256. 997 pages. $70. 877-762-2974. www.wiley.com.

Conducting a Successful Major Gifts and Planned Giving Program: A Comprehensive Guide and Resource. 2002. Kent E. Dove, Alan M. Spears, and Thomas W. Herbert. John Wiley & Sons, Inc., 10475 Crosspoint Blvd., Indianapolis, IN 46256. 576 pages. $55. 877-762-2974. www.wiley.com.

Creative Stewardship for the Local Congregation: Introducing Planned Giving into Our Stewardship Awareness. 1992. David Schmeling, CFRE. Deferred Giving Services/Creative Stewardship Strategies, 1517 Turnberry Circle, Oconomowoc, WI 53066. $42. 262-567-6452. www.deferredgivingservices.com.

Family Foundation Handbook. Kathryn W. Miree and Jerry, J. McCoy. Aspen Publishers, 7201 McKinney Circle, Frederick, MD 21701. 301-698-7100. $185. www.aspenpublishers.com.

Finders Keepers: Lessons I've Learned About Dynamic Fundraising. Jerold Panas. Bonus Books, Inc., 875 N. Michigan Ave., Suite 1416, Chicago, IL 60611. 280 pages. 800-225-3775. $31.96. www.bonus-books.com.

The First Legal Answer Book for Fund Raisers. 2000. Bruce R. Hopkins. John Wiley & Sons, Inc., 10475 Crosspoint Blvd., Indianapolis, IN 46256. 288 pages. $65. 877-762-2974. www.wiley.com.

From Grantmaker to Leader: Emerging Strategies for Twenty-First Century Foundations. 2002. Frank L. Ellsworth and Joe Lumarda, Editors. John Wiley & Sons, Inc., 10475 Crosspoint Blvd., Indianapolis, IN 46256. 268 pages. $70. 877-762-2974. www.wiley.com. Also in e-book format.

Fundraising for Dummies. John Mutz and Katherine Murray. 2000. IDG Books Worldwide, Inc., 919 E. Hillsdale Blvd., Suite 400, Foster City, CA 94404. $21.99. 800-762-2974. www.dummies.com.

Fundraising in Times of Crisis. Kim Klein. 2003. 192 pages. John Wiley & Sons, Inc., 10475 Crosspoint Blvd., Indianapolis, IN 46256. $24.95. 877-762-2974. www.wiley.com.

Giving USA. Updated annually. AAFRC Trust for Philanthropy, 10293 N. Meridian Street, Suite 175, Indianapolis, IN 46290. 225 pages. 888-544-8464. $65. (Also **Giving USA CD and Update Subscription** $195) www.aafrc.org.

The Harvard Manual on Tax Aspects of Charitable Giving. Carolyn Osteen and Martin Hall. 1999. Harvard University, Planned Giving, 124 Mt. Auburn Street, Cambridge, MA 02138. $105. 800-446-1277. 617-495-4647. pgo@harvard.edu. www.haa.harvard.edu/pgo.

Gospels of Wealth: How the Rich Portray their Lives. Paul G. Schervish, Platon Coutsoukis, and Ethan Lewis. 1994. 304 pages. Praeger Publishers, Greenwood Publishing Group, Inc., 88 Post Road West, Westport, CT 06881. 203-226-3571. $80.95. Paperback $25. www.greenwood.com.

High Impact Philanthropy: How Donors, Boards, and Nonprofit Organizations Can Transform Communities. 2000. John Wiley & Sons, Inc., 10475 Crosspoint Blvd., Indianapolis, IN 46256. 208 pages. $34.95. 877-762-2974. www.wiley.com.

Inspired Philanthropy: Your Step-by-Step Guide to Creating a Giving Plan, Second Edition. Tracy Gary and Melissa Kohner. John Wiley & Sons, Inc., 10475 Crosspoint Blvd., Indianapolis, IN 46256. 2002. 304 pages. 877-762-2974. $24.95. www.wiley.com.

Invest in Charity: A Donor's Guide to Charitable Giving. 2001. Ron Jordan and Katelyn L. Quynn. John Wiley & Sons, Inc., 10475 Crosspoint Blvd., Indianapolis, IN 46256. 264 pages. $29.95. 877-762-2974. www.wiley.com. Also in e-book format.

Making the Case: The No-Nonsense Guide to Writing the Perfect Case Statement. Jerold Panas. 2003. Institutions Press, 500 North Michigan Ave., 20th Floor, Chicago, IL 60611. 138 pages. 800-234-7777.

Mega Gifts: Who Gives Them, Who Gets Them. Jerold Panas. Bonus Books, Inc., 875 N. Michigan Ave., Suite 1416, Chicago, IL 60611. 231 pages. 800-225-3775. $32. www.bonus-books.com.

New Directions for Philanthropic Fundraising, The Role of the Planned Giving Professional: Serving Nonprofit Organizations and Their Donors. 2001. Gordon D. Chavers, editor. John Wiley & Sons, Inc., 10475 Crosspoint Blvd., Indianapolis, IN 46256. 120 pages. $29. 877-762-2974. www.wiley.com.

Nonprofit Kit for Dummies. 2001. Stan Hutton and Frances Phillips. 384 pages. IDG Books Worldwide, Inc., 919 E. Hillsdale Blvd., Suite 400, Foster City, CA 94404. $29.99. 800-762-2974. www.dummies.com.

The Nonprofit Membership Toolkit. Ellis M. Robinson and Kim Klein. 2003. John Wiley & Sons, Inc., 10475 Crosspoint Blvd., Indianapolis, IN 46256. 320 pages. $35. www.wiley.com.

The PGT Resource Library. Lots of books on planned giving. Planned Giving Today®, 100 Second Avenue South, Suite 180, Edmonds, WA 98020. 800-525-7748. www.pgtoday.com.

Planned Giving Essentials: A Step-by-Step Guide to Success, Second Edition. Richard D. Barrett and Molly E. Ware. 2002. Jones & Bartlett Publishers, 40 Tall Pine Drive, Sudbury, MA 01776. 187 pages. $73.95. 800-832-0034. www.jbpub.com.

Planned Giving for Small Nonprofits. 2002. Ronald R. Jordan and Katelyn L. Quynn. John Wiley & Sons, Inc., 10475 Crosspoint Blvd., Indianapolis, IN 46256. 324 pages. $39.95. 877-762-2974. www.wiley.com.

Planned Giving for the One Person Development Office: Taking the First Steps. David Schmeling, CFRE. 2003. 228 pages. Deferred Giving Services/Creative Stewardship Strategies, 1517 Turnberry Circle, Oconomowoc, WI 53066. $44 print. $69 electronic. 262-567-6452. www.deferredgivingservices.com.

Planned Giving: Management, Marketing, and Law, Third Edition. 2003. Ronald R. Jordan and Katelyn L. Quynn. John Wiley & Sons, Inc., 10475 Crosspoint Blvd., Indianapolis, IN 46256. 624 pages. $195. 877-762-2974. www.wiley.com.

Planned Giving Simplified: The Gift, The Giver, and the Gift Planner. 1998. Robert F. Sharpe. John Wiley & Sons. 10475 Crosspoint Blvd., Indianapolis, IN 46256. 240 pages. $34.95. 877-762-2974. www.wiley.com.

Planned Giving Workbook. 2002. Ronald R. Jordan and Katelyn L. Quynn. John Wiley & Sons. 10475 Crosspoint Blvd., Indianapolis, IN 46256. 199 pages. $39.95. 877-762-2974. www.wiley.com.

Portable Planned Giving Manual. Conrad Teitell, LL.B., LL.M. Taxwise Giving, 13 Arcadia Road, Old Greenwich, CT 06870. 700 pages. $195. 800-243-9122 or 203-637-4553. www.taxwisegiving.com.

A Practitioner's Guide to Estate Planning: Guidance and Planning Strategies. Douglas H. Moy. CCH INC., 4025 W. Peterson Avenue, Chicago, IL 60646. $310. http://tax.cchgroup.com. 800-TELL-CCH.

PricewaterhouseCoopers Guide to Charitable Giving. 2002. PricewaterhouseCoopers LLP, Michael B. Kennedy, Evelyn M. Capassakis, Richard S. Wagman. John Wiley & Sons, Inc., 10475 Crosspoint Blvd., Indianapolis, IN 46256. 202 pages. $19.95. 877-762-2974. www.wiley.com.

Professional Advisor's Guide to Planned Giving. (updated annually) Kathryn W. Miree. Aspen Publishers, 7201 McKinney Circle, Frederick, MD 21701. 301-698-7100. $215. www.aspenpublishers.com.

Tax Aspects of Charitable Giving, Second Edition. Carolyn Osteen and Martin Hall. 2000. Ropes & Gray, One International Place, Boston, MA 02110. 617-951-7000. $190. www.ropesgray.com.

Tax Economics of Charitable Giving. Wealth and Tax Services, Inc., Joseph P. Toce, Jr., Byrle M. Abbin, William M. Pace and Mark L. Vorsatz. 2003. 670 pages. Warren, Gorham and Lamont, Research Institute of America (RIA), 395 Hudson Street, New York, NY 10014. 800-950-1216. $200. www.riahome.com.

The Ultimate Do-It-Yourself Bequest Book. Betsy A. Mangone and Lynn Thomas. 2002. Mangone & Company, 12687 West Cedar Drive, Suite 210, Lakewood, CO 80228. $125. 866-814-0794. 303-980-0800. www.mangoneandco.com.

Wealth in Families. Charles W. Collier. 2001. Harvard University, 124 Mount Auburn Street, Cambridge, MA 02138. 617-495-5040. $15.

Appendix IV

PLANNED GIVING/FUND RAISING CONSULTANTS

Whether you need help with your feasibility study, brochures or newsletters for your donors, booklets, technical expertise, planned giving training, research, planned giving web content or other services related to planned giving or general fund raising, there are many people and firms ready to help you. While there are many excellent advisors, attorneys, or others serving the charitable giving community, this listing is primarily limited to people or firms who provide services specifically in fund raising or in some other capacity of consulting for nonprofit organizations. I am not listing the many terrific firms or people who are charitable gift planning attorneys or advisors, managers of assets or administrators of charitable trusts and other deferred gifts.

Many of the firms or individuals listed below have been in the planned giving or fund raising field for a long time and were listed in my last two books. Others are new to this listing. Some of the listings in my last book are missing in action and could not be found with either an Internet search or through calling the phone number I had before. Some have merged with other firms, changed their name, or don't exist any longer.

Some "consultants" (and I use this term loosely) formerly worked as a director of planned giving somewhere and are now consultants. In any evaluation of a consultant, you should get references. You should also read the short Chapter I-3 about whether you need a planned giving consultant. Not only should you get references, you should also get the names of clients who terminated services with these vendors or people.

If I have omitted you or your firm, forgive me. Send an e-mail to debra@debraashton.com and I will add you to the Revised Fourth Edition if your services fall within the guidelines for this appendix.

I pulled the descriptions of services from the consultants' web sites or promotional materials. This is what they say about themselves and this is neither an evaluation by me nor an endorsement by me. The list is alphabetical. Bear in mind that the many listings appear equal in legitimacy due to their inclusion in this book. That is not true. This is simply a listing of some people or firms holding themselves out as consultants of one form or another to the charitable giving community.

In every case, the web sites of the consultants provide much more detail, often with lists of current or past clients, and lots of information about the various services they offer. For an extensive list of consultants together with descriptions of their services, go to www.aafrc.org and download the Member Directory for free.

American City Bureau, Inc.
33 West Higgins Road, Suite 520
South Barrington, IL 60010

224-293-3000
800-786-4625
224-293-3012 (Fax)
success@acb-inc.com
www.acb-inc.com

Since 1913, American City Bureau's mission has been to help your organization advance its mission. With our fund raising touch, American City Bureau has been able to help raise necessary funds for thousands of organizations throughout the United States.

American City Bureau is one of the country's premier fund-raising consulting firms which specializes in major gift development. In fact, we are considered the most experienced firm of our kind in the nation. Our longevity—nearly nine decades of service—and our track record—over three billion dollars raised for not-for-profit organizations, is a story that speaks for itself...and to what we can do for you.

The American College
270 S. Bryn Mawr Avenue
Bryn Mawr, PA 19010

888-263-7265
610-526-1490
610-526-1465 (Fax)
studentservices@amercoll.edu
www.amercoll.edu

The American College is the nation's oldest and largest nontraditional institution for higher learning devoted exclusively to academic studies of life insurance and related financial services. Founded in 1927 and accredited by the Commission on Higher Education of the Middle States Association of Colleges and Schools, the College administers a variety of professional designation programs and continuing education programs for those seeking career growth in life insurance and financial services. Provides courses and training to receive the following designations:

CLU: Chartered Life Underwriter
ChFC: Chartered Financial Consultant
CFP™: Certified Financial Planner
RHU: Registered Health Underwriter
CAP: Chartered Advisor in Philanthropy®

REBC: Registered Employee Benefits Consultant
CLF: Chartered Leadership Fellow
MSFS: Master of Science in Financial Services
LUTCF: LUTC Fellow

American Fund Raising Institute
c/o William L. "Bill" Doyle, C.F.R.P.
7004 Comanche Drive
North Little Rock, AR 72116

501-834-8188
800-496-2374
afri88@aol.com
www.afri.org

Ronald C. "Ron" Harding, C.F.R.P.
179 Country Club Drive
Hiram, GA 30141

770-443-0932
profundraiser@hotmail.com

American Fund Raising Institute, Inc. (AFRI) is recognized nationally as an innovative and client-sensitive fundraising firm. Known for providing the greatest value in development counsel, AFRI was founded in 1987 as a partnership of highly seasoned development professionals with many years of collective fundraising experience. AFRI professionals have helped raise millions of dollars for leading non-profits in the areas of education, health and human services, culture and arts, youth services, and economic development. We are a firm large enough to deliver cost-effective fundraising counsel, yet small enough to personally provide these services by the senior principals of the firm.

The stated part of American Fund Raising Institute's mission is to assist non-profit organizations to secure private sector funding in a cost-effective manner, on time, under budget, and over goal. We adhere to a high standard of accountability and measurable results, and pursue a pragmatic no-nonsense management style.

(Note: the AFRI web site has dozens of reasonably priced booklets on every conceivable topic you can think of in the area of boards, campaigns, events, fund raising, annual giving, sample letters, volunteers, writing proposals, among others. There are too many to list. Check it out.)

American Institute for Philanthropic Studies
California State University
Long Beach Foundation
CSU Chancellor's Office
401 Golden Shore
Long Beach, CA 90802

562-985-8466
562-985-5660
ddavis@csulb.edu
www.plannedgivingedue.com

The Institute provides training in planned giving and offers a designation of Certified Specialist in Planned Giving℠. The program encompasses the entire syllabus recommended by the National Committee on Planned Giving. It includes in-depth coverage and sophisticated treatment of pertinent topics and issues in the field of planned giving. Participants must complete all six modules to receive the CSPG℠ designation. C.E.

credits are available for CPA, CFP, MCLE, CLU, and ChFC. Modules are offered every year beginning in September.

Art & Science Group, LLC	**410-377-7880**
6115 Falls Road, Suite 101	**410-377-7955 (Fax)**
Baltimore, MD 21209	**consult@artsci.com**
	www.artsci.com

114 Swift Avenue	**919-286-4821**
Durham, NC 27705	**919-286-4932**
	consult@artsci.com
	www.artsci.com

The range of marketing and communications consulting services we offer is both multifaceted and focused. We can provide informed, incisive advice and guidance for every major area of institutional marketing activity, from fundraising and corporate relations to student recruitment and retention. Many of our assignments, in fact, integrate several of these services within a single project.

Even though we have considerable expertise in many institutional marketing realms, since our firm's practice is not narrowly focused on any single area—enrollment management or alumni relations, for example—we bring a breadth of experience and understanding to each assignment that raises the quality, imagination, and insight of the advice we provide to a higher level.

Barnes & Roche, Inc.	**610-527-3244**
Rosemont Business Campus	**610-527-0381**
Building Three, Suite 302	**consult@brnsrche.com**
919 Conestoga Road	**www.barnesroche.com**
Rosemont, PA 19010	

Also, Philadelphia, Washington, and San Francisco

Provides comprehensive consulting services tailored to the specific needs of your fundraising program, either on an individual aspect or project or as part of an integrated consulting relationship. Services include strategic planning, program audits and consulting, capital campaign counsel, feasibility studies, case statements and campaign materials, electronic database screening, prospect research, prospect management, proposal writing, board development and solicitor training, planned giving, fund raising financial business planning.

Marketing: Achieving your goals depends on clear and effective marketing and communications programs. Our comprehensive approach to marketing will help you understand your markets, identify your institution's most important messages, and implement the most effective way to reach your audiences. Services include marketing communications, market research, public relations, publications, membership services, enrollment management.

Barrett Planned Giving, Inc.	**202-349-3812**
1721 I Street, NW, Suite 300	**800-332-9132**
Washington, DC 20006	**202-349-3813 (Fax)**
	Richard@BarrettPlannedGiving.com
	www.BarrettPlannedGiving.com

Comprehensive services in planned giving program development including evaluation of all pertinent elements of an organization's planned giving potential; creation of a step-by-step marketing plan; interactive workshops for board, staff, and volunteers; custom tailored slide shows; telephone consulting with charity's staff and the donor; and preparation of relevant gift illustrations. Also, the principal, Richard D. Barrett, is author of the book *Planned Giving Essentials: A Step-by-Step Guide to Success, Second Edition* (listed in Appendix III).

Bentz Whaley Flessner
7215 Ohms Lane
Minneapolis, MN 55439

952-921-0111
952-921-0109 (Fax)
bwf@bwf.com
www.bwf.com

5272 River Road, Suite 500
Bethesda, MD 20816

301-656-7823
301-656-2156 (Fax)
bethesda@bwf.com

Bentz Whaley Flessner is a national fund-raising consulting firm founded by a group of development officers who sought to create a new kind of consulting practice. From the beginning, we have pursued a philosophy that seeks to help our clients meet their current fund-raising challenges while helping them to develop strategies, skills, and systems that will plant the seeds for future success.

With an average of over twenty years of experience, our consultants bring the broad range of expertise needed to make the most impact in the immediate need and for the future. As a result, our clients not only succeed in creating new sources of funding, but also improve their ability to manage their advancement programs in the process.

Campaigns, feasibility studies, audits, client counsel, board development, staff development, alumni relations, prospecting, systems, and more.

(Note: BWF has a "Publications" link on its web site with lots of free PDF documents on philanthropy and other fund raising topics.)

Boyd's City Dispatch
185 Millerton Road
P.O. Box 860
Millerton, NY 12546

518-789-8500
800-458-7664
518-789-0559 (Fax)
boyds@boydscity.com
www.boydscity.com

Provides alumni search services plus prospecting leads service to locate high income prospects, affluent seniors, annuity prospects, small business owners, turning 65 file and homeowners with children, some of which is targeted to the insurance industry.

Brakeley Inc.
86 Prospect Street
Stamford, CT 06901

203-348-8100
203-978-0114 (Fax)
info@brakeley.com
www.brakeley.com

Established in the United States in 1919, we have grown to serve clients globally in education, arts and cultural, health, religious, environmental, social and humanitarian sectors. We provides services in major gift fund raising; capital campaign planning and management; audits, feasibility and planning studies; training and executive coaching; strategic planning; communication strategies; information technology; prospect research; international fundraising; annual campaigns and planned giving; board development and governance; executive search; alumni, constituency and public relations.

Brakeley Inc. serves North and South America. Brakeley Ltd., based in London, serves Europe, Asia, Southern Africa and other regions of the world.

The Breton Group
2504 Ardmore, SE
Grand Rapids, MI 49506

616-975-9907
616-975-9909 (Fax)
tbg@bretongroup.com
www.bretongroup.com

Serving organizations in Michigan, The Breton Group is a full service development consulting firm devoted to assisting libraries, churches, church-affiliated organizations, and non-profit community organizations.

Services include feasibility studies, capital campaign counsel, capital stewardship campaign counsel, library needs assessment and facility planning, resource development planning and implementation, annual giving counsel and support, and grant writing.

John Brown Limited, Inc.	603-924-3834
P.O. Box 296	603-924-7998 (Fax)
Peterborough, NH 03458	info@johnbrownlimited.com
	www.johnbrownlimited.com

Provides personalized campaign counsel, strategy for planned giving and major gifts programs, marketing/feasibility studies, and development audits. Counsel on outright and planned gifts, gift arrangements, donor prospects, marketing, expanded relationship-building and solicitation teams, donor research, proposal preparation, solicitation presentations and planned giving calculations. Campaign counsel including gift policies and procedures, volunteer and board presentations, individual donor strategies, and review of all collateral materials. Multimedia seminars, 3-day seminars in major cities, and on-site seminars for donors, trustees, or volunteers.

Browning Associates	973-746-5960
209 Cooper Avenue	973-760-0189 (Fax)
Upper Montclair, NJ 07043	info@browning-associates.com
	www.browning-associates.com

A full-service development consulting firm that also specializes in strategic planning, board governance, and retreats. Browning Associates has dedicated itself since 1966 to assisting independent schools and other not-for-profit organizations in realizing their missions. Provides counsel on all aspects of fundraising including capital gift programs, annual funds, and planned giving.

Campbell & Company	312-644-7100
1 E. Wacker Drive, Suite 2525	877-957-0000
Chicago, IL 60601	info@campbellcompany.com
	www.campbellcompany.com
Other offices:	
Gloucester, MA	978-281-1235
Washington, DC	202-756-4788
Beachwood, OH	216-766-5730
Scottsdale, AZ	480-513-8001
Laguna Hills, CA	949-470-4555
Seattle, WA	206-505-7989

Founded in 1976, Campbell & Company is a national philanthropic consulting firm offering a full range of fundraising services, including capital and endowment campaign counsel, annual and planned giving program counsel, feasibility studies and development audits, volunteer and staff training, marketing and communications plans and materials, case statements, board development, and executive search. With a record of success in working with over 700 clients over the past 25 years, Campbell and Company has the experience and expertise to assist in all your fundraising needs.

Cargill Associates	800-433-2233
4701 Altamesa Blvd.	Church@Cargillfw.com
Fort Worth, TX 76133	Institution@Cargillfw.com
	www.cargillassociates.com

Cargill Associates is a full-service stewardship development firm with two key areas: churches and institutions.

We can help your church or parish with all aspects of stewardship, using a faith perspective in place of a dollar perspective. Our services are based on insightful planning, partner relationship, continuous hands-on involvement, record-breaking outcomes. With more than 80 employees, Cargill Associates has served churches and

Christian causes in all fifty states, as well as Canada, Brazil and Australia. The consultants of Cargill Associates are all committed Christians with a unique calling to the stewardship ministry.

In addition, Cargill Associates develops fund raising programs for a wide variety of non profit organizations through our Institution Division, ranging from church related colleges, schools and seminaries to state universities, agencies and national charities. Our commitment is to design a unique fund raising program that will enlist individuals, corporations, and foundations who will make your cause their concern.

The Center on Philanthropy	317-274-4200
at Indiana University	317-684-8900 (Fax)
550 W. North Street, #301	**iucop@iupui.edu**
Indianapolis, IN 46202	**www.philanthropy.iupui.edu**

The Center on Philanthropy increases the understanding of philanthropy and improves its practice through programs in research, teaching, public service, and public affairs. The Center has academic and research programs on the IUPUI and the IU-Bloomington campuses. Academic programs, research programs, The Fund Raising School (see listing below), partnership programs, conferences and institutes, publications and newsletters on philanthropy and fund raising.

Charitable Solutions, LLC	866-993-8501
4880 Lower Roswell Road	770-993-8501 / 404-375-5496
Suite 165-109	678-623-5697 (Fax)
Atlanta, GA 30068	**info@charitablesolutionsllc.com**
	www.charitablesolutionsllc.com

Charitable Solutions, LLC provides technical solutions to non-profit organizations by focusing on three primary areas of interest—noncash donations, charitable gift annuities and donor advised funds. Principals Bryan Clontz and Mack Johnston designed their business so that services are available "cafeteria-style" which allows non-profits to fill in the gaps in their own services where and when needed.

Charitable Solutions, LLC's services for non-cash donations allow charities to more readily accept gifts of non-cash assets either directly into their own non-profit or *via* Dechomai Foundation, Inc., a national donor advised fund for which Charitable Solutions, LLC provides all administrative services. Non-cash assets accepted (subject to Dechomai Foundation Board approval) include both commercial and residential real estate, restricted and closely held stock, net leased properties, LLCs, limited partnerships, operating partnership units, mortgages, S-corporation stock, seats on financial market exchanges, timber deeds, installment notes, mineral rights including oil and gas partnerships and royalties. Other non-cash assets will be considered on a case-by-case basis.

Charitable Solutions, LLC's services for charitable gift annuities provide charities with expertise in all facets of gift annuity programs including risk analysis and risk management plans on existing programs and for large individual annuities. This analysis can determine how much risk to retain and appropriate investment and longevity risk strategies as well as the exhaustion probabilities for new or existing individual annuities. Charitable Solutions, LLC has a collaborative relationship with Planned Giving Services for charities wishing to start a new program, develop policies and procedures or a comprehensive marketing strategy.

Charitable Solutions, LLC's services for donor advised funds enable charities to establish a donor advised fund program from scratch or in partnership with another charity. We specialize in helping financial services companies develop donor advised funds with community foundations and other charities.

Charles W. Collier	617-495-5218
Senior Philanthropic Advisor	617-495-0521 (Fax)
Harvard University	**ccollier@harvard.edu**
124 Mount Auburn Street	
Cambridge, MA 02138	

Specializes in presentations for trustees and major donors on topics surrounding family, wealth, and philanthropy. Will work with institutions' major prospects in structuring tax wise gifts. Also, author of *Wealth in Families*, listed in Appendix III.

Helen Colson Development Associates	301-652-7819
4725 Dorset Avenue	301-652-7916 (Fax)
Chevy Chase, MD 20815	hcolson@hcda.com
	www.hcda.com

Development and management consultants for independent schools. Services include institutional plans; program assessments; annual, capital and planned gift counsel; board development and retreats; and executive search.

Community Counseling Service	212-695-1175
461 Fifth Avenue	800-223-6733
New York, NY 10017	212-967-6451 (Fax)
	ccsnewyork@ccsfundraising.com
	www.ccsfundraising.com
Other offices:	
Chicago, IL	800-832-4060
San Francisco, CA	800-227-3834
Washington, DC	888-451-4080
Towson, MD	800-249-2680
Atlanta, GA	800-510-0944
Boston, MA	617-619-3971
Fort Lauderdale, FL	800-510-9148
Detroit, MI	800-231-6183
Seattle, WA	800-227-3834
Toronto, Ontario, Canada	416-368-5902
London, England	011-44-20-7731-3439
Dublin, Ireland	011-353-1-676-0041

Since, 1947, CCS provides comprehensive fund raising counsel and campaign management services including campaign planning, management, and direction; prospect screening; trustee development and orientation (training, role playing, and retreats); public relations and communications; planned giving; feasibility studies and development audits. Also provides assistance with major gift strategies, case statement development, and recruiting of key leadership.

Copley Harris Company, Inc.	978-750-1028
106 High Street	978-750-6709 (Fax)
Danvers, MA 01923	chc@copleyharris.com
	www.copleyharris.com

Copley Harris Company, Inc. provides counsel to non-profit health care, education, cultural and human service organizations seeking to advance their mission through philanthropy. Provides comprehensive services including feasibility studies, capital endowment campaigns, development program startups, formation of new foundations, development audits, board retreats, planned giving counsel, general fund raising counsel, interim services, and executive search.

Corporate DevelopMint	843-853-9999
49 Calhoun Street, Suite C	843-853-9993
Charleston, SC 29401	cdm@corporatedevelopmint.com
	www.corporatedevelopmint.com

Offers a comprehensive range of services including campaign planning studies, strategic planning studies, foundation implementation, capital campaign counsel, annual giving, board retreats, workshops and seminars, presentations and speeches, and executive recruitment.

Cross Associates
Consultants in Fundraising and Development
P.O. Box 1075
Niwot, CO 80544

303-652-8186
303-652-3455
c.cross@crossassociates.net
www.dimensional.com

Cross Associates is a full-service fundraising firm offering programs tailored to meet the special needs of each client. We help nonprofit organizations achieve their fundraising objectives *via* capital campaigns, major and planned gift programs, and annual funding plans. Our clients include a wide variety of nonprofit institutions ranging from small, community-based institutions to large, established national charitable organizations with endowments in excess of $50 million. Cross Associates brings years of professional experience to all phases of fundraising development. Combining national experience and local expertise, Cross Associates is a client-focused firm in which the principals do all the work. Few organizations can offer solutions quite the way we do. Clients bring us compelling objectives. We respond with in-depth understanding, thoughtful analysis, and a strong creative process, resulting in innovative solutions.

Services include capital campaigns, feasibility studies, development and fund raising evaluations, annual giving, major gift programs, planned giving programs, foundation solicitations, board development, corporate gifts, board and solicitor training, strategic and operational programs, prospect research identification and cultivation, public relations, special events, earned income programs, direct mail, commemorative opportunities, and contributor recognition.

Cunneen Fundraising
24 Rossotto Drive
Hamden, CT 06514

800-842-4488
203-407-5858 (Fax)
info@cunneencompany.com
www.cunneencompany.com

A veteran with 30 years of experience in philanthropy, Avery Tillinghast, Of Counsel, brings extensive success in annual giving, planned giving, capital campaigns and long range planning to his position. Cunneen provides comprehensive services including general fund raising counsel; development audits, feasibility and planning studies; annual fund counsel; full or part-time resident counsel for capital campaigns.

Custom Development Solutions (CDS)
1470 Ben Sawyer Blvd., Suite 3
Mt. Pleasant, SC 29464

843-971-8801
800-761-3833
843-971-8788 (Fax)
info@cdsfunds.com
www.cdsfunds.com

CDS is a full-service fundraising consulting firm specializing in the strategic planning and tactical execution of capital campaigns for non-profits large and small. We offer capital campaign counsel and fund raising consultants to organizations throughout the United States and Canada. Our site is a resource for philanthropy, non-profit, and fund-raising professionals, and people interested in hiring a fundraising consultant.

Feasibility and planning studies, full-time on-site campaign director, development audits, general fund raising advice, and many auxiliary services such as creating brochures, donor research, training, and executive search.

DAV Navion
3525 Habersham at Northlake
Building A
Tucker, GA 30084

404-688-4410
404-688-3916 (Fax)
atlanta@dvanavion.com
www.dvanavion.com

Other offices:
Auckland, New Zealand
Calgary, Alberta, Canada
Cape Town, South Africa
Dallas, TX
Melbourne, Australia

64 9 523 1403
403-216-8470
27 21 6740803
214-618-3435
61 3 9853 5111

Perth, Australia	61 8 9486 4447
Sydney, Australia	61 2 9241 4066
Toronto, Canada	416-544-9700
Vancouver, Canada	604-467-5402

An international fund raising firm providing comprehensive services in all areas of fund raising. Services include feasibility and planning study, capital campaigns, Total Development™, direct mail, bequest programs, planned giving, telemarketing, annual giving, prospect research, marketing and communications. Volunteer recruitment and development, board training, endowment, and strategic planning. Also, executive search.

M. Davenport Associates	802-649-8333
P.O. Box 333	802-649-8282 (Fax)
Hanover, NH 03755	Mike@consultmda.com
	Karen.barr@valley.net
	www.consultmda.com

The principals, Michael E. Davenport and Karen Adams Barr, bring many years of development and volunteer experience together to assist a wide range of not-for-profit institutions. M. Davenport Associates provides fund raising development services and individualized fundraising counsel including capital campaign planning, feasibility studies, capital campaign management, planned giving program design and implementation, foundations research, grant funding strategy development, board and trustee education, and start up development programs. Additional services include interim development counsel, development program assessments, special events, donor cultivation and recognition, foundation development, executive search and placement services for development professionals.

DeChenne Company	310-643-4466
5230 Pacific Concourse Drive, Suite 200	310-643-4499 (Fax)
Los Angeles, CA 90045	sdechenne@dechenneco.com
	www.dechenneco.com

Provides comprehensive services including development program assessment and counsel, campaign counsel, board development, fundraising and advancement workshops, staff evaluation, gift annuity license procurement, interim executive leadership services, prospect research, information technology and communications.

Deferred Giving Services	262-567-6452 (phone and Fax)
1517 Turnberry Circle	schmeling@aol.com
Oconomowoc, WI 53066	www.deferredgivingservices.com

Deferred Giving Services is a fund development consulting firm specializing in helping charitable organizations, especially the smaller to mid-size development office, build endowment through planned giving programs. Services include planned giving audits, financial and estate planning newsletters, customized or personalized planned giving brochures, tax update newsletters for advisors, written illustration of proposed gift benefits, training sessions and seminars, on-site or off-site retainer agreements, and seminars for donors.

The principal, David G. Schmeling, has over 21 years of experience as a planned giving practitioner and has written *Planned Giving for the One Person Development Office: Taking the First Steps* and an adapted version for churches called *Creative Stewardship: Introducing Planned Giving into Our Stewardship Awareness* (see Appendix III).

The Development Exchange (DEI)	888-454-2314
1645 Hennepin Avenue, Suite 312	612-677-1508 (Fax)
Minneapolis, MN 55403	deichten@deiworksite.org
	www.deiworksite.org

DEI specializes in services for public radio stations. Services include on-air fund raising; membership, direct mail and telemarketing; online revenue generation; underwriting sales and sales management; mid-level, major and planned giving; foundation and grant support; marketing and promotion; management; small station resources; and interdisciplinary resources. Holds an annual conference covering all areas of public radio operations and fund raising.

The Development Guild (DDI)	617-277-2112 x239
233 Harvard Street, Suite 107	800-537-9011
Brookline, MA 02446	617-277-2116 (Fax)
	wweber@developmentguild.com
	www.developmentguild.com

Development Guild/DDI is a consulting firm founded in 1978 to work with nonprofit leaders committed to aligning vision and strategic priorities, building organizational capacity, and strengthening philanthropic support. We have helped over 500 nonprofits create and evaluate their strategic plans, recruit and retain key leadership, and raise the significant philanthropy required to advance their missions. Our clients include a broad spectrum of national and international leaders in their fields as well as highly respected locally based nonprofits. We believe our clients are among the most committed, innovative and results-oriented cultural, education, foundation, health and human service nonprofits in the country.

Strategic planning, leadership development, transition planning, program evaluation and impact assessment, evaluation of foundation initiatives. Strategic planning for fund raising, campaign planning and counsel, audits and assessments, feasibility studies, board and leadership development, interim on-site counsel, major gift program design and implementation. Executive search.

The Dini Partners	713-942-8110
2727 Allen Parkway, Suite 700	713-942-8708 (Fax)
Houston, TX 77019	infor@dinipartners.com
	www.dinipartners.com
Other offices:	
374 Jefferson Street, Suite 302	512-302-1943
Austin, TX 78731	512-302-5424 (Fax)
3400 Carlisle Street, Suite 348	214-754-9393
Dallas, TX 75204	214-754-9363 (Fax)

Campaign cultivation, feasibility and planning studies; counseling and managing capital campaigns; designing and counseling major gift fund raising programs; assessing and planning development programs; training development staff. Long-term planning, building commitment to strategic plans, developing vision and mission statements, setting goals and objectives, facilitating board retreats and meetings. Analyzing board membership and recruitment strategies, organizing the board for peak performance, developing board policies, training board members and volunteers. Managing sponsor solicitation process, guiding program and entertainment details, coordinating site selection, menu, catering, printed materials, and invitations. Developing record keeping and gift acknowledgement systems. Executive search, consultant surveys, team building and other services to enhance your organization's operation.

Donovan Slone	800-370-0036
Five Appleton Street, Suite 1A	617-574-8787
Boston, MA 02116	617-574-9267 (Fax)
	philanthropy@donovanslone.com
	www.donovanslone.com
Other offices:	
Warwick, RI	401-941-3805
Fort Oglethorpe, GA	800-370-0036

Donovan Slone has been serving not-for-profit clients since 1983 and has managed or consulted on more than 175 campaigns, raising more than $500 million. Campaign Services: Marketing, planning, and feasibility studies; capital campaign management/consultation; pre-feasibility study assistance; post-campaign counsel. Program Services: Philanthropy strategic planning; development program assessments/audits; annual program development and support; major gift program implementation and training; planned giving program start up and planning; developing a culture of philanthropy; donor relations/stewardship; prospect research; grant writing; and executive search.

Also provides services for new foundation formation and interim development services. Plus, board development, board retreats, and staff training, comprehensive communications support and case statement development.

Endowment Development Services (EDS)	317-542-9829
5546 Shorewood Drive	317-549-9470 (Fax)
Indianapolis, IN 46220	eds@pgiresources.com

EDS specializes in marketing planned giving programs. Provides promotional literature, videos, training programs and consultation. Much of their promotional materials can be personalized or customized with your organization's logo and branding.

Their newest product is Planned Giving Answers Online, an electronic reference library with easy-to-use, point-and-click design. It provides concise, highly understandable explanations of all gift plans, supplemented by charts, graphs, examples, and valuable marketing tips. Use it with development staff, volunteers, board members, and allied professionals in the estate planning community.

Estes Associates	203-393-3159
41 Spoke Drive	203-393-3857
Woodbridge, CT 06525	ellen.estes@juno.com
	www.ellenestes.com

Ellen Estes provides expert advice and counsel in the area of major and planned giving to organizations nationwide including the arts, education, religion, health care, social services and other endeavors. Provides personal hands-on consulting; board, volunteer and staff training; estate planning seminars for donors or advisors. Runs a series of one-day, basic comprehensive seminars on planned giving. Feasibility studies, audits, planning, marketing, strategizing, proposals, and helping clients build their programs.

Ford & Associates	404-897-3456
1372 Peachtree Street, NE, Suite 207	404-897-3452 (Fax)
Atlanta, GA 30309	info@fordassociates.com
	www.fordassociates.com

Other offices: Marshall. MI

Provide comprehensive development services with a special focus on independent schools in the U.S. and abroad. Services include annual giving, capital campaign direction, development office assessments, feasibility studies, general development counsel, and prospect research. Also has publications for purchase and consults on the institution's publications. Development office retreats, fund raising seminars, strategic planning, trustee development leadership, and volunteer training.

Ford Thompson Consulting	727-823-7282
P.O. Box 76011	727-823-8852 (Fax)
St. Petersburg, FL 33734	LJPauley@aol.com
	www.fordthompson.com

A national fund raising consulting firm founded in 1984. We have helped executives of charitable institutions plan, market, manage, and evaluate their development and planned giving programs. Primary emphasis is on current and deferred planned giving, we understand its integral role in the entire development effort. Services include program evaluation, planned giving audits, feasibility studies, board presentations, direct mail, planned giving consulting, and executive search.

Products include: Development Policies and Procedures Manual, Professional Enrichment Series (for financial and estate planners), Professional Notebook Series (for attorneys, financial and estate planners), Planned Giving Newsletters (for donors), and Planned Giving Brochures.

The Fund Raising School
550 W. North St., Suite 301
Indianapolis, IN 46202-3272

800-962-6692
tfrs@iupui.edu
www.philanthropy.iupui.edu

The Fund Raising School is run by Indiana University's Center on Philanthropy. For 29 years, The Fund Raising School has helped thousands of fundraising professionals around the world achieve new levels of success. At the School, we teach the historical and philanthropic context, the current issues, the art and the science of fundraising and philanthropy. You take back knowledge needed to build your organization's resources with confidence and success in an ever-changing society.

Fusco & Four
One Murdock Terrace
Brighton, MA 02135

617-787-2637
617-782-4430 (Fax)
fuscofour@aol.com

Founded in 1979 as the first full-service Marketing and Public Relations Agency in New England specializing in non-profit clients, we also provide a range of Organizational Development and Fund Raising/Campaign support services. Over 300 non-profit clients have been served. We are happy to provide a no obligation assessment of your current needs and how we might help your organization.

Annual campaigns, capacity building, change management, organizational development/assessment, program development, public relations/marketing, and strategic planning.

Future Focus
3282 Stone Valley Road
Alamo, CA 94509

800-737-3437
925-820-9238
925-855-1170 (Fax)
mail@futurefocus.net
www.futurefocus.net

Since 1997, Future Focus provides personalized web-based planned giving content for charitable organizations designed to enhance the donor/organization relationship and foster personal contact. Future Focus is affiliated with Hardisty and Hardisty—estate planning attorneys who assist in providing planned giving content and legal expertise. George Hardisty is the author of *Plan Your Estate*, now in its seventh printing. The content is personalized to your organization, pictures of your facilities and/or services populate the site, and the content is subject to your review and edit.

The Franklin Consulting Group
248 West Sheridan Avenue
Annville, PA 17003

717-867-0417
717-867-0419 (Fax)
www.franklingroup.com

Principals:
Richard F. Charles
Thomas H. Bamford, APR
Thomas R. Stone, Ph.D., CFRE

charles@FranklinGroup.com
bamford@FranklinGroup.com
stone@FranklinGroup.com

Serves cultural, educational and religious organizations in capital and annual fund raising, governing board development, organizational planning and decision-making. Strategic planning including board retreats and counseling senior staff and volunteer leadership. Comprehensive fund raising services include internal development and advancement audits, feasibility studies and campaign planning, capital campaign counsel and services, annual giving and special projects funding, endowment fund development and planned giving, donor research and development.

Gonser Gerber Tinker Stuhr, LLP
400 East Diehl Road, Suite 380
Naperville, IL 60563

630-505-1433
630-505-7710 (Fax)
ckayton@ggts.com
www.ggts.com

GGTS was the first firm specifically organized to provide a complete and comprehensive development consulting service to educational, cultural, religious, and health care organizations. Since 1950, we have helped more than 550 client institutions build comprehensive, continuing, long-term programs for obtaining greater understanding and acceptance from those publics most vital to the institutions and increased financial support for annual operations, capital growth, and long-term financial viability.

Services include advancement counsel, campaign counsel, campaign readiness study, advancement audit, strategic planning, board and volunteer development. Provides free client workshops semiannually in Chicago for top management, advancement staff, board members and volunteers.

The Greenwood Company
2351 Powell Street, Suite 505
San Francisco, CA 94133

415-837-5858
415-837-5850 (Fax)
RHG@thegreenwoodcompany.com
www.thegreenwoodcompany.com

Specializes in the design and management of comprehensive development programs and campaigns that support the capital and endowment needs of not-for-profit organizations. Founded in 1979, it operates throughout the United States. Primary services are capital and endowment campaign management, campaign planning and feasibility studies, development audits, comprehensive long range development plans, gift approach training programs, constituent education programs, case development, board development, board retreats and executive recruitment.

Grenzebach Glier & Associates, Inc.
55 West Wacker Drive, Suite 1500
Chicago, IL 60601

313-372-4040
312-372-7911 (Fax)
gga@grenzglier.com
www.grenzebachglier.com

Other offices:
London and Glasgow

GG&A is a full-service philanthropic management consulting firm with more than 40 years of experience. With a complete project and support staff headquartered in Chicago, GG&A provides counsel to many of the largest capital campaigns today, offering its services throughout the campaign effort, from the planning stages, through campaign management, to post-campaign analysis.

GG&A clients include educational, medical, cultural, and other not-for-profit organizations located throughout the United States, Canada, and Europe. Client campaigns have included significant building and endowment objectives as well as a broad range of special purpose programs and projects. Current client campaign goals total more than $18 billion.

Support and services for chief development/advancement officer, major gifts programs, corporate/foundation relations programs, the case for support, annual giving programs, planned giving, constituent-based programs, alumni relations programs, public relations/communications, fundraising progress, volunteer and institutional leadership, prospect/donor research, records, staff and volunteer training, research, and systems support functions. Electronic screening.

John J. Havens
Research Director
Social Welfare Research Institute
515 McGuinn Hall
Boston College
Chestnut Hill, MA 02478

617-552-4070
havens@bc.edu
www.bc.edu/swri

Consults on the patterns of wealth and philanthropy and on the forthcoming intergenerational transfer of wealth to financial institutions and fundraising professionals. Havens developed the microsimulation model that projected the $41 trillion transfer of wealth. He has been selected three times to the *NonProfit Times* annual "Power and Influence Top 50."

Henry & Associates	217-529-1958
Vaughn W. Henry	800-879-2098
Gift and Estate Planning	217-529-1959 (Fax)
Resources for Professionals	vwhenry@aol.com
22 Hyde Park	www.gift-estate.com
Springfield, IL 62703	

As an independent advisor to charitable organizations on planned giving, Vaughn's clients include some of the Forbes 400 and large U.S. corporations. His consultancy specializes in gifting, estate planning and wealth conservation resources to professional advisors. Since 1977, Vaughn has been a widely recognized and popular presenter to charitable groups, business owners, accountants, attorneys and financial services providers. He specializes in deferred gifting and the Economic Citizenship concept, and creative gifting for the Reluctant Donor. He helps charities learn how to develop larger gifts from difficult prospects and to work more cooperatively with donor advisors.

(Note: This web site has massive numbers of free articles, case analysis, resources, and helpful links for planned giving or estate planning professionals.)

Tom Herren & Company, Inc.	713-789-6535
4615 Post Oak Place, Suite 293	713-850-0821
Houston, TX 77027	tomhherren@aol.com
	www.tomherrencompany.com

Tom Herren & Company, Inc., has served a cross section of nonprofit charitable organizations since 1984. If your organization is contemplating a capital campaign (most often $1 million or more), we are experienced in guiding you through the planning phase and then the campaign. Also, does feasibility studies. A hallmark of the firm is Tom's personal involvement with every client. The firm provides creative problem-solving with a systematic approach, and has a proven track record.

Institute for Charitable Giving	800-234-7777
500 North Michigan Avenue, Suite 2008	312-222-9411
Chicago, IL 60611	icg@pop.net
	www.instituteforgiving.org

Runs a comprehensive range of seminars for fund raisers in many cities around the country for fund raising staff, board members, and volunteers. In order to encourage CEOs to attend, registration fees are waived for a CEO who accompanies a registrant. (cost of meals and materials required). Offers a limited number of partial scholarships. Also has many books, videos, and tapes. Seminars given by the Institute qualify for C.E. credits for CFRE status.

Ketchum, Inc.	800-242-2161
Three Gateway Center, Suite 1726	info@rsi-ketchum.com
Pittsburgh, PA 15222	www.rsi-ketchum.com

5151 Belt Line Road, Suite 900
Dallas, TX 75254

Provides varying levels of service during intensive campaigning as well as limited counsel when appropriate. Services include development audits, planning studies (to facilitate campaign planning and to determine fundraising potential), campaign management, major gift and planned gift development, board and volunteer leadership development, communications counsel, staff development, access to research, strategic and long-range development planning, annual giving programs, funding proposals and presentations to foundations and corporations, donor relations and stewardship development, post-campaign counsel.

KetchumConnection   Ketchumconnection.com

This is an online service for providing all the necessary resources to manage day-to-day tasks, as well as to develop long-range goals and objectives. The service provides small- and mid-sized non-profit organizations access to online counsel, fund raising resources and reference materials, a worldwide online community to encourage interaction with peers, access to a number of other industry resources geared specifically to development issues. The service is designed for agency executives, development directors, volunteers, and other non-profit professionals from small shops. There are several levels of service to suit even those with limited budgets.

Liebold & Associates, Inc.   410-544-3655
14 White Oak Court   414-544-4249
Severna Park, MD 21146   Linda@LieboldAssociates.com
                                                        www.lieboldassociates.com

Strategic planning, marketing, communications and team building consulting and training. Seminars, workshops and intensive coaching on leadership and management; all areas of development and fund raising, sales, and interpersonal effectiveness.

LMNOP Seminars and Publications   760-804-8058
701 Palomar Airport Road, Suite 110   888-818-8861
Carlsbad, CA 92009   info@LMNOPstuff.com
                                                        www.LMNOPstuff.com

LMNOP presents motivational keynote, half-day and full-day programs for nonprofits and their sponsors on marketing, building an endowment, creating an effective board/management team, and on gift structuring for best effect for donor and donee. It also presents a series of seminars for women on developing women leaders, creating financial success and becoming a woman philanthropist. Publications are also available on the web site. Software available includes Charitable Docs in a Box, research and document assembly software for all the planned gift vehicles, plus many other document necessities for the major gift office, such as endowment policies and agreements, investment policies and spending rules, donor advised finds, bequests, marketing and "business" plans for fundraising and much more in easy to use software format.

Marriott Consulting, Inc.   336-945-3151, ext. 314
P.O. Box 219   hankbattle@marriottinc.com
Lewisville, NC 27023   www.marriottnc.com

Marriott Consulting provides services to independent schools and churches in areas of fund raising, strategic planning, and executive search. Services include feasibility studies, grant writing, publications support, prospect research, as well as services in information technology.

Marts & Lundy, Inc.   800-526-9005
1200 Wall Street West   201-460-1660 (outside US)
Lyndhurst, NJ 07071   201-460-0680 (Fax)
                                                        info@martsandlundy.com
                                                        www.martsandlund.com

Marts & Lundy is a full-service consulting firm serving the not-for-profit community since 1926. Services include counsel on annual giving, campaigns, major gifts, and planned giving. Assessments on the advancement program, campaign planning, campaign progress, communications, gift planning, information technology, prospect research. Consulting on communications including assessments, branding, campaign, marketing, planning, and writing. Data analysis and Electronic Screening®, ePhilanthropy, feasibility studies, gift planning, governance and leadership, prospect management, and strategic planning.

MGI Fund-Raising Consulting, Inc.   800-387-9840
145 King Street West, Suite 1000   800-587-5579 (Fax)
Toronto, Ontario M5H 1J8   mgi@mgifundraising.com
        wwwmgifundraising.com

Other offices:
Minneapolis, MN   612-801-5149
Washington, DC   202-625-8370
Hilton Head, SC   843-342-9779

MGI is a full service fund-raising and communications consulting firm operating across North America. Services include philanthropic market (feasibility) studies, development program audits, prospect identification and research, volunteer identification and training, telemarketing and capital-by-phone programs, data management and computer support, management audits, strategic and long-range planning, board and leadership development, staff recruitment, evaluation and development, market research and image studies, constituent development programs, communication strategies and implementation, collateral material including direct mail and case brochures, marketing and public relations counsel.

Lynda S. Moerschbaecher   760-804-8058
701 Palomar Airport Road, Suite 110   lsm@LMNOPstuff.com
Carlsbad, CA 92009   www.LyndaM.com

Other location: 505 Montgomery Street, Fifth Floor, San Francisco, CA 94911. 415-485-2908.

Lynda S. Moerschbaecher is one of the leading attorney/consultants in the country on the philanthropic transfer of wealth, planned giving and endowments. She consults to fund raising and funds administration offices on all aspects of endowment and planned giving, and to private and supporting foundations, individuals of wealth and vendors to the charitable market. Her consulting covers areas ranging from developing a strategic plan, creating and implementing a dynamic marketing plan, identifying prospects with high likelihood of close for sophisticated gift structures, to structuring complex gifts and board/management and staff training. See also her seminar company LMNOP in this Appendix.

National Planned Giving Institute   800-249-0179
College of William and Mary   757-221-2090 (Fax)
Gabrial Galt Building, 2nd Floor   npgi@wm.edu
Dillard Complex   http://fsweb.wm.edu/npgi
P.O. Box 8795
Williamsburg, VA 12187

NPGI offers a series of eight seminars covering all aspects of gift development through major current and deferred planned giving. Seminars are open to full-time employees of not-for-profit institutions and accompanying trustees. NPGI also runs GoodWorks-L (listserv for past and present students or graduates). CEOs, CFOs, and trustees pay half price when accompanying a full-paying registrant.

Jerold Panas, Linzy & Partners   800-234-7777
500 North Michigan Avenue, Suite 2008   312-222-9411 (Fax)
Chicago, IL 60611   ideas@pop.net
        www.panaslinzy.com

Other offices: Boston, MA; Sydney and Melbourne, Australia

This is a full service firm engaged in all phases of financial development including feasibility studies, development office audits, public relations and design communications, foundation research and grants, resident campaign services, and consultation for strategic, governance, and leadership attainment. Since its founding in 1968, the firm has served over 1,600 client institutions.

Pentera, Inc.
8650 Commerce Park Place, Suite G
Indianapolis, IN 46268

317-875-0910
317-875-0912 (Fax)
info@pentera.com
www.pentera.com

Produces a wide variety of donor booklets, donor newsletters, advisor newsletters, planned giving brochures, and target mailers. Newsletters can be customized to suit the client's needs. Also, provides training seminars for beginner to advanced. Customized staff training, board presentations, and donor seminars, including document preparation when needed. Customized planned giving content for the charity's web site.

PG Calc
129 Mount Auburn Street
Cambridge, MA 02138

617-497-4970
617-497-4974 (Fax)
info@pgcalc.com
www.pgcalc.cm

PG Calc is listed in Appendix II for software, but they are also listed here for planned giving consulting. They not only sell software, they can guide you through setting up your own planned giving program. From identifying the basic resources you need to solicit planned gifts, to marketing your program to prospects, to compliance with state and federal regulations, PG Calc can guide you. One size does not fit all, so we tailor our recommendations to your objectives and resources. Their staff members have personally led successful planned giving efforts. They also have experienced planned gift administrators who can use their real life experience to teach you to keep your donors happy once the gift is closed. In addition, they have more than 17 years experience guiding the nation's leading non-profits in their planned giving efforts. Staff is available for telephone consultation, can review or provide written guidelines and resources and, if warranted, come to your facility for a site visit. Services include program assessment, gift administration implementation, gift processing assessment, planned giving web page design assessment, and planned giving web site marketing analysis.

Planned Giving Resources, Inc.
James B. Potter, Planned Giving Consultant
P.O. Box 665
Baker, LA 70704

225-774-6700
225-775-6910 (Fax)
JimBPotter@aol.com
www.pgresources.com

Overnight only: 3022 Ray Weiland Drive, Baker, LA 70714

Planned Giving Resources assists charities in starting or expanding their Planned Giving Program, with help in starting and/or improving a Charitable Gift Annuity Program, including compliance with state regulations, as well as developing, accepting, processing and managing a gift annuity fund. Help and guidance is also available in the areas of Bequest Solicitation and Wills Emphasis, Donor Cultivation, Charitable Remainder Trusts, Charitable Lead Trusts, Pooled Income Funds and Endowment Funds.

We can help with compliance of state insurance/securities laws that regulate Charitable Gift Annuity Funds by assisting in the filing for State Permits and State Notifications of annuity gift activity to the various state regulators, now required by at least 22 states, together with calculating the state mandated Required Reserve obligations and the FASB Liabilities for a charity's existing annuity agreements (and other life income plans).

(Note: This web site has enormous amounts of free information on numerous aspects of planned giving, including links to the state regulations for gift annuities for all 50 states.)

Planned Giving Design Center, LLC
10800-D Independence Point Parkway
Matthews, NC 28105

704-849-0731
704-849-2279 (Fax)
info@pgdc.net
www.pgdc.com

The PGDC is the largest online community for gift planners. The PGDC consists of a series of customized web sites that are hosted by nonprofit organizations in geographically exclusive areas throughout the U.S. The sites are designed to assist hosting organizations in cultivating relationships with professional advisors by providing the latest in up-to-date news, articles, planning and implementation tools specific to charitable gift planning. When an advisor registers on the site, they are matched by zip code with the PGDC in their local area. Once registered, members receive period email newsletters that include the latest news from Treasury, Congress and the courts affecting charitable giving, as well as timely articles on a broad spectrum of planned giving topics. The site includes a powerful search engine that makes it an invaluable research tool for advisors.

In addition to providing the largest body of content specific to gift planning on the web, the site includes discussion boards, a national directory of members, and free online gift deduction calculations.

Most importantly, membership and access to site content is free! The cost of providing the site is underwritten by hosting organizations and corporate sponsors.

(Note: The charitable gift planning content on the PGDC web site is monstrously large.)

Planned Giving Services
1910 Fairview Avenue East, Suite 102
Seattle, WA 98102

206-329-8144
206-329-8230 (Fax)
info@PlannedGivingServices.com
http://plannedgivingservices.com

Comprehensive services in all areas of planned giving for charities, donors, and their advisors in both the U.S. and Canada. Services include assisting the charity to start a new planned giving program, providing ongoing support to a planned giving program, and conducting an audit of an existing planned giving program. Specialized services include auditing your gift annuity program to ensure compliance or helping you establish a gift annuity program. Also can assist with proposals or illustrations, drafting documents, or facilitating gifts with individual donors.

Also provides presentations for staff, board and volunteer training, seminars for donors and for allied professionals. *Charitable Gift Annuities: The Complete Resource Manual* (See Appendix III).

Planned Giving Startup
P.O. Box 925
Middlebury, VT 05753

802-759-3203 (Vermont)
781-718-5629 (Massachusetts)
tomsmithw@aol.com
www.plannedgivingstartup.com

Planned Giving Startup is designed as a low-cost way for charitable organizations to add a bequest and planned giving element to their fund raising programs. We serve primarily organizations that currently do not have the personnel or financial resources to launch a complete planned giving program.

Thomas W. Smith, the principal, has 29 years of planned giving experience, including eight years as Director of Gift and Estate Planning at the California Institute of Technology in Pasadena, CA, and eleven years at the University of Vermont, in Burlington, VT.

We offer your organization a part-time skilled senior planned giving officer who can assist you in areas such as the following: development of policies and procedures; presentations to board members, staff, volunteers, and prospects; preparation of customized text for brochures and newsletters; planned gift calculations; development of a marketing plan; personal cultivation and solicitation visits; valuation and strategic planning assistance; planned giving audit; counsel for unusual or difficult planned gift opportunities; planned giving executive search.

Ravenel and Associates, Inc.
Katharine Ravenel, President
225 East Pearson Street, Suite 1203
Chicago, IL 60611

312-943-6203
312-943-6284 (Fax)
katravenel@aol.com

Specializes in comprehensive services for annual and capital campaigns and school capacity-building: board development, staff training, and creation of key institutional messages.

R&R Newkirk
8695 South Archer, Suite #10
Willow Springs, IL 60480

800-342-2375
708-839-9207 (Fax)
inquiries@rrnewkirk.com
www.rrnewkirk.com

R&R Newkirk has been providing planned gift promotional programs and training since 1967, serving more than 1,400 clients annually in all 50 states and Canada. Provides a wide variety of planned giving publications, planned giving response booklets, donor newsletters, advisors newsletter, targeted newsletters (physicians), wills program, Investment Planning and Estate Planning Home Study Courses for donors, seminars for donors and advisors, staff training (basic to advanced), and board presentations. Seminar Leader's Notebook with overhead transparencies and PowerPoint™ presentation, and donor seminar kit.

Charitable Giving Tax Service, a loose-leaf tax service with quarterly updates (see Appendix III).

Resource Development Group
P.O. Box 1115
Dublin, OH 43017

614-792-8814
617-789-9348 (Fax)
cholcombe@rdgusa.net
www.rdgusa.net

Provides comprehensive services for nonprofit organizations including pre-campaign planning and readiness, training staff, developing case statements, funding recommendations and campaign strategy. RDG implements a proven turnkey approach to developing all of the necessary logistical and administrative systems in preparation for a broad-based funding campaign. Assisting with recruiting campaign leadership, creating the campaign brochure and collateral material, creating all of the campaign correspondence, creating a master prospect list, sector funding analysis and prospect rating.

Retriever Development Counsel, LLC
Kevin Johnson, Principal
4183 SE Division Street
Portland, OR 97202

503-736-1102
info@RetrieverDevelopment.com
www.RetrieverDevelopment.com

Retriever Development Counsel specializes in 1) starting or expanding gift planning programs or campaigns; and 2) integrating gift planning into capital and endowment campaigns; 3) working collaboratively with you and your key donors to help maximize philanthropic opportunities.

Specific services include development and planned giving audits, planning studies (to facilitate endowment or capital campaign planning and to determine fundraising potential), campaign management, major gift and planned gift development, board and volunteer leadership development, staff development, strategic and long-range development planning, on-going one-on-one coaching, and training or motivating presentations to boards, staff and donors. Its primary focus is on organizations and individual clients in the western United States.

Paul G. Schervish
Professor and Director
Social Welfare Research Institute
515 McGuinn Hall
Boston College
Chestnut Hill, MA 02478

617-552-4070
paul.Schervish@bc.edu
www.bc.edu/swri

Serves financial institutions, development offices, community foundations, and fundraising organizations as a speaker and consultant on how to surface and analyze the moral biographies of wealth holders on the patterns and motivations for charitable giving, on the spirituality of financial life, and on a discernment methodology for guiding wealth holders through a self-reflective process of conscientious decision-making about their finances and philanthropy. He is co-author of *Gospels of Wealth: How the Rich Portray Their Lives*, listed in Appendix III, and has been selected four times to the *NonProfit Times* annual "Power and Influence Top 50."

Robert F. Sharpe & Company, Inc.	800-238-3253
6401 Poplar Avenue, Suite 700	901-680-5300
Memphis, TN 38119	901-761-4268 (Fax)
	infor@rfsco.com
	www.rfsco.com

2303 Haddon Place	301-352-4002
Bowie, MD 20716	301-352-4003 (Fax)
	d-c@rfsco.com

Since 1963, communicating estate and gift planning ideas to the people who support education, social services, health care, the arts and many more charitable endeavors. Services include a wide variety of donor publications, booklets for donors and advisors, planned giving newsletters, and planned giving brochures. Runs many training seminars for development officers in beginner, intermediate, and advanced planned giving.

Newsletter, *Give and Take*, free on e-mail or $89 by U.S. mail. Free to clients.

Sinclair, Townes & Company	770-988-8111
Building 19, 670 Village Trace	770-988-8665 (Fax)
Atlanta, GA 30067	info@sinclairtownes.com
	www.sinclairtownes.com
Mailing address:	
P.O. Box 2816, Atlanta, GA 30358	

Since 1980, provides comprehensive fund raising consulting services for non-profit organizations. Services include capital campaign counsel, feasibility studies, planned giving consulting, annual giving consulting, membership programs, board development, program assessments, executive search, board retreats, prospect research, multi-media case development, and internal readiness assessments. Also provides fund raising publications and products—such as planned giving brochures, planned giving newsletters, year-end giving publications, and fund raising deskbooks—for the benefit of donors, prospective donors, and fund raising professionals. Seminars for professional and volunteer fund raisers, donors, and prospective donors.

Social Welfare Research Institute	617-552-4070
515 McGuinn Hall	swri508@bc.edu
Boston College	www.bc.edu/swri
Chestnut Hill, MA 02478	

The Social Welfare Research Institute (SWRI) is a recognized authority on the meaning and motivations of philanthropy, the spiritual underpinnings of financial life, the patterns and trends in individual charitable giving, philanthropy of wealth holders, and the forthcoming $41 trillion wealth transfer. SWRI designs and carries out survey and interview research on the trends, motivations, and meanings of charitable giving, especially among wealth holders. It provides workshops, seminars, presentations and published research on a donor-centered approach to fundraising and financial planning.

Susan D. Smith	315-896-8524
Consultant in Philanthropy	315-896-9869 (Fax)
8466 Old Poland Road	suefish@borg.com
Barneveld, NY 13304	

Susan D. Smith has been involved with nonprofit organizations for over 29 years. She has worked with a variety of nonprofit groups and organizations handling everything from marketing communications and public relations to fund development, grant making and nonprofit management. Provides services to nonprofit organizations that encompass board training and governance, strategic planning, fund development, and nonprofit administration.

Winton Smith and Associates
2670 Union Extended, Suite 1200
Memphis, TN 38112

800-727-1040
901-327-5875 (Fax)
wsa@wintonsmith.com
www.wintonsmith.com

Combining practical development experience and legal expertise in tax law, Winton Smith & Associates offers services to help charitable organizations establish and improve planned giving programs, build endowments through planned gifts, and help donors give more than they ever dreamed possible to charitable organizations. Services include intensive planned giving training workshops; seminars for donors, professional advisors, planned giving officers, or board members; consulting to charities wishing to develop or enhance a planned giving program; personal visits with prospects; proposal preparation; specimen agreements to assist the donor's counsel; and telephone consultation. Also provides planned giving brochures, booklets and newsletters for donors or advisors.

StaleyRobeson
733 Summer Street, Suite 204
Stamford, CT 06901

800-659-7247
203-358-9262 (Fax)
uwin@staleyrobeson.com
www.staleyrobeson.com

Serving a diverse client base since 1976 including independent schools, health care, arts, higher education, and many others. Services include annual giving, comprehensive campaign counsel, feasibility studies, special young alumni/ae giving program, and *The Navigator*, a free set of online articles on current fund raising issues and responses to client questions.

The Stelter Company
10435 New York Avenue
DeMoines, IA 50322

800-331-6881
515-278-5851 (Fax)
larry@stelter.com
www.stelter.com

The Stelter Company is a leading publisher of planned giving direct mail marketing programs, currently serving more than 1,500 clients nationally, with a staff of 55 individuals. A seven-person field staff conducts face-to-face, on-site marketing consultations with clients and prospects. Stelter products include high-quality, custom-designed newsletters, targeted newsletters (women, seniors, physicians, church endowment, professional advisors), an interactive WEB product for planned giving, as well as its unique Relationship Building Workshop, training for development professionals held in several cities or on-site for staff development. To complete their full-service objective, Stelter also offers donor research, testimonial writing service, mail processing and an on-site printing facility.

A Strategic Alliance of
Planned Giving Consultants

www.giftplanners.com

Kathryn W. Miree & Associates, Inc.
P.O. Box 130846
Birmingham, AL 35213
205-939-0003
205-939-3781 (Fax)
kwmiree@giftplanners.com

Davidson Gift Design
3940 Walcott Lane
Blooming, IN 47404
812-876-8646
812-876-9484 (Fax)
pjdavidson@giftplanners.com

Mangone & Company
12687 West Cedar Drive, Suite 210
Lakewood, CO 80228
303-980-0800
303-980-9158 (Fax)
bamangone@giftplanners.com

Wilson & Krause
3224 Basil Court
Dallas, TX 75204
214-823-8729
214-824-8409 (Fax)
cwkrause@giftplanners.com

A Strategic Alliance is an informal coalition of four independent planned giving consulting firms: Davidson Gift Design, Mangone & Company, Kathryn W. Miree & Associates, Inc. and Wilson & Krause. The consultants are colleagues who work independently—and sometimes collaboratively—to serve a client base comprised of local, regional and national nonprofits. These working relationships bring additional professional resources to each firm's clients and allow the companies to leverage their marketing dollars.

The firms provide a full range of planned giving consulting services including audits/readiness assessment; planned giving program design and implementation; charitable gift annuity program advice and design, gift design, computations and illustrations; board, staff and volunteer training; motivational seminars for donors and prospects; professional advisor seminars; endowment building; new and existing planned giving program support.

Other services include:
Office Personnel Analysis and Team Building (Wilson & Krause)
Planned Giving Printed Materials/Web site Design Concept and Text (Mangone)
Private Foundations Support and Gift/Grant Programs (Mangone, Miree)
Planned Giving Job Search (Davidson, Miree, Wilson & Krause)

Strategic Fundraising Consultants   401-274-3863
J. Richard Ely, Jr., President   401-274-3194 (Fax)
86 Lorraine Avenue   info@planned-giving.com
Providence, RI 02096   www.planned-giving.com

Comprehensive services to start and revitalize planned giving and major gifts programs: marketing, policies, training, closing gifts with donors and advisors. Specializes in capital campaigns, endowment development, planned giving and major gifts.

Taxwise Giving &   800-243-9122
Philanthropy Tax Institute   203-637-4572 (Fax)
13 Arcadia Road   info@taxwisegiving.com
Old Greenwich, CT 06870   www.taxwisegiving.com

Taxwise Giving: Monthly tax newsletters (*Taxwise Giving*) and textbooks for development officers and professional advisors. See Appendix III for listings of books and loose-leaf tax services. Donor newsletter (*Amicus*). Philanthropy Tax Institute: Planned giving seminars for development officers, professional advisors, volunteers, and board members. Numerous donor booklets and brochures.

VirtualGiving, Inc.   610-631-8913
133 Commons Court   610-631-8915 (Fax)
Chadds Ford, PA 19317   info@virtualgiving.com
                                               www.virtualgiving.com

VirtualGiving has one prime goal: To help planned giving programs close more and larger gifts faster and easier. We do this by harnessing the power of the Internet through our turnkey planned giving web sites.

VirtualGiving offers several web site levels for different needs and budgets. Designed by our team of planned giving experts, Web designers, marketing specialists, content developers and others, VirtualGiving web sites are customized to reflect each client's program and gift plans.

But VirtualGiving offers more than just web sites: We offer a robust, Web-centric approach to marketing that minimizes expense while maximizing response. This frees our clients to focus on what they do best: Raise money. VirtualGiving gives development offices a critical advantage in today's highly competitive fundraising industry.

Among others, VirtualGiving clients include Williams, Oberlin and Macalaster colleges, as well as World Vision, the Smithsonian, Phillips Exeter, The Philadelphia Zoo and Wycliffe of Canada.

Howard Walker & Associates
11529 Wild Hawthorn Court
Reston, VA 20194

703-787-8525
703-787-7587 (Fax)
vhowardwalker@aol.com
www.howardwalker.com

Provides full fund raising service to independent schools, including annual, capital and planned giving counsel, board retreats, development audits, strategic planning and feasibility studies. Also facilitates board retreats, computer consultation and training, communications audit, development office retreats, and solicitor training.

Young-Preston Associates, Inc.
P.O. Box 280
Cloverdale, VA 24077

800-344-5701
540-966-4905 (Fax)
info@youngpreston.com
www.youngpreston.com

Provides a wide range of services to nonprofit organizations. Personal and professional development and relationships for board, staff, and administration; staff team development; personal and professional development; relationship building between the organization, staff, volunteers, prospects and donors; development program audits; strategic planning; feasibility studies; capital campaigns including case statement, campaign plan, prospect identification, volunteer recruitment, training and prospect pairing, day-to-day management; seminars, workshops, and talks; on-site seminars and retreats; planned giving copy on disk; print-on-demand booklets; planned giving content for web site or newsletter; inspirational photo art, note cards, and posters for donors.

Appendix V

SPECIMEN AGREEMENTS

Following are sample specimen agreements so that you can see what a typical gift document looks like. As I cautioned you in the Introduction to Part IV, do not use these agreements. Don't send them to a donor or to a donor's attorney. They are legally correct, but they are intended only as samples. Each donor or situation deserves his or her own attorney to craft the document required under applicable federal and state law.

SAMPLE INTERVIVOS CHARITABLE REMAINDER UNITRUST

THE *(TRUST NAME)*
CHARITABLE REMAINDER UNITRUST

This TRUST AGREEMENT is made and is effective on this _____ day of *(MONTH)*, *(YEAR)*, by and between *(DONOR)*, residing at *(DONOR'S ADDRESS)*, as the Donor and *(TRUSTEE)*, located/residing at *(TRUSTEE'S ADDRESS)*, and its successor(s), as the Trustee.

I.
AGREEMENT OF TRUST

The Donor is irrevocably assigning, transferring and delivering on the date hereof to the Trustee all right, title and interest in and to the property described in Exhibit A, a copy of which is attached hereto and specifically made a part hereof by this reference. The Trustee hereby accepts such irrevocable gift and agrees to hold, administer and distribute such property, together with any other property which is or shall become an asset of this Trust, in accordance with the provisions of the Trust Agreement. The Trust Agreement is intended to create a charitable remainder unitrust within the meaning of Revenue Procedure 89-20 and Section 664(d)(2) of the Code. Certain terms throughout this Trust Agreement are defined in Article XII.

II.
DISTRIBUTIONS

A. <u>Income and Principal</u>. During the Unitrust Period, the Trustee shall distribute the income and principal of this Trust as follows:

1. In each taxable year of this Trust, the Trustee shall pay the Unitrust Amount to *(RECIPIENT)* during the Unitrust Period.

2. The Unitrust Amount shall mean an amount equal to *(FMV PERCENT)* percent (*(FMV PERCENT)*%) of the Net Fair Market Value of the Trust Assets, as modified by Paragraphs C and D of this Article II.

3. The Unitrust Amount shall be paid in equal installments at the end of each calendar quarter of each taxable year of this Trust from Net Income, and to the extent Net Income is insufficient, from principal. Any Net Income in excess of the Unitrust Amount shall be added to principal. Notwithstanding any existing or hereafter enacted state law, no amount other than the Unitrust Amount may be paid to or for the use of any person or entity other than a Charitable Organization. However, an amount shall not be deemed to be paid to or for the use of any person other than a Charitable Organization if the amount is transferred for full and adequate consideration.

4. The Trustee may pay the Unitrust Amount to the Recipient by payment directly to him or her or by deposit in any bank designated by him or her. If the Recipient should at any time be under a Disability, the Trustee may pay the Unitrust Amount to the Custodian. Any such payment for the benefit of the Recipient shall release the Trustee from its obligation to pay the Unitrust Amount, and the Trustee shall have no duty to supervise or inquire into the application of any funds so paid.

5. Upon the expiration of the Unitrust Period, the Trustee shall distribute the then principal and income of this Trust in accordance with Article III herein.

B. <u>Valuation Date</u>. The Net Fair Market Value of the Trust Assets shall be determined annually on the first day of each taxable year of this Trust (including any short taxable year), in accordance with the provisions of Paragraph E of this Article II.

C. <u>Taxable Year and Short Taxable Years</u>. The first taxable year of this Trust shall commence on the date this Trust is first funded and shall end on December 31st of that year. Subsequent taxable years shall be on a calendar year basis, except that the last taxable year of this Trust shall end on the date that this Trust terminates pursuant to Article III herein. In the case of a taxable year which is for a period of less than twelve (12) months (other than the taxable year in which the Unitrust Period ends), the amount described in Paragraph A.2 of this Article II shall be such amount multiplied by a fraction the numerator of which is the number of days in the taxable year of this Trust and the denominator of which is 365 (366 if February 29 is a day included in the numerator). In the case of the taxable year in which the Unitrust Period ends, the amount described in Paragraph A.2 of this Article II shall be such amount multiplied by a fraction the numerator of which is the number of days in the period beginning on the first day of such taxable year and ending on the date the Unitrust Period ends and the denominator of which is 365 (366 if February 29 is a day included in the numerator). Notwithstanding the foregoing, the obligation of the Trustee to pay the Unitrust Amount shall terminate with the regular periodic payment next preceding the date the Unitrust Period ends.

D. <u>Additional Contributions</u>. Any person may contribute property to this Trust, with the consent of the Trustee, either during life or at death. For the taxable year of this Trust in which any additional contribution is made, the additional property shall be valued at the time of contribution and in accordance with Paragraph E of this Article II, and the amount described in Paragraph A.2 of this Article II shall be *(FMV PERCENT)* percent (*(FMV PERCENT)*%) of the sum of the following components:

1. The Net Fair Market Value of the Trust Assets determined on the first day of the taxable year (and thus excluding the value of the additional property, and earned income from, and any appreciation on, such property after its contribution); and

2. That proportion of the value of the additional property (that was excluded under Paragraph D.1 of this Article II immediately above) which the number of days in the period that begins with the date of contribution and ends with the earlier of the last day of such taxable year or the date the Unitrust Period ends bears to the number of days in the period that begins on the first day of such taxable year and ends with the earlier of the last day of such taxable year or the date the Unitrust Period ends.

If an additional contribution is made by Will, the obligation to pay the Unitrust Amount payable with respect to the additional contribution shall commence with the date of death of the person under whose Will the additional contribution is made. Payment of that portion of the Unitrust Amount may be deferred, however, from such date of death to the end of the taxable year in which occurs the complete funding of the additional contribution. Within a reasonable time following such complete funding of the additional contribution, the Trustee shall pay to the Recipient, in the case of an underpayment, or receive from the Recipient, in the case of an overpayment, the difference between: (i) the Unitrust Amount with respect to such additional contribution actually paid to the Recipient, plus interest on such amounts, compounded annually, computed for any period at the rate of interest that the Regulations under Section 664 of the Code prescribe for this Trust for such computation for such period; and (ii) the Unitrust Amount with respect to such additional contribution payable, determined under the method described in Section 1.664-1(a)(5)(ii) of the Regulations. Any payments required to be made because of an underpayment shall be paid to the Recipient (or such Recipient's estate) who received the underpayment. Any repayments required to be made because of an overpayment shall be repaid by the Recipient (or such Recipient's estate) who received the overpayment.

E. _Fair Market Value._ The Trustee shall compute the Net Fair Market Value of the Trust Assets considering all assets and liabilities without regard to whether particular items are taken into account in determining the Net Income; provided, however, in the event an Unmarketable Asset is transferred to or held by this Trust, and whenever this Trust is required to value such asset, the valuation shall be either performed exclusively by an Independent Special Trustee or determined by a current qualified appraisal, as defined in Regulation Section 1.170A-13(c)(3), from a qualified appraiser, as defined in Regulation Section 1.170A-13(c)(5). All determinations of the Net Fair Market Value of the Trust Assets shall be in accordance with generally accepted fiduciary accounting principles and any United States Treasury requirements governing charitable remainder unitrusts. In any conflict, Treasury requirements shall prevail over generally accepted fiduciary accounting principles and any inconsistent provisions of this Trust Agreement. In the event that the Net Fair Market Value of the Trust Assets is determined incorrectly for any taxable year, the Trustee shall pay to the Recipient or the Recipient's estate (in the case of an undervaluation), or be repaid by the Recipient or the Recipient's estate (in the case of an overvaluation), an amount equal to the difference between the Unitrust Amount which the Trustee should have paid to the Recipient if the correct values were used, and the Unitrust Amount which the Trustee actually paid to the Recipient. Such payments or repayments shall be made within a reasonable period after the final determination of the correct value.

III.
TERMINATION

This Trust shall terminate within a reasonable time after the expiration of the Unitrust Period; provided, however, that such reasonable time shall not extend beyond the last day of the month in which occurs the ninetieth (90th) day following the date the Unitrust Period ends. Upon termination, the Trustee shall distribute all of the then principal and income of this Trust, free of trust, other than any amount due to the Recipient or the Recipient's estate, to _(REMAINDERMAN)_.

Notwithstanding any contrary provision of the Trust Agreement, prior to the expiration of the Unitrust Period, the Donor shall retain the right, by acknowledged written instrument delivered to the Trustee, to change the Donee by adding or substituting new Charitable Organization(s) and/or omitting certain Charitable Organization(s) or by altering the share each is to receive. If more than one written instrument is so delivered to the Trustee, the written instrument bearing the latest date shall control and shall be deemed to revoke all prior written instruments unless the most recent one shall provide otherwise.

If any Donee is not a Charitable Organization at the time when any principal or income of this Trust is to be distributed to it, the Trustee shall distribute such principal or income in proportion to the relative shares of the Donees which are so described and, if none of the Donees is so described, to one or more Charitable Organizations as the Trustee shall select and in such shares as it shall determine.

IV.
FIDUCIARY PROVISIONS

A. _Appointment of Trustee._ _(TRUSTEE)_ shall serve as Trustee of this Trust. In the event that _(TRUSTEE)_ for any reason shall fail to serve as Trustee, then _(ALTERNATE TRUSTEE)_ shall serve in the place and stead of _(TRUSTEE)_.

B. _Appointment of Independent Special Trustee._

1. In the event an Unmarketable Asset is transferred to or held by this Trust, an Independent Special Trustee may be appointed by the Trustee. If so appointed, the Independent Special Trustee shall exclusively determine the fair market value of each Unmarketable Asset in accordance with such appointment.

2. The Trustee shall also have the right and option to appoint an Independent Special Trustee to take such action as the Trustee shall clearly define and delegate.

3. When (i) the sole Trustee is an Independent Trustee or (ii) more than one person is acting as Trustee hereunder and one of such Trustees is an Independent Trustee, such Independent Trustee shall

have the right and option to act as an Independent Special Trustee hereunder. However, no Trustee (other than an acting Independent Special Trustee) shall have any power, duty or liability hereunder with respect to matters described in this Paragraph B.

4. The Independent Special Trustee shall have no powers, duties, or liabilities hereunder, except with respect to matters specifically described in this Paragraph B, and solely with respect to such matters, the Independent Special Trustee may exercise the rights, powers, authority and discretion, and be subject to the restrictions, obligations and duties, accorded to a Trustee pursuant to Article V herein. However, the Independent Special Trustee may not function in a manner which would jeopardize the status of this Trust as a charitable remainder trust as defined in Section 664 of the Code, the Regulations thereunder and Internal Revenue Service rulings governing the operation thereof.

C. <u>Resignation of Fiduciary</u>. Any Fiduciary may resign at any time by giving a notice to any other Fiduciary and to the Recipient, or if the Recipient is Disabled, to the Custodian. Such resignation shall be effective upon the sooner to occur of: (i) sixty (60) days after the date of the notice of resignation, or (ii) the appointment of and acceptance by the successor Fiduciary. Notwithstanding the above, in the event (i) a Fiduciary dies or is Disabled or (ii) an Independent Special Trustee ceases to be an Independent Trustee, notice of resignation is deemed given, and the resignation shall be effective as of the date of such death, Disability or ceasing to be an Independent Trustee, as the case may be. The resigning Fiduciary (or its representative) shall file a final accounting and deliver all Trust assets under its charge and control to the successor Fiduciary as soon as possible, but in no event later than sixty (60) days following the date of the resignation notice being given or deemed given. Upon the relinquishment and delivery of all Trust assets and the final accounting to the successor Fiduciary, the resigning Fiduciary shall be discharged of all further duties and obligations hereunder.

D. <u>Removal of Fiduciary</u>. The Recipient shall have the right, with or without cause, to replace or discharge any acting Fiduciary. Upon the Disability of the Recipient, this right may be exercised by the Custodian. Such removal shall be effective upon the sooner to occur of: (i) sixty (60) days after giving the Fiduciary being removed notice of such removal, or (ii) the appointment of and acceptance by the successor Fiduciary. The Fiduciary being removed shall file a final accounting and deliver all Trust assets under its charge and control to the successor Fiduciary within such sixty (60) day period. Upon the relinquishment and delivery of all Trust assets and the final accounting to the successor Fiduciary, the Fiduciary being removed shall be discharged of all further duties and obligations hereunder.

E. <u>Appointment of Successor Fiduciary</u>. In the event any vacancy at any time occurs in the office of a Fiduciary hereunder, regardless of how caused, the Recipient shall have the right to fill such vacancy. Upon the Disability of the Recipient, the Custodian shall exercise such right. At the earliest possible date, all Trust assets and a final accounting shall be delivered to the successor Fiduciary. At such time as any successor Fiduciary delivers notice of acceptance to the Recipient, such successor Fiduciary shall have the rights, powers, authority and discretion, and be subject to the restrictions, obligations and duties, regarding this Trust within the appointed capacity.

F. <u>Liability of Successor Fiduciary</u>. A successor Fiduciary shall not be responsible to any beneficiary of this Trust or to this Trust for any act or omission of a former Fiduciary, and shall not be required to audit or investigate the acts or administration of any former Fiduciary and shall be charged, upon issuing a simple receipt, with only the Trust assets so received. In addition, unless requested in writing by a beneficiary of this Trust and indemnified adequately (in such Fiduciary's discretion therefor), no successor Fiduciary shall have any duty to take action to seek redress for breach of trust by a former Fiduciary.

G. <u>Appointment of Co-Fiduciary</u>. The Recipient shall have the right to appoint additional persons to act as Co-Fiduciaries hereunder. At such time as the newly-appointed Co-Fiduciary delivers notice of acceptance to the Recipient, the newly-appointed Co-Fiduciary shall have the rights, powers, authority and discretion, and be subject to the restrictions, obligations and duties, regarding this Trust within the appointed capacity. In granting the foregoing right, it is not the intention of the Donor to require that any specific number of Fiduciaries serve in any one capacity hereunder simultaneously.

H. <u>Want of Trustee</u>. If at any time for any reason this Trust shall be without a Trustee, *(CORPORATE TRUSTEE)* shall be and become the Trustee.

I. _Fiduciary Actions._ When more than two persons are acting as Trustees (or Independent Special Trustees), the concurrence and joinder of a majority of them shall control in all matters pertaining to the administration hereunder. When two persons are acting as Trustees (or Independent Special Trustees), the concurrence and joinder of both Trustees (or Independent Special Trustees) shall be required. Such actions by the Fiduciaries shall be made either by vote at a meeting (in person or by telephone) or by written concurrence. When more than two persons are acting as Trustees (or Independent Special Trustees), any dissenting or abstaining Fiduciary may be absolved from personal liability by registering a written dissent or abstention with the records of this Trust. Such dissenting Fiduciary shall thereafter act with the other Fiduciaries in any manner necessary or appropriate to effectuate the decision of the majority.

J. _Compensation._ A Fiduciary, and any agents of or successors to any Fiduciary, shall be entitled to reasonable compensation for services rendered in connection with this Trust. The amount of compensation shall be an amount equal to the customary and prevailing charges for services of a similar nature during the same period of time and in the same geographic locale. Any Fiduciary may waive any compensation at any time, by providing notice of such waiver to the Recipient and another Fiduciary, if then serving.

K. _Retention of Agents._ A Fiduciary may delegate investment and management functions to an agent as is prudent under the circumstances, but shall exercise reasonable care in selecting such agent. The duties of the agent shall be consistent with the terms and intent of this Trust, and the Fiduciary shall periodically review the agent's performance.

L. _Liability for Retaining Property._ The Fiduciary shall not be liable for any loss or depreciation in value sustained by this Trust as a result of the Fiduciary accepting or retaining any property upon which hazardous materials or substances are discovered, unless the Fiduciary contributed to the loss or depreciation in value through willful default, willful misconduct or gross negligence.

M. _Indemnification._ The Donor shall indemnify the Fiduciary against any claims (except for claims due to the Fiduciary's willful default, willful misconduct or gross negligence) filed against the Fiduciary (i) as an "owner" or "operator" under the federal Comprehensive Environmental Response, Compensation and Liability Act of 1980 (as from time to time amended) or any regulation thereunder and (ii) under any other federal, state or local environmental law, rule, regulation or order relating to the property contributed to this Trust by the Donor.

N. _Jurisdiction and Bond._ This Trust shall not be administered under the jurisdiction of any court. Should a question or issue be submitted to a court of competent jurisdiction at any time or from time to time, such court shall acquire jurisdiction of only the question or issue submitted to it, and the jurisdiction of such court shall terminate upon the conclusion or settlement of such question or issue. No bond or other security shall be required of any person acting as a Fiduciary, whether serving jointly or alone.

V.
POWERS OF THE TRUSTEE

All rights, powers, authority and discretion exercisable by the Trustee under this Trust or by law shall be binding and conclusive on all interested parties; shall be exercisable by the Trustee in its sole and absolute discretion; shall be exercisable only in a fiduciary capacity and in the best interests of the beneficiaries; shall be construed in the broadest possible manner; and shall be exercisable without prior or subsequent application to any court under the jurisdiction of which this Trust may be administered.

The Trustee is under a duty to the beneficiaries to invest and manage the funds of the Trust as a prudent investor would, in a manner that is fair to all beneficiaries as a reflection of the Trust's purposes, terms, and obligations and in light of the circumstances of the Trust and the relevant circumstances of its beneficiaries. The investment decisions of a Trustee shall be evaluated not in isolation, but in the context of the investment portfolio as a whole and as part of an overall investment strategy reasonably suited to the Trust.

Not in derogation of or in limitation upon the powers, authority and discretion conferred by law upon a trustee, the Trustee is vested with the following rights, powers, authority and discretion:

A. To alter, repair, improve, erect buildings upon, demolish, manage, partition, mortgage, lease for any period, including a period in excess of any fixed by statute or extending beyond the duration of this Trust, exchange, grant options to lease or to buy, and sell or dispose of, at public or private sale, and upon such conditions and such terms as to cash and credit as it deems advisable, any of the Trust assets;

B. To compromise, settle, subordinate, arbitrate, extend, renew, modify, or release, in whole or in part, any claim held by it or held against any of the Trust assets;

C. To continue to hold the property transferred to it hereunder in the form in which it shall be when transferred or as the form thereof may be changed pursuant to the other provisions of the Trust Agreement, without regard to the limitations imposed by law upon the investment of trust funds;

D. To borrow money and to encumber or hypothecate Trust assets whether by mortgage, deed of trust, pledge or otherwise;

E. To commence or defend litigation with respect to the Trust assets, at the expense of the Trust assets;

F. To employ any person, firm, corporation, bank, or trust company for advice with respect to investment policy or any other matter; but the Trustee may follow or refrain from following any recommendation so obtained and such recommendations shall not in any way limit the discretionary power and authority conferred upon the Trustee hereunder with respect to investments or other matters;

G. To retain or discharge accountants, attorneys, administrators, brokers, investment advisers, investment counselors and other agents, and to pay reasonable compensation for their services;

H. To enter into any and all agreements with the Internal Revenue Service or any other governmental body and to execute, from time to time, any declarations of policy or disclaimers restricting the powers, authority and discretion granted to the Trustee;

I. To invest and to reinvest the Trust assets in every kind of property, real, personal or mixed, and every kind of investment; and nothing in the Trust Agreement shall be construed to restrict the Trustee from investing the Trust assets in a manner which could result in the annual realization of a reasonable amount of income or gain from the sale or disposition of Trust assets;

J. With respect to any investment held by the Trustee, to participate in and consent to any corporate or financial reorganization, dissolution, liquidation, merger, consolidation, sale or lease, or in and to any other change in its financial structure; and to become a depositor with any protective, reorganization, or similar committee, and to make any necessary payments incident to the foregoing; to organize or participate in the organization of corporations or other business entities, and to transfer to them any part or all of the Trust assets in exchange for an investment therein; to exercise or to sell any conversion, subscription, or similar rights; and in general to exercise in respect to any investment the unrestricted rights of a personal owner, including voting in person and granting proxies, discretionary, general, or otherwise;

K. In any case in which the Trustee makes any payments or other distribution of Trust assets, to make such payment or distribution in money or in kind, including undivided interests in any property, or partly in money and partly in kind; and in the case of any distribution in kind to any Donee, the adjusted basis of the Trust property distributed shall be fairly representative of the adjusted bases of all Trust properties available for distribution on the date of distribution;

L. To apportion and allocate Trust receipts and expenses between Net Income and principal accounts (provided that no pre-gift appreciation shall be allocable to Net Income);

M. To retain the services of an independent appraiser to assist in valuing assets of this Trust and to reasonably compensate such appraiser for such services;

N. If required by the Code, the Regulations or any Internal Revenue Service rulings thereunder to maintain the status of the Trust as a charitable remainder unitrust, to set aside a reserve or allowance from Trust income for the depreciation or depletion of any property transferred to or invested in by the Trust; otherwise, the Trustee shall have discretion whether or not to set aside such a reserve;

O. With respect to any environmental hazards on Trust property:

1. To take all appropriate actions to prevent, identify or respond to actual or threatened violations of any environmental law, rule or regulation, including compliance with any federal, state or local agency or court order directing an assessment, abatement or cleanup of any environmental hazard;

2. To disclaim, in whole or in part, any interests in property for any reason, including but not limited to, a concern that such property could cause potential liability under any federal, state, or local environmental law, rule or regulation; and/or

3. To set aside any interests in property, which could cause potential liability under any federal, state, or local environmental law, rule or regulation as a separate trust to be held and administered upon the same terms as those governing the remaining Trust assets;

P. To designate as custodian of any Trust property any business entity authorized and engaged in the business of brokers or dealers in securities;

Q. To the extent permitted by law, to register any of such property in its name as Trustee or in the names of nominees, or to take and keep the same unregistered or in bearer form, or in such condition as to pass by delivery; and/or

R. Whenever the Trust acquires an Annuity Contract, to exercise with respect to such Annuity Contract any rights and discretion as owner thereof, as limited hereby, including but not limited to the right or discretion to:

1. Making partial or total withdrawals or surrenders from the Annuity Contract; provided however, the Trustee gives due regard to any withdrawal or partial surrender penalties that may be imposed and to the best interest of all Trust beneficiaries;

2. Electing any annuity option(s) which guarantees the payment to the Trust by or upon the death of the annuitant of an amount at least equal to the surrender value of the Annuity Contract(s) as of the day before the day the annuity payments commence;

3. Designating the day the annuity payments commence; and/or

4. Seeing to the allocation of any payments of any type received from the Annuity Contract between principal and income as is required by this Trust.

Anything in the Trust Agreement to the contrary notwithstanding, it is the intention of the Donor to create a qualifying charitable remainder unitrust under Section 664 of the Code; therefore, no rights, powers, authority or discretion either otherwise granted by the Trust Agreement or by applicable state law that exceed or are inconsistent with those allowed under Section 664 of the Code and the Regulations thereunder are to be possessed or exercised by the Trustee. At no time and under no circumstances shall a Donor serving as a Trustee exercise any power that would result in this Trust being treated as a grantor trust under Subpart E of the Code.

VI.
APPLICABLE LAW

The validity of this Trust shall be controlled by the laws of the State of *(STATE LAW)* The construction and administration of this Trust shall be controlled by the laws of the State of *(STATE LAW)*. However, in any conflict with Section 664 of the Code, the Regulations thereunder or any other existing or hereafter promulgated legislative or Treasury requirements for the qualification of this Trust and for the Donor's obtaining the full benefit of any income, gift and estate tax charitable deductions to which the Donor (and the Donor's estate) may be entitled, Section 664 of the Code, the Regulations thereunder and the legislative and Treasury requirements shall govern.

VII.
IRREVOCABILITY AND AMENDMENT

This Trust shall be irrevocable. However, the Trustee shall have the power, acting alone, to amend the Trust Agreement in any manner required for the sole purpose of ensuring that this Trust qualifies and continues to qualify as a charitable remainder unitrust within the meaning of Section 664 of the Code and the Regulations thereunder.

VIII.
PROHIBITED ACTS

Notwithstanding any other provision of the Trust Agreement, no Fiduciary shall (except for the payment of the Unitrust Amount) engage in any act of self-dealing (as defined in Section 4941(d) of the Code), retain any excess business holdings (as defined in Section 4943(c) of the Code) which would subject this Trust to tax under Section 4943 of the Code, make any investments which would subject this Trust to tax under Section 4944 of the Code, or make any taxable expenditure (as defined in Section 4945(d) of the Code). If Section 4942 of the Code is deemed applicable to this Trust by reason of Section 508(e) of the Code or otherwise, then the Trustee shall make distributions at such times and in such manner as not to subject this Trust to tax under Section 4942 of the Code.

IX.
INTENTION TO CREATE UNITRUST

It is the Donor's intention to obtain the full benefit of any income, gift and estate tax charitable contribution deductions to which the Donor (and the Donor's estate) may be entitled to under the Code and for this Trust to qualify as a charitable remainder unitrust within the meaning of Section 664(d)(2) of the Code and the Regulations thereunder. Accordingly, the Trust Agreement shall be interpreted and administered, and the Trust assets shall be valued, managed and invested, in a manner consistent with the Donor's intent and the provisions of such Section, the Regulations thereunder and the Internal Revenue Service rulings relating thereto.

X.
DEATH TAXES

No Death Taxes with respect to this Trust shall be allocated to or be recoverable from this Trust. The Donor agrees to provide in the Donor's Will, or any other appropriate estate planning documents, that any Death Taxes arising from the creation of this Trust, or the interest of the Donor therein, shall be payable from the estate of the Donor, excluding the assets of this Trust. The Donor hereby imposes an affirmative obligation on the Donor's estate to pay all of such Death Taxes (if any) from sources other than this Trust and agrees that this obligation may be enforced by the Trustee or any Donee, acting alone or together. Should Death Taxes with respect to this Trust become due as a result of additional contributions by any person other than the Donor, then the provisions of this Article X shall apply to such other person as if the other person were the Donor for purposes of this Article X.

XI.
MISCELLANEOUS

A. <u>Construction</u>. Unless the context requires otherwise, words in the singular may be construed as denoting the plural, and words in the plural may be construed as denoting the singular. Words of one gender may be construed as denoting another gender as is appropriate within such context.

B. <u>Headings</u>. Titles and headings in the Trust Agreement are added for convenient reference, and shall not be deemed to alter or affect the meaning of any provision hereof.

C. <u>Severability</u>. If any provision or part of any provision of the Trust Agreement shall for any reason be held invalid, illegal or unenforceable in any respect by a court of competent jurisdiction, such invalidity, illegality or unenforceability shall not affect any other provision of the Trust Agreement and the Trust Agreement shall be construed as if such invalid, illegal or unenforceable provision or part thereof had never been contained herein, but only to the extent of its invalidity, illegality or unenforceability.

D. <u>Counterparts</u>. The Trust Agreement has been executed in triplicate, each of which shall be an original and each of which shall constitute the entire Trust Agreement without reference to or the necessity of producing the other counterparts.

E. <u>Spendthrift</u>. The Recipient shall not have any power to sell, transfer, assign, pledge, mortgage, or alienate all or any part of the Recipient's beneficial interest in this Trust in any manner whatsoever. The interest of the Recipient shall not be subject to the claims of the Recipient's creditors or to attachment, execution, bankruptcy proceedings or any other legal process.

XII.
DEFINITIONS

For purposes of the Trust Agreement, the following words and phrases shall have the meanings ascribed to them in this Article XII, as follows:

"Annuity Contract" shall mean any kind of annuity to be paid by an insurance company or by an organization regularly engaged in issuing annuity contracts.

"Charitable Organization" shall mean an organization described in each of Sections 170(b)(1)(A), 170(c), 2055(a) and 2522(a) of the Code.

"Code" shall mean the Internal Revenue Code of 1986, as amended from time to time, and references to a Section of the Code shall include any successor provisions to the Section referred to and to any corresponding provisions of any subsequent federal tax laws.

"Custodian" shall mean a trustee of any trust established exclusively for the benefit of the Recipient, if such a trust has been established, or the conservator, custodian, person holding an effective durable power of attorney or legally appointed guardian of the person or estate of the Recipient.

"Death Taxes" shall mean any and all federal estate taxes, state death taxes or any other estate, death, inheritance or welfare transfer taxes.

"Disability" or "Disabled" shall mean when (i) a guardian or conservator of an individual's person or estate is duly appointed by a court of competent jurisdiction and continues to serve in such capacity, (ii) two physicians (licensed to practice under the laws of the state where the person is domiciled) certify that such person is unable to properly care for his or her person or property, (iii) an individual is a minor under the laws of the state where he or she is domiciled, or (iv) an individual disappears for an unreasonable period of time with no apparent explanation for such disappearance.

"Donee" or "Donees" shall mean any Charitable Organization selected to be a charitable remainderman (or remaindermen) pursuant to Article III of this Trust Agreement.

"Donor" shall mean the settlor of this Trust as named on the first page of the Trust Agreement, who has signed the Trust Agreement.

"Fiduciary" or "Fiduciaries" shall mean, as the context requires, each Trustee and/or Independent Special Trustee, and their successor(s).

"Independent Special Trustee" or "Independent Special Trustees" shall mean each individual and/or entity who or which is appointed as a fiduciary of this Trust, solely for the specific purposes provided in Paragraph B of Article IV, and who or which is an "Independent Trustee", and any successor(s) thereto.

"Independent Trustee" shall have the meaning ascribed to it in Regulation Section 1.664-1(a)(7)(iii).

"Net Fair Market Value of the Trust Assets" shall mean the net fair market value of the assets owned by the Trust as described in Paragraphs B and E of Article II of this Trust.

"Net Income" shall mean the net income of this Trust as determined by the Trustee pursuant to the terms of the Trust Agreement, Section 643(b) of the Code and the Regulations thereunder.

"Notice" or "notify" shall mean a communication in writing, signed by the party sending such communication, mailed by certified mail, return receipt requested, or personally hand delivered, dated receipt obtained. The effective date of such notice shall be deemed to be the date of mailing of such certified mail or the actual date of had delivery, as the case may be. Notice shall be addressed to such person(s) at such person(s) last known address.

"Recipient" shall mean the individual who is entitled to receive the Unitrust Amount pursuant to Paragraph A.1 of Article II of this Trust.

"Regulations" shall mean the regulations published under 26 Code of Federal Regulations as in effect on the date of execution of this Trust Agreement, or, in the event that any such regulation is amended or superseded thereafter, to the regulation (or any successor regulation) as so amended.

"Trust" shall mean the charitable remainder unitrust established under the Trust Agreement, otherwise known as "THE *(TRUST NAME)* CHARITABLE REMAINDER UNITRUST".

"Trust Agreement" shall mean this trust instrument signed by all parties hereto.

"Trustee", "it" or "its" shall mean each individual or entity acting in a fiduciary capacity who or which is named on the first page of the Trust Agreement, and who or which signed the Trust Agreement, and its successor(s).

"Unitrust Amount" shall mean the amount described in Paragraph A.2 of Article II of this Trust.

"Unitrust Period" shall mean the period of time which begins on the date this Trust is first funded and ends on the date upon which the Recipient dies.

"Unmarketable Asset" shall have the meaning ascribed to it in Regulation Section 1.664-1(a)(7)(ii).

IN WITNESS WHEREOF, the parties hereto have executed this Trust Agreement on the date first above written.

DONOR:

_____
(DONOR)

TRUSTEE:

_____
(TRUSTEE)

[ACKNOWLEDGMENT & WITNESS AS REQUIRED UNDER STATE LAW]

EXHIBIT A

THE *(TRUST NAME)*
CHARITABLE REMAINDER UNITRUST

Item No.   Date of Transfer   Description

Receipt of the above described assets is hereby acknowledged this _____ day of *(MONTH)*, *(TAX YEAR)*.

TRUSTEE:

_____
(TRUSTEE)

SAMPLE INTERVIVOS CHARITABLE REMAINDER ANNUITY TRUST

THE *(TRUST NAME)*
CHARITABLE REMAINDER ANNUITY TRUST

This TRUST AGREEMENT is made and is effective on this _____ day of *(MONTH)*, *(TRUSTEE)*, by and between *(DONOR)*, residing at *(DONOR'S ADDRESS)*, as the Donor and *(TRUSTEE)*, located/residing at *(TRUSTEE'S ADDRESS)*, and its successor(s), as the Trustee.

I.
AGREEMENT OF TRUST

The Donor is irrevocably assigning, transferring and delivering on the date hereof to the Trustee all right, title and interest in and to the property described in Exhibit A, a copy of which is attached hereto and specifically made a part hereof by this reference. The Trustee hereby accepts such irrevocable gift and agrees to hold, administer and distribute such property, together with any other property which is or shall become an asset of this Trust, in accordance with the provisions of the Trust Agreement. The Trust Agreement is intended to create a charitable remainder annuity trust within the meaning of Revenue Procedure 2003-53 and Section 664(d)(1) of the Code. Certain terms throughout this Trust Agreement are defined in Article XII.

II.
DISTRIBUTIONS

A. <u>Income and Principal</u>. During the Annuity Period, the Trustee shall distribute the income and principal of this Trust as follows:

1. In each taxable year of this Trust, the Trustee shall pay the Annuity Amount to *(RECIPIENT)* during the Annuity Period.

2. The Annuity Amount shall mean an amount equal to *(ANNUAL DOLLAR AMOUNT)* Dollars ($*(ANNUAL DOLLAR AMOUNT)*).

3. The Annuity Amount shall be paid in equal installments of *(QUARTERLY DOLLAR AMOUNT)* Dollars ($*(QUARTERLY DOLLAR AMOUNT)*) at the end of each calendar quarter of each taxable year of this Trust from Net Income, and to the extent Net Income is insufficient, from principal. Any Net Income in excess of the Annuity Amount shall be added to principal. The Trustee's obligation to make payments is limited to Trust assets. Notwithstanding any existing or hereafter enacted state law, no amount other than the Annuity Amount may be paid to or for the use of any person or entity other than a Charitable Organization. However, an amount shall not be deemed to be paid to or for the use of any person other than a Charitable Organization if the amount is transferred for full and adequate consideration.

4. The Trustee may pay the Annuity Amount to the Recipient by payment directly to him or her or by deposit in any bank designated by him or her. If the Recipient should at any time be under a Disability, the Trustee may pay the Annuity Amount to the Custodian. Any such payment for the benefit of the Recipient shall release the Trustee from its obligation to pay the Annuity Amount, and the Trustee shall have no duty to supervise or inquire into the application of any funds so paid.

5. Upon the expiration of the Annuity Period, the Trustee shall distribute the then principal and income of this Trust in accordance with Article III herein.

B. <u>Taxable Year and Short Taxable Years</u>. The first taxable year of this Trust shall commence on the date this Trust is first funded and shall end on December 31st of that year. Subsequent taxable years shall be on a calendar year basis, except that the last taxable year of this Trust shall end on the date that this Trust terminates pursuant to Article III herein. In the case of a taxable year which is for a period of less than twelve (12) months (other than the taxable year in which the Annuity Period ends), the amount described in Paragraph A.2 of this Article II shall be such amount multiplied by a fraction the numerator of which is the number of days in the taxable year of this Trust and the denominator of which is 365 (366 if February 29 is a day included in the numerator). In the case of the taxable year in which the Annuity Period ends, the amount described in Paragraph A.2 of this Article II shall be such amount multiplied by a fraction the numerator of which is the number of days in the period beginning on the first day of such taxable year and ending on the date the Annuity Period ends and the denominator of which is 365 (366 if February 29 is a day included in the numerator). Notwithstanding the foregoing, the obligation of the Trustee to pay the Annuity Amount shall terminate with the regular periodic payment next preceding the date the Annuity Period ends.

C. <u>Additional Contributions</u>. No additional contributions shall be made to this Trust after the initial contribution.

III.
TERMINATION

This Trust shall terminate within a reasonable time after the expiration of the Annuity Period; provided, however, that such reasonable time shall not extend beyond the last day of the month in which occurs the ninetieth (90th) day following the date the Annuity Period ends. Upon termination, the Trustee shall distribute all of the then principal and income of this Trust, free of trust, other than any amount due to the Recipient or the Recipient's estate, to *(REMAINDERMAN)*.

Notwithstanding any contrary provision of the Trust Agreement, prior to the expiration of the Annuity Period, the Donor shall retain the right, by acknowledged written instrument delivered to the Trustee, to change the Donee by adding or substituting new Charitable Organization(s) and/or omitting certain Charitable Organization(s) or by altering the share each is to receive. If more than one written instrument is so delivered to the Trustee, the written instrument bearing the latest date shall control and shall be deemed to revoke all prior written instruments unless the most recent one shall provide otherwise.

If any Donee is not a Charitable Organization at the time when any principal or income of this Trust is to be distributed to it, the Trustee shall distribute such principal or income in proportion to the relative shares of the Donees which are so described and, if none of the Donees is so described, to one or more Charitable Organizations as the Trustee shall select and in such shares as it shall determine.

IV.
FIDUCIARY PROVISIONS

A. <u>Appointment of Trustee</u>. *(TRUSTEE)* shall serve as Trustee of this Trust. In the event that *(TRUSTEE)* for any reason shall fail to serve as Trustee, then *(ALTERNATE TRUSTEE)* shall serve in the place and stead of *(TRUSTEE)*.

B. <u>Appointment of Independent Special Trustee</u>.

1. In the event an Unmarketable Asset is transferred to or held by this Trust, an Independent Special Trustee may be appointed by the Trustee. If so appointed, the Independent Special Trustee shall exclusively determine the fair market value of each Unmarketable Asset in accordance with such appointment. If not so appointed, the valuation shall be determined by a current qualified appraisal, as defined in Regulation Section 1.170A-13(c)(5).

2. The Trustee shall also have the right and option to appoint an Independent Special Trustee to take such action as the Trustee shall clearly define and delegate.

3. When (i) the sole Trustee is an Independent Trustee or (ii) more than one person is acting as Trustee hereunder and one of such Trustees is an Independent Trustee, such Independent Trustee shall have the right and option to act as an Independent Special Trustee hereunder. However, no Trustee (other than an acting Independent Special Trustee) shall have any power, duty or liability hereunder with respect to matters described in this Paragraph B.

4. The Independent Special Trustee shall have no powers, duties, or liabilities hereunder, except with respect to matters specifically described in this Paragraph B, and solely with respect to such matters, the Independent Special Trustee may exercise the rights, powers, authority and discretion, and be subject to the restrictions, obligations and duties, accorded to a Trustee pursuant to Article V herein. However, the Independent Special Trustee may not function in a manner which would jeopardize the status of this Trust as a charitable remainder trust as defined in Section 664 of the Code, the Regulations thereunder and Internal Revenue Service rulings governing the operation thereof.

C. <u>Resignation of Fiduciary</u>. Any Fiduciary may resign at any time by giving a notice to any other Fiduciary and to the Recipient, or if the Recipient is Disabled, to the Custodian. Such resignation shall be effective upon the sooner to occur of: (i) sixty (60) days after the date of the notice of resignation, or (ii) the appointment of and acceptance by the successor Fiduciary. Notwithstanding the above, in the event (i) a Fiduciary dies or is Disabled or (ii) an Independent Special Trustee ceases to be an Independent Trustee, notice of resignation is deemed given, and the resignation shall be effective as of the date of such death, Disability or ceasing to be an Independent Trustee, as the case may be. The resigning Fiduciary (or its representative) shall file a final accounting and deliver all Trust assets under its charge and control to the successor Fiduciary as soon as possible, but in no event later than sixty (60) days following the date of the resignation notice being given or deemed given. Upon the relinquishment and delivery of all Trust assets and the final accounting to the successor Fiduciary, the resigning Fiduciary shall be discharged of all further duties and obligations hereunder.

D. <u>Removal of Fiduciary</u>. The Recipient shall have the right, with or without cause, to replace or discharge any acting Fiduciary. Upon the Disability of the Recipient, this right may be exercised by the Custodian. Such removal shall be effective upon the sooner to occur of: (i) sixty (60) days after giving the Fiduciary being removed notice of such removal, or (ii) the appointment of and acceptance by the successor Fiduciary. The Fiduciary being removed shall file a final accounting and deliver all Trust assets under its charge and control to the successor Fiduciary within such sixty (60) day period. Upon the relinquishment and delivery of all Trust assets and the final accounting to the successor Fiduciary, the Fiduciary being removed shall be discharged of all further duties and obligations hereunder.

E. <u>Appointment of Successor Fiduciary</u>. In the event any vacancy at any time occurs in the office of a Fiduciary hereunder, regardless of how caused, the Recipient shall have the right to fill such vacancy. Upon the Disability of the Recipient, the Custodian shall exercise such right. At the earliest possible date, all Trust assets and a final accounting shall be delivered to the successor Fiduciary. At such time as any successor Fiduciary delivers notice of acceptance to the Recipient, such successor Fiduciary shall have the rights, powers, authority and discretion, and be subject to the restrictions, obligations and duties, regarding this Trust within the appointed capacity.

F. <u>Liability of Successor Fiduciary</u>. A successor Fiduciary shall not be responsible to any beneficiary of this Trust or to this Trust for any act or omission of a former Fiduciary, and shall not be required to audit or investigate the acts or administration of any former Fiduciary and shall be charged, upon issuing a simple receipt, with only the Trust assets so received. In addition, unless requested in writing by a beneficiary of this Trust and indemnified adequately (in such Fiduciary's discretion therefor), no successor Fiduciary shall have any duty to take action to seek redress for breach of trust by a former Fiduciary.

G. <u>Appointment of Co-Fiduciary</u>. The Recipient shall have the right to appoint additional persons to act as Co-Fiduciaries hereunder. At such time as the newly-appointed Co-Fiduciary delivers notice of acceptance to the Recipient, the newly-appointed Co-Fiduciary shall have the rights, powers, authority and discretion, and be subject to the restrictions, obligations and duties, regarding this Trust within the appointed capacity. In granting the foregoing right, it is not the intention of the Donor to require that any specific number of Fiduciaries serve in any one capacity hereunder simultaneously.

H. <u>Want of Trustee</u>. If at any time for any reason this Trust shall be without a Trustee, *(CORPORATE TRUSTEE)* shall be and become the Trustee.

I. <u>Fiduciary Actions</u>. When more than two persons are acting as Trustees (or Independent Special Trustees), the concurrence and joinder of a majority of them shall control in all matters pertaining to the administration hereunder. When two persons are acting as Trustees (or Independent Special Trustees), the concurrence and joinder of both Trustees (or Independent Special Trustees) shall be required. Such actions by the Fiduciaries shall be made either by vote at a meeting (in person or by telephone) or by written concurrence. When more than two persons are acting as Trustees (or Independent Special Trustees), any dissenting or abstaining Fiduciary may be absolved from personal liability by registering a written dissent or abstention with the records of this Trust. Such dissenting Fiduciary shall thereafter act with the other Fiduciaries in any manner necessary or appropriate to effectuate the decision of the majority.

J. <u>Compensation</u>. A Fiduciary, and any agents of or successors to any Fiduciary, shall be entitled to reasonable compensation for services rendered in connection with this Trust. The amount of compensation shall be an amount equal to the customary and prevailing charges for services of a similar nature during the same period of time and in the same geographic locale. Any Fiduciary may waive any compensation at any time, by providing notice of such waiver to the Recipient and another Fiduciary, if then serving.

K. <u>Retention of Agents</u>. A Fiduciary may delegate investment and management functions to an agent as is prudent under the circumstances, but shall exercise reasonable care in selecting such agent. The duties of the agent shall be consistent with the terms and intent of this Trust, and the Fiduciary shall periodically review the agent's performance.

L. <u>Liability for Retaining Property</u>. The Fiduciary shall not be liable for any loss or depreciation in value sustained by this Trust as a result of the Fiduciary accepting or retaining any property upon which hazardous materials or substances are discovered, unless the Fiduciary contributed to the loss or depreciation in value through willful default, willful misconduct or gross negligence.

M. <u>Indemnification</u>. The Donor shall indemnify the Fiduciary against any claims (except for claims due to the Fiduciary's willful default, willful misconduct or gross negligence) filed against the Fiduciary (i) as an "owner" or "operator" under the federal Comprehensive Environmental Response, Compensation and Liability Act of 1980 (as from time to time amended) or any regulation thereunder and (ii) under any other federal, state or local environmental law, rule, regulation or order relating to the property contributed to this Trust by the Donor.

N. <u>Jurisdiction and Bond</u>. This Trust shall not be administered under the jurisdiction of any court. Should a question or issue be submitted to a court of competent jurisdiction at any time or from time to time, such court shall acquire jurisdiction of only the question or issue submitted to it, and the jurisdiction of such court shall terminate upon the conclusion or settlement of such question or issue. No bond or other security shall be required of any person acting as a Fiduciary, whether serving jointly or alone.

V.
POWERS OF THE TRUSTEE

All rights, powers, authority and discretion exercisable by the Trustee under this Trust or by law shall be binding and conclusive on all interested parties; shall be exercisable by the Trustee in its sole and absolute discretion; shall be exercisable only in a fiduciary capacity and in the best interests of the beneficiaries; shall be construed in the broadest possible manner; and shall be exercisable without prior or subsequent application to any court under the jurisdiction of which this Trust may be administered.

The Trustee is under a duty to the beneficiaries to invest and manage the funds of the Trust as a prudent investor would, in a manner that is fair to all beneficiaries as a reflection of the Trust's purposes, terms, and obligations and in light of the circumstances of the Trust and the relevant circumstances of its beneficiaries. The investment decisions of a Trustee shall be evaluated not in isolation, but in the context of the investment portfolio as a whole and as part of an overall investment strategy reasonably suited to the Trust.

Not in derogation of or in limitation upon the powers, authority and discretion conferred by law upon a trustee, the Trustee is vested with the following rights, powers, authority and discretion:

A. To alter, repair, improve, erect buildings upon, demolish, manage, partition, mortgage, lease for any period, including a period in excess of any fixed by statute or extending beyond the duration of this Trust, exchange, grant options to lease or to buy, and sell or dispose of, at public or private sale, and upon such conditions and such terms as to cash and credit as it deems advisable, any of the Trust assets;

B. To compromise, settle, subordinate, arbitrate, extend, renew, modify, or release, in whole or in part, any claim held by it or held against any of the Trust assets;

C. To continue to hold the property transferred to it hereunder in the form in which it shall be when transferred or as the form thereof may be changed pursuant to the other provisions of the Trust Agreement, without regard to the limitations imposed by law upon the investment of trust funds;

D. To borrow money and to encumber or hypothecate Trust assets whether by mortgage, deed of trust, pledge or otherwise;

E. To commence or defend litigation with respect to the Trust assets, at the expense of the Trust assets;

F. To employ any person, firm, corporation, bank, or trust company for advice with respect to investment policy or any other matter; but the Trustee may follow or refrain from following any recommendation so obtained and such recommendations shall not in any way limit the discretionary power and authority conferred upon the Trustee hereunder with respect to investments or other matters;

G. To retain or discharge accountants, attorneys, administrators, brokers, investment advisers, investment counselors and other agents, and to pay reasonable compensation for their services;

H. To enter into any and all agreements with the Internal Revenue Service or any other governmental body and to execute, from time to time, any declarations of policy or disclaimers restricting the powers, authority and discretion granted to the Trustee;

I. To invest and to reinvest the Trust assets in every kind of property, real, personal or mixed, and every kind of investment; and nothing in the Trust Agreement shall be construed to restrict the Trustee from investing the Trust assets in a manner which could result in the annual realization of a reasonable amount of income or gain from the sale or disposition of Trust assets;

J. With respect to any investment held by the Trustee, to participate in and consent to any corporate or financial reorganization, dissolution, liquidation, merger, consolidation, sale or lease, or in and to any other change in its financial structure; and to become a depositor with any protective, reorganization, or similar committee, and to make any necessary payments incident to the foregoing; to organize or participate in the organization of corporations or other business entities, and to transfer to them any part or all of the Trust assets in exchange for an investment therein; to exercise or to sell any conversion, subscription, or similar rights; and in general to exercise in respect to any investment the unrestricted rights of a personal owner, including voting in person and granting proxies, discretionary, general, or otherwise;

K. In any case in which the Trustee makes any payments or other distribution of Trust assets, to make such payment or distribution in money or in kind, including undivided interests in any property, or partly in money and partly in kind; and in the case of any distribution in kind to any Donee, the adjusted basis of the Trust property distributed shall be fairly representative of the adjusted bases of all Trust properties available for distribution on the date of distribution;

L. To apportion and allocate Trust receipts and expenses between Net Income and principal accounts (provided that no pre-gift appreciation shall be allocable to Net Income);

M. To retain the services of an independent appraiser to assist in valuing assets of this Trust and to reasonably compensate such appraiser for such services;

N. If required by the Code, the Regulations or any Internal Revenue Service rulings thereunder to maintain the status of the Trust as a charitable remainder annuity trust, to set aside a reserve or allowance from Trust income for the depreciation or depletion of any property transferred to or invested in by the Trust; otherwise, the Trustee shall have discretion whether or not to set aside such a reserve;

O. With respect to any environmental hazards on Trust property:

    1. To take all appropriate actions to prevent, identify or respond to actual or threatened violations of any environmental law, rule or regulation, including compliance with any federal, state or local agency or court order directing an assessment, abatement or cleanup of any environmental hazard;

    2. To disclaim, in whole or in part, any interests in property for any reason, including but not limited to, a concern that such property could cause potential liability under any federal, state, or local environmental law, rule or regulation; and/or

    3. To set aside any interests in property, which could cause potential liability under any federal, state, or local environmental law, rule or regulation as a separate trust to be held and administered upon the same terms as those governing the remaining Trust assets;

P. To designate as custodian of any Trust property any business entity authorized and engaged in the business of brokers or dealers in securities;

Q. To the extent permitted by law, to register any of such property in its name as Trustee or in the names of nominees, or to take and keep the same unregistered or in bearer form, or in such condition as to pass by delivery; and/or

R. Whenever the Trust acquires an Annuity Contract, to exercise with respect to such Annuity Contract any rights and discretion as owner thereof, as limited hereby, including but not limited to the right or discretion to:

    1. Making partial or total withdrawals or surrenders from the Annuity Contract; provided however, the Trustee gives due regard to any withdrawal or partial surrender penalties that may be imposed and to the best interest of all Trust beneficiaries;

    2. Electing any annuity option(s) which guarantees the payment to the Trust by or upon the death of the annuitant of an amount at least equal to the surrender value of the Annuity Contract(s) as of the day before the day the annuity payments commence;

    3. Designating the day the annuity payments commence; and/or

    4. Seeing to the allocation of any payments of any type received from the Annuity Contract between principal and income as is required by this Trust.

Anything in the Trust Agreement to the contrary notwithstanding, it is the intention of the Donor to create a qualifying charitable remainder annuity trust under Section 664 of the Code; therefore, no rights, powers, authority or discretion either otherwise granted by the Trust Agreement or by applicable state law that exceed or are inconsistent with those allowed under Section 664 of the Code and the Regulations thereunder are to be possessed or exercised by the Trustee. At no time and under no circumstances shall a Donor serving as a Trustee exercise any power that would result in this Trust being treated as a grantor trust under Subpart E of the Code.

VI.
APPLICABLE LAW

The validity of this Trust shall be controlled by the laws of the State of *(STATE LAW)*. The construction and administration of this Trust shall be controlled by the laws of the State of *(STATE LAW)*. However, in any conflict with Section 664 of the Code, the Regulations thereunder or any other existing or hereafter promulgated legislative or Treasury requirements for the qualification of this Trust and for the Donor's obtaining the full benefit of any income, gift and estate tax charitable deductions to which the Donor (and the Donor's estate) may be entitled, Section 664 of the Code, the Regulations thereunder and the legislative and Treasury requirements shall govern.

VII.
IRREVOCABILITY AND AMENDMENT

This Trust shall be irrevocable. However, the Trustee shall have the power, acting alone, to amend the Trust Agreement in any manner required for the sole purpose of ensuring that this Trust qualifies and continues to qualify as a charitable remainder annuity trust within the meaning of Section 664 of the Code and the Regulations thereunder.

VIII.
PROHIBITED ACTS

Notwithstanding any other provision of the Trust Agreement, no Fiduciary shall (except for the payment of the Annuity Amount) engage in any act of self-dealing (as defined in Section 4941(d) of the Code), retain any excess business holdings (as defined in Section 4943(c) of the Code) which would subject this Trust to tax under Section 4943 of the Code, make any investments which would subject this Trust to tax under Section 4944 of the Code, or make any taxable expenditure (as defined in Section 4945(d) of the Code). If Section 4942 of the Code is deemed applicable to this Trust by reason of Section 508(e) of the Code or otherwise, then the Trustee shall make distributions at such times and in such manner as not to subject this Trust to tax under Section 4942 of the Code.

IX.
INTENTION TO CREATE ANNUITY TRUST

It is the Donor's intention to obtain the full benefit of any income, gift and estate tax charitable contribution deductions to which the Donor (and the Donor's estate) may be entitled to under the Code and for this Trust to qualify as a charitable remainder annuity trust within the meaning of Section 664(d)(1) of the Code and the Regulations thereunder. Accordingly, the Trust Agreement shall be interpreted and administered, and the Trust assets shall be valued, managed and invested, in a manner consistent with the Donor's intent and the provisions of such Section, the Regulations thereunder and the Internal Revenue Service rulings relating thereto.

X.
DEATH TAXES

No Death Taxes with respect to this Trust shall be allocated to or be recoverable from this Trust. The Donor agrees to provide in the Donor's Will, or any other appropriate estate planning documents, that any Death Taxes arising from the creation of this Trust, or the interest of the Donor therein, shall be payable from the estate of the Donor, excluding the assets of this Trust. The Donor hereby imposes an affirmative obligation on the Donor's estate to pay all of such Death Taxes (if any) from sources other than this Trust and agrees that this obligation may be enforced by the Trustee or any Donee, acting alone or together.

XI.
MISCELLANEOUS

A. Construction. Unless the context requires otherwise, words in the singular may be construed as denoting the plural, and words in the plural may be construed as denoting the singular. Words of one gender may be construed as denoting another gender as is appropriate within such context.

B. Headings. Titles and headings in the Trust Agreement are added for convenient reference, and shall not be deemed to alter or affect the meaning of any provision hereof.

C. Severability. If any provision or part of any provision of the Trust Agreement shall for any reason be held invalid, illegal or unenforceable in any respect by a court of competent jurisdiction, such invalidity, illegality or unenforceability shall not affect any other provision of the Trust Agreement and the Trust Agreement shall be construed as if such invalid, illegal or unenforceable provision or part thereof had never been contained herein, but only to the extent of its invalidity, illegality or unenforceability.

D. Counterparts. The Trust Agreement has been executed in triplicate, each of which shall be an original and each of which shall constitute the entire Trust Agreement without reference to or the necessity of producing the other counterparts.

E. Spendthrift. The Recipient shall not have any power to sell, transfer, assign, pledge, mortgage, or alienate all or any part of the Recipient's beneficial interest in this Trust in any manner whatsoever. The interest of the Recipient shall not be subject to the claims of the Recipient's creditors or to attachment, execution, bankruptcy proceedings or any other legal process.

XII.
DEFINITIONS

For purposes of the Trust Agreement, the following words and phrases shall have the meanings ascribed to them in this Article XII, as follows:

"Annuity Amount" shall mean the amount described in Paragraph A.2 of Article II of this Trust.

"Annuity Contract" shall mean any kind of annuity to be paid by an insurance company or by an organization regularly engaged in issuing annuity contracts.

"Annuity Period" shall mean the period of time which begins on the date this Trust is first funded and ends on the date upon which the Recipient dies.

"Charitable Organization" shall mean an organization described in each of Sections 170(b)(1)(A), 170(c), 2055(a) and 2522(a) of the Code.

"Code" shall mean the Internal Revenue Code of 1986, as amended from time to time, and references to a Section of the Code shall include any successor provisions to the Section referred to and to any corresponding provisions of any subsequent federal tax laws.

"Custodian" shall mean a trustee of any trust established exclusively for the benefit of the Recipient, if such a trust has been established, or the conservator, custodian, person holding an effective durable power of attorney or legally appointed guardian of the person or estate of the Recipient.

"Death Taxes" shall mean any and all federal estate taxes, state death taxes or any other estate, death, inheritance or welfare transfer taxes.

"Disability" or "Disabled" shall mean when (i) a guardian or conservator of an individual's person or estate is duly appointed by a court of competent jurisdiction and continues to serve in such capacity, (ii) two physicians (licensed to practice under the laws of the state where the person is domiciled) certify that such person is unable to properly care for his or her person or property, (iii) an individual is a minor under the laws of the state where he or she is domiciled, or (iv) an individual disappears for an unreasonable period of time with no apparent explanation for such disappearance.

"Donee" or "Donees" shall mean any Charitable Organization selected to be a charitable remainderman (or remaindermen) pursuant to Article III of this Trust Agreement.

"Donor" shall mean the settlor of this Trust as named on the first page of the Trust Agreement, who has signed the Trust Agreement.

"Fiduciary" or "Fiduciaries" shall mean, as the context requires, each Trustee and/or Independent Special Trustee, and their successor(s).

"Independent Special Trustee" or "Independent Special Trustees" shall mean each individual and/or entity who or which is appointed as a fiduciary of this Trust, solely for the specific purposes provided in Paragraph B of Article IV, and who or which is an "Independent Trustee", and any successor(s) thereto.

"Independent Trustee" shall have the meaning ascribed to it in Regulation Section 1.664-1(a)(7)(iii).

"Net Income" shall mean the net income of this Trust as determined by the Trustee pursuant to the terms of the Trust Agreement, Section 643(b) of the Code and the Regulations thereunder.

"Notice" or "notify" shall mean a communication in writing, signed by the party sending such communication, mailed by certified mail, return receipt requested, or personally hand delivered, dated receipt obtained. The effective date of such notice shall be deemed to be the date of mailing of such certified mail or the actual date of hand delivery, as the case may be. Notice shall be addressed to such person(s) at such person(s) last known address.

"Recipient" shall mean the individual who is entitled to receive the Annuity Amount pursuant to Paragraph A.1 of Article II of this Trust.

"Regulations" shall mean the regulations published under 26 Code of Federal Regulations as in effect on the date of execution of this Trust Agreement, or, in the event that any such regulation is amended or super-seded thereafter, to the regulation (or any successor regulation) as so amended.

"Trust" shall mean the charitable remainder annuity trust established under the Trust Agreement, otherwise known as "THE *(TRUST NAME)* CHARITABLE REMAINDER ANNUITY TRUST".

"Trust Agreement" shall mean this trust instrument signed by all parties hereto.

"Trustee", "it" or "its" shall mean each individual or entity acting in a fiduciary capacity who or which is named on the first page of the Trust Agreement, and who or which signed the Trust Agreement, and its successor(s).

"Unmarketable Asset" shall have the meaning ascribed to it in Regulation Section 1.664-1(a)(7)(ii).

IN WITNESS WHEREOF, the parties hereto have executed this Trust Agreement on the date first above written.

DONOR:

_____

(DONOR)

TRUSTEE:

_____

(TRUSTEE)

[ACKNOWLEDGMENT & WITNESS AS REQUIRED UNDER STATE LAW]

EXHIBIT A

THE *(TRUST NAME)*
CHARITABLE REMAINDER ANNUITY TRUST

<u>Item No.</u>   <u>Date of Transfer</u>   <u>Description</u>

Receipt of the above described assets is hereby acknowledged this _____ day of *(MONTH)*, *(TAX YEAR)*.

TRUSTEE:

_____
(TRUSTEE)

SAMPLE INTERVIVOS NET INCOME CHARITABLE REMAINDER UNITRUST

THE *(TRUST NAME)*
CHARITABLE REMAINDER UNITRUST

This TRUST AGREEMENT is made and is effective on this _____ day of *(MONTH)*, *(YEAR)*, by and between *(DONOR)*, residing at *(DONOR'S ADDRESS)*, as the Donor and *(TRUSTEE)*, located/residing at *(TRUSTEE'S ADDRESS)*, and its successor(s), as the Trustee.

I.
AGREEMENT OF TRUST

The Donor is irrevocably assigning, transferring and delivering on the date hereof to the Trustee all right, title and interest in and to the property described in Exhibit A, a copy of which is attached hereto and specifically made a part hereof by this reference. The Trustee hereby accepts such irrevocable gift and agrees to hold, administer and distribute such property, together with any other property which is or shall become an asset of this Trust, in accordance with the provisions of the Trust Agreement. The Trust Agreement is intended to create a charitable remainder unitrust within the meaning of Section 4 of Revenue Procedure 90-31 to the extent applicable and Section 664(d)(2) and (3) of the Code. Certain terms throughout this Trust Agreement are defined in Article XII.

II.
DISTRIBUTIONS

A. <u>Income and Principal</u>. During the Unitrust Period, the Trustee shall distribute the income and principal of this Trust as follows:

1. In each taxable year of this Trust, the Trustee shall pay the Unitrust Amount to *(RECIPIENT'S NAME)* during the Unitrust Period.

2. The Unitrust Amount shall mean an amount equal to the lesser of: (a) the Net Income for each taxable year of this Trust; or (b) *(FMV PERCENT)* percent (*(FMV PERCENT NUMBER)*%) of the Net Fair Market Value of the Trust Assets, as modified by Paragraphs C and D of this Article II.

3. The Unitrust Amount shall be paid in equal installments at the end of each calendar quarter of each taxable year of this Trust. Any Net Income in excess of the Unitrust Amount shall be added to principal. Notwithstanding any existing or hereafter enacted state law, no amount other than the Unitrust Amount may be paid to or for the use of any person or entity other than a Charitable Organization. However, an amount shall not be deemed to be paid to or for the use of any person other than a Charitable Organization if the amount is transferred for full and adequate consideration.

4. The Trustee may pay the Unitrust Amount to the Recipient by payment directly to him or her or by deposit in any bank designated by him or her. If the Recipient should at any time be under a Disability, the Trustee may pay the Unitrust Amount to the Custodian. Any such payment for the benefit of the Recipient shall release the Trustee from its obligation to pay the Unitrust Amount, and the Trustee shall have no duty to supervise or inquire into the application of any funds so paid.

5. Upon the expiration of the Unitrust Period, the Trustee shall distribute the then principal and income of this Trust in accordance with Article III herein.

B. <u>Valuation Date</u>. The Net Fair Market Value of the Trust Assets shall be determined annually on the first day of each taxable year of this Trust (including any short taxable year), in accordance with the provisions of Paragraph E of this Article II.

C. <u>Taxable Year and Short Taxable Years</u>. The first taxable year of this Trust shall commence on the date this Trust is first funded and shall end on December 31st of that year. Subsequent taxable years shall be on a calendar year basis, except that the last taxable year of this Trust shall end on the date that this Trust terminates pursuant to Article III herein. In the case of a taxable year which is for a period of less than twelve (12) months (other than the taxable year in which the Unitrust Period ends), the amount described in Paragraph A.2(b) of this Article II shall be such amount multiplied by a fraction the numerator of which is the number of days in the taxable year of this Trust and the denominator of which is 365 (366 if February 29 is a day included in the numerator). In the case of the taxable year in which the Unitrust Period ends, the amount described in Paragraph A.2(b) of this Article II shall be such amount multiplied by a fraction the numerator of which is the number of days in the period beginning on the first day of such taxable year and ending on the date the Unitrust Period ends and the denominator of which is 365 (366 if February 29 is a day included in the numerator). Notwithstanding the foregoing, the obligation of the Trustee to pay the Unitrust Amount shall terminate with the regular periodic payment next preceding the date the Unitrust Period ends.

D. <u>Additional Contributions</u>. Any person may contribute property to this Trust, with the consent of the Trustee, either during life or at death. For the taxable year of this Trust in which any additional contribution is made, the additional property shall be valued at the time of contribution and in accordance with Paragraph E of this Article II, and the amount described in Paragraph A.2(b) of this Article II shall be *(FMV PERCENT)* percent (*(FMV PERCENT NUMBER)*%) of the sum of the following components:

1. The Net Fair Market Value of the Trust Assets determined on the first day of the taxable year (and thus excluding the value of the additional property, and earned income from, and any appreciation on, such property after its contribution); and

2. That proportion of the value of the additional property (that was excluded under Paragraph D.1 of this Article II immediately above) which the number of days in the period that begins with the date of contribution and ends with the earlier of the last day of such taxable year or the date the Unitrust Period ends bears to the number of days in the period that begins on the first day of such taxable year and ends with the earlier of the last day of such taxable year or the date the Unitrust Period ends.

If an additional contribution is made by Will, the obligation to pay the Unitrust Amount payable with respect to the additional contribution shall commence with the date of death of the person under whose Will the additional contribution is made. Payment of that portion of the Unitrust Amount may be deferred, however, from such date of death to the end of the taxable year in which occurs the complete funding of the additional contribution. Within a reasonable time following such complete funding of the additional contribution, the Trustee shall pay to the Recipient, in the case of an underpayment, or receive from the Recipient, in the case of an overpayment, the difference between: (i) the Unitrust Amount with respect to such additional contribution actually paid to the Recipient, plus interest on such amounts, compounded annually, computed for any period at the rate of interest that the Regulations under Section 664 of the Code prescribe for this Trust for such computation for such period; and (ii) the Unitrust Amount with respect to such additional contribution payable, determined under the method described in Section 1.664-1(a)(5)(ii) of the Regulations. Any payments required to be made because of an underpayment shall be paid to the Recipient (or such Recipient's estate) who received the underpayment. Any repayments required to be made because of an overpayment shall be repaid by the Recipient (or such Recipient's estate) who received the overpayment.

E. <u>Fair Market Value</u>. The Trustee shall compute the Net Fair Market Value of the Trust Assets considering all assets and liabilities without regard to whether particular items are taken into account in determining the Net Income; provided, however, in the event an Unmarketable Asset is transferred to or held by this Trust, and whenever this Trust is required to value such asset, the valuation shall be either performed exclusively by an Independent Special Trustee or determined by a current qualified appraisal, as defined in Regulation Section 1.170A-13(c)(3), from a qualified appraiser, as defined in Regulation Section 1.170A-13(c)(5). All determinations of the Net Fair Market Value of the Trust Assets shall be in accordance with generally accepted fiduciary accounting principles and any United States Treasury requirements governing charitable remainder unitrusts. In any conflict, Treasury requirements shall prevail over generally accepted fiduciary accounting principles and any inconsistent provisions of this Trust Agreement. In the event that the Net Fair Market Value of the Trust Assets is determined incorrectly for any taxable year, the Trustee shall pay to the Recipient or the Recipient's estate (in the case of an undervaluation), or be repaid by the Recipient or the Recipient's estate (in the case of an overvaluation), an amount equal to the difference between the Unitrust

Amount which the Trustee should have paid to the Recipient if the correct values were used, and the Unitrust Amount which the Trustee actually paid to the Recipient. Such payments or repayments shall be made within a reasonable period after the final determination of the correct value.

III.
TERMINATION

This Trust shall terminate within a reasonable time after the expiration of the Unitrust Period; provided, however, that such reasonable time shall not extend beyond the last day of the month in which occurs the ninetieth (90th) day following the date the Unitrust Period ends. Upon termination, the Trustee shall distribute all of the then principal and income of this Trust, free of trust, other than any amount due to the Recipient or the Recipient's estate, to *(REMAINDERMAN)*.

Notwithstanding any contrary provision of the Trust Agreement, prior to the expiration of the Unitrust Period, the Donor shall retain the right, by acknowledged written instrument delivered to the Trustee, to change the Donee by adding or substituting new Charitable Organization(s) and/or omitting certain Charitable Organization(s) or by altering the share each is to receive. If more than one written instrument is so delivered to the Trustee, the written instrument bearing the latest date shall control and shall be deemed to revoke all prior written instruments unless the most recent one shall provide otherwise.

If any Donee is not a Charitable Organization at the time when any principal or income of this Trust is to be distributed to it, the Trustee shall distribute such principal or income in proportion to the relative shares of the Donees which are so described and, if none of the Donees is so described, to one or more Charitable Organizations as the Trustee shall select and in such shares as it shall determine.

IV.
FIDUCIARY PROVISIONS

A. <u>Appointment of Trustee</u>. *(TRUSTEE)* shall serve as Trustee of this Trust. In the event that *(TRUSTEE)* for any reason shall fail to serve as Trustee, then *(ALTERNATE TRUSTEE)* shall serve in the place and stead of *(TRUSTEE)*.

B. <u>Appointment of Independent Special Trustee</u>.

1. In the event an Unmarketable Asset is transferred to or held by this Trust, an Independent Special Trustee may be appointed by the Trustee. If so appointed, the Independent Special Trustee shall exclusively determine the fair market value of each Unmarketable Asset in accordance with such appointment.

2. The Trustee shall also have the right and option to appoint an Independent Special Trustee to take such action as the Trustee shall clearly define and delegate.

3. When (i) the sole Trustee is an Independent Trustee or (ii) more than one person is acting as Trustee hereunder and one of such Trustees is an Independent Trustee, such Independent Trustee shall have the right and option to act as an Independent Special Trustee hereunder. However, no Trustee (other than an acting Independent Special Trustee) shall have any power, duty or liability hereunder with respect to matters described in this Paragraph B.

4. The Independent Special Trustee shall have no powers, duties, or liabilities hereunder, except with respect to matters specifically described in this Paragraph B, and solely with respect to such matters, the Independent Special Trustee may exercise the rights, powers, authority and discretion, and be subject to the restrictions, obligations and duties, accorded to a Trustee pursuant to Article V herein. However, the Independent Special Trustee may not function in a manner which would jeopardize the status of this Trust as a charitable remainder trust as defined in Section 664 of the Code, the Regulations thereunder and Internal Revenue Service rulings governing the operation thereof.

C. <u>Resignation of Fiduciary</u>. Any Fiduciary may resign at any time by giving a notice to any other Fiduciary and to the Recipient, or if the Recipient is Disabled, to the Custodian. Such resignation shall be effective upon the sooner to occur of: (i) sixty (60) days after the date of the notice of resignation, or (ii) the appointment of and acceptance by the successor Fiduciary. Notwithstanding the above, in the event (i) a Fiduciary dies or is Disabled or (ii) an Independent Special Trustee ceases to be an Independent Trustee, notice of resignation is deemed given, and the resignation shall be effective as of the date of such death, Disability or ceasing to be an Independent Trustee, as the case may be. The resigning Fiduciary (or its representative) shall file a final accounting and deliver all Trust assets under its charge and control to the successor Fiduciary as soon as possible, but in no event later than sixty (60) days following the date of the resignation notice being given or deemed given. Upon the relinquishment and delivery of all Trust assets and the final accounting to the successor Fiduciary, the resigning Fiduciary shall be discharged of all further duties and obligations hereunder.

D. <u>Removal of Fiduciary</u>. The Recipient shall have the right, with or without cause, to replace or discharge any acting Fiduciary. Upon the Disability of the Recipient, this right may be exercised by the Custodian. Such removal shall be effective upon the sooner to occur of: (i) sixty (60) days after giving the Fiduciary being removed notice of such removal, or (ii) the appointment of and acceptance by the successor Fiduciary. The Fiduciary being removed shall file a final accounting and deliver all Trust assets under its charge and control to the successor Fiduciary within such sixty (60) day period. Upon the relinquishment and delivery of all Trust assets and the final accounting to the successor Fiduciary, the Fiduciary being removed shall be discharged of all further duties and obligations hereunder.

E. <u>Appointment of Successor Fiduciary</u>. In the event any vacancy at any time occurs in the office of a Fiduciary hereunder, regardless of how caused, the Recipient shall have the right to fill such vacancy. Upon the Disability of the Recipient, the Custodian shall exercise such right. At the earliest possible date, all Trust assets and a final accounting shall be delivered to the successor Fiduciary. At such time as any successor Fiduciary delivers notice of acceptance to the Recipient, such successor Fiduciary shall have the rights, powers, authority and discretion, and be subject to the restrictions, obligations and duties, regarding this Trust within the appointed capacity.

F. <u>Liability of Successor Fiduciary</u>. A successor Fiduciary shall not be responsible to any beneficiary of this Trust or to this Trust for any act or omission of a former Fiduciary, and shall not be required to audit or investigate the acts or administration of any former Fiduciary and shall be charged, upon issuing a simple receipt, with only the Trust assets so received. In addition, unless requested in writing by a beneficiary of this Trust and indemnified adequately (in such Fiduciary's discretion therefor), no successor Fiduciary shall have any duty to take action to seek redress for breach of trust by a former Fiduciary.

G. <u>Appointment of Co-Fiduciary</u>. The Recipient shall have the right to appoint additional persons to act as Co-Fiduciaries hereunder. At such time as the newly-appointed Co-Fiduciary delivers notice of acceptance to the Recipient, the newly-appointed Co-Fiduciary shall have the rights, powers, authority and discretion, and be subject to the restrictions, obligations and duties, regarding this Trust within the appointed capacity. In granting the foregoing right, it is not the intention of the Donor to require that any specific number of Fiduciaries serve in any one capacity hereunder simultaneously.

H. <u>Want of Trustee</u>. If at any time for any reason this Trust shall be without a Trustee, *(CORPORATE TRUSTEE)* shall be and become the Trustee.

I. <u>Fiduciary Actions</u>. When more than two persons are acting as Trustees (or Independent Special Trustees), the concurrence and joinder of a majority of them shall control in all matters pertaining to the administration hereunder. When two persons are acting as Trustees (or Independent Special Trustees), the concurrence and joinder of both Trustees (or Independent Special Trustees) shall be required. Such actions by the Fiduciaries shall be made either by vote at a meeting (in person or by telephone) or by written concurrence. When more than two persons are acting as Trustees (or Independent Special Trustees), any dissenting or abstaining Fiduciary may be absolved from personal liability by registering a written dissent or abstention with the records of this Trust. Such dissenting Fiduciary shall thereafter act with the other Fiduciaries in any manner necessary or appropriate to effectuate the decision of the majority.

J. <u>Compensation</u>. A Fiduciary, and any agents of or successors to any Fiduciary, shall be entitled to reasonable compensation for services rendered in connection with this Trust. The amount of compensation shall be an amount equal to the customary and prevailing charges for services of a similar nature during the same period of time and in the same geographic locale. Any Fiduciary may waive any compensation at any time, by providing notice of such waiver to the Recipient and another Fiduciary, if then serving.

K. <u>Retention of Agents</u>. A Fiduciary may delegate investment and management functions to an agent as is prudent under the circumstances, but shall exercise reasonable care in selecting such agent. The duties of the agent shall be consistent with the terms and intent of this Trust, and the Fiduciary shall periodically review the agent's performance.

L. <u>Liability for Retaining Property</u>. The Fiduciary shall not be liable for any loss or depreciation in value sustained by this Trust as a result of the Fiduciary accepting or retaining any property upon which hazardous materials or substances are discovered, unless the Fiduciary contributed to the loss or depreciation in value through willful default, willful misconduct or gross negligence.

M. <u>Indemnification</u>. The Donor shall indemnify the Fiduciary against any claims (except for claims due to the Fiduciary's willful default, willful misconduct or gross negligence) filed against the Fiduciary (i) as an "owner" or "operator" under the federal Comprehensive Environmental Response, Compensation and Liability Act of 1980 (as from time to time amended) or any regulation thereunder and (ii) under any other federal, state or local environmental law, rule, regulation or order relating to the property contributed to this Trust by the Donor.

N. <u>Jurisdiction and Bond</u>. This Trust shall not be administered under the jurisdiction of any court. Should a question or issue be submitted to a court of competent jurisdiction at any time or from time to time, such court shall acquire jurisdiction of only the question or issue submitted to it, and the jurisdiction of such court shall terminate upon the conclusion or settlement of such question or issue. No bond or other security shall be required of any person acting as a Fiduciary, whether serving jointly or alone.

V.
<u>POWERS OF THE TRUSTEE</u>

All rights, powers, authority and discretion exercisable by the Trustee under this Trust or by law shall be binding and conclusive on all interested parties; shall be exercisable by the Trustee in its sole and absolute discretion; shall be exercisable only in a fiduciary capacity and in the best interests of the beneficiaries; shall be construed in the broadest possible manner; and shall be exercisable without prior or subsequent application to any court under the jurisdiction of which this Trust may be administered.

The Trustee is under a duty to the beneficiaries to invest and manage the funds of the Trust as a prudent investor would, in a manner that is fair to all beneficiaries as a reflection of the Trust's purposes, terms, and obligations and in light of the circumstances of the Trust and the relevant circumstances of its beneficiaries. The investment decisions of a Trustee shall be evaluated not in isolation, but in the context of the investment portfolio as a whole and as part of an overall investment strategy reasonably suited to the Trust.

Not in derogation of or in limitation upon the powers, authority and discretion conferred by law upon a trustee, the Trustee is vested with the following rights, powers, authority and discretion:

A. To alter, repair, improve, erect buildings upon, demolish, manage, partition, mortgage, lease for any period, including a period in excess of any fixed by statute or extending beyond the duration of this Trust, exchange, grant options to lease or to buy, and sell or dispose of, at public or private sale, and upon such conditions and such terms as to cash and credit as it deems advisable, any of the Trust assets;

B. To compromise, settle, subordinate, arbitrate, extend, renew, modify, or release, in whole or in part, any claim held by it or held against any of the Trust assets;

C. To continue to hold the property transferred to it hereunder in the form in which it shall be when transferred or as the form thereof may be changed pursuant to the other provisions of the Trust Agreement, without regard to the limitations imposed by law upon the investment of trust funds;

D. To borrow money and to encumber or hypothecate Trust assets whether by mortgage, deed of trust, pledge or otherwise;

E. To commence or defend litigation with respect to the Trust assets, at the expense of the Trust assets;

F. To employ any person, firm, corporation, bank, or trust company for advice with respect to investment policy or any other matter; but the Trustee may follow or refrain from following any recommendation so obtained and such recommendations shall not in any way limit the discretionary power and authority conferred upon the Trustee hereunder with respect to investments or other matters;

G. To retain or discharge accountants, attorneys, administrators, brokers, investment advisers, investment counselors and other agents, and to pay reasonable compensation for their services;

H. To enter into any and all agreements with the Internal Revenue Service or any other governmental body and to execute, from time to time, any declarations of policy or disclaimers restricting the powers, authority and discretion granted to the Trustee;

I. To invest and to reinvest the Trust assets in every kind of property, real, personal or mixed, and every kind of investment; and nothing in the Trust Agreement shall be construed to restrict the Trustee from investing the Trust assets in a manner which could result in the annual realization of a reasonable amount of income or gain from the sale or disposition of Trust assets;

J. With respect to any investment held by the Trustee, to participate in and consent to any corporate or financial reorganization, dissolution, liquidation, merger, consolidation, sale or lease, or in and to any other change in its financial structure; and to become a depositor with any protective, reorganization, or similar committee, and to make any necessary payments incident to the foregoing; to organize or participate in the organization of corporations or other business entities, and to transfer to them any part or all of the Trust assets in exchange for an investment therein; to exercise or to sell any conversion, subscription, or similar rights; and in general to exercise in respect to any investment the unrestricted rights of a personal owner, including voting in person and granting proxies, discretionary, general, or otherwise;

K. In any case in which the Trustee makes any payments or other distribution of Trust assets, to make such payment or distribution in money or in kind, including undivided interests in any property, or partly in money and partly in kind; and in the case of any distribution in kind to any Donee, the adjusted basis of the Trust property distributed shall be fairly representative of the adjusted bases of all Trust properties available for distribution on the date of distribution;

L. To apportion and allocate Trust receipts and expenses between Net Income and principal accounts (provided that no pre-gift appreciation shall be allocable to Net Income);

M. To retain the services of an independent appraiser to assist in valuing assets of this Trust and to reasonably compensate such appraiser for such services;

N. If required by the Code, the Regulations or any Internal Revenue Service rulings thereunder to maintain the status of the Trust as a charitable remainder unitrust, to set aside a reserve or allowance from Trust income for the depreciation or depletion of any property transferred to or invested in by the Trust; otherwise, the Trustee shall have discretion whether or not to set aside such a reserve;

O. With respect to any environmental hazards on Trust property:

1. To take all appropriate actions to prevent, identify or respond to actual or threatened violations of any environmental law, rule or regulation, including compliance with any federal, state or local agency or court order directing an assessment, abatement or cleanup of any environmental hazard;

2. To disclaim, in whole or in part, any interests in property for any reason, including but not limited to, a concern that such property could cause potential liability under any federal, state, or local environmental law, rule or regulation; and/or

3. To set aside any interests in property, which could cause potential liability under any federal, state, or local environmental law, rule or regulation as a separate trust to be held and administered upon the same terms as those governing the remaining Trust assets;

P. To designate as custodian of any Trust property any business entity authorized and engaged in the business of brokers or dealers in securities;

Q. To the extent permitted by law, to register any of such property in its name as Trustee or in the names of nominees, or to take and keep the same unregistered or in bearer form, or in such condition as to pass by delivery; and/or

R. Whenever the Trust acquires an Annuity Contract, to exercise with respect to such Annuity Contract any rights and discretion as owner thereof, as limited hereby, including but not limited to the right or discretion to:

1. Making partial or total withdrawals or surrenders from the Annuity Contract; provided however, the Trustee gives due regard to any withdrawal or partial surrender penalties that may be imposed and to the best interest of all Trust beneficiaries;

2. Electing any annuity option(s) which guarantees the payment to the Trust by or upon the death of the annuitant of an amount at least equal to the surrender value of the Annuity Contract(s) as of the day before the day the annuity payments commence;

3. Designating the day the annuity payments commence; and/or

4. Seeing to the allocation of any payments of any type received from the Annuity Contract between principal and income as is required by this Trust.

Anything in the Trust Agreement to the contrary notwithstanding, it is the intention of the Donor to create a qualifying charitable remainder unitrust under Section 664 of the Code; therefore, no rights, powers, authority or discretion either otherwise granted by the Trust Agreement or by applicable state law that exceed or are inconsistent with those allowed under Section 664 of the Code and the Regulations thereunder are to be possessed or exercised by the Trustee. At no time and under no circumstances shall a Donor serving as a Trustee exercise any power that would result in this Trust being treated as a grantor trust under Subpart E of the Code.

VI.
APPLICABLE LAW

The validity of this Trust shall be controlled by the laws of the State of *(STATE LAW)*. The construction and administration of this Trust shall be controlled by the laws of the State of *(STATE LAW)*. However, in any conflict with Section 664 of the Code, the Regulations thereunder or any other existing or hereafter promulgated legislative or Treasury requirements for the qualification of this Trust and for the Donor's obtaining the full benefit of any income, gift and estate tax charitable deductions to which the Donor (and the Donor's estate) may be entitled, Section 664 of the Code, the Regulations thereunder and the legislative and Treasury requirements shall govern.

VII.
IRREVOCABILITY AND AMENDMENT

This Trust shall be irrevocable. However, the Trustee shall have the power, acting alone, to amend the Trust Agreement in any manner required for the sole purpose of ensuring that this Trust qualifies and continues to qualify as a charitable remainder unitrust within the meaning of Section 664 of the Code and the Regulations thereunder.

VIII.
PROHIBITED ACTS

Notwithstanding any other provision of the Trust Agreement, no Fiduciary shall (except for the payment of the Unitrust Amount) engage in any act of self-dealing (as defined in Section 4941(d) of the Code), retain any excess business holdings (as defined in Section 4943(c) of the Code) which would subject this Trust to tax under Section 4943 of the Code, make any investments which would subject this Trust to tax under Section 4944 of the Code, or make any taxable expenditure (as defined in Section 4945(d) of the Code). If Section 4942 of the Code is deemed applicable to this Trust by reason of Section 508(e) of the Code or otherwise, then the Trustee shall make distributions at such times and in such manner as not to subject this Trust to tax under Section 4942 of the Code.

IX.
INTENTION TO CREATE UNITRUST

It is the Donor's intention to obtain the full benefit of any income, gift and estate tax charitable contribution deductions to which the Donor (and the Donor's estate) may be entitled to under the Code and for this Trust to qualify as a charitable remainder unitrust within the meaning of Section 664(d)(2) and (3) of the Code and the Regulations thereunder. Accordingly, the Trust Agreement shall be interpreted and administered, and the Trust assets shall be valued, managed and invested, in a manner consistent with the Donor's intent and the provisions of such Section, the Regulations thereunder and the Internal Revenue Service rulings relating thereto.

X.
DEATH TAXES

No Death Taxes with respect to this Trust shall be allocated to or be recoverable from this Trust. The Donor agrees to provide in the Donor's Will, or any other appropriate estate planning documents, that any Death Taxes arising from the creation of this Trust, or the interest of the Donor therein, shall be payable from the estate of the Donor, excluding the assets of this Trust. The Donor hereby imposes an affirmative obligation on the Donor's estate to pay all of such Death Taxes (if any) from sources other than this Trust and agrees that this obligation may be enforced by the Trustee or any Donee, acting alone or together. Should Death Taxes with respect to this Trust become due as a result of additional contributions by any person other than the Donor, then the provisions of this Article X shall apply to such other person as if the other person were the Donor for purposes of this Article X.

XI.
MISCELLANEOUS

A. <u>Construction</u>. Unless the context requires otherwise, words in the singular may be construed as denoting the plural, and words in the plural may be construed as denoting the singular. Words of one gender may be construed as denoting another gender as is appropriate within such context.

B. <u>Headings</u>. Titles and headings in the Trust Agreement are added for convenient reference, and shall not be deemed to alter or affect the meaning of any provision hereof.

C. <u>Severability</u>. If any provision or part of any provision of the Trust Agreement shall for any reason be held invalid, illegal or unenforceable in any respect by a court of competent jurisdiction, such invalidity, illegality or unenforceability shall not affect any other provision of the Trust Agreement and the Trust Agreement shall be construed as if such invalid, illegal or unenforceable provision or part thereof had never been contained herein, but only to the extent of its invalidity, illegality or unenforceability.

D. <u>Counterparts</u>. The Trust Agreement has been executed in triplicate, each of which shall be an original and each of which shall constitute the entire Trust Agreement without reference to or the necessity of producing the other counterparts.

E. <u>Spendthrift</u>. The Recipient shall not have any power to sell, transfer, assign, pledge, mortgage, or alienate all or any part of the Recipient's beneficial interest in this Trust in any manner whatsoever. The interest of the Recipient shall not be subject to the claims of the Recipient's creditors or to attachment, execution, bankruptcy proceedings or any other legal process.

XII.
DEFINITIONS

For purposes of the Trust Agreement, the following words and phrases shall have the meanings ascribed to them in this Article XII, as follows:

"Annuity Contract" shall mean any kind of annuity to be paid by an insurance company or by an organization regularly engaged in issuing annuity contracts.

"Charitable Organization" shall mean an organization described in each of Sections 170(b)(1)(A), 170(c), 2055(a) and 2522(a) of the Code.

"Code" shall mean the Internal Revenue Code of 1986, as amended from time to time, and references to a Section of the Code shall include any successor provisions to the Section referred to and to any corresponding provisions of any subsequent federal tax laws.

"Custodian" shall mean a trustee of any trust established exclusively for the benefit of the Recipient, if such a trust has been established, or the conservator, custodian, person holding an effective durable power of attorney or legally appointed guardian of the person or estate of the Recipient.

"Death Taxes" shall mean any and all federal estate taxes, state death taxes or any other estate, death, inheritance or welfare transfer taxes.

"Disability" or "Disabled" shall mean when (i) a guardian or conservator of an individual's person or estate is duly appointed by a court of competent jurisdiction and continues to serve in such capacity, (ii) two physicians (licensed to practice under the laws of the state where the person is domiciled) certify that such person is unable to properly care for his or her person or property, (iii) an individual is a minor under the laws of the state where he or she is domiciled, or (iv) an individual disappears for an unreasonable period of time with no apparent explanation for such disappearance.

"Donee" or "Donees" shall mean any Charitable Organization selected to be a charitable remainderman (or remaindermen) pursuant to Article III of this Trust Agreement.

"Donor" shall mean the settlor of this Trust as named on the first page of the Trust Agreement, who has signed the Trust Agreement.

"Fiduciary" or "Fiduciaries" shall mean, as the context requires, each Trustee and/or Independent Special Trustee, and their successor(s).

"Independent Special Trustee" or "Independent Special Trustees" shall mean each individual and/or entity who or which is appointed as a fiduciary of this Trust, solely for the specific purposes provided in Paragraph B of Article IV, and who or which is an "Independent Trustee", and any successor(s) thereto.

"Independent Trustee" shall have the meaning ascribed to it in Regulation Section 1.664-1(a)(7)(iii).

"Net Fair Market Value of the Trust Assets" shall mean the net fair market value of the assets owned by the Trust as described in Paragraphs B and E of Article II of this Trust.

"Net Income" shall mean the net income of this Trust as determined by the Trustee pursuant to the terms of the Trust Agreement, Section 643(b) of the Code and the Regulations thereunder.

"Notice" or "notify" shall mean a communication in writing, signed by the party sending such communication, mailed by certified mail, return receipt requested, or personally hand delivered, dated receipt obtained. The effective date of such notice shall be deemed to be the date of mailing of such certified mail or the actual date of hand delivery, as the case may be. Notice shall be addressed to such person(s) at such person(s) last known address.

"Recipient" shall mean the individual entity who is entitled to receive the Unitrust Amount pursuant to Paragraph A.1 of Article II of this Trust.

"Regulations" shall mean the regulations published under 26 Code of Federal Regulations as in effect on the date of execution of this Trust Agreement, or, in the event that any such regulation is amended or superseded thereafter, to the regulation (or any successor regulation) as so amended.

"Trust" shall mean the charitable remainder unitrust established under the Trust Agreement, otherwise known as "THE *(TRUST NAME)* CHARITABLE REMAINDER UNITRUST."

"Trust Agreement" shall mean this trust instrument signed by all parties hereto.

"Trustee", "it" or "its" shall mean each individual or entity acting in a fiduciary capacity who or which is named on the first page of the Trust Agreement, and who or which signed the Trust Agreement, and its successor(s).

"Unitrust Amount" shall mean the amount described in Paragraph A.2 of Article II of this Trust.

"Unitrust Period" shall mean the period of time which begins on the date this Trust is first funded and ends on the date upon which the Recipient dies.

"Unmarketable Asset" shall have the meaning ascribed to it in Regulation Section 1.664(a)(7)(ii).

IN WITNESS WHEREOF, the parties hereto have executed this Trust Agreement on the date first above written.

DONOR:

_____

(DONOR)

TRUSTEE:

_____

(TRUSTEE)

[ACKNOWLEDGMENT & WITNESS AS REQUIRED UNDER STATE LAW]

EXHIBIT A

THE *(TRUST NAME)*
CHARITABLE REMAINDER UNITRUST

<u>Item No.</u>   <u>Date of Transfer</u>   <u>Description</u>

Receipt of the above described assets is hereby acknowledged this _____ day of *(MONTH)*, *(TAX YEAR)*.

TRUSTEE:

_____

(TRUSTEE)

SAMPLE INTERVIVOS FLIP UNITRUST

THE *(TRUST NAME)*
CHARITABLE REMAINDER UNITRUST

This TRUST AGREEMENT is made and is effective on this _____ day of *(MONTH)*, *(YEAR)*, by and between *(DONOR 1)* and *(DONOR 2)*, residing at *(DONORS' ADDRESS)*, as the Donors, and *(TRUSTEE)*, located at *(TRUSTEE'S ADDRESS)*, and its successor(s), as the Trustee.

I.
AGREEMENT OF TRUST

The Donors are irrevocably assigning, transferring and delivering on the date hereof to the Trustee all right, title and interest in and to the property described in Exhibit A, a copy of which is attached hereto and specifically made a part hereof by this reference. The Trustee hereby accepts such irrevocable gift and agrees to hold, administer and distribute such property, together with any other property which is or shall become an asset of this Trust, in accordance with the provisions of the Trust Agreement. The Trust Agreement is intended to create a charitable remainder unitrust within the meaning of Regulation Section 1.664-3(c) and Section 664(d)(2) and (3) of the Code. Certain terms throughout this Trust Agreement are defined in Article XII.

II.
DISTRIBUTIONS

A. <u>Income and Principal</u>. During the Unitrust Period, the Trustee shall distribute the income and principal of this Trust as follows:

1. In each taxable year of this Trust, the Trustee shall pay, in equal installments at the end of each calendar quarter, the Unitrust Amount to *(DONOR 1)* and *(DONOR 2)*, jointly and then to the survivor of them during the Unitrust Period.

2. (a) During the Initial Period, the term "Unitrust Amount" shall mean an amount equal to the lesser of: (i) the Net Income of this Trust for such taxable year or (ii) _____ percent (___%) of the Net Fair Market Value of the Trust Assets, as modified by Paragraphs C and D of this Article II. If the Net Income for any taxable year exceeds the amount determined under Paragraph A.2(a)(ii) of this Article II, the Unitrust Amount shall also include such excess Net Income to the extent that the aggregate of the amounts paid to the Recipients and the survivor of them in prior years is less than _____ percent (___%) of the aggregate Net Fair Market Value of the Trust assets for such years. During the Initial Period, any Net Income of this Trust in excess of the Unitrust Amount shall be added to principal. Any Makeup Amount accrued during the Initial Period shall be forfeited at the termination of the Initial Period.

(b) During the Remaining Period, the term "Unitrust Amount" shall mean an amount equal to _____ percent (___%) of the Net Fair Market Value of the Trust Assets, as modified by Paragraphs C and D of this Article II and not any amount described in Paragraph A.2(a) of this Article II. During the Remaining Period, the Unitrust Amount shall be paid from Net Income, and to the extent Net Income is insufficient, from principal. Any Net Income in excess of the Unitrust Amount shall be added to principal.

3. Notwithstanding any existing or hereafter enacted state law, no amount other than the Unitrust Amount may be paid to or for the use of any person or entity other than a Charitable Organization. However, an amount shall not be deemed to be paid to or for the use of any person other than a Charitable Organization if the amount is transferred for full and adequate consideration."

4. The Trustee may pay the Unitrust Amount to the Recipients by payment directly to him or her or by deposit in any bank designated by him or her. If any Recipient should at any time be under a Disability, the Trustee may pay the Unitrust Amount to his or her Custodian. Any such payment for the

benefit of such Recipient shall release the Trustee from its obligation to pay the Unitrust Amount, and the Trustee shall have no duty to supervise or inquire into the application of any funds so paid.

    5. Upon the expiration of the Unitrust Period, the Trustee shall distribute the then principal and income of this Trust in accordance with Article III herein.

    B. <u>Valuation Date</u>. The Net Fair Market Value of the Trust Assets shall be determined annually on the first day of each taxable year of this Trust (including any short taxable year), in accordance with the provisions of Paragraph E of this Article II.

    C. <u>Taxable Year and Short Taxable Years</u>. The first taxable year of this Trust shall commence on the date this Trust is first funded and shall end on December 31st of that year. Subsequent taxable years shall be on a calendar year basis, except that the last taxable year of this Trust shall end on the date that this Trust terminates pursuant to Article III herein. In the case of a taxable year which is for a period of less than twelve (12) months (other than the taxable year in which the Unitrust Period ends), the amount described in Paragraph A.2(a)(ii) of this Article II or Paragraph A.2(b) of this Article II shall be such amount multiplied by a fraction the numerator of which is the number of days in the taxable year of this Trust and the denominator of which is 365 (366 if February 29 is a day included in the numerator). In the case of the taxable year in which the Unitrust Period ends, the amount described in Paragraph A.2(a)(ii) of this Article II or Paragraph A.2(b) of this Article II shall be such amount multiplied by a fraction the numerator of which is the number of days in the period beginning on the first day of such taxable year and ending on the date the Unitrust Period ends and the denominator of which is 365 (366 if February 29 is a day included in the numerator). Notwithstanding the foregoing, the obligation of the Trustee to pay the Unitrust Amount shall terminate with the regular periodic payment next preceding the date the Unitrust Period ends.

    D. <u>Additional Contributions</u>. Any person may contribute property to this Trust, with the consent of the Trustee, either during life or at death. For the taxable year of this Trust in which any additional contribution is made, the additional property shall be valued at the time of contribution and in accordance with Paragraph E of this Article II, and the amount described in Paragraph A.2(a)(ii) of this Article II or Paragraph A.2(b) of this Article II shall be five percent (5%) of the sum of the following components:

    1. The Net Fair Market Value of the Trust Assets determined on the first day of the taxable year (and thus excluding the value of the additional property, and earned income from, and any appreciation on, such property after its contribution); and

    2. That proportion of the value of the additional property (that was excluded under Paragraph D.1 of this Article II immediately above) which the number of days in the period that begins with the date of contribution and ends with the earlier of the last day of such taxable year or the date the Unitrust Period ends bears to the number of days in the period that begins on the first day of such taxable year and ends with the earlier of the last day of such taxable year or the date the Unitrust Period ends.

    If an additional contribution is made by Will, the obligation to pay the Unitrust Amount payable with respect to the additional contribution shall commence with the date of death of the person under whose Will the additional contribution is made. Payment of that portion of the Unitrust Amount may be deferred, however, from such date of death to the end of the taxable year in which occurs the complete funding of the additional contribution. Within a reasonable time following such complete funding of the additional contribution, the Trustee shall pay to the Recipients, in the case of an underpayment, or receive from the Recipients, in the case of an overpayment, the difference between: (i) the Unitrust Amount with respect to such additional contribution actually paid to the Recipients, plus interest on such amounts, compounded annually, computed for any period at the rate of interest that the Regulations under Section 664 of the Code prescribe for this Trust for such computation for such period; and (ii) the Unitrust Amount with respect to such additional contribution payable, determined under the method described in Section 1.664-1(a)(5)(ii) of the Regulations. Any payments required to be made because of an underpayment shall be paid to each Recipient (or each Recipient's estate) who received the underpayment. Any repayments required to be made because of an overpayment shall be repaid by each Recipient (or each Recipient's estate) who received the overpayment.

E. <u>Fair Market Value</u>. The Trustee shall compute the Net Fair Market Value of the Trust Assets considering all assets and liabilities without regard to whether particular items are taken into account in determining the Net Income; provided however, in the event an Independent Special Trustee shall be appointed to value any Trust asset pursuant to Paragraph B of Article IV herein, the Independent Special Trustee shall so value each such asset. All determinations of the Net Fair Market Value of the Trust Assets shall be in accordance with generally accepted fiduciary accounting principles and any United States Treasury requirements governing charitable remainder unitrusts. In any conflict, Treasury requirements shall prevail over generally accepted fiduciary accounting principles and any inconsistent provisions of this Trust Agreement. In the event that the Net Fair Market Value of the Trust Assets is determined incorrectly for any taxable year, the Trustee shall pay to the Recipients or their respective estates (in the case of an undervaluation), or be repaid by the Recipients or their respective estates (in the case of an overvaluation), an amount equal to the difference between the Unitrust Amount which the Trustee should have paid to the Recipients if the correct values were used, and the Unitrust Amount which the Trustee actually paid to the Recipients. Such payments or repayments shall be made within a reasonable period after the final determination of the correct value. If necessary to maintain this Trust as a tax-exempt charitable remainder unitrust under Section 664 of the Code, the Trustee shall (only for purposes of determining the deficiency payable pursuant to the second sentence of Paragraph A.2 of this Article II and not for any other reason): (i) treat as a liability on each annual valuation date the sum of any accrued (but unrealized) gain on a hypothetical sale or exchange of any capital asset held in this Trust to the extent this sum is less than or equal to any such deficiency payable balance; and (ii) subtract such liability from the Net Fair Market Value of the Trust Assets on such date when computing the Unitrust Amount.

F. <u>Right to Revoke</u>. Notwithstanding any of the foregoing provisions of this Trust Agreement:

1. *(DONOR 1)* hereby expressly reserves the power, exercisable only by her Will, to revoke and terminate the survivorship payments for *(DONOR 2)* from her interest in the property in this Trust. If she effectively exercises her testamentary power:

(a) the Trustee shall upon her death distribute one-half of the then income and principal of this Trust, other than any amounts due to the Recipients, to the Donee(s) as set forth in Article III hereof;

(b) the Trustee's obligation to make payments to her shall cease with the payment next preceding her death and one-half of the accruals for the period beginning with the payment date next preceding her death and ending with the date of her death shall on her death be paid to the Donee(s) as set forth in Article III hereof; and

(c) the Trustee shall thereafter pay the Unitrust Amount to *(ALTERNATE RECIPIENT 1)* for the remainder of the Unitrust Period.

2. *(DONOR 2)* hereby expressly reserves the power, exercisable only by his Will, to revoke and terminate the survivorship payments for *(DONOR 1)* from his interest in the property in this Trust. If he effectively exercises his testamentary power:

(a) the Trustee shall upon his death distribute one-half of the then income and principal of this Trust, other than any amounts due to the Recipients, to the Donee(s) as set forth in Article III hereof;

(b) the Trustee's obligation to make payments to him shall cease with the payment next preceding his death and one-half of the accruals for the period beginning with the payment date next preceding his death and ending with the date of his death shall on his death be paid to the Donee(s) as set forth in Article III hereof; and

(c) the Trustee shall thereafter pay the Unitrust Amount to *(ALTERNATE RECIPIENT 2)* for the remainder of the Unitrust Period.

III.
TERMINATION

This Trust shall terminate within a reasonable time after the expiration of the Unitrust Period; provided, however, that such reasonable time shall not extend beyond the last day of the month in which occurs the ninetieth (90th) day following the date the Unitrust Period ends. Upon termination, the Trustee shall distribute all of the then principal and income of this Trust, free of trust, other than any amount due to the surviving Recipient or the surviving Recipient's estate, to a Donee.

Notwithstanding any contrary provision of the Trust Agreement, prior to the expiration of the Unitrust Period, the Donors, and the survivor of them, shall retain the right, by acknowledged written instrument delivered to the Trustee, to designate the Donee(s) and to change the Donee(s) by adding or substituting new Charitable Organization(s) and/or omitting certain Charitable Organization(s) or by altering the share each is to receive. If more than one written instrument is so delivered to the Trustee, the written instrument bearing the latest date shall control and shall be deemed to revoke all prior written instruments unless the most recent one shall provide otherwise.

If any Donee is not a Charitable Organization at the time when any principal or income of this Trust is to be distributed to it, the Trustee shall distribute such principal or income in proportion to the relative shares of the Donees which are so described and, if none of the Donees is so described, to one or more Charitable Organizations as the Trustee shall select and in such shares as it shall determine.

IV.
FIDUCIARY PROVISIONS

A. <u>Appointment of Trustee</u>. *(TRUSTEE)* shall serve as Trustee of this Trust. In the event that *(TRUSTEE)* for any reason shall fail to serve as Trustee, then *(ALTERNATE TRUSTEE)* shall serve in the place and stead of *(TRUSTEE)*.

B. <u>Appointment of Independent Special Trustee</u>.

1. In the event this Trust acquires or owns any asset which does not have an objective, ascertainable market value, such as closely held stock or real estate, an Independent Special Trustee shall, if required by law, be appointed by the Trustee. If so appointed, the Independent Special Trustee shall determine the fair market value of such asset at the time of contribution or acquisition and for purposes of the annual determination of the Net Fair Market Value of the Trust Assets.

2. The Trustee shall also have the right and option to appoint an Independent Special Trustee to take such action as the Trustee shall clearly define and delegate.

3. When (i) the sole Trustee is Independent or (ii) more than one person is acting as Trustee hereunder and one of such Trustees is Independent, the Independent Trustee shall have the right and option to act as an Independent Special Trustee hereunder. However, no Trustee (other than an acting Independent Special Trustee) shall have any power, duty or liability hereunder with respect to matters described in this Paragraph B.

4. The Independent Special Trustee shall have no powers, duties, or liabilities hereunder, except with respect to matters specifically described in this Paragraph B, and solely with respect to such matters, the Independent Special Trustee may exercise the rights, powers, authority and discretion, and be subject to the restrictions, obligations and duties, accorded to a Trustee pursuant to Article V herein. However, the Independent Special Trustee may not function in a manner which would jeopardize the status of this Trust as a charitable remainder trust as defined in Section 664 of the Code, the Regulations thereunder and Internal Revenue Service rulings governing the operation thereof.

C. <u>Resignation of Fiduciary</u>. Any Fiduciary may resign at any time by giving a notice to any other Fiduciary and to the Recipients, or if either or both of the Recipients are Disabled, to their respective

Custodian(s). Such resignation shall be effective upon the sooner to occur of: (i) sixty (60) days after the date of the notice of resignation, or (ii) the appointment of and acceptance by the successor Fiduciary. Notwithstanding the above, in the event (i) a Fiduciary dies or is Disabled or (ii) an Independent Special Trustee ceases to be Independent, notice of resignation is deemed given, and the resignation shall be effective as of the date of such death, Disability or ceasing to be Independent, as the case may be. The resigning Fiduciary (or its representative) shall file a final accounting and deliver all Trust assets under its charge and control to the successor Fiduciary as soon as possible, but in no event later than sixty (60) days following the date of the resignation notice being given or deemed given. Upon the relinquishment and delivery of all Trust assets and the final accounting to the successor Fiduciary, the resigning Fiduciary shall be discharged of all further duties and obligations hereunder.

D. <u>Removal of Fiduciary</u>. The Recipients (or the survivor thereof) shall have the right with or without cause, to replace or discharge any acting Fiduciary. Upon the Disability of either Recipient, this right may be exercised by the Recipient who is not Disabled. Upon the Disability of the surviving Recipient or the Disability of both Recipients, this right may be exercised by his or her respective Custodian(s). Such removal shall be effective upon the sooner to occur of: (i) sixty (60) days after giving the Fiduciary being removed notice of such removal, or (ii) the appointment of and acceptance by the successor Fiduciary. The Fiduciary being removed shall file a final accounting and deliver all Trust assets under its charge and control to the successor Fiduciary within such sixty (60) day period. Upon the relinquishment and delivery of all Trust assets and the final accounting to the successor Fiduciary, the Fiduciary being removed shall be discharged of all further duties and obligations hereunder.

E. <u>Appointment of Successor Fiduciary</u>. In the event any vacancy at any time occurs in the office of a Fiduciary hereunder, regardless of how caused, the Recipients (or the survivor thereof) shall have the right to fill such vacancy. Upon the Disability of either Recipient, this right may be exercised by the Recipient who is not Disabled. Upon the Disability of the surviving Recipient or the Disability of both Recipients, his or her respective Custodian(s) shall exercise such right. At the earliest possible date, all Trust assets and a final accounting shall be delivered to the successor Fiduciary. At such time as any successor Fiduciary delivers notice of acceptance to the Recipients, such successor Fiduciary shall have the rights, powers, authority and discretion, and be subject to the restrictions, obligations and duties, regarding this Trust within the appointed capacity.

F. <u>Liability of Successor Fiduciary</u>. A successor Fiduciary shall not be responsible to any beneficiary of this Trust or to this Trust for any act or omission of a former Fiduciary, and shall not be required to audit or investigate the acts or administration of any former Fiduciary and shall be charged, upon issuing a simple receipt, with only the Trust assets so received. In addition, unless requested in writing by a beneficiary of this Trust and indemnified adequately (in such Fiduciary's discretion therefor), no successor Fiduciary shall have any duty to take action to seek redress for breach of trust by a former Fiduciary.

G. <u>Appointment of Co-Fiduciary</u>. The Recipients (or the survivor thereof) shall have the right to appoint additional persons to act as Co-Fiduciaries hereunder. At such time as the newly-appointed Co-Fiduciary delivers notice of acceptance to the Recipients, the newly-appointed Co-Fiduciary shall have the rights, powers, authority and discretion, and be subject to the restrictions, obligations and duties, regarding this Trust within the appointed capacity. In granting the foregoing right, it is not the intention of the Donors to require that any specific number of Fiduciaries serve in any one capacity hereunder simultaneously.

H. <u>Fiduciary Actions</u>. When more than two persons are acting as Trustees (or Independent Special Trustees), the concurrence and joinder of a majority of them shall control in all matters pertaining to the administration hereunder. When two persons are acting as Trustees (or Independent Special Trustees), the concurrence and joinder of both Trustees (or Independent Special Trustees) shall be required. Such actions by the Fiduciaries shall be made either by vote at a meeting (in person or by telephone) or by written concurrence. When more than two persons are acting as Trustees (or Independent Special Trustees), any dissenting or abstaining Fiduciary may be absolved from personal liability by registering a written dissent or abstention with the records of this Trust. Such dissenting Fiduciary shall thereafter act with the other Fiduciaries in any manner necessary or appropriate to effectuate the decision of the majority.

I. <u>Compensation</u>. A Fiduciary, and any agents of or successors to any Fiduciary, shall be entitled to reasonable compensation for services rendered in connection with this Trust. The amount of compensation shall be an amount equal to the customary and prevailing charges for services of a similar nature during the same period of time and in the same geographic locale. Any Fiduciary may waive any compensation at any time, by providing notice of such waiver to the Recipients and another Fiduciary, if then serving.

J. <u>Retention of Agents</u>. A Fiduciary may delegate investment and management functions to an agent as is prudent under the circumstances, but shall exercise reasonable care in selecting such agent. The duties of the agent shall be consistent with the terms and intent of this Trust, and the Fiduciary shall periodically review the agent's performance.

K. <u>Liability for Retaining Property</u>. The Fiduciary shall not be liable for any loss or depreciation in value sustained by this Trust as a result of the Fiduciary accepting or retaining any property upon which hazardous materials or substances are discovered, unless the Fiduciary contributed to the loss or depreciation in value through willful default, willful misconduct or gross negligence.

L. <u>Indemnification</u>. The Donors shall indemnify the Fiduciary against any claims (except for claims due to the Fiduciary's willful default, willful misconduct or gross negligence) filed against the Fiduciary (i) as an "owner" or "operator" under the federal Comprehensive Environmental Response, Compensation and Liability Act of 1980 (as from time to time amended) or any regulation thereunder and (ii) under any other federal, state or local environmental law, rule, regulation or order relating to the property contributed to this Trust by the Donors.

M. <u>Jurisdiction and Bond</u>. This Trust shall not be administered under the jurisdiction of any court. Should a question or issue be submitted to a court of competent jurisdiction at any time or from time to time, such court shall acquire jurisdiction of only the question or issue submitted to it, and the jurisdiction of such court shall terminate upon the conclusion or settlement of such question or issue. No bond or other security shall be required of any person acting as a Fiduciary, whether serving jointly or alone.

V.
<u>POWERS OF THE TRUSTEE</u>

All rights, powers, authority and discretion exercisable by the Trustee under this Trust or by law shall be binding and conclusive on all interested parties; shall be exercisable by the Trustee in its sole and absolute discretion; shall be exercisable only in a fiduciary capacity and in the best interests of the beneficiaries; shall be construed in the broadest possible manner; and shall be exercisable without prior or subsequent application to any court under the jurisdiction of which this Trust may be administered.

The Trustee is under a duty to the beneficiaries to invest and manage the funds of the Trust as a prudent investor would, in a manner that is fair to all beneficiaries as a reflection of the Trust's purposes, terms, and obligations and in light of the circumstances of the Trust and the relevant circumstances of its beneficiaries. The investment decisions of a Trustee shall be evaluated not in isolation, but in the context of the investment portfolio as a whole and as part of an overall investment strategy reasonably suited to the Trust.

Not in derogation of or in limitation upon the powers, authority and discretion conferred by law upon a trustee, the Trustee is vested with the following rights, powers, authority and discretion:

A. To alter, repair, improve, erect buildings upon, demolish, manage, partition, mortgage, lease for any period, including a period in excess of any fixed by statute or extending beyond the duration of this Trust, exchange, grant options to lease or to buy, and sell or dispose of, at public or private sale, and upon such conditions and such terms as to cash and credit as it deems advisable, any of the Trust assets;

B. To compromise, settle, subordinate, arbitrate, extend, renew, modify, or release, in whole or in part, any claim held by it or held against any of the Trust assets;

C. To continue to hold the property transferred to it hereunder in the form in which it shall be when transferred or as the form thereof may be changed pursuant to the other provisions of the Trust Agreement, without regard to the limitations imposed by law upon the investment of trust funds;

D. To borrow money and to encumber or hypothecate Trust assets whether by mortgage, deed of trust, pledge or otherwise;

E. To commence or defend litigation with respect to the Trust assets, at the expense of the Trust assets;

F. To employ any person, firm, corporation, bank, or trust company for advice with respect to investment policy or any other matter; but the Trustee may follow or refrain from following any recommendation so obtained and such recommendations shall not in any way limit the discretionary power and authority conferred upon the Trustee hereunder with respect to investments or other matters;

G. To retain or discharge accountants, attorneys, administrators, brokers, investment advisers, investment counselors and other agents, and to pay reasonable compensation for their services;

H. To enter into any and all agreements with the Internal Revenue Service or any other governmental body and to execute, from time to time, any declarations of policy or disclaimers restricting the powers, authority and discretion granted to the Trustee;

I. To invest and to reinvest the Trust assets in every kind of property, real, personal or mixed, and every kind of investment, specifically including, but not limited to, corporate and government obligations of every kind, stocks (preferred or common), partnerships (general or limited), limited liability companies, options, shares or interests in common trust funds, or Annuity Contracts, regardless of any laws or rules of law governing the investment of trust funds; to lawfully disregard any laws or rule of law that, in the absence of contrary trust provisions, would limit the amount any trustee can invest in or pay for any Annuity Contract; with respect to unproductive property (*i.e.*, property which is not producing fiduciary income currently for distribution to the Recipients), the Trustee is hereby authorized to continue to hold or to acquire such property, especially when such unproductive property is appreciating or may appreciate in value; and carrying charges for such property shall be paid first out of income and then out of principal; and upon the sale of such property, the Trustee shall allocate fiduciary income and principal as set forth in Paragraph L of this Article V; and nothing in the Trust Agreement shall be construed to restrict the Trustee from investing the Trust assets in a manner which could result in the annual realization of a reasonable amount of income or gain from the sale or disposition of Trust assets;

J. With respect to any investment held by the Trustee, to participate in and consent to any corporate or financial reorganization, dissolution, liquidation, merger, consolidation, sale or lease, or in and to any other change in its financial structure; and to become a depositor with any protective, reorganization, or similar committee, and to make any necessary payments incident to the foregoing; to organize or participate in the organization of corporations or other business entities, and to transfer to them any part or all of the Trust assets in exchange for an investment therein; to exercise or to sell any conversion, subscription, or similar rights; and in general to exercise in respect to any investment the unrestricted rights of a personal owner, including voting in person and granting proxies, discretionary, general, or otherwise;

K. In any case in which the Trustee makes any payments or other distribution of Trust assets, to make such payment or distribution in money or in kind, including undivided interests in any property, or partly in money and partly in kind; and in the case of any distribution in kind to any Donee, the adjusted basis of the Trust property distributed shall be fairly representative of the adjusted bases of all Trust properties available for distribution on the date of distribution;

L. To apportion and allocate Trust receipts and expenses between income and principal accounts (provided that no pre-gift appreciation shall be allocable to fiduciary income); and to treat as fiduciary income the increase in value of an obligation for the payment of money, payable at a future time in accordance with a fixed, variable or discretionary schedule of appreciation in excess of the fair market value on the date of contribution or the price at which it was issued, or the increase in value of an interest in a partnership or other investment in excess of the fair market value on the date of contribution or the price paid, as the case may be, including but not limited to a bond, a zero coupon bond, an Annuity Contract before annuitization, a life insurance contract before the death of the insured and/or an interest in a common trust fund as defined under Section 584 of the Code; and such increase in value of an obligation for the payment of money or the increase in value of an interest in a partnership or other investment shall be available for distribution only when the Trustee receives cash on account of the obligation, partnership interest or other investment;

M. To retain the services of an independent appraiser to assist in valuing assets of this Trust and to reasonably compensate such appraiser for such services;

N. If required by the Code, the Regulations or any Internal Revenue Service rulings thereunder to maintain the status of the Trust as a charitable remainder unitrust, to set aside a reserve or allowance from Trust income for the depreciation or depletion of any property transferred to or invested in by the Trust; otherwise, the Trustee shall have discretion whether or not to set aside such a reserve;

O. With respect to any environmental hazards on Trust property:

1. To take all appropriate actions to prevent, identify or respond to actual or threatened violations of any environmental law, rule or regulation, including compliance with any federal, state or local agency or court order directing an assessment, abatement or cleanup of any environmental hazard;

2. To disclaim, in whole or in part, any interests in property for any reason, including but not limited to, a concern that such property could cause potential liability under any federal, state, or local environmental law, rule or regulation; and/or

3. To set aside any interests in property, which could cause potential liability under any federal, state, or local environmental law, rule or regulation as a separate trust to be held and administered upon the same terms as those governing the remaining Trust assets;

P. To designate as custodian of any Trust property any business entity authorized and engaged in the business of brokers or dealers in securities;

Q. To the extent permitted by law, to register any of such property in its name as Trustee or in the names of nominees, or to take and keep the same unregistered or in bearer form, or in such condition as to pass by delivery; and/or

R. Whenever the Trust acquires an Annuity Contract, to exercise with respect to such Annuity Contract any rights and discretion as owner thereof, as limited hereby, including but not limited to the right or discretion to:

1. Making partial or total withdrawals or surrenders from the Annuity Contract; provided however, the Trustee gives due regard to any withdrawal or partial surrender penalties that may be imposed and to the best interest of all Trust beneficiaries;

2. Electing any annuity option(s) which guarantees the payment to the Trust by or upon the death of the annuitant of an amount at least equal to the surrender value of the Annuity Contract(s) as of the day before the day the annuity payments commence;

3. Designating the day the annuity payments commence; and/or

4. Seeing to the allocation of any payments of any type received from the Annuity Contract between principal and income as is required by this Trust.

Anything in the Trust Agreement to the contrary notwithstanding, it is the intention of the Donors to create a qualifying charitable remainder unitrust under Section 664 of the Code; therefore, no rights, powers, authority or discretion either otherwise granted by the Trust Agreement or by applicable state law that exceed or are inconsistent with those allowed under Section 664 of the Code and the Regulations thereunder are to be possessed or exercised by the Trustee. At no time and under no circumstances shall a Donor serving as a Trustee exercise any power that would result in this Trust being treated as a grantor trust under Subpart E of the Code.

VI.
APPLICABLE LAW

The validity of this Trust shall be controlled by the laws of the State of *(STATE)*. The construction and administration of this Trust shall be controlled by the laws of the State of *(STATE)*, or if the Trustee designates in writing to the contrary, by the laws of the Commonwealth or State in which this Trust is administered. However, in any conflict with Section 664 of the Code, the Regulations thereunder or any other existing or hereafter promulgated legislative or Treasury requirements for the qualification of this Trust and for the Donors' obtaining the full benefit of any income, gift and estate tax charitable deductions to which the Donors and the Donors' estates may be entitled, Section 664 of the Code, the Regulations thereunder and the legislative and Treasury requirements shall govern.

VII.
IRREVOCABILITY AND AMENDMENT

This Trust shall be irrevocable. However, the Trustee shall have the power, acting alone, to amend the Trust Agreement in any manner required for the sole purpose of ensuring that this Trust qualifies and continues to qualify as a charitable remainder unitrust within the meaning of Section 664 of the Code and the Regulations thereunder.

VIII.
PROHIBITED ACTS

Notwithstanding any other provision of the Trust Agreement, no Fiduciary shall (except for the payment of the Unitrust Amount) engage in any act of self-dealing (as defined in Section 4941(d) of the Code), retain any excess business holdings (as defined in Section 4943(c) of the Code) which would subject this Trust to tax under Section 4943 of the Code, make any investments which would subject this Trust to tax under Section 4944 of the Code, or make any taxable expenditure (as defined in Section 4945(d) of the Code). If Section 4942 of the Code is deemed applicable to this Trust by reason of Section 508(e) of the Code or otherwise, then the Trustee shall make distributions at such times and in such manner as not to subject this Trust to tax under Section 4942 of the Code.

IX.
INTENTION TO CREATE UNITRUST

It is the Donors' intention to obtain the full benefit of any income, gift and estate tax charitable contribution deductions to which the Donors and their estates may be entitled to under the Code and for this Trust to qualify as a charitable remainder unitrust within the meaning of Regulation 1.664-3(c), and Section 664(d)(2) and (3) of the Code and the Regulations thereunder. Accordingly, the Trust Agreement shall be interpreted and administered, and the Trust assets shall be valued, managed and invested, in a manner consistent with the Donors' intent and the provisions of such Section, the Regulations thereunder and the Internal Revenue Service rulings relating thereto.

X.
DEATH TAXES

No Death Taxes with respect to this Trust shall be allocated to or be recoverable from this Trust. The Donors agree to provide in their Wills, or any other appropriate estate planning documents, that any Death

Taxes arising from the creation of this Trust, or the interest of any Donor therein, shall be payable from the estates of the Donors, excluding the assets of this Trust. The Donors hereby impose an affirmative obligation on their respective estates to pay all of such Death Taxes (if any) from sources other than this Trust and agree that this obligation may be enforced by the Trustee or any Donee, or by each Donor, acting alone or together.

Each of the Donors has provided for the payment of any death taxes from sources other than this Trust Agreement. Nevertheless, if for any reason, this Trust becomes liable for death taxes on the death of the first of the Donors to die, the interest of the surviving Recipient in the one-half interest of the deceased Donor in this Trust shall take effect only if the surviving Recipient furnishes the funds for payment of any death taxes for which this Trust may be liable. If the surviving Recipient fails to furnish those funds, it shall be deemed for all purposes of this Trust Agreement that the first of the Donors to die exercised the right in his or her Will described in Paragraphs F(1) or F(2) of Article II herein. This Article X is included herein specifically to comply with the intent and provisions of Revenue Ruling 82-128. Should Death Taxes with respect to this Trust become due as a result of additional contributions by any person other than the Donors, then the provisions of this Article X shall apply to such other person as if the other person were a Donor for purposes of this Article X.

XI.
MISCELLANEOUS

A. <u>Construction</u>. Unless the context requires otherwise, words in the singular may be construed as denoting the plural, and words in the plural may be construed as denoting the singular. Words of one gender may be construed as denoting another gender as is appropriate within such context.

B. <u>Headings</u>. Titles and headings in the Trust Agreement are added for convenient reference, and shall not be deemed to alter or affect the meaning of any provision hereof.

C. <u>Severability</u>. If any provision or part of any provision of the Trust Agreement shall for any reason be held invalid, illegal or unenforceable in any respect by a court of competent jurisdiction, such invalidity, illegality or unenforceability shall not affect any other provision of the Trust Agreement and the Trust Agreement shall be construed as if such invalid, illegal or unenforceable provision or part thereof had never been contained herein, but only to the extent of its invalidity, illegality or unenforceability.

D. <u>Counterparts</u>. The Trust Agreement has been executed in triplicate, each of which shall be an original and each of which shall constitute the entire Trust Agreement without reference to or the necessity of producing the other counterparts.

E. <u>Spendthrift</u>. The Recipients shall not have any power to sell, transfer, assign, pledge, mortgage, or alienate all or any part of their beneficial interest in this Trust in any manner whatsoever. The interest of the Recipients shall not be subject to the claims of their creditors or to attachment, execution, bankruptcy proceedings or any other legal process.

XII.
DEFINITIONS

For purposes of the Trust Agreement, the following words and phrases shall have the meanings ascribed to them in this Article XII, as follows:

"Annuity Contract" shall mean any kind of annuity to be paid by an insurance company or by an organization regularly engaged in issuing annuity contracts.

"Charitable Organization" shall mean an organization described in each of Sections 170(b)(1)(A), 170(c), 2055(a) and 2522(a) of the Code.

"Code" shall mean the Internal Revenue Code of 1986, as amended from time to time, and references to a Section of the Code shall include any successor provisions to the Section referred to and to any corresponding provisions of any subsequent federal tax laws.

"Custodian" shall mean a trustee of any trust established exclusively for the benefit of a Recipient, if such a trust has been established, or the conservator, custodian, person holding an effective durable power of attorney or legally appointed guardian of the person or estate of a Recipient.

"Death Taxes" shall mean any and all federal estate taxes, state death taxes or any other estate, death, inheritance or welfare transfer taxes.

"Disability" or "Disabled" shall mean when (i) a guardian or conservator of an individual's person or estate is duly appointed by a court of competent jurisdiction and continues to serve in such capacity, (ii) two physicians (licensed to practice under the laws of the state where the person is domiciled) certify that such person is unable to properly care for his or her person or property, (iii) an individual is a minor under the laws of the state where he or she is domiciled, or (iv) an individual disappears for an unreasonable period of time with no apparent explanation for such disappearance.

"Donee" or "Donees" shall mean any Charitable Organization selected to be a charitable remainderman (or remaindermen) pursuant to Article III of this Trust Agreement.

"Donor" or "Donors" shall mean the settlor(s) of this Trust as named on the first page of the Trust Agreement, who have signed the Trust Agreement.

"Fiduciary" or "Fiduciaries" shall mean, as the context requires, each Trustee and/or Independent Special Trustee, and their successor(s).

"Independent" shall mean any person or entity other than the Donors, or persons or entities no more than half of whom are Related or Subordinate Parties who are subservient to the wishes of the Donors, and as further defined in Section 674(c) of the Code.

"Independent Special Trustee" or "Independent Special Trustees" shall mean each individual and/or entity who or which is appointed as a fiduciary of this Trust, solely for the specific purposes provided in Paragraph B of Article IV, and who or which is "Independent", and any successor(s) thereto.

"Initial Period" shall commence on the first day of the first taxable year of this Trust and shall terminate on the last day of the taxable year in which the Triggering Event occurs.

"Makeup Amount" shall mean the amount described in the second sentence of Paragraph A.2(a) of Article II of this Trust.

"Net Fair Market Value of the Trust Assets" shall mean the net fair market value of the assets owned by the Trust as described in Paragraphs B and E of Article II of this Trust.

"Net Income" shall mean the net income of this Trust as determined by the Trustee pursuant to the terms of the Trust Agreement, Section 643(b) of the Code and the Regulations thereunder.

"Notice" or "notify" shall mean a communication in writing, signed by the party sending such communication, mailed by certified mail, return receipt requested, or personally hand delivered, dated receipt obtained. The effective date of such notice shall be deemed to be the date of mailing of such certified mail or the actual date of hand delivery, as the case may be. Notice shall be addressed to such person(s) at such person(s) last known address.

"Recipient" or "Recipients" shall mean each individual who is entitled to receive the Unitrust Amount pursuant to Paragraph A.1 of Article II of this Trust.

"Regulations" shall mean the regulations published under 26 Code of Federal Regulations as in effect on the date of execution of this Trust Agreement, or, in the event that any such regulation is amended or superseded thereafter, to the regulation (or any successor regulation) as so amended.

"Related or Subordinate Parties" shall have the same meaning as defined in Section 672(c) of the Code.

"Remaining Period" shall commence on the first day of the taxable year that immediately follows the taxable year in which the Triggering Event occurs and shall terminate on the date of death of the survivor of the Recipients.

"Triggering Event" shall occur on December 30, 2006, and it is intended that the Triggering Event qualifies as a permissible event under Regulation Section 1.664-3(c)(1).

"Trust" shall mean the charitable remainder unitrust established under the Trust Agreement, otherwise known as "THE *(TRUST NAME)* CHARITABLE REMAINDER UNITRUST."

"Trust Agreement" shall mean this trust instrument signed by all parties hereto.

"Trustee", "it", or "its" shall mean each individual or entity acting in a fiduciary capacity who or which is named on the first page of the Trust Agreement, and who or which signed the Trust Agreement, and its successor(s).

"Unitrust Period" shall mean the period of time which begins on the date this Trust is first funded and ends on the date upon which the last surviving Recipient dies.

"Unitrust Amount" shall mean the amount described in Paragraph A.2(a) during the Initial Period and the amount described in Paragraph A.2(b) during the Remaining Period.

IN WITNESS WHEREOF, the parties hereto have executed this Trust Agreement on the date first above written.

WITNESS: DONORS:

_____   _____

_____   _____

ATTEST: TRUSTEE:

_____   By:_____

[ACKNOWLEDGMENT & WITNESS AS REQUIRED UNDER STATE LAW]

EXHIBIT A

THE *(TRUST NAME)*
CHARITABLE REMAINDER UNITRUST

<u>Item No.</u>   <u>Date of Transfer</u>   <u>Description</u>

Receipt of the above described assets is hereby acknowledged this _____ day of *(MONTH), (YEAR).*

TRUSTEE:

By:_____

SAMPLE INTERVIVOS NET INCOME WITH MAKE-UP CHARITABLE REMAINDER UNITRUST

THE *(TRUST NAME)*
CHARITABLE REMAINDER UNITRUST

This TRUST AGREEMENT is made and is effective on this _____ day of *(MONTH)*, *(YEAR)*, by and between *(DONOR)*, residing at *(DONOR'S ADDRESS)*, as the Donor and *(TRUSTEE)*, located/residing at *(TRUSTEE'S ADDRESS)*, and its successor(s), as the Trustee.

I.
AGREEMENT OF TRUST

The Donor is irrevocably assigning, transferring and delivering on the date hereof to the Trustee all right, title and interest in and to the property described in Exhibit A, a copy of which is attached hereto and specifically made a part hereof by this reference. The Trustee hereby accepts such irrevocable gift and agrees to hold, administer and distribute such property, together with any other property which is or shall become an asset of this Trust, in accordance with the provisions of the Trust Agreement. The Trust Agreement is intended to create a charitable remainder unitrust within the meaning of Section 4 of Revenue Procedure 90-31 and Section 664(d)(2) and (3) of the Code. Certain terms throughout this Trust Agreement are defined in Article XII.

II.
DISTRIBUTIONS

A. <u>Income and Principal</u>. During the Unitrust Period, the Trustee shall distribute the income and principal of this Trust as follows:

1. In each taxable year of this Trust, the Trustee shall pay the Unitrust Amount to *(RECIPIENT'S NAME)* during the Unitrust Period.

2. The Unitrust Amount shall mean an amount equal to the lesser of: (a) the Net Income for each taxable year of this Trust; or (b) *(FMV PERCENT)* percent (*(FMV PERCENT NUMBER)* %) of the Net Fair Market Value of the Trust Assets, as modified by Paragraphs C and D of this Article II. If the Net Income for any taxable year exceeds the amount determined under Paragraph A.2(b) of this Article II, the Unitrust Amount shall also include such excess Net Income to the extent that the aggregate of the amounts paid to the Recipient in prior years is less than *(FMV PERCENT)* percent (*(FMV PERCENT NUMBER)* %) of the aggregate Net Fair Market Value of the Trust Assets for such years.

3. The Unitrust Amount shall be paid in equal installments at the end of each calendar quarter of each taxable year of this Trust. Any Net Income in excess of the Unitrust Amount shall be added to principal. Notwithstanding any existing or hereafter enacted state law, no amount other than the Unitrust Amount may be paid to or for the use of any person or entity other than a Charitable Organization. However, an amount shall not be deemed to be paid to or for the use of any person other than a Charitable Organization if the amount is transferred for full and adequate consideration.

4. The Trustee may pay the Unitrust Amount to the Recipient by payment directly to him or her or by deposit in any bank designated by him or her. If the Recipient should at any time be under a Disability, the Trustee may pay the Unitrust Amount to the Custodian. Any such payment for the benefit of the Recipient shall release the Trustee from its obligation to pay the Unitrust Amount, and the Trustee shall have no duty to supervise or inquire into the application of any funds so paid.

5. Upon the expiration of the Unitrust Period, the Trustee shall distribute the then principal and income of this Trust in accordance with Article III herein.

B. <u>Valuation Date</u>. The Net Fair Market Value of the Trust Assets shall be determined annually on the first day of each taxable year of this Trust (including any short taxable year), in accordance with the provisions of Paragraph E of this Article II.

C. <u>Taxable Year and Short Taxable Years</u>. The first taxable year of this Trust shall commence on the date this Trust is first funded and shall end on December 31st of that year. Subsequent taxable years shall be on a calendar year basis, except that the last taxable year of this Trust shall end on the date that this Trust terminates pursuant to Article III herein. In the case of a taxable year which is for a period of less than twelve (12) months (other than the taxable year in which the Unitrust Period ends), the amount described in Paragraph A.2(b) of this Article II shall be such amount multiplied by a fraction the numerator of which is the number of days in the taxable year of this Trust and the denominator of which is 365 (366 if February 29 is a day included in the numerator). In the case of the taxable year in which the Unitrust Period ends, the amount described in Paragraph A.2(b) of this Article II shall be such amount multiplied by a fraction the numerator of which is the number of days in the period beginning on the first day of such taxable year and ending on the date the Unitrust Period ends and the denominator of which is 365 (366 if February 29 is a day included in the numerator). Notwithstanding the foregoing, the obligation of the Trustee to pay the Unitrust Amount shall terminate with the regular periodic payment next proceeding the date the Unitrust Period ends.

D. <u>Additional Contributions</u>. Any person may contribute property to this Trust, with the consent of the Trustee, either during life or at death. For the taxable year of this Trust in which any additional contribution is made, the additional property shall be valued at the time of contribution and in accordance with Paragraph E of this Article II, and the amount described in Paragraph A.2(b) of this Article II shall be *(FMV PERCENT)* percent *(FMV PERCENT NUMBER)* %) of the sum of the following components:

1. The Net Fair Market Value of the Trust Assets determined on the first day of the taxable year (and thus excluding the value of the additional property, and earned income from, and any appreciation on, such property after its contribution); and

2. That proportion of the value of the additional property (that was excluded under Paragraph D.1 of this Article II immediately above) which the number of days in the period that begins with the date of contribution and ends with the earlier of the last day of such taxable year or the date the Unitrust Period ends bears to the number of days in the period that begins on the first day of such taxable year and ends with the earlier of the last day of such taxable year or the date the Unitrust Period ends.

If an additional contribution is made by Will, the obligation to pay the Unitrust Amount payable with respect to the additional contribution shall commence with the date of death of the person under whose Will the additional contribution is made. Payment of that portion of the Unitrust Amount may be deferred, however, from such date of death to the end of the taxable year in which occurs the complete funding of the additional contribution. Within a reasonable time following such complete funding of the additional contribution, the Trustee shall pay to the Recipient, in the case of an underpayment, or receive from the Recipient, in the case of an overpayment, the difference between: (i) the Unitrust Amount with respect to such additional contribution actually paid to the Recipient, plus interest on such amounts, compounded annually, computed for any period at the rate of interest that the Regulations under Section 664 of the Code prescribe for this Trust for such computation for such period; and (ii) the Unitrust Amount with respect to such additional contribution payable, determined under the method described in Section 1.664-1(a)(5)(ii) of the Regulations. Any payments required to be made because of an underpayment shall be paid to the Recipient (or such Recipient's estate) who received the underpayment. Any repayments required to be made because of an overpayment shall be repaid by the Recipient (or such Recipient's estate) who received the overpayment.

E. <u>Fair Market Value</u>. The Trustee shall compute the Net Fair Market Value of the Trust Assets considering all assets and liabilities without regard to whether particular items are taken into account in determining the Net Income; provided, however, in the event an Unmarketable Asset is transferred to or held by this Trust, and whenever this Trust is required to value such asset, the valuation shall be either performed exclusively by an Independent Special Trustee or determined by a current qualified appraisal, as defined in Regulation Section 1.170A-13(c)(3), from a qualified appraiser, as defined in Regulation Section 1.170-13(c)(5). All determinations of the Net Fair Market Value of the Trust Assets shall be in accordance with generally accepted fiduciary accounting principles and any United States Treasury requirements governing charitable remainder unitrusts. In any conflict, Treasury requirements shall prevail over generally accepted fiduciary accounting principles and any inconsistent provisions of this Trust Agreement. In the event that the Net Fair Market Value of the Trust Assets is determined incorrectly for any taxable year, the Trustee shall pay to the Recipient or the Recipient's estate (in the case of an undervaluation), or be repaid by the Recipient or the Recipient's estate (in the case of an overvaluation), an amount equal to the difference between the Unitrust Amount which the Trustee should have paid to the Recipient if the correct values were used, and the Unitrust Amount which the Trustee actually paid to the Recipient. Such payments or repayments shall be made within a reasonable period after the final determination of the correct value.

III.
TERMINATION

This Trust shall terminate within a reasonable time after the expiration of the Unitrust Period; provided, however, that such reasonable time shall not extend beyond the last day of the month in which occurs the ninetieth (90th) day following the date the Unitrust Period ends. Upon termination, the Trustee shall distribute all of the then principal and income of this Trust, free of trust, other than any amount due to the Recipient or the Recipient's estate, to *(REMAINDERMAN)*.

Notwithstanding any contrary provision of the Trust Agreement, prior to the expiration of the Unitrust Period, the Donor shall retain the right, by acknowledged written instrument delivered to the Trustee, to change the Donee by adding or substituting new Charitable Organization(s) and/or omitting certain Charitable Organization(s) or by altering the share each is to receive. If more than one written instrument is so delivered to the Trustee, the written instrument bearing the latest date shall control and shall be deemed to revoke all prior written instruments unless the most recent one shall provide otherwise.

If any Donee is not a Charitable Organization at the time when any principal or income of this Trust is to be distributed to it, the Trustee shall distribute such principal or income in proportion to the relative shares of the Donees which are so described and, if none of the Donees is so described, to one or more Charitable Organizations as the Trustee shall select and in such shares as it shall determine.

IV.
FIDUCIARY PROVISIONS

A. <u>Appointment of Trustee</u>. *(TRUSTEE)* shall serve as Trustee of this Trust. In the event that *(TRUSTEE)* for any reason shall fail to serve as Trustee, then *(ALTERNATE TRUSTEE)* shall serve in the place and stead of *(TRUSTEE)*.

B. <u>Appointment of Independent Special Trustee</u>.

1. In the event an Unmarketable Asset is transferred to or held by this Trust, an Independent Special Trustee may be appointed by the Trustee. If so appointed, the Independent Special Trustee shall exclusively determine the fair market value of each Unmarketable Asset in accordance with such appointment.

2. The Trustee shall also have the right and option to appoint an Independent Special Trustee to take such action as the Trustee shall clearly define and delegate.

3. When (i) the sole Trustee is an Independent Trustee or (ii) more than one person is acting as Trustee hereunder and one of such Trustees is an Independent Trustee, such Independent Trustee shall have the right and option to act as an Independent Special Trustee hereunder. However, no Trustee (other than an acting Independent Special Trustee) shall have any power, duty or liability hereunder with respect to matters described in this Paragraph B.

4. The Independent Special Trustee shall have no powers, duties, or liabilities hereunder, except with respect to matters specifically described in this Paragraph B, and solely with respect to such matters, the Independent Special Trustee may exercise the rights, powers, authority and discretion, and

be subject to the restrictions, obligations and duties, accorded to a Trustee pursuant to Article V herein. However, the Independent Special Trustee may not function in a manner which would jeopardize the status of this Trust as a charitable remainder trust as defined in Section 664 of the Code, the Regulations thereunder and Internal Revenue Service rulings governing the operation thereof.

C. <u>Resignation of Fiduciary</u>. Any Fiduciary may resign at any time by giving a notice to any other Fiduciary and to the Recipient, or if the Recipient is Disabled, to the Custodian. Such resignation shall be effective upon the sooner to occur of: (i) sixty (60) days after the date of the notice of resignation, or (ii) the appointment of and acceptance by the successor Fiduciary. Notwithstanding the above, in the event (i) a Fiduciary dies or is Disabled or (ii) an Independent Special Trustee ceases to be an Independent Trustee, notice of resignation is deemed given, and the resignation shall be effective as of the date of such death, Disability or ceasing to be an Independent Trustee, as the case may be. The resigning Fiduciary (or its representative) shall file a final accounting and deliver all Trust assets under its charge and control to the successor Fiduciary as soon as possible, but in no event later than sixty (60) days following the date of the resignation notice being given or deemed given. Upon the relinquishment and delivery of all Trust assets and the final accounting to the successor Fiduciary, the resigning Fiduciary shall be discharged of all further duties and obligations hereunder.

D. <u>Removal of Fiduciary</u>. The Recipient shall have the right, with or without cause, to replace or discharge any acting Fiduciary. Upon the Disability of the Recipient, this right may be exercised by the Custodian. Such removal shall be effective upon the sooner to occur of: (i) sixty (60) days after giving the Fiduciary being removed notice of such removal, or (ii) the appointment of and acceptance by the successor Fiduciary. The Fiduciary being removed shall file a final accounting and deliver all Trust assets under its charge and control to the successor Fiduciary within such sixty (60) day period. Upon the relinquishment and delivery of all Trust assets and the final accounting to the successor Fiduciary, the Fiduciary being removed shall be discharged of all further duties and obligations hereunder.

E. <u>Appointment of Successor Fiduciary</u>. In the event any vacancy at any time occurs in the office of a Fiduciary hereunder, regardless of how caused, the Recipient shall have the right to fill such vacancy. Upon the Disability of the Recipient, the Custodian shall exercise such right. At the earliest possible date, all Trust assets and a final accounting shall be delivered to the successor Fiduciary. At such time as any successor Fiduciary delivers notice of acceptance to the Recipient, such successor Fiduciary shall have the rights, powers, authority and discretion, and be subject to the restrictions, obligations and duties, regarding this Trust within the appointed capacity.

F. <u>Liability of Successor Fiduciary</u>. A successor Fiduciary shall not be responsible to any beneficiary of this Trust or to this Trust for any act or omission of a former Fiduciary, and shall not be required to audit or investigate the acts or administration of any former Fiduciary and shall be charged, upon issuing a simple receipt, with only the Trust assets so received. In addition, unless requested in writing by a beneficiary of this Trust and indemnified adequately (in such Fiduciary's discretion therefor), no successor Fiduciary shall have any duty to take action to seek redress for breach of trust by a former Fiduciary.

G. <u>Appointment of Co-Fiduciary</u>. The Recipient shall have the right to appoint additional persons to act as Co-Fiduciaries hereunder. At such time as the newly-appointed Co-Fiduciary delivers notice of acceptance to the Recipient, the newly-appointed Co-Fiduciary shall have the rights, powers, authority and discretion, and be subject to the restrictions, obligations and duties, regarding this Trust within the appointed capacity. In granting the foregoing right, it is not the intention of the Donor to require that any specific number of Fiduciaries serve in any one capacity hereunder simultaneously.

H. <u>Want of Trustee</u>. If at any time for any reason this Trust shall be without a Trustee, *(CORPORATE TRUSTEE)* shall be and become the Trustee.

I. <u>Fiduciary Actions</u>. When more than two persons are acting as Trustees (or Independent Special Trustees), the concurrence and joinder of a majority of them shall control in all matters pertaining to the administration hereunder. When two persons are acting as Trustees (or Independent Special Trustees), the concurrence and joinder of both Trustees (or Independent Special Trustees) shall be required. Such actions by the Fiduciaries shall be made either by vote at a meeting (in person or by telephone) or by written concurrence.

When more than two persons are acting as Trustees (or Independent Special Trustees), any dissenting or abstaining Fiduciary may be absolved from personal liability by registering a written dissent or abstention with the records of this Trust. Such dissenting Fiduciary shall thereafter act with the other Fiduciaries in any manner necessary or appropriate to effectuate the decision of the majority.

J. Compensation. A Fiduciary, and any agents of or successors to any Fiduciary, shall be entitled to reasonable compensation for services rendered in connection with this Trust. The amount of compensation shall be an amount equal to the customary and prevailing charges for services of a similar nature during the same period of time and in the same geographic locale. Any Fiduciary may waive any compensation at any time, by providing notice of such waiver to the Recipient and another Fiduciary, if then serving.

K. Retention of Agents. A Fiduciary may delegate investment and management functions to an agent as is prudent under the circumstances, but shall exercise reasonable care in selecting such agent. The duties of the agent shall be consistent with the terms and intent of this Trust, and the Fiduciary shall periodically review the agent's performance.

L. Liability for Retaining Property. The Fiduciary shall not be liable for any loss or depreciation in value sustained by this Trust as a result of the Fiduciary accepting or retaining any property upon which hazardous materials or substances are discovered, unless the Fiduciary contributed to the loss or depreciation in value through willful default, willful misconduct or gross negligence.

M. Indemnification. The Donor shall indemnify the Fiduciary against any claims (except for claims due to the Fiduciary's willful default, willful misconduct or gross negligence) filed against the Fiduciary (i) as an "owner" or "operator" under the federal Comprehensive Environmental Response, Compensation and Liability Act of 1980 (as from time to time amended) or any regulation thereunder and (ii) under any other federal, state or local environmental law, rule, regulation or order relating to the property contributed to this Trust by the Donor.

N. Jurisdiction and Bond. This Trust shall not be administered under the jurisdiction of any court. Should a question or issue be submitted to a court of competent jurisdiction at any time or from time to time, such court shall acquire jurisdiction of only the question or issue submitted to it, and the jurisdiction of such court shall terminate upon the conclusion or settlement of such question or issue. No bond or other security shall be required of any person acting as a Fiduciary, whether serving jointly or alone.

V.
POWERS OF THE TRUSTEE

All rights, powers, authority and discretion exercisable by the Trustee under this Trust or by law shall be binding and conclusive on all interested parties; shall be exercisable by the Trustee in its sole and absolute discretion; shall be exercisable only in a fiduciary capacity and in the best interests of the beneficiaries; shall be construed in the broadest possible manner; and shall be exercisable without prior or subsequent application to any court under the jurisdiction of which this Trust may be administered.

The Trustee is under a duty to the beneficiaries to invest and manage the funds of the Trust as a prudent investor would, in a manner that is fair to all beneficiaries as a reflection of the Trust's purposes, terms, and obligations and in light of the circumstances of the Trust and the relevant circumstances of its beneficiaries. The investment decisions of a Trustee shall be evaluated not in isolation, but in the context of the investment portfolio as a whole and as part of an overall investment strategy reasonably suited to the Trust.

Not in derogation of or in limitation upon the powers, authority and discretion conferred by law upon a trustee, the Trustee is vested with the following rights, powers, authority and discretion:

A. To alter, repair, improve, erect buildings upon, demolish, manage, partition, mortgage, lease for any period, including a period in excess of any fixed by statute or extending beyond the duration of this Trust, exchange, grant options to lease or to buy, and sell or dispose of, at public or private sale, and upon such conditions and such terms as to cash and credit as it deems advisable, any of the Trust assets;

B. To compromise, settle, subordinate, arbitrate, extend, renew, modify, or release, in whole or in part, any claim held by it or held against any of the Trust assets;

C. To continue to hold the property transferred to it hereunder in the form in which it shall be when transferred or as the form thereof may be changed pursuant to the other provisions of the Trust Agreement, without regard to the limitations imposed by law upon the investment of trust funds;

D. To borrow money and to encumber or hypothecate Trust assets whether by mortgage, deed of trust, pledge or otherwise;

E. To commence or defend litigation with respect to the Trust assets, at the expense of the Trust assets;

F. To employ any person, firm, corporation, bank, or trust company for advice with respect to investment policy or any other matter; but the Trustee may follow or refrain from following any recommendation so obtained and such recommendations shall not in any way limit the discretionary power and authority conferred upon the Trustee hereunder with respect to investments or other matters;

G. To retain or discharge accountants, attorneys, administrators, brokers, investment advisers, investment counselors and other agents, and to pay reasonable compensation for their services;

H. To enter into any and all agreements with the Internal Revenue Service or any other governmental body and to execute, from time to time, any declarations of policy or disclaimers restricting the powers, authority and discretion granted to the Trustee;

I. To invest and to reinvest the Trust assets in every kind of property, real, personal or mixed, and every kind of investment; and nothing in the Trust Agreement shall be construed to restrict the Trustee from investing the Trust assets in a manner which could result in the annual realization of a reasonable amount of income or gain from the sale or disposition of Trust assets;

J. With respect to any investment held by the Trustee, to participate in and consent to any corporate or financial reorganization, dissolution, liquidation, merger, consolidation, sale or lease, or in and to any other change in its financial structure; and to become a depositor with any protective, reorganization, or similar committee, and to make any necessary payments incident to the foregoing; to organize or participate in the organization of corporations or other business entities, and to transfer to them any part or all of the Trust assets in exchange for an investment therein; to exercise or to sell any conversion, subscription, or similar rights; and in general to exercise in respect to any investment the unrestricted rights of a personal owner, including voting in person and granting proxies, discretionary, general, or otherwise;

K. In any case in which the Trustee makes any payments or other distribution of Trust assets, to make such payment or distribution in money or in kind, including undivided interests in any property, or partly in money and partly in kind; and in the case of any distribution in kind to any Donee, the adjusted basis of the Trust property distributed shall be fairly representative of the adjusted bases of all Trust properties available for distribution on the date of distribution;

L. To apportion and allocate Trust receipts and expenses between Net Income and principal accounts (provided that no pre-gift appreciation shall be allocable to Net Income);

M. To retain the services of an independent appraiser to assist in valuing assets of this Trust and to reasonably compensate such appraiser for such services;

N. If required by the Code, the Regulations or any Internal Revenue Service rulings thereunder to maintain the status of the Trust as a charitable remainder unitrust, to set aside a reserve or allowance from Trust income for the depreciation or depletion of any property transferred to or invested in by the Trust; otherwise, the Trustee shall have discretion whether or not to set aside such a reserve;

O. With respect to any environmental hazards on Trust property:

    1. To take all appropriate actions to prevent, identify or respond to actual or threatened violations of any environmental law, rule or regulation, including compliance with any federal, state or local agency or court order directing an assessment, abatement or cleanup of any environmental hazard;

    2. To disclaim, in whole or in part, any interests in property for any reason, including but not limited to, a concern that such property could cause potential liability under any federal, state, or local environmental law, rule or regulation; and/or

    3. To set aside any interests in property, which could cause potential liability under any federal, state, or local environmental law, rule or regulation as a separate trust to be held and administered upon the same terms as those governing the remaining Trust assets;

P. To designate as custodian of any Trust property any business entity authorized and engaged in the business of brokers or dealers in securities;

Q. To the extent permitted by law, to register any of such property in its name as Trustee or in the names of nominees, or to take and keep the same unregistered or in bearer form, or in such condition as to pass by delivery; and/or

R. Whenever the Trust acquires an Annuity Contract, to exercise with respect to such Annuity Contract any rights and discretion as owner thereof, as limited hereby, including but not limited to the right or discretion to:

    1. Making partial or total withdrawals or surrenders from the Annuity Contract; provided however, the Trustee gives due regard to any withdrawal or partial surrender penalties that may be imposed and to the best interest of all Trust beneficiaries;

    2. Electing any annuity option(s) which guarantees the payment to the Trust by or upon the death of the annuitant of an amount at least equal to the surrender value of the Annuity Contract(s) as of the day before the day the annuity payments commence;

    3. Designating the day the annuity payments commence; and/or

    4. Seeing to the allocation of any payments of any type received from the Annuity Contract between principal and income as is required by this Trust.

Anything in the Trust Agreement to the contrary notwithstanding, it is the intention of the Donor to create a qualifying charitable remainder unitrust under Section 664 of the Code; therefore, no rights, powers, authority or discretion either otherwise granted by the Trust Agreement or by applicable state law that exceed or are inconsistent with those allowed under Section 664 of the Code and the Regulations thereunder are to be possessed or exercised by the Trustee. At no time and under no circumstances shall a Donor serving as a Trustee exercise any power that would result in this Trust being treated as a grantor trust under Subpart E of the Code.

VI.
APPLICABLE LAW

The validity of this Trust shall be controlled by the laws of the State of *(STATE LAW)*. The construction and administration of this Trust shall be controlled by the laws of the State of *(STATE LAW)*. However, in any conflict with Section 664 of the Code, the Regulations thereunder or any other existing or hereafter promulgated legislative or Treasury requirements for the qualification of this Trust and for the Donor's obtaining the full benefit of any income, gift and estate tax charitable deductions to which the Donor (and the Donor's estate) may be entitled, Section 664 of the Code, the Regulations thereunder and the legislative and Treasury requirements shall govern.

VII.
IRREVOCABILITY AND AMENDMENT

This Trust shall be irrevocable. However, the Trustee shall have the power, acting alone, to amend the Trust Agreement in any manner required for the sole purpose of ensuring that this Trust qualifies and continues to qualify as a charitable remainder unitrust within the meaning of Section 664 of the Code and the Regulations thereunder.

VIII.
PROHIBITED ACTS

Notwithstanding any other provision of the Trust Agreement, no Fiduciary shall (except for the payment of the Unitrust Amount) engage in any act of self-dealing (as defined in Section 4941(d) of the Code), retain any excess business holdings (as defined in Section 4943(c) of the Code) which would subject this Trust to tax under Section 4943 of the Code, make any investments which would subject this Trust to tax under Section 4944 of the Code, or make any taxable expenditure (as defined in Section 4945(d) of the Code). If Section 4942 of the Code is deemed applicable to this Trust by reason of Section 508(e) of the Code or otherwise, then the Trustee shall make distributions at such times and in such manner as not to subject this Trust to tax under Section 4942 of the Code.

IX.
INTENTION TO CREATE UNITRUST

It is the Donor's intention to obtain the full benefit of any income, gift and estate tax charitable contribution deductions to which the Donor (and the Donor's estate) may be entitled to under the Code and for this Trust to qualify as a charitable remainder unitrust within the meaning of Section 664(d)(2) and (3) of the Code and the Regulations thereunder. Accordingly, the Trust Agreement shall be interpreted and administered, and the Trust assets shall be valued, managed and invested, in a manner consistent with the Donor's intent and the provisions of such Section, the Regulations thereunder and the Internal Revenue Service rulings relating thereto.

X.
DEATH TAXES

No Death Taxes with respect to this Trust shall be allocated to or be recoverable from this Trust. The Donor agrees to provide in the Donor's Will, or any other appropriate estate planning documents, that any Death Taxes arising from the creation of this Trust, or the interest of the Donor therein, shall be payable from the estate of the Donor, excluding the assets of this Trust. The Donor hereby imposes an affirmative obligation on the Donor's estate to pay all of such Death Taxes (if any) from sources other than this Trust and agrees that this obligation may be enforced by the Trustee or any Donee, acting alone or together. Should Death Taxes with respect to this Trust become due as a result of additional contributions by any person other than the Donor, then the provisions of this Article X shall apply to such other person as if the other person were the Donor for purposes of this Article X.

XI.
MISCELLANEOUS

A. <u>Construction</u>. Unless the context requires otherwise, words in the singular may be construed as denoting the plural, and words in the plural may be construed as denoting the singular. Words of one gender may be construed as denoting another gender as is appropriate within such context.

B. <u>Headings</u>. Titles and headings in the Trust Agreement are added for convenient reference, and shall not be deemed to alter or affect the meaning of any provision hereof.

C. <u>Severability</u>. If any provision or part of any provision of the Trust Agreement shall for any reason be held invalid, illegal or unenforceable in any respect by a court of competent jurisdiction, such invalidity, illegality or unenforceability shall not affect any other provision of the Trust Agreement and the Trust Agreement shall be construed as if such invalid, illegal or unenforceable provision or part thereof had never been contained herein, but only to the extent of its invalidity, illegality or unenforceability.

      D. <u>Counterparts</u>. The Trust Agreement has been executed in triplicate, each of which shall be an original and each of which shall constitute the entire Trust Agreement without reference to or the necessity of producing the other counterparts.

      E. <u>Spendthrift</u>. The Recipient shall not have any power to sell, transfer, assign, pledge, mortgage, or alienate all or any part of the Recipient's beneficial interest in this Trust in any manner whatsoever. The interest of the Recipient shall not be subject to the claims of the Recipient's creditors or to attachment, execution, bankruptcy proceedings or any other legal process.

XII.
DEFINITIONS

For purposes of the Trust Agreement, the following words and phrases shall have the meanings ascribed to them in this Article XII, as follows:

"Annuity Contract" shall mean any kind of annuity to be paid by an insurance company or by an organization regularly engaged in issuing annuity contracts.

"Charitable Organization" shall mean an organization described in each of Sections 170(b)(1)(A), 170(c), 2055(a) and 2522(a) of the Code.

"Code" shall mean the Internal Revenue Code of 1986, as amended from time to time, and references to a Section of the Code shall include any successor provisions to the Section referred to and to any corresponding provisions of any subsequent federal tax laws.

"Custodian" shall mean a trustee of any trust established exclusively for the benefit of the Recipient, if such a trust has been established, or the conservator, custodian, person holding an effective durable power of attorney or legally appointed guardian of the person or estate of the Recipient.

"Death Taxes" shall mean any and all federal estate taxes, state death taxes or any other estate, death, inheritance or welfare transfer taxes.

"Disability" or "Disabled" shall mean when (i) a guardian or conservator of an individual's person or estate is duly appointed by a court of competent jurisdiction and continues to serve in such capacity, (ii) two physicians (licensed to practice under the laws of the state where the person is domiciled) certify that such person is unable to properly care for his or her person or property, (iii) an individual is a minor under the laws of the state where he or she is domiciled, or (iv) an individual disappears for an unreasonable period of time with no apparent explanation for such disappearance.

"Donee" or "Donees" shall mean any Charitable Organization selected to be a charitable remainderman (or remaindermen) pursuant to Article III of this Trust Agreement.

"Donor" shall mean the settlor of this Trust as named on the first page of the Trust Agreement, who has signed the Trust Agreement.

"Fiduciary" or "Fiduciaries" shall mean, as the context requires, each Trustee and/or Independent Special Trustee, and their successor(s).

"Independent Special Trustee" or "Independent Special Trustees" shall mean each individual and/or entity who or which is appointed as a fiduciary of this Trust, solely for the specific purposes provided in Paragraph B of Article IV, and who or which is an "Independent Trustee", and any successor(s) thereto.

"Independent Trustee" shall have the meaning ascribed to it in Regulation Section 1.664-1(a)(7)(iii).

"Net Fair Market Value of the Trust Assets" shall mean the net fair market value of the assets owned by the Trust as described in Paragraphs B and E of Article II of this Trust.

"Net Income" shall mean the net income of this Trust as determined by the Trustee pursuant to the terms of the Trust Agreement, Section 643(b) of the Code and the Regulations thereunder.

"Notice" or "notify" shall mean a communication in writing, signed by the party sending such communication, mailed by certified mail, return receipt requested, or personally hand delivered, dated receipt obtained. The effective date of such notice shall be deemed to be the date of mailing of such certified mail or the actual date of hand delivery, as the case may be. Notice shall be addressed to such person(s) at such person(s) last known address.

"Recipient" shall mean each individual who is entitled to receive the Unitrust Amount pursuant to Paragraph A.1 of Article II of this Trust.

"Regulations" shall mean the regulations published under 26 Code of Federal Regulations as in effect on the date of execution of this Trust Agreement, or, in the event that any such regulation is amended or superseded thereafter, to the regulation (or any successor regulation) as so amended.

"Trust" shall mean the charitable remainder unitrust established under the Trust Agreement, otherwise known as "THE *(TRUST NAME)* CHARITABLE REMAINDER UNITRUST".

"Trust Agreement" shall mean this trust instrument signed by all parties hereto.

"Trustee", "it" or "its" shall mean each individual or entity acting in a fiduciary capacity who or which is named on the first page of the Trust Agreement, and who or which signed the Trust Agreement, and its successor(s).

"Unitrust Amount" shall mean the amount described in Paragraph A.2 of Article II of this Trust.

"Unitrust Period" shall mean the period of time which begins on the date this Trust is first funded and ends on the date upon which the Recipient dies.

"Unmarketable Asset" shall have the meaning ascribed to it in Regulation Section 1.664-1(a)(7)(ii).

IN WITNESS WHEREOF, the parties hereto have executed this Trust Agreement on the date first above written.

DONOR:

_____

(DONOR)

TRUSTEE:

_____

(TRUSTEE)

[ACKNOWLEDGMENT & WITNESS AS REQUIRED UNDER STATE LAW]

EXHIBIT A

THE *(TRUST NAME)*
CHARITABLE REMAINDER UNITRUST

Item No.   Date of Transfer   Description

Receipt of the above described assets is hereby acknowledged this _____ day of *(MONTH)*, *(TAX YEAR)*.

TRUSTEE:

_____

(TRUSTEE)

F:\FORMS\DEBRA ASHTON FORMS\007 - INTERVIVOS NIMCRUT.DOC

SAMPLE GRANTOR CHARITABLE LEAD ANNUITY TRUST

CHARITABLE LEAD ANNUITY TRUST AGREEMENT
by and between
(DONOR), DONOR
and
(TRUSTEE), TRUSTEE

This CHARITABLE LEAD ANNUITY TRUST AGREEMENT (hereinafter referred to as "Agreement") is made this _____ day of *(MONTH)*, *(YEAR)*, by and between *(DONOR)*, as Donor (hereinafter referred to as "Donor") and *(TRUSTEE)*, of *(CITY)*, *(STATE)* and its successor(s), as Trustee (hereinafter referred to as the "Trustee" and sometimes as "it" or "its").

WITNESSETH:

WHEREAS, Donor has a deep interest in the Donee (as defined below in paragraph F of ITEM SECOND herein, hereinafter referred to as the "Donee"); and

WHEREAS, Donor desires to establish a trust to benefit the Donee for *(LENGTH OF ANNUITY)* years, and at the end of such period, to benefit his/her *(RELATIONSHIP TO REMAINDER BENEFICIARY)*, *(REMAINDER BENEFICIARY)* (hereinafter referred to as "Remainder Beneficiary"); and

WHEREAS, Donor desires to make a gift to the Donee of the income interest in the trust created hereunder; and

WHEREAS, this Agreement is executed for the purpose of defining the terms and conditions of the trust created hereby.

NOW THEREFORE, in consideration of the premises, the mutual covenants and agreements contained herein, and intending to be legally bound thereby, and in consideration of other good and valuable consideration (the receipt and sufficiency of which are hereby acknowledged), the Donor, contemporaneously with the execution of this Agreement is irrevocably assigning, transferring and delivering to the Trustee all his/her right, title and interest in and to the property listed in Schedule A, attached hereto and specifically made a part hereof by this reference. The Trustee hereby accepts such irrevocable gift and agrees to hold and administer the same for the uses, purposes and trusts hereinafter set forth.

__ITEM FIRST__: It is agreed that the trust created by this Agreement shall be referred to as "THE *(TRUST NAME)* CHARITABLE LEAD ANNUITY TRUST" (hereinafter referred to as "Trust").

__ITEM SECOND__: The "Annuity Period" as used herein shall mean that period of time which begins on the date that the property listed in Schedule A is contributed to this Trust by the Donor and ends *(LENGTH OF ANNUITY)* years thereafter. During the Annuity Period, the Trustee shall administer and dispose of the income and principal of the Trust as follows:

A. During the Annuity Period, in each taxable year of the Trust, the Trustee shall pay to the Donee, the Annuity Amount as defined in paragraph B of this ITEM SECOND.

B. The term "Annuity Amount" as used herein shall mean a guaranteed annuity equal to_____ percent (___%) of the initial net fair market value of the assets constituting the Trust, payable in cash, in kind or partly in each. The Annuity Amount shall be decreased as provided in paragraph C of this ITEM SECOND in the case where the taxable year is a short taxable year or is the taxable year in which the Annuity Period ends. In determining such initial net fair market value, the assets constituting the Trust shall be valued at their values as finally determined for federal tax purposes. If the initial net fair market value of the assets constituting the Trust is incorrectly determined by the Trustee, then within a reasonable period after the correct determination, the Trustee shall pay to the Donee in the case of an undervaluation or shall receive from the Donee in the case of an overvaluation an amount equal to the difference between the Annuity Amount properly payable and the Annuity Amount actually paid. The Annuity Amount shall be paid in annual installments at the end of each calendar year, with the first such installment as of *(ANNUITY DATE)*. The payments to the Donee shall be paid first from ordinary income (excluding unrelated business income), then from short-term capital gain, then from long-term capital gain, then from unrelated business income, then from tax-exempt income, and to the extent that the foregoing items for the taxable year are not sufficient, from principal. Any income of the Trust in excess of the Annuity Amount shall be added to principal. The Trustee's obligation to make payments is limited to the Trust assets. Notwithstanding any existing or hereafter enacted state law, no amount may be paid by the Trust for a private purpose before the expiration of the Annuity Period. However, an amount shall not be deemed to be so paid if the amount is transferred for full and adequate consideration.

C. The first taxable year of the Trust begins with the date of this Agreement and shall end on December 31, *(YEAR)*. Subsequent taxable years shall be on a calendar year basis. In the case of a taxable year which is for a period of less than 12 months (other than the taxable year in which the Annuity Period ends), the Annuity Amount shall be such amount multiplied by a fraction the numerator of which is the number of days in the taxable year of the Trust and the denominator of which is 365 (366 if February 29 is a day included in the numerator). In the case of the taxable year in which the Annuity Period ends, the Annuity Amount shall be such amount multiplied by a fraction the numerator of which is the number of days in the period beginning on the first day of such taxable year and ending on the date of the last day of the Annuity Period and the denominator of which is 365 (366 if February 29 is a day included in the numerator).

D. No additional contributions shall be made to the Trust after the initial contribution.

E. Upon the expiration of the Annuity Period, the Trustee shall distribute all of the then remaining principal and income of the Trust (other than any amount due to the Donee) to the Remainder Beneficiary.

F. For purposes of this Agreement, the Donee shall be *(CHARITY)*, a Section *(CHARITABLE STATUS)* organization, currently with its principal offices at *(CHARITY'S ADDRESS)*. The designation may be amended or revoked by a specific written instrument provided by the Remainder Beneficiary ("written instrument"), adding or substituting other charitable beneficiaries (such original charitable beneficiary and any additional and/or substitute charitable beneficiaries shall herein be collectively referred to as "Donee"). If more than one written instrument is so delivered to the Trustee, the written instrument bearing the latest date shall control and shall be deemed to revoke all prior written instruments unless the most recent one shall provide otherwise. If any Donee is not an organization described in each of Sections 170(b)(1)(A), 170(c), 2055(a) and 2522(a) of the Code at the time when any principal or income of the Trust is to be distributed to it, then the Trustee shall distribute such principal or income in proportion to the relative shares of the Donee(s) which are so described and, if none of the Donee(s) is so described, to one or more organizations then so described as the Trustee in its sole and absolute discretion shall select and in such shares as it shall determine.

ITEM THIRD: In addition to the authority, power and discretion conferred upon a trustee by the laws of the State of *(STATE)*, the Trustee shall have the following authority, power and discretion:

A. To make distribution, when distribution is authorized under the provisions hereof, either wholly or partly in kind, at market value. The adjusted basis for federal income tax purposes of any Trust property which the Trustee distributes in kind to the Donee during the Annuity Period must be fairly representative of the adjusted basis for such purposes of all Trust property available for distribution on the date of distribution.

B. To alter, repair, improve, erect buildings upon, demolish, manage, partition, lease for any period, including a period in excess of any fixed by statute or extending beyond the duration of the Trust, exchange, grant options to lease or to buy, and sell or dispose of, at public or private sale, and upon such conditions and such terms as to cash and credit as it deems advisable, any of such property.

C. To compromise, settle, subordinate, arbitrate, extend, renew, modify, or release, in whole or in part, any claim held by it or held against any of the property hereunder.

D. To continue to hold the property transferred to it hereunder in the form in which it shall be when transferred or as the form thereof may be changed pursuant to the other provisions of this Agreement so long as it, in its sole and absolute discretion, deems it advisable, without regard to the limitations imposed by law upon the investment of trust funds.

E. As to investments, (i) to allocate receipts and expenditures between principal and income as it, in its sole and absolute discretion, may determine; (ii) to sell, exchange or otherwise dispose of any of the property hereunder; and (iii) to invest and reinvest the funds of the Trust in any kind of property, real or personal, regardless of any laws or rules of law governing the investment of trust funds or diversification of trust funds.

F. To employ any person, firm, corporation, bank, or trust company for advice with respect to investment policy or any other matter; but the Trustee may, in its absolute discretion, follow or refrain from following any recommendation so obtained and such recommendations shall not in any way limit the discretionary power and authority conferred upon the Trustee hereunder with respect to investments or other matters.

G. To participate in and consent to any corporate reorganization, dissolution, liquidation, merger, consolidation, corporate sale or lease, or in and to any other change in any corporation or in its financial structure; and to become a depositor with any protective, reorganization, or similar committee, and to make any necessary payments incident to the foregoing; to organize or participate in the organization of corporations, and to transfer to them any part or all of the property hereunder in exchange for securities thereof which it may retain so long as it deems it advisable; to exercise or to sell any conversion, subscription, or similar rights; and in general to exercise in respect to any securities the unrestricted rights of a personal owner, including voting in person and granting proxies, discretionary, general, or otherwise.

H. To designate any partnership engaged in the business of brokers or dealers in securities, or any corporation authorized so to act, as custodian of any of such property.

I. To the extent permitted by law, to register any of such property in its name as Trustee or in the names of nominees, or to take and keep the same unregistered or in bearer form, or in such condition as to pass by delivery.

J. Nothing in this Agreement shall be construed to restrict the Trustee from investing the Trust property in a manner which could result in the annual realization of a reasonable amount of income or gain from the sale or disposition of Trust property.

K. Any other provisions of this Agreement notwithstanding, if Section 4942 of the Code is deemed applicable to the Trust by reason of Section 508(e) of the Code or otherwise, the Trustee shall make distributions at such time and in such manner as not to subject the Trust to tax under Section 4942 of the Code.

L. Any other provisions of this Agreement notwithstanding, the Trustee shall not engage in any act of self-dealing as defined in Section 4941(d) of the Code; nor retain any excess business holdings as defined in Section 4943(c) of the Code which would subject the Trust to tax under Section 4943 of the Code; nor acquire any assets which would subject the Trust to tax under Section 4944 of the Code, nor retain any assets which would, if acquired by the Trustee, subject the Trust to tax under Section 4944 of the Code; nor make any taxable expenditures as defined in Section 4945(d) of the Code.

M. It is expected that the Trustee will allocate any depreciation deductions to the Trust, and in that regard, the Trustee shall, in its sole and absolute discretion, have the authority to allocate any depreciation deductions to the Trust.

Anything in this Agreement to the contrary notwithstanding, no authority, discretion or power either otherwise granted by this Agreement or by state law that exceed or are inconsistent with the fulfillment of the Donor's Intentions (as defined below in ITEM FIFTH) are to be possessed or exercised by the Trustee.

ITEM FOURTH: As to the Trustee:

A. If *(TRUSTEE)* fails to qualify or for any reason ceases to serve as Trustee, the Remainder Beneficiary shall have the authority to appoint a successor Trustee.

B. The Remainder Beneficiary shall have the power and authority to remove at any time any Trustee and to appoint in the place and stead thereof a successor Trustee; provided, however, that the Donor shall never have the authority to appoint and remove any Trustee hereunder nor be appointed or serve as a Trustee hereunder.

Such removal and appointment shall be accomplished by an instrument in writing, executed in triplicate by the person having the aforesaid removal power and acknowledged before a Notary Public; and one of such executed counterparts shall be delivered to the Trustee that is being removed, a second counterpart shall be delivered to the individual or bank or trust company that is appointed as a successor Trustee here-under, and a third counterpart shall be filed in the permanent records of the Trustee. Upon receiving such executed counterpart, together with receiving an instrument in writing from the successor Trustee accepting such appointment, the Trustee that is being removed shall no longer act as a Trustee hereunder and shall transfer, pay over and deliver the Trust property then in its hands to such successor Trustee, against the latter's simple receipt.

C. Any individual or corporate Trustee serving hereunder shall have the right and privilege to resign as a Trustee under this Agreement upon giving ninety (90) days notice in writing to the other Trustee(s) serving hereunder at the time (if any) and also to the Remainder Beneficiary.

D. No such successor shall be required to investigate the administration or demand an accounting from a predecessor Trustee or the personal representative of a predecessor Trustee and each such successor, upon issuing a simple receipt, shall be charged with only the trust assets so received and shall not be liable or responsible for the acts and deeds of any predecessor Trustee.

E. The Trust shall not be administered under the jurisdiction of any court. Should a question or issue be submitted to a court of competent jurisdiction at any time or from time to time, such court shall acquire jurisdiction of only the question or issue submitted to it, and the jurisdiction of such court shall terminate upon the conclusion or settlement of such question or issue.

F. No Trustee, other than a corporate Trustee, shall receive any compensation for services rendered under this Agreement. No Trustee shall be required to post a bond or other security for the faithful performance of its fiduciary duty in any jurisdiction. Any fees that are paid to an independent Trustee or any of the Trustee's agents in administering this Trust shall be charged to income.

G. The Trustee shall exercise or perform every authority, right, or duty, including discretionary powers, acting alone, and if more than one Trustee is appointed, by majority vote, with the same effect as if all had joined therein.

H. The undersigned Trustee accepts the Trust herein created and consents and agrees that it will carry out the provisions hereof and will faithfully perform and discharge all the duties of its office as Trustee.

ITEM FIFTH: In creating this Trust, the Donor intends (i) to obtain the full benefit of any income, gift and estate tax charitable contribution deductions to which he/she (and his/her estate) may be entitled to under the Code, (ii) for the Annuity Amount to qualify as a guaranteed annuity interest under Sections 170(f)(2)(B), 2522(c)(2)(B) and 2055(e)(2)(B) of the Code and other applicable provisions of the Code and the

Treasury Regulations, and (iii) for the Trust to be treated as a "grantor trust" under Sections 671-679 of the Code ("Donor's Intentions"). Accordingly, this Trust shall be interpreted, valued, managed, invested, administered and in all other respects governed in a manner which is consistent with the Donor's Intentions.

ITEM SIXTH: At any time(s) during the Annuity Period, the Grantor, acting alone and in a non-fiduciary capacity, may acquire or reacquire any portion of the Trust assets by substituting therefor other property of an equivalent value, valued on the date of substitution. The substitution can be effected by the Grantor without the consent of the Trustee. In order to effect the substitution, the Grantor must certify in writing to the Trustee that the substituted property is of equivalent value to the property for which it is substituted, and the Trustee may independently verify such certification of value. Any dispute as to whether the substituted assets are of equivalent value shall be resolved by a court of proper jurisdiction. The Grantor directs that this retained power of substitution is not assignable, and any attempted assignment will make this power void. The Grantor may at any time(s) during the Term by delivery of a written, acknowledged instrument to the Trustee, release such power, in whole or in part, and any such release shall be irrevocable. [Insert other language as appropriate to insure that the Trust will be treated as a Grantor Trust.]

ITEM SEVENTH: No federal estate taxes, state death taxes or any other estate, death or inheritance taxes ("death taxes") with respect to the Trust shall be allocated to or be recoverable from the Trust. The Donor hereby imposes an obligation on his/her estate to pay any death taxes from sources other than the Trust and agrees to so provide in his/her Will or in another way. This provision may be enforced by a Donee in its capacity as charitable beneficiary or the Trustee, acting alone or together.

ITEM EIGHTH: Throughout this Agreement, the word "Code" shall mean the Internal Revenue Code of 1986, as amended from time to time, and references to a Section of the Code shall include any successor provisions to the Section referred to and to any corresponding provisions of any subsequent federal tax laws.

ITEM NINTH: This Agreement is irrevocable. However, the Trustee, acting alone, shall have the power to amend this Agreement in any manner required for the sole purpose of ensuring that the Trust complies with the requirements of Sections 170(f)(2)(B), 2522(c)(2)(B) and 2055(e)(2)(B) of the Code and other applicable provisions of the Code and the corresponding Treasury Regulations.

ITEM TENTH: This Agreement is made pursuant to, and shall be interpreted in accordance with, the laws of the State of *(STATE)*. However, in any conflict with the Code and the Treasury Regulations specified herein, or any other existing or hereafter promulgated legislative or Treasury requirements in order to fulfill the Donor's Intentions, the Code, the Treasury Regulations thereunder and the legislative and Treasury requirements shall govern.

IN WITNESS WHEREOF, the parties hereto have executed this Charitable Lead Annuity Trust Agreement the date first above written.

WITNESS: DONORS:

_____   _____(SEAL)
                                              (DONOR)

                                              TRUSTEE:

_____   _____(SEAL)
                                              (TRUSTEE)

[ACKNOWLEDGMENT & WITNESS AS REQUIRED UNDER STATE LAW]

SCHEDULE A

This Schedule A is the one referred to in the CHARITABLE LEAD ANNUITY TRUST AGREE-MENT dated *(DATE)*, by and between *(DONOR)*, as Donor and *(TRUSTEE)*, as Trustee. The Donor, concurrent with the signing of this Agreement, hereby transfers to the Trustee and the Trustee hereby recognizes and accepts receipt of the following:

[DESCRIPTION OF PROPERTY]

_____ _____(SEAL)
(DONOR)

TRUSTEE:

_____ _____(SEAL)
(TRUSTEE)

SAMPLE GRANTOR CHARITABLE LEAD UNITRUST

CHARITABLE LEAD UNITRUST TRUST AGREEMENT
by and between
(DONOR), DONOR
and
(TRUSTEE), TRUSTEE

This CHARITABLE LEAD UNITRUST TRUST AGREEMENT (hereinafter referred to as "Agreement") is made this _____ day of *(MONTH)*, *(YEAR)*, by and between *(DONOR)*, as Donor (hereinafter referred to as "Donor") and *(TRUSTEE)*, of *(CITY)*, *(STATE)* and its successor(s), as Trustee (hereinafter referred to as the "Trustee" and sometimes as "it" or its").

W I T N E S S E T H :

WHEREAS, Donor has a deep interest in the Donee (as defined below in paragraph F of ITEM SECOND herein, hereinafter referred to as the "Donee"); and

WHEREAS, Donor desires to establish a trust to benefit the Donee for *(LENGTH OF UNITRUST)* years, and at the end of such period, to benefit his/her *(RELATIONSHIP TO REMAINDER BENEFICIARY)*, *(REMAINDER BENEFICIARY)* (hereinafter referred to as "Remainder Beneficiary"); and

WHEREAS, Donor desires to make a gift to the Donee of the income interest in the trust created hereunder; and

WHEREAS, this Agreement is executed for the purpose of defining the terms and conditions of the trust created hereby.

NOW THEREFORE, in consideration of the premises, the mutual covenants and agreements contained herein, and intending to be legally bound thereby, and in consideration of other good and valuable consideration (the receipt and sufficiency of which are hereby acknowledged), the Donor, contemporaneously with the execution of this Agreement is irrevocably assigning, transferring and delivering to the Trustee all his/her right, title and interest in and to the property listed in Schedule A, attached hereto and specifically made a part hereof by this reference. The Trustee hereby accepts such irrevocable gift and agrees to hold and administer the same for the uses, purposes and trusts hereinafter set forth.

ITEM FIRST: It is agreed that the trust created by this Agreement shall be referred to as "THE *(TRUST NAME)* CHARITABLE LEAD UNITRUST" (hereinafter referred to as "Trust").

ITEM SECOND: The "Unitrust Period" as used herein shall mean that period of time which begins on the date that the property listed in Schedule A is contributed to this Trust by the Donor and ends *(LENGTH OF UNITRUST)* years thereafter. During the Unitrust Period, the Trustee shall administer and dispose of the income and principal of the Trust as follows:

A. During the Unitrust Period, in each taxable year of the Trust, the Trustee shall pay to the Donee, the Unitrust Amount as defined in paragraph B of this ITEM SECOND.

B. The term "Unitrust Amount" as used herein shall mean an amount equal to _____ percent (___%) of the net fair market value of the Trust assets valued as of the first day of each taxable year of the Trust except as otherwise provided in paragraph C of this ITEM SECOND in the case where the taxable year is a short taxable year or is the taxable year in which the Unitrust Period ends. The Unitrust Amount shall be paid in annual installments at the end of each calendar year, with the first such installment as of *(UNITRUST DATE)*. The payments to the Donee shall be paid first from ordinary income (excluding unrelated business income), then from short-term capital gain, then from long-term capital gain, then from unrelated business income, then from tax-exempt income, and to the extent that the foregoing items for the taxable year are not sufficient, from principal. Any income of the Trust in excess of the Unitrust Amount shall be added to principal. The Trustee's obligation to make payments is limited to the Trust assets. Notwithstanding any existing or hereafter enacted state law, no amount may be paid by the Trust for a private purpose before the expiration of the Unitrust Period. However, an amount shall not be deemed to be so paid if the amount is transferred for full and adequate consideration.

C. The first taxable year of the Trust begins with the date of this Agreement and shall end on December 31, *(YEAR)*. Subsequent taxable years shall be on a calendar year basis. In the case of a taxable year which is for a period of less than 12 months (other than the taxable year in which the Unitrust Period ends), the Unitrust Amount shall be such amount multiplied by a fraction the numerator of which is the number of days in the taxable year of the Trust and the denominator of which is 365 (366 if February 29 is a day included in the numerator). In the case of the taxable year in which the Unitrust Period ends, the Unitrust Amount shall be such amount multiplied by a fraction the numerator of which is the number of days in the period beginning on the first day of such taxable year and ending on the date of the last day of the Unitrust Period and the denominator of which is 365 (366 if February 29 is a day included in the numerator).

D. The Donor may, from time to time, add property acceptable to the Trustee to the Trust. If any additional contributions are made to the Trust after the initial contribution, the Unitrust Amount for the taxable year in which the assets are added to the Trust shall be ___ percent (___%) of the sum of (a) the net fair market value of the Trust assets (excluding the assets so added and any income from or appreciation on such assets), and (b) that proportion of the value of the assets so added that was excluded under (a) which the number of days in the period which begins with the date of contribution and ends with the earlier of the last day of the taxable year or the last day of the Unitrust Period bears to the number of days in the period which begins on the first day of such taxable year and ends with the earlier of the last day in such taxable year or the last day of the Unitrust Period. The assets so added shall be valued at the time of contribution.

E. Upon the expiration of the Unitrust Period, the Trustee shall distribute all of the then remaining principal and income of the Trust (other than any amount due to the Donee) to the Remainder Beneficiary.

F. For purposes of this Agreement, the Donee shall be *(CHARITY)*, a Section *(CHARITABLE STATUS)* organization, currently with its principal offices at *(CHARITY'S ADDRESS)*. The designation may be amended or revoked by a specific written instrument provided by the Remainder Beneficiary ("written instrument"), adding or substituting other charitable beneficiaries (such original charitable beneficiary and any additional and/or substitute charitable beneficiaries shall herein be collectively referred to as "Donee"). If more than one written instrument is so delivered to the Trustee, the written instrument bearing the latest date shall control and shall be deemed to revoke all prior written instruments unless the most recent one shall provide otherwise. If any Donee is not an organization described in each of Sections 170(b)(1)(A), 170(c), 2055(a) and 2522(a) of the Code at the time when any principal or income of the Trust is to be distributed to it, then the Trustee shall distribute such principal or income in proportion to the relative shares of the Donee(s) which are so described and, if none of the Donee(s) is so described, to one or more organizations then so described as the Trustee in its sole and absolute discretion shall select and in such shares as it shall determine.

<u>ITEM THIRD:</u> In addition to the authority, power and discretion conferred upon a trustee by the laws of the State of *(STATE)*, the Trustee shall have the following authority, power and discretion:

A. To make distribution, when distribution is authorized under the provisions hereof, either wholly or partly in kind, at market value. The adjusted basis for federal income tax purposes of any Trust property which the Trustee distributes in kind to the Donee during the Unitrust Period must be fairly representative of the adjusted basis for such purposes of all Trust property available for distribution on the date of distribution.

B. To alter, repair, improve, erect buildings upon, demolish, manage, partition, lease for any period, including a period in excess of any fixed by statute or extending beyond the duration of the Trust, exchange, grant options to lease or to buy, and sell or dispose of, at public or private sale, and upon such conditions and such terms as to cash and credit as it deems advisable, any of such property.

C. To compromise, settle, subordinate, arbitrate, extend, renew, modify, or release, in whole or in part, any claim held by it or held against any of the property hereunder.

D. To continue to hold the property transferred to it hereunder in the form in which it shall be when transferred or as the form thereof may be changed pursuant to the other provisions of this Agreement so long as it, in its sole and absolute discretion, deems it advisable, without regard to the limitations imposed by law upon the investment of trust funds.

E. As to investments, (i) to allocate receipts and expenditures between principal and income as it, in its sole and absolute discretion, may determine; (ii) to sell, exchange or otherwise dispose of any of the property hereunder; and (iii) to invest and reinvest the funds of the Trust in any kind of property, real or personal, regardless of any laws or rules of law governing the investment of trust funds or diversification of trust funds.

F. To employ any person, firm, corporation, bank, or trust company for advice with respect to investment policy or any other matter; but the Trustee may, in its absolute discretion, follow or refrain from following any recommendation so obtained and such recommendations shall not in any way limit the discretionary power and authority conferred upon the Trustee hereunder with respect to investments or other matters.

G. To participate in and consent to any corporate reorganization, dissolution, liquidation, merger, consolidation, corporate sale or lease, or in and to any other change in any corporation or in its financial structure; and to become a depositor with any protective, reorganization, or similar committee, and to make any necessary payments incident to the foregoing; to organize or participate in the organization of corporations, and to transfer to them any part or all of the property hereunder in exchange for securities thereof which it may retain so long as it deems it advisable; to exercise or to sell any conversion, subscription, or similar rights; and in general to exercise in respect to any securities the unrestricted rights of a personal owner, including voting in person and granting proxies, discretionary, general, or otherwise.

H. To designate any partnership engaged in the business of brokers or dealers in securities, or any corporation authorized so to act, as custodian of any of such property.

I. To the extent permitted by law, to register any of such property in its name as Trustee or in the names of nominees, or to take and keep the same unregistered or in bearer form, or in such condition as to pass by delivery.

J. Nothing in this Agreement shall be construed to restrict the Trustee from investing the Trust property in a manner which could result in the annual realization of a reasonable amount of income or gain from the sale or disposition of Trust property.

K. Any other provisions of this Agreement notwithstanding, if Section 4942 of the Code is deemed applicable to the Trust by reason of Section 508(e) of the Code or otherwise, the Trustee shall make distributions at such time and in such manner as not to subject the Trust to tax under Section 4942 of the Code.

L. Any other provisions of this Agreement notwithstanding, the Trustee shall not engage in any act of self-dealing as defined in Section 4941(d) of the Code; nor retain any excess business holdings as defined in Section 4943(c) of the Code which would subject the Trust to tax under Section 4943 of the Code; nor acquire any assets which would subject the Trust to tax under Section 4944 of the Code, nor retain any assets which would, if acquired by the Trustee, subject the Trust to tax under Section 4944 of the Code; nor make any taxable expenditures as defined in Section 4945(d) of the Code.

M. It is expected that the Trustee will allocate any depreciation deductions to the Trust, and in that regard, the Trustee shall, in its sole and absolute discretion, have the authority to allocate any depreciation deductions to the Trust.

Anything in this Agreement to the contrary notwithstanding, no authority, discretion or power either otherwise granted by this Agreement or by state law that exceed or are inconsistent with the fulfillment of the Donor's Intentions (as defined below in ITEM FIFTH) are to be possessed or exercised by the Trustee.

ITEM FOURTH: As to the Trustee:

A. If *(TRUSTEE)* fails to qualify or for any reason ceases to serve as Trustee, the Remainder Beneficiary shall have the authority to appoint a successor Trustee.

B. The Remainder Beneficiary shall have the power and authority to remove at any time any Trustee and to appoint in the place and stead thereof a successor Trustee; provided, however, that the Donor shall never have the authority to appoint and remove any Trustee hereunder nor be appointed or serve as a Trustee hereunder.

Such removal and appointment shall be accomplished by an instrument in writing, executed in triplicate by the person having the aforesaid removal power and acknowledged before a Notary Public; and one of such executed counterparts shall be delivered to the Trustee that is being removed, a second counterpart shall be delivered to the individual or bank or trust company that is appointed as a successor Trustee here-under, and a third counterpart shall be filed in the permanent records of the Trustee. Upon receiving such executed counterpart, together with receiving an instrument in writing from the successor Trustee accepting such appointment, the Trustee that is being removed shall no longer act as a Trustee hereunder and shall transfer, pay over and deliver the Trust property then in its hands to such successor Trustee, against the latter's simple receipt.

C. Any individual or corporate Trustee serving hereunder shall have the right and privilege to resign as a Trustee under this Agreement upon giving ninety (90) days notice in writing to the other Trustee(s) serving hereunder at the time (if any) and also to the Remainder Beneficiary.

D. No such successor shall be required to investigate the administration or demand an accounting from a predecessor Trustee or the personal representative of a predecessor Trustee and each such successor, upon issuing a simple receipt, shall be charged with only the trust assets so received and shall not be liable or responsible for the acts and deeds of any predecessor Trustee.

E. The Trust shall not be administered under the jurisdiction of any court. Should a question or issue be submitted to a court of competent jurisdiction at any time or from time to time, such court shall acquire jurisdiction of only the question or issue submitted to it, and the jurisdiction of such court shall terminate upon the conclusion or settlement of such question or issue.

F. No Trustee, other than a corporate Trustee, shall receive any compensation for services rendered under this Agreement. No Trustee shall be required to post a bond or other security for the faithful performance of its fiduciary duty in any jurisdiction. Any fees that are paid to an independent Trustee or any of the Trustee's agents in administering this Trust shall be charged to income.

G. The Trustee shall exercise or perform every authority, right, or duty, including discretionary powers, acting alone, and if more than one Trustee is appointed, by majority vote, with the same effect as if all had joined therein.

H. The undersigned Trustee accepts the Trust herein created and consents and agrees that it will carry out the provisions hereof and will faithfully perform and discharge all the duties of its office as Trustee.

ITEM FIFTH: In creating this Trust, the Donor intends (i) to obtain the full benefit of any income, gift and estate tax charitable contribution deductions to which he/she (and his/her estate) may be entitled to under the Code, (ii) for the Unitrust Amount to qualify as a guaranteed unitrust interest under Sections 170(f)(2)(B), 2522(c)(2)(B) and 2055(e)(2)(B) of the Code and other applicable provisions of the Code and the

Treasury Regulations, and (iii) for the Trust to be treated as a "grantor trust" under Sections 671-679 of the Code ("Donor's Intentions"). Accordingly, this Trust shall be interpreted, valued, managed, invested, administered and in all other respects governed in a manner which is consistent with the Donor's Intentions.

ITEM SIXTH: At any time(s) during the Unitrust Period, the Grantor, acting alone and in a non-fiduciary capacity, may acquire or reacquire any portion of the Trust assets by substituting therefor other property of an equivalent value, valued on the date of substitution. The substitution can be effected by the Grantor without the consent of the Trustee. In order to effect the substitution, the Grantor must certify in writing to the Trustee that the substituted property is of equivalent value to the property for which it is substituted, and the Trustee may independently verify such certification of value. Any dispute as to whether the substituted assets are of equivalent value shall be resolved by a court of proper jurisdiction. The Grantor directs that this retained power of substitution is not assignable, and any attempted assignment will make this power void. The Grantor may at any time(s) during the Term by delivery of a written, acknowledged instrument to the Trustee, release such power, in whole or in part, and any such release shall be irrevocable. [Insert other language as appropriate to insure that the Trust will be treated as a Grantor Trust.]

ITEM SEVENTH: No federal estate taxes, state death taxes or any other estate, death or inheritance taxes ("death taxes") with respect to the Trust shall be allocated to or be recoverable from the Trust. The Donor hereby imposes an obligation on his/her estate to pay any death taxes from sources other than the Trust and agrees to so provide in his/her Will or in another way. This provision may be enforced by a Donee in its capacity as charitable beneficiary or the Trustee, acting alone or together.

ITEM EIGHTH: Throughout this Agreement, the word "Code" shall mean the Internal Revenue Code of 1986, as amended from time to time, and references to a Section of the Code shall include any successor provisions to the Section referred to and to any corresponding provisions of any subsequent federal tax laws.

ITEM NINTH: This Agreement is irrevocable. However, the Trustee, acting alone, shall have the power to amend this Agreement in any manner required for the sole purpose of ensuring that the Trust complies with the requirements of Sections 170(f)(2)(B), 2522(c)(2)(B) and 2055(e)(2)(B) of the Code and other applicable provisions of the Code and the corresponding Treasury Regulations.

ITEM TENTH: This Agreement is made pursuant to, and shall be interpreted in accordance with, the laws of the State of *(STATE)*. However, in any conflict with the Code and the Treasury Regulations specified herein, or any other existing or hereafter promulgated legislative or Treasury requirements in order to fulfill the Donor's Intentions, the Code, the Treasury Regulations thereunder and the legislative and Treasury requirements shall govern.

IN WITNESS WHEREOF, the parties hereto have executed this Charitable Lead Unitrust Trust Agreement the date first above written.

WITNESS: DONORS:

_____   _____(SEAL)
                                                                (DONOR)

                                                                TRUSTEE:

_____   _____(SEAL)
                                                                (TRUSTEE)

[ACKNOWLEDGMENT & WITNESS AS REQUIRED UNDER STATE LAW]

SCHEDULE A

This Schedule A is the one referred to in the CHARITABLE LEAD UNITRUST AGREEMENT dated *(DATE)*, by and between *(DONOR)*, as Donor and *(TRUSTEE)*, as Trustee. The Donor, concurrent with the signing of this Agreement, hereby transfers to the Trustee and the Trustee hereby recognizes and accepts receipt of the following:

[DESCRIPTION OF PROPERTY]

_____   _____(SEAL)
                                          (DONOR)

                                          TRUSTEE:

_____   _____(SEAL)
                                          (TRUSTEE)

SAMPLE NONGRANTOR CHARITABLE LEAD ANNUITY TRUST

CHARITABLE LEAD ANNUITY TRUST AGREEMENT
by and between
(DONOR), DONOR
and
(TRUSTEE), TRUSTEE

This CHARITABLE LEAD ANNUITY TRUST AGREEMENT (hereinafter referred to as "Agreement") is made this _____ day of *(MONTH)*, *(YEAR)*, by and between *(DONOR)*, as Donor (hereinafter referred to as "Donor") and *(TRUSTEE)*, of *(CITY)*, *(STATE)* and its successor(s), as Trustee (hereinafter referred to as the "Trustee" and sometimes as "it" or "its").

W I T N E S S E T H :

WHEREAS, Donor has a deep interest in the Donee (as defined below in paragraph F of ITEM SECOND herein, hereinafter referred to as the "Donee"); and

WHEREAS, Donor desires to establish a trust to benefit the Donee for *(LENGTH OF ANNUITY)* years, and at the end of such period, to benefit his/her *(RELATIONSHIP TO REMAINDER BENEFICIARY)*, *(REMAINDER BENEFICIARY)* (hereinafter referred to as "Remainder Beneficiary"); and

WHEREAS, Donor desires to make a gift to the Donee of the income interest in the trust created hereunder; and

WHEREAS, this Agreement is executed for the purpose of defining the terms and conditions of the trust created hereby.

NOW THEREFORE, in consideration of the premises, the mutual covenants and agreements contained herein, and intending to be legally bound thereby, and in consideration of other good and valuable consideration (the receipt and sufficiency of which are hereby acknowledged), the Donor, contemporaneously with the execution of this Agreement is irrevocably assigning, transferring and delivering to the Trustee all his/her right, title and interest in and to the property listed in Schedule A, attached hereto and specifically made a part hereof by this reference. The Trustee hereby accepts such irrevocable gift and agrees to hold and administer the same for the uses, purposes and trusts hereinafter set forth.

ITEM FIRST: It is agreed that the trust created by this Agreement shall be referred to as "THE *(TRUST NAME)* CHARITABLE LEAD ANNUITY TRUST" (hereinafter referred to as "Trust").

ITEM SECOND: The "Annuity Period" as used herein shall mean that period of time which begins on the date that the property listed in Schedule A is contributed to this Trust by the Donor and ends *(LENGTH OF ANNUITY)* years thereafter. During the Annuity Period, the Trustee shall administer and dispose of the income and principal of the Trust as follows:

A. During the Annuity Period, in each taxable year of the Trust, the Trustee shall pay to the Donee, the Annuity Amount as defined in paragraph B of this ITEM SECOND.

B. The term "Annuity Amount" as used herein shall mean a guaranteed annuity equal to _____ percent (_____ %) of the initial net fair market value of the assets constituting the Trust, payable in cash, in kind or partly in each. The Annuity Amount shall be decreased as provided in paragraph C of this ITEM SECOND in the case where the taxable year is a short taxable year or is the taxable year in which the Annuity Period ends. In determining such initial net fair market value, the assets constituting the Trust shall be valued at their values as finally determined for federal tax purposes. If the initial net fair market value of the assets constituting the Trust is incorrectly determined by the Trustee, then within a reasonable period after the correct determination, the Trustee shall pay to the Donee in the case of an undervaluation or shall receive from the Donee in the case of an overvaluation an amount equal to the difference between the Annuity Amount properly payable and the Annuity Amount actually paid. The Annuity Amount shall be paid in annual installments at the end of each calendar year, with the first such installment as of *(ANNUITY DATE)*. The payments to the Donee shall be paid first from ordinary income (excluding unrelated business income), then from short-term capital gain, then from long-term capital gain, then from unrelated business income, then from tax-exempt income, and to the extent that the foregoing items for the taxable year are not sufficient, from principal. Any income of the Trust in excess of the Annuity Amount shall be added to principal. The Trustee's obligation to make payments is limited to the Trust assets. Notwithstanding any existing or hereafter enacted state law, no amount may be paid by the Trust for a private purpose before the expiration of the Annuity Period. However, an amount shall not be deemed to be so paid if the amount is transferred for full and adequate consideration.

C. The first taxable year of the Trust begins with the date of this Agreement and shall end on December 31, *(YEAR)*. Subsequent taxable years shall be on a calendar year basis. In the case of a taxable year which is for a period of less than 12 months (other than the taxable year in which the Annuity Period ends), the Annuity Amount shall be such amount multiplied by a fraction the numerator of which is the number of days in the taxable year of the Trust and the denominator of which is 365 (366 if February 29 is a day included in the numerator). In the case of the taxable year in which the Annuity Period ends, the Annuity Amount shall be such amount multiplied by a fraction the numerator of which is the number of days in the period beginning on the first day of such taxable year and ending on the date of the last day of the Annuity Period and the denominator of which is 365 (366 if February 29 is a day included in the numerator).

D. No additional contributions shall be made to the Trust after the initial contribution.

E. Upon the expiration of the Annuity Period, the Trustee shall distribute all of the then remaining principal and income of the Trust (other than any amount due to the Donee) to the Remainder Beneficiary.

F. For purposes of this Agreement, the Donee shall be *(CHARITY)*, a Section *(CHARITA-BLE STATUS)* organization, currently with its principal offices at *(CHARITY'S ADDRESS)*. The designation may be amended or revoked by a specific written instrument provided by the Remainder Beneficiary ("written instrument"), adding or substituting other charitable beneficiaries (such original charitable beneficiary and any additional and/or substitute charitable beneficiaries shall herein be collectively referred to as "Donee"). If more than one written instrument is so delivered to the Trustee, the written instrument bearing the latest date shall control and shall be deemed to revoke all prior written instruments unless the most recent one shall provide otherwise. If any Donee is not an organization described in each of Sections 170(b)(1)(A), 170(c), 2055(a) and 2522(a) of the Code at the time when any principal or income of the Trust is to be distributed to it, then the Trustee shall distribute such principal or income in proportion to the relative shares of the Donee(s) which are so described and, if none of the Donee(s) is so described, to one or more organizations then so described as the Trustee in its sole and absolute discretion shall select and in such shares as it shall determine.

ITEM THIRD: In addition to the authority, power and discretion conferred upon a trustee by the laws of the State of *(STATE)*, the Trustee shall have the following authority, power and discretion:

A. To make distribution, when distribution is authorized under the provisions hereof, either wholly or partly in kind, at market value. The adjusted basis for federal income tax purposes of any Trust property which the Trustee distributes in kind to the Donee during the Annuity Period must be fairly representative of the adjusted basis for such purposes of all Trust property available for distribution on the date of distribution.

B. To alter, repair, improve, erect buildings upon, demolish, manage, partition, lease for any period, including a period in excess of any fixed by statute or extending beyond the duration of the Trust, exchange, grant options to lease or to buy, and sell or dispose of, at public or private sale, and upon such conditions and such terms as to cash and credit as it deems advisable, any of such property.

C. To compromise, settle, subordinate, arbitrate, extend, renew, modify, or release, in whole or in part, any claim held by it or held against any of the property hereunder.

D. To continue to hold the property transferred to it hereunder in the form in which it shall be when transferred or as the form thereof may be changed pursuant to the other provisions of this Agreement so long as it, in its sole and absolute discretion, deems it advisable, without regard to the limitations imposed by law upon the investment of trust funds.

E. As to investments, (i) to allocate receipts and expenditures between principal and income as it, in its sole and absolute discretion, may determine; (ii) to sell, exchange or otherwise dispose of any of the property hereunder; and (iii) to invest and reinvest the funds of the Trust in any kind of property, real or personal, regardless of any laws or rules of law governing the investment of trust funds or diversification of trust funds.

F. To employ any person, firm, corporation, bank, or trust company for advice with respect to investment policy or any other matter; but the Trustee may, in its absolute discretion, follow or refrain from following any recommendation so obtained and such recommendations shall not in any way limit the discretionary power and authority conferred upon the Trustee hereunder with respect to investments or other matters.

G. To participate in and consent to any corporate reorganization, dissolution, liquidation, merger, consolidation, corporate sale or lease, or in and to any other change in any corporation or in its financial structure; and to become a depositor with any protective, reorganization, or similar committee, and to make any necessary payments incident to the foregoing; to organize or participate in the organization of corporations, and to transfer to them any part or all of the property hereunder in exchange for securities thereof which it may retain so long as it deems it advisable; to exercise or to sell any conversion, subscription, or similar rights; and in general to exercise in respect to any securities the unrestricted rights of a personal owner, including voting in person and granting proxies, discretionary, general, or otherwise.

H. To designate any partnership engaged in the business of brokers or dealers in securities, or any corporation authorized so to act, as custodian of any of such property.

I. To the extent permitted by law, to register any of such property in its name as Trustee or in the names of nominees, or to take and keep the same unregistered or in bearer form, or in such condition as to pass by delivery.

J. Nothing in this Agreement shall be construed to restrict the Trustee from investing the Trust property in a manner which could result in the annual realization of a reasonable amount of income or gain from the sale or disposition of Trust property.

K. Any other provisions of this Agreement notwithstanding, if Section 4942 of the Code is deemed applicable to the Trust by reason of Section 508(e) of the Code or otherwise, the Trustee shall make distributions at such time and in such manner as not to subject the Trust to tax under Section 4942 of the Code.

L. Any other provisions of this Agreement notwithstanding, the Trustee shall not engage in any act of self-dealing as defined in Section 4941(d) of the Code; nor retain any excess business holdings as defined in Section 4943(c) of the Code which would subject the Trust to tax under Section 4943 of the Code; nor acquire any assets which would subject the Trust to tax under Section 4944 of the Code, nor retain any assets which would, if acquired by the Trustee, subject the Trust to tax under Section 4944 of the Code; nor make any taxable expenditures as defined in Section 4945(d) of the Code.

M. It is expected that the Trustee will allocate any depreciation deductions to the Trust, and in that regard, the Trustee shall, in its sole and absolute discretion, have the authority to allocate any depreciation deductions to the Trust.

Anything in this Agreement to the contrary notwithstanding, no authority, discretion or power either otherwise granted by this Agreement or by state law that exceed or are inconsistent with the fulfillment of the Donor's Intentions (as defined below in ITEM FIFTH) are to be possessed or exercised by the Trustee.

<u>ITEM FOURTH:</u> As to the Trustee:

A. If *(TRUSTEE)* fails to qualify or for any reason ceases to serve as Trustee, the Remainder Beneficiary shall have the authority to appoint a successor Trustee.

B. The Remainder Beneficiary shall have the power and authority to remove at any time any Trustee and to appoint in the place and stead thereof a successor Trustee; provided, however, that the Donor shall never have the authority to appoint and remove any Trustee hereunder nor be appointed or serve as a Trustee hereunder.

Such removal and appointment shall be accomplished by an instrument in writing, executed in triplicate by the person having the aforesaid removal power and acknowledged before a Notary Public; and one of such executed counterparts shall be delivered to the Trustee that is being removed, a second counterpart shall be delivered to the individual or bank or trust company that is appointed as a successor Trustee here-under, and a third counterpart shall be filed in the permanent records of the Trustee. Upon receiving such executed counterpart, together with receiving an instrument in writing from the successor Trustee accepting such appointment, the Trustee that is being removed shall no longer act as a Trustee hereunder and shall transfer, pay over and deliver the Trust property then in its hands to such successor Trustee, against the latter's simple receipt.

C. Any individual or corporate Trustee serving hereunder shall have the right and privilege to resign as a Trustee under this Agreement upon giving ninety (90) days notice in writing to the other Trustee(s) serving hereunder at the time (if any) and also to the Remainder Beneficiary.

D. No such successor shall be required to investigate the administration or demand an accounting from a predecessor Trustee or the personal representative of a predecessor Trustee and each such successor, upon issuing a simple receipt, shall be charged with only the trust assets so received and shall not be liable or responsible for the acts and deeds of any predecessor Trustee.

E. The Trust shall not be administered under the jurisdiction of any court. Should a question or issue be submitted to a court of competent jurisdiction at any time or from time to time, such court shall acquire jurisdiction of only the question or issue submitted to it, and the jurisdiction of such court shall terminate upon the conclusion or settlement of such question or issue.

F. No Trustee, other than a corporate Trustee, shall receive any compensation for services rendered under this Agreement. No Trustee shall be required to post a bond or other security for the faithful performance of its fiduciary duty in any jurisdiction. Any fees that are paid to an independent Trustee or any of the Trustee's agents in administering this Trust shall be charged to income.

G. The Trustee shall exercise or perform every authority, right, or duty, including discretionary powers, acting alone, and if more than one Trustee is appointed, by majority vote, with the same effect as if all had joined therein.

H. The undersigned Trustee accepts the Trust herein created and consents and agrees that it will carry out the provisions hereof and will faithfully perform and discharge all the duties of its office as Trustee.

<u>ITEM FIFTH:</u> In creating this Trust, the Donor intends (i) to obtain the full benefit of any gift and estate tax charitable contribution deductions to which he/she (and his/her estate) may be entitled to under the Code, (ii) for the Annuity Amount to qualify as a guaranteed annuity interest under Sections 2522(c)(2)(B) and 2055(e)(2)(B) of the Code and other applicable provisions of the Code and the Treasury Regulations thereunder, (iii) that the Trust be allowed charitable income tax deductions under Section 642(c) of the Code for all payments of the Annuity Amount to a Donee (including but not limited to, capital gains or other gross income allocated to Trust principal), (iv) that none of the income of this Trust be included in the Donor's personal taxable income and (v) that no part of the Trust be included in the Donor's gross estate for federal estate tax purposes ("Donor's Intentions"). Accordingly, this Trust shall be interpreted, valued, managed, invested, administered and in all other respects governed in a manner which is consistent with the Donor's Intentions.

ITEM SIXTH: No federal estate taxes, state death taxes or any other estate, death or inheritance taxes ("death taxes") with respect to the Trust shall be allocated to or be recoverable from the Trust. The Donor hereby imposes an obligation on his/her estate to pay any death taxes from sources other than the Trust and agrees to so provide in his/her Will or in another way. This provision may be enforced by a Donee in its capacity as charitable beneficiary or the Trustee, acting alone or together.

ITEM SEVENTH: Throughout this Agreement, the word "Code" shall mean the Internal Revenue Code of 1986, as amended from time to time, and references to a Section of the Code shall include any successor provisions to the Section referred to and to any corresponding provisions of any subsequent federal tax laws.

ITEM EIGHTH: This Agreement is irrevocable. However, the Trustee, acting alone, shall have the power to amend this Agreement in any manner required for the sole purpose of ensuring that the Trust complies with the requirements of Sections 2522(c)(2)(B) and 2055(e)(2)(B) of the Code and other applicable provisions of the Code and the corresponding Treasury Regulations. Except as provided above in this ITEM EIGHTH, neither the Donor nor any other person shall have any power, either alone or in conjunction with any other person, to alter, amend, revoke or terminate this Trust or any of its terms in any manner whatsoever. Except as provided above in paragraph F of ITEM SECOND, neither the Donor nor any other person shall have any power, either alone or in conjunction with any other person, to designate the persons who shall possess or enjoy the Trust property, or the income therefrom.

ITEM NINTH: No income or principal of the Trust shall be distributed, accumulated or used for the benefit of the Donor or to pay premiums on any policy of insurance on the life of the Donor; no loans shall be made, directly or indirectly, from the Trust hereunder to the Donor; no property shall be bought from, sold to, exchanged with or leased to -or from any person for less than an adequate consideration in money or money's worth; no person, other than the Trustee acting in a fiduciary capacity, shall have or exercise the power to vote or direct the voting of any stock or securities of this Trust, or to control the investment of this Trust either by directing investments or reinvestments or by vetoing proposed investments or reinvestments; no person, other than the Trustee acting in a fiduciary capacity, shall have or exercise the power to reacquire or exchange any property of this Trust by substituting other property of an equivalent value; and the Donor shall not have the power to control in any manner the administration of the Trust hereunder.

ITEM TENTH: This Agreement is made pursuant to, and shall be interpreted in accordance with, the laws of the State of *(STATE)*. However, in any conflict with the Code and the Treasury Regulations specified herein, or any other existing or hereafter promulgated legislative or Treasury requirements in order to fulfill the Donor's Intentions, the Code, the Treasury Regulations thereunder and the legislative and Treasury requirements shall govern.

IN WITNESS WHEREOF, the parties hereto have executed this Charitable Lead Annuity Trust Agreement the date first above written.

WITNESS: DONORS:

_____   _____(SEAL)
                                                  (DONOR)

                                                 TRUSTEE:

_____   _____(SEAL)
                                                  (TRUSTEE)

[ACKNOWLEDGMENT & WITNESS AS REQUIRED UNDER STATE LAW]

SCHEDULE A

      This Schedule A is the one referred to in the CHARITABLE LEAD ANNUITY TRUST AGREE-MENT dated *(DATE)*, by and between *(DONOR)*, as Donor and *(TRUSTEE)*, as Trustee. The Donor, concurrent with the signing of this Agreement, hereby transfers to the Trustee and the Trustee hereby recognizes and accepts receipt of the following:

[[DESCRIPTION OF PROPERTY]

_____   _____(SEAL)
                                                   (DONOR)

                                                   TRUSTEE:

_____   _____(SEAL)
                                                   (TRUSTEE)

SAMPLE NONGRANTOR CHARITABLE LEAD UNITRUST

CHARITABLE LEAD UNITRUST TRUST AGREEMENT
by and between
(DONOR), DONOR
and
(TRUSTEE), TRUSTEE

This CHARITABLE LEAD UNITRUST TRUST AGREEMENT (hereinafter referred to as "Agreement") is made this _____ day of *(MONTH)*, *(YEAR)*, by and between *(DONOR)*, as Donor (hereinafter referred to as "Donor") and *(TRUSTEE)*, of *(CITY)*, *(STATE)* and its successor(s), as Trustee (hereinafter referred to as the "Trustee" and sometimes as "it" or its").

WITNESSETH:

WHEREAS, Donor has a deep interest in the Donee (as defined below in paragraph F of ITEM SECOND herein, hereinafter referred to as the "Donee"); and

WHEREAS, Donor desires to establish a trust to benefit the Donee for *(LENGTH OF UNITRUST)* years, and at the end of such period, to benefit his/her *(RELATIONSHIP TO REMAINDER BENEFICIARY)*, *(REMAINDER BENEFICIARY)* (hereinafter referred to as "Remainder Beneficiary"); and

WHEREAS, Donor desires to make a gift to the Donee of the income interest in the trust created hereunder; and

WHEREAS, this Agreement is executed for the purpose of defining the terms and conditions of the trust created hereby.

NOW THEREFORE, in consideration of the premises, the mutual covenants and agreements contained herein, and intending to be legally bound thereby, and in consideration of other good and valuable consideration (the receipt and sufficiency of which are hereby acknowledged), the Donor, contemporaneously with the execution of this Agreement is irrevocably assigning, transferring and delivering to the Trustee all his/her right, title and interest in and to the property listed in Schedule A, attached hereto and specifically made a part hereof by this reference. The Trustee hereby accepts such irrevocable gift and agrees to hold and administer the same for the uses, purposes and trusts hereinafter set forth.

ITEM FIRST: It is agreed that the trust created by this Agreement shall be referred to as "THE *(TRUST NAME)* CHARITABLE LEAD UNITRUST" (hereinafter referred to as "Trust").

ITEM SECOND: The "Unitrust Period" as used herein shall mean that period of time which begins on the date that the property listed in Schedule A is contributed to this Trust by the Donor and ends *(LENGTH OF UNITRUST)* years thereafter. During the Unitrust Period, the Trustee shall administer and dispose of the income and principal of the Trust as follows:

A. During the Unitrust Period, in each taxable year of the Trust, the Trustee shall pay to the Donee, the Unitrust Amount as defined in paragraph B of this ITEM SECOND.

B. The term "Unitrust Amount" as used herein shall mean an amount equal to _____ percent (___%) of the net fair market value of the Trust assets valued as of the first day of each taxable year of the Trust except as otherwise provided in paragraph C of this ITEM SECOND in the case where the taxable year is a short taxable year or is the taxable year in which the Unitrust Period ends. The Unitrust Amount shall be paid in annual installments at the end of each calendar year, with the first such installment as of *(UNITRUST DATE)*. The payments to the Donee shall be paid first from ordinary income (excluding unrelated business income), then from short-term capital gain, then from long-term capital gain, then from unrelated business income, then from tax-exempt income, and to the extent that the foregoing items for the taxable year are not sufficient, from principal. Any income of the Trust in excess of the Unitrust Amount shall be added to principal. The Trustee's obligation to make payments is limited to the Trust assets. Notwithstanding any existing or hereafter enacted state law, no amount may be paid by the Trust for a private purpose before the expiration of the Unitrust Period. However, an amount shall not be deemed to be so paid if the amount is transferred for full and adequate consideration.

C. The first taxable year of the Trust begins with the date of this Agreement and shall end on December 31, *(YEAR)*. Subsequent taxable years shall be on a calendar year basis. In the case of a taxable year which is for a period of less than 12 months (other than the taxable year in which the Unitrust Period ends), the Unitrust Amount shall be such amount multiplied by a fraction the numerator of which is the number of days in the taxable year of the Trust and the denominator of which is 365 (366 if February 29 is a day included in the numerator). In the case of the taxable year in which the Unitrust Period ends, the Unitrust Amount shall be such amount multiplied by a fraction the numerator of which is the number of days in the period beginning on the first day of such taxable year and ending on the date of the last day of the Unitrust Period and the denominator of which is 365 (366 if February 29 is a day included in the numerator).

D. The Donor may, from time to time, add property acceptable to the Trustee to the Trust. If any additional contributions are made to the Trust after the initial contribution, the Unitrust Amount for the taxable year in which the assets are added to the Trust shall be _____ percent (___%) of the sum of (a) the net fair market value of the Trust assets (excluding the assets so added and any income from or appreciation on such assets), and (b) that proportion of the value of the assets so added that was excluded under (a) which the number of days in the period which begins with the date of contribution and ends with the earlier of the last day of the taxable year or the last day of the Unitrust Period bears to the number of days in the period which begins on the first day of such taxable year and ends with the earlier of the last day in such taxable year or the last day of the Unitrust Period. The assets so added shall be valued at the time of contribution.

E. Upon the expiration of the Unitrust Period, the Trustee shall distribute all of the then remaining principal and income of the Trust (other than any amount due to the Donee) to the Remainder Beneficiary.

F. For purposes of this Agreement, the Donee shall be *(CHARITY)*, a Section *(CHARITA-BLE STATUS)* organization, currently with its principal offices at *(CHARITY'S ADDRESS)*. The designation may be amended or revoked by a specific written instrument provided by the Remainder Beneficiary ("written instrument"), adding or substituting other charitable beneficiaries (such original charitable beneficiary and any additional and/or substitute charitable beneficiaries shall herein be collectively referred to as "Donee"). If more than one written instrument is so delivered to the Trustee, the written instrument bearing the latest date shall control and shall be deemed to revoke all prior written instruments unless the most recent one shall provide otherwise. If any Donee is not an organization described in each of Sections 170(b)(1)(A), 170(c), 2055(a) and 2522(a) of the Code at the time when any principal or income of the Trust is to be distributed to it, then the Trustee shall distribute such principal or income in proportion to the relative shares of the Donee(s) which are so described and, if none of the Donee(s) is so described, to one or more organizations then so described as the Trustee in its sole and absolute discretion shall select and in such shares as it shall determine.

ITEM THIRD: In addition to the authority, power and discretion conferred upon a trustee by the laws of the State of *(STATE)*, the Trustee shall have the following authority, power and discretion:

A. To make distribution, when distribution is authorized under the provisions hereof, either wholly or partly in kind, at market value. The adjusted basis for federal income tax purposes of any Trust property which the Trustee distributes in kind to the Donee during the Unitrust Period must be fairly representative of the adjusted basis for such purposes of all Trust property available for distribution on the date of distribution.

B. To alter, repair, improve, erect buildings upon, demolish, manage, partition, lease for any period, including a period in excess of any fixed by statute or extending beyond the duration of the Trust, exchange, grant options to lease or to buy, and sell or dispose of, at public or private sale, and upon such conditions and such terms as to cash and credit as it deems advisable, any of such property.

C. To compromise, settle, subordinate, arbitrate, extend, renew, modify, or release, in whole or in part, any claim held by it or held against any of the property hereunder.

D. To continue to hold the property transferred to it hereunder in the form in which it shall be when transferred or as the form thereof may be changed pursuant to the other provisions of this Agreement so long as it, in its sole and absolute discretion, deems it advisable, without regard to the limitations imposed by law upon the investment of trust funds.

E. As to investments, (i) to allocate receipts and expenditures between principal and income as it, in its sole and absolute discretion, may determine; (ii) to sell, exchange or otherwise dispose of any of the property hereunder; and (iii) to invest and reinvest the funds of the Trust in any kind of property, real or personal, regardless of any laws or rules of law governing the investment of trust funds or diversification of trust funds.

F. To employ any person, firm, corporation, bank, or trust company for advice with respect to investment policy or any other matter; but the Trustee may, in its absolute discretion, follow or refrain from following any recommendation so obtained and such recommendations shall not in any way limit the discretionary power and authority conferred upon the Trustee hereunder with respect to investments or other matters.

G. To participate in and consent to any corporate reorganization, dissolution, liquidation, merger, consolidation, corporate sale or lease, or in and to any other change in any corporation or in its financial structure; and to become a depositor with any protective, reorganization, or similar committee, and to make any necessary payments incident to the foregoing; to organize or participate in the organization of corporations, and to transfer to them any part or all of the property hereunder in exchange for securities thereof which it may retain so long as it deems it advisable; to exercise or to sell any conversion, subscription, or similar rights; and in general to exercise in respect to any securities the unrestricted rights of a personal owner, including voting in person and granting proxies, discretionary, general, or otherwise.

H. To designate any partnership engaged in the business of brokers or dealers in securities, or any corporation authorized so to act, as custodian of any of such property.

I. To the extent permitted by law, to register any of such property in its name as Trustee or in the names of nominees, or to take and keep the same unregistered or in bearer form, or in such condition as to pass by delivery.

J. Nothing in this Agreement shall be construed to restrict the Trustee from investing the Trust property in a manner which could result in the annual realization of a reasonable amount of income or gain from the sale or disposition of Trust property.

K. Any other provisions of this Agreement notwithstanding, if Section 4942 of the Code is deemed applicable to the Trust by reason of Section 508(e) of the Code or otherwise, the Trustee shall make distributions at such time and in such manner as not to subject the Trust to tax under Section 4942 of the Code.

L. Any other provisions of this Agreement notwithstanding, the Trustee shall not engage in any act of self-dealing as defined in Section 4941(d) of the Code; nor retain any excess business holdings as defined in Section 4943(c) of the Code which would subject the Trust to tax under Section 4943 of the Code; nor acquire any assets which would subject the Trust to tax under Section 4944 of the Code, nor retain any assets which would, if acquired by the Trustee, subject the Trust to tax under Section 4944 of the Code; nor make any taxable expenditures as defined in Section 4945(d) of the Code.

M. It is expected that the Trustee will allocate any depreciation deductions to the Trust, and in that regard, the Trustee shall, in its sole and absolute discretion, have the authority to allocate any depreciation deductions to the Trust.

Anything in this Agreement to the contrary notwithstanding, no authority, discretion or power either otherwise granted by this Agreement or by state law that exceed or are inconsistent with the fulfillment of the Donor's Intentions (as defined below in ITEM FIFTH) are to be possessed or exercised by the Trustee.

ITEM FOURTH: As to the Trustee:

A. If *(TRUSTEE)* fails to qualify or for any reason ceases to serve as Trustee, the Remainder Beneficiary shall have the authority to appoint a successor Trustee.

B. The Remainder Beneficiary shall have the power and authority to remove at any time any Trustee and to appoint in the place and stead thereof a successor Trustee; provided, however, that the Donor shall never have the authority to appoint and remove any Trustee hereunder nor be appointed or serve as a Trustee hereunder.

Such removal and appointment shall be accomplished by an instrument in writing, executed in triplicate by the person having the aforesaid removal power and acknowledged before a Notary Public; and one of such executed counterparts shall be delivered to the Trustee that is being removed, a second counterpart shall be delivered to the individual or bank or trust company that is appointed as a successor Trustee here-under, and a third counterpart shall be filed in the permanent records of the Trustee. Upon receiving such executed counterpart, together with receiving an instrument in writing from the successor Trustee accepting such appointment, the Trustee that is being removed shall no longer act as a Trustee hereunder and shall transfer, pay over and deliver the Trust property then in its hands to such successor Trustee, against the latter's simple receipt.

C. Any individual or corporate Trustee serving hereunder shall have the right and privilege to resign as a Trustee under this Agreement upon giving ninety (90) days notice in writing to the other Trustee(s) serving hereunder at the time (if any) and also to the Remainder Beneficiary.

D. No such successor shall be required to investigate the administration or demand an accounting from a predecessor Trustee or the personal representative of a predecessor Trustee and each such successor, upon issuing a simple receipt, shall be charged with only the trust assets so received and shall not be liable or responsible for the acts and deeds of any predecessor Trustee.

E. The Trust shall not be administered under the jurisdiction of any court. Should a question or issue be submitted to a court of competent jurisdiction at any time or from time to time, such court shall acquire jurisdiction of only the question or issue submitted to it, and the jurisdiction of such court shall terminate upon the conclusion or settlement of such question or issue.

F. No Trustee, other than a corporate Trustee, shall receive any compensation for services rendered under this Agreement. No Trustee shall be required to post a bond or other security for the faithful performance of its fiduciary duty in any jurisdiction. Any fees that are paid to an independent Trustee or any of the Trustee's agents in administering this Trust shall be charged to income.

G. The Trustee shall exercise or perform every authority, right, or duty, including discretionary powers, acting alone, and if more than one Trustee is appointed, by majority vote, with the same effect as if all had joined therein.

H. The undersigned Trustee accepts the Trust herein created and consents and agrees that it will carry out the provisions hereof and will faithfully perform and discharge all the duties of its office as Trustee.

ITEM FIFTH: In creating this Trust, the Donor intends (i) to obtain the full benefit of any gift and estate tax charitable contribution deductions to which he/she (and his/her estate) may be entitled to under the Code, (ii) for the Unitrust Amount to qualify as a guaranteed unitrust interest under Sections 2522(c)(2)(B) and 2055(e)(2)(B) of the Code and other applicable provisions of the Code and the Treasury Regulations thereunder, (iii) that the Trust be allowed charitable income tax deductions under Section 642(c) of the Code for all payments of the Unitrust Amount to a Donee (including but not limited to, capital gains or other gross income allocated to Trust principal), (iv) that none of the income of this Trust be included in the Donor's personal taxable income and (v) that no part of the Trust be included in the Donor's gross estate for federal estate tax purposes ("Donor's Intentions"). Accordingly, this Trust shall be interpreted, valued, managed, invested, administered and in all other respects governed in a manner which is consistent with the Donor's Intentions.

ITEM SIXTH: No federal estate taxes, state death taxes or any other estate, death or inheritance taxes ("death taxes") with respect to the Trust shall be allocated to or be recoverable from the Trust. The Donor hereby imposes an obligation on his/her estate to pay any death taxes from sources other than the Trust and agrees to so provide in his/her Will or in another way. This provision may be enforced by a Donee in its capacity as charitable beneficiary or the Trustee, acting alone or together.

ITEM SEVENTH: Throughout this Agreement, the word "Code" shall mean the Internal Revenue Code of 1986, as amended from time to time, and references to a Section of the Code shall include any successor provisions to the Section referred to and to any corresponding provisions of any subsequent federal tax laws.

ITEM EIGHTH: This Agreement is irrevocable. However, the Trustee, acting alone, shall have the power to amend this Agreement in any manner required for the sole purpose of ensuring that the Trust complies with the requirements of Sections 2522(c)(2)(B) and 2055(e)(2)(B) of the Code and other applicable provisions of the Code and the corresponding Treasury Regulations. Except as provided above in this ITEM EIGHTH, neither the Donor nor any other person shall have any power, either alone or in conjunction with any other person, to alter, amend, revoke or terminate this Trust or any of its terms in any manner whatsoever. Except as provided above in paragraph F of ITEM SECOND, neither the Donor nor any other person shall have any power, either alone or in conjunction with any other person, to designate the persons who shall possess or enjoy the Trust property, or the income therefrom.

ITEM NINTH: No income or principal of the Trust shall be distributed, accumulated or used for the benefit of the Donor or to pay premiums on any policy of insurance on the life of the Donor; no loans shall be made, directly or indirectly, from the Trust hereunder to the Donor; no property shall be bought from, sold to, exchanged with or leased to or from any person for less than an adequate consideration in money or money's worth; no person, other than the Trustee acting in a fiduciary capacity, shall have or exercise the power to vote or direct the voting of any stock or securities of this Trust, or to control the investment of this Trust either by directing investments or reinvestments or by vetoing proposed investments or reinvestments; no person, other than the Trustee acting in a fiduciary capacity, shall have or exercise the power to reacquire or exchange any property of this Trust by substituting other property of an equivalent value; and the Donor shall not have the power to control in any manner the administration of the Trust hereunder.

ITEM TENTH: This Agreement is made pursuant to, and shall be interpreted in accordance with, the laws of the State of *(STATE)*. However, in any conflict with the Code and the Treasury Regulations specified herein, or any other existing or hereafter promulgated legislative or Treasury requirements in order to fulfill the Donor's Intentions, the Code, the Treasury Regulations thereunder and the legislative and Treasury requirements shall govern.

IN WITNESS WHEREOF, the parties hereto have executed this Charitable Lead Unitrust Trust Agreement the date first above written.

WITNESS: DONORS:

_____   _____(SEAL)
                                                                (DONOR)

                                                                 TRUSTEE:

_____   _____(SEAL)
                                                                (TRUSTEE)

[ACKNOWLEDGMENT & WITNESS AS REQUIRED UNDER STATE LAW]

SCHEDULE A

      This Schedule A is the one referred to in the CHARITABLE LEAD UNITRUST AGREEMENT dated *(DATE)*, by and between *(DONOR)*, as Donor and *(TRUSTEE)*, as Trustee. The Donor, concurrent with the signing of this Agreement, hereby transfers to the Trustee and the Trustee hereby recognizes and accepts receipt of the following:

[[DESCRIPTION OF PROPERTY]

_____   _____(SEAL)
                                                           (DONOR)

TRUSTEE:

_____   _____(SEAL)
                                                          (TRUSTEE)

SAMPLE QUITCLAIM DEED

QUITCLAIM DEED

THIS QUITCLAIM DEED, dated *(MONTH) (DAY), (YEAR)*, from *(GRANTOR)*, of the County of *(COUNTY)*, State of *(STATE)* ("Grantor"), to *(CHARITY)*, ("Grantee").

The Grantor, for no consideration, hereby grants, conveys, releases, assigns and quitclaims to the Grantee, its successors and assigns, forever, all such right, title, interest, property, possession, claim and demand, as it has or ought to have in or to the following described premises:

See Exhibit "A" attached hereto and made a part hereof.

Provided, however, that Grantor reserves to itself the right to reside in the real property during its lifetime. Such right to reside in the described real property shall be terminated prior to Grantor's death if written notice of voluntary termination of Grantor's right to reside in such real property in a form suspectable of recordation in the official records of the County Recorder of *(COUNTY)* County, State of *(STATE)*, is given to Grantee by Grantor personally, or by a person authorized by a duly executed Power of Attorney to give such notice on Grantor's behalf, or by any conservator or guardian appointed by a court of competent jurisdiction to manage Grantor's estate.

TO HAVE AND TO HOLD the said land and premises above described and conveyed hereby, together with the buildings and improvements thereupon erected, and every and all title, right, privileges, appurtenances and advantages thereunto belonging or in any way appertaining, unto and to the use and benefit of the Grantee, its successors and assigns.

SUBJECT to the covenants, easements and restrictions of record insofar as they may apply to the property conveyed hereby.

AND the Grantor covenants that it will execute such other and further assurances as may be requisite.

IN WITNESS WHEREOF, the Grantor has signed and sealed this Quitclaim Deed as of the date first above written.

WITNESS: GRANTOR:

_____   _____(SEAL)
                                                              (GRANTOR)

SAMPLE ACKNOWLEDGMENT FOR QUITCLAIM DEED (previous page)

COUNTY OF *(COUNTY)*
STATE OF *(STATE)*, to-wit:

BEFORE ME, the undersigned Notary Public, personally appeared on this ___ day of *(MONTH)*, *(YEAR)*, *(GRANTOR)*, known to me or satisfactorily proven to be the person whose name is signed to the foregoing Quitclaim Deed as Grantor, and acknowledged that he/she executed the same as his/her free act and deed for the purposes therein contained.

_____
Notary Public

My Commission Expires: _____

I HEREBY CERTIFY that the within instrument was prepared an attorney, under such attorney's supervision, or by one of the parties named in this instrument.

_____

EXHIBIT "A"

SAMPLE ONE-LIFE GIFT ANNUITY AGREEMENT (Massachusetts)

<Charity Name>
GIFT ANNUITY AGREEMENT
Immediate Payments

This Agreement is made between (Donor name), of (Legal Address) (hereinafter "the Donor"), and <Charity Name>, of <Charity Address> (hereinafter "Charity").

1. Transfer of Property by Donor: Charity certifies that the Donor, as an evidence of his/her desire to support the work of Charity and to make a charitable gift, on (month day, year) contributed to Charity the property described in Schedule A attached hereto, the fair market value of which is (fair market value of gift).

2. Payment of Annuity: In consideration of the property transferred by the Donor, Charity shall pay an annual annuity of (annual dollar amount) from the date of this Agreement and shall pay such amount to the Donor so long as he/she is living.

3. Payment Dates; First Installment: The annuity shall be paid in quarterly installments of (quarterly payment amount). The first installment shall be payable on (date of first partial payment) in the amount of (dollar amount of partial payment), prorated on the basis of the number of days in the initial payment period. Subsequent installments beginning on (date of next regular quarterly payment) and continuing every quarter thereafter shall be in the full amount of (regular quarterly payment amount).

4. Birth Date of Donor: The Donor's date of birth is (month day, year).

5. Irrevocability; Non-assignability; Termination: This annuity is irrevocable and non-assignable, except that it may be assigned to Charity. Charity's obligation under this Agreement shall terminate with the regular payment preceding the Donor's death.

6. Uses and Purposes of Gift: Upon Charity's satisfaction of its obligation under this Agreement, an amount equal to the residuum of the gift shall be used by Charity for its (general purposes, or state other purposes).

7. Entire Agreement; Governing Law: This Agreement, together with Schedule A attached hereto, constitutes the entire agreement of the parties. This Agreement shall be governed by the laws of the Commonwealth of Massachusetts.

This Agreement is effective as of (month day, year).

DONOR: <Charity Name>:

_____   By: _____
Donor   <Name of Signing Officer>,
                                          <Title>

Gift Annuity Agreement between (Donor name) and <Charity Name>

SCHEDULE A

Description of Property

<Description of gift asset(s)>

SAMPLE POOLED INCOME FUND LANGUAGE

Following are the I.R.S. suggested terms for a prototype Pooled Income Fund document including a one-life Instrument of Transfer. This is provided by Charitable Giving Tax Service by R&R Newkirk, listed in Appendix III.

REV. PROC. 88-53

SECTION 1. PURPOSE.

This revenue procedure makes available a sample form of declaration of trust and instruments of transfer that meet the requirements for a pooled income fund as described in section 642(c)(5) of the Internal Revenue Code.

SEC. 2. BACKGROUND.

The Internal Revenue Service receives and responds to many requests for rulings dealing with the qualification of trusts as pooled income funds and the availability of deductions for contributions made to such trusts. In many of these requests, the trust instruments and charitable objectives are very similar. Consequently, in order to provide a service to taxpayers and to save the time and expense involved in requesting and processing a ruling on a proposed pooled income fund, taxpayers who make transfers to a trust that substantially follows the model trust instrument contained herein can be assured that the Service will recognize the trust as meeting all of the requirements of a qualified pooled income fund, provided the trust operates in a manner consistent with the terms of the trust instrument and provided it is a valid trust under applicable local law.

SEC. 3. SCOPE AND OBJECTIVE.

The sample declaration of trust and instruments of transfer made available by this revenue procedure meet all of the applicable requirements for a pooled income fund under section 642(c)(5) of the Code, if the trust document also creates a valid trust under local law. If the public charity responsible for the creation and maintenance of a pooled income fund makes reference in the trust instrument of the fund to this revenue procedure, and adopts substantially similar documents, the Service will recognize the trust documents as satisfying all of the applicable requirements of section 642(c)(5) of the Code and the corresponding regulations. Moreover, for transfers to a qualifying pooled income fund, the remainder interest will be deductible under sections 170(f)(2)(A), 2055(e)(2)(A), and 2522(c)(2)(A) of the Code for income, estate, and gift tax purposes, respectively. Therefore, it will not be necessary for a taxpayer to request a ruling as to the qualification of a substantially similar trust, and the Service generally will not issue such a ruling. See Rev. Proc. 88-54, page 16, this Bulletin.

SEC. 4. SAMPLE DECLARATION OF TRUST.

On this ____ day of ____, 19__, the Board of Trustees of the ____ Public Charity (hereinafter referred to as "Public Charity") desiring to establish a pooled income fund within the meaning of Rev. Proc. 88-53 and section 642(c)(5) of the Internal Revenue Code (hereinafter referred to as "the Code"), hereby creates the ____ Public Charity Pooled Income Fund (hereinafter referred to as "the Fund") and designates ____ as the initial trustee to hold, manage, and distribute such property hereinafter transferred to and accepted by it as part of the Fund under the following terms and conditions.

1. Gift of Remainder Interest. Each donor transferring property to the Fund shall contribute an irrevocable remainder interest in such property to Public Charity.

2. Retention of Life Income Interest. Each donor transferring property to the Fund shall retain for himself or herself an income interest in the property transferred, or create an income interest in such property for the life of one or more named beneficiaries, provided that each income beneficiary must be a living person at the time of the transfer of property to the Fund by the donor. If more than one beneficiary of the income interest is named, such beneficiaries may enjoy their shares concurrently and/or consecutively. Public Charity

may also be designated as one of the beneficiaries of the income interest. The donor need not retain or create a life interest in all of the income from the property transferred to the Fund and any income not payable to an income beneficiary shall be contributed to, and within the taxable year of the Fund in which it is received paid to. Public Charity.

3. Commingling of Property. The property transferred to the Fund by each donor shall be commingled with, and invested or reinvested with, other property transferred to the Fund by other donors satisfying the requirements of this instrument and of section 642(c)(5) of the Code or corresponding provision of any subsequent federal tax law. The Fund shall not include property transferred under arrangements other than those specified in this instrument and satisfying the said provisions of the Code.

All or any portion of the assets of the Fund may, however, be invested or reinvested jointly with other properties not a part of the Fund that are held by, or for the use of, Public Charity. When joint investment or reinvestment occurs, detailed accounting records shall be maintained by the Trustee specifically identifying the portion of the jointly invested property owned by the Fund and the income earned by, and attributable to such portion.

4. Prohibition Against Exempt Securities. The property transferred to the Fund by any donor shall not include any securities whose income is exempt from taxation under subtitle A of the Code or the corresponding provisions of any subsequent federal tax law. The Trustee of the Fund shall not accept or invest in such securities as part of the assets of the Fund.

5. Maintenance by Public Charity. Public Charity shall always maintain the Fund or exercise control, directly or indirectly, over the Fund. Public Charity shall always have the power to remove any Trustee or Trustees and to designate a new Trustee or Trustees.

6. Prohibition Against Donor or Beneficiary Serving as Trustee. The Fund shall not have as a Trustee a donor to the Fund or a beneficiary (other than Public Charity) of an income interest in any property transferred to the Fund. No donor or beneficiary (other than Public Charity) shall have, directly or indirectly, general responsibilities with respect to the Fund that are ordinarily exercised by a Trustee.

7. Income of Beneficiary to be Based on Rate of Return of Fund. The taxable year of the Fund shall be the calendar year. The Trustee shall pay income to each beneficiary entitled thereto in any taxable year of the Fund in the amount determined by the rate of return earned by the Fund for the year with respect to the beneficiary's income interest. Payments must be made at least once in the year in which the income is earned. Until the Trustee determines that payments shall be made more or less frequently or at other times, the Trustee shall make income payments to the beneficiary or beneficiaries entitled to them in four quarterly payments on or about March 31, June 30, September 30, and December 31 of each year. An adjusting payment, if necessary, will be made during the taxable year or within the first 65 days following its close to bring the total payment to the actual income to which the beneficiary or beneficiaries are entitled for that year.

On each transfer of property by a donor to the Fund, there shall be assigned to the beneficiary or beneficiaries of the income interest retained or created in the property the number of units of participation equal to the number obtained by dividing the fair market value of the property transferred by the fair market value of a unit in the Fund immediately before the transfer. The fair market value of a unit in the Fund immediately before the transfer shall be determined by dividing the fair market value of all property in the Fund at that time by the number of units then in the Fund. The initial fair market value of a unit in the Fund shall be the fair market value of the property transferred to the Fund divided by the number of units assigned to the beneficiaries of the income interest in that property. All units in the Fund shall always have equal value.

If a transfer of property to the Fund by a donor occurs on other than a determination date, the number of units of participation assigned to the beneficiary or beneficiaries of the income interest in the property shall be determined by using the average fair market value of the property in the Fund immediately before the transfer, which shall be deemed to be the average of the fair market values of the property in the Fund on the determination dates immediately preceding and succeeding the date of transfer. For the purpose of determining the average fair market value, the property transferred by the donor and any other property transferred to the Fund between the preceding and succeeding dates, or on such succeeding date, shall be excluded. The fair market value of a unit in the Fund immediately before the transfer shall be determined by dividing the average fair market value of the property in the Fund at that time by the number of units then in the Fund. Units of participation assigned with respect to property transferred on other than a [determination] date shall be deemed to be assigned as of the date of the transfer.

A determination date means each day within a taxable year of the Fund on which a valuation is made of the property in the Fund. The property of the Fund shall be valued on January 1, April 1, July 1, and October 1 of each year; provided, however, that where such date falls on a Saturday, Sunday or legal holiday (as defined in section 7503 of the Code and the regulations thereunder), the valuation shall be made on the next succeeding day which is not a Saturday, Sunday or legal holiday.

The amount of income allocated to each unit of participation in the Fund shall be determined by dividing the income of the Fund for the taxable year by the outstanding number of units in the Fund at the end of the year, except that income shall be allocated to units outstanding during only part of the year by taking into consideration the period of time the units are outstanding during the year.

For purposes of this instrument, the term "income" has the same meaning as it does under section 643(b) of the Code or corresponding provision of any subsequent federal tax law and the regulations thereunder.

The income interest of any beneficiary of the Fund shall terminate with the last regular payment of income that was made before the death of the beneficiary. The Trustee of the Fund shall not be required to prorate any income payment to the date of the beneficiary's death.

8. Termination of Life Income Interest. Upon the termination of the income interest of the designated beneficiary (or, in the case of successive income interests, the survivor of the designated beneficiaries) entitled to receive income pursuant to the terms of a transfer to the Fund, the Trustee shall sever from the Fund an amount equal to the value of the remainder interest in the property upon which the income interest is based. The value of the remainder interest for severance purposes shall be its value as of the date on which the last regular payment was made before the death of the beneficiary. The amount so severed from the Fund shall be paid to Public Charity. If at the time of severance of the remainder interest Public Charity has ceased to exist or is not a public charity (an organization described in clauses (i) through (vi) of section 170(b)(1)(A) of the Code), the amount severed shall be paid to an organization selected by the Trustee that is a public charity.

9. Prohibited Activities. The income of the Fund for each taxable year shall be distributed at such time and in such manner as not to subject the Fund to tax under section 4942 of the Code. Except for making the required payments to the life income beneficiaries, the Trustee shall not engage in any act of self-dealing as defined in section 4941(d) and shall not make any taxable expenditures as defined in section 4945(d). The Trustee shall not make any investments that jeopardize the charitable purpose of the Fund within the meaning of section 4944 or retain any excess business holdings within the meaning of section 4943.

10. Depreciable or Depletable Assets. The Trustee shall not accept or invest in any depreciable or depletable assets.

11. Incorporation by Reference. The provisions of this document may be, and are intended to be, incorporated by reference in any will, trust, or other instrument by means of which property is transferred to the Fund. Any property transferred to the Fund whereby an income interest is retained or created for the life of one or more named beneficiaries, where this document is not incorporated by reference, shall become a part of the Fund and shall be held and managed under the terms and conditions of this document, unless the instrument of transfer is inconsistent with such terms and conditions, in which case the Trustee shall not accept the property.

12. Governing Law. The operation of the Fund shall be governed by the laws of the State of ____. However, the Trustee is prohibited from exercising any power or discretion granted under said laws that would be inconsistent with the qualification of the Fund under section 642(c)(5) of the Code and the corresponding regulations.

13. Power of Amendment. The Fund is irrevocable. However, Public Charity shall have the power, acting alone, to amend this document and the associated instruments of transfer in any manner required for the sole purpose of ensuring that the Fund qualifies and continues to qualify as a pooled income fund within the meaning of section 642(c)(5).

IN WITNESS WHEREOF ____ [PUBLIC CHARITY] and ____. [TRUSTEE] by their duly authorized officers have signed this agreement the day and year first above written.

[PUBLIC CHARITY]
By _____

[TRUSTEE]
By _____
[Acknowledgements, Witnesses, *etc.*]

SEC. 5. SAMPLE INSTRUMENT OF TRANSFER: ONE LIFE.

On this ____ day of ____, 19__, I hereby transfer to the ____ Public Charity Pooled Income Fund, under the terms and conditions set forth in its Declaration of Trust, the following property: ____.

The income interest attributable to the property transferred shall be paid as follows:

____ A. To me during my lifetime.

____ B. To ____ during his or her life. However, I reserve the right to revoke, solely by will, this income interest.

Upon the termination of the income interest, the Trustee of the Fund will sever from the Fund an amount equal to the value of the remainder interest in the transferred property and transfer it to Public Charity:

____ A. For its general uses and purposes.

____ B. For the following charitable purpose(s): ____.

However, if it is not possible for Public Charity in its sole discretion to use the severed amount for the specified purpose(s), then it may be used for the general purposes of Public Charity.

This instrument and the transfer of property made pursuant thereto shall be effective after acceptance by both the Donor and the Trustee.

IN WITNESS WHEREOF ____ and ____, [TRUSTEE] by its duly authorized officer have signed this agreement the day and year first above written.

_____
[DONOR]

_____
[TRUSTEE]

by _____

(Acknowledgements, Witnesses, *etc.*)

SEC. 8. APPLICATION.

The Service will recognize a trust as meeting all of the requirements of a qualified pooled income fund under section 642(c)(5) of the Code if the public charity responsible for the creation and maintenance of the trust makes reference in the trust instrument of the fund to this revenue procedure and adopts substantially similar documents, provided the trust operates in a manner consistent with the terms of the trust instrument, and provided it is a valid trust under applicable local law. A trust that contains substantive provisions in addition to those provided by this revenue procedure (other than provisions necessary to establish a valid trust under applicable local law) or that omits any of those provisions will not necessarily be disqualified, but neither will it qualify under the provisions of this revenue procedure.

SEC. 9. EFFECTIVE DATE.

This revenue procedure is effective for ruling requests received in the National Office after November 28, 1988, the date of publication of this revenue procedure in the Internal Revenue Bulletin.

INDEX

This index is nonconventional in that I added items that are not included in this book. Maybe they will get into the next edition. However, I didn't want my readers to go crazy searching for things that I didn't cover. The book is big enough and I simply couldn't cover everything. Therefore, if something is not covered, there is a listing that says "not included." You won't waste any time trying to find something that isn't here. I apologize for the few entries like that, but I figured it would save you time. There is a lot more in this book than could be covered in the Index, but I tried very hard to cover the bases. Further, if anybody looked up a topic and couldn't find it, send me an e-mail at debra@debraashton.com and I will include your search words in the next edition. I want to make this book as helpful as possible to you.

ABOUT THE AUTHOR

Debra Ashton has had a stellar career in planned giving since 1975. If you know the words "planned giving," you know her name and her book, "The Blue Bible" of planned giving, first published in 1988. Generations of new and experienced planned giving officers have relied on her wise advice and keen insight on creating and running a planned giving program that really works!

Debra runs one of the top three, exclusively planned giving consulting firms in the nation. She has consulted to every type of nonprofit—educational, health, environmental, social service, religious, you name it. They all come to her to learn not only WHAT to do, but HOW TO DO IT.

She knows how to take a planned giving office from the doldrums at the very bottom to the heights of success with millions of dollars in closed and matured gifts. She accomplished that for Boston College, Boston University, Wheaton College, and WGBH in Boston.

And she has painstakingly put that wealth of expertise into her book, not once, not twice, but three times with this Revised Third Edition. As she has gained insight through the years from her own professional positions and in her consulting role with clients, she has shared the depths of her secrets to success, no holds barred. She doesn't just tantalize the reader with highlights or half-information. She gives you all the goods....every single thing you need to know to start, operate and succeed in planned giving.

The most valuable thing about Debra's wealth of information is that it is EASY TO READ, and, if you will do the simple things she suggests, it will GUARANTEE YOUR SUCCESS. Don't pass up her knowledge and wisdom—in a format that is AFFORDABLE to every nonprofit and development officer. YOU DON'T HAVE TO BE EXPERIENCED TO LEARN FROM HER BOOK. She gives you her experience from her heart so that the very beginner can benefit from her, and the wizened old planned giving officer will glean more than just a little new knowledge. It's the A to Z of planned giving.

Debra is a long-time friend of so many of us in planned giving. She is a sought-after speaker and consultant. Her writing style is crystal clear, her speeches engaging and her commitment to professionalism beyond compare.

Take it from me—you could have no better a mentor than Debra Ashton.

——Lynda S. Moerschbaecher 2003

THE COMPLETE GUIDE TO BECOMING A FUND RAISER

How to Break Into Development

by Debra Ashton

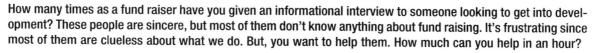

How many times as a fund raiser have you given an informational interview to someone looking to get into development? These people are sincere, but most of them don't know anything about fund raising. It's frustrating since most of them are clueless about what we do. But, you want to help them. How much can you help in an hour?

How many times have you gone on an informational interview to start networking to get a job in development? But, it's frustrating because you're getting nowhere. Yet, you desperately want to leave your job and become a fund raiser. This is a noble goal. Fund raising is a terrifically rewarding profession.

The book you both want is coming. If someone calls you for an informational interview, wouldn't it be great to tell them that there is a book they should read first? Wouldn't you love to buy the one book that can prepare you to go on your informational interview or a real interview?

Nobody has ever written a book on this subject and you need this book.

This book covers:

- Little known hiring secrets of charities;
- How to evaluate good and bad development office cultures;
- Questions to ask on your interview;
- Paying your dues to get into fund raising;
- What you give up and what you gain by working for a charity;
- Evaluating the reality of what different fund raising jobs require;
- Going on an informational interview and not saying something stupid;
- Selecting the right charitable industry to suit your personality;
- "I'm really good with people." Why you should never say this and other dumb things to not say;
- Ways to convince charities you can do the job when you have no clue;
- The truth about working with volunteers;
- Understanding the pure torture of not being able to make a decision without a committee vote;
- How to network to meet the right people;
- Creating a resume that will get you an interview;
- How to evaluate a potential charity employer and stay clear of a nightmare.

Sign the guest book at **www.debraashton.com** to be notified when this book is ready to buy. No obligations and you'll never be spammed nor will your e-mail ever be sold or traded.

COMING IN 2005

PG Calc Incorporated

History

PG Calc was founded in 1985 by Gary M. Pforzheimer with three colleagues from the Harvard University Planned Giving Office. Their experience there included significant development work with alumni, as well as on-going coordination with the investment management professionals for Harvard's endowment and charitable trusts. All continue to provide leadership and expertise in various areas at PG Calc today. The company has grown steadily each year and is located in offices in Cambridge, Massachusetts.

PG Calc is the leading provider of software and services for planned gift calculations, marketing, reporting, administration, and planned giving on the web. Our clients include charities of every size and description as well as service providers, banks, attorneys, consultants, and financial service companies.

Gift Planning Software

Our *Planned Giving Manager* software for gift proposals is used nationwide as part of successful planned gift fundraising efforts by thousands of gift planners, trust officers, attorneys, and planned giving consultants. *GiftCalcs*, our planned gift calculator for the web, helps hundreds of charities cultivate and identify new planned gift prospects.

Gift Administration Software and Services

Our *GiftWrap* and *Pooled Fund Organizer* software enables hundreds of charities, banks and service providers to provide accurate and professional gift administration for their income beneficiaries and clients. Through our *Gift Administration Services*, our experienced staff processes income distributions and tax reports for hundreds of pooled income funds and thousands of gift annuities and remainder trusts on behalf of charities across the U.S.

Consulting, Training, Reporting

In addition, PG Calc offers consulting services, group or individual training, custom programming, and FASB liability and state annuity reserve report production.

Outstanding Customer Service

PG Calc supports our clients with advice and expertise in all areas of planned giving. Our staff members bring valuable experience to PG Calc from prior work as gift planners at charities, trust officers at banks, and attorneys in private practice. Our intimate understanding of donors and charities combined with a passionate dedication to client support allows us to provide our clients with a truly exceptional level of service.

PG Calc Incorporated
Your partner in planned giving ℠

129 Mount Auburn Street
Cambridge, MA 02138
888-497-4970
www.pgcalc.com